The Kingdom of
León-Castilla Under King Alfonso VII
1126–1157

THE MIDDLE AGES SERIES

Ruth Mazo Karras, General Editor
Edward Peters, Founding Editor

A complete list of books in the series
is available from the publisher.

The
Kingdom of León-Castilla
Under King Alfonso VII
1126–1157

Bernard F. Reilly

PENN

University of Pennsylvania Press

Philadelphia

Publication of this volume was assisted by a subvention from
the Program for Cultural Cooperation between Spain's Ministry of
Education and Culture and United States' Universities.

10 9 8 7 6 5 4 3 2 1

Published by
University of Pennsylvania Press
Philadelphia, Pennsylvania 19104–4011

Library of Congress Cataloging-in-Publication Data
Reilly, Bernard F., 1925–
The Kingdom of León-Castilla under King Alfonso VII, 1126–1157 / Bernard F. Reilly.
p.   cm. — (The Middle Ages series)
Includes bibliographical references and index.
ISBN 0-8122-3452-9 (cloth)
1. Castile (Spain) — History — Alfonso VII, 1126–1157.   2. Leon (Kingdom) — History.
3. Alfonso VII, The Emperor, King of Castile, 1104–1157.   I. Title.   II. Series.
DP138.3.R45   1998
946'.202 — dc21
98-6677
CIP

To
Kenneth M. Setton
David Herlihy
C. Julian Bishko
mentors all

Contents

Abbreviations

AA	*Anthologica Annua*
AC	Archivo de la Catedral de . . .
ACA	Archivo de la Coroña de Aragón, Barcelona
Acad. Hist.	Real Academia de la Historia, Madrid
AD	Archivo Diocesano de . . .
AEM	*Anuario de Estudios Medievales*
AGN	Archivo General de Navarra
AGS	Archivo General de Simancas
AGWG	*Abhandlungen der Gesellschaft der Wissenschaft zur Göttingen. Philologisch-historische Klase. Neue Folge*
AHDE	*Anuario de la Historia del Derecho Espanol*
AHN, Lisbon	Archivo Histórico Nacional, Lisbon
AHN, Madrid	Archivo Histórico Nacional, Madrid
AHP	Archivo Histórico Provincial de . . .
AHR	*American Historical Review*
AL	*Archivos Leoneses*
AM	*Asturiensia Medievalia*
AMon	Archivo Monastico de . . .
AMun	Archivo Municipal de . . .
ARG	Archivo del Reino de Galicia, La Coruña
ASI	Archivo de San Isidoro, León
AU	*Archiv für Urkundenforschungen*
BCM	*Boletín de la Comision Monumental de . . .*
BIEA	*Boletín del Instituto de Estudios Asturianos*
BIFG	*Boletín de la Institución Fernán González*
BN	Biblioteca Nacional, Madrid
BRAH	*Boletín de la Real Academia de Historia*
CAI	*Chronica Adefonsi Imperatoris*
CEG	*Cuadernos de Estudios Gallegos*
CH	*Cuadernos de Historia*
CHE	*Cuadernos de Historia de España*
DHE	*Diccionario de Historia de España*

DHEE	*Diccionario de Historia Eclesiástica de España*
DHGE	*Dictionnaire d'Histoire et de Géographie Ecclésiastiques*
DMP	*Documentos Medievais Portugueses*
EEMCA	*Estudios de la Edad Media de la Corona de Aragón*
EDMP	*Estudios dedicados a Menéndez Pidal*
EHR	*English Historical Review*
ES	*España Sagrada*
GAKS	*Gesammelte Aufsätze zur Kulturgeschichte Spaniens*
HC	*Historia Compostellana*
HS	*Hispania Sacra*
JMH	*Journal of Medieval History*
J-W	Jaffé-Wattembach, *Regesta Pontificium Romanorum*
PL	*Patrologiae Latinae*
PMH	*Portugaliae Monumenta Histórica*
RABM	*Revista de Archivos, Bibliotecas, y Museos*
RPH	*Revista Portuguesa de História*

Preface

THIS BOOK HAS BEEN in preparation for better than a quarter of a century. Its roots lay in my decision to write a wider work on the general history of the church in eleventh- and twelfth-century Iberia after having finished my doctoral thesis on the church of Santiago de Compostela under Bishop-archbishop Diego Gelmírez (1100–1140) in 1965. The reform movement in the medieval church had been a major preoccupation of historians such as Geoffrey Barraclough in England, Augustin Fliche in France, and Gerd Tellenbach in Germany during my days as a graduate student. The predisposition they had fostered was then reinforced by the current ferment in the Catholic community occasioned by the startling changes legislated by the Second Vatican Council (1962–1965) to move me to decide to investigate further that reform in the local churches that had been the particular focus of my thesis interest.

But my earliest reconnaissance of the Iberian church soon acquainted me with two major problems. The first of these was that, with a few honorable exceptions, the history of the medieval church in Iberia had not progressed beyond the point reached with the publication of the volumes of the *España Sagrada* in the late eighteenth and nineteenth centuries. In turn that meant that I should have to do virtually all of the archival, paleographic, and diplomatic groundwork myself.

The second problem impressed itself on me almost as soon as I began those preparatory investigations. Briefly, I found it impossible to separate the documents or the history of the eleventh-century church from the documents or the history of the contemporary monarchy. But when I sought some useful orientation to the Leonese monarchy of the period, I discovered the modern bibliography as scant as that regarding the church. For the crucial reigns of Fernando I (1037–1065), Alfonso VI (1065–1109), Urraca I (1109–1126), and Alfonso VII (1126–1157) there were, literally, no modern histories and almost no critical studies even of their documents. If I were to write the history of the Iberian church of the period, clearly I should have to write the history of the contemporary monarchy of León-Castilla first, and there was much to suggest that both might well be accomplished under the latter rubric.

Because of my prior acquaintance with him as ward, associate, and antagonist of Archbishop Gelmírez and because some very solid, if partial, study of his charters had already been done by Peter Rassow in the late 1920s, the reign of Alfonso VII recommended itself immediately. However, after some preliminary studies of his charters designed to supplement that of Rassow, I found myself embroiled in questions that could not be satisfactorily resolved without recourse to the reign of his mother. That, in short, is how I came to publish *The Kingdom of León-Castilla under Queen Urraca, 1109–1126* (Princeton University Press, 1982).

Not that that undertaking was without problems of its own. I was acutely aware of questions raised therein that could only, it appeared to me, be satisfactorily attacked by a thoroughgoing examination of the reign of her father. Subsequently then, I studied them and eventually published *The Kingdom of León-Castilla under King Alfonso VI, 1065–1109* (Princeton University Press, 1988).

Obviously the danger, or perhaps temptation, of an infinite regression loomed here, but this book is evidence that it was averted or resisted. It does still seem to me that despite his obvious claim to be father and forebear of the dynasty, the realm of Fernando I belongs rather more to the preceding period of the old Leonese and Navarrese monarchies than it does to the monarchy of León-Castilla that emerges in the late eleventh century and the first half of the twelfth century. This may be a trick of my own perspective, of course, or the function of our continuing lack of a critical study of his documents or, indeed, of a sufficient body of surviving Fernandine documents to allow the formation of a final judgment on his place in that development. It is probably better altogether to avoid that cursed word "transitional" to describe Fernando's reign and to state frankly that the policy and institutions that dominate the evolution of that greatest of the Christian Iberian monarchies during the High Middle Ages were set and largely inaugurated with the reign of his son, Alfonso VI.

The sources for the reign of Alfonso VII are far superior to those for any of his predecessors. That peculiar text, the *Chronica Adefonsi Imperatoris*, supplies in various formats a description of many of the events of the period up until 1147.[1] Only rarely, however, do any of the literary forms employed therein comment directly on the person of the emperor. The other major narrative source, the *Historia Compostellana*, treats many of the circumstances of

---

1. Antonio Maya Sánchez and Juan Gil, eds., *CAI*, in *Chronica Hispana Saeculi XII*, pp. 109–296 (Turnholt, 1990).

the youth of Alfonso and of his early reign up until 1139.[2] Nevertheless, the king himself is always tangential to the purposes of its episcopal biographer, and royal motives are misinterpreted if not always, one suspects, misunderstood. Thus, while both sources furnish invaluable material to the historian of the reign, it is not the stuff of biography. As a result, this book is no more a biography of Alfonso VII than were my earlier treatments of Urraca or Alfonso VI biographies of those worthies.

This book does draw on a great deal of archival material collected or happened on in the course of my varied researches over the past thirty years in the major national and ecclesiastical collections of the peninsula. At the present moment, my notes draw upon something like a thousand royal and another thousand private documents of the period proper and a fair scattering of earlier ones from my past enterprises. For no portion of this century, roughly, are they exhaustive, of course, but the reader should be advised that early on I began to concentrate on all royal documents and any private ones that were dated and that mentioned the name of a bishop, abbot, noble, or official. Doubtless that kind of discrimination allowed some materials to fall through the cracks, but it did facilitate getting on with the job and produced a useful and random sample of such matters as the then current terminology, the currency in circulation, and even urban institutions.

My hope, then, is that this volume will supply the lack of an adequate history for Alfonso's reign. Certainly it marks an advance over Prudencio de Sandoval, *Chronica del inclito y bienaventurado famoso emperador de España, Don Alfonso VII de este nombre, Rey de Castilla y León, hijo de Don Ramón de Borgoña y Doña Urraca, reyna proprietaria de Castilla* (Madrid, 1600), or Manuel Risco, *Historia de Alfonso VII el Emperador* (Madrid, 1792). It is also, I must regretfully note, a far more comprehensive and accurate history than that of Manuel Recuero Astray, *Alfonso VII, Emperador* (León, 1979). The latter work represented some considerable advance in exploitation of the archival materials but remains inadequate to what might have been reasonably expected. The author drew on hardly more than that half of the Alfonsine diplomas already known to Rassow in the 1920s and a mere scattering of the private documents. The fundamental framework of his history was supplied therefore by that of the *Chronica Adefonsi Imperatoris*. That meant that his account ended substantially in 1147, as did the *Chronica* itself. It also meant that the institutional development of the kingdom was virtually ignored.

To be fair it must be pointed out that, writing in the 1970s, Recuero

2. Emma Falque Rey, ed., *HC* (Turnholt, 1988).

Astray preceded some of the advances in medieval studies in Iberia of which I have been able to take advantage and that I must gratefully acknowledge. Basic in this respect has been the reorganization and recataloging of most of the national and ecclesiastical collections of the peninsula as well as the provision of regular and more complete access to them. That process continues even now. Moreover, the trickle of editions of documents and specialized studies deriving from them has swelled into a blessed flood. In addition to the work of independent scholars, my particular researches have been facilitated in major fashion by the publications of the Centro de estudios y investigación "San Isidoro" of León, by those of the series Documentos y estudios para la historia del occidente peninsular durante la Edad Media of the University of Salamanca, and by those done under the patronage of the Departmento de Historia Medieval del Colegio Universitario de Burgos.

Given the particular parentage of this volume, at least two observations are necessary as to the fashion in which it would reflect on its predecessors. First, I would not now take such a sanguine view of the situation of the crown of León-Castilla at the end of her reign as I did in my Urraca book in 1982. Seen in detail, the struggle of Alfonso VII to secure his hold on the throne between 1126 and 1131 was much more burdened by the freight of his mother's necessities than I had previously understood.

Second, and more important, my conception of the nature of the county in the kingdom of León-Castilla may have changed more than anything else. In the Urraca book I assumed more than discovered that it was the ordinary territorial and administrative unit thereof. When I looked closely at the reign of Alfonso VI, the county, in that sense, became harder and harder to find. A yet closer look, in the light of more plentiful documents, at the countship of the time of Alfonso VII has convinced me that it was then simply a court dignity and a fiscal device. I now believe that it had never been anything different. With the atypical and exceptional instances of the countship of Portugal and that of Castilla, both of which owed their particular incarnation to sucessful revolts, the county in the realm of León-Castilla and its predecessor realms of Asturias and León was never a unit of territorial administration. The reader should keep that in mind especially in utilizing my Urraca book, also, although to lesser extent my Alfonso VI book, and finally for the whole of the early history of the kingdom.

In this entire work of a quarter of a century, I have been the benefactor of countless people and institutions. The shortest of lists must include my dear friends and colleagues of the American Academy of Research Historians of Medieval Spain, who have shared their own studies and suffered through the early versions of mine with patience and a heartening show of interest. Special grants from the American Council of Learned Societies, the Comité Conjunto Hispano-Norteamericano para la Cooperación Cultura y Educativa, the American Philosophical Society, and a variety of sabbaticals, grants, and travel funds from Villanova University supplied the essential material support. Finally, the longest heat of the longest days has still been borne by my beloved wife, Marge. None of this would have been done without her.

I

The Political Organization of
Christian Iberia: 1035–1126

IN THE YEAR 1035 both Muslims and Christians in Spain were undergoing crises that would eventuate in the emergence of a vastly different state of affairs in each community ninety years later. That these crises would be related was inevitable. The disintegration of the Caliphate of Córdoba provided the optimum condition for the emergence of a new political order in the Christian north. At the same time, the emergence of that new Christian order made a restoration of the old order in al-Andalus virtually impossible. Instead, it facilitated the reduction of Iberian Islamic political society to a mere province of a North African empire.

By contrast, the end of the tenth century and the outset of the eleventh century had still been marked, politically, by that state of affairs customary between the two societies for the past three centuries, almost since the Islamic invasion of the peninsula in the eighth century. The raids of the great al-Mansūr had resulted in the sack of Barcelona in 985, of León in 988, of Santiago de Compostela in 997, and of Burgos in 1000. On his death in 1002 al-Mansūr's policies and successes were continued by his son, Abd al-Mālik. Each year until his own decease in 1008 the latter launched new raids on the north up to the very slopes of the Pyrenees, the Cantabrians, and the mountains of Galicia. Then, abruptly, the succession of his half-brother, Abd al-Rāhman ibn Abī Amir, and his assassination scarcely a year later plunged the south into a civil war from which there was to be no recovery. It eventuated in the short run in the emergence of the *taifa*, or party kingdoms, and finally exposed the Iberian Islamic world to conquest from North Africa.[1]

Against this background there played out the surprising, brief hege-

---

1. The premier guide in English to this evolution in the south is David Wasserstein, *The Rise and Fall of the Party-Kings: Politics and Society in Islamic Spain, 1002–1086* (Princeton, 1985).

mony of the Navarrese monarchy under Sancho III el Mayor (1000–1035) in the north. That king incorporated the tiny worlds of Aragón, Ribagorza, and Sobrarbe into the Navarrese realm, allied himself with the small county of Barcelona farther east, and cannibalized the realm of the unfortunate Vermudo III of León-Castilla in the west. By 1035 he had installed his own son, Fernando, as count in Castilla and had wrested León itself as well as Asturias away from his opponent, Vermudo III (1028–1037). The Leonese monarch retreated into Galicia in the far west.[2]

The prize that Sancho III sought was the wealth and resources of the northern half of the Duero river basin. Since the end of the ninth century that plain had been gradually reclaimed by the overflow of population from beyond the mountains in Asturias and Cantabria in the north and Galicia in the west. Descending small rivers, such as the Pisuerga, the Carrión, the Esla, and the Orbigo, flowing south into the Duero and colonizing their banks, a new peasant farming population transformed that area into the demographic center of gravity of the Christian north. It had been further enriched by the flow from the Muslim south of Mozarab Christian peasants, who for the first time perceived a viable alternative to their permanent minority and subject status in the home of their ancestors. The importance of this emerging society had first been grasped by the Asturian dynasty of kings who, in the person of Ordoño II (910–925), removed their royal city from Oviedo in the sheltered redoubt beyond the Cantabrians to León on the northern edge of that plain. Having done so, the kings of León-Castilla secured a natural primacy among the Christian princes of the north of Iberia.

The threat implicit in the development of this new society north of the Duero was soon perceived by the caliphs of Córdoba. Nonetheless, they lacked an effective counter to it. The population of al-Andalus was itself stationary if not contracting. Some portion of its Mozarab component was even emigrating north to swell the ranks of this new world taking shape. The caliphs lacked, therefore, the ability to permanently occupy or colonize the basin of the Duero themselves. They were limited to launching great raids to overawe and channel the actions of the Leonese kings. Finally, even their ability to do that was destroyed by the collapse of the caliphate after 1009.

It was into this momentary vacuum created by the collapse of political Islam and the disarray of the Leonese monarchy that Sancho el Mayor of Navarra had moved. But it was inherently unlikely that the growing society

---

2. Sancho and his realm badly need a new history. Justo Pérez de Urbel, *Sancho el Mayor de Navarra* (Madrid, 1950), needs to be rethought to draw on the flood of research done in Iberian history in the last half century.

of the entire northern Duero basin could be permanently dominated from the diminutive plain of Pamplona. His death in 1035, accompanied by the division of his lands among his several sons, allowed the young Vermudo III to reclaim León and Asturias easily.

The renewed preeminence of León-Castilla in the world of the Christian north was to take place under the tutelage of the house of Navarra if not under its kings, however. Sancho had married his son, Fernando, to the sister of Vermudo III and endowed the pair with the countship of Castilla. When the Leonese attempted to reassert his authority in those eastern lands about Burgos, he was defeated and killed by Fernando at the battle of Tamarón in 1037. Fernando and his wife, Sancha, then secured his entire kingdom. The decline of the kingdom of Navarra was further hastened by Fernando's subsequent defeat of his elder brother, García III, and the latter's death at Atapuerca in 1054.

The rule of Fernando I el Magno (1037–1065) and Sancha restored the control of the Leonese monarchy over the thriving plain north of the Duero as well as what increasingly were becoming its appendages in Asturias and Galicia. Toward the end of his reign, the accession of strength secured thereby allowed him to take advantage of the continuing division and disorder of Iberian Islam. In the west Fernando captured Lamego in 1057, Viseu in 1058, and finally Coimbra in 1064. Those campaigns cleared the lower valley of the Duero and then the basin of the Mondego River farther south of Muslim rule and laid the territorial base for the subsequent emergence of a Portuguese kingdom. In the east he campaigned similarly to liberate the headwaters of the Duero around Berlanga and San Esteban de Gormaz. Additional campaigns enabled him to reduce the three northernmost Muslim *taifas* of Zaragoza, Toledo, and Badajoz to the position of tributary kingdoms. In return for the cessation of campaigns against them, their kings agreed to pay León-Castilla annual tribute, or *parias*, whose future nonpayment would furnish continuing excuse for intervention in their affairs and the financial sinews to do so when desired.[3]

This commanding position so dramatically constructed by Fernando was threatened with dissolution on his death in 1065. He had provided for the division of his realms among his three sons, the eldest, Sancho II (1065–1072),

---

3. The reign of Fernando I is currently without an adequate history. Recent publication of a host of documents, public and private, especially from the cathedral archives of León and the former archives of the monastery of Sahagún in the Archivo Histórico Nacional of Madrid, have opened the way to the realization of such a task. In addition, the printing by Pilar Blanco Lozano, ed., *Colección diplomática de Fernando I, 1037–1065* (León, 1987), is a major resource for such a project. Justo Pérez de Urbel and Atilano González Ruiz-Zorrilla, eds., *Historia Silense* (Madrid, 1959), is the sole extended and near-contemporary account of his career.

receiving the eastern lands about Burgos and the Sorian highlands together with rights to the *parias* of Zaragoza. Alfonso VI (1065–1109), the second son, was given León, Asturias, and the *parias* of Toledo. García I (1065–1072), the youngest, was ceded Galicia, the Portuguese territories, and the *parias* of Badajoz. Typically such an inheritance pleased no one, and a seven year struggle between the heirs ended only with the assassination of Sancho in 1072 and the lifelong imprisonment of García in the same year. The reconstitution of the kingdom of León-Castilla by Alfonso VI after 1072, the end of the disarray within its ruling house, and the thirty-seven years of his sole rule thereafter resulted in yet more spectacular developments. The primacy in Iberia of that kingdom became rather a hegemony.[4]

One should not overestimate the contribution of the monarch himself to this process. Just as the division of the dynasty had not greatly retarded the continuing development of the society of the north, its positive role consisted largely in coordinating and channeling that growth. Government at the time had few means adequate to the active direction of society. But the division of Islamic Iberia remained beyond the remedy of any of its governors and could be manipulated to advantage. Then, too, the inherently superior resources of the government of León-Castilla, no matter how ramshackle by modern standards, could be utilized against its less powerful Christian neighbors.

Even so, the talent and tenacity of Alfonso VI must be recognized. Like his father before him, he appreciated the growing importance of the great Burgundian monastery of Cluny and Cluniac Benedictine monasticism in Europe and cooperated with it more fully so that an Iberian province of the Cluniac order began to take shape. To secure that monastery's assistance and good will the king paid it an annual *cens* rising after 1090 from 1,000 to 2,000 gold *morabetinos* a year. Alfonso recruited and then installed a Cluniac monk, Bernard, as archbishop of Toledo after 1086, and between them the two contrived to fill much of the episcopacy of the expanding church of the realm with other former Cluniac monks. With the assistance of Cluny he managed to secure and retain the friendship and cooperation of the reforming papacy at Rome, avoiding the prolonged and sterile conflicts that often distracted and exhausted his contemporaries among the monarchs of western Europe.

In this fashion, a reorganized, reformed, and loyal secular and monastic

---

4. Bernard F. Reilly, *The Kingdom of León-Castilla under King Alfonso VI, 1065–1109* (Princeton, 1988), treats the reign in appropriate detail. The treatment of Alfonso by near-contemporary and subsequent major Spanish historians in the Middle Ages is reviewed thoroughly in Bernard Reilly, "Rodrigo Giménez de Rada's Portrait of Alfonso VI of León-Castile in the 'De Rebus Hispaniae': Historical Methodology in the Thirteenth Century," in *Estudios en Homenaje a Don Claudio Sánchez Albornoz en sus 90 años*, 3:87–97 (Buenos Aires, 1985).

church became a major instrument of government to a crown virtually without a bureaucracy of its own. Bishops and abbots were preferred instruments of local government and managers and repositories of the dynastic wealth. They tempered the near absolute authority of the burgeoning nobility in the countryside. In addition, he had reclaimed the *parias* from Toledo, Zaragoza, and Granada that furnished him with an annual income of 30,000 gold dinars. The careful orchestration of these assets made Alfonso VI the most powerful monarch in the peninsula and added substance to his preferred title, *Totius Hispaniae Imperator*. His prestige was reflected in his choice of consorts. Of his six wives over a long reign, only one was drawn from within the peninsula and none of them from within his own kingdom.

In 1076 the assassination of his cousin, Sancho IV of Navarra, gave the Leonese monarch the opportunity to annex the 4,000 square kilometers of the Rioja district, some of the most fertile agricultural land in Iberia. At the same time he gained suzerainty over the adjoining Basque districts of Alava, Vizcaya, and Guipúzcoa. Another cousin, Sancho Ramírez I of Aragón (1063–1094), annexed the districts about Pamplona, Estella, and the east bank of the upper Ebro River, doing homage for these territories to Alfonso VI. The kingdom of Navarra then disappeared from the political life of the north for almost seventy years and, even when it reappeared, was never to be more than a minor player. Its road to expansion to the south was blocked permanently by a yet more puissant León-Castilla on the one hand and by a newly important Aragón on the other.

But it is for his achievements in the center of the peninsula that Alfonso is chiefly remembered. His father's offensives in Portugal and the Sorian highlands had already created the conditions prerequisite to the annexation by León-Castilla of the 50,000 square kilometers between these two, south of the Duero River and north of the Guadarrama Mountains. Those lands most obviously lay in the path of the expanding agricultural society north of the Duero, long a no-man's-land of wandering shepherds and occasional homesteads.[5] Under the caliphate its southern border had been formed by the march of Toledo, now independent as the *taifa* of Toledo. Alfonso VI, his daughter, and his grandson were to devote a substantial portion of their reigns to the repopulation and reorganization of this area. The restoration of the episcopal sees of Segovia, Salamanca, and Avila and the emergence of the

---

5. Claudio Sánchez-Albornoz, *Despoblación y repoblación del valle del Duero* (Buenos Aires, 1966), is the classic study that touched off a controversy over the extent of the depopulation of the Duero basin between the eighth and eleventh centuries that continues still. The brute fact is indisputable, however.

medieval Christian cities synonymous with them are but the most obvious results of that long effort.

The protection of the proliferating new settlements south of the Duero involved Alfonso VI ever more deeply in the politics of al-Andalus. Of first importance was the defense of the kings of Toledo, first al-Mamūn and then al-Qādir, his tributaries. The assassination of the first in 1075 and a series of revolts in Toledo itself against the latter convinced Alfonso that more drastic steps were necessary. After a dramatically staged siege, al-Qādir surrendered his *taifa* at Toledo to the Leonese monarch on May 25, 1085. Troops of the latter escorted him to Valencia on the Mediterranean and installed him there in a new *taifa* kingdom. At Toledo the lives, property, and rights of Muslims, Jews, and Mozarabs were quickly guaranteed, while an influx of northern Christians was encouraged.

The fall of the *taifa* of Toledo, one of the five greatest Muslim kingdoms of Iberia, whose lands comprised some 90,000 square kilometers reaching from the Guadarrama Mountains south to the Sierra Morena, made León-Castilla a true behemoth in Iberian terms. No other realm, Muslim or Christian, compared to it in extent or power. The full consolidation of its position in the lands of Toledo and the simultaneous task of facilitating new Christian settlement there and in the lands south of the Duero would be the work of more than a century.[6] In addition, diminutive Aragón in the Christian north was a vassal realm, as were Muslim Valencia in the east and Granada in the extreme south. Alfonso VI busied himself in 1085 and 1086 with embassies to Zaragoza, Badajoz, and Sevilla. He sought the recognition of their tributary status and the consequent payment of *parias* from all three.

That pressure, unwise given the already enormously enhanced position of León-Castilla, moved the remaining *taifa* kings to desperate remedies. Led by al-Mutamid of Sevilla, they appealed for assistance to the leader of the North African fundamentalist Almoravids, Yūsuf ibn Tāshufīn. That Berber sect had been consolidating its power in Morocco and in western Algeria for a quarter of a century. Promised funds and troops by the *taifa* kings, Yūsuf agreed to cross the Straits of Gibraltar in 1086 and marched north to Badajoz, where in October he defeated Alfonso VI at Zalaca.

Over the ensuing twenty-five years the struggle in Iberia developed into a war between two empires. Whatever his original intentions, Yūsuf ibn Tāshufīn soon decided that his *taifa* allies were largely useless or treacherous

6. Julio González, *Repoblación de Castilla La Nueva*, 2 vols. (Madrid, 1975), explores that process in detail for the lands south of the Guadarrama. To date no one has attempted the same for all those lands to the north of the mountains.

by turn. He set about their deposition and the outright annexation of their territories. Granada came first in 1090, followed by Sevilla in 1092, and Badajoz in 1094. At Valencia when al-Qādir was murdered in 1092 the city was temporarily kept from Almoravid hands by the great vassal of Alfonso VI, Rodrigo Díaz de Vivar, el Cid, who captured it in 1094 and held it until his death in 1099. Until 1102 his widow, Jimena, maintained herself there but finally in the spring of that year withdrew west with the remaining Christian population. In 1110 an Almoravid governor was received even by the leaders of Muslim Zaragoza.

The struggle outlived both of its initiators. Yūsuf had died already in 1106 and his place was taken by his son, Alī ibn Yūsuf. Despite the defeat at Zalaca, Alfonso VI fought a long, bitter defensive struggle. He aided the *taifa* kings while they lasted. He supported el Cid and then Jimena at Valencia as long as possible. He raided into Andalucía itself when opportunity offered and hastened the repopulation of Avila, Salamanca, and Segovia, north of the Guadarrama, to guard the vital passes into the Duero basin if Toledo should be lost. Still he was pressed back in Portugal and had to concede all of the territory of Toledo south of the Tajo River. The great city itself became a frontier post and remained such for almost a century. In 1108 at Uclés only thirty kilometers south of the Tajo he lost an army and his only son and heir, Sancho Alfónsez, to the Almoravids. The old king himself died in July 1109 in Toledo, strengthening the city for its defense.

Shortly before his death, the Leonese monarch had settled the kingdom upon his oldest daughter, Urraca, and arranged her marriage to Alfonso I, king of Aragón. His hope was to preserve both the dynasty and the realm. Alfonso I was the eldest surviving son of Sancho Ramírez I and the great-grandson of Sancho el Mayor of Navarra. He already had a reputation as a formidable warrior, Alfonso *el Batallador*, and would possess the united resources of almost the entire Christian north. The marriage took place in the fall of 1109 but its promise was never realized. Shortly, the realm of León-Castilla was embroiled in both civil war and war with Aragón in addition to the ongoing conflict with the Almoravids.[7]

---

7. Bernard F. Reilly, *The Kingdom of Leon-Castilla under Queen Urraca, 1109–1126* (Princeton, 1982), is the best current guide to the affairs of those years and forms the basis of the account given here. Cristina Monterde Albiac, ed., *Diplomatario de la Reina Urraca de Castilla y León, 1109–1126* Zaragoza, 1996), is a valuable edition of her documents. Urraca was largely ignored by contemporary historians except for the hostile biographers of Archbishop Gelmírez of Santiago de Compostela. There is a long-needed edition of it in Emma Falque Ray, ed., *HC* (Turnholt, 1988). Lucas de Túy, "Chronicon Mundi ab Origine Mundi usque ad Eram MCCLXXIV," in *Hispaniae Illustratae*, edited by Andrea Schottus, 4:1–116 (Frankfurt, 1608), writing more than a century later included a brief, garbled account that became something of a standard thereafter.

From the first, the marriage of Urraca and Alfonso I was freighted with a host of disabilities whose relative importance is difficult to weigh. The greatest of these, in law, was that Urraca like her husband was a descendant of Sancho el Mayor, a great-granddaughter to be exact. The episcopacy of the realm found consanguinity a bar to the marriage in canon law and, when they appealed to him, so did Pope Paschal II at Rome. That might have been gotten over, but apparently Alfonso I was either sterile or impotent and a child to seal the union and to promise an eventual undisputed succession was not forthcoming.[8]

Other heirs were plentiful. Urraca's half sister, Teresa, had been married to Count Henry of Burgundy in about 1096 and the two were entrusted with the oversight of the county of Portugal. By 1109 they had, or were just about to have, a son. He was to be Afonso Henriques (1128–1185), the first king of Portugal. After the death of Alfonso VI, Count Henry and Teresa withdrew from court to the isolation of Coimbra. They never recognized Urraca as queen and heir. Count Henry fought against her until his death in 1112. Teresa eventually took the title of queen herself in 1117, ruled the county of Portugal independently, and until Urraca's death in 1126, fought her sister for the control of southern Galicia.

Urraca, too, had been married previously. Her husband, Count Raymond of Burgundy, had died in late 1107, but there were two surviving children of the marriage. The eldest, Sancha Raimúndez, born about 1095, and a son, Alfonso Raimúndez, born on March 1, 1105. *Infanta* Sancha seems to have been careful to avoid involvement in the dynastic intrigues of the period, but *Infante* Alfonso was a piece on the board if long too young to be himself a player. In fact, even before his death the old Leonese king had arranged a settlement that stipulated that the *infante* would become independent ruler of Galicia should his mother remarry. A number of reasons made that pact a weighty one. One was that it was witnessed by Archbishop Guy of Vienne, brother of the late Count Raymond and so the boy's uncle, who in 1120 was to become Pope Calixtus II. Equally important, guardians were appointed for the boy in the persons of Count Pedro Froílaz, head of the potent Trastámara lineage of Galicia, and Diego Gelmírez, bishop of Santiago de Compostela, future archbishop, and a power in Galicia in his own right. Such principals had a vested interest in opposing the marriage of the queen with Alfonso of Aragón. Additionally, even before the marriage was

---

8. Like most of his family, Alfonso has no adequate historian. José María Lacarra, *Vida de Alfonso el Batallador* (Zaragoza, 1971), is a bare sketch. José Angel Lema Pueyo, ed., *Colección diplomática de Alfonso I de Aragón y Pamplona, 1104–1134* (San Sebastián, 1990), has performed the necessary first step.

arranged, some of the Castilian nobility had opposed it in hopes of becoming Urraca's husband themselves.

That the marriage survived even briefly was due to the inability of the various parties of the opposition to agree among themselves. Alfonso of Aragón attempted to suppress rebellion in Galicia by force in 1110 but failed. Urraca vacillated between her rebel son and her bishops and, in the absence of a pregnancy, sought further allies among the Castilian nobility. Alfonso of Aragón now resorted to outright war and defeated the queen's forces at Candespina in 1111. His ally in that battle was Count Henry of Portugal but, in its aftermath, Urraca managed to divide them by diplomatic means. She briefly allied herself with Count Henry but the pretensions of her sister, Teresa, were too great. Urraca fled into Galicia but a Galician force marching against Alfonso of Aragón was roundly defeated. The latter then seems to have come to terms with Henry of Portugal and the two divided the realm of León-Castilla between them.

Further hostilities in 1112 resulted in but another reconciliation between Urraca and the Aragonese king, who were jointly laying siege to the count of Portugal when he died in May 1112. Teresa herself soon ceased to be a serious contender except in southern Galicia. Nevertheless negotiations between Urraca, her husband, the bishops, and the nobility of the realm repeatedly broke down. More and more, Alfonso of Aragón resorted to outright force. He seized control of the Rioja and most of Castilla including Burgos and established a long salient into León itself, reaching from Castrojeriz through Carrión de los Condes and to the royal monastery at Sahagún itself, where he installed his brother, Ramiro, as abbot. Far to the south, he was recognized in Toledo and adopted the style of "emperor" in his diplomas. Over the next five years, the fortunes of war swayed back and forth.

Finally in 1117 at Burgos the couple negotiated the first of a series of three-years truces, renewed in 1120 and again in 1123. The pact, which had the blessing of a papal legate, left the Rioja, the Sorian highlands, and most of Castilla as far west as Carrión de los Condes in the hands of the Aragonese on a de facto basis, but Alfonso made no further effort to reassert his control at Sahagún or in León generally. Instead el Batallador returned to the already traditional practice of his house of trenching on the territories of the great *taifa* of Zaragoza whenever opportunity offered. His grandfather, Ramiro I (1035–1063), had brought his tiny kingdom to the edge of the great plain of the central Ebro but was killed in an attempt on Muslim Graus, a fortress controlling one of the entrances onto that plain itself. Alfonso's father, Sancho Ramírez (1063–1094), after participating in the dismemberment of the Navarrese kingdom of his cousin in 1076 had returned to the attack on Zaragozan lands and took Graus in 1083. To bolster his larger ambitions he surrendered his land to the papacy and received it back as papal vassal. In addition, he had allied his house by marriage with the house of the viscounts of Béarn and Bigorre just across the Pyrenees. Further success followed in 1089 with the capture of Monzón but met his death in 1094 in an attempt on Muslim Huesca, the second city of the *taifa*.

His eldest son, Pedro I (1094–1104), continued his policies and with considerable French help captured Huesca in 1096 despite the despatch by Alfonso VI of León-Castilla of forces of his own to aid his vassal-king at Zaragoza. Pedro was also able to take the Muslim town of Barbastro in 1100, but further progress was blocked by the surge of Almoravid power into the northeast of the peninsula and the final incorporation of Zaragoza into its empire in 1110. Succeeding his brother, Alfonso I continued to root out the Muslim string of fortresses that barred Aragón from the plain of Zaragoza. In 1106 he took Ejea de los Caballeros only fifty-five kilometers northeast of the great city. In 1110 his defeat of the *taifa* king, al-Mustaín, had precipitated the Almoravid occupation of the city. The Aragonese had been fully involved for the next seven years in the attempt to make good his marriage claim on León-Castilla. The truce at Burgos freed his hands for the great final assault on the metropolis on the middle Ebro.

Pope Gelasius II blessed the effort as a crusade. Count Rotrou of Perche in Normandy, Viscounts Gaston of Béarn and Centulle of Bigorre, Count Bernard of Comminges, Viscount Bernard Atto of Carcassone and Béziers, and a host of other French warriors joined the Aragonese army that besieged Zaragoza from May 1118 until it fell in December. The momentum was kept up with the capture of Tarazona and Borja in early 1119. An Almoravid counterattack from Andalucía was routed at Cutanda in 1120 and Muslim Calatayud and Daroca surrendered shortly thereafter. By 1124 Alfonso had extended his control as far south as Monreal del Campo. The Almoravid power had experienced its first irreversible loss of territory in the peninsula at his hands, and the lands of the old *taifa* of Zaragoza on the middle Ebro were lost to Islam forever. In so doing Alfonso had more than doubled the size of the kingdom of Aragón and swelled its population to something like a half million. Aragón became the second Christian kingdom of Iberia in terms of power, and remained such down until the emergence of a united Spain at the end of the Middle Ages.[9]

9. The growth of Aragón from the time of Pedro I through that of Alfonso I requires a history. A beginning on the sort of thing that needs to be done was illustrated by Clay Stalls, *Posssessing the Land: Aragón's Expansion into Islam's Ebro Frontier under Alfonso the Battler, 1104–*

With the fall of Zaragoza the limits on what the North African Almoravid empire could achieve in Iberia were becoming apparent. In Portugal they had retaken Santarém in 1111 from Count Henry, but in 1117 they had failed to retake Coimbra from Queen Teresa. In the center of the peninsula they retook Coria in 1111 and threatened to turn the western flank of the Duero Basin, but in campaign after campaign the great city of Toledo on the middle Tajo defied their every effort. Instead, in 1118 Leonese forces retook Alcalá de Henares, safeguarding the eastern approaches to Madrid, and in 1124 Urraca was able to recapture Sigüenza, flanking their route north to Zaragoza. Something less than a quarter of the old lands of the *taifa* of Toledo remained in her hands by this time but the initiative was beginning to swing back to León-Castilla.

In retrospect what seems to have been occurring was a slow withdrawal toward the south of much of the indigenous Muslim population everywhere. The portion that remained in its ancestral lands now was subject to an increasingly numerous Christian population immigrating from the north and their allies among the old Mozarab populations of these districts. Such a fundamental demographic shift could not be combated with the scant mechanisms available to governments of that period. The Almoravid empire could sometimes commit North African armies in considerable numbers and over impressive distances, but, without the ability to occupy and colonize the ground taken, such victories as were achieved proved ephemeral.

Her former husband neutralized by his preoccupation with the conquest of Zaragoza, Urraca utilized the truce effected at Burgos to restore order in her dynasty and her realm. Her son, who had been annointed and crowned king in the cathedral of Santiago de Compostela in 1111, had since sometimes appeared formally associated with her in her diplomas. In late 1116 the queen acted both to clarify and to alter the position of the future Alfonso VII. In a general council of the kingdom she created an appanage for the eleven-year-old in the territories of Toledo and the lands south of the Duero. The point of these dispositions was to remove her scion from the day-to-day control of his guardians, the Galician house of Trastámara and the bishop of Santiago de Compostela. In his new lands to the south, Alfonso would not so much rule as he would instead now fall under the tutelege of Archbishop Bernard of Toledo. Bernard, a loyal servant of both her father Alfonso and of Urraca herself for thirty-five years and a bitter rival of Bishop Gelmírez of Compostela, was a safe choice.

1134 (New York, 1995), but that work is too limited in scope and method. Antonio Ubieto Arteta, *Historia de Aragón: La formación territorial* (Zaragoza, 1981), supplies some of the data, but confines itself largely to the political and military aspects.

Of course the young king had to be provided with the trappings of power if not with much of its substance. For the period between late 1116 and his own accession in 1126, some thirty of his diplomas survive (D1–35).[10] Most deal with the alienation to his supporters of lands of the royal fisc south of the Duero. Irregularities raise questions regarding some of these documents, but collectively they testify to the real inclusion of the young man in the then most fundamental instrument of royal government. They also show the growth about his person of an entourage, a court. Various charters demonstrate that he had his own scribe, chaplain, butler, as well as a majordomo and *alférez*, to direct his household and his bodyguard, respectively.

About the same date, in all likelihood, independent provision was also made for two other major members of the dynasty. Alfonso's sister, *Infanta* Sancha Raimúndez now about twenty-two years old, was entrusted with important holdings from the fisc including the castle at Grajal just south of Sahagún. Four of her diplomas from the period before 1126 survive (D8, 11–12, 26). Doubtless she also had her own court, and a majordomo is attested. A single diploma of *infanta* Elvira, sister of Teresa of Portugal, like her illegitimate, half sister of Urraca and aunt of Alfonso and Sancha, indicates that she, too, was included in the sharing out of dynastic resources (D32).

Opponents of Urraca in Galicia, the count of Traba and the bishop of Compostela, insisted that the queen had also agreed to cede control of that territory to her son in 1116. Whether she had or had not, clearly the queen had no intention of permitting such a thing. The remainder of her reign was spent fighting bitterly for control in Galicia. By 1122 she had to settle for joint sovereignty with her sister Teresa over the valley of the lower Miño and its episcopal cities of Orense and Túy. She attempted the deposition of the Archbishop Diego Gelmírez of Compostela in 1120 and came to near disaster. Only the intervention of Archbishop Bernard of Toledo and of the young Alfonso Raimúndez with Pope Calixtus II, the boy's uncle, prevented her excommunication and likely deposition. Nonetheless, about 1123 the queen had so far been able to divide her enemies in Galicia that she was able to arrest and imprison the Count of Traba and his sons.

To further strengthen her own delicate position, Urraca had had to seek allies among the nobility of the realm. Chief among these in the east were the two brothers of the Lara lineage. Rodrigo González was raised by her to the comital dignity, entrusted with the protection of the royal interests in

10. Throughout references such as these refer to documents listed by number in An Annotated Guide to the Documents of Alfonso VII and His Dynasty, 1107–1157, following Chapter 11.

Asturias de Santillana, and, perhaps about the same time, married to *Infanta* Sancha Alfónsez, half sister of Urraca. By 1125 that marriage had produced two daughters. Count Rodrigo's jurisdiction lay to the north of that salient held in Castilla by Alfonso of Aragón, forming a most useful counterpoise. Rodrigo's elder brother was the Count Pedro González, who had had a distinguished career in her father's time. His own patrimony and the royal positions with which he was entrusted lay in the south of Castilla and of the Aragonese salient. Pedro became the queen's favorite and lover, in all probability sometime after her definitive break with her Aragonese husband in 1112. The queen bore him two children. The eldest was seemingly *Infanta* Elvira Pérez, who first appears in the documents in 1117. The second was a son, *Infante* Fernando Pérez, who was first noticed in a document of 1123. The position of Count Pedro seems to have become so powerful that there was an abortive coup in 1119, whose alleged purpose was to free the queen from his influence.

Notwithstanding, events testify to Urraca's continuing central position in the realm. Her heir, Alfonso Raimúndez, was often at her court until the late spring of 1125, where he confirmed her documents and her sovereignty. He participated in her successful campaign against Sigüenza in 1124 and was knighted in the spring of that year in Compostela, with her permission. The two of them are likely to have agreed on the knighting of his cousin, Afonso Henriques of Portugal, in Zamora in the spring of 1125.

The few surviving documents suggest that in the summer and fall of 1125 Urraca was in Castilla. By this time she may have been approximately forty-five, if the marriage of her father and Constance of Burgundy is properly fixed in late 1079. There is no contemporary reference to her having been in ill health until an embassy of Archbishop Gelmírez of Compostela seeking the royal support found her on the point of death in Saldaña north of Carrión in early 1126. She died there on March 8. A later and generally hostile witness reported that she died during the birth of a child conceived in adultery.

However that may be, Urraca left her heir a realm at peace and with its central core intact. Asturias, León, the lands south of the Duero, and the northernmost portions of the territories of the old *taifa* of Toledo were solidly united under the authority of the crown. In Galicia its writ was more respected than it had been in almost two decades, but the south was still disputed with Teresa of Portugal. That split of the dynasty was on its way to becoming permanent, thereby creating a new principality, which was a problem to be addressed by Urraca's heir.

In the east the position of the crown was similarly challenged. Like Teresa, Alfonso of Aragón was himself a member of the dynasty. Like her, he

2

Succession and Empire:
1126–1135

AT HIS MOTHER'S DEATH, Alfonso was at the royal monastery of Sahagún, thirty kilometers southwest of the scene of her demise in Saldaña and roughly fifty-five kilometers southeast of the city of León.[1] He was in the presence of a small but influential court consisting of his sisters, Sancha and Elvira, his cousin, Count Alfonso Jordan of Toulouse, and the bishops of León, Astorga, and Mondoñedo (D37).[2] He must have heard of Urraca's death swiftly for on the following day Alfonso traveled swiftly to León where Bishop Diego presided over the popular recognition of the new king in the cathedral.

The young king found additional partisans in one of the oldest lineages of the Leonese realm. Within four days Count Suero Vermúdez together with his brother, Count Alfonso Vermúdez, the latter's son, Pedro Alfónsez, and another brother, Rodrigo Alfónsez, all rode in to proffer their allegiance. These magnates were related to the royal house through the female line. Just as important, between them they controlled the territories west and north-

1. Contrary to the usual conditions, we have two dramatic literary descriptions of the change of reigns. One is Emma Falque Rey, ed., *HC* (Turnholt, 1988), pp. 382–95. The text has been newly edited as vol. 70 of the "Corpus Christianorum: Continuatio Medievalis." It was written within twenty years of the events. The other text is the *Chronica Adefonsi Imperatoris*, in *Chronica Hispana Saeculi XII*, pp. 111–296, ed. Antonio Maya Sánchez and Juan Gil (Turnholt, 1990), pp. 149–53. This portion of the *Chronica* is likely contemporary, at least to Alfonso's reign. My account of the early moments of the reign essentially follows these two sources.

The reign of Alfonso VII has lacked a modern historian. The Augustinian scholar Manuel Risco, *Historia de Alfonso VII el Emperador* (Madrid, 1792), gave us a mere sketch. Manuel Recuero Astray, *Alfonso VII, Emperador* (León, 1979), is essentially a translation of the *Chronica Adefonsi Imperatoris*, which is followed uncritically, bolstered by a certain familiarity with some of the documents and the literature.

2. Independent confirmation of the presence of Count Alfonso Jordan of Toulouse and his bishop, Aemelian, in Iberia at this time is found in Eloy Benito Ruano, "Alfonso Jordan, Conde de Toulouse," in *Estudios sobre Alfonso VI y la reconquista de Toledo*, 83–98 (Toledo, 1987), p. 91. He was the son of Alfonso VI's natural daughter, Elvira, and of Count Raymond IV, born in the Holy Land during the First Crusade. Hence the sobriquet.

west of León from Astorga north though the castles of Luna and Gordón, much of the Bierzo and eastern Galicia, and far western Asturias as well. They also possessed significant land in Castilla, although they held no royal appointments there.[3] Their adhesion brought a solid bloc of experience and support from the former court circle of Urraca into Alfonso's camp and their rapidity of choice must have heightened its impact on others.

The *Chronica Adefonsi Imperatoris* also singles out the support of the nobles Pedro Rodríguez, Pedro Braólez, and Rodrigo González, the last not to be confused with the contemporary Lara count of the same name. The first was probably an Asturian with ties to the monastery of Corias who figured often in the charters of Urraca.[4] The latter two were Leonese magnates of lesser rank but with solid experience already in court circles and an important local following.[5]

This rapid rallying to Alfonso had its effect in surmounting the first problem of the succession. The castellan and garrison of the "towers of León," that royal fortress that bestrode the north gate of the city, refused to surrender it to the new king and his partisans. So long as they did not, they were in a position to admit enemies to the royal city itself. The king first attempted to treat with his opponents utilizing the good offices of Bishop Diego of León and of Counts Suero and Alfonso Vermúdez. When that course failed, he displayed that forthrightness of action that ordinarily would mark his rule. An assault was launched on the towers, and resistance collapsed quickly in the face of this royal determination.

Success built upon success. The remaining holders of royal honors in the region of León flocked to pledge their allegiance. Rodrigo Martínez and his brother, Osorio, who held the strategic Melgar de Arriba fifteen kilometers south of Sahagún, rode in as did Ramiro Froílaz, who held the important castle of Ulver in the Bierzo.[6] They were joined by one Count Ramiro, otherwise unidentifiable, and by Gonzalo Peláez, styled "count" in the chronicle, although he did not then hold that title. Gonzalo held central Asturias around Oviedo itself and had been long a rival of Count Suero Vermúdez.[7] The momentum in favor of the new king had now become such that the time for

3. Bernard F. Reilly, *The Kingdom of León-Castilla under Queen Urraca, 1109–1126* (Princeton, 1982), pp. 219–20.

4. The latest document of Urraca that he confirms was granted to the cathedral of Oviedo in May 1120. Reilly, *Urraca*, p. 143.

5. Ibid, pp. 300–1, for Pedro Braólez. For Rodrigo González see Luis Sánchez Belda, ed., *Chronica Adefonsi Imperatoris* (Madrid, 1950), p. 252. Unfortunately the latest edition of the *Chronica* lacks the useful index and notes of Sánchez Belda.

6. Reilly, *Urraca*, pp. 302–3 and 293.

7. Ibid., pp. 286–88 and 311.

fence-sitting had passed. From the east adjoining Castilla, the castellan of Saldaña, Pedro López, came in with his brother, Lop López, who had perhaps been sent to persuade him. Lop López had been *alférez* of the young heir since 1123, as he had earlier been of Urraca herself.[8] Both were scions of the noble house of Haro, of Riojan origin.

All of this maneuvering had taken less than a month. By the time a great delegation from Galicia arrived in León on Holy Saturday, April 10, young Alfonso was no longer there. The position of the king had so far developed that he had felt free to journey west to Zamora. There he met his royal aunt, Teresa, in little Ricobayo, twenty kilometers west of Zamora and fifteen kilometers east of the modern border of Portugal.[9] The nature of their agreement is unknown but undoubtedly Alfonso VII's purpose was to buy time to consolidate his position in Castilla free of worry about the always explosive border of Portugal and Galicia.

The Galician delegation overtook the king in Zamora, where Archbishop Gelmírez confirmed a royal donation to the cathedral of Salamanca on April 13, 1126 (D39, 40). The prelate was accompanied by a large number of the Galician nobility. Count Rodrigo Vélaz of strategic Lemos and Sarria was there, as was Guter Vermúdez who controlled the castles of Montenegro and Monterroso in central Galicia. He was another brother of Count Suero Vermúdez. Most important of all, the Trastámara clan, sons of Count Pedro Froílaz, who controlled the north and west of that province, made their submission. The old count, now deceased, had been an early guardian of the young Alfonso and sometimes opponent of Urraca, who had finally imprisoned him in 1123. One son, Fernando Pérez, was the lover and then the husband of Teresa of Portugal and another, Vermudo Pérez, was married to Teresa's daughter, Urraca.[10] Count Gómez Nuñez and his son-in-law, Fernando Yañez, who dominated southern Galicia between them also pledged their support.[11] The castellans of Cea west of León and those of Toro and of Salamanca did the same.

Within two months the new king had managed to secure the recognition of virtually the entire west of his realm. The next problem was to obtain that of the east. León and Asturias had been steadfastly loyal to the dynasty, and

8. Ibid., pp. 285 and 213–14.

9. Ibid., pp. 117–18. Torquato de Sousa Soares, "O governo de Portugal pela Infante-Rainha D. Teresa," in *Colectanea de estudios im honra do Prof-Doutor Damiao Peres* (Lisbon, 1974), p. 117, believed that the meeting took place in the fall of the year but he was unaware of the full documentary record.

10. Belda, *CAI*, pp. 230–31 and 257, is a handy guide, but the early Trastamara badly need a modern historian.

11. Reilly, *Urraca*, p. 291.

he inherited their support. Galicia had often been more his than it had been his mother's, and its allegiance came naturally. Castilla, on the other hand, had been a bone of contention for years, and its affairs would resist settlement for some time yet. Alfonso I of Aragón had never surrendered the hold that he had secured there. Other areas were largely dominated by the Lara lineage, and Count Pedro González de Lara had been Urraca's lover, perhaps to the last months of her life. From that irregular union at least two children survived who had not too distant a claim to the throne and a father capable of, and interested in, pursuing it.

Thus far the Laras had held aloof, but the young king had now been so widely recognized that their isolation was becoming pronounced. The *Chronica Adefonsi Imperatoris*, which is frankly hostile to the Laras, imputes the resistance of the castellan of León to them and suggests that they already sought alliance with the king of Aragón to sustain their fortunes. Nevertheless, a reconciliation with Alfonso VII was demanded by the circumstances, and we can see it in process by May 3, 1126. On that date, probably at Sahagún, the widow of Count Pedro Froílaz, Mayor Rodríguez, made a bequest to the monastery for the soul of her husband.[12] The king may not have been present, for he did not confirm but major supporters did, including Archbishop Raymond of Toledo and Bishop Pedro of Palencia, both making their first appearances at court. That negotiations were in train is indicated by the confirmation of Count Pedro of Lara. The recognition of León-Castilla's new king had become ostensibly universal.[13]

The king spent a year in the heart of the realm about the city of León working to consolidate his position. As always, that meant largesse (D41–47). A recent historian asserted that Alfonso held a major curia in León in mid-July in which he confirmed the decrees of a council held by his mother, Urraca, in Oviedo in 1115. There is no good reason to accept any such event (D48).[14] Some evidence suggests his presence as far east as Palencia and the area about the monastery of San Pedro de las Dueñas (D49–51). Alfonso nec-

12. AHN, Clero, Carpeta 894, nos. 18 and 19, pub. José Antonio Fernández Flórez, ed., *Colección diplomática del monasterio de Sahagún, 1110–1199*, vol. 4 (León, 1991), pp. 98–102. The first is the original.

13. A private donation of June 17, 1126, José María Fernández Catón, ed., *Catálogo del archivo del monasterio de San Pedro de las Dueñas* (León, 1977), p. 21, cites Count Pedro González and his brother Rodrigo González as holding Lara, the *Campos Goticos* and Asturias de Santillana. To their east, the very political Count Bertrán held Oca, for whom it would be hard to say, but he was related to Alfonso of Aragón by marriage. *Infanta* Sancha is shown dominating the crucial castle of Grajal south of Sahagún. Its confirmations suggest that it was drawn up at court.

14. Recuero Astray, *Alfonso VII*, p. 80. For a brief introduction into the subject of the supposed Council of Oviedo of 1115 see Reilly, *Urraca*, p. 107, n. 57.

essarily continued to be wary about the Galicia, where fighting was endemic. Two charters touch on affairs in that territory, and the second of them indicates that Archbishop Gelmírez of Santiago de Compostela paid a visit to the royal court in late fall. Other charters, dated less securely, may indicate his attention about this time to places as scattered as Segovia and Avila (D35–36).

Alfonso also must have been busy with the search for a bride from the first moments of his reign. Only a male heir would guarantee his partisans against the prospect of a sudden failure of their hopes resulting from the king's possible death and the succession of another of the only-too-numerous claimants to the crown. Alfonso was twenty-one, long past the canonical age for legitimate marriage of fourteen, and the likelihood is that his mother had prevented any marriage until now precisely to forestall the too rapid growth of his party. Count Ramon Berenguer III (1097–1131) was the logical ally if the Leonese monarch's eastern policy was to succeed at the expense of his former stepfather, Alfonso of Aragón. The Barcelonan had witnessed the extraordinary growth of Aragonese power in the basin of the Ebro after its conquest of the *taifa* of Zaragoza. Alfonso of Aragón clearly had further ambitions directed at the absorption of the eastern lands about Lérida and Tortosa, and these had long been marked as their own by the counts of Barcelona. Ramon was, therefore, more than willing to conclude a marriage alliance with León once its new king had demonstrated the capacity to put his house in that order needed in a major ally.

The best of fortunes enables us to follow the diplomacy preceding the marriage and so to gauge the concern of the Ramon and his estimate of what would be necessary to a beneficial alliance. A diplomatic memorandum survives and reveals that one Pedro, archdeacon of the church of Barcelona, traveled through the eastern territories of Alfonso VII in the summer of 1127 administering an oath designed to ensure the general acceptance of Berengaria, the count's daughter, as queen of León-Castilla.[15] In this account, on June 23 Alfonso himself swore on the altar of the monastery of Sahagún and in the name of God and of His saints to receive Berengaria as his bride in a formal church wedding and to keep her as his wife so long as he should live. The Leonese magnate Rodrigo Martínez swore to uphold the royal oath. Six days later, on June 29 in the church of San Pedro in San Zoil de Carrión,

---

15. ACA, Cancillería, Pergaminos, Ramon Berenguer III, Carpeta 33, no. 28. The document is written on an irregular piece of parchment in the caroline script. I would make it a thirteenth-century copy that is abstracted from a longer and more formal account by a scribe who was not too familiar with the earlier script of the original. The document does not specify the year and indeed lacks any final protocol.

Count Suero of Asturias and his nephew, Pedro Alfónsez, Ramiro Froílaz of the Bierzo, and Count Latro of Alava and Vizcaya did the same. By July 2 Archdeacon Pedro of Barcelona had reached Frómista where Count Pedro of Lara swore on the altar of San Martín. On July 4 the archdeacon was in Palencia of the Counts and there administered the oath to Lop Díaz of Alava and to García García of Nájera. July 9 found him in Burgos, where the other Lara count, Rodrigo of Asturias, and Count Bertrán swore. At month's end the archdeacon of Barcelona was still there, and Rodrigo Gómez, son of Count Gómez Gómez, took the oath on July 25.

This extraordinary survival indicates that the count of Barcelona was aware of the fragility of the young Leonese monarch's rule and understood which of the magnates must support the marriage of his daughter if it were to endure. He exacted all that he himself could to perpetuate it and the alliance it sealed.

These negotiations finally bore fruit in late November 1127 when Alfonso and Berengaria were wed at Saldaña (D75).[16] The choice of little Saldaña is striking, especially since Alfonso had to travel from Galicia through the royal city of León to reach it. The *Chronica* says that Berengaria had come by sea, but that would have been practical only by way of southern France and ship to Asturias and Oviedo and thence overland south again through León itself. It is possible, but not likely, that she had accompanied the legation of Peter of Barcelona and herself witnessed the oaths in her support. The place of the nuptials surely was determined by its proximity to those lands of Castilla with whose recovery the Leonese king had been busy earlier in the year, and the opportunity it thereby afforded to display the royal power and magnificence to new and prospective subjects in that crucial area.

If Berengaria had to travel to her nuptials by a roundabout route to avoid interception by the irate king of Aragón, her inconvenience was but petty revenge for the latter. Alfonso I had enjoyed an unparalleled triumph between September 1125 and June 1126 when he had not only led a great army deep into Andalucía but had even wintered there.[17] The point of the expedition had been to forestall Almoravid attack from that direction while he consolidated control over his much-swollen realm with its Muslim majority. Unfortunately, he therefore had been absent at Urraca's death and during the

16. The *CAI* places the marriage in Saldaña rather in November of 1128 but is clearly wrong in the year since the earliest subsequent and complete charters of January 1128 have begun to cite Berengaria as queen routinely. Maya Sánchez and Gil, *CAI*, p. 155. There is a variant that reads 1127.

17. Bernard F. Reilly, *The Contest of Christian and Muslim Spain, 1031–1157* (Cambridge, Mass., 1992), pp. 163–67, for a brief account.

first critical months while his former stepson was consolidating his control. Moreover, the intentions of the latter were evident. His rapprochement with Teresa of Portugal boded ill for Aragonese fortunes as did his assumption of the title "Imperator Totius Hispaniae" so early in his documents. There could be but one "imperator" in the peninsula.

Early in 1127 the fortunes of the Aragonese suffered a further major blow. Something like the traditional order of things was bound to reemerge in Castilla with the accession of a direct, male heir of the dynasty. The strength of that feeling seemed to surprise even Alfonso VII himself. During late winter and early spring 1127 his charters display no particularly significant activity (D57–62). Then, on April 30, a possibly original charter of the Leonese is dated "the same day when God gave the castle of Burgos to the king of Spain" (D63).[18] The chronicle account of these events is more explicit and registers the return not just of Burgos but of Carrión de los Condes and of Villafranca de Oca.[19] The latter village controlled the best pass over the Sierra de la Demanda from the Rioja into Castilla. The development threatened the collapse of the position that Alfonso of Aragón had maintained there from 1114.

Our chronicle dates his counterstroke only to July 1127. The charter record allows a bit more precision, but it is difficult to read (D64–66) We do better to credit the account of the marriage negotiations that put Alfonso VII in Sahagún on June 23 and then followed the emissary of Barcelona through Carrión, Frómista, Palencia, and by July 9 reached Burgos. From there he went out to give battle. Charters of the Aragonese show him moving slowly west from Sos to Huesca to Uncastillo and thence to Pamplona, Entrena near Logroño, and finally to Briviesca between February and June 1127.[20] Briviesca is roughly forty kilometers northeast of Burgos, and that suggests that the Aragonese king was attempting to swing past that town to join forces with his remaining garrison in Castrojeriz. Apparently the Leonese was able to

18. April 6, 1127. Pub. Saturnino Ruiz de Loizaga, ed., *Los Cartularios Gótico y Galicano de Santa María de Valpuesta, 1090–1140* (Alava, 1995), pp. 121–22, is a private document that cites Alfonso VII as already ruling in Burgos. There is a problem, however, with its year.
19. Maya Sánchez and Gil, *CAI*, pp.152–53.
20. Only rarely does Aragonese diplomatic usage employ the day in the dating formula. February 1127. Sos. Pub. José Angel Lema Pueyo, ed., *Colección diplomática de Alfonso I de Aragón y Pamplona, 1104–1134* (San Sebastián, 1990), pp. 248–50. A copy of the fourteenth century that gives the year as 1124. February 1127. Huesca. AHN, Clero, Carpeta 712, no. 7, a copy of the twelfth century, pub. ibid., pp. 245–47. February 1127. Uncastillo. Biblioteca Central de Cataluña, Manuscritos, pergaminos sueltos, no. 4.586, pub. ibid., pp. 247–48, calling it an original. March 1127. Pamplona. AHN, Códices, 1.296B, fol. 20v, a copy of the thirteenth century, pub. ibid., pp. 250–51. April 1127. "Antelena super Logronio." AC Pamplona, *Libro Redondo*, fol. 68v, a copy of the thirteenth century that gives the year as 1124, pub. ibid., pp. 254–55, with correction. June 1127. Briviesca. AC Zaragoza, *Cartoral pequeno*, ff. 17v-18r under date of 1124, pub. ibid., pp. 255–56, with correction.

prevent the juncture for the two met, according to the chronicle, in the valley of Támara between Castrojeriz and Fornellos.[21] A charter of Alfonso I, dated July 31, 1127, places him at Isar in the valley of the Fornellos "where the oaths and terms were made" between the two.[22]

The matter did not come to combat. The circumstances deduced above and the tenor of the chronicle both suggest that Alfonso of Aragón was taken at a disadvantage and, on the advice of two of his major supporters, sued to be allowed to retreat to his own lands. These were Viscount Gaston of Béarn and the latter's brother, Viscount Centule of Bigorre. The southern French magnates had originally entered Aragón in 1118 to help with the siege of Muslim Zaragoza. That city taken, it had been granted as a honor to Gaston while his brother, by this time, held Tarazona. The interest of neither would have been served by a war with León while the resettlement and aggrandizement of a greater Aragón was still the pressing need. The chronicle also suggests that Alfonso VII could not be sure of the loyalty of Count Pedro of Lara if the matter came to battle and so was willing to make terms.

According to the admittedly partial chronicle, the Aragonese agreed to return within forty days all those lands that had been held in hereditary right by the parents of the Leonese king. These could not have been the precise terms, of course, even if the *Batallador* had been soundly outmaneuvered. An Aragonese source, the *Crónica de San Juan de la Peña*, reports rather that Alfonso I agreed to return those Castilian lands as they existed before 1065 but retained all of the Rioja and even those parts of "Castilla La Vieja" that had been held by the Navarrese monarchs up until that time. In addition, the king of Aragón would cease to employ the title of "emperor."[23] The Leonese chronicler complains that the Aragonese did not comply with the terms, as he himself had given them. Certainly Alfonso I did not surrender the fortress of Castrojeriz and its supporting castles. As for the mountainous districts of the Bureba and the Sorian highlands, both kingdoms had claims and dispute was inevitable. In the matter of the imperial title, if indeed it was a concern

---

21. Maya Sánchez and Gil, *CAI*, pp. 154–55.

22. AHN, Clero, Carpeta 800, no. 7, a copy of the twelfth century, pub. Lema Pueyo, *Colección*, pp. 257–59.

23. The matter was explored in detail by Ramón Menéndez Pidal, "Sobre un tratado de paz entre Alfonso el Batallador y Alfonso VII," *BRAH* 111 (1943), pp. 115–31, who incorrectly placed the entire incident in 1124. José Maria Lacarra, "Alfonso el Batallador y las paces de Tamara," *EEMCA* 3 (1947–48): 461–73, corrected the date but by and large accepted Menéndez Pidal's assertion that the Aragonese chronicler and Rodrigo Jiménez de Rada, *De Rebus Hispaniae* (Turnholt, 1987), pp. 223–24, both had access to the treaty document itself. Certainly the latter knew the *CAI*, or shared a common source with it, although his description varies in some respects. It is much closer to the *CAI* than to the Aragonese source.

of the treaty, the verdict is unclear, but I incline to believe that Alfonso I of Aragón did not use that title subsequent to the Peace of Támara.[24]

The first trial by campaign had been essayed, and the Leonese king had held his newly reclaimed lands around Burgos and Carrión de los Condes. Nevertheless, he could not have accepted with equanimity the continued Aragonese presence in the advance fortress at Castrojeriz or the permanent loss of the Rioja and the lands about Soria. The matter could hardly rest there. Alfonso of Aragón now also understood that he could not underestimate the ability of his former stepson. He spent the remainder of the year strengthening his new frontier.[25]

The Leonese king spent early August in Castilla, where his position depended in marked degree on its unreliable magnates. Two of his charters are confirmed by the counts of Lara, Pedro and Rodrigo González, and by Count Bertrán of Risnel (D68–69). The latter enjoyed the confidence of Alfonso of Aragón and had acted as guarantor of his interests in eastern Castilla since 1117. He now held Burgos for the Leonese king.[26] Farther north, neither monarch could be sure of the independent Count Latro of Alava and Vizcaya who, together with his relatives, controlled the fate of the northern Rioja as well.[27] Nevertheless, Alfonso VII refused to be paralyzed by the situation and departed for Galicia in September.[28] Apparently, from the narrative in the *Historia Compostellana*, Teresa had again been acting to consolidate her power in the south of Galicia.[29] The young king now launched a counteroffensive and spent some six weeks ravaging the north of Portugal. That campaign sufficed to bring the Portuguese queen to terms.

24. On the basis of Aragonese diplomatic, as we currently know it, Alfonso I began to employ the imperial title after his marriage to Urraca of León-Castilla in late 1109. After both spouses agreed to respect one another's de facto holdings at Burgos in 1117, Alfonso seems to have employed it somewhat less frequently. Subsequent to July 1127 there are only four known instances of its occurrence in his charters, all in thirteenth-century copies, and two of them bear a manifestly incorrect date, corrected by the editor, while a third has no date at all. See Lema Pueyo, *Colección*, pp. 341–43, 331–32, 328–29, and 318–20.

25. Ibid., pp. 259–73, publishes no fewer than eight of his charters given in Tudela in August and one in each of the latter places. More detailed treatment of his precautions at this time can be found in Antonio Ubieto Arteta, *Historia de Aragón: La formación territorial* (Zaragoza, 1981), pp. 181–84.

26. Reilly, *Urraca*, p. 122. Also, July 16, 1127. Pub. Fernández Flórez, *Colección*, 4:114–15.

27. Gregorio de Balparda y las Herrarias, *Historia crítica de Vizcaya y de sus fueros*, 2 vols. (Madrid, 1924, and Bilbao, 1933–34) 2:319–20.

28. Apparently he left after August 26, 1127, from León. In a charter of that date his sister, *Infanta* Sancha, and he appear together with the bishops of León and Oviedo and other members of his court exchanging properties with a local Leonese convent. ASI, Reales, no. 137, pub. María Amparo Valcarce, *El dominio de la real colegiata de S. Isidoro de León hasta 1189* (Leon, 1985), pp. 101–2. The *infanta* will subsequently with him appear in a charter granted in Galicia.

29. Falque Rey, *HC*, pp. 395–410.

The royal effort had been assisted by rebels against Teresa in the north of Portugal, troops recruited in Galicia, and the city militia of Santiago de Compostela, for the terrain of the province ordinarily prohibited the transport of an army there from the *meseta* of León. Notwithstanding the utilization of mostly local resources, Alfonso VII found himself badly in need of funds as a result of active campaigning on two fronts. What followed on the triumphant return to Santiago de Compostela was a serious quarrel between the king and the lordly Archbishop Diego Gelmírez as the young monarch tried to raise funds out of the patrimony of the cathedral church itself. The archbishop, the most powerful magnate in the south of Galicia and *señor* of the pilgrim city and its environs, had not a few enemies who were more than willing to bring charges of misconduct against him before the king. The bargaining was hard and extended even to the threat of royal confiscation of the properties held in fief by the cathedral and of its secular jurisdiction. Gelmírez urged his long service to the king during the latter's minority and in the reign of his mother. The prelate doubtless understood as well as Alfonso himself did that royal power in Galicia would continue to need some effective prop there in the royal absence. Although our account speaks in terms of moral outrage, the question from the beginning was the final amount of the contribution and the terms on which it would be made.

Finally, both the burghers of the city and the canons of the cathedral chapter contributed to the royal needs and Archbishop Gelmírez added to those unspecified sums an additional 1,000 silver marks. In return, the king not only left the status quo untouched but made a donation of a royal castle, himself became a canon of the cathedral, and promised that his body would be buried there on his death. These terms are partially recorded in a series of three royal charters dated to November (D72–74). For good measure *Infanta* Sancha also agreed that she would be buried there. The charters reveal the presence of Alfonso's cousin, *Infante* Afonso of Portugal. That eighteen-year-old heir was unhappy about the marriage of his mother to a magnate of the Trastámara and the latter's influence in the realm. The issue would shortly come to outright war.[30] Meanwhile, Alfonso VII could improve his own position by playing off son against mother.

Victorious over his enemies, his purse repaired by the reluctant generosity of the citizens and clergy of Compostela, Alfonso VII proceeded to Saldaña for his wedding. He must have traveled fast and light to reach the

---

30. Sousa Soares, "O governo D. Teresa," pp. 116–19. Joaquim Verissimo Serrao, *História de Portugal*, 3 vols. (Lisbon, 1976), 1:80.

latter town by November 22 if he left Santiago only on November 13. Sometime that same month the young king was so confident of his new strength that he risked being the guest of the very person who had the most to gain from any royal mishap, Count Pedro González of Lara (D71).

As was customary, Alfonso wintered in the area around the city of León (D76–80). His attempts at this time to woo the Lara clan led to the appointment of Count Rodrigo González as *alférez*, commander of the royal bodyguard.[31] Charters of the spring of this year also reveal the presence of Count Pedro González at court. Moreover, most of the personnel of the royal chancery were now being drawn from the cathedral chapter of Santiago de Compostela, in accord with arrangements worked out the previous fall. But a royal charter of March 26, 1128, illuminates the reason for Alfonso's journey to Zamora just then. It was confirmed by no less than Teresa, queen of Portugal (D82). In addition, some six days earlier, Alfonso VII had appeared as a confirmant to a charter of Teresa to the Templars.[32] The interview between the two monarchs was prompted by the increasing unrest of Teresa's son. The queen sought the aid of her Leonese nephew to restrain him. Even so, the dynamic of events escaped them both.

In Portugal the unity of the incipient dynasty had long been precarious and now was to fracture entirely. The marriages of Traba magnates, Fernando Pérez to his mother and Vermudo Pérez to his sister Urraca, could not but raise up rivals to the young Afonso for the new throne. The young *infante* openly began to build a faction by the traditional means in the spring of 1128. That is, he began to issue charters that dispensed regalian rights and lands to those who would support him.[33] Such practice could not be tolerated, and the issue was joined on the battlefield of São Mamede south of Guimarães on June 24, 1128. The forces of the young Afonso triumphed, and Teresa and Count Fernando fled north into Galicia.

Afonso Henriques was destined to a long rule as Afonso I of Portugal (1128–1185). But initially he did not issue an open challenge to his cousins of León as had his mother when she adopted the royal "queen." After some hesitation, he was content with the modest dignity of *infante* and an assertion of

31. AHN, Clero, Carpeta 977, no. 4, a thirteenth-century copy of a private document; pub. Guillermo Castán Lanaspa and Javier Castán Lanaspa, eds., *Documentos del monasterio de Santa María de Trianos, siglos XII–XIII* (Salamanca, 1992), pp. 16–17.

32. March 19,1128. Pub. Marquis D'Albon, ed., *Cartulaire general de l'Ordre du Temple, 1119–1150* (Paris, 1913), p. 7.

33. April 27, 1128. Pub. Luiz Maria da Camara Pina, "A batalha de S. Mamede (24-VI-1128): Subsidios para su historia militar," *RPH* 17 (1977): 223–24. May 15, 1128. Pub. Rui Pinto de Azevedo, ed., *Documentos Medievais Portugueses*, vol. 1 (Lisbon, 1958), 1-1:110–11. May 27, 1128. Ibid., 1-1:111–12.

his own emparentage with the Leonese dynasty as a grandson of Alfonso VI.[34] Nevertheless, by the end of the year the Portuguese ruler had enforced the choice of Bernard, the former archdeacon of the church of Braga, as the new bishop of Coimbra. Such selections were a royal prerogative. Even in 1128 the greatest likelihood was that the two young cousins would inherit the respective rivalries of their mothers, for their disparity of interests would be the same.

While Portuguese matters were taking their fateful course, the king of León first turned to his frontier with the Muslims. In April he swung south from Palencia, to Maqueda just beyond the Guadarramas in May, where he confirmed the exemptions of the clergy of Toledo from military service and then returned north to Segovia (D83–85). Alfonso spent the summer and fall mending fences in Castilla before returning to the area about León for the winter (D86–94). Late that fall, however, the conflicting interests of León-Castilla and Aragón almost erupted into open war. After his reverse in 1127, the Aragonese monarch devoted much attention to his western frontier. High on the Sierra de la Demanda he fortified the hamlet of Agreda on the route west to Soria. He resettled Almazán, thirty kilometers south of Soria itself, and fortified Monreal de Ariza, some fifty kilometers southeast of the former. Also in 1128 he was engaged in the siege of Muslim Molina de Aragón, another fifty kilometers to the south of Monreal, which town dominated a secondary pass that gave access to the Aragonese kingdom just north of the Sierra de Albarracín.[35] In December 1128 Molina surrendered to him.

Such vigor had repercussions in the Castilian towns of the area, and the inhabitants of Medinaceli and of Morón de Almazán appealed to Alfonso VII for support.[36] The Leonese king responded, marching first to Atienza and then to Morón. He surprised the Aragonese who shut themselves up in Almazán. Perhaps Alfonso I had only a few troops drawn off from the siege of Molina. At any rate, he asked for terms, but the Leonese monarch demanded

---

34. July 8, 1128. Ibid., pp. 114–16. August 3, 1128. Ibid., pp. 116–17. September 3, 1128. Ibid., pp. 117–18. December 4, 1128. Ibid., pp. 118–19.

35. For his activities during the year see Lema Pueyo, *Colección*, pp. 284–97. Antonio Ubieto Arteta, "Los primeros años de la diócesis de Sigüenza," in *Homenaje a Johannes Vincke*, vol. 1, pp. 135–48 (Madrid, 1962–63), pp. 144–45, discusses the Aragonese activities of 1128 in some detail.

36. *CAI*, pp. 156–58. This source places the campaign of Alfonso VII in 1129 without further specification as to time or duration. In his account Manuel Recuero Astray, *Alfonso VII, Emperador* (León, 1979), pp. 98–102, follows the dating of the *Chronica*. Although the year 1129 cannot be ruled out definitively, the greater probability lies with 1128. Certainly the accuracy of the *Chronica* is far from unimpeachable. One of the actors in the drama is given as Bishop Pedro of Pamplona, but Bishop Sancho had long held that post. Possibly some of the events recounted stretched well into 1129.

the return of Castrojeriz in Castilla and La Rioja, promised he believed, at the Peace of Támara.

Alfonso I was strong enough to refuse such terms, and Alfonso VII was too weak to press his initial advantage. Our account makes Counts Pedro González and Rodrigo González responsible by denying their sovereign their aid. The king of León busied himself fortifying Morón and Medinaceli before withdrawing. The Aragonese in turn further fortified Almazán before returning to his ultimately successful siege of Molina de Aragón. The chronicler describes the whole incident as a major diplomatic triumph for Alfonso VII, but the reality was that he had been publicly humiliated for want of resources and by the refusal of the Lara family to honor their commitments. The royal impotence was underlined by the fact that Count Rodrigo González held the post of *alférez*, at the very time when he scanted his monarch's necessities. Such insubordination unrepressed was shortly to lead to yet more direct challenges.

The mounting difficulties of the young king are indicated by the survival of a document that reveals a major council of the realm, held in or near León in December 1128. This private charter of the magnate Count Suero Vermúdez and his wife, the Countess Enderquina, records his donation of the Asturian monastery of San Salvador de Cornellana to the church of Oviedo.[37] The act was confirmed by no less than seventeen of the then eighteen bishops of the realm. The Portuguese bishops of Porto and Coimbra, and the archbishop of Braga joined the archbishops of Toledo and Compostela in this extraordinary assembly. The king himself does not appear in the document, but he must have been present. Otherwise, such a meeting would have been tantamount to rebellion. The business of the council is unknown, but subsequent events make it likely that the succession and the recent royal marriage were the major topic. That these matters were unresolved is indicated by the events of the next two years.

The recent royal marriage may have become a major issue owing to the birth of a male heir to Alfonso and Berengaria. Since he did not survive to reign, the birth of their son Ramón has largely been overlooked by historians. Nevertheless, in April 1136 there is a record that the men of Zamora did homage to him at the behest of Alfonso VII (D248).[38] A birthdate of about

37. AC Oviedo, Serie B, Carpeta 3, no. 3; pub. Santos García Larragueta, ed., *Colección de documentos de la catedral de Oviedo* (Oviedo, 1962), pp. 377–80. The editor does not specify whether the document is a copy or an original.

38. Hilda Grassotti, "Dos problemas de historia Castellano-leonesa, siglo XII," *CHE* 49–50 (1969): 144, first pointed out the existence of the child Raymond. Enrique Flórez, *Memorias de las reinas católicas de España*, 2 vols. 1761 (Madrid, 1964): 1:279, established the existence of yet

1128 would therefore be likely. Now, if a healthy successor had just been born to the royal couple, other possible heirs would have been pressed to act. A childless marriage was no threat and the birth of a daughter or a sickly male not much more a threat. But a healthy male child made prudent an immediate attack on the marriage to protect other's own claims. The marriage could only have been assailed on grounds of consanguinity. But that Alfonso VII was the great-grandson of Fernando I (1037–1065) and that Berengaria was the great-great-granddaughter of the latter's half brother, Ramiro I of Aragón (1035–1063), were slim grounds to range against the influence of a reigning monarch. Early in the new year Alfonso summoned another council at Palencia for the first week of Lent. Ash Wednesday that year fell on February 27. Before then the king's whereabouts are less than clear (D96–100).

The *Historia Compostellana* is the major source for the Council of Palencia of 1129. It furnishes us with the conciliar decrees and a copy of the royal charter of March 25, 1129, by which Alfonso recognized the jurisdiction of the church of Santiago over the city of Mérida when the latter should be reconquered from the Muslims (D101). The account is written both to commemorate that bequest and to celebrate the eminence of Archbishop Gelmírez in the council, where the *Historia* says that the latter was guiding spirit at the behest of the king. Nevertheless, the decrees were issued by Archbishop Raymond of Toledo as primate and papal legate for the peninsula. Unfortunately, neither the lists of those who confirmed the decrees nor the charter survive, but fairly general attendance can be presumed.

If the issuance of the charter followed the close of the council, then its sessions had lasted about three weeks. Such unusual duration argues a difficult problem, such as the politics of the legitimation of a royal marriage. In all likelihood both sides agreed to suspend their considerations pending an appeal to Rome. According to the *Historia*, after the close of the council at Palencia, the king went north to Carrión de los Condes where Archbishop Gelmírez left him. From that time the documents tell us little about the royal itinerary until late fall when the court was again at Carrión (D102–12).

At that time the Muslim emir, Alī ibn Yūsuf, had begun to take steps to reinvigorate his empire and the Christian-Muslim frontier in Iberia saw heightened activity in 1129. In León-Castilla this meant a series of border raids and counterraids in which the king was not directly involved. For Aragón the Muslim vigor was more serious. Alfonso of Aragón chose the offen-

---

another early male child of the marriage. Named Alfonso, the boy was buried at in the choir of the monastery of San Clemente in Toledo.

sive and launched a preemptive siege of Valencia from at least May into July. The new Almoravid governor in Sevilla advanced to meet the challenge only to be resoundingly defeated by *el Batallador* at Cullera forty kilometers south of Valencia.[39] This victory forestalled a general Muslim offensive against Aragonese positions but limited the efforts of Alfonso I along his western border. In October, however, the Aragonese monarch was at Briviesca and in November just south of Soria.[40] Tensions along that frontier through 1129 may explain some later dating of events by the *Chronica Adefonsi Imperatoris*.

Before León could take advantage of the mounting preoccupations of Aragón it had to endure a major convulsion. The settlement of all challenges to the succession of Alfonso VII followed on a round of international diplomacy, a royal coup, and an outright revolt against the two former. The central events were enacted at the Council of Carrión in February. Before that time royal documents tell us little (D113–14).[41] In the major source, the *Historia Compostellana*,[42] the account begins with three papal letters addressed severally to the archbishop of Braga, the archbishop de Compostela, and Alfonso VII. They are datable to 1129 from the fact that the prelate of Braga is called to account for having consecrated Bishop Bernard of Coimbra, a suffragan of Compostela since 1120. The letter to Alfonso is marked by its warmth and is obviously written as a reply to a royal letter. Honorius II (1124–1130) informed the king that he was despatching a legate to deal with the general well-being of the kingdom. In receipt of such a letter the young king could hardly have had many misgivings as to the resolution of the challenge to his marriage.

When Humbert, cardinal-priest of San Clemente, arrived in Iberia is unknown. He went first to visit for eight days with Archbishop Gelmírez and then to Portugal before returning to Carrión. Alfonso VII himself had spent no less than five weeks with Gelmírez in Compostela, celebrating the Christmas season there in 1129–1130. Even given the partisan nature of our source, the conclusion that the prelate of Compostela was the essential support and

39. Ambrosio Huici Miranda, *Historia musulmana de Valencia y su región*, 3 vols. (Valencia, 1969–70), 3:67–68, and also "Contribución al estudio de la dinastía almorávides: el gobierno de Tasfin ben Ali ben Yusuf in al-Andalus," *Études d'orientalisme dédiés à la mémoire de Lévi-Provençal*, vol. 2 (Paris, 1962), pp. 606–9.

40. Lema Pueyo, *Colección*, pp. 315–25. There are numerous hamlets called Ribota but the reference "super Sancto Saturnino" would seem to refer to the hermitage of that name just about two kilometers south of Soria.

41. January 4, 1130. Pub. Muñoz y Romero, *Colección*, pp. 485–89, is a *fuero* granted by Diego and Domingo Alvarez to the men of Escalona apparently confirmed by Alfonso VII since it has a royal *signum*. This eighteenth-century copy has been much interpolated.

42. Falque Rey, *HC*, pp. 435–43.

intermediary of the crown in the matter of papal validation of the royal marriage is inescapable.

Archbishop Gelmírez made the winter trip from Galicia, although the *Historia* underscores his ill health, and was received in León by the king with great pomp. Later, the two met privately and the king requested the aid of his old mentor in defending his marriage against the charge of consanguinity. It is difficult to believe that all this had not been largely concerted before and that only the quid pro quo still at issue. The pair now continued to the council at Carrión. There they joined the cardinal legate and the archbishop of Tarragona, Oleguer Bonestruga, in a secret meeting where the agenda was set. The *Historia* relates that the council began on February 4, but of its documents only one is dated (D115).[43] The records indicate that no less than seventeen bishops, in addition to the legate, attended and that Portugal was represented by the bishops of Coimbra and Oporto. The bishops of Aragón, of course, did not attend.

Formal *acta* of the council have not survived, but we are fairly well informed of its activities. The question of the legitimacy of the king's marriage was quashed for good, although that is indicated only indirectly; that is, the council authorized the deposition of three bishops, Diego of León, Pelayo of Oviedo, and Muño of Salamanca, and the abbot of Samos, all of whom we suppose to have been party to the appeal to Rome. Archbishop Gelmírez realized substantial rewards for his help; one of his canons, Arias, became the new bishop of León, another, Alfonso Pérez, became the new bishop of Salamanca, and the royal support for yet another, the Martín already mentioned in Pope Honorius's letter of 1129, secured for him the bishopric of Orense. The council likely ended before Ash Wednesday, February 12.

Archbishop Gelmírez's triumphs had their costs. The prelate's aid to the crown was not limited to public support and private influence at Rome and in Carrión. The *Historia* relates hard bargaining before the council in which the archbishop agreed to pay the king an annual subsidy of 100 silver marks out of the revenues of his church in order to retain the royal favor and to avoid outright spoliation. Shortly after the closing of the council, the king made a grant already promised that set seal on his gratitude (D116).

Diplomacy and politics had contributed hugely to the consolidation of the young king's power, but their verdict had to be confirmed by direct action. In the late winter or spring 1130 a series of revolts broke out in the realm as

43. For the others see Bernard F. Reilly, "On Getting to Be a Bishop in León-Castile: The 'Emperor' Alfonso VII and the Post-Gregorian Church," *Studies in Medieval and Renaissance History*, ns, 1 (1978): 48–51.

those vanquished at the council table sought to redeem their fortunes in the field. The *Chronica Adefonsi Imperatoris* describes these episodes in good detail, but its dating of them is not precise.[44]

Some of the conspirators may have withdrawn from court earlier as it became clear that a final break was inevitable. Alfonso VII had relieved Count Rodrigo González of his post as *alférez* when that magnate refused to participate in the campaign against Alfonso of Aragón in 1129. That crucial position was then given to Pedro Alfónsez, nephew of Count Suero Vermúdez and an early supporter of the king.[45] Nor are the Lara counts visible at the royal court from that time. Some could hardly absent themselves, such as the bishop of León, but others such as Bishop Pelayo of Oviedo could. The latter seems not to have attended the council of Carrión whose result, he probably suspected, would be a foregone conclusion.

Since absenting oneself from court without royal approval was generally regarded as incipient rebellion, the dating of the revolts to January 1130 by the *Chronica* may be roughly accurate, even if they took the better part of the year to repress. However, their active phases were a reaction to the royal coup at Carrión. The most serious focus was in Castilla, where Count Pedro of Lara and his son-in-law, Count Bertrán, seized the episcopal city of Palencia and declared against the king. Pedro was supported by his brother, Count Rodrigo González, who rose in Asturias de Santillana. Given the extensive holdings of the Lara family there and the control of Burgos by Count Bertrán, the whole of the eastern quarter of the realm was at risk. In addition, the rebels appealed to Alfonso of Aragón.

Fortunately the latter was occupied elsewhere and Alfonso VII marched promptly against the major threat. The city of Palencia rose against the rebels and opened its gates. Alfonso never lost the support of Bishop Pedro of Palencia who was at Carrión, and who regarded the action of the counts as a usurpation of his *señorial* authority. Moreover, the city had never been friendly to *el Batallador* and the appeal to him by the rebels would have made few friends. The most important nexus of the rebellion collapsed, and Counts Pedro and Bertrán were captured and carried off to León, where they were deprived of their honors and possessions. The king did release them subsequently, whereupon Count Pedro fled to the camp of the king of Aragón in

44. Maya Sánchez and Gil, *CAI*, pp. 158–61. They appear under the heading for 1130 "in the month of January."

45. February 16, 1129. AHN, Clero, Carpeta 895, no. 4; pub. Fernández Flórez, *Colección*, 4:118–20, a private document, is the last known citation of Rodrigo. For the first citation of Pedro Alfonso as *alférez* (D108).

the south of France, where that king was besieging Bayonne. There he was challenged to a duel by Count Alfonso Jordan of Toulouse, the first cousin of Alfonso VII. Alfonso of Aragón permitted the encounter, and Count Pedro González was killed. The date of his death, October 16, 1130, was recorded in the *Obituario* of the cathedral of Burgos where he was interred.[46]

Before marching to Palencia, the Leonese monarch had entrusted the reduction of the rebels in the territory of León itself to his castellan, Rodrigo Martínez, and the latter's brother, Osorio. But Pedro Díaz, an important Leonese magnate, and his ally Pelayo Froílaz, held out successfully against them in the former's castle at Valle. The place must have been strong, although its identity eludes us, and continued to resist even after the king had returned triumphant from Palencia and joined the besiegers. At length, the rebels did surrender and, while Pedro Díaz's life was spared and he was set at liberty, he was disgraced and died in poverty. His supporters were treated rather more harshly. On the collapse of the rebellion, another prominent magnate with close ties to the king of Aragón, Jimeno Jiménez, made his submission and surrendered the key fortress of Coyanza forty kilometers south of León. Unfortunately, the royal charters of the period are of no help in dating its episodes more closely. In May one of them reveals the presence at court again of the bishops of Santiago de Compostela and of Mondoñedo, so it may be that support had to be summoned from Galicia (D117–21). In early June Alfonso is missing from the court when we should expect his presence, so one campaign or another may be in progress.[47]

Finally, the king was ready to deal with Count Rodrigo González and personally led an army northeast into Asturias de Santillana. There he wasted the lands of the rebel and reduced his castles until the count was forced to ask for terms. In a personal interview under an arranged truce, Rodrigo managed so to enrage the king that Alfonso attacked him bodily, seizing him by the throat, and both fell from their horses. The count's escort fled and he himself was carried off in chains and deprived of honors and possessions. Although the enduring influence of the Lara family later led to a partial restoration of his fortunes, the enmity between the two remained. The campaign can be partially dated by a royal charter of August 26, 1130, granted to the church of Burgos in Asturias (D122). This document also reveals the action of the king

---

46. Luciano Serrano, *El obispado de Burgos y Castilla primitiva desde el siglo V al XIII*, 3 vols. (Madrid, 1935), 3:390.

47. June 10, 1130. AHN, Clero, Carpeta 895, no. 10; pub. Fernández Flórez, *Colección*, 4:124–26. This is a private document confirmed by a good many court figures but not by Alfonso himself.

to restore order and to create a better balance in Castilla. Pedro Alfónsez has been replaced by Rodrigo Fernández as *alférez*. The new standard bearer was a member of the Castro family, rivals of the Laras for influence in the realm and long to continue as such.[48] Two months later a notice indicates the king's favor bestowed on another Castilian, soon to be count, and member of a lineage rival to the Laras, Rodrigo Gómez. No other genuine royal document for the year survives (D123–24).

The revolts occasioned by Alfonso VII's coup at the Council of Carrión had now been repressed everywhere with one exception. Bishop Pelayo of Oviedo had been deposed, probably in absentia, at the council and a successor named. But this new Bishop Alfonso had serious problems in taking control of the see from his predecessor, who had presided there for thirty years, had advanced the fortunes of the church of Oviedo in major fashion, and was no stranger to the byways of political life and intrigue.[49] Pelayo surely appealed to Rome against the actions of legate and council. After the death of Bishop Alfonso and before the election of his successor, Pelayo reappears as the bishop of Oviedo in a number of private documents, although he was never recognized in royal documents.[50]

Moreover, there was danger that Bishop Pelayo would make common cause with the adventurer, Gonzalo Peláez. The latter had almost as long a career as a magnate in Asturias as the bishop. His rise from obscure origins to almost total power in Asturias was a function of the reign of Urraca and its troubles. He had adhered faithfully to her party, although the queen never rewarded him with the comital title.[51] The *Chronica Adefonsi Imperatoris* mentions him as a great magnate, *dux*, in Asturias and an early supporter of

48. Belda, *CAI*, p. 251.

49. He had been the biographer of Alfonso VI, see Benito Sánchez Alonso, ed., *Crónica del Obispo Don Pelayo* (Madrid, 1924). He was a court figure during the latter part of the reign of Alfonso VI and during that of Urraca as well. He is infamous as the man who authorized wholesale adulteration and outright forgery of documents to enhance the resources and position of the cathedral of Oviedo, especially against the rising star of Santiago de Compostela. A detailed study of his career is needed and may now be possible. Marcos G. Martínez, "Regesta de Don Pelayo, obispo de Oviedo," *BIEA* 18 (1964): 211–48, is quite inadequate to its subject.

50. March 1142. A Mon San Vicente, no. 272; pub. Pedro Floriano Llorente, ed., *Colección diplomática del monasterio de San Vicente de Oviedo* (Oviedo, 1968), pp. 328–29. April 1142. Ibid., no. 271; pub. Floriano Llorente, *Colección*, pp. 329–31. March 11, 1143. Ibid., no. 167; pub. Floriano Llorente, *Colección*, pp. 333–35. The editor styles all of these documents originals. It should be noted that since legitimate title to property was being conveyed by these documents the citing of the bishop of the see at the time was not an action to be lightly taken if he did not have a serious claim to recognition.

51. Reilly, *Urraca*, pp. 286–87. Antonio C. Floriano Cumbreno, *Estudios de Historia de Asturias* (Oviedo, 1962), pp. 153–69, has a useful study as has Elida García García, "El conde asturiano Gonzalo Peláez," *Asturiansia medievalia* 2 (1975): 39–64.

Alfonso VII in 1126 and states that the king raised him to comital rank.[52] But that action was not taken immediately, for it was the policy of the dynasty to avoid the creation of a strong regional power in Asturias de Oviedo. In that territory closely identified with the origin of the dynasty itself and whose support, joined to that of the Leonese heartland, was so critical to its well-being, the crown sought to rule rather more directly and would long continue to do so.[53] In the late medieval period the heir to the throne came to be titled the "Prince of Asturias."

Gonzalo Peláez had reason to be unhappy with royal policy after 1126. The increasing reliance by the king on the family of Suero Vermúdez could not have been welcome, as they were his principal rivals in western Asturias. The promotion of Suero's nephew, Pedro Alfónsez, to *alférez* in 1129 would have been even more disturbing. It is not likely to be a coincidence then that in winter of 1130 Gonzalo first appears with the title of count (D116).[54] Under the press of emergency, Alfonso yielded to what may be regarded as severe pressure from the magnate and bestowed the countship on him. Doubtless the king resented such compulsion. What had transpired was something less than rebellion, surely, but the threat was implicit. Alfonso would yield yet further in the following year when he was engaged with still more pressing matters that required internal peace and assistance against Aragón by all parties. By the fall of 1131, Count Gonzalo Peláez appears as *alférez* and remains in that capacity the late winter of 1132 (D131, 137, 146). The Asturian had reached the zenith of his influence, but his position was, in the nature of things, precarious.

While Alfonso's realm was torn by internal strife he was fortunate that his major Christian rival was yet more preoccupied. Alfonso *el Batallador* was at war with Ramon Berenguer and early in that year took the town of Monzón from the Catalan.[55] While he was so engaged the Muslim frontier burst into new life. The Almoravid governor of Valencia routed a strong Aragonese force in early May, killing Bishop Stephen of Huesca and Viscount Gaston of Béarn, whose head was carried in triumph through the streets of Córdoba and then sent on to Marrakesh. The latter had long been a major vassal and the king had to sue for peace.[56] Fortunately the Muslims, planning a major offensive against León-Castilla, were willing to grant it.

---

52. Maya Sánchez and Gil, *CAI*, p. 151.
53. Reilly, *Urraca*, pp. 286–88.
54. The first private document to do so is of June 15, 1130. A Mon San Vicente, no. 33; pub: Floriano Llorente, *Colección*, pp. 280–82. The editor calls it an original.
55. Ubieto Arteta, *Historia de Aragón: La formación territorial*, p. 187.
56. Huici Miranda, "Contribución," p. 609.

The Aragonese monarch was also preparing a campaign in the south of France and in the spring of 1130 made a foray into the Vale of Arán, which sat astride a secondary route north. He then may have returned to Zaidín near Fraga in August and later gone on to Bayonne in Gascony. Possibly, the king returned to Aragón in winter 1131, rejoining his army before Bayonne in April 1131.[57] The reasons for this intervention in the south of France are not known, although it has been asserted that it was intended to prop up the rule of Gaston of Béarn's son, Centule V, against pressure from the duke of Aquitaine.[58] The old claims of the house of Pamplona may have entered into the matter as well. Nevertheless, the Aragonese monarch was tied down there into the fall of 1131.[59]

In his turn, Alfonso VII had little time in 1130 to spare for his southern frontier.[60] Left to rely on their own strength, the Toledans were badly cut up by the Almoravids. The castle of Aceca northeast of Toledo was taken by the latter with great loss to its defenders, and the governor of Toledo, Tello Fernández, was captured. Other districts were overrun, and the outpost of Toledo just beyond the Tajo, the castle of San Servando, was attacked though not taken. Toledo, fortress city and symbol, defied capture.[61]

Internal disorder denied Alfonso the luxury of immediate attention to Portugal as well. True, Afonso Henriques was largely preoccupied with establishing his own authority after the victory at São Mamede in 1128, but he found time by the fall of 1130 to politic in the Miño valley. This territory might eventually have become part of either kingdom given its geography. In September the Portuguese was in Villaza, a hamlet presently in the Spanish province of Orense, where he issued a charter confirmed by Bishop Diego

57. Lema Pueyo, *Colección*, pp. 331–52. Such an itinerary would be unusual but not impossible. Given the present state of criticism of the diplomas of Alfonso I it is not possible to reject any of the critical documents whose place of issuance suggests the route.

58. Marcelin Defourneaux, *Les français en Espagne aux XI et XII siècles*. (Paris, 1949), pp. 161–63, who is the only French historian to take the incident as historical.

59. Lema Pueyo, *Colección*, pp. 353–68.

60. Prudencio de Sandoval, *Chronica del inclito y bienaventurado famoso emperador de España, Don Alfonso VII deste nombre, rey de Castilla y León, hijo de Don Ramón de Borgona, y de Doña Urraca, reyna proprietaria de Castilla* (Madrid, 1600), p. 53, cites in some detail a charter of Alfonso VII that he connects with a campaign of the king in the south in 1130. This charter is otherwise unknown, and no place of issuance or date beyond the simple year is given. Sandoval seems to have been relying on the *CAI*, or some source related to it, in immediately adjacent portions of his *Chronica*, but the *CAI* places these events rather in 1131 and suggests no royal campaign against the Muslims in 1130. The charter could hardly have been of any other year than the latter, however, for it is confirmed by Arias as bishop-elect of Leon and by Tello Fernández. This last was a prisoner in Morocco by the late fall of that year. In general, the charter seems closely related to that of *Infanta* Sancha of May 15, 1130, for most of the same people confirm it. See note 78 above.

61. Maya Sánchez and Gil, *CAI*, pp. 201–2. Huici Miranda, "Contribución," pp. 609–10.

of Orense and by Abbot Pelayo of the monastery of Celanova.[62] These were major defections, but the options of the Leonese monarch were reduced when his aunt and the former queen of Portugal, Teresa, died on November 1, 1130, in her stronghold of Lanhoso, northeast of Braga.[63] No longer could Alfonso VII count on an incipient party of rebellion in the realm of his cousin.

But for the present, priority was given to the restoration of his kingdom's old borders with Aragón in the east. Alfonso perceived that his most important objectives and the most favorable opportunities then lay in that quarter. Even today it is difficult to quarrel with that political assessment.

Although a claim to preeminence among the Christian principalities of Iberia may have been implicit in the actions of the early kings of Asturias, clearly it was Alfonso VI of León-Castilla who initiated the practice of styling himself "Totius Hispaniae Imperator" early in his reign and had never ceased to use that title. Queen Urraca, after some early experimentation with the imperial title, preferred to call herself "Totius Hispaniae Regina." Her sometime husband, Alfonso I of Aragón, employed the imperial title at least occasionally for almost a decade and a half after his marriage to her. Alfonso VII adopted it from the outset of his reign. The title had never been less than an assertion of preeminence of rule on the part of León-Castilla over the miscellany of Iberian powers. It was at once the most compact of political manifestos and a practical declaration of the superior strength of that realm.[64] But from the irruption of the Almoravid empire there in 1086, the opportunity to translate the claim into reality had been denied by the necessarily defensive posture of León vis-à-vis both that power and the ambitions of Aragón. Although he asserted the title, Alfonso VII had been preoccupied by the challenges to his succession for five years. Now he began to seek its realization.

Conditions at the beginning of 1131 precluded exclusive concentration of effort, but the major target was the kingdom of Aragón. Symptomatic of this intent, by March 1131 the post of majordomo had passed from the Leonese Rodrigo Vermúdez to Lop López of the Riojan house of Haro. The new appointee might be expected to share more fully the desire of reclaiming those lost lands. Nevertheless, Alfonso spent the late winter of 1130–1131 at Compostela. Alfonso was engaged in shoring up his position in that far province (D125, 129). His intervention probably led to revolt in Portugal. Vermudo Pérez chose that year to rebel in his castle at Seia, roughly sixty-five kilometers

---

62. AHN, Códices, 986B, fol. 96; pub. *DMP*, 1–1:136. Sandoval, *Chronica*, p. 54, cites another charter of Afonso of the same date to the monastery of Celanova itself.

63. Monica Blocker-Walter, *Alfons I von Portugal* (Zurich, 1966), p. 152. Serrao, *História*, 1:81.

64. For a brief introduction to a tangled history see Bernard F. Reilly, *The Kingdom of León-Castilla under King Alfonso VI, 1065–1109* (Princeton, 1988), pp. 103–4.

northeast of Coimbra.[65] The Trastámara magnate was brother-in-law to the former queen, married to her daughter, Urraca Henriques, and brother-in-law to the Portuguese ruler. But Alfonso of León was too far away to intervene and Afonso Henriques acted vigorously, reducing the castle and forcing his sister and her husband into Galicia. Meanwhile, the Leonese king had journeyed to Palencia (D126–29). The town was but forty kilometers southeast of Castrojeriz and was the most convenient staging area for an attack.

Castrojeriz, a hamlet and fortress perched upon a rock rising out of the *meseta*, was the key to the remaining Aragonese position in Castilla. It lay athwart communications from Burgos, thirty-five kilometers to its east and north, and Palencia, as it did also on those from Burgos to Carrión de los Condes, another thirty-five kilometers to its west. Surrounded by a network of supporting castles, it was held for Alfonso of Aragón by a veteran castellan, Oriel García. The expulsion of Aragonese power from Castilla logically began there.

In May Alfonso VII moved against this complex, setting close siege to Castrojeriz by means of a wall built entirely about the position.[66] For the next five months he lay before the enemy stronghold, closing it off from supply and reinforcement. The Aragonese castellan finally sued to be permitted to send messengers to his king asking either to be reinforced or to be allowed to surrender. The Leonese agreed to these usual terms of the times, but Alfonso of Aragón, tied down before Bayonne in Gascony, could send no help. In October the Aragonese commander surrendered the complex (D132–33). Aragonese power west of the Sierra de la Demanda had been eradicated and La Rioja was the next objective.

Aragon held a strong position at Belorado on the lowest pass over the sierra and the road that led to Nájera and Logroño.[67] To the south a more arduous route over the Sorian highlands was defended by a complex of positions. The heart of the latter was Soria on the western side. The Aragonese king planned to include it in the jurisdiction of Bishop Michael of Tarazona. Soria was bolstered by the castle of San Esteban de Gormaz, on the Duero sixty kilometers to the west, and by Almazán, thirty-five kilometers to the south. To its rear on the highland road to Tarazona lay the fortified hamlet of Agreda.[68]

---

65. Blocker-Walter, *Alfons I*, p. 152.

66. We have a description of the campaign in Maya Sánchez and Gil, *CAI*, pp. 161–62. For once the *Chronica* dovetails closely with what we can see in the charters.

67. October 1131. Pub. Lema Pueyo, *Colección*, pp. 356–70.

68. May 11, 1132. Ibid., pp. 395–96. This diploma of Alfonso of Aragón is dated to 1136 in the thirteenth-century copy but its editor assigns it rather to this year on the basis of those who are cited.

Either route to the coveted lands of La Rioja promised hard fighting, but in late 1131 Alfonso VII found a way to flank the southern one partially. The Muslim princeling, Saif al-Dawla, was heir of the native Hūddid dynasty of Zaragoza, displaced by the Almoravids in 1110. From that time Saif al-Dawla had become a vassal of Alfonso *el Batallador*, cooperated in the Aragonese conquest of Zaragoza in 1118, and now held lands in and about Rueda de Jalón, only thirty-five kilometers from Zaragoza. The Muslim now chose to abandon his allegiance to Aragón and to cast his lot with León-Castilla. Accordingly, Zafolda, as the Christian chroniclers call him, surrendered his lands about Rueda to Alfonso VII in return for others south of the Duero and about Toledo.[69] If Alfonso VII could make good his occupation of Rueda de Jalón, he could bypass the Sorian complex and gain entrance to the valley of the Ebro. On the other hand, to attempt to occupy Rueda would be a daring undertaking with so many enemy positions to his rear. By the time that negotiations had been concluded, the year was far advanced and the Leonese wintered about León (D134–38).[70]

In May 1132, a month after Easter, the king was at Carrión de los Condes on the way to the east (D139–48). The rendezvous for the army was at Atienza, from which the king could strike either northeast against Almazán and Soria or east toward Rueda de Jalón. Alfonso of Aragón obviously anticipated a Leonese offensive that spring. From March through April he hovered in the Rioja about Logroño in case the enemy thrust should come by way of Belorado. In May he took up a position in Soria, aware by that time of Alfonso VII's concentration at Atienza. But by June the danger had passed and the Aragonese now busied himself elsewhere.[71]

What had disrupted the Leonese plans was a conspiracy discovered in camp at Atienza.[72] The object of the plot is not stated but the culprits are identified as Count Gonzalo Peláez of Asturias de Oviedo and Count Rodrigo Gómez of Asturias de Santillana, reputedly the former's kinsman. Count Gonzalo managed to escape and fled back to his province, but Count

69. Maya Sánchez and Gil, *CAI*, pp. 162–64. The account reads like an portion of a popular tale, is inserted under the annalistic account of 1131, and follows that of the siege of Castrojeriz. Apparently the submission took place sometime after October. The episode is also reported in Muslim sources. Francisco Codera, *Decadencia y desaparición de los almorávides en España* (Zaragoza, 1899), pp. 24–25.

70. A contemporary diploma of Afonso Henriques, October 26, 1131, pub. *DMP*, 1–1:142–43, has the Leonese still besieging Castrojeriz but one assumes that news of its fall had not yet reached the far west.

71. March-June, 1132. Pub. Lema Pueyo, *Colección*, pp. 388–401. The fifth of these six charters is obviously a forgery but the place of issuance, Novellas, may be accurate.

72. Maya Sánchez and Gil, *CAI*, pp. 164–65.

Rodrigo was arrested and deprived of his honors. So the tale goes, but it is difficult to see what the rebels had hoped to achieve. Moreover, if Count Rodrigo Gómez was implicated and disgraced it must have been a remarkably brief episode since he confirmed royal charters as late as May 28, 1132, and already again in January 1133 (D148, 160). Rodrigo had been a court figure from the beginning of the reign and had been entrusted with the province and elevated to comital rank after the fall of Count Rodrigo González in 1130.[73] He would enjoy a successful career at court and eventually become guardian of the youngest of the king's sons, García. The count was the son of Count Gómez González and member of a family long and solidly based in the north of Castilla and rivals to the Laras.[74] For his kinship to Gonzalo Peláez there is only the testimony of the *Chronica* although it may well be real.

More probably, the rebellion of Gonzalo Peláez consisted in the pressure that he had exerted when the king was busy with the revolt of the Lara counts, exacting comital status and the post of royal *alférez*. Alfonso VII may have chosen the occasion of the mustering of the host in Atienza, far from Asturias de Oviedo, to deprive him of the latter or both on the grounds of lèse-majesté. Count Rodrigo's guilt may have consisted in a protest against the arbitrariness of such a decision. Whatever the real substance of the matter, it had to be subsequent to March 8, 1132, when Gonzalo last appears as *alférez* (D146).

Clearly the king misjudged the mettle of his antagonist. Count Gonzalo's successful flight meant that Alfonso now had an actual rebellion on his hands, and more than likely there was sympathy for the rebel in other quarters. The king decided against pursuing the war with Aragón under those circumstances. Instead he moved north to Oviedo (D142, 150–52). That cathedral town was central to castles held by the rebel in the countryside. Its selection as a base of operations by Alfonso VII implies that he had moved into that province in such overwhelming strength as not to have to fear being besieged. Notwithstanding, the rebels offered stiff resistance. Some castles were taken by the royal forces, but others defied capture. Finally, the king was reduced to the humiliating expedient of extending a one-year's truce to the count. The king then repaired his position there by taking a daughter of one of its magnates as a mistress. This was Guntroda Pérez, daughter of Pedro Díaz and María Ordoñez, by whom he was to have his natural daughter Urraca Alfónsez. Guntroda's parents are identified with the western district of Asturias de

---

73. 1131 AHN, Códices, 105B, fol. 136r-v. This private document cites him with the comital title in Asturias de Santillana.

74. Julio González, *El reino de Castilla en la época de Alfonso VIII*, 3 vols. (Madrid, 1960), 1:336–37.

Oviedo about Tineo. A Pedro Díaz, distinct from the earlier rebel Pedro Díaz de Valle, frequently confirmed in the documents of Alfonso VII, and so the parents may have been court figures.

Afterward, the king returned to winter in the center of the realm (D154–55). In the east his father-in-law, Ramon Berenguer, had died in July 1131. The latter's son and successor was then seventeen and time must elapse before he became a valuable ally against Aragón. In the west his cousin, Afonso of Portugal, continued to seek to consolidate his position in the south of Galicia. For the moment, however, local forces had checked his advance.[75]

The campaign of the coming year was directed against the valley of the Tajo where the Almoravids had followed up the capture of the castle of Aceca in 1130 with a close harrying of Toledo in 1131. An ambush in its environs resulted in the defeat and death of the alcalde of Toledo, Guter Ermíldez, and the capture of the alcalde of the fortress of Mora, thirty kilometers to the south, Muño Alfónsez.[76] The crisis forced Alfonso VII to rehabilitate his old foe, Rodrigo González de Lara, and that formidable warrior was put in charge of the southern frontier as the new alcalde of Toledo (D153).[77] In the summer of 1132 the count led the local Christian forces deep into Almoravid territory, defeating and killing the governor of Sevilla not far from his own capital. A victory in La Mancha by the Almoravid heir, ibn Tāshufīn, over a small Toledan force later in the summer hardly redressed the balance. While the situation thus had righted itself to some extent, the king needed to give evidence of his own concern with the frontier and his role as chief warrior of the realm and paladin of the *reconquista*. He could not permit himself to be outshone by a mere vassal, and a recently rebellious one at that.

In 1133 Alfonso first tended his defenses in the northeast of Castilla (D156–62). From mid-January to mid-March the Leonese monarch was about León politicing and preparing to celebrate Easter on March 26. Three days after that feast, he was on his way south (D163–69). Fortunately, Alfonso VII was free from worry about his eastern frontier. Aragón's king had also set in motion a campaign against the Muslims. From the early spring of 1133 until

75. Serrao, *História*, 1:82.

76. The events of these two summers are related in both Christian and Muslim sources, not without some confusion. For a sure guide cf. Julio González, *Repoblación de Castilla la Nueva*, 2 vols. (Madrid, 1975–76), 1:136–38. The best guide to the Arabic sources is Ambrosio Huici Miranda, "Contribución," pp. 610–13. The accounts in Maya Sánchez and Gil, *CAI*, pp. 202–3 and 206–9, are chronologically difficult to follow because the author was probably reworking a popular tale.

77. A private document of February 3, 1133. Pub. Luis-Miguel Villar García, ed., *Documentación medieval de la catedral de Segovia, 1115–1300* (Salamanca, 1990), pp. 59–60, cites him as commanding there as well.

his defeat and death in the late summer of 1134, the Aragonese king was occupied with an attempt to overrun and annex the territories of Lérida.

The coincidence of Aragonese and Leonese interests and the complementary nature of their actions in 1133 suggest the possibility that their plans were concerted. One cannot be sure but Alfonso of León was in a location to communicate with the Aragonese in January 1133. Alfonso of Aragón, too, may have been in the same vicinity.[78] In March the latter was launching a river fleet on the Ebro at Zaragoza to transport and supply his troops busy with the sieges of Mequinenza and Fraga on the approaches to Lérida.[79]

The Leonese campaign was a brilliant success. Joined by his new ally Saif al-Dawla, the army invaded Andalucía in two wings, one commanded by Alfonso personally and the other by Count Rodrigo González. They swept the middle and lower valley of the Guadalquivir, from the lands about Córdoba, Carmona, and Sevilla, and proceeded on to Jérez de la Frontera and finally to Algeciras and the shores of the Mediterranean. They took no cities, except Jérez very briefly, but looted and burned through the countryside, carrying off livestock and other movables. Almoravid forces made little effort to oppose them and none to bring the main bodies to decisive combat. So marked was that fact that local Muslims made overtures to Saif al-Dawla to join forces and expel their impotent masters from Andalucía, upon which they would become tributaries of the Leonese king.[80] Alfonso returned to the north by perhaps by September (D176–77).

He now decided to put an end to the rebellion in Asturias de Oviedo. This initiative was made more necessary by the action of Pope Innocent II, who had excommunicated Bishop Alfonso of Oviedo. That prelate had been Alfonso VII's choice at the Council of Carrión, but the deposed Bishop Pelayo appealed to Rome. Despite that fact and in disregard of the immedi-

78. 1133. Pub. Lema Pueyo, *Colección*, pp. 428–30. It is a grant to the church of Santo Domingo de la Calzada without further date or place of issue, but the church itself lay on the pilgrimage road west from Aragonese to Leonese territory. On the other hand, Lema Pueyo, ibid., pp. 403–7, gives the text of three charters of January 1133, whose place of issuance is Fraga. The second two of these are unreliable for they give the Aragonese magnate García Ramírez as commanding in Tudela and Calatayud, but those towns were held by Count Rotrou of Perche and Jimeno Jiménez respectively at that date. The first of the charters seems unexceptionable, and it is possible that Alfonso I made a preliminary reconnaissance about Fraga.

79. March 1133. Pub. ibid., pp. 407–8. April 29, 1133. Pub. ibid., pp. 408–11, is a private document that would place the king, along with the Roman Cardinal Boso, in Pamplona at that date. The document is false, there being no record of a legation of the cardinal to Iberia so late. Some copies are dated rather to 1113 or 1123 but these are too early for Bishop Arnold of Huesca who also appears.

80. Maya Sánchez and Gil, *CAI*, pp. 165–68. The *Chronica* relates the events after the fashion of a popular tale. The episode as reported in the Muslim sources can be had from Huici Miranda, "Contribución," pp. 613–14.

ate jurisdiction of Rome over Oviedo, an exempt see, the king had allowed the consecration of Alfonso. Which of his bishops presided in that piece of effrontery is not clear, but Archbishop Raymond of Toledo was the probable culprit. Pope Innocent reacted by excommunicating the hapless Bishop Alfonso, which fact he announced in two letters to the bishops of the peninsula on March 1, 1133. It is probable that the king found this most unwelcome news awaiting him on his return from Andalucía.[81]

In late summer Alfonso VII traveled over the Cantabrians to resolve his difficulties in Asturias (D175–78).[82] There he served formal demand on Count Gonzalo for the surrender of the latter's three castles but was met by a blunt refusal. In the following battle for one of them at Proaza, twenty kilometers southwest of Oviedo, the king himself narrowly escaped serious injury. Alfonso decided that he could not tarry longer in Asturias, entrusting the struggle to Count Suero Vermúdez and Pedro Alfónsez. These magnates met with no more success and their sieges turned into a bloody guerrilla warfare in the territory. Two years later, the problem had again to be temporarily resolved by diplomacy.[83]

At this point both the *Chronica* and the charter record fail. What occupied the king during the winter of 1133–1134 is unknown The former occupies itself with the story of the last days of Alfonso of Aragón and the latter is largely a tissue of forgeries (D180–85). Most likely Alfonso VII was in Galicia during the early spring. In the preceding three years Afonso of Portugal had made constant inroads on the Miño valley. At first, he had been repelled by local forces but more recently he had constructed a castle at Celmes south of Orense that threatened the southerly route into Galicia from León. That was intolerable and Alfonso VII launched a quick stroke against the offending position, catching its defenders unprepared. The castle was taken within a few days along with numerous prisoners, and the king returned to León

81. The text of the letters appears in Falque Rey, *HC*, pp. 468–69. Doubtless Honorius's decision in this case had also been influenced by the similar disregard of his rights over the bishopric of León for Bishop Arías had also been consecrated by Archbishop Raymond. For a fuller treatment of this tangled aftermath of the Council of León of 1130 see Reilly, "On Getting to Be a Bishop," pp. 50–52.

82. The exact timing is difficult to resolve. Recuero Astray, *Alfonso VII*, pp. 115–18, has the king make two expeditions to Asturias, one before and one after his campaign in Andalucía. However, he does not take into account that charters concerning Asturias may be made in a court far distant from that territory. The narration in Maya Sánchez and Gil, *CAI*, pp. 170–71, places the entire matter after the Andalusian campaign.

83. Maya Sánchez and Gil, *CAI*, p. 170. Recuero Astray does violence to the text when he associates the later surrender of Count Gonzalo with the fall of 1133. As a result he then has to treat the private document of May 1, 1134, Pub. Floriano Llorente, *Colección*, pp. 300–301, as if it refers to a new revolt when in fact it describes the continuance of that of 1133.

in triumph. This episode is narrated in the *Chronica* in a section basically ordered on thematic rather than chronological grounds, but it is stated that the events occurred before the imperial coronation. The few royal charters of this period allow time for the episode in the spring of either 1134 or 1135, but the former seems more likely.[84]

Meanwhile, Alfonso I had first taken Mequinenza, on the Ebro forty kilometers south of Lérida, and then had advanced to lay siege to Fraga, some twenty-five kilometers south of the former. The Muslims of Lérida appealed to the governor of Valencia, ibn Gāniya, for assistance. He advanced to the attack and was initially repelled, but on July 17 a renewed attack, coupled with a sally on the part of the Fragans, overwhelmed the Aragonese. Viscount Centulle of Bigorre, castellan of Zaragoza, Bishop Pedro of Roda, and Bishop Arnold of Huesca all died on the field. Alfonso I himself barely escaped, mortally wounded. The king and his remaining followers found refuge in the castle of Poleñino, hard by the little hamlet of Sariñena, where Alfonso died on September 7, 1134.[85] Now Sariñena was only fifty-five kilometers from Fraga and no defensive positions of any account lay between the two. That the king should have lain there for seven weeks indicates two important facts. One is that the king's wounds were so serious that to move him to a militarily more secure position would have killed him outright. The other is that, even after their almost crushing victory, the enemy feared to take the offensive.

Despite the fears of contemporaries, the Almoravids were unable to exploit the rout at Fraga. The late winter of 1133–1134 had seen more Leonese and Castilian forces invade the Extremadura, advancing practically to Badajoz and gathering great booty before they were brought to bay and defeated by ibn Tāshufīn. Nothing discouraged by that repulse, the same sort of Christian forces once again invaded Extremadura in September and were again repulsed by ibn Tāshufīn in October.[86] These perhaps tied down forces that might have exploited the victory at Fraga.

In Aragón the death of its childless king and the simultaneous loss of most of its capable leadership threw that newly constructed kingdom into

84. Maya Sánchez and Gil, *CAI*, pp. 185–86. Recuero Astray, *Alfonso VII*, pp. 118–19, seems to place it rather in the spring of 1135.

85. Maya Sánchez and Gil, *CAI*, pp. 173–81, is the prime narrative source for this disaster and the confusion that ensued in the political affairs of the northeastern peninsula. Nonetheless, the need for caution in its use is emphasized by the fact that it lists as one of the fallen at Fraga Viscount Gaston of Bearn who had perished four years earlier in 1130 in another defeat. It also misdates the death of Alfonso I by some two weeks and places it in the monastery of San Juan de la Peña in old Aragón, far to the north of where it occurred.

86. Huici Miranda, "Contribución," pp. 616–17, supplies more of the details about these raids and corrects the chronology of the *CAI* on the basis of the various Muslim sources.

three years of confusion. But there was no rising of what must have been its still Muslim majority nor any threat from its Muslim neighbors to the east or south. The disintegration, partition, and absorption of the kingdom of Alfonso *el Batallador* was to be a function of its Christian neighbors. Even as Alfonso lay dying, his imperious nature brooked no reconsideration of the dispositions that he had already made for the future of his realm. The great king was childless, without wife, concubines, or mistress. While besieging Bayonne in October 1131 he had made a will dividing the realm he had spent his life so painstakingly aggrandizing between three religious bodies: the Templars, Hospitallers, and the canons of the Holy Sepulchre. On September 4, 1134, at Sariñena, he formally restated those provisions.[87] Contemporaries must have found such a project bizarre. All of these were new. No one knew what future they might have, particularly in the peninsula.

But if the king had died childless, he was not without heirs.[88] Of the four heirs of the blood who survived, the first claim to the realm was that of his brother, Ramiro. He had been closely associated with Alfonso's career and often had been an instrument of his policy. When the Aragonese monarch had been pursuing his hope of dominating León-Castilla he tried to install Ramiro first as abbot of Sahagún, and then as bishop of Burgos. Later he may have nominated him to the see of Pamplona. Certainly Ramiro had been a monk of the monastery of San Pedro el Viejo in Huesca. In 1134 he may have been at Fraga or may have joined his dying brother at Sariñena. In any event, subsequent to that battle, he was nominated by his brother to the episcopacy at Huesca left vacant with the death Bishop Arnold.[89]

Ramiro's immediate future, nevertheless, was to be anything but ecclesiastical. The *Chronica Adefonsi Imperatoris* tells us that the Aragonese nobles, soldiers, clergy, and people came together in Jaca after the death of Alfonso and elected Ramiro their king. They did this out of their perceived need for

---

87. Lema Pueyo, *Colección*, pp. 356–70, and 446–48. His personal life and the testament at its end have been the subject of much interpretation, but both remain something of a puzzle. See Elena Lourie, "The Will of Alfonso I, *el Batallador*, King of Aragón and Navarre: A Reassessment," *Speculum* 50 (1975): 635–51, and the critique of her argument by A. J. Forey, "The Will of Alfonso I of Aragón and Navarre," *Durham University Journal* 73 (1980): 59–65.
88. Antonio Ubieto Arteta, *Historia de Aragón; Creación y desarrollo de la corona de Aragón* (Zaragoza, 1987), pp. 80–81, for these and for much of the events that follow. For Ramiro II see Szabolcs de Vajay, "Ramire le moine et Agnès de Poitou," in *Mélanges offerts à René Crozet*, 2 vols. (Poitiers, 1966), 2:727–50.
89. ACA, Cancillería, Pergaminos, RB3, Carpeta 32, no. 262, is a possible original diploma of Alfonso I dated only to August 1134. It cites Bishop-elect Dodo of Roda who replaced Bishop Stephen also fallen in that bloody defeat. Lema Pueyo, *Colección*, pp. 443–44, published it from a twelfth-century copy in the cathedral archive of Roda. It is troubling that the place of issue is given as an unknown spot, Lizana.

a protector against the Muslims. Although the *Chronica* may be putting too formal a face on what may have been little more than a decision of survivors gathered about the body of *el Batallador*, in fact the first hard date we have for his reign is a charter that Ramiro II issued on September 11, 1134 in Jaca.[90] By the month's end the new king was in the greatest city of his realm, Zaragoza, acting very much the monarch.[91]

His rule was challenged almost immediately. García Ramírez, former castellan of the fortress of Monzón, was the great-great-grandson of Sancho el Mayor, although not in the legitimate line. He had survived the disaster of Fraga and accompanied his dying king to Sariñena. Probably he dissented from the first in the choice of Ramiro but needed to dissimulate his real feelings until he could find a course of action. Among the leading towns of the polyglot kingdom of the new Aragón was Pamplona, once the royal city of an independent Navarra but now increasingly a backwater in the age of Jaca, Huesca, and Zaragoza. It took García longer to reach Pamplona from Sariñena than it did Ramiro to reach Jaca, especially since he could not betray his purpose. But reach it he did, and before the end of the year he was himself granting diplomas as "king of the Pamplonans" and claiming the rule as well of Nájera, Alava, Vizcaya, Tudela, and Monzón.[92]

Yet a third claimant remained to be considered. Alfonso VII was, after all, a great-great-grandson of Sancho el Mayor. In addition, the Leonese monarch had a separate claim to La Rioja, going back to the partitions of 1076, and a lively interest in acquiring the city of Zaragoza and its territories, as had his predecessors.

Someone of those who surrounded the Aragonese king at his death on September 7 would have perceived a possible personal advantage in courting a predictable Leonese interest. But prudence would have been in order, and the distance was great; for example, from Sariñena to Carrión de los Condes, for example, it amounted to some 450 kilometers. Allowing for some initial hesitation, a reasonable estimate is that Alfonso VII could hardly have

90. Maya Sánchez and Gil, *CAI*, pp. 177–79. For the charter, Antonio Ubieto Arteta, ed., *Documentos de Ramiro II de Aragón* (Zaragoza, 1988), pp. 22–23.

91. Ibid., pp. 30–38. The first of these diplomas, that of September 30, 1134, bears the confirmation of Alfonso VII but it was done subsequently and not likely by any Leonese notary for it calls him "imperator Leonensis."

92. 1134. ACA, Cancillería, Registro 310, fol. 78r; pub. José María Lacarra, ed., "Documentos para el estudio de la reconquista y repoblación del valle del Ebro," *EEMCA* 5 (1952): 558–59. There is one other known charter of García dated 1134 but it is false. 1134. Pub. José Antonio Munita Loínaz, ed., *Libro Becerro del monasterio de Sta. Maria de La Oliva (Navarra); Colección documental, 1132–1500* (San Sebastián, 1984), pp. 38–39. Maya Sánchez and Gil, *CAI*, p. 179, speaks of García Ramírez as the choice of the Pamplonans and the Navarrese.

had the news much before the beginning of October. Preparations made, an adequate force would have required at least another two weeks to cover the ground from central León to Nájera.

Before departing, the king gave the orders necessary to mend the stubborn rebellion in Asturias de Oviedo; terms must be reached in the face of major problems and opportunities in the valley of the Ebro. Bishop Arías of León was despatched to join Suero Vermúdez and Pedro Alfónsez. The three then negotiated with the rebel and Gonzalo agreed to surrender his castles and return to court. Our narrative does not say when precisely this took place, but the fall of 1134 is likely. A private document of November 17 cites "Fernandus Gutterrez Iudex in Asturias" and Fernando was a curial official.[93] Moreover, none of the three royal negotiators accompanied the king to the east, although they were court figures. Count Gonzalo reappears at court in May of 1135.

Alfonso VII meanwhile departed for the east and by mid-November he was already at Nájera (D186–88).[94] There García Ramírez IV of Pamplona met him, did homage to Alfonso, and was recognized as legitimately holding the territories of Pamplona, Basque Alava and Vizcaya, and perhaps Tudela.[95] The Leonese monarch retained Nájera and the other lands on the west bank of the Ebro, Leonese from 1076 until 1112, and now definitively reverted to it. Alfonso diplomas began immediately to include Nájera in the list of realms appended to their dating formulas.

From Nájera, the Leonese king advanced down the Ebro to Zaragoza. He was met by Ramiro II of Aragón who gladly received Alfonso's promises of aid against the Muslims and ceded to him the "regnum Caesaraugustanum" in perpetuity. Possibly Alfonso did homage for these lands although that is a matter of dispute.[96] Likely Ramiro accompanied him to Zaragoza, although he does not appear in charters Alfonso granted there in December (D189–91). The Leonese was received in the city with great pomp but it was immediately apparent that the affairs of the disintegrating Aragón were of interest

93. Maya Sánchez and Gil, *CAI*, pp. 170–71, without specification of date. Floriano Llorente, *Colección*, pp. 303–4. The editor calls the private document an original but the orthography makes that doubtful. The terms for administrators of the royal fisc in this period are flexible. *Iudex, merinus,* and *villicus* all seem to be used interchangeably. Such fiscal officials usually enjoyed authority over adjacent districts as well.

94. Ferran Soldevila, ed., *Historia dels Catalans*, 2nd ed., 3 vols. (Barcelona, 1964), 1:150, has Alfonso enter Aragón by way of Agreda and Tarazona but gives no authority for it.

95. Maya Sánchez and Gil, *CAI*, p. 179.

96. Ibid., pp. 179–80. The charters of Ramiro II show him in and near Jaca in November but at some date in December he was in the village of Ejea de los Caballeros, northwest of Zaragoza, taking the route down the Ebro from Nájera to that metropolis. Antonio Ubieto Arteta, *Documentos*, pp. 44–58. On the question of the homage see Antonio Ubieto Arteta, *Historia de Aragon: Creación*, p. 108.

far beyond that kingdom. The diplomas show that the Leonese monarch had been joined by a considerable contingent of south French princes: his cousin Alfonso Jordan, Count of Toulouse, Count Bernard of Comminges, Count Roger II of Foix, and Count William of Montpellier. The powers of the northeast of the peninsula were represented by Count Armengol of Urgel and Count Arnau Mir of Pallars and the ecclesiastical interests by Archbishop Oleguer Bonestruga of Tarragona and by Bishop Guido of Lescar.

What these potentates discussed or decided is unknown, but, when their opinions and interests had been duly noted, Alfonso VII emerged as the master of the "regnum Caesaraugustana." The Viscountess Talesa, the widow of Viscount Gaston of Béarn, who had held that honor since the death of Centulle of Béarn at Fraga was replaced in December by Count Armengol VI of Urgel. As the grandson of the a Leonese magnate, the deceased Pedro Ansúrez, the count was doubtless acceptable to Alfonso of León. At least as early as January 20, 1135, however, the tenancy of that great city passed to Lop López, brother of Count Pedro López of Haro, a trusted member of the Leonese court.[97] In addition to the city itself, the lands west about Soria and Almazán, so often in dispute between Aragón and León-Castilla, passed now to the latter. Unlike Zaragoza, the latter were never to be reclaimed. In like fashion the territories to the west of Nájera about Oca and Belorado had already passed to León-Castilla. After two decades, the imperial domain of Aragón in the west was finally liquidated.

The question as to precisely how extensive a kingdom of Aragón he had been crowned must have disturbed Ramiro II in the winter of 1134–1135. In January 1135, in addition to the losses to León-Castilla, a new kingdom of Navarra centered about Pamplona and stretched south to Tudela, a mere seventy-five kilometers north of Zaragoza. García Ramírez was married to Margaret, either the daughter or the niece of that French Count Rotru of Perche who had been tenant of Tudela before his death at Fraga. That alone may have won him the city in the frenzied days immediately after the battle, or it may be that Alfonso of León had recognized him there. However it had occurred, the valley of the middle Ebro seemed lost to Aragón. Thus far, Ramiro II had been most cautious. He did not try to dispute the "regnum Caesaraugustana" with Alfonso VII nor had he formally claimed the old Navarrese lands. His diplomas claimed only Aragón, whatever that might be, and the eastern Pyrenaen counties of Sobrarbe and Ribagorza. In January Ramiro was ready to attempt something more.

97. Luis Rubio, ed., *Documentos del Pilar* (Zaragoza, 1971), p. 18.

That month his deputies and García Ramírez met at the little hamlet of Vadaluengo on the border of their then territories and near the heights of Leire, whose crags delimited the lands of old Aragón from those of the Pamplonese *contado*. They agreed that García Ramírez should continue to hold those lands actually in his possession but as the vassal of Ramiro II, to whom he now should be as a "son," presumably with the right of succession.[98] This solution agreed, Ramiro II was accepted in Pamplona with fitting ceremony. The arrangement endured from January until May of that year as the documents of Ramiro II attest. He styles himself king in Pamplona, which city García Ramírez rules "sub meum imperium."[99] Such a settlement could hardly have been fully pleasing to either party and was bound to raise questions in the Leonese kingdom. There is no evidence that Alfonso VII was party to its negotiation.

That monarch had remained in the northeast during January and into February (D194–95, 197–99). About that time, he confirmed an earlier charter of Alfonso I of Aragón. The latter indicates the presence in his entourage of Count Armengol VI of Urgel, destined to move into the Leonese orbit. Also present was Pedro Taresa, another great-great-grandson of Sancho el Mayor, and at least a potential claimant to the throne of Aragón.[100] Yet, unlike his rivals, the Leonese monarch could not devote his sole attention to that region. Between February and April he swung west as far as Zamora (D193, 200–203).

May found the king again in the Burgos area, moving toward La Rioja (D204–5, 207–8). There, probably shortly after May 5, Alfonso VII met with García Ramírez and the Navarrese yielded to either threat or persuasion. He deserted his recent alliance with Ramiro II and again became Alfonso's vassal. Beyond the now repeated Leonese recognition of García Ramírez as legitimate holder of Pamplona, the Basque provinces, and such other of the possessions of Ramiro beyond the Ebro that he should seize, the major concession that Alfonso appears to have made was to guarantee his possession of the town of Logroño on the middle Ebro. That budding monarch thus strengthened his hold on the east bank of the river down to his advance position at Tudela. But Alfonso required of García specifically military aid in return, and the former extended his protection to the possessions of Count Latro in the Basque country, to Lop Díaz of the house of Haro, and to Pedro Taresa. These magnates are explicitly said to have done the Leonese monarch homage.[101]

---

98. The details and the narratives that record and, one thinks, embellish them may be found in Antonio Ubieto Arteta, *Historia de Aragón: Creación*, pp. 114–18.

99. January 1135. Pub. Ubieto Arteta, *Documentos*, pp. 65–66. May 1135. Ibid., pp. 82–83.

100. January 10, 1135. Pub. Balparda, *Historia*, 2:353, n. 279.

101. The undated documents were subsequently copied into a thirteenth-century cartulary

Doubtless more particular dispositions were made at the same time, but we are only partially informed of them. For example, in May at Nájera the king made a grant to the influential magnate Fortún García confirmed by a wide variety of the local nobility. On May 14 a settlement of a dispute between the church of Tudela, controlled by García Ramírez, and the church of Tarazona, controlled by Alfonso, was concluded. The likelihood is that it was reached at Nájera and formed part of a more general adjudication of issues outstanding in the area. If this hypothesis is correct, then the meeting of the two monarchs at Nájera was attended as well by the archbishop of Tarragona, and the bishops of Nájera, Zaragoza, and Pamplona, in whose presence the latter accord was made.[102]

Then the Leonese monarch was ready to depart the Rioja for León where preparations were being made for his imperial coronation. This central declaration of the authority and might of the kingdom of León-Castilla in the peninsula took place in solemn council in the royal city on the days of May 25, 26, and 27, 1135, as we are informed by the *Chronica*.[103] On the opening day, the participants gathered in the cathedral of León, dedicated to the Blessed Virgin, for the liturgy and mass of conciliar initiation and to treat of spiritual matters. The following day was Pentecost. In the cathedral a golden and jeweled crown was placed on Alfonso's head, a scepter was placed in his hands, and he was led in procession to the high altar by King García Ramírez IV on his right hand and by Bishop Arías of León on his left to the chanting of "Te Deum laudantes."[104] Then the assembled multitude hailed him with the cry, "Vivat Adefonsus Imperator." The *Chronica* here says that he was blessed but does not specifically say that he was anointed. Afterward, the mass of the Holy Spirit was celebrated and all then repaired to their "tents." A great feast followed with the distribution of gifts to those in attendance, the clergy, and the poor.

On Monday, May 27, we are told, everyone gathered in the royal palaces to treat of the well-being of the "kingdom of all Spain." The "palaces" meant that complex of structures usually styled in the documents as the "towers of Leon" on the north side of the city. No formal acts of the council survive, but

---

of the church of Toledo. AHN, Códices, 996B, fol. 82r-v; pub. Hilda Grassotti, "Homenaje de García Ramírez a Alfonso VII," *CHE* 37–38 (1963), pp. 328–29.

102. May 1135. AGN, Documentos, signatura 11.019, Cartulario 3, pt. 2, pp. 205–6. May 14, 1135. Pub. José María Lacarra, "La iglesia de Tudela ante Tarazona y Pamplona," *EEMCA* 5 (1952): 423.

103. Maya Sánchez and Gil, *CAI*, pp. 182–84.

104. Writing a century later, Lucas of Túy, "Chronicon Mundi ab Origine Mundi usque ad Eram MCCLXXIV," in *Hispaniae Illustratae*, ed. Andreas Schottus, vol. 4 (Frankfurt, 1608), p. 103, will say that Alfonso placed the crown on his head himself. The *CAI* is vague.

the *Chronica* tells us that the good old laws of the days of Alfonso VI were restored, evil doing was forbidden, confiscated goods were ordered returned, justice was enjoined, and the officers and inhabitants of border districts were directed to make annual war on the Muslims. Then all departed rejoicing.

To this stylized and abbreviated account, important data can be added from the documents. First, the council was a council not simply of the realm of León-Castilla but of the new Leonese empire. The *Chronica* itself relates that, in addition to King García Ramírez IV of Pamplona, it was attended by Count Ramon Berenguer of Barcelona, Count Alfonso Jordan of Toulouse, the Muslim Saif al-Dawla, and by a multitude of the counts and dukes of France and Gascony. To the latter we can add with assurance only Count Armengol VI of Urgel. Among clerics, however, Bishop Guido of the Bearnese see of Lescar, Bishop García of Zaragoza, and Bishop Michael of Tarazona were in attendance. It is a safe assumption that Counts Bernard of Comminges, William of Montpellier, and Arnau Mir of Pallars, were there and perhaps even Count Roger of Foix. The political and familial histories of the north and south slopes of the Pyrenees had long been interlocked and now Alfonso VII hoped to become a major actor in that theater.

From the kingdom of León-Castilla proper, the council was attended by Queen Berengaria, by *infanta* Sancha, his sister, and by *infanta* Elvira, his aunt, by the archbishops of Toledo and of Santiago de Compostela, and by ten other bishops. At least ten counts were in attendance as well. In some strict sense, the council may have been terminated after three days, but few there would have seen the event in such legalistic terms. The documents indicate a great gathering still in process five days later on June 2. If some had departed, García Ramírez and the bishop of Lescar were still there (D206, 209–15, 218–20).

A contested election to the see of Salamanca was taken up and the king's chancellor, Archdeacon Berenguer of Toledo, was imposed as its new bishop. In this connection, we learn of the presence at León of the Roman cardinal-legate Guido, who does not otherwise appear in the documents. The council may also have seen the selection of a bishop to the vacant Galician see of Lugo.[105] Finally, with both dioceses now lying within his own kingdom, Alfonso was able to settle a longstanding dispute over the borders of the sees of Zaragoza and Sigüenza.

After the council, the newly made emperor began a tour of the center

105. Falque Rey, *HC*, pp. 499–502. The chronology seems correct for Berenguer begins to appear as bishop-elect of Salamanca in late summer of the year. For detailed commentary see Reilly, "Getting to Be a Bishop," pp. 53–56.

of his realm from Toro through Burgos. He was on his way to Pradilla del Ebro, northwest of Zaragoza, at the end of September. There Alfonso made a grant to the church of Zaragoza and García Ramírez confirmed it (D227). There as well he surrendered Zaragoza to the Navarrese monarch, who did homage for it.[106] The rationale behind such an extreme decision is impossible to recover. One can only speculate that Alfonso sought local aid against the growing strength of Ramiro II. But the exaction of so major a price would have been bitterly resented by the Leonese monarch whose only consolation would have been that the grant would bring García Ramírez into permanent reliance on León-Castilla. That monarch now faced the problem of attempting to control and defend a realm consisting of a long and narrow strip of land in the Ebro Valley, from Pamplona to Zaragoza against a more compact Aragón, which kingdom bordered it at every point on that frontier. Alfonso VII then retired though Nájera to Saldaña, Palencia, and finally to the royal castle of Coca, fifty kilometers south of Valladolid, where he remained into January (D228, 231, 233–41).

For fifteen months, the king had been largely preoccupied with the problems and opportunities arising from the sudden death of the king of Aragón and the disintegration of the latter's realm. These events had contributed to make his imperial coronation in León splendid and significant, but they had also made his presence beyond the Sierra de La Demanda more and more necessary. Given the virtual absence of any institutional frame of central government other than the royal court itself in León-Castilla at the time, these circumstances created a political vacuum in the other portions of the kingdom in which local initiatives, for better or worse, had free rein. Over an extended period of time, the latter would tend toward a practical anarchy which king and counselors could only regard with dismay and frustration. Nevertheless the only remedy at hand, the constant movement of the royal curia from one end of a kingdom now some 200,000 kilometers square to the other as necessity arose, created a strain on king and counselors that would ultimately prove insupportable.

The Leonese imperium then, as it had taken shape by the end of 1135, was inherently unstable. The hegemony to which it pretended was simply unenforceable in any practical sense. *Merinos*, castellans, counts, abbots, or bishops, even nobles, might well be royal officers but there existed no hier-

106. The first notice of the transfer of the city is a private document dated November 13, 1135, pub. Rubio, *Documentos*, p. 21. The first charter in which García himself cites his lordship in Zaragoza is dated March 1136. Pub. José María Jimeno Jurio, ed., *Documentos medievales artajoneses* (Pamplona, 1968), p. 205.

archy among them nor a royal officialdom responsible for their coordination. Their respective jurisdictions were, in fact, a jumble of custom and precedents, of property rights and claims of blood, of royal privilege and of canon law. Under such conditions, government was an art and a divination reserved to the king alone or to such as he expressly appointed for judgment of a particular controversy. If the personal attention of the king were too long diverted, these heterogeneous instruments became part of the problem, rather than its possible solution.

Assuredly, the crown was a moral force in the age. The entire history of the period testifies to that fundamental fact. That kingdoms should have had any political content at all under such conditions demonstrates that compliance and obedience need not always be enforced but could ordinarily be assumed. But direction was essential for continuing political cohesion, and it could come only from the person of the king. Social and political conflict increased anywhere in direct proportion to the length of time he was absent. These were the conditions that proved insuperable finally for the "empire" of León-Castilla in the middle of the twelfth century. In the long run, Alfonso VII had to depend too much on the moral authority of his crown. While it might hold together the already unwieldy bulk of Galicia, Asturias, León, and Castilla, and while it might find energy to reclaim the Rioja and add the developing new lands along the Toledan border, it could not simultaneously absorb the long-desired lands about the great city of Zaragoza, hold off the ambitions of Navarra and Aragón, and prevent the gradual but final secession of its Portuguese cousin. At such point as he should come to accept the inevitability of those limitations, Alfonso VII would have to devise a new policy to substitute for the dream of empire as he first seems to have envisioned it in 1135.

3

Toward a Concert of
Christian Princes: 1136–1145

WITHIN FOUR MONTHS of his imperial coronation Alfonso VII had begun to experience the chasm between his ambitions and his abilities to direct the course of events. On September 18, 1135, his cousin, Alfonso Jordan, count of Toulouse, did homage to Ramon Berenguer IV of Barcelona.[1] True enough, both princes were his allies and the form of the homage specifically safeguarded the obligations of the count to Alfonso VII, nevertheless, the drawing together of the two could not but react against the interests of León.

Worse, at Jaca on November 13, 1135, Ramiro II of Aragón had married Agnès of Poitou, the daughter of Duke William IX of Aquitaine. Given the most irregular status of the king himself and the power of his adversaries, only the promise of an heir of the blood would suffice to reassure his supporters that theirs was not a quixotic position. The fertility of Agnès seemed assured. She had already given birth to three sons by a former marriage to Viscount Aimery of Thouars (d. 1127). Then, too, her father was one of only two important supporters in the western Christian world of Pope Anacletus II against Pope Innocent II in the schism that had erupted at Rome in 1130. The latter could be expected, soon or late, to raise the question of Ramiro's claim to a kingdom willed by his brother to three religious bodies. As the weaker candidate to the papacy, Anacletus might be persuaded to take a reasonable view of the practicalities.[2]

---

1. Ferran Soldevila, *Historia dels Catalans*, 2nd ed., 3 vols. (Barcelona, 1962–64), 1:156.
2. Antonio Ubieto Arteta, *Historia de Aragón: Creación y desarrollo de la Corona de Aragón* (Zaragoza, 1987), pp. 128–32. This is the indispensable source for the details of the unlikely union of the two principalities. Szabolcs de Vajay, "Ramire le moine et Agnès de Poitou," *Mélanges offerts à René Crozet*, 2 vols. (Poitiers, 1966), 1:727–50, remains the basic study of the marriage itself. However, the first known royal diploma in which Agnès appears as queen is dated January 29, 1136, pub. Antonio Ubieto Arteta, ed., *Documentos de Ramiro II de Aragón* (Zaragoza, 1988), pp. 104–5, from what he styled an original.

Those most immediately affected by the marriage of Ramiro and Agnes were the allies of 1135, García Ramírez of Pamplona and Alfonso VII. The latter was in the center of his realm where news of the marriage had certainly reached him and possibly even the intelligence that the new queen of Aragón was pregnant. By that point, consultations between the kings of León and Pamplona were already in process. On March 15 Alfonso VII's sister, *Infanta* Sancha, made a grant to Bishop Sancho and the cathedral of Pamplona and the document was drawn up by one Arnold, canon of Pamplona (D241–46).[3] Alfonso confirmed the charter, so it was likely drawn up in Sahagún.

Subsequently, Alfonso and Berengaria traveled west to Zamora, where they celebrated their own important dynastic event. The men of Zamora were required to do homage to their firstborn son, Ramón, who was probably about seven or eight by then. This son did not survive until adulthood (D247–49). Quite possibly the recognition of the child as heir to the throne had begun in León at Easter and was being repeated in a circuit of the realm.

By the end of the month Alfonso was on the eastern frontier and spent the next five months the general area (D250–62). On August 24, 1136, a private document reveals his presence in Alagón, northwest of Zaragoza. There, he fundamentally reshaped his policy for the valley of the Ebro. The dating protocol cites a new bishop, William, as elect in Zaragoza and that Alfonso had returned that territory to Ramiro II of Aragón and his wife. The Leonese monarch confirmed the document.[4] Reflected here is the conclusion reached by Alfonso VII that his Navarrese ally of the previous year would be unable to defend Zaragoza against Ramiro, newly strengthened by the imminent birth of an heir to the crown.[5] It had become preferable to recognize Ramiro's title, to take control of its rich lands himself, and to do the Aragonese homage for them.

It has been argued that the essential stimulus to the Leonese change of policy was a bull of Innocent II calling on Alfonso to see that the will of the late Alfonso I was honored and the Aragonese kingdom distributed among the three religious claimants. But if that bull is dated to June 1136 rather than June 1135 then it is extremely unlikely that it had yet reached Iberia.[6] Given

---

3. AC Pamplona, Libro Redondo, fol. 62r-63r.

4. Pub. Luis Rubio, ed., *Documentos del Pilar* (Zaragoza, 1971), p. 22, who dated it to July 3, 1136. A copy of the twelfth century, this private document is confirmed by Alfonso VII and is strangely dated to both Monday, the feast of Saint Bartholomew, and to July 3, 1136. These cannot be reconciled, but the feast was celebrated on August 24 and that was a Monday in 1136.

5. If indeed the child had not already been born. We cannot be sure of the exact date of the accord and Ubieto Arteta, *Historia de Aragón: Creación*, p. 131, places the birth exactly on August 11, 1136.

6. Ibid., pp. 132–33. It is a rehearsal of his argument earlier in "Navarra-Aragón y la idea

the earlier date, it is difficult to detect any anxiety about papal wishes reflected in the policy of León in late 1135 and early 1136. It has been suggested alternatively that Alfonso's actions were the result of an attack on him by García Ramírez of Navarra in the spring of 1136. There is no evidence for such an event in the documents.[7] Rather Alfonso carried an offensive north against Navarra that produced only modest results. A private document, dated October 28, 1136, reveals that there had been a Leonese penetration as far north as Estella.[8] At this juncture, the Basque Count Latro defected to the Leonese. In 1136 García's charters cease to refer to the Basque provinces and only resume doing so in 1143.

At Burgos in the fall, a great council of the realm was held under the presidency of the cardinal-legate Guido (D263–64). The archbishops of Toledo and of Santiago de Compostela attended as did all fifteen living bishops of the realm proper. In addition, the newly reclaimed Ebro Valley was represented by the prelates of Calahorra and Tarazona and the bishop-elect of Zaragoza. The interests of the northern slope of the Pyrenees found voice in the person of the bishop of Oléron in Béarn certainly and perhaps the bishop of Tarbes, while the archbishop of Arles may have journied from the far-off valley of the Rhone.[9] The problems of the far west were discussed, for the archbishop of Braga and the bishop of Coimbra attended, while a new bishop of Oporto, João Peculiar, was elected there. An attempt to depose the archbishop of Santiago de Compostela failed, and a new bishop was chosen for the see of Mondoñedo.

A letter of the papal legate, Cardinal Guido, outlines the settlement of the boundary disputes between the episcopates of Burgos, Osma, Sigüenza, and Tarazona.[10] Another document cites the recognition by Alfonso VII of the new divisions established between the lands of the episcopates of Burgos, Osma, Sigüenza, and Zaragoza (D261). The see of Zaragoza received a new bishop, and its military defenses were addressed when on October 4

imperial de Alfonso VII de Castilla," *EEMCA* 6 (1956), pp. 41–82. For the bull of Innocent II see Paul Kehr, ed., "Papsturkunden in Spanien, I; Katalonien," *AGWG* 18 (1926): p. 318.

7. Alan John Forey, *The Templars in the Corona de Aragón* (London, 1973), p. 19, who bases his argument on the implications of his readings of the *Chronica Adefonsi Imperatoris* and of the *Historia Compostelana*.

8. Pub. José María Lacarra, ed., "Documentos para el estudio de la reconquista y la repoblación del valle de Ebro," *EEMCA* 3 (1947–48): 340–41.

9. The confirmations to the charter of Belchite by the prelates of Zaragoza, Tarbes, Arles, Palencia, and the cardinal-legate himself are all in a different ink, but it appears to me, the same hand. Nevertheless, we know from Guido's own letter that he and Bishop Pedro of Palencia were present so that these others probably were as well.

10. Pub. José Manuel Garrido Garrido, ed., *Documentación de la catedral de Burgos, 804–1133* (Burgos, 1983), pp. 205–6.

Alfonso VII renewed the privileges of the Confraternity of Belchite head-quartered forty kilometers southeast of the great city on the Ebro. That Iberian military order initially had been established by Alfonso I of Aragón in 1122 or 1123 not long after his conquest of Zaragoza. Apparently, it had not taken root, but in the aftermath of Fraga in 1134 there was a new urgency to see that it did (D264).[11]

Whatever dispositions the Leonese king made for the government of his lands in the valley of the Ebro continued to be challenged by Aragón and Navarra. In October the doughty king of Navarra was in Tudela at the southern edge of his realm. He apparently felt no need to retreat to the more defensible area about Pamplona in the north. There he entrusted the castle of Alfaro to Fortún López.[12] That fortress was situated about twenty kilometers north of Tudela on the western side of the Ebro, a prime position for the defense of that town against an attack from the Leonese center at Nájera. The noble whom García chose for that key position was the same man who, as tenant of Alfonso I of Aragón at Soria from 1127 to 1134 had been responsible for its defense against Alfonso VII. Another charter of García of 1136, granted to the Templars, suggests that he sought some settlement of their claim to his lands.[13]

Ramiro II of Aragón had internal interests to attend. The Almoravid governor of Valencia laid siege to Mequinenza on the lower Ebro at summer's end. A relief force from Zaragoza thought better of attempting to break the blockade, and the castellan at Mequinenza surrendered on the guarantee of safe conduct for himself and the garrison.[14]

Alfonso VII withdrew to Palencia to attend matters internal to the realm (D265–74). It is just possible that he moved south to Toledo to reorganize the defenses, for it had been a bad year there. Alī ibn Tāshufīn had surprised and defeated a force intended to establish a base south of Mora in La Mancha.[15] This rout could have served as the occasion to remove Count Rodrigo González from command. When exactly that change occurred is not clear, but the last known reference to Count Rodrigo holding Toledo is a private document of March 31, 1136. By April 1, 1137, another cites him as a tenant of Aguilar on the northern *meseta*.[16] On the other hand, it may be that the

11. For the dating and context of the original charter of Alfonso I see Bernard F. Reilly, *The Kingdom of León-Castilla under Queen Urraca, 1109–1126* (Princeton, 1982), pp. 171–73.

12. Pub. Ildefonso Rodríguez de Lama, ed., *Colección diplomática medieval de La Rioja: Documentos, 923–1168*, vol. 2 (Logroño, 1976), 2:175–76.

13. ACA, Cancillería, Registro 310, fol. 62r.

14. María J. Viguera, *Aragón musulmán* (Zaragoza, 1988), p. 244.

15. Julio González, *Repoblación de Castilla la Nueva*, 2 vols. (Madrid, 1975), 1:139.

16. Pub. José Antonio Fernández Flórez, ed., *Colección diplomática del monasterio de Sahagún, 1110–1199*, vol. 4 (León, 1991), pp. 151–52, who calls it an original. The second is published in José

removal of the old conspirator had to do with the internal politics of the realm. The king never trusted him, although he was sometimes forced to employ him. The count was dangerous because of his close relationship to the crown. He had been married to *Infanta* Sancha, daughter of Alfonso VI. His nephew and niece, Fernando and Elvira Pérez, were half brother and half sister to Alfonso VII by virtue of the marriage of Urraca to his deceased brother. Then on September 5, 1135, Rodrigo had married again, this time to Estefanía Armengol, daughter of Count Armengol VI of Urgel. Probably at the same time, Armengol married the daughter of Count Rodrigo by Sancha, Elvira Rodríguez de Lara. The Castilian magnate continued to be uncomfortably close to the throne.[17]

For two years after April 1137 the count disappears from the documents, although he had been a curial figure. The chronicler tells us that he went on crusade to the Holy Land after incurring royal disfavor. There he distinguished himself in battle and also raised a castle called "Toron" before the walls of Ascalon that he subsequently turned over to the Templars. When the count returned he was not received in León-Castilla, but spent his days first with Ramon Berenguer and then with García Ramírez, and finally with the Almoravid governor of Valencia, ibn Gāniya. There he contracted leprosy and returned to the Holy Land to die. This account is roughly accurate, if compressed.[18]

By the end of December, king and court had returned to Burgos where they remained for three months (D276–85). It is a gauge of the seriousness of the situation in the east that the court lingered in that area for such a length of time. But once more the affairs of his sprawling empire prevented full attention to any one point. Sometime after September 1136 Alī ibn Tāshufīn had led another army into the valley of the Tajo and had overrun and sacked Escalona, fifty kilometers northwest of Toledo.[19] Alfonso had to respond,

María Fernández Catón, ed., *Catalógo del archivo del monasterio de San Pedro de las Dueñas* (León, 1977), pp. 21–22. March 1, 1137. AD León, monasterio de Gradefes, no. 38, places him in Aguilar, but the dating formula is defective.

17. September 5, 1135. Pub. Manuel Mañueco Villalobos and José Zurita Nieto, eds., *Documentos de la Iglesia Colegial de Santa María la Mayor de Valladolid*, 2 vols. (Valladolid, 1917–20), 1:170–77, for the marriage contract of Count Rodrigo and Estefanía. José María Canal Sanchéz-Pagín, "Casamientos de los condes de Urgel en Castilla," *AEM* 19 (1989): 119–35, develops that relationship. Although most historians of the period have had something to say about Count Rodrigo, much of it is erroneous.

18. Antonio Maya Sánchez and Juan Gil, eds., *CAI*, p. 172 in *Chronica Hispana Saeculi XII* (Turnholt, 1990). Unfortunately the order of the chronicle is as often topical as chronological so that it is of little use in dating the affair.

19. González, *Repoblación*, 1:139–40. The campaign was dated only by year in the Muslim chronicle but it could hardly have been immediately subsequent to the campaign of Alfonso in early 1137.

and in mid-March he may already have been on his way south (D286). Muslim sources report his entry into the lands of the upper Guadalquivir about Baeza and Ubeda, where the army was much hampered by spring rains that went on continuously for twenty days.[20] The cavalry was unable to conduct its regular sweeps of the countryside because of the omnipresent mud. Rafts constructed to cross the river broke up and their occupants drowned. The operation had to be abandoned with little accomplished and by mid-May the emperor had moved north to Toledo (D287).

The two major chronicles of the time agree that García Ramirez of Navarra and Afonso Henriques of Portugal plotted to launch concerted attacks on León-Castilla in the spring of 1137.[21] At what point Alfonso became aware of them we do not know, but he dealt first with the Portuguese. Afonso I had been preparing the road north. Over a year earlier, he had made a generous grant to the Galician monastery of Tojos Outos only thirty kilometers southwest of Santiago de Compostela itself.[22] We must not suppose that it was the only instance of his penetration. Now he was able to secure the defection of two major Galician magnates, Count Gómez Nuñez who held the crucial territory of Toroño just north of Túy and Count Rodrigo Pérez of Trastámara.[23] With their assistance, Afonso captured Túy and overran the lower valley of the Miño.

The Portuguese leader may also have made his plans in concert with yet another Leonese defector. Since his surrender and return to court in the spring of 1135 matters had not gone well for Count Gonzalo Peláez, the old rebel of Asturias. Although he retained his comital dignity, at least some of his possessions had been confiscated and granted away by July of that year (D222). In December he was once more in rebellion in the castle of Buanga in Asturias, but he no longer posed the threat that he had earlier.[24] By March 9, 1136, he had returned to court (D243). He then appeared regularly in the royal charters, perhaps even so late as March 18, 1137 (D286). The *Chronica* tells us that during the period after 1135, Gonzalo was a court figure and was made tenant of the castle of Luna only to rebel again and to be put in chains

20. Ambrosio Huici Miranda, "Contribución al estudio de la dinastía almorávides: el gobierno de Tasfin ben Ali ben Yusuf en al-Andalus," pp. 605–21 in *Études d'orientalisme dédiés à la mémoire de Lévi-Provençal*, vol. 2 (Paris, 1962), p. 619.

21. Falque Rey, *HC*, pp. 519–20. Maya Sánchez and Gil, *CAI*, 184–87. The account of the Portuguese campaigns in the latter source is quite convoluted.

22. AHN, Clero, Carpeta 556, no. 2; and Códices, 1.002B, fol. 36r-v; pub. *DMP*, I–I:183–84.

23. For the identity of the latter see Simon Barton, "Sobre el conde Rodrigo Pérez 'el Velloso,'" *Estudios Mindonienses* 5 (1989): 653–61.

24. December, 1135. Pub. Pedro Floriano Llorente, ed., *Colección diplomática del monasterio de San Vicente de Oviedo* (Oviedo, 1968), pp. 305–7.

in the castle of Aguilar. Alfonso then exiled him and the count proceeded to the court of Afonso Henriques, which prince employed him in Galicia and Asturias until Gonzalo finally died in Portugal. His body was returned and buried in Oviedo.[25]

The Leonese king was probably at Palencia in early June when he received the news of the Portuguese attack (D288–89). If he left the former on the very day of June 2 and arrived in the latter on June 27, 500 kilometers later, he managed twenty kilometers a day over country rougher as one travels west. But the facts may have been even more remarkable. The *Historia Compostellana* tells of the last leg of the trip from Zamora to Túy, a distance of 352 kilometers by any feasible route. Alfonso traveled night and day with an escort of only a few knights and arrived in Túy in three days (D291–92). If accurate, that was a remarkable and daring feat. The sudden presence of the king must have abashed his enemies and rallied his allies for he entered that city without opposition. There he sent messengers summoning the magnates of the realm for he intended to invade and lay waste Portugal. His subjects in Galicia largely chose not to respond. Nevertheless, Alfonso rallied adequate forces without them for Afonso of Portugal abruptly agreed on July 4, 1137, to a treaty that put an end to all his gains of that season (D293).

The Portuguese prince became a "fidelis" of the emperor and guaranteed the security of all the latter's lands. He further accepted responsibility should any of his nobles violate the terms of peace and pledged aid to the emperor against the attack of any Christian or pagan king. The treaty was to be perpetual, the *infante* and 150 of his followers were to swear to it, and the archbishop of Braga, the bishop of Oporto, and the bishops of Segovia, Orense, and Túy, witnessed it. The audacity of the Leonese king had carried all before it. Moreover, the troublesome Portuguese prince had suddenly found troubles of his own. The Almoravid had launched an attack on the frontier fortress of Leiria and its fall would threaten the safety of Coimbra. During June and July Afonso Henriques was preoccupied there, but in October he was again courting the always receptive bishop of Túy.[26]

The Portuguese frontier quiet, the king rode north to Santiago de Compostela, where Archbishop Gelmírez received him with pomp and feasting. While Alfonso was still at Túy his emissaries had visited the archbishop to solicit military assistance and no less than 2,000 solidi for the campaign. Cer-

25. Maya Sánchez and Gil, *CAI*, pp. 170–71. None of this can be verified from the documents but likely it is roughly true.

26. Joaquim Veríssimo Serrão, *História de Portugal*, 3rd ed., vol. 1 (Lisbon, 1979), pp. 82–83. June 1137. *DMP*, 1–1:190–91. July 1137. Ibid., pp. 192–93. October 31, 1137. Ibid., pp. 199–200. Maya Sánchez and Gil, *CAI*, p. 187, puts the Portuguese losses at more than 250.

tainly the archepiscopal army never marched, and it is unclear that the subsidy was paid. When the king arrived at the shrine city he proceeded to raise funds at the expense of those who had conspired against the archbishop in the preceding spring. A royal grant to the cathedral of the properties of one of them, a "John the Lombard," dated July 17, 1137, was made for the payment by the archbishop to the king of 100 silver marks. We should not assume that this was an isolated sale. Indeed the king raised so much money that in a fit of euphoria, he excused the church of Santiago from the annual contribution that it owed to the cost of his government. Moreover, he himself promised to contribute some 200 gold pieces annually towards the cost of constructing the cloister of the cathedral.[27] This splendid act of generosity probably took place on Sunday, July 25, the feast day of Santiago. King and court continued in the city through July 29, 1137 (D294–97). Then he set out for Navarra to deal with the second princely invader of his realm. By October the emperor had reached Logroño (D278–79, 298–99). From that point, Leonese forces savaged the countryside of Navarra, taking castles and strongpoints, and burning grapevines and trees. The Basque Count Latro was captured and swore loyalty to Alfonso.[28]

This campaign lasted only four weeks, for by October 20 García Ramírez had sued for peace. The victor then moved though Nájera to San Millán de La Cogolla, where he participated in the consecration of the new monastic church, and finally back to Burgos by mid-November (D281, 302–8). There we find the first notice of Alfonso's son, Sancho, for a charter is granted to his *ayos* or guardians, Rodrigo Pérez and his wife, Marina Laínez. If Sancho was born in 1132, the timing would have been right for him to have been separated from the family proper for his early training.[29] At year's end the court moved west to Segovia and Salamanca (D309–10).

Alfonso VII must have been moderately pleased with the resolution of the conflicts with Portugal and Navarra but frustrated by his inability to establish firm control over the Ebro valley and Zaragoza. While he strained every resource to secure victory on the battlefield, such terms as he could command were too limited to be effective, given the political and geographical arenas in which he now must operate.

The summer of 1136 had seen the birth of a daughter, Petronila, to Ramiro II of Aragón and Agnès of Aquitaine, and 1137 had seen Petronila's betrothal to Ramon Berenguer of Barcelona and his recognition as regent for

27. Falque Rey, *HC*, pp. 520–23.
28. Maya Sánchez and Gil, *CAI*, p. 187.
29. Luciano Serrano, "Bérengère," *DHGE* 8 (1935), cols. 411–13.

Aragón. If the infant lived to consummate the marriage, any children born to them might rule a new political hybrid, Aragón-Barcelona, second only to León-Castilla among the Christian realms of the peninsula. Such a realm would have roughly half the size of the latter and about half the population. Unlike Navarra, it could not be pinned against the Pyrenees but would march south, more or less in concert with León-Castilla, as the reconquest progressed. Although the two realms would be only infrequently at war with one another, the mere existance of Aragón-Barcelona henceforth constituted the most powerful single determinant of political life in León-Castilla.

When the negotiations for the marriage pact had begun is impossible to say. Perhaps in the spring when Agnès's brother, Count William X of Aquitaine, was in the peninsula on pilgrimage to Santiago de Compostela where he died on April 3, 1137.[30] Although there is no record of the count's presence in the diplomas of Ramiro II, to consider his wishes would have been natural. Beginning August 11 and continuing through November 13, a number of documents record first the giving in marriage of the infant Petronila, the taking of oaths by the men of the realm to their new lord, and finally the formal grant of the governing power in Aragón on November 13, 1137, at El Castellar near Zaragoza.[31] Following these events, Queen Agnès returned to France and busied herself with the affairs of her sons by previous marriage. Sancho II retired into private life, although he did leave a subsequent documentary record.[32]

There is no evidence that Alfonso VII participated in these momentous decisions. The best hypothesis is that Ramiro and Ramon Berenguer seized the opportunity presented by the simultaneous invasion of Alfonso's lands by the Portuguese and the Navarrese to fashion a settlement. By the time Alfonso returned to the east, he was presented with a fait accompli while still at the war with Navarra. The Leonese king then recognized what he could not prevent and ceded the city of Zaragoza and some of its territories to the count of Barcelona, who did homage.[33] Subsequently the exact delimitation of these territories became a matter of much dispute.

30. Paul Marchegay and Emile Mabille, eds., "Chronicon Sancti Maxentii Pictavensis," *Chroniques des églises D'Anjou* (Paris, 1869), p. 432.

31. Ubieto Arteta, *Historia de Aragón: Creación*, pp. 138–55, relates the initiation of the union and prints all of the documents. Most of the latter are currently in the ACA in Barcelona and unfortunately none of them are originals. They were drafted by the count's notary, Pons, in a peculiar mixture of Aragonese and Barcelonan practice. While the large outlines of what took place in 1137 are clear, it is hard to avoid the suspicion that some of the particular terms were a product of later invention.

32. Ubieto Arteta, *Documentos*, pp. 147–50.

33. Vajay, "Ramire le moine," p. 745, n. 143. This is a private document of December 5, 1137,

The complicated politics of the reign of Aragón again tempted García Ramírez of Pamplona into action. He had, after all, a perfectly good claim of his own there and the new settlement might yet be disrupted. In the winter of 1137–1138 he made an attempt to seize the old royal city, Jaca.[34] Sometime in that year he also had the effrontery to grant a charter to San Juan de la Peña, the chief monastery and the pantheon of the Aragonese kings. In it he styled himself "king in Pamplona, Tudela, Logroño, in all of Navarra and in all the mountains."[35] Not yet "king of Aragón," but clearly García had hopes. By July of the same year it appeared that the Basque Count Latro had returned to the Aragonese camp.[36]

Where the king of León wintered is unknown. Such charters as exist are unreliable but may collectively place him at Carrión de los Condes. There he was waited on by a large delegation from Galicia, including the archbishop of Compostela, the bishop of Mondoñedo, and the abbots of Anteltares and of Tojos Outos (D311–18). Their business may have been those long negotiations described in the *Historia Compostellana*, the substance of which was that Alfonso VII again needed funds. He had come to regret the exemption he had so cavalierly made in Compostela in 1136. The revenues of the shrine were an obvious target and he was eventually to get some 500 silver marks from them.[37] The *Historia* does not mention the visit of Archbishop Diego to he court but it does specify the lapse of time between the imperial exemption and the new exactions in a way that would make that trip reasonable. Moreover, there is a reference in the imperial letter that ends the matter both to a council to be held in Palencia in October and to the royal intention subsequently to visit Archbishop Gelmírez in Compostela. Both of these events take place in 1138.

The king's need for funds was, of course, directly related to the problems of the eastern frontier and of Aragón. The charter of May 10 suggests the presence of the king's cousin, Count Alfonso Jordan of Toulouse, at court. Just the previous fall, the Toulousan had done homage to Count Ramon Berenguer and Alfonso VII was his liege lord. He had the perfect credentials for a mediator and was most likely the agent who arranged the conference that was to take place in September.

---

that cites Alfonso as having given the "potestas" there to the Barcelonan. Maya Sánchez and Gil, *CAI*, p. 181, mentions the enfeoffment of the count of Barcelona but typically puts it far too early.

34. Antonio Ubieto Arteta, ed., *Cartulario de Sant Cruz de la Serós* (Valencia, 1966), pp. 54–55. That monastery is just west of Jaca.

35. AHN, Clero, Carpeta 714, no. 1; a possible original.

36. July 1138. Pub. Santos A. García Larragueta, *El gran priorado de la Orden de San Juan de Jerusalén*, 2 vols. (Pamplona, 1957), 2:23–24.

37. Falque Rey, *HC*, pp. 523–29.

In the meantime, the king conducted a fairly extensive series of attacks on the Muslims of the south. The Alfonsine chronicle describes them in a way that would include that campaign about Ubeda and Baeza dated to 1137 in Muslim sources.[38] However, it also narrates an unsuccessful attack by Alfonso on Coria at the entrance to Muslim Extremadura, said to have occurred the same year. Certainly the latter campaign could not have taken place in 1137 when the Leonese monarch was busy with Portuguese affairs immediately after returning from upper Andalucía. It is doubtful as well that both could have been squeezed into 1138.

Alfonso VII surely attacked Coria during July 1138 without success. The chronicler vividly describes the initiation of the siege, the wasting by the besiegers of the countryside about Coria, and the sallies of its defenders that forced their attackers to draw off and to send for reinforcements. The siege lines were then drawn tight about the town, and machines were constructed to press it aggressively. Yet the siege went no better, and, in what may well have been a wider defeat than our source reveals, the Leonese magnate, Rodrigo Martínez, was killed while pressing the attack from a siege tower. Count Rodrigo had long been the castellan of the royal fortress in León and, practically speaking, the civil and military governor of the city. At this point, the king abandoned the siege and retired to Salamanca.

In mid-September he was in Almazán on the upper Duero south of Soria for an interview with Ramon Berenguer and García Ramírez. That conference of at least three days was attended by the bishops of Zaragoza, Tarazona, and Bearnese Lescar (D320–22).[39] Doubtless their considerations elaborated a temporary status quo in the Iberian northeast. Ramon Berenguer then passed to Zaragoza, where he granted a *fuero* to the men of that city and its territories with the counsel and consent of the barons of Aragón and of the *concejo* of the town. This is the first instance preserved of the Barcelonan acting alone and in his own name as "prince of the Aragonese." It also mentions that the city continued under the tenancy of Lop López of Haro, Alfonso VII's choice, who presumably retained the latter's confidence. That arrangement of ultimate suzerainty of León, the homage of Aragón-Barcelona for it, and its

38. Maya Sánchez and Gil, *CAI*, pp. 212–16. González, *Repoblación*, 1:141, accepts the 1138 date.

39. All of these individuals are among those who confirm these three grants to the cathedral of Sigüenza. Even before this interview, the parties were drawing together. June 5, 1138. Pub. Antonio Durán Gudiol, "La Santa Sede y los obispados de Huesca y Roda en la primera mitad del siglo XII," *AA* 13 (1965): 101, n. 25. This is an agreement between the bishops of Pamplona, Nájera, Tarazona, Huesca, and Gerona to create a confraternity for the defense of the peace and of Christianity. It is unlikely that the bishops would have dared to act without the approval of the three princes to whom they severally owed allegiance.

subinfeudation to someone acceptable to Alfonso VII endured through the remainder of the year.[40]

Alfonso VII moved to Burgos where the Basque Count Latro attended him and then to Villafranca de Oca in the Sierra de la Demanda. There he confirmed a *fuero* that his mother had made to the men of Atapuerca (D323–24). Later, Alfonso VII spent about two months in the center of his realm and at Palencia, presumably to hold that council of which Alfonso had written to Archbishop Gelmírez (D325–29). The monarch then undertook his promised journey to Santiago. Unfortunately the *Historia Compostellana* abruptly ends before that journey, and the historical trail grows singularly poorer. Possibly the king wintered there (D330–32).[41]

The modus vivendi in the northeast held for the year of 1139. The temporary reasonableness of other parties is displayed by a charter of Pedro Taresa, possible claimant to the throne of Aragón himself, yielding up a castle to the Templars, also claimants to a third of Aragón. In the dating formula, Pedro cites both García in Navarra and Count Ramon in Aragón.[42] Most surprising of all, a letter of Pope Innocent II of April 19, 1139, settling a dispute between the churches of Zaragoza and Huesca is addressed to Lop López and the citizens of Zaragoza. Implicitly the pontiff recognizes the jurisdiction of Alfonso VII's agent there and ignores the claims of the three religious groups of the will of *el Batallador*.[43]

Alfonso VII's decision to risk a major siege during the summer may reflect this calm in the northeast. At the same time, his Portuguese cousin, Afonso Henriques, would be fully occupied. The old chronicles allege that the Almoravids gathered forces from both Andalucía and Morocco for an invasion of Christian Portugal. Faced with intelligence of that fact, Afonso went over to the offensive himself and struck into the Muslim Alentejo. On July 25, 1139, the feast of Saint James "the Moorslayer," he was said to have scored a complete victory at Ourique.[44] Their inability to identify this place

40. October 18, 1138. Zaragoza. Pub. José María Lacarra, ed., "Documentos para el estudio de la reconquista y repoblación del valle del Ebro," *EEMCA* 2 (1946): 543–44. This is the *fuero* of Ramon Berenguer from a fourteenth-century copy in the archive of the city. November 1138. Ibid., 3 (1947–48), p. 593. A private document from the cartularies of the cathedral.

41. Earlier in the year, on February 28, 1138, the bishop of Túy had issued a charter reforming the life of his cathedral chapter. Possibly it was confirmed by Alfonso VII at this time (D313).

42. Marquis D'Albon, ed., *Cartulaire général de l'Ordre du Temple, 1119–1150* (Paris, 1913), p. 122.

43. Paul Kehr, ed., "Papsturkunden in Spanien, II: Navarra und Aragon," *AGWG* vol. 22 (1928),: 328–29.

44. Monica Blocker-Walter, *Alfons I von Portugal* (Zurich, 1966), pp. 153–54. The very location of "Aulic" or "Ourique" as well as the reality of the battle remains a matter of debate however. Serrão, *História*, pp. 83–84. Most recently, Ana Osabel Buescu, "O mito das origens da nacionalidade: O milagre de Ourique," *A Memória da Naçao* (Lisbon, 1991), pp. 49–69.

has long troubled Portuguese historians and the recent tendency has been to reject the entire incident. Still, it is difficult to imagine that the episode has no historical fundament.

Departing Palencia, Alfonso VII spent the spring, summer, and early fall of this year in the siege of the powerful Almoravid fortress of Colmenar de Oreja (D334–52). Located sixty kilometers northeast of Toledo and forty kilometers southeast of Madrid, it had been a standing threat to the supply lines of Toledo for the previous thirty years. The Alfonsine chronicle relates the siege at length.[45] Earlier in the year the king had ordered the local commanders, his former majordomo, Guter Fernández, and the latter's brother, Rodrigo Fernández, to assemble the troops of Toledo and those of the trans-Duero region, such as Salamanca, Avila, and Segovia, and open the siege. These scions of the house of Castro did so in April. Alfonso himself collected forces from León, Castilla, and Galicia and joined the siege in progress. He had arrived before the end of July and stayed until it fell in October.

The Almoravid governors of Córdoba, Sevilla, and Valencia, in turn, assembled their forces to waste the country about Toledo to compel Alfonso to lift the siege. Those efforts were unavailing, however, and they declined a direct assault on the strongly fortified Leonese positions about Colmenar de Oreja. They made a feint at Toledo to force Alfonso to draw off or to commit himself to battle in the open field, but he did neither. The chronicle also details a chivalric but unlikely episode in which Queen Berengaria verbally assailed their forces from the walls of Toledo for unmanly behavior in concentrating their forces against a mere woman.

Finally, the castellan of Oreja asked for a truce of one month, during which he would request help from Tāshufīn ibn Alī. Failing such relief, he would surrender. Such arrangements were quite usual and Alfonso agreed readily on the receipt of fifty hostages. The defenders were suffering from a scarcity of water but had acquitted themselves manfully, and the likelihood of taking their position by storm was remote. To bring the long siege to a

---

45. Maya Sánchez and Gil, *CAI*, pp. 218–24, dates the beginning of the siege in April and its end in October. Both the virtues and the vices of the chronicle lie (in my opinion which I may undertake to demonstrate fully one day) in the fact that the second book of the *CAI* is made up largely of a series of popular tales orignally composed separately and only subsequently tacked together in a literary, Latin text appended to the more traditional and staid annals that form most of its first book. The compiler has often scarcely bothered to reconcile his materials, much less treat them critically. For present purposes, its account of the siege of Oreja must be supplemented by Ambrosio Huici Miranda, *Historia musulmana de Valencia y de su región* 3 vols. (Valencia, 1969–70), 3:92–98. Randall Rogers, *Latin Siege Warfare in the Twelfth Century* (Oxford, 1992), p. 175, has an account of this siege and also of the later ones of Coria, Lisbon, Almeria, and Tortosa. Although he does not adduce new source materials he does place Iberian siege technologies in a wider context.

quick conclusion was increasingly desirable. When the messengers returned with news that no help was forthcoming, the surrender was duly made. The garrison was allowed to march south to the Muslim fortress at Calatrava and Alfonso provided an escort under Rodrigo Fernández, for the Toledans wished to massacre the defeated. Toledo and the emperor then celebrated with great rejoicing.

Colmenar de Oreja surrendered sometime between October 18, the date of the last imperial diploma granted before its walls, and October 26, when the latter had already returned to Toledo. The following day *Infanta* Sancha granted a charter to the monastery of Sahagún "in the year and month in which Oreja was captured" (D353–54). Since she probably had the news at Sahagún, a date close to October 20 is likely.

After two weeks, the king moved north and, in January, to Burgos, where he may have overseen the installation of its new bishop, Pedro Domín-guez (D355–61). The major concern of the coming year is indicated by his grant of a *fuero* to the hamlet of Salinas de Añana in Basque Alava. Count La-tro confirmed (D362). Routine occupied Alfonso until in February the main business for the coming year was concerted at Carrión de los Condes (D363–70). There a pact reached on February 21 provided for the partition of the kingdom of Navarra. Those of its territories held by Alfonso VI after 1076 should go to Alfonso VII. Those held by Aragón under Sancho Ramírez I and Pedro I were to go to Ramon Berenguer. The remainder was to be divided with one-third for León and two-thirds for Aragón-Barcelona. León would receive the portions about Estella and Pamplona. For his two-thirds, Ramon Berenguer would do such homage to Alfonso VII as Sancho Ramírez and Pedro I had done to Alfonso VI. The monarchs of the two major Christian powers were preparing a radical simplification of affairs in the northeast. Navarra was to disappear (D371).[46]

The execution of this design was then left for the fall and for his Barce-lonan ally, for by May Alfonso was in Berlanga near the Duero and then in Atienza, thirty kilometers farther south (D372–75). Even so, he was busy with the affairs of the northeast. A charter granted at the latter location re-

---

46. ACA, Cancillería, Ramon Berenguer IV, Carpeta 35, no. 96, a twelfth-century copy; Carpeta 36, no. 134, a thirteenth-century copy. The first is dated to A.D. 1139 but to 1140 in the Spanish Era. The latter is dated to A.D. 1139 but to 1141 in the Spanish Era. Because Bishop-elect Pedro Domínguez of Burgos is a confirmant, 1139 is impossible. Because Berenguer confirmed as bishop of Salamanca, 1141 is impossible. By then, Berenguer was claimant to the see of Santiago de Compostela. Francisco M. Rosell, ed., *Liber Feudorum Maior* (Barcelona, 1945), pp. 37–38, published it under the date of 1141. Antonio Ubieto Arteta, "Homenaje de Aragón a Castilla por el condado de 'Navarra,'" *EEMCA* 3 (1947–48): 14, n. 13, said that the original was then in the cathedral archive of Jaca, Legajo 1, no. 13, but I have not been able to verify that fact.

veals the presence at his court of the grand master of the Hospitalers, Ramon. Doubtless the terms of the surrender of that order's rights in Aragón under the will of Alfonso I were being negotiated. To facilitate matters, the king was prepared to be generous as Ramon continued at court for a month (D376–79). Not before the end of July was the Leonese back in the northeast.[47]

There his lieutenants had been harrying the territories of García Ramírez, up to Pamplona itself, with great effect. These activities had been coordinated with that of Ramon Berenguer, whose troops had also penetrated the environs of Pamplona.[48] Subsequently, however, the Barcelonan suffered defeat at the hands of the Navarrese near Ejea de los Caballeros. Alfonso thus was forced personally to campaign in the middle Rioja until peace was reached with Navarra at the end of October (D390–94).[49] As so frequently was the case, the reconciliation was dynastic. Margaret, daughter of Rotrou of Perche, wife of García Ramírez, had recently died.[50] Her decease left the Navarrese free to hold out a valuable marriage alliance to interested parties. The Leonese king found the eventual prospect of the peaceful acquisition of Navarra an acceptable alternative to outright conquest. It was agreed that García Rámirez would be wed to the daughter of Alfonso VII by his Asturian mistress Guntroda Pérez, Urraca. The young *infanta* may then have been as much as eight years old. That age would accord well with the date of the actual marriage, which took place in 1144 at which time Urraca would have reached twelve years, the canonical age for the marriage of women.

47. July 29, 1140. Logroño. Pub. Luciano Serrano, *El obispado de Burgos y Castilla primitiva desde el siglo V al XIII*, 3 vols. (Madrid, 1935), 3:181–82, who dated it to 1141 on the basis of the confirmation of Pedro of Burgos and Juan of León, both as bishops-elect. The dating formula of the twelfth-century copy of the royal grant to the monastery of San Miguel de Escalada actually reads 1133 but it also is dated to the sixth year since Alfonso's imperial coronation in late May 1135, which event yields rather 1140 (D389). Both bishops were already elect in that year.
48. The account of this campaign in the Alfonsine chronicle is rivaled only by its contemporary treatment of matters in Portugal for sheer chronological confusion. It here has Alfonso returning from Galicia to begin it and later will have the count of Toulouse intervening to bring about a royal marriage alliance. There is no record of the presence of Alfonso Jordan in Iberia in 1140, nor is there any reliable record of the Leonese monarch in Galicia unless he spent the Christmas season there which seems unlikely. Maya Sánchez and Gil, *CAI*, pp. 190–91. For the participation of Aragón-Barcelona, October 8, 1140, Lacarra, "Documentos," 3:598–99. November 1141. Pub. Antonio Durán Gudiol, ed., *Colección diplomática de la catedral de Huesca*, vol. 1 (Zaragoza, 1965), p. 178, is a copy of a private document that is dated "in the year when that count and that emperor were with their army in Pamplona." It should be redated to 1140, for the known itinerary of Alfonso VII precludes his having been again in or near Pamplona after November 1140.
49. For the setback of Ramón Berenguer, September 2, 1140. Pub. Lacarra, "Documentos," 3:598. It is possible that this document is dated a year too early. The *CAI* also mentions a resounding defeat of his ally that had to be remedied by Alfonso VII.
50. May 1141. Pub. Angel J. Martín Duque, ed., *Documentación medieval de Leire; siglos IX al XII* (Pamplona, 1983), pp. 413–14, a charter of García Ramírez mentions in its dating formula the death of the queen within the past year. May 20–31, 1141. Ibid., pp. 412–13, another grant of that king mentions the queen as still living. It is false.

This treaty marked the end of Alfonso's immediate plans for the dismemberment of Navarra, although that was an idea to which he and his successors periodically returned. García did do homage to the Leonese king. Perhaps as a result Alfonso VII agreed that the Basque provinces be returned to Navarra, although it was not for another two years that García began to cite them in his charters.[51]

While this development could not have been pleasing to Ramon Berenguer IV, it did not work directly to his prejudice. His hold on old Aragón or on Zaragoza was not called into question. He himself was not yet reconciled with García Rámirez IV and the two continued to wage war, without any great effect, for two years. The Barcelonan was busier settling the claims of the Hospitallers and the canons of the Holy Sepulcher to his new realm. On September 16, 1140, those organizations surrendered their legal rights under the will of Alfonso I.[52] The position of the new Prince of Aragón thus went from strength to strength and this could not but come to strain his relations with his brother-in-law. For the moment, however, no conflict was evident, and Lop López continued in control of the Zaragozan lands. Alfonso VII continued in the east about Soria during the month of November (D394–96).

By the close of 1140 the king of León-Castilla had spent the five years since his imperial coronation attempting to find a legal and practical framework within which the new political realities of Christian Iberia could be subsumed. He had managed by that date to create circumstances in which the princes of Portugal, Navarra, and Aragón-Barcelona had all agreed to do him homage. Nevertheless, it must have become increasingly clear that such feudal restraint had little practical effect on their several ambitions. The most recent attempt to simply absorb, even jointly with Aragón-Barcelona, the realm of Navarra had proved beyond the resources that either of the aggrandizing parties could reasonably devote to it. Ramon Berenguer, while sometimes an ally, went on gradually strengthening his own control over most of the territories of Aragón. In Portugal, Afonso Henriques behaved as an independent monarch.

At the same time, in León-Castilla itself, the king-emperor possessed an

51. Gregorio de Balparda y las Herrarias, *Historia crítica de Vizcaya y de sus fueros*, 2 vols. (Madrid, 1924, and Bilbao, 1933–34), 2:349–51. It should be noted that the diplomas of García are very few for 1141 and 1142.
52. García Larragueta, *Gran Priorado*, p. 41. Negotiations were helped along by the fact that the prior of the canons of the Holy Sepulchre at the time was Pedro of Barcelona (1130–1158). William, Archbishop of Tyre, *A History of Deeds Done beyond the Sea*, vol. 1, trans. Emily Atwater Babcock and A. C. Krey (New York, 1943), p. 9.

increasingly unwieldy landmass to whose four diverse and constituent parts, Asturias, Galicia, the Duero Basin, and the Tajo Basin, La Rioja had now been reannexed. These he must attempt to rule without benefit of an organized officialdom, in competition with a nobility of growing strength and confidence, and sometimes in concert with a church engaged in its own reorganization and newly in contact with a revitalized papacy. To none of these realities did the imperial conception have a significant relevance. The fundamental allegiance of all of them was rather to a dynasty legitimate in and of itself. Moreover, as Alfonso was cousin of the Portuguese ruler, brother-in-law to the prince of Aragón-Barcelona, and soon-to-be father-in-law of the king of Navarra, the dynasty was central to Christian affairs in the peninsula as well as in the kingdom. The empire was an episode. No more than his predecessors or his successors for long centuries could Alfonso VII escape the ineluctable finality of dynastic politics.

As the new year began, the peace restored through exhaustion and compromise the previous fall proved more durable than perhaps anyone expected. García Ramírez of Navarra must have been happy for a respite, although he had acquitted himself valiantly in the year just past. His diplomas betray no new claims or initiatives. He did mend affairs with the monastery of Leire on his eastern border.[53] He was also generous to the Templars. Indeed there was something of a rash of donations to the Temple.[54] We suspect that these are individual contributions to a general settlement being worked out with the Templar claims under the will of Alfonso I.

Ramon Berenguer was content to let his legitimacy in his new realms grow with time. Private documents of Zaragoza routinely acknowledge both the suzerainty of the Barcelonan and the practical control of Lop López. One reveals that the hold of Alfonso of León over Rueda de Jalón on the very doorstep of Zaragoza continued.[55] At the end of the year, the prince of Aragón granted the castle of Bascués to Lop López, indicating that his confidence in him remained high.[56] While it has been asserted that the former continued hostilities with Navarra, even again penetrating to Pamplona itself, the evidence is slight and more likely refers to the campaign of the preced-

---

53. 1141. Pub. Martín Duque, *Documentación*, pp. 415–16.

54. February 2, 1141. Tudela. Pub. Lacarra, "Documentos," 5:568. March 1141. Cited Albon, *Cartulaire*, p. 155, is a grant by Pedro Teresa and his mother. June 3, 1141. Cited ibid., p. 160, is a grant by Pedro Pérez and his wife.

55. March 2, 1141. Pub. Rubio, *Documentos*, p. 30.

56. December, 1141. Huesca. Pub. Rubio, *Documentos*, pp. 29–30, who calls it an original and dates it to 1140. Lacarra, "Documentos," 3:604–5, dated it to 1141. I think it must be a copyist's error for it cites the ferial day but not the day itself. Moreover, the citation of Count Rodrigo González of Lara as commanding in Huesca is better reconciled with 1141.

ing year.[57] Despite this quiet, Alfonso VII made a substantial tour of the area early in the year (D397–405).

Major events of the year, however, took place in the far west. In April Alfonso began to move from Carrión de los Condes through León to Zamora and there made a grant to the monastery of Celanova (D406–8). Now that house is located in the hills south of Orense in Galicia and north of the Limia, which river flows southwestward into Portugal. This route from Galicia into Portugal was not easy, but it was practical for a mounted raiding party. For that reason the loyalty of the abbot of Celanova was a matter of concern to both realms. In all probability the grant of the castle of Sandi to Celanova followed on the appearance at the court of the abbot or some of his monks, in the company of the Galician magnate Fernándo Yáñez bearing disquieting news about the activities of Afonso Henriques. Possibly as early as February of the preceding year, he had begun to style himself *rex* and then *rex Portugalensium* in his diplomas.[58] Previously, he had been content to employ the title of *infante* and to stress his lineage as scion of the royal house of León-Castilla. It is just possible that the change was made following his major victory over the Muslims, one cited by the old chronicles, at Ourique in July 1139. On the other hand, his mother, Teresa, had made the same change in 1117 when the reconciliation of her sister Urraca with the future Alfonso VII had distanced her yet further from the throne of León-Castilla.[59] Thus the attainment of six years of age by Alfonso's son Sancho or the birth of another male heir, Fernando, had convinced their Portuguese uncle that he no longer had a real prospect of inheriting the greater throne, and so he set about fashioning a lesser one.

Such a change of policy would have been reported to Alfonso VII fairly swiftly for important people fished in these troubled waters. The Galician magnates, Count Rodrigo Pérez and Count Gómez Nuñez, were negotiating with the new king. Count Gómez would subsequently go into exile and end a monk at Cluny after a new round of fighting between the princes had resulted in a patched up peace. The Count Rodrigo would be pardoned, for the power of his family was so great that a major affront to it was almost unthink-

---

57. July 1, 1141. Pub. Lacarra, "Documentos," 3:601–2, from a thirteenth-century copy. The document is a strange mixture of a private and a comital one.

58. Rui Pinto de Azevado, ed., *DMP*, vol. 1 (Lisbon, 1958) 1–1:214–24. Much depends upon the rigor with which the Portuguese royal charters are assessed when one attempts to divine Afonso's precise intentions. Maria João Violante Branco Marques da Silva, "Portugal no reino de León. Etapas de uma relação (866–1179)," in *El Reino de León en la Alta Edad Media*, vol. 4, *La Monarquia, 1109–1230* (León, 1993), pp. 604–21, synthesizes the more recent opinions of Portuguese historians.

59. Bernard F. Reilly, *The Kingdom of León-Castilla under Queen Urraca, 1109–1126* (Princeton, 1982), pp. 117–18.

able, but he was kept at court, isolated from the intrigues of the northwest.[60] The treason that eventually brought the two counts into royal disfavor issued in an invasion north of the Miño River by the Portuguese prince in 1141. The Leonese monarch learned of this activity at Zamora and shortly advanced into Portugal.

Both accounts of the campaign agree that the Leonese monarch crossed the Miño and established his base camp about modern Arcos de Valdevez, not far north of the Limia River. From there his troops fanned out in raiding parties that wasted the land in an effort to force his Portuguese cousin to commit to battle. But Afonso Henriques contrived to isolate and soundly defeat a major party of Leonese troops, perhaps returning from just such a raid. The *Chronica Adefonsi Imperatoris* admits to the capture of Count Ramiro Froílaz, but the Portuguese source speaks of the capture as well of the magnates Pons de Cabrera, Vermudo Pérez, and others including the half brother of Alfonso VII, Fernando Pérez.

Clearly, the Leonese had suffered a major setback and the Portuguese king prepared to lay siege to his cousin's camp. Alfonso VII chose to request the good offices of the archbishop of Braga to arrange a peace. Fortunately, the Almoravid had taken advantage of the preoccupation of the Portuguese to attack and reduce the castle of Leiria south of Coimbra. Its fall laid the valley of the Mondego and Coimbra itself open to Muslim raids. Under these circumstances peace was concluded in the north with a mutual exchange of positions and persons captured.

On that unhappy note, Alfonso VII evacuated Portugal and moved north to Santiago de Compostela, to pray, we are told. Negotiations negotiations were surely part of the reason of his visit, however, since the question of a new archbishop for that see was still unsettled. The Compostelan was as much a power as a prelate in Galicia, and since the Portuguese frontier obviously would remain critical, that office must be filled as quickly as possible. Nevertheless, we know only that Alfonso was there in late September when he made a grant to the monastery of Antealtares in Compostela. The king was still supporting his own candidate as evidenced by the confirmation of the grant by Berenguer as archbishop-elect (D413).

In October the king returned to the center of his realm about Palencia

60. Maya Sánchez and Gil, *CAI*, pp. 188–90. The *Chronica* seems well informed of the details of this episode although at an almost complete loss as to its chronology. To compound the difficulty, the major Portuguese source, most recently edited in Blocker-Walter, *Alfons I*, pp. 154–55, dates it a year too soon. For an account in the light of most recent Portuguese scholarship see Serrão, *História*, 1:86.

(D414–15). After that date, the whereabouts of the king become problematic. The *Chronica* said that from the Portuguese campaign and the visit to Compostela Alfonso proceeded to the northeast frontier, where he wasted the territories of Navarra once more. But that section of the *Chronica* is notoriously unreliable so far as chronology is concerned, there is no other confirmation of a Leonese campaign against Navarra in that year and, given the peace arranged the previous year, one is unlikely. Nevertheless, there is a royal charter granting *fueros* to the inhabitants of Santo Domingo de la Calzada dated in November 3, 1141, in Nájera (D416).

This charter is confirmed by that old rebel, Count Rodrigo González. The *Chronica* asserted that after his departure on crusade in 1137 that count never returned to León-Castilla. But there are two other documents of this year that place the count in Castilla and La Rioja briefly. One is a private charter in which he and others of his family made a donation to the Castilian monastery of Arlanza.[61] The other is the royal grant to the monastery of San Millán, dated only to 1141 (D397). Moreover, a third document of December 1141 cites the count as castellan in Aragonese Huesca.[62] The *Chronica Adefonsi Imperatoris* states that Rodrigo did visit the realms of Ramon Berenguer and García Ramírez, but these are the first documentary confirmations of that assertion. Count Rodrigo was dead by February 15, 1143, when his widow made a grant to the monastery of Valbuena.[63] He may then have been fishing in the troubled waters of the northeast and, finding no prospect of rehabilitation, attended to some family affairs before departing for Valencia to explore possibilities. If that premise is accepted, then the likelihood of Alfonso's presence in La Rioja, to politic if not to fight, is much enhanced.

The respite allowed Alfonso to remove another Muslim salient in the south through the conquest of Coria in the Leonese Extremadura. His Portuguese cousin was simultaneously very active strengthening Leiria, its all-important castle, and the castle at Penela closer yet to Coimbra.[64] During that year as well, a flotilla of crusaders and pilgrims from the north of Europe appeared off the coast of Portugal and a bargain was struck with them for a joint attack on Muslim Lisbon. The venture did not issue in success, as a similar venture did some five years later, but Afonso Henriques kept the initiative throughout the year.[65] Possibly the efforts of the cousins against the

61. Luciano Serrano, ed., *Cartulario de San Pedro de Arlanza* (Madrid, 1925), pp. 187–89.
62. Pub. Rubio, *Documentos*, pp. 29–30.
63. See note 4 and Maya Sánchez and Gil, *CAI*, p. 172. For the charter of his widow see Julio González, *El reino de Castilla en la época de Alfonso VIII*, 3 vols. (Madrid, 1960), 1:262.
64. *DMP*, 1-1:233–36.
65. Serrao, *História*, pp. 86–87.

Almoravids were coordinated. In late March the sister of the Portuguese king was at Zamora, where she made a grant of lands that she held in León to Albertino and his wife. Albertino was one of Alfonso VII's trusted aides and father to the new bishop, Juan, of León. Surely some sort of negotiations were in train.[66]

The king of León is invisible before he appears at the siege of Coria in the spring (D417–24). Probably the time for the assembly of the army was Easter on April 19 and the place Valladolid, a town central to the realm yet on the way to the objective. Alfonso VII had reached Coria by the early part of May or well before, for hunger was swiftly to become a major problem for the besieged. That means that the attackers invested the city before the winter wheat crop was harvested (D425–28).[67] Quickly camps were established about the town, and towers and siege machines were constructed. There was to be no repetition of the fiasco of 1138, and this time the garrison of Coria did not attempt to sally beyond the walls. Before the end of May, they had decided that resistance out of their own resources would be futile and had asked for a thirty-day truce on condition that they would surrender the city if help did not arrive. Alfonso agreed and the usual embassy was despatched to make the rounds of the governors of al-Andalus and even to visit the emir Alī ibn Yūsuf in Morocco to plead for help. None was forthcoming, and the city surrendered before the end of June.[68]

The fall of that city, whose position controlled the entry from the plains of the lower Tajo and the territories of Badajoz onto the plain of the Duero, was a matter for great rejoicing. The chronicle implies that the Muslim population was expelled immediately and a bishop was elected to a restored see of Coria on the spot. King and court then moved northeast to Salamanca from which the repopulation of that town would be organized.

There the king met with Abbot Peter the Venerable of Cluny who had traveled to Iberia at the royal invitation. From the time of Fernando I, the kingdom had been pledged to an annual payment of 1,000 gold dinars to the

66. March 23, 1142. Zamora. Pub. Fernández Catón, *Colección*, 5:207–8. It is probably an original. The lands donated were former possessions of her grandmother, Jimena Múñoz, mistress of Alfonso VI.

67. The campaign is described in some detail in Maya Sánchez and Gil, *CAI*, pp. 224–25. July 1141. Partially pub. Francisco J. Hernandez, ed., *Los cartularios de Toledo* (Madrid, 1985), p. 46, as an original is a private document whose dating formula reads in part "when the emperor took Coria." Obviously it is anything but original. There is a late copy of it in BN, manuscritos, 13.093, ff. 103r-4r.

68. June 6, 1142. Coria. AC Zamora, *Tumbo Negro*, ff. 12v-3r; a royal grant to that see. It is the only other documentary record that bears on the chronology. Fortunately the dating of the *CAI* is here surprisingly good. June 19, 1142. AHN, Códices, 1.195B, fol. 402r; a grant of *Infanta* Elvira to the see of Astorga. It is a very rough copy and Alfonso does not confirm.

great Burgundian abbey in return for its spiritual intercession for king and realm and sometimes for mundane uses of its influence. Alfonso VI had renewed and doubled that annual subsidy in 1090 at the time of the visit to Iberia of another Cluniac abbot, the great Hugh of St.-Maur. The time of troubles after Alfonso VI's death and during the reign of Urraca had seen the lapse of that subsidy for want of funds. Now finances of the Burgundian abbey were in disarray and Alfonso VII could hope for a reasonable settlement. In addition, the king had wished to secure the influence of Cluny for the advance of his candidate, Bishop Berenguer of Salamanca, to the vacant see of Santiago de Compostela in the face of the appeal of the cathedral chapter to Rome on behalf of its choice.[69] For the cession of the annual subsidy, Abbot Peter agreed to accept the royal grant to Cluny of the Castilian monastery of San Pedro de Arlanza, an annual rent of 200 *morabetinos* drawn from the revenues of the public baths in Burgos, and a variety of lesser concessions (D431–32).

In August Alfonso, accompanied by Peter the Venerable, proceeded to Burgos where he endowed the newly recovered see of Coria (D421–22, 433–39). The tenor of the latter diploma suggests that Bishop Navarro may have been formally consecrated there. That location would have been fitting for a prelate whose very name betrays his origins in that region. The court remained at Burgos at least through the first week of September as did Abbot Peter.

Purely domestic concerns may have called Alfonso into Castilla, but a certain wariness about affairs in the valley of the Ebro may also have played a part. The precise activities of Navarra and of Aragón-Barcelona can seldom be followed continuously during these years but hostilities between them were more ordinary than not. A private document of October 1142 informs that at sometime in the previous twelve months Ramon Berenguer had made an unsuccessful attempt on Pamplona.[70] Still another tells us that he was sufficiently secure in 1142 to pass some fifteen days in Lombers in the south of France.[71] In November, on the other hand, the Barcelonan was in the ex-

---

69. On the general subject of the relationship between León-Castilla and Cluny the fundamental authority is Charles Julian Bishko, "Fernando I and the Origins of the Leonese-Castilian Alliance with Cluny," in *Studies in Medieval Spanish Frontier History*, 1–136 (London, 1980). First pub. in Spanish in *CHE* 47–48 (1968): 31–135, and 49–50 (1969): 50–116. For this particular episode, Charles Julian Bishko, "Peter the Venerable's Journey to Spain," in *Petrus Venerabilis (1156–1196): Studies and Texts Commemorating the Eighth Century of His Death* (Rome, 1956), pp. 163–75. The latter is volume 40 of the *Studia Anselmiana*. James Kritzeck, *Peter the Venerable and Islam* (Princeton, 1964), pp. 10–14, is a useful résumé.

70. Durán Gudiol, *Colección*, 1:180.

71. Cited José Goñi Gaztambide, ed., *Catálogo del archivo catedral de Pamplona; Tomo I (829–1500)* (Pamplona, 1965), p. 54. That Ramon should have been so far north (Lombers is sixty kilometers northeast of Toulouse and only ten kilometers south of Albi) seems extraordinary and we have no explanation for it.

treme south of his Aragonese domains at Daroca.[72] Some sort of peace had probably been arranged by Alfonso VII that included both monarchs.[73] Relations between Aragón-Barcelona and León-Castilla also continued cordial. Lop López of Haro still held Zaragoza as the Barcelonan's tenant and, at years end, received a substantial grant from the former.[74] Reassured, the Leonese monarch turned south to Toledo (D440–42). From that vantage, he may either have encouraged the men of Avila and Salamanca to destroy the castle of Albalat or have learned of their success in so doing.

After the fall of Coria during the preceding spring, the Muslim defenders of Albalat, an advance position overlooking a ford on the Tajo, decided it was indefensible and abandoned it. Local Christians lacked the resources to occupy it and chose simply to raze the fortress to prevent the return of their adversaries.[75] Such developments coincided nicely with the new determination of the king for a general offensive in the south the following year.

For a decade the Moroccan rulers of al-Andalus had been experiencing increasing difficulties maintaining their position against new challengers at home. In a mirror image of the rise of the Almoravids themselves, this challenge had taken the shape of an Islamic reform. It too, would gather strength in a particular Berber confederation before washing over the plains of Morocco, Algeria, and finally Tunisia. Its founder was ibn Tūmart, a Masmūda Berber born about 1075. About 1110, in the context of a pilgrimage that took him east to Bougie in modern Algeria, his particular doctrine began to take recognizable shape. A decade later ibn Tūmart returned to Almoravid Marrakesh to proclaim his message of repentance and renewal. At the court of Emir Alī ibn Yūsuf, he urged a renewed observance of the traditional practices of the strict segregation of the sexes, abstinence from alcohol, and avoidance of music, poetry, and dance. All of that puritanism once preached with enthusiasm by the Almoravids themselves and employed by them as their means of appeal to the simple, the disgruntled, and the enthusiasts, against their then leaders, now reemerged to drive a new wave of reform. Ibn Tūmart denounced the slackness of the Almoravids, and their

---

72. Tomas Muñoz y Romero, ed., *Colección de fueros y cartas pueblas.* (Madrid, 1847), pp. 534–43. The fact of the grant may be accepted, but the text as we have it is certainly considerably embellished despite the editor's assertion that he had it from the original in the municipal archive of that town.

73. 1143. Pub. Lacarra, "Documentos," 5:572–73, is a document of Bishop Miguel of Tarazona whose dating formula cites just such a general peace as having been agreed within the past year. Given the context of the times, late 1142 seems more likely than early 1143.

74. September 1142. Pub. Rubio, *Documentos*, p. 33. December 1142. AHN, Códices, 595B, ff. 132r-3r.

75. González, *Repoblación*, 1:144.

lack of recent success in the obligatory struggle of Islam against the infidel. Worse still, the Almoravids, their judges and scholars, and the Malikite jurists were the heretic. The literal interpretation of the Koran championed by them ended, in the eyes of the reformers, by asserting division within the godhead, a scarcely disguised polytheism. A proper theology, that of ibn Tūmart and his followers, insisted above all on the absolute unity of Allah. They were *al-Muwwahidūn*, the Almohads, the believers in the one God.

In 1120 this new orthodoxy found no foothold at Alī's court in Marrakesh and ibn Tūmart took refuge at Tinmal in the Atlas Mountains to preach his doctrine among the simple peoples. In that retreat he found courage to declare himself the *mahdī*, the chosen one of Allah, and discovered that he was, in fact, a blood descendant of the prophet, Muhammad. This development gave new impetus to his cause in its appeal to Shiite tradition. So, too, did his practice of writing and preaching in the Berber tongue of the hill folk as well as Arabic of the court and city. The unflinching rigorism of this *mahdī*, *imām*, and *amīr-al-muminīn*, together with a high order of skill at political organization, had made the Almohads masters of the mountainous spine of Morocco by his death in 1130.

Nevertheless, attempts to challenge the control of the Almoravids on the plains had failed, just as had the latter's attempts to reduce the mountain redoubts of the Almohads. The death of ibn Tūmart had given the Almoravids some respite but their challengers found a new champion in Abd al-Mūmin, his faithful disciple for more than two decades. Taking the titles of caliph and *amīr al-muminīn*, but not that of *mahdī*, al-Mūmin gradually consolidated his power. He proved quite as adept as his old mentor, and by 1141 the Almohads were ready to emerge at last onto the plains of Morocco for a climactic tilt with their old enemies. From that date until the death of Alī ibn Yūsuf, the Almoravids were in continuous retreat in their own heartland.

That Alfonso VII should have known nothing of these developments is impossible. Christian merchants and mercenaries in Morocco as well as Iberian Muslims who looked to their own well-being as bound up in cooperation with the new Christian powers of the Iberian north were all sources of information. While he doubtless understood little of the complex dynamic at work in North Africa, its significance for Iberia would not have been lost on him. Opportunity for aggrandizement in al-Andalus was greater than it had been in two generations.

At the beginning of 1143 an already famous frontier warrior of Galician origin, Muño Alfónsez, organized a major raid into the Muslim south by the combined forces of Avila, Segovia, and Toledo. In Andalucía they ravaged the countryside about Córdoba and took numerous captives. Because they had struck so early in the season, surprise magnified their success.[76] But the Almoravid governors of Córdoba and Sevilla recovered and organized a pursuit, following the raiders north through La Mancha and into the valley of the Tajo. Encumbered by their booty, the Christian army was overtaken and forced into an engagement that it would have preferred to avoid. Their good fortune persisted nonetheless, and the governors of both Córdoba and Sevilla were slain in a rout of the pursuers. The victors marched into Toledo bearing not only their plunder but the severed head of the governor of Córdoba.

The same days had seen the death of Emir Alī ibn Yūsuf in Morocco on January 28, 1143. He was succeeded by his son, Tāshufin ibn Alī (1143–1145), in the North African provinces but in Iberia a vacuum in leadership suddenly had been produced by the Christian victory at Montellos. To fill it, Tāshufin chose the victor of Fraga and the governor of Valencia, ibn Gāniya, to become his viceroy for all of al-Andalus. The latter, too, was a scion of the Almoravid dynasty, however, neither was able to stem the tide now running so strongly against them in North Africa and in Iberia.[77]

Alfonso VII was at Palencia in late January 1143 where a charter cited Ramon Berenguer as present. Unfortunately that portion has either been retouched or simply amended (D447). The likelihood is strong that Alfonso VII had been seeking reassurance from Aragón-Barcelona that the northeast frontier was not about to erupt. At the end of the month the Leonese marched south, reaching Toledo in mid-April (D448–52).[78] The assembly of the army may have been set for the feast of Pentecost on May 23. Meanwhile, Alfonso was busy collecting the royal fifth to which he was entitled from the raid just completed. He sent some of the spoils north to the shrine of Santiago at Compostela in thanksgiving for the victory. The head of the governor of Córdoba and the captured princesses of the fallen Muslim leaders were graciously returned to that city.

When the army had assembled, the king first provided against a possible counterstroke. Muño Alfónsez and Martín Fernández of Fita were entrusted

76. Maya Sánchez and Gil, *CAI*, pp. 226–38, gives the account of the campaigns of the year with great verve and much literary embellishment. González, *Repoblación*, 1:145–47, is a briefer, drier summary.

77. Francisco Codera, *Decadencia y desaparición de los Almorávides en España* (Zaragoza, 1899), remains the classic study.

78. Maya Sánchez and Gil, *CAI*, pp. 231–32. The accounts of the remaining campaigns of the year follow. April 13, 1143. Pub. Fernández Flórez, *Colección*, 4:181–83, as an original but it is a copy. This private will in favor of the monastery of Sahagún was confirmed by many of the members of the royal court but not by the king himself. Since no place of issuance is given it could have been done at Toledo.

with the garrisoning of the castle of Peña Negra, a new construction designed to blockade the Muslim castle at Mora southwest of Toledo. From it, the two veteran warriors could both harass the Muslim position and prevent it from being used as a staging area for an attack on the that city.

Then Alfonso departed with the main army into the heart of al-Andalus. For weeks he ravaged the territories about Córdoba, Carmona, and Sevilla, apparently without challenge from the Almoravid forces, which remained secure behind the walls of those cities. The cost of such a defensive posture was heavy however. It left the Christian forces free to sweep the countryside, gathering up the useful population, livestock, and anything else of value that happened to be moveable. At the same time, they destroyed what, in the nature of things, must be left behind. Fruit and fig trees, olive trees and grape vines were cut down and put to the torch. Doubtless so, too, were houses, barns, and stables along with waterwheels and mills. This sort of destruction could cripple or even depopulate a district for a decade or more when the attacking force had the undisputed leisure to carry it out thoroughly. In an area whose population was already in decline, the results were even more devastating.

Having penetrated west to the lands about Sevilla, the Leonese returned by way of Badajoz. That was the shortest route and one not already despoiled by the previous passage of his forces. Nor had it many garrisons ready to fall upon an army burdened by spoils and tired from months of campaigning. The king reentered Christian territory at Talavera de la Reina west of Toledo. There he found that in his absence an attack had been launched by the enemy. The commander of the major Muslim fortress of Calatrava, determined on a major resupply of Mora with an eye to readying it for continuing harassment of the lands of Toledo. From Peña Negra the Christian commanders learned of his approach during routine reconnoitering of the countryside and intercepted and dispersed at least one food convoy. Then on August 1, they unwisely decided to contest the advance of the main enemy force. Martín Fernández was wounded in the engagement but managed to escape back to Peña Negra with some troops. Muño Alfónsez and another portion of the Christian force was trapped while attempting to cover their withdrawal and annihilated. The old warrior's body was dismembered by the Muslim commander and parts of it, along with the heads of his fallen companions, came to grace the fortress of Calatrava and the turrets of Córdoba, Sevilla, and even far Morocco. Nonetheless the Christian blocking force had served its purpose. The lands of Toledo were protected, and the following year Mora would fall to what had doubtless been a continuous Christian siege from about this time.

Further consequences were to follow from the victorious campaign of Alfonso VII. The inability of the Almoravids to defeat him, or even seriously to limit the scope of his operations and so protect their subjects, contributed to the outbreak of the first revolts against their rule in Iberia. Initially, these took place in the Algarve, but they soon found echoes elsewhere. At the same time, the full dimensions of the weakness of the Almoravids had been discovered by the Leonese monarch, and before leaving Toledo he announced his plans for a yet greater effort in the following year. The date for the assembly of the army was set for mid-September 1144.

Alfonso VII had returned to Toledo by the third week of August (D454). After a rest, he moved north to Valladolid for a major council of the realm and indeed of the peninsula. The best idea of its dimensions is revealed by the decree of the papal legate, Cardinal Guido, who there published the canons of the Second Lateran Council of 1139. The beginning of that text rehearsed the two archbishops and the sixteen bishops of León-Castilla who attended as well as the archbishop of Braga and the bishop of Coimbra from the vassal kingdom of Portugal, the bishop of Pamplona from the vassal kingdom of Navarra, and the ubiquitous Bishop Arnold of Oléron in Béarn.[79]

When precisely the council began is unknown, but it was before September 19 when a notice informs us that one Martín had been elected there to the disputed see of Oviedo.[80] This was one of the many ecclesiastical disputes that had troubled the kingdom, often for more than a decade. Given the nature of both royal and ecclesiastical authority at the time, they were inevitably political disputes as well. If Alfonso VII was formulating major new initiatives to the south, the resolution of these disruptive conflicts was especially desireable.

Possibly Alfonso VII had requested the appointment of a papal legate for Iberia with the authority to settle all outstanding matters. One of these conflicts may have had to do with a major secular figure of the peninsula. The previous spring Pope Innocent II had excommunicated Count Armengol VI of Urgel and placed that county under interdict because the count had resorted to violence against the canons of the cathedral there. Since the count was also one of the more important magnates of León-Castilla, the papal action concerned Alfonso. An echo of this affair may be reflected in a *mandatum* of the count to the inhabitants of Valladolid informing them of

79. Pub. Carl Erdmann, ed., "Papsturkunden in Portugal," *AGWG* 20 (1927), 198–203, from the copy in the *Livro Preto* of the cathedral of Coimbra. The text has its corruptions including the clearly erroneous date of 1144.

80. Manuel Risco, ed., *ES*, vols. 28–42 (Madrid, 1774–1801), 38:145, from a notice in an old chronicle of that church.

an agreement between himself and the bishop of Palencia, recognizing the latter's jurisdiction over that collegiate church. Weakened by the papal ban, Count Armengol may have chosen to settle all of his outstanding differences with churchmen. The mandate is dated only to 1143, but probably represents another result of Cardinal Guido's legatine mediation.[81]

The oldest ecclesiastical dispute that had required attention was the contention for the see of Oviedo, originating from the removal of Bishop Pelayo in 1130. Alfonso VII's support for his bishop for such an extended period is quite extraordinary even if it grew out of political necessity. A new bishop, Martín II (1143–1156), was chosen at Valladolid. The settlement of the succession at Oviedo was linked to the settlement as well of the succession to Santiago de Compostela. In the documents of Valladolid Pedro Elias appears as the archbishop (D455–57). Cardinal Guido listed him in the publication of the canons and Pedro also confirmed royal charters. Finally, a document of Archbishop Pedro himself of the same period shows him functioning in that office.[82] Certainly at Valladolid, the king was persuaded to recognize Pedro finally and may have made additional amends with the acceptance of Bishop Martín for the see of Oviedo. The latter was connected with the church of Compostela and would become its archbishop in 1156.[83]

The council thus put an end to many of the outstanding problems that had had the potential to distract Alfonso at a time when he was contemplating a massive assault on al-Andalus. But the king intended more than simply a general reconciliation within León-Castilla. In October he invited Afonso Henriques to a conference at Zamora. The Leonese monarch wished not only to secure his own border with Portugal in the coming months but also to obtain the collaboration of his cousin in simultaneous attacks on the Almoravids and he was willing to make the greatest concessions to achieve such cooperation.

The evidence for what transpired between the two at Zamora is certainly less than we should wish. In the first instance, it consists in two royal charters, one to a Martín Cidez and another to Pons de Cabrera (D458–59). Although the Portuguese ruler does not appear as a confirmant of either he is cited in the dating formula of both. They speak of the Council of Valla-

81. Pub. Teresa Abajo Martín, ed., *Documentación de la catedral de Palencia* (Palencia, 1986), pp. 86–87.

82. September 16, 1143. AC Compostela; pub. Antonio López-Ferreiro, *Historia de la Santa Apostólica Metropolitana Iglesia de Santiago de Compostela*, 11 vols. (Santiago de Compostela, 1898–1911), 4:32–36. It is a grant of the archbishop to the Galician monastery of San Juan da Coba. Though it bears no place of issuance it was probably done at Valladolid after Pedro's recognition.

83. Richard A. Fletcher, *The Episcopate of the Kingdom of León in the Twelfth Century* (Oxford, 1978), p. 74.

dolid celebrated by Cardinal Guido and of the "king of Portugal" who came to hold a conference with the emperor. Since the charters were drafted by Alfonso VII's chancery, the recognition of the new royal status of Afonso Henriques is implicit. Nevertheless, as in the case of Navarra, such recognition did not imply absolute independence, at least in theory. The king of Portugal remained the vassal of the Leonese king as he had been since the treaty of 1137. To reinforce that bond Afonso Henriques now may have been entrusted symbolically with the important city of Astorga. A charter of *Infanta* Sancha, dated December 4, 1143, cites the king of Portugal as castellan there and a Leonese noble, Fernando Captivo, as his agent (D461).[84]

But it seems that Afonso Henriques did not do, or felt that he did not do, homage for the kingdom of Portugal itself. In a charter of December 13, 1143, the Portuguese king surrendered that realm to the papacy, by the hand of Cardinal Guido, promising to become a "miles beati Petri" and to pay an annual *census* of four ounces of gold. The pope himself may have been uneasy with this latter bargain. Although in his charter of donation Afonso Henriques styled himself "rex Portugalensis" it will be many years yet before the papacy will address him as anything but "dux Portugalensis" in its correspondence.[85]

His business finished at Zamora, Alfonso VII turned east in the company of the legate to Nájera, which town he had reached by late October. There he granted the monastery of San Vicente in Salamanca to Cluny (D460).[86] But though we are ignorant of his other initiatives in that quarter doubtless they dealt with the still unsettled relations of García Ramírez and Ramon Berenguer. In 1143 the former had laid successful siege to the episcopal city of Tarazona. That action ran clearly counter to the desires of Alfonso VII for peace on the frontier but the Leonese monarch was occupied in Andalucía and Ramon Berenguer in the south of France.

Alfonso VII may have paid a price in the northeast to prop up a fragile peace there. Lop López lost control in Zaragoza and in February 1143 one Ato Sanz is cited as justiciar. In the same November the papal legate, Cardinal Guido, continued his Iberian itinerary with a general council of the realm of

84. July 20, 1144. AD Astorga, Carpeta 1, no. 5. This private document, although defective in some particulars, also cites Pelayo Captivo, the son of the Galician magnate, Fernando Yáñez, as holding the royal palace there. Pelayo had also been cited in the former document as subordinate to Fernando Captivo.

85. Pub. Pinto de Azevado, *DMP*, 1–1:250–51. For commentary see Serrão, *História*, 1: 87–90.

86. Pub. Alexandre Bruel, ed. *Recueil des chartes de l'Abbaye de Cluny* 6 vols. (Paris, 1876–1903),5:428–30, from what he called an original in the Bibliothèque Nationale, Paris. The orthography makes that unlikely and the premature appearance of García Rodríguez as *merino* in Burgos raises more doubts.

Aragón-Barcelona held in Gerona. In attendance were the newly elect archbishop of Tarragona, the newly elect bishops of Rota and of Urgel, the bishops of Gerona, Vich, Huesca, and Bishop Bernard of Zaragoza. In fact, the document that informs us of their presence is an agreement made between Bishop Bernard and his cathedral chapter. The principality of Zaragoza was being increasingly integrated into the new hybrid kingdom.[87]

Once again events over which he had scant control were moving Alfonso VII's new policy of merely dynastic hegemony in the peninsula along rather faster than he may have cared. Also in November, Ramon Berenguer finally managed to secure a general agreement with the Templars. The delicate matter of their claim to a one-third of the realm was settled with a generous grant of castles and a variety of other revenues and possessions.[88] The resolution of that nagging problem improved the bargaining position of the Barcelonan vis-à-vis the Leonese monarch. Whether or not these matters had been previously discussed with Alfonso VII is simply unknown, but the probability that they had been is strong. In any event, the king was in Castrojeriz shortly before Christmas where he granted a *fuero* to the men of Roa (D462). He then returned to León for the holiday season. The growing strength of the Portuguese and the Aragonese may have been the incentive for Alfonso VII to bolster his own dynasty, at least symbolically, at this time. His oldest male heir, Sancho, who would have been about ten, was brought to court and began to confirm royal charters when he was actually present. Over the next two years Sancho confirmed roughly one-third of all of the surviving, reliable charters of his father. He is occasionally listed in their intitulation along with his mother, Berengaria. The inference is that the heir was kept rather more often at court and sometimes involved in its official acts in order to display physically the stability of the dynasty.

The whereabouts of the court in early 1144 is difficult to specify (D463–67).[89] The problem is also complicated by the assertion of the chronicle of Cardeña that it was in this year that the king visited the monastery and introduced French Cluniac monks, expelling the native community. It is tempting

---

87. February 1143. Pub. Rubio, *Documentos*, pp. 34–35. November 16, 1143. Pub. Kehr, "Papsturkunden," 2:337–38.

88. November 27, 1143. ACA, Cancillería, Pergaminos, Ramon Berenguer IV, Carpeta 37, no. 159; a copy of the fourteenth century. Pub. Albon, *Cartulaire*, pp. 204–5.

89. January 24, 1144. León. Pub. Fernández Catón, *Colección*, 5:223–24, who called it an original. This is a royal charter to one Martín Díaz and Jimena Pérez, his wife. The orthography and diplomatic make it unlikely that it is original and the premature appearance of García Rodríguez as *merino* in Burgos raises further doubts. February 25, 1144. ASI, no. 98; pub. ibid., pp. 225–28, as an original. This is a private document of Bishop Juan Albertínez of León confirmed by Alfonso VII. Certainly it is not original for it cites the long-dead Bernard as then archbishop of Toledo. The place of issuance is not given, but most probably it was the episcopal city, placing the court there if the document can be trusted at all.

to assign this event rather to the latter part of 1143 when Alfonso VII was clearly in the northeast. However, two other documents exist and suggest that the chronicle is accurate.[90] If so, the early part of the year seems the most likely time. From March through May a progress through the center of the realm is indicated (D468–72).

A major event in the history of the dynasty and of the realm was in the offing that spring, the marriage between García Ramírez and Urraca, daughter of Alfonso. The union would seal the uneasy peace between the two realms and hopefully prepare the way for the eventual incorporation of the Pyrenaen kingdom in the patrimony of the dynasty of León-Castilla. In June the emperor went out to receive the bridegroom with proper honors, and before the wedding García was in the company of Alfonso at Carrión de los Condes, whence they traveled to León (D473–80). The festivities surrounding the nuptials, which went on for two weeks, are described in detail in the *Chronica Adefonsi Imperatoris*.[91] Alfonso had summoned the magnates from throughout his kingdom to attend. García Ramírez came with a suitable entourage, of course. The bride entered the city in the company of her aunt, *Infanta* Sancha, in whose court she had been educated. The marriage itself took place on June 24. Music, games, and feasting marked the days that followed. Noble horsemen displayed their ability at target-shooting from horseback, and others fought and killed bulls while mounted. Less dangerous and less serious were the contests at pigsticking.

The newlyweds departed, showered with gifts by the emperor and his sister, and they were accompanied back to Pamplona by an honor guard of the nobility of León-Castilla among whom Count Rodrigo Gómez and the Castro magnate Guter Fernández were prominent. In Pamplona the festivities were duplicated. The *Chronica* also informs us that Guntroda Pérez, royal mistress and mother of Urraca, satisfied with the honors and position accorded to her daughter, now retired to a convent in Oviedo.

But much grimmer endeavors awaited Alfonso and his nobles in al-Andalus that fall. In August he moved south to Salamanca on his way to Toledo (D484–88). The great *razzia* or raid of Alfonso VII in al-Andalus was virtually a repetition of the raid of 1143.[92] The major difference was that now it struck Upper Andalucía. Beginning in the lands of La Mancha and about Calatrava, the army crossed the Sierra Morena to Baeza and Ubeda, then up into the foothills of the Sierra Nevada, worrying the territories of Granada

90. Ambrosio Huici Miranda, ed., *Las crónicas latinas de la reconquista*, 2 vols. (Valencia, 1913), 1:375.
91. Maya Sánchez and Gil, *CAI*, pp. 191–94.
92. Ibid., pp. 238–40.

and even penetrating to the fringes of the of the district of Almería. The technique was familiar. Everywhere residents who had not fled was rounded up and carried off, along with livestock from horses to mules to cattle and even to pigs. Livestock became walking provisions for the continuing campaign. Most damaging of all to those Muslims who survived the raid, vineyards, olive groves, fig and fruit trees were cut down and put to the torch. Most probably the terrified population was itself driven to that task. Houses, entire villages, and strong points (the chronicle calls them castles) were destroyed, but they could be rebuilt fairly quickly. The herds would take years to rebuild and the vines and trees easily ten to twenty years.

The Almoravid forces were powerless to interfere with this systematic destruction. Even before it had begun the general disaffection with their rule, outrage at their growing ineffectuality against Christian expeditions, and a growing awareness of the precariousness of their domination in the imperial homeland in North Africa had resulted in revolts against their authority in the Portuguese Algarve. Led by ibn Qasi, a native of Silves and a devotee of the mystic Sufic tradition, which found appealing the Almohad call to reform, the rebellion had secured the town of Mértola by August 1144. From there it spread to Silves and to Evora and then farther east to Huelva, Niebla, and up to the very gates of Sevilla. Ibn Qasi, who had taken the title of *imām*, also recognized the authority of the North African Almohad caliph, Abd al-Mūmin.

The seriousness of this challenge prevented the Almoravid governor from responding to the invasion of Alfonso VII. Unable to secure support from Tāshufīn ibn Alī, who was himself locked in a mortal struggle with the Almohads for control of Oran and Tlemcen in Algeria, Yahya ibn Gāniya was forced to choose between two theaters of operation: the rebellion in the west that menaced Sevilla itself or the less critical raid on Upper Andalucía. Consequently resistance to the Leonese expedition was minimal. Ibn Gāniya husbanded his forces and launched a counterattack against the rebels before Sevilla, defeating them soundly. He then took the offensive, driving toward Niebla. There, however, resistance stiffened and he found himself forced to an ultimately unsuccessful siege that lasted three months. However defensible such a strategy, it dismayed those sectors that must bear the brunt of the Leonese onslaught unaided. The reaction was not long delayed. At the very end of 1144 or in January 1145, while ibn Gāniya was tied down before Niebla, revolt broke out in Córdoba itself. Its leader was ibn Hamdin, *qādī* of the city and member of a prominent local family.[93]

---

93. Ibid., pp. 239–46, provides a rough account of these and subsequent events of the demise of Murabit power in Muslim Iberia. The Muslim histories are fuller, of course, Codera,

By this time Alfonso VII had long since returned to Toledo. From there, the army disbanded and king and court struck north to Segovia and thence to Valladolid (D485–92). Existing information does not allow us to be sure that Alfonso VII had had intelligence of the anti-Almoravid revolts in the Portuguese Algarve prior to his raid into Upper Andalucía in mid-September. Certainly he would have heard something of them during the raid itself, and more information would have become available after his return to Toledo. But both the season and the exhaustion of his forces prevented any immediate direct response of his own to that emerging opportunity. Nevertheless, he may have been able to inspire mischief in the south.

The one-time Hūddite heir to the *taifa* of Zaragoza, Saif al-Dawla, was known to the rebel leaders of al-Andalus. Now they invited his intervention, appealing to Alfonso VII for aid and offering to renew the *parias* in return for Leonese protection.[94] Alfonso's vassal accepted the invitation and in February and March 1145 ruled in Córdoba. Doubtless he began what ultimately proved to be a fruitless and hectic career in the volatile politics of the south with the blessing of Alfonso VII. More, for the moment, the Leonese monarch could not do although the news continued to get better and better for his purposes. Desperate and on the defensive in the face of a sweeping Almohad offensive in North Africa, Tāshufīn ibn Alī in December 1144 had recalled his heir, the young Ibrahim, from his studies at Sevilla and then had despatched the youth to Marrakesh to safeguard the fidelity of that capital in his own absence. But shortly thereafter, on March 23, 1145, the Almoravid emir met his death attempting to escape from the Almohad siege of Oran. The Almoravid cause in North Africa now was lost.

Meanwhile, in al-Andalus, the strength of their party was draining away. Málaga, Murcia, and Valencia all declared themselves independent in March 1145, even before the news of Alī's death had arrived from Africa. One possibility inherent in this new state of affairs was the emergence of a new group of *taifas*, as susceptible of exploitation and dominance by León-Castilla as those of the period of Fernando I and Alfonso VI. At best, the developing near-anarchy might permit large portions of al-Andalus simply to be absorbed. Alfonso VII's first concern was to concert the initiatives of the Christian north to make the best use of these opportunities.

To the west cooperation was largely self-generating. The Portuguese crown was already locked in a struggle with the Muslims of Santarém in

---

Decadencia, older but still useful, and Jacinto Bosch Vilá, *Los Almorávides* (Granada, 1990), pp. 255–95, have mined them thoroughly.

94. Maya Sánchez and Gil, *CAI*, p. 240.

which the latter raided north toward Coimbra itself. Such offensive actions redoubled the determination of the Portuguese king finally to have done with that danger. Any energies left over from that problem were, in 1145, directed to marriage negotiations with Count Amadeus III of Savoy. Afonso married the count's daughter, Matilda, in 1146.

The relationships of Navarra and Aragón-Barcelona in the northeast were, on the other hand, like quicksilver. No sooner was a peace patched up than one or the other party found itself unable to resist a momentary opportunity and the entire process had to begin again. During the summer of 1143 Ramon Berenguer had marched north into the Midi, where his vassal, Count William of Montpellier, was attempting to subdue the revolt of the commune. Ramon's aid put an end to the rebellion but García Ramírez had seized on Ramon's absence to overrun both Tarazona and Sos, strengthening his hold on the valley of the middle Ebro. The challenge was met, for by April 1144 the Barcelonan had retaken both Tarazona and Sos.[95] The status quo was thus restored only to be threatened again by the death of Count Berenguer Ramon II of Provence, brother of Ramon. The deceased left only a son of minor years, and the Barcelonan became the latter's guardian and regent. Challenges to the young heir were immediately mounted by the Provencal house of Baux, which had its own claims to the county and which could ordinarily bank on the support of Alfonso Jordan, count of Toulouse, who also had ambitions for the area. These developments ensured that for the forseeable future Aragón-Barcelona would be burdened by cares for the defense of Provence.

In these circumstances, Ramon wrote to Alfonso VII expressing his own willingness to conclude a truce with Navarra, to pursue the common struggle with the Muslims, and to seek a further marriage alliance with León-Castilla.[96] However, the count showed no inclination to relax one whit his own claims to Aragon. In a contemporary charter he cited his rule in Aragón, Ribagorza, Sobrarbe, Barbastro, Huesca, Zaragoza, Calatayud, and Daroca.[97] Alfonso's response was delayed. In 1145 his itinerary tell us little beyond the ordinary. He reached Toledo in May (D493–500). As the situation in al-Andalus was changing almost monthly that city furnished the most convenient seat for observation.

95. April 1144. Pub. Lacarra, "Documentos," 5:573–74. If another private document is to be trusted the turmoil in Montpellier was probably related as well to the continuing intrigues of Count Alfonso Jordan of Toulouse in the Midi. November 1144. Pub. Durán Gudiol, *Colección*, 1:184.
96. ACA, Cancillería, Pergaminos, Ramon Berenguer IV, Carpeta 41, no. 23. It is undated as letters of the period ordinarily are.
97. July 1145. Ibid., Carpeta 37, no. 181.

His ally, vassal, and (we may think) pawn, Saif al-Dawla had been expelled from Córdoba, and the native *qādī*, ibn Hamdin, resumed power. The rejected Hūddite prince traveled east from that city to the fortress town of Jaén where he was more welcome. His nephew became governor of that strategic center between Córdoba and Granada, while Saif al-Dawla himself continued on to Granada where he was welcomed by those elements opposed to the Almoravids. His power proved sufficiently strong for him to appoint a governor for the outlying town of Guadix. Nevertheless, it never extended to the town or district of Málaga, which center had also risen in revolt in March.

Meanwhile, Valencia too had risen against its Almoravid governor and the garrison had retired down the coast to Játiva. After some hesitation the local *qādī*, Marwān, assumed control and the Almoravids were besieged in Játiva. Farther south in Murcia the same process had taken place and had resulted in a wild melee with a variety of claimants to power, all of whom seemed to have begun to mint their own coinage.[98] The rebels were not to have things all their own way, however. Sometime during the early summer, Saif al-Dawla informed Alfonso of the refusal of the Upper Andalusian cities of Baeza and Ubeda to recognize him or to pay *parias* to León. The latter responded by despatching a strong force under Counts Manrique of Lara, Armengol of Urgel, Pons of Cabrera, and Martín Fernández of León, to assist his ally.[99] But as experience began to erode the first confidence that all would be well if only the control of North Africa were thrown off, the Almoravids and their supporters began to recoup support and they regained control of Granada in late August 1145. Saif al-Dawla was compelled to retreat to Jaén, was unable to maintain himself there, and withdrew into Murcia, with one of whose contestants for power he had made an alliance. Alfonso could not have been impressed with his performance.

The king traveled north in August, called by his other responsibilities (D501–07).[100] That Alfonso was still trying to arrange a general peace between Navarra and Aragón-Barcelona is indicated by a document of Archbishop Raymond of Toledo dated October 3, 1145.[101] From the confirmants

98. Huici Miranda, *Historia*, 3:103–6.

99. Maya Sánchez and Gil, *CAI*, p. 242. As usual the chronicle is not precise. In full context, early summer of 1145, seems most probable.

100. October 1145. Pub. Gonzalo Martínez, "Diplomatario de San Cristobal de Ibeas," *BIFG* 55 (1975): 698–99, a private grant to the Castilian monastery of La Vid that claims to have been done in Burgos in the presence of *Infanta* Sancha. It was witnessed by a variety of members of the royal court if not Alfonso himself. The copy is dated to October 1151, but the witness list makes 1145 the only possible date.

101. Pub. Kehr, "Papsturkunden," 22:351–53, from an original in the cathedral archive of Pamplona.

it was obviously done at court, although the king was not among them. In it Raymond settled a dispute between the Navarrese see of Pamplona and the Aragonese see of Jaca. In mid-November the king and court were at Valladolid (D508–10).

As the year closed the larger currents of western European politics were to impinge on affairs in Iberia. In distant Syria at the end of 1144 the Muslim emir, Zenghi, had surprised and taken the town of Edessa. That success signaled the end of the County of Edessa, first of the Latin principalities established by the First Crusade. When the conquest became known in the west, it would provoke the Second Crusade. The news was delayed for ordinarily the seas were devoid of shipping during the winter in the Middle Ages and the road by land would have been arduous.

At Rome the first evidence of knowledge of Edessa's fall came in the crusading bull *Quantum Praedecessores* of December 1, 1145. But then the papal mills grind slowly and much consultation and discussion doubtless preceded its issuance. Probably the news of the fall of Edessa arrived in Rome sometime in April or May. On that hypothesis, the same news, and the reports of the first reactions to it in the papal court, should have become available to Alfonso VII during the summer when he was at Toledo. By this period, legations from the Iberian church waited regularly on the Roman pontiff. In March 1145 Bishop Martín of Oviedo was pursuing the resolution of a local dispute there and in May a representative of Alfonso secured a judgment against Archbishop João of Braga for ignoring the primatial authority of Toledo in the peninsula.[102]

From that point forward, the king of León-Castilla must have been occupied with measures that would call to the attention of the papacy and Europe the relevance of the new crusading enthusiasm to affairs in Iberia. Neither the concept nor the experience of crusades was entirely foreign there. Some of the earliest applications of the idea had been to Iberia and, despite papal recommendations to the contrary, the participation of individual Iberians in crusades to the Levant was frequent.[103] If some of the energy aroused by a new, general preaching of a crusade could be diverted into Iberian channels the disarray of Muslim Andalucía promised particularly rich returns.

The first formal royal legations must wait on news of the promulga-

102. March 17, 1145. Pub. Risco, *ES*, 41:307. May 1145. Pub. J. V. Pflugk-Harttung, ed., *Acta Pontificum Romanorum Inedita*, 3 vols. (Graz, 1958), 2:341–42.

103. See Charles Julian Bishko, "The Spanish and the Portuguese Reconquest, 1095–1492," in *A History of the Crusades*, ed. Kenneth M. Setton, vol. 3 (Madison, Wis., 1975), pp. 396–456, or Derek W. Lomax, *The Reconquest of Spain* (London, 1978), for reliable surveys. More particularly, José Goñi Gaztambide, *Historia de la Bula de la Cruzada en España* (Vitoria, 1958), is authoritative.

tion of the papal bull of crusade in December. News of it would hardly have reached the west of the peninsula before February or March 1146. But surely clerics despatched to Rome in the interim on other business were counseled to pay close attention to developing opinion. As came to pass, Iberia and the Second Crusade were to be closely interrelated.

4

Crusade, *Reconquista*, and Dynasty: 1146–1157

THE RESPONSE OF WESTERN EUROPE to the fall of the crusading principality of Edessa developed momentum in 1146. The papal bull of December 1145, perhaps moved Louis VII of France to propose an eastern expedition in his Christmas court at Bourges. Influential voices there spoke against that notion. Nevertheless the king pursued the idea at his Easter court in March at Vézelay. Meanwhile negotiations began both with Eugenius III at Rome and with Bernard of Clairvaux.

As a result, the pope reissued *Quantum Praedecessores* on March 1, 1146, and Bernard himself attended the Easter court to preach a crusade. The dynamic so initiated not only set western armies marching toward the Holy Land in 1147 but raised up hosts in Iberia. When Louis VII took the cross, one witness who followed the royal lead was Count Alfonso Jordan of Toulouse, premier vassal of France and first cousin of Alfonso VII. It is likely that the Leonese king had encouraged his kinsman to attend. The count surely informed Alfonso of his decision to crusade and of what had transpired at the French court.

Another interested party was Ramon Berenguer IV, since Toulouse and Barcelona were related in various ways. For one, Alfonso Jordan was Ramon's vassal, although for what lands we do not know. For another, the two were major rivals about whom the politics of the Midi revolved. The ambitions of the county of Toulouse stretched to Comminges, Foix, Carcassone, Béziers, and Montpellier and each of those was important to Barcelona. Moreover, since count of Barcelona had become prince of Aragón, he contested the influence of Toulouse in Béarn and Bigorre. These two viscounties had been intimately associated with Aragón for a half century. Finally, in 1145 the death of his younger brother had obliged Ramon Berenguer to assume responsibility for the county of Provence. There, too, Toulouse was involved, being allied informally with the house of Baux, rivals of Barcelona.

Surely Ramon greeted Alfonso Jordan's decision to take the cross with rejoicing. His problems beyond the Pyrenees would be much moderated in the absence of their major author. Perhaps, as did happen, Alfonso Jordan would not return alive and an even longer respite might be anticipated. Ramon could yield more safely to the importunities of the king of León, for a joint effort against the Muslims of Iberia. A new archbishop for the ancient see of Tarragona, Bernard Tort, had just been despatched to Italy to be consecrated. Eugenius III performed that office in Viterbo on May 26, 1146, and the new prelate was charged with the pursuit of that offensive against the Muslims of the area, urged by popes since Pope Urban II.[1]

Farther west, García Ramírez would have been apprised of what was happening in Italy. In 1146 he was to despatch his daughter Margaret to that quarter to become the bride of the future William I (1154–1166) of Norman Sicily.[2] The latter's father, Roger II, had an active interest in a crusade. García's ambassadors at the Sicilian court or Roger II's ambassadors at the Navarrese court hardly avoided the topic. Even the far-off king of Portugal may have been passably informed. In early 1146 his diplomas begin to mention his new wife, Matilda, daughter of Count Amadeo III of Savoy. The count took the cross and departed for the Levant in 1147. The first diploma in which the princess of Savoy appears as bride of Afonso Henriques is a confirmation by the latter of an earlier donation by his mother to the great Burgundian monastery of Cluny.[3] Such confirmations were ordinarily solicited, so we may presume that the Portuguese monarch was in contact with that center of influence and information as well.

Alfonso VII was busy meanwhile with ordinary affairs. By late March he was in Avila (D511–21). There *Infante* Sancho was inducted as a regular member of the court. For two years his attendance had been frequent, but now it becomes nearly invariable. At twelve, on the verge of manhood as the age counted, Sancho's name was added as a confirmant to all royal charters. At this same time, his younger brother, Fernando, began to be occasionally at court, and to confirm. The younger son was about seven or eight.

Had Alfonso VII preferred to wait clarification of the crusading impulse in France, he was denied that luxury by the speed of developments in al-

1. Lawrence J. McCrank, "Norman Crusaders in the Catalan Reconquest: Robert Burdet and the Principality of Tarragona, 1129–1155," *JMH* 7 (1981): 73.

2. May 1146. AGN, Sección de Comptos, Cajón 1, O. 8; a private and possibly original document. Pub. Fritz Baer, *Die Juden im Christlichen Spanien*, vol. 1 (Berlin, 1929), p. 924. The information is seconded in a Templar document dated to 1146, pub. Marquis D'Albon, ed., *Cartulaire general de l'Ordre du Temple, 1119–1150* (Paris, 1913), p. 246. It also is supported by the chronicler Romuald of Salerno, see Ferdinand Chalandon, *Histoire de la domination Normande en Italie et en Sicile*, 2 vols. 1907 (New York, 1969), 2:107.

3. May 23, 1146. Pub. Rui de Azevado, ed., *DMP*, vol. 1 (Lisbon, 1958), 1–1: 263–64.

Andalus. On February 5 the combined Muslim forces of Valencia and Murcia were defeated by his lieutenants, presumably that force he had despatched to aid Saif al-Dawla the previous summer. We must conjecture that the anti-Almoravid forces of the southeast had taken alarm at the actions of their Christian allies and contested the latters' control in the area around Chinchilla, southeast of Albacete in La Mancha. Saif al-Dawla met his death in the encounter. Alfonso was suspected of having acted radically to simplify the affairs of the southeast and found it necessary later to deny premeditation in the demise of his vassal.[4]

In Córdoba too the balance of forces was fluid. Ibn Ganiya, had returned from his bootless siege of Niebla and expelled ibn Hamdin from that city by February. The former *qāḍī* retreated up the Guadalquivir to Andújar, seventy-five kilometers to the east. Ibn Gāniya pursued and began a siege while ibn Hamdin appealed to Alfonso VII. Preparing a full descent into al-Andalus, Alfonso despatched his Galician vassal, Fernando Yáñez, to his relief. At his appearance, ibn Gāniya retired on Córdoba.[5]

In Toledo Alfonso had tarried for two months, but now he joined ibn Hamdin (D522–28). Their combined armies then proceeded to Córdoba which city they took, save for its *Madinat* into which ibn Gāniya retreated. By late May the Leonese ruler was faced by a dilemma. Word reached him that the Almohads had responded to an appeal from the rebels of the Algarve and an expeditionary force from Morocco had landed. At word of it, the populace of Sevilla had again thrown off Almoravid rule. Suddenly it was in the interest of both Alfonso and ibn Gāniya to reach an accommodation. Deserting ibn Hamdin, Alfonso recognized ibn Gāniya as the ruler of most of the city on condition that the latter become his vassal. A portion of the city became a Christian enclave and its mosque, probably the great central mosque, was converted into a Christian church.[6] Ibn Hamdin in desperation fled to the Algarve and later passed over to Morocco where he conferred with Abd al-Mūmin. The *qāḍī* was received kindly and permitted to return to the penin-

---

4. Antonio Maya Sánchez and Juan Gil, eds., *CAI*, in *Chronica Hispana: Saeculi XII* (Turnholt, 1990), pp. 242–44, describes these affairs vividly but not very exactly. Ambrosio Huici Miranda, *Historia musulmana de Valencia y su región*, 3 vols. (Valencia, 1969–70), 3:112–13, clarifies the death of Saif al-Dawl on the basis of Muslim accounts.

5. Francisco Codera, *Decadencia y desaparición de los Almorávides en España* (Zaragoza, 1899), pp. 59–62, treats this episode and the subsequent campaign of Alfonso.

6. The timing of these events is difficult to establish. Codera, *Decadencia*, pp. 59–63, fixes the entrance of Alfonso into Córdoba as between May 10 and May 12, but the charters make that impossible. A royal charter (D529) is dated to Córdoba for May 21, 1147, but the known itinerary of the king and the reference to a siege in process make 1146 more likely. Maya Sánchez and Gil, *CAI*, p. 246, says that the fighting for Córdoba still continued on June 24.

sula. There he became the independent ruler of the rebels of Málaga until his death in November 1151. Ibn Hamdin made at least one subsequent attempt to regain Córdoba. One or the other of these actions seemingly went beyond his understandings with Abd al-Mumin for, when the Almohads took Málaga in 1153, his bones were disinterred and crucified.

While Alfonso VII made his peace with ibn Gāniya, another consideration had arisen. In the spring of 1146 the forces of Genoa had launched a series of raids against Muslim Minorca and Almería. It may or may not have been coordinated with the papacy or the evolving crusade. The Genoese chronicler, Caffaro, is not interested in any but Genoese exploits and introduces third parties almost dismissively.[7] But the descent on Almería had gone sufficiently well to prompt the Genoese to send a legation overland to Córdoba where the Leonese was besieging the *Madinat*. They proposed a joint attack on Almería the following year. Alfonso was receptive and a rendezvous was set for August 1147. The king agreed as well to appeal to the rulers of Aragón-Barcelona and Montpellier for their collaboration.[8]

Alfonso returned to Toledo in August (D531–32).[9] Before then, he initiated negotiations with the other Christian princes. The Alfonsine chronicle gives the impression that the king had despatched Bishop Arnold of Astorga directly from Córdoba to seek the participation of Ramon Berenguer IV and of Count William VI of Montpellier.

Formal agreement with Genoa was reached in September 1146. For their assistance, the Leonese agreed to pay 10,000 *morabetinos* within thirty-one days and another 10,000 by Easter, to be delivered to the Genoese envoys at Barcelona. In addition, the Genoese were to have one-third of all the lands and goods that either or both were to conquer in 1147. In such territories, they could maintain their own factories, markets, churches, baths, and ovens. Moreover, Genoese subjects would be granted safe-conduct throughout the kingdom of León-Castilla and exemption from all tolls. The levels of armed forces that each party would provide are not stipulated in the treaty but were likely contained in a companion agreement. The entire pact was made contingent on a similar agreement with Barcelona. The forces of Genoa were to be ready the following May (D533). The list of those persons who joined

7. Caffaro, *De Captione Almerie et Tortuose*, ed. Antonio Ubieto Arteta (Valencia, 1973).
8. Maya Sánchez and Gil, *CAI*, pp. 246–77.
9. August 6, 1146. Pub. Manuel Lucas Alvarez, ed., *El Tumbo de San Julián de Samos, siglos VIII–XII* (Santiago de Compostela, 1986), pp. 144–45, is an *agnitio* between Bishop Guido of Lugo and Abbot Juan of Samos reached in the presence of the king. The date given is 1145 but the dating formula makes it a Tuesday and August 6 fell on Tuesday in 1146. It may have been drawn at Toledo although it does not say so.

Alfonso VII in swearing to the pact reads like a roster of the secular magnates of his kingdom. Surely all were not physically present, but their adhesion must have been solicited much as it had been to the oath preceding Alfonso's marriage to Berengaria in 1127. Curiously, no archbishop or bishop of the realm swore.

The king now set about recruiting the participation of the other Christian princes. In October he was at the monastery of Santa María de Niencebas near Tudéjen in La Rioja. Alfonso was accompanied by his eldest son, Sancho, and many barons and the charter to the monastery was confirmed by García Ramírez, accompanied by barons of his kingdom (D534). It may have been simpler to meet first with the king of Navarra or perhaps it was necessary to bring pressure on him first. In any event, such an agreement was reached at San Esteban de Gormaz in mid-November, when the dating formulas of two royal grants inform that a general peace had been agreed by García Ramírez and by Count Ramon (D537–38).

Subsequently Ramon signed a treaty with the Genoese quite like that of Alfonso VII. The Genoese pledged that, after the expedition to Almeria, they would assist the count with a siege of Muslim Tortosa on the Lower Ebro. If successful, there too they would be rewarded with one-third of the city and in it would be able to maintain their own churches, factories, ovens, and baths. They would be rewarded as well by the free passage of their goods and subjects throughout the territories of the count, including Provence. The major difference between the two treaties is that the Barcelonan pledged no money.[10]

Alfonso VII then visited Burgos briefly. There he and his wife made a grant to the Castilian monastery of Oña for the eternal welfare of their youngest son, García, who had recently died. Later in the year they were at Arévalo and perhaps Atienza (D535–36, 539–40). But this was not the usual Christmas season, spent about León with its respite from the yearly round of travel, politics, and campaigning. Instead, the king plunged south to seize the Almoravid fortress of Calatrava La Vieja by January 9, 1147 (D541). Given its speed of execution the initiative must have been concerted earlier. The grant that Alfonso made in the captured fortress was confirmed by no fewer than three bishops, four counts, and the alcalde of Toledo as well as his son, Sancho, indicating an army of considerable size.[11]

---

10. 1146. ACA, Cancillería, pergaminos, RB IV, Carpeta 41, nos. 6 and 10; pub. Caesare Imperiale de Sant' Angelo, ed., *Codice diplomatico della Republica di Genova*, vol. 1 (Rome, 1936), pp. 204–17.

11. In this same campaign Alfonso may have taken Almodóvar del Campo, thirty-five kilometers to the west. Three years later he would bestow property in Toledo on one Guter Pérez,

This success was important, for Calatrava had long been the major Almoravid base north of the Sierra Morena, controlling the routes south into the upper valley of the Guadalquivir and west into the higher reaches of the Guadiana basin. From it a series of Almoravid commanders long directed raids north into the valley of the Tajo. The seizure of that stronghold was critical to a protracted campaign in al-Andalus. Its sudden collapse requires explanation. Surprise may have been a factor for a campaign during the Christmas season was certainly not usual in peninsular warfare, but the disarray of the garrison most likely was crucial. The disintegration of the Almoravid position, the secession of Muslim Valencia, Murcia, Granada, and Málaga and continuing revolt in the Algarve would have demoralized a frontier garrison. The Almohad expeditionary force and the rebels in January laid siege to Sevilla, which opened its doors on January 17 or 18, while Almoravid adherents fled east to Carmona. In addition, the Almoravid prince, ibn Gāniya, had become a vassal of Alfonso VII. Small wonder then that Calatrava surrendered. Probably, the Leonese monarch had but to appear unexpectedly with a major force to effect an immediate submission. Nor did Alfonso feel a necessity of tarrying on the frontier to strengthen his new acquisition. From February until May he was in the north (D543–52).[12]

Now Easter was the scheduled departure date for the Second Crusade but we have no evidence that Alfonso was in touch with its leaders. Continuing contact with the papacy there was. In 1145 both Bishop Martín of Oviedo and Archbishop Raymond of Toledo had visited Rome but seemingly on ecclesiastical business.[13] When the pope reissued the bull of crusade in March 1146 Iberia went unmentioned. Moreover, three papal letters addressed to various Iberian figures during the year contained no reference to a crusade.[14] Only on April 11, 1147, in the bull *Divina Dispositione* did he mention the preparations for an attack on the Muslims of the peninsula.[15] At some time during the summer or fall of 1146 the pope had been informed of Alfonso VII's plans and

---

which had previously belonged to a Pedro Sánchez, a traitor who had surrendered it presumably to the Almohads (D653).

12. February 14, 1147. Pub. Alfredo Herrara Nogal, *El concejo de la villa de Tardajos: Fueros e Historia* (Burgos, 1980), pp. 25–39. Alfonso supposedly then reconfirmed this much interpolated *fuero* but that likelihood is small.

13. Carl Erdmann, *Das Papsttum und Portugal in ersten Jahrhundert der portugiesichen Geschicte* (Berlin, 1928), p. 34.

14. March 29, to Bishop Bernard of Sigüenza. Pub. Toribio Minguella y Arnedo, *Historia de la diócesis de Sigüenza y de sus obispos*, vol. 1 (Madrid, 1910), pp. 378–80. April 28, to Bishop Lop of Pamplona. Pub. Paul Kehr, ed. "Papsturkunden in Spanien, II: Navarra und Aragon," in *AGWG* 22 (1928): 353–54. June 14, to Ramon Berenguer. Ibid., pp. 357–58.

15. *PL* 180:1203–4.

approved them. The pontiff cooperated by working for peace in the north of Italy and encouraging the Genoese to honor their Iberian commitment.[16] The search for support in Iberia also may be indicated by a grant extended at this time by *Infanta* Sancha to Bernard of Clairvaux (D542).[17]

Peninsular events were moving rapidly forward. A private document indicates that by the end of April, the king of Navarra and the count of Barcelona were conferring, or mobilizing, south of Tudela.[18] In a month the count had retaken the castle of Ontiñena on the western edge of the territories of Lérida.[19] Events in the far west were more spectacular. In a sudden march and a night descent on March 11, the Portuguese king captured the fortress of Santarém, key to the approaches of Lisbon from the east. That strategic town had changed hands before, but this time it was to prove irrevocably lost to Islam. In April the king granted much of its goods to the military order of the Templars in a charter indicating his planned descent upon Lisbon.[20] Nevertheless, the city was an enormously strong position and Afonso I disposed of precious slim resources for such an enterprise.

What now transpired was entirely unexpected. A fleet of Germans, Flemings, and English bound for the Second Crusade in the Levant made landfall in Asturias at the end of May. It then coasted round Galicia to put in at Padrón and to celebrate Pentecost on June 8 at Santiago de Compostela. Sailing from there it touched at Oporto in Portugal to water and revictual. By this time, Afonso Henriques was alert to their presence. At his behest the bishop of Oporto approached the leaders of the fleet, asking them to consider a joint assault on Lisbon. The crusaders were interested and the fleet moved south to rendezvous with Afonso where the latter had begun harassing that city. A treaty was concluded, probably in late June, and the mixed force settled down to a long and arduous summer siege.[21]

16. Virginia Berry, "The Second Crusade," in *A History of the Crusades*, ed. Kenneth M. Setton, vol. 1 (Philadelphia, 1955), p. 469.

17. Berry, "Second Crusade," p. 476, n. 12, mentions a letter of Bernard of Clairvaux addressed *Ad Peregrinantes Ierusalem* as existing in the ACA at Barcelona. However, that letter, ACA, Códices, Ripoll 56, fol. 58r-v, is part of a collection of the fourteenth century and is addressed in fact to the clergy and people of eastern France.

18. April 27, 1147. AHN, Códices, 595B, fol. 29r-v; pub. Albon, ed. *Cartulaire*, p. 279.

19. Antonio Ubieto Arteta, *Historia de Aragón: La formación territorial* (Zaragoza, 1981), p. 223.

20. Monica Blocker-Walker, *Alfons I von Portugal* (Zurich, 1966), pp. 156–57. April 1147. Pub. DMP, 1-1:272–73. A detailed and more lively account of the capture of the town exists in the "De Expugnatione Scalabris," *PMH, Scriptores*, 1:93–95, but it is much later in origin and literary in nature although it draws on popular accounts of what clearly had become a folk epic of sorts.

21. Fortunately the laconic Portuguese chronicles are richly supplemented by Charles Wendell David, ed., *De Expugnatione Lyxbonensi* (New York, 1936). An account by an English cleric and member of the expedition.

By the end of May Alfonso VII was in Toledo, favored jumping-off point for offensives into al-Andalus (D553–56). For the campaign of 1147 a variety of sources survive, the most authoritative of which are imperial diplomas. The so-called "Poema de Almería" appended to the *Chronica Adefonsi Imperatoris* breaks off abruptly after furnishing little more than an extended encomium to the notables who did battle there.[22] A complementary account is that of the Genoese Caffaro, *De Captione Almerie et Tortuose*.[23] The thirteenth-century histories of Lucas of Túy and of Rodrigo Jiménez de Rada add only misinformation.

On the basis of the royal charters and the "Poema" we can estimate the army with which Alfonso VII began the campaign at about 5,000 men. That figure is based on the presumption that each of the identified fifteen major lay nobles of León-Castilla, plus the nine archbishops and bishops who appear in the charters and in the "Poema," would have been responsible for providing one squadron of heavy cavalry. Such squadrons averaged about forty to sixty horses in the military practice of the day. Each of these 1,200 horsemen would have required at least a squire and a groom with some experience of arms so that the total effectives would number some 3,600. Finally, we must add to that figure a minimum of 1,400 support personnel: footmen first, then drovers, carters, blacksmiths, cooks, and all that miscellany of hands and backs that made the maintenance, movement, and fighting of an army possible.[24]

The army moved south from Toledo in late May and reached Calatrava by June 4. Thereafter the charters are ambiguous. Some indicate that the army delayed about Calatrava until mid-July. On the other hand, the "Poema de Almería" speaks of a grueling and unsuccessful siege of Andújar, where we find the army on July 17, 1147 (D557–61).[25]

The possession of that fortress northwest of Jaén and southwest of the vital pass of Despeñaperros through the Sierra Morena would have furnished the maximum protection for Alfonso's line of advance and retreat. However, the defenders fought valiantly and eventually the Leonese could afford no more time. The army marched east and forced the surrender of Baeza and Úbeda sixty kilometers west of Andújar. Those hill towns furnished some security against attack on Alfonso's rear as he advanced toward Almería.

---

22. Juan Gil, ed., "Prefatio de Almeria," in *Chronica Hispana Saeculi XII* (Turnholt, 1990), pp. 249–67.

23. Ed. Antonio Ubieto Arteta (Valencia, 1973).

24. On military practice and logistics of the period one could handily consult Bernard F. Reilly, *The Kingdom of León-Castilla under King Alfonso VI, 1065–1109* (Princeton, 1988), pp. 148–60, and 180–90.

25. Gil, "Prefatio," p. 265.

In mid-August the king was in Baeza, joined by García Ramírez, who had been at Tudela as late as the end of May and probably did not participate in the assault on Andújar (D562).[26] The Navarrese likely brought on the order of fifty men-at-arms and another 250 infantry and support personnel. Meanwhile, the Genoese had arrived off Cape Gato on the Gulf of Almería only to find that their Leonese ally had not yet arrived. An embassy was despatched overland to seek him, the Genoese were concerned with their exposed anchorage, and found Alfonso at Baeza.[27]

Caffaro complains that the Leonese monarch had allowed a good portion of his army to return home from Baeza and eventually proceeded to the rendezvous with a mere 400 horsemen and a 1,000 infantry. To evaluate the Genoese complaint, several factors need to be examined. First, the army had been two and a half months in the field, most of it in full summer, had been roughly treated in one siege, and had conducted another almost immediately thereafter. Supposing that the usual premodern factors of disease in camp, exhaustion, and simple desertion had been at work, it seems likely that the original force of 5,000 had already been reduced by at least 20 percent. Moreover, substantial forces must be detached to guard Baeza and Ubeda. In addition, among the volunteer forces of the medieval army any success that yielded substantial booty tended automatically to terminate the campaign. Captains all too often had the choice of thanking their troops for their services and parting on friendly terms for the future, trying to woo them to further exertions with glowing descriptions of what more might yet be gained, or storming and sulking while good numbers of their recalcitrant squadrons melted away as opportunity offered. Something of this sort may have taken place even with so important a figure as Count Armengol of Urgel, who confirmed the charter of Alfonso at Baeza but did not figure in the later ones of the campaign. Instead that count made a grant to the Templars on October 28, 1147, at Agramunt in Urgel.[28]

But the most important reason for Alfonso's departure from Baeza for Almería with but 400 horse, 1,000 foot, and perhaps another 1,000 support personnel was logistic. The 110 kilometers from Baeza to Guadix are difficult ground for an army encumbered by a supply train of carts and donkeys. The last 100 kilometers from Guadix to Almería were a nightmare for such a force in the month of August. Foraging would have provided little relief, if some opportunities to water the stock, until Guadix was reached. Beyond that

26. May 30, 1147. Tudela. AGN, Documentos, Signatura 11.019, vol. 3, pt. 1, pp. 76–77.
27. Caffaro, *De Captione*, pp. 23–24.
28. Albon, *Cartulaire*, pp. 296–97.

point, the road winds southeast between the Sierra Nevada and the Sierra de Baza, with water almost nonexistent at that season, until the one true desert in Iberia was crossed and the seacoast gained. The route threatened disaster to the unwary commander. An army of that size, requiring on the order of 1,500 head of horse, donkeys, and oxen to remain both mobile and formidable, was optimum for such a passage.

Fortunately, some of the hazards attendant on this advance were minimized by the actions of the new Muslim master of Valencia, ibn Mardanish. This native Iberian, perhaps a former Christian, had managed to fasten his control on that important city and *taifa* with the assistance of Ramon Berenguer in 1146.[29] Now in 1147, possibly in concert with the Christian attack on Almería, he set about the reduction of the *taifa* of Murcia. His efforts that year had the effect of paralyzing any attack by Murcian forces on the exposed Leonese line of march to the south.[30]

From Baeza on, precise dates are long unavailable. If Alfonso left Baeza on August 19, the day after the date of his diploma, he may have reached the coast by about September 1. There he joined a Genoese force consisting, according to Caffaro, of 63 galleys and 163 lesser vessels.[31] If such figures can be trusted, and calculating at a complement of 100 for each galley and 40 for the supporting ships, the Genoese contingent alone would have numbered close to 13,000 persons. Finally, at some point, Count Ramon arrived with 53 knights.[32] Count William of Montpellier is not mentioned by Caffaro but likely brought another forty or so knights. Combined support troops of the two might have brought their contingents to 600 or 700 hundred.

The entire attacking force then would have numbered some 15,000 foot, less those detailed to maintain the fleet, and a covering force of 500 heavy cavalry to form a reserve against possible sallies of the besieged. The city of Almería has a strong position on heights above the Mediterranean. Level ground from which to assault it was limited largely to the beachfront and severely limited lateral access on either flank. But assault from the landward northwest was even more impractical and the beachfront became the main avenue of attack. The role of cavalry was necessarily limited and it is likely that the Genoese, who disposed of by far the greatest number of footmen, bore the brunt of the fighting just as Caffaro insists.

29. Ubieto Arteta, *Historia, Formación*, p. 222.
30. Mariano Gaspar Remiro, *Historia de Murcia musulmana* (Zaragoza, 1905), p. 188.
31. Cafffaro, *De Captione*, pp. 21–29, constitutes the sole surviving Christian narrative of the siege.
32. As late as August 5, 1147, it would appear that he was still in the north conducting the ordinary business of the realm. ACA, Cancillería, Pergaminos, RB IV, Carpeta 41, no. 3.

We have no figures for the garrison but Almeria's total population may have been near 30,000.[33] The town covered some 200 acres and was heavily fortified. Even given the numbers of its assailants, such a city could make a strong defense from behind its walls. And that was how the fight developed for the Almerians do not seem to have made major sallies once the full army of the allies was deployed. Instead, the nastiest sort of siegework ensued and dragged on for seven weeks. At one point, the defenders approached Alfonso, Ramon Berenguer, and García Ramírez, offering to ransom their city for 100,000 *morabetinos*. According to Caffaro, the Iberian leaders were ready to accept those terms but the Genoese forestalled them by preparing to attack the city alone. The resulting storm did carry the walls on October 17, 1147, and what resulted in its course was quite usual when a medieval city under siege resisted to the very end. Caffaro says that 20,000 Muslims died that day and that the survivors were given the option of ransoming themselves or being sold into slavery. Thirty thousand *morabetinos* are asserted to have been extorted in ransoms, doubtless over and above casual plunder. If there is some hyperbole here, still the punishment of Almería was dire.

The Genoese writes that government of the city went to the Genoese captain, Otto of Bonovillano, and a garrison of 1,000 men but it is unlikely that it was so simple. A series of documents testify that Otto was representative of Genoa in Almería although a garrison of 300 is mentioned. But the agreement of the previous year with Alfonso VII remained in effect, for provision was made in one of them for a Genoese share in the former's future conquests in the entire area from Denia on the east coast to Sevilla on the lower Guadalquivir.[34] In all probability, the final conquest of the town had not been so purely a Genoese affair as Cafffaro implies and what resulted was the sort of condominium envisioned in the initial agreement of 1146.

After the necessary negotiation, rest, and diversions, Alfonso returned through Baeza, where he established a government as well. His charter indicates that Count Manrique became tenant there and the king's majordomo, Count Pons of Cabrera, became tenant of Almería. From Baeza the monarch went on to Toledo for the remainder of the year (D564–68).

At Toledo, if not before, the king would have learned of the success of

33. Leopoldo Torres Balbás, "Almería islámica," *Al-Andalus* 22 (1957): 452, put its population in the middle of the eleventh century at 28,000 and said that it did not thereafter grow in size. José Angel Tapía Garrido, *Historia general de Almeria y su provincia*, 3 vols. (Almeria, 1976–78), 2:433–34, suggests 50,000, but his numbers are generally high.

34. Imperiale, *Codice*, pp. 228–30. Tapía Garrido, *Historia*, 3:10–12, asserts that the city never fully recovered from the effects of the siege and that the Mozarab community there vanished. His support for this conclusion is not evident.

his cousin, Afonso Henriques. On October 24, after seventeen weeks of fierce resistance, the city of Lisbon had surrendered to the mixed force of Portuguese and crusaders. For three days thereafter, it had been given over to spoil and rapine. Little heed was paid to persons or position and even the aged, Mozarab Christian bishop of the city was killed. After a carnival of destruction the city passed to the Portuguese king and a new bishop was selected, an English cleric, Gilbert of Hastings. Our source implies that the Muslims of Lisbon were expelled and that the city became purely Christian. Moreover, it describes a general pestilence in the neighboring countryside that probably should be seen as the effect of a long period of hunger and privation among the expelled that resulted in a further depletion of the former population of Muslims and Mozarabs. Lesser Muslim strongholds such as Cintra hastened to surrender and the entire north bank of the Tajo from Santarém down to the Atlantic passed definitively into Christian hands.[35]

Eugenius III had reason to rejoice at the news from the, west even as he pondered the near destruction of Conrad III's army by the Seljuk Turks in Anatolia and increasingly ominous news concerning that of Louis VII. But there is little evidence that the Roman pontiff busied himself with the Christian offensive in Iberia. For the entire year of 1147, only three papal bulls addressed to the peninsula are known. None of them mentions a crusade or related matters. At best, it can be noted that one of the three was directed to the abbot of the monastery of Fitero, where Alfonso VII had met with García Ramírez the preceding fall to concert their campaign.[36]

In 1148, with the successes of the previous year still fresh, the princes of Iberia secured rather more attention. Eugenius III held a major council in France at Rheims in March and April, and extant papal letters indicate major attention to the peninsula. They also demonstrate the attendance there of the bishops of Segovia, Coria, and Oviedo. Of course, most of these bulls dealt with properly ecclesiastical affairs.[37] But doubtless the episcopal delegation

---

35. David, *De Expugnatione*, pp. 173–81.

36. May 9, 1147. AHN, Carpeta 526, no. 14; pub. Pilar Loscertales de García de Valdeavellano, ed., *Tumbos del monasterio de Sobrado de los monjes*, 2 vols. (Madrid, 1976), 2:19–20, a likely original. June 28, 1147. Pub. Luciano Serrano, *El obispado de Burgos y Castilla primitiva desde el siglo V al XIII*, 3 vols. (Madrid, 1935), 3:188. September 17, 1147. AHN, Clero, Carpeta 1.397, no. 8; pub. Cristina Monterde Albiac, ed., *Colección diplomático del monasterio de Fitero: 1140–1210* (Zaragoza, 1978), pp. 360–65, a likely original.

37. Juan Francisco Rivera Recio, *La Iglesia de Toledo en el siglo XII*, vol. 1 (Rome, 1966), p. 340, argued that the delegation was led by Archbishop Raymond of Toledo but it seems to me that the reasoning of Angel González Palencia, *El Arzobispo D. Raimundo de Toledo* (Barcelona, 1942), pp. 94–96, carries more conviction. April 7, 1148. Pub. Kehr, "Papsturkunden," 2:362–63. It confirms the privileges of the see of Calahorra. April 7, 1148. AHN, Códices, 988B, fol. 6r-v; pub. Luis Fernández Martín, "Villafrades de Campos: Señorío del abad de Sahagún," *AL* 27

despatched by Alfonso VII had other requests and Pope Eugenius responded
by blessing the king's proposed expedition against the Muslims. By the hand
of Bishop Pedro of Segovia, the pontiff also despatched the golden rose indicating high papal favor. In addition, Eugenius promised to see that the
archbishop of Braga recognized the primatial rights of Toledo and counseled
reconciliation between León and Portugal to facilitate their military plans.[38]
Finally, Pope Eugenius forwarded to Ramon Berenguer a bull bestowing all
the benefits of a crusade on that ruler's planned assault on Muslim Tortosa.[39]
With that aim, the Genoese fleet had wintered at Barcelona. However, the attack on Tortosa was delayed until midsummer. The tardy beginning resulted
from the opportunism of García of Navarra who utilized Barcelona's preoccupation to seize Tauste, forty kilometers northwest of Zaragoza. Our sole
notice of it is dated only by year, but it probably occurred in March.[40]

The Leonese king had been busy with domestic affairs and a great council of the realm at Palencia (D569–79). When word of the new falling-out
reached him, he again set out to repair a fragile truce in the northeast. March
found him in Soria and April in Almazán (D580–82). From these Alfonso
negotiated a new understanding between the belligerents. Ramon Berenguer
was present at Soria and in April met with his Aragonese rival at Gallur near
Tauste.[41] The settlement effected is unknown, but it sufficed to allow Ramon
to pick up the threads of the Tortosa enterprise. In May he signed a pact with
Count Armengol of Urgel that granted that magnate a third of the territories
of Muslim Lérida on its capture.[42] Armengol had also been present in Soria in
March. Alfonso VII may have undertaken to guarantee the good behavior of
the Navarrese monarch who subsequently attended on his court (D583–89).

(1973): 253–55. It reaffirmed the privileges of the latter monastery. April 9, 1148. Pub. Miguel C.
Vivancos Gómez, ed., *Documentación del monasterio de Santo Domingo de Silos, 954–1254* (Burgos,
1988), pp. 72–74. This likely original confirmed that abbey's rights. April 9, 1148. Pub. Luis-
Miguel Villar García, ed., *Documentación medieval de la catedral de Segovia, 1115–1300* (Salamanca,
1990), pp. 89–91, a probable original that confirmed the possessions and exemptions of the monastery of Oña. April 9, 1148. Pub. Carl Erdmann, ed., "Papsturkunden in Portugal," *AGWG* 20
(1927): 210–11. It settled a boundary dispute between the sees of Oviedo and Lugo. April 15,
1148. Pub. José María Fernández Catón, ed., *Colección documental de la catedral de León, 1109–1187*,
vol. 5 (León, 1990), pp. 244–46. Again it is a possible original that reaffirms some possessions of
the cathedral of León.
        38. April 27, 1148. Pub. Demetrio Mansilla, ed., *La documentación pontificia hasta Inocen-
cio III, 965–1216* (Rome, 1955), pp. 94–96. Later in the year the pope confirmed the rights of the
see of Braga. September 8, 1148. Pub. Erdmann, "Papsturkunden," pp. 211–13.
        39. June 22, 1148. Cited in José Goñi Gaztambide, *Historia de la Bula de la Cruzada en
España* (Vitoria, 1958), p. 86.
        40. AHN, Códices, 595B, fol. 31r; pub. Albon, *Cartulaire*, p. 307.
        41. April 15, 1148. Pub. José María Lacarra, "Documentos para el estudio de la reconquista
y repoblación del valle del Ebro," *EEMCA* 3 (1947–48): 623–24.
        42. May 1148. Monzón. ACA, Cancillería, Pergaminos, RB IV, Carpeta 37, no. 164. May 25,
1148. Pub. Francisco M. Rosell, ed., *Liber Feudorum Maior* (Barcelona, 1945), pp. 168–69.

The forces of Barcelona and Genoa sailed for Tortosa on June 29 and arrived in the delta of the Ebro on July 1, 1148.[43] They were joined there by Count Armengol of Urgel, Count William of Montpellier, the Count Bertrán of Toulouse, the viscounts of Béarn and of Narbonne, the Templars and Hospitallers of the realm, and even by some contingents of the fleet that had assisted at the reduction of Lisbon the previous fall. Those adventurers had coasted round the peninsula to join the assault on hapless Tortosa.[44]

The Ebro was then navigable by seagoing vessels all the way up to the city. Nevertheless, Tortosa was a formidable position and had had ample warning to secure provisions. The allies disposed of sufficient forces to surround the city, but its walls were strong and its citadel of formidable height. The siege was arduous and protracted. Caffaro makes the capture of Tortosa almost entirely the work of the Genoese, but the strenuous siegework dragged on through summer into early winter. Finally the Muslim requested a truce of forty days while they appealed for help, surrendered hostages, and swore to surrender if aid were not forthcoming. The truce was granted but no help appeared. On December 31, 1148, therefore, Tortosa capitulated. The monarch of Barcelona then bestowed a third of it on the Genoese, who were to have their own officials, churches, ovens, baths, and commercial rights. A fifth went to the Templars and something less to the count's seneschal, Guillem Ramon de Montcada, out of that portion the count secured for himself. The Muslim population was guaranteed rights to its religion, officials, and property, save that houses held within the city proper were to be surrendered within a year. Meanwhile, the Christian offensive in Andalucía slowed to a halt. After his interview with García Ramírez, Alfonso VII traveled south, reaching Toledo by the end of May (D590). For the results of the campaign we depend on late Muslim sources.

By midyear ibn Gāniya despaired of maintaining himself and arranged to surrender Córdoba and Jaén to the Almohads, he himself retiring to Granada. Alfonso VII, whose vassal he had been since 1146, was forced to dispute a transfer so dangerous to his position on the upper Guadalquivir. He did manage to seize Córdoba briefly but had to yield it to a combination of Almohad and local forces. Alfonso seems even to have campaigned so far south as Alcalá la Real, forty kilometers below Jaén, but finally had to accept the new status quo along the Guadalquivir. While a major defeat is not reported, the

---

43. Caffaro, *De Captione*, pp. 31–35.
44. Rudof Hiestand, "Reconquista, Kreuzzug und heiliges Grab," *GAKS* 31 (1984): 136–57, but see also Giles Constable, "A Note on the Route of the Anglo-Flemish Crusaders of 1147," *Speculum* 28 (1953): 525–26, Marcelin Defourneaux, *Les Français en Espagne aux XI et XIII siècles* (Paris, 1949), p. 177, and Alan J. Forey, *The Templars in the Corona de Aragón* (London, 1973), pp. 24–25.

setback may have been quite serious because the royal *alférez*, Nuño Pérez, fell captive and was held for a time at Jaén.⁴⁵ The Leonese monarch's movements for the remainder of the year are obscure. Surviving charters, taken together, suggest that he may have been in the vicinity of León as early as the end of August and as late as December (D591–96).⁴⁶

There are indications that the Leonese monarch planned an active year in 1149. Early in January he was at Toledo and spent a month there, preparing important negotiations with potential Muslim allies in Valencia and Murcia. He granted a portion of the tolls from the bridge of Logroño to the monastery of Cluny at the request of its treasurer, Boso, who was also prior of the monastery of Santa María de Nájera (D597–603). One suspects that significant diplomatic business was being transacted with that Burgundian center, too. Then Alfonso departed Toledo to rendezvous with the Muslim rulers ibn Mardanish of Valencia and the latter's lieutenant in Murcia, ibn Hamusk. The trio met at Zorita, seventy kilometers east of Madrid on the Valencian frontier. Plans laid for the campaign, Alfonso traveled to Madrid in February, where he learned that his wife had died in his absence (D604–6). Since the queen had been at Toledo on January 30 and died in Palencia some 250 kilometers to the north before February 15, we should place her demise about February 8–9.

The death of Berengaria of Barcelona after more than twenty years of marriage immediately posed political and diplomatic problems. The youth of the king (he was not yet forty-four) made it certain that he would remarry. To keep up the more-than-ever important Aragón-Barcelona alliance suggested some other scion of that house. But if the new preeminence of the crown of León-Castilla in the peninsula were to be underlined, perhaps a bride from beyond the Pyrenees might be preferable. Then, too, the offensive against Muslim al-Andalus had reached a critical point. The current needs of the crusade in Iberia reinforced the utility of a marriage beyond the Pyrenees if it

45. Codera, *Decadencia*, pp. 64–65, and Rafael Gerardo Peinado Santaella and José Enrique López de Coca Castañer, *Historia de Granada*, vol. 2 (Granada, 1987), p. 232. October 22, 1148. AD León, Gradefes, nos. 60, 61; pub. Aurelio Calvo, *El monasterio de Gradefes* (León, 1936), pp. 306–7. This private charter reported the *alférez* captive. There is some difficulty with it since it also cites Diego Muñoz as *merino* in León but it is unlikely that such a detail as the former was fabricated.

46. September 4, 1148. Pub. José Antonio Fernández Flórez, ed., *Colección diplomático del monasterio de Sahagún, 1110–1199*, vol. 4 (León, 1991), pp. 209–10, as an original. This private donation to the monastery of Sahagún, confirmed by court figures, is probably false since one of them is Nuño Pérez, captive in Jaén. November 7, 1148. AHN, Orden militares, Carpeta 455, no. 2; and Acad. Hist., Colección Salazar, I-38, fol. 276r. This private exchange of land among the members of the Lara family is also confirmed by court figures including Nuño, who conceivably had been ransomed by this time.

could generate aid for that project. But a new marriage carried with it the promise of new births and thus of new heirs. If dynastic rivalries were to be minimized, then the position of the present *infantes*, Sancho and Fernando, needed to be clarified. The superior position of the first, Sancho, had been signaled already since 1146 by his association with the king and queen in the intitulation of royal diplomas. Berengaria was scarcely dead when such intitulation begins to cite the king and both surviving sons. The change is striking and is hardly mere coincidence. Decisions forced by the death of the queen began to be made almost immediately.

Some evidence suggests that an appanage was erected for the eldest, Sancho, about Nájera in La Rioja and that he then controlled some portion of the royal fisc from which to make alienations of land with paternal consent. But most of the charters adduced are dubious, probably interpolated, and late copies. The strongest evidence is contained in his charter of February 1149 (D607). However, that charter conferred a portion of the bridge tolls at Logroño on the church of Santa María de Nájera, and this privilege had already been conferred by an Alfonsine charter of January 30, 1149, just mentioned. The diploma of the young *infante* shows him with a court of his own including a chancellor, notary, majordomo, and *alférez*. Alfonso VII confirms it, but so does Archbishop Bernard of Toledo (who had been dead for two dozen years). A scattering of other documents point in the same direction but cannot be taken at face value (D599).

On the news of Berengaria's death, the court proceeded north to León for the obsequies. Then the body of the queen was entrusted, on March 8, to Archbishop Pedro of Santiago de Compostela who conducted thence where it was interred with great ceremony (D608–9).[47] The evidence indicates a substantial gathering of prelates and magnates at León and doubtless preliminary discussions on the question of marriage and the succession were held. If so, the king's journey east in March would have explored the views of the prelates and magnates there concerning decisions tentatively considered at León. The two *infantes* accompanied the king. The Castilian bishops of Burgos and Osma and the Riojan bishops of Tarazona and Calahorra attended him in Burgos as did Count Armengol of Urgel and García Ramírez

47. March 6, 1149. This is an inscription recording the consecration of the shrine church of San Isidoro of León reported in *ES*, 35:207, and independently in BN, Manuscritos, 712, fol. 81v. It records the presence of Alfonso, the two *infantes*, and the *infantas* Sancha and Constanza, along with the archbishops of Toledo and Compostela and nine other bishops. Unfortunately one of the latter is a Pedro of Avila but the incumbent was then one Jimeno. Antonio López Ferreiro, *Historia de la Santa Apostica Metropolitana Iglesia de Santiago de Compostela*, 11 vols. (Santiago de Compostela, 1898–1911), 4:239, describes the funeral.

of Navarra (D610–14). The death of Berengaria particularly concerned the latter, for it might dissolve the close alliance of León and Aragón-Barcelona. That tie had blocked García's ambitions in the Ebro valley since 1137.

Possibly the arrangements made at León were modified. In the charters of March 24 and 25 Martín Muñoz confirms as *Infante* Sancho's majordomo, and this time there is no good reason to question the designation. Possibly Castilian influence at Burgos resulted in a certain preeminence for the older of the two sons rather than their strict equality. In any event, henceforth one can speak of the existence of a court of the young Sancho.

Alfonso next moved west, probably again to parade his heirs and solicit the adhesion of the prelates and magnates of those regions (D615–18). Collectively, the diplomas show the archbishop of Compostela and the bishops of León, Astorga, Zamora, Túy, Orense, and Salamanca at court, as well as many of the secular magnates of Galicia. A grant to Clairvaux surely was accompanied by a request for support from its abbot, Bernard, for the developing royal concerns.

From Salamanca the king proceeded to Toledo in June. Then he disappears until mid-October when he is again at Toledo (D619–24). All of this irresistibly suggests a campaign in Andalucía. The opportunity would have been there for the most able of the native Muslim leaders, ibn Gāniya, had died at the beginning of the year. Granada and Málaga continued to oppose Almohad power. Alfonso's recent pact with the independent Muslim rulers of Valencia and Murcia was designed to take advantage of such division. If, however, there was a campaign it was not decisive and was unrecorded.

With winter the king moved north to Salamanca (D626–28). During this period a noticeable irregularity developed in the intitulation of royal charters. It may be the character of the record, but subsequent developments incline one to suspect rather more. *Infante* Fernando disappears, sometimes Alfonso VII appears alone, and other times *Infante* Sancho acts in concert with him. Possibly in Toledo and the vicinity, an area of strong Castilian character by this time, the crown again found it necessary to stress the primacy of the eldest son. In coming months that emphasis emerges yet more clearly.

Infanta Sancha seems to have held clear of this family struggle. In mid-September she was in Compostela, perhaps to inspect the work on the Berengaria's tomb and possibly to sidestep involvement in the dynastic question (D623). But her presence there alerted her to the failing health of its archbishop who died on November 9, 1149.[48] The king had been bilked of his

---

48. Richard A. Fletcher, "The Archbishops of Santiago de Compostela between 1140 and 1173: A New Chronology," *Compostellanum* 17 (1972): 49.

choice there in 1140–1141 but was not to be again and early notice from his sister would allow him to steal a march on any local opposition. By the end of December his ambassador had reached Pope Eugenius III in Rome and the pope wrote the king in support of the latter's request to regulate matters between the peninsular archbishops of Toledo, Braga, and Santiago de Compostela.[49] One suspects that royal solicitation for the translation of his candidate of 1140, Berenguer of Salamanca, to the archepiscopal see was also made.

Meanwhile Aragón-Barcelona scored another of the major triumphs of the *reconquista*. For a full century the great Muslim city, and sometimes *taifa*, of Lérida had dominated the fertile plains of the lower Ebro basin. In 1090 at the height of his power the Cid had briefly intervened in its life as protector of its young heirs. In 1134 Alfonso *el Batallador* had lost his life at Fraga in a vain attempt to conquer the city. In 1149 Count Ramon enjoyed the momentum imparted by the just completed conquest of Tortosa. But before he could commit his full strength there, he had to be sure of a neutral Navarra. That precaution was especially necessary now that Alfonso VII was no longer Ramon's brother-in-law but rather the father-in-law of García. On July 1, 1149, the Barcelonan signed a treaty with García that has troubled historians ever since. In brief, Ramon would marry Blanca, daughter of García, before September 29, 1149, perpetual peace would follow between their houses, conquests of either or both in the Muslim lands south of Zaragoza would be partitioned between the two, and a mutual exchange of castles would accompany the marriage ceremonies.[50]

Had he implemented this extraordinary treaty, Ramon Berenguer would have had to disavow his twelve-year-old betrothal to Petronila of Aragón. Such an action would have forfeited his claim to that regnum, except perhaps secondarily through the claims of the bastard line of García, to whom he would now be affiliated by marriage. In short, the treaty is unbelievable now and probably was incredible then as well; that is, it is not likely that either signatory ever expected that it would be consumated. The Barcelonan was essentially playing for time during which he could reduce Lérida unhindered. The Navarrese expected no more than that, in itself, publication of the pact would destroy Aragonese confidence in the good faith of their new prince and open the road to future Navarrese gains.

---

49. *PL*, 180, cols. 1, 405–6.

50. ACA, Cancillería, Pergaminos, RB IV, Carpeta 38, no. 214; pub. Antonio Ubieto Arteta, *Historia de Aragón. Creación y desarollo de la Corona de Aragón* (Zaragoza, 1987), pp. 165–69, who called it an original. It is rather a thirteenth-century copy on the basis of the script but its integrity seems guaranteed by the fact that the Aragonese rulers would have had no reason to fabricate or to preserve such a potentially damaging document.

Ramon began the siege of Lérida in June with the aid of Templars of his realm, the count of Urgel, and the Bearnese señor of Huesca, Pierre de Gabaret. It endured until late October, complicated by the simultaneous blockades of the satellite fortresses of Fraga and Mequinenza on its western and southern approaches. The burden was arduous, but the neutralization of Valencia under ibn Mardanish and the general hopelessness engendered by the loss of Almería and Tortosa in the two preceding years had taken their toll. On October 24, 1149, the discouraged defenders surrendered all three positions. Ramon Berenguer now became marquess of Tortosa and of Lérida as well as count of Barcelona and prince of Aragón. He took two-thirds of the city for himself, endowing Count Armengol with the other third, and then granted the Templars a fifth of the city from his own portion. Perre de Gabaret was rewarded with the tenancy of Fraga. The Muslim population was guaranteed life, freedom, property, law, and religion, so long as an annual royal tribute was paid.[51]

The fall of Lérida marked the final passage of the basin of the Ebro, the greatest river system of Iberia, into the hands of Aragón-Barcelona. That river became the its major artery and was lost forever to Iberian Islam. Independent but isolated Muslim populations persisted in the rugged sierras south of the Ebro, but to their south ibn Mardanish was a tributary of Ramon Berenguer to whom he promised annual *parias* of 100,000 dinars. In January 1149 he had signed a ten-year treaty with the republic of Pisa, granting that city factories in Valencia and Denia. In June he signed an almost identical pact with the Genoese and agreed in addition to respect the latter's trading stations in Almería and Tortosa.[52]

Ramon Berenguer's conquests in 1148 and 1149 were the last great geographical gains of the kingdom during his reign. Their very extent militated against further advance. They mirrored the triumph of Alfonso I of Aragón in 1118–1120 that suddenly had incorporated the lands of Zaragoza, Calatayud, and Daroca into the kingdom and, with those territories, a large and sophisticated Muslim population that could neither simply be displaced nor diluted with Christian settlers at any very rapid rate. Now the river valleys of the lower Segre, the lower Cinca, and the lower Ebro had to be organized. Consolidation rather than aggrandizement was ordained by the new circumstances.

51. See the notices collected in Antonio Ubieto Arteta, *Historia. Formación*, pp. 229–32.
52. Michele Amari, ed., *I diplomi arabi del R. Archivio Fiorentini* (Florence, 1863), pp. 239–40, and Imperiale, *Codice*, 1:247–49. Ramon Berenguer himself continued to court the presence of the Genoese, as evidenced by his exemption of their trade with the west of the peninsula where it entered his realms at Tamarite. Ibid., pp. 238–40.

Ramon spent the first three months of the new year in Lérida, joining with the count of Urgel in the grant of a *fuero* to its inhabitants.[53] In that city he was married in August of 1150, but not, of course, to Blanca of Navarra. As a consequence, the letter of congratulation, despatched by Pope Eugenius III on July 25, 1150, hailing the salutary results to be expected from the projected perpetual peace of July 1149 between Navarra and Aragón-Barcelona spoke to events long dead in the peninsula.[54] Such was the handicap usually imposed on papal diplomacy in Iberia by the problems of distance and time. When the missive arrived, Ramon was celebrating his nuptials with the heiress of Aragón, Petronila, the latter having attained her fourteenth year. The match consolidated that most fortuitous union of Aragón and Barcelona that had somehow endured against all odds since 1137. Marriage to its heiress and male issue was requisite to the survival of that unlikely political hybrid.[55]

Eugenius's letter looked to a renewed offensive against the Muslim south that was out of date. Events were drawing the interests of Ramon north. Alfonso Jordan of Toulouse had perished in the Near East in April 1148. His demise focused attention at Barcelona on possibilities inherent in the succession of the young Raymond V. The county of Toulouse had long been a powerful check on the influence of Barcelona in the Midi. After his marriage in Lérida, Ramon journeyed to Provence. By September he had effected a general treaty with the house of Baux, the major opponents of his own dynasty in that county, now deprived of support from Toulouse.[56] In November at Narbonne he secured the homage of Viscount Raymond Trencavell for Carcassonne and Razès. The passage down the valley of the River Aude toward the Narbonnais and the Mediterranean was now secure. The good fortune of Aragón-Barcelona in the Midi deprived Alfonso VII of a major ally. For the remaining six and a half years of his reign, the Leonese worked only with such help as Navarra, Portugal, and his own Muslim allies could sometimes afford him. Ultimately, that aid proved insufficient.

At Burgos Alfonso VII was finding his initiatives limited to the peninsula (D632–36). There he may have learned of the crusading debacles in the Holy Land, Emperor Conrad III's plans for joint war with Emperor Manuel of Byzantium against Roger II of Sicily, the revolt against the former by Welf faction at home, and Louis VII's project for a new crusade against Byzantium

53. January 1150. ACA, Cancillería, Pergaminos, RB IV, Carpeta 38, no. 225; pub. Francisco M. Rosell, ed., *Liber Feudorum Maior* (Barcelona, 1945), pp. 170–72. January 8, 1150. Lérida. ACA, Cancillería, Registro 2, ff. 115r-16r. March 1150. Lérida. AHN, Clero, Carpeta 714, no. 11.
54. Paul Kehr, ed., "Papsturkunden in Spanien, I: Katalonien," *AGWG* 18 (1926): 327–28.
55. Antonio Ubieto Arteta, *Historia. Creación*, pp. 170–71.
56. September 1150. Arles. Pub. Rosell, *Liber Feudorum*, pp. 351–53.

in concert with William I. Clearly this was no time to rush into marriage alliances with any of them. One step was possible. If the supporters of the accession of *Infante* Sancho were restive, they could be mollified by arrangements for that prince's marriage; one that would promise to provide him with both an heir of his own and the additional prestige of a royal bride. At the same time, the Iberian interests of the Leonese crown could be furthered. If it is doubtful that Alfonso VII took seriously the short-lived project for the marriage of Ramon Berenguer and Blanca of Navarra, the random initiatives of her father must have been disturbing. One way to neutralize the princess was to marry her to Sancho, so the king invited García to Burgos later in the winter.

Meanwhile, the court seems to have moved southwest (D637–39). On Ash Wednesday the court had returned to Burgos and King García was there. Likely the negotiations that eventuated in the marriage of the *infante* Sancho and of Blanca in less than a year began then. In addition, the campaign of the approaching season in Andalucía and García's participation were also topics (D640–44).

From March until April the king was in Toledo (D645–60). A major effort, both military and diplomatic, was being planned. We are told that while Alfonso VII was in the city a deaf-mute was miraculously cured in the cathedral in the presence of many spectators. The king, the primate, and a number of bishops testified to the veracity of the miracle and perhaps took it as an augury of success.[57]

The major design of the summer, the capture of the key city of Córdoba, now required the king's departure. As a crucial factor in the reduction of such a populous city was famine, if the initiation of a siege were delayed longer, the winter wheat crop could be harvested, depriving the attackers of a major advantage. Alfonso departed Toledo in April and began the siege of Córdoba in May. He had already taken the strategic stronghold of Montoro, forty-five kilometers upstream. The count of Urgel had also joined the army (662–67).

Not long after his departure, on May 16, 1150, the expected Portuguese embassy arrived. It was led by the archbishop of Braga, present to negotiate an alliance and to make his own religious obedience to the primate of Toledo in response to repeated papal commands. In the absence of the king, the embassy was received by Archbishop Raymond, by the bishops of Sigüenza and Salamanca, and by the Leonese *infante*, Fernando.[58] The two powers agreed

---

57. April 21, 1150. Cited, Francisco J. Hernández, ed., *Los cartularios de Toledo* (Madrid, 1985), p. 74.
58. Cited ibid., p. 74; pub. Fidel Fita, "Primera legación del Cardenal Jacinto en España.

to despatch embassies to the major realms of western Europe to secure aid for a transcendent effort in Iberia. One of these embassies was led by Bishop Gilbert of Lisbon, himself an Englishman and a crusader in 1147 who could testify firsthand to the rewards likely to follow on success. Gilbert's efforts in England were noticed by John of Hexham in his *Historia*.[59] Alfonsine charters of the summer of 1151 tell us that another embassy was sent to France.

Alfonso VII lay before Córdoba for three months during the spring and summer of 1150. From June he had the aid there of García Ramírez, but the city resisted valiantly and an Almohad force was sent from Sevilla. The charters of Alfonso speak of 30,000 warriors but claim victory nonetheless. The sole Muslim source speaks of the 40,000 horsemen of the Leonese monarch and the inability of the relief force to meet them in the open field. Yet the Almohads managed to throw reinforcements into the city by a strategem. Despite the incredible numbers alleged we can accept the general depiction of events as likely, given their aftermath. Faced with the probability that the reinforced garrison of Córdoba would now resist indefinitely, Alfonso gave up the siege in favor of a quick strike against Jaén. Control of that rocky fastness would have made much more difficult any further Almohad advance toward Alfonso's chief operational center at Baeza. It also would have flanked any African advance overland on Granada, which *taifa* had still not accepted their dominance.

The attitude of the populace of Jaén must have been mixed. The prospect of a Leonese protectorate rather than outright Almohad rule might have been preferrable, but Jaén saw no immediate need to make a choice. Their fortified position was almost impregnable and the army of Alfonso became discouraged after three months of hard campaigning. Little more than a week after his arrival before the city in mid-August, he had withdrawn to Baeza (D668–71). The campaign was over and by September 1 the king had reached Toledo. Frontier concerns dominated the royal actions there through October and November and his charters show his preoccupation with encouraging settlements (D672–76).

Then pressing matters summoned him north. On November 21, 1150, García Ramírez of Navarra died at Lorca near Estella and the independent existence of Navarra was again a question. The work of García Ramírez *el Restaurador* was only sixteen years old and before that León-Castilla and Aragón had shared out its territories between them for almost sixty years. The Nava-

Bulas inéditas de Anastasio IV. Nuevas luces sobre el concilio nacional de Valladolid (1155) y otros datos inéditos," *BRAH* 14 (1889): 544.

59. T. Arnold, ed., *Symeonis monachi opera omni* (Rolls Series), vol. 2 (1885), p. 324.

rrese left an heir, Sancho VI (1150–1194), who came to be known as *el Sabio*, a title earned in the struggle to prevent a new partition of his tiny realm. In December Sancho met with Ramon Berenguer who, as prince of Aragón, had an obvious interest in lands formerly part of that realm. We do not know what transpired, but clearly graver negotiations followed.[60]

Alfonso VII could have learned of the García's death in a mere ten days. It would have been in someone's interest to report that news to him, and the journey from Estella to Toledo was easily completed in that time. The king hurried north to Burgos, there to confer with as many of the great prelates and magnates of the realm as could be reached, for crucial decisions must be made. The new heir of Navarra was summoned to do homage for Navarra was a fief of León-Castilla (D679–81).

Before the third week of January 1151 had ended, the decisive steps had been taken. Sancho VI had done homage and been recognized as the new king of Navarra. In addition, the future Sancho III of Castilla had been married to Blanca of Navarra, daughter of the deceased García. Thus it was ensured that the latter kingdom would continue as a Leonese client realm and, should Sancho VI die without an heir, become a possession outright of the house of León (D682). Nevertheless, no options were being neglected and one of them can only be described as Machiavellian. Before the month was out, agents of Alfonso VII had negotiated a treaty with Ramon Berenguer for the partition of Navarra.[61] Meeting with the Barcelonan at the fortress of Tudéjen near Fitero in La Rioja, they agreed that lands about the Navarrese nucleus of Pamplona and Estella and the newer acquisitions about Tudela would both be divided between Alfonso and Ramon. The latter would do the Leonese homage for his portion. The future Sancho III, for his part, would repudiate the Navarrese princess Blanca by the following Michaelmas, September 29.

The treaty further provided for joint action against the Muslims of the Mediterranean coast. After their conquest, Ramon was to hold the kingdom of Valencia and Murcia, the latter save the district about Lorca, from Alfonso VII on the same conditions as he already held the territories of Zaragoza. He further agreed to hold all of these lands, Navarrese and Valencian-Murcian, from the future Sancho III after the death of Alfonso VII and from the future Fernando II if Sancho should die. The Leonese monarch had

---

60. December 1150. Sos. AGN, Comptes, Cajón 1, no. 26; a private document. See also Antonio Ubieto Arteta, "Navarra-Aragón y la idea imperial de Alfonso VII de Castilla," *EEMCA* 6 (1956): 67.

61. January 27, 1151. Tudején. Pub. Rosell, *Liber Feudorum*, pp. 39–42. The document was prepared by Pons, the regular scribe of Ramon Berenguer, and follows the form of that chancery, including the date, which is given by year of the Incarnation, not the Spanish era. The copy's date is incorrect. It is given as 1150, impossible because García Ramírez still lived.

provided himself with two possible courses of action. If the untried king of Navarra managed to establish his authority, then that kingdom would continue closely tied to León-Castilla with the possibility of its eventual absorption. If by the end of September he proved unable to control his inheritance, then Alfonso and Ramon Berenguer could partition it. At the same time, the treaty held out the maximum incentives to the Barcelonan in return for his renewed participation in the war against the Muslims. While the latter's share in any partition of Navarra was not explicitly related to his resumption of the *reconquista*, it is likely that Alfonso's agents made clear that their sovereign must have one ally or the other, Navarra if not Aragón-Barcelona.

The text also indicates that at this time *Infante* Sancho was seen as the prospective heir of Alfonso VII. Sancho alone is associated everywhere with his father. It is to Sancho that Ramon will do homage for his territories in Navarra and Valencia-Murcia in the event of the death of the Leonese monarch. *Infante* Fernando is entitled king but is mentioned only as the possible heir of Sancho. The eventual division of the realm into a kingdom of León and another of Castilla, which so radically altered the political realities of Iberia in 1157, was not yet envisioned.

In the aftermath of these negotiations Alfonso spent the next six weeks in the northeast. With him were the king of Navarra, the Basque Count Latro and his heir Vela, and the border magnate Rodrigo Pérez of Azagra and his brother Gonzalo (D684–87). Alfonso was still in a position to intervene quickly in Navarra if necessary (D688–93).[62]

Ramon Berenguer, who had quite as much interest in what was to transpire in Navarra if not so much influence, hung about Zaragoza.[63] For the time being he held back, but, when Alfonso VII moved south, the Barcelonan contributed what he could to the troubles of the new king. He attacked and took the castle of Borja, twenty-five kilometers south of Navarrese Tudela, and also assaulted the strongpoint of Cascante, ten kilometers southwest of that city.[64] Nevertheless, neither initiative succeeded in destabilizing the developing reign of Sancho.

During the winter of 1150–1151 the king of León despatched an embassy to Conrad III of Germany in search of a new wife. The German had dropped

62. February 20, 1151. AHN, Clero, Carpeta 249, no. 3; pub. Gonzalo Martínez, "Diplomatario de San Cristóbal de Ibeas," *BIFG* 55 (1975): 697–98, who calls it an original. Actually this is a copy of a private donation of Guter Fernández and his wife to that monastery and is confirmed by Alfonso and many of his court.

63. January 31, 1151. Zaragoza. Pub. Luis Rubio, ed., *Documentos del Pilar* (Zaragoza, 1971), p. 51. It is a donation of the Barcelonan to the men of Mamblas. March 1151. Zaragoza. AHN, Códices,95B, ff. 11r-12r. This is a donation of that count to the Templars.

64. April 26, 1151. Borja. ACA, Cancillería, Pergaminos, RB IV, Carpeta 38, no. 249. See Ubieto Arteta, "Navarra-Aragón," pp. 69–70.

his projected alliance with Roger II of Sicily and sought a rapprochement with Eugenius III and the imperial coronation. Alfonso VII may have had word of this when his newly consecrated Archbishop Berenguer of Compostela returned from Rome through Burgos. The archbishop could have brought the news that a marital alliance arranged by Conrad would now be acceptable at Rome.[65] An embassy from Alfonso VII reached Conrad III that winter and was dismissed by the latter on Pentecost, May 27, 1151, after having been long at his court, according to Otto of Freising.[66] They had arranged for a marriage between Alfonso and the Polish princess called Rica in the peninsula. She was the granddaughter of Boleslaus III of Poland and the daughter of Ladislaus I, once prince of Cracow but since driven into exile, and Agnes, daughter of Leopold, Margrave of Austria. Rica was probably in her late teens and without great prospects because of her family's circumstances.[67] Doubtless the match was attractive to her. As far as Alfonso was concerned, her chief recommendation was the imperial approbation that the marriage would demonstrate. However, the imperial connection proved cause for delay when Conrad died the following February.

Despite these grand plans, there are indications that uncertainty about the future of the dynasty was causing concern in León-Castilla. Queen Berengaria was close to two years dead, Alfonso VII had not yet remarried, *Infante* Sancho had found a royal bride, but the future was not clearly to be descried in any of this. One result of this concern may be found in the change of intitulation in the royal charters. The association there of the "emperor" Alfonso and "my son King Sancho" that had been usual since Berengaria's death now gives way for a time to Alfonso and "my sons and daughters and everyone of my blood." Presumably the rationale of the change is that the title conveyed will thus stand, no matter who should eventually succeed. But while that change might serve the particular good of the grantee, it did little to stabilize the realm. In that latter respect the new practice now of having the *infante* Fernando confirm each charter as "king" as *Infante* Sancho had been doing for years may speak to the polite jostling beginning about the person of the widower-king.

Yet the demands of the south could not wait. By April the king was in Toledo (D694–701). From there he marched to Jaén, which fastness he be-

65. Fletcher, "Archbishops," p. 50. Berenguer died at Torquemada on the road to Palencia.
66. *Gesta Frederici*, ed. Franz-Josef Schmale (Berlin, 1965), p. 286.
67. Maria Dembińska, "A Polish Princess-Empress of Spain and Countess of Provence in the 12th Century," *Frauen in Spatantike und Fruhmittelalter*, ed. Werner Affeldt (Sigmaringen, 1990), pp. 283–84 and 286.

sieged in July and August. Contemporary charters describe him as awaiting the arrival of a French fleet before Sevilla (D702–6). Possibly during the same period, Afonso of Portugal launched an unsuccessful attack on Alcácer do Sal, as agreed in the negotiations of 1150, but it is difficult to be sure. The Portuguese king did secure the momentary acceptance of tributary status by a local Muslim leader in Silves but a revolt developed, the latter was overthrown, and the city passed to the Almohads.[68]

By August 25 Alfonso VII had withdrawn from Jaén to Baeza, although he had still not given up hope of French aid (D707–8). Moreover, the siege of Jaén continued through the following winter, although the king himself was otherwise occupied. Subsequently he withdrew to Toledo and remained there into 1152(710–28). One should also remark that royal charters of the preceding spring and summer had been issued in Alfonso's name and that of his sons Sancho and Fernando. Now in the late fall and winter, they begin again to cite all of his offspring. Possibly this reversion to the fuller formula meant the arrival of news from the Germanies that the projected marriage had been approved by the new emperor, Frederick Barbarossa. Therefore, grantees once again desired the fullest hedge they could get against future dynastic squabbles. There is a charter of Sancho III cited as reigning in Castilla that would have a bearing, but it is false (D704).

In February Alfonso reached Valladolid and remained there until March (D729–38). The major business was the induction of the *infante* Sancho into knighthood. Sancho, born about 1133 or 1134, may have been nineteen, and evidently his knighting had been considerably delayed. Fourteen would have been more usual. But the act was freighted with political and dynastic implications. The official entrance of the eldest male heir into manhood made him the second political authority in the realm. He became a potential challenger to the king himself if the two should fall out or if the king should suffer severe reverses. Alfonso VII, whose own knighting had been just such a challenge to the authority of his mother, was scarcely unaware of that potential. After the death of Berengaria, Alfonso had routinely associated Sancho with himself in the charters. Further he had not gone, and increasingly he had taken, as well, to so associating *Infante* Fernando and sometimes even all living members of his family. But by early 1152, remaining roadblocks to the remarriage of Alfonso VII had been cleared. New royal nuptials would create the possibility of the birth of further rivals to *Infante* Sancho and political stability

68. Charles Julian Bishko, "The Spanish and Portuguese Reconquest, 1095–1492," in *The History of the Crusades*, vol. 3, p. 413, ed. Kenneth Setton (Madison, Wis., 1975). Joaquim Veríssimo Serrão, *História de Portugal*, vol. 1 (Lisbon, 1976), p. 100. Codera, *Decadencia*, pp. 50–51.

now demanded some further step toward recognition of his premier position as successor.

Sancho was knighted at Valladolid on February 27, in the midst of a council of the realm. The archbishop of Toledo and ten bishops were present. Two of the remaining eight bishoprics, Sigüenza and Lugo, were probably vacant at the time and the archbishop of Compostela, the former Bernard of Sigüenza, had just returned from seeking recognition in Rome.[69] Secular magnates of the kingdom were more scantily represented. Likely most were occupied with the ongoing siege of Jaén in the south. Following his recognition, Sancho was granted an appanage in La Rioja and a portion of the territories in Soria, Daroca, and Calatayud. Some private documents suggest that similar provision was simultaneously made for *Infante* Fernando in the west but they are misdated.[70]

Additional conciliar business concerned the organization of men and funds for the successful conclusion of the siege at Jaén. Accordingly, Alfonso then moved south, ending at Toledo, where he remained through May (D739–49). Then, apparently, Alfonso received disturbing news about the actions of Sancho of Navarra on the Ebro. Alfonso's son Sancho was dispatched north, arriving in Soria on May 27 (D750). With him were Raymond, archbishop of Toledo, and the bishops of Palencia, Burgos, Segovia, and Calahorra in addition to Count Manrique of Lara and Guter Fernández. The explanation for this diversion of forces in the face of an impending campaign is provided by a private document of July 6, 1152, that puts Sancho of Castilla in Calahorra with a large army to combat a blood relative. This latter could only have been Sancho of Navarra.[71] Subsequent quiet in La Rioja suggests the show of force sufficed to deter the Navarrese.

Nevertheless the delay cost Alfonso VII dearly. When those forces rejoined him we do not know. As late as July 12 the *infantes*, Sancho and

69. Fletcher, "Archbishops," pp. 49–50.
70. 1152. AHN, Clero, Carpeta 1.509, no. 18, cites Fernando ruling in León and Galicia. March 12, 1152. AHN, Códices, 1.044B, fol. 37r-v, cites Fernando ruling in Galicia. Both are copies and also cite Bishop Juan of Lugo who does not appear in that see before July 1152. May 1152. AHN, Clero, Carpeta 1.568, no. 10, cites Fernando ruling in León. But it also cites Bishop Gonzalo in the see of Oviedo, there from late 1161. July 6, 1152. AHN, Clero, Carpeta 1.126, no. 5, cites Fernando as king. However, it also incorrectly cites one Count Pedro as holding Astorga and one Ramiro as tenant in Galicia. December 3, 1152. AHN, Códices, 1.047B, fol. 5r. This private document cites Fernando as king in Galicia but it also cites Bishop Pedro of Mondoñedo who only acceded to that office in 1155 and Archbishop Martín of Compostela who was elected in 1156. December 25, 1152. AHN, Clero, Carpeta 275, no. 4; pub. Serrano, *Obispado*, 3:256, who called it false. This private document cites both Sancho and Fernando as ruling jointly in Castile.
71. May 27, 1152. Soria. Pub. Julio González, *El reino de Castilla en la época de Alfonso VIII*, 3 vols. (Madrid, 1960), 2:19–21. July 6, 1152. Pub. Ildefonso Rodríguez de Lama, ed., *Colección diplomática medieval de La Rioja: Documentos, 923-1168*, vol. 2 (Logroño, 1976), pp. 236–37.

Fernando, seem to have been in the company of Alfonso's sister, Queen Sancha, when she granted a charter to one Pedro de Tolosa. Also with the queen
were counts Manrique and Pons (D751, 753). Perhaps these events led the
king to dispatch young Sancho to make one last attempt on Jaén, while he
himself assaulted the tiny city and *taifa* of Guadix (D752, 755). That Muslim principality lay athwart the main road from Baeza to Almería and was a
major nuisance to communication and supply. But the loss of time and the
weakening of Alfonso's army that resulted from the Navarrese episode made
it possible for Guadix to hold out through the summer. Moreover, the *taifa's*
prince, Ahmad ibn Milhan, decided that his unaided survival in the dangerous world of Iberia was unlikely. He traveled to Morocco and surrendered
his little realm to Abd al-Mūmin, receiving it back as governor.[72]

In August Alfonso VII left the siege of Guadix and traveled northeast to
Lorca in Murcia to confer with his ally, ibn Mardanish. He then returned to
Toledo by way of Júcar and Uclés (D754, 758–62).[73] During the second and
third weeks of September the king saw to the selection of a new archbishop of
Toledo for Archbishop Raymond had died while the king was on campaign.
Alfonso then rode north for the most portentous of undertakings during the
age of monarchy. Passing through San Esteban de Gormaz in mid-November
he came to Agreda high in the Sierra del Moncayo (D763–70), where he met
his betrothed, the Polish princess Rica.

Probably the princess had traveled down the Rhone, by sea to Barcelona
and perhaps then up the Ebro to Zaragoza, Tarazona, and so to Agreda. That
they wed there is unlikely. In all probability, they traveled to Burgos to be
wed, possibly on November 22 or 23. By November 25, 1152, the couple were
in Castrojeriz where Rica appears in a charter as Alfonso's wife (D771). The
court continued west, through Carrión de los Condes, Grajal, and Sahagún,
to Palencia where it celebrated Christmas (D772–77). The festivities attendant on the new marriage and the season must have been interspersed with
concerns over changing conditions in the peninsula. The Almohad threat
continued to grow as the time left to contain it dwindled. Alfonso had tried
to recruit aid from France and England but neither had responded. While
relations with the papacy remained close, Eugenius III's own interest in

72. Ambrosio Huici Miranda, *Historia musulmana de Valencia y su región* 3 vols. (Valencia,
1969–70), 3:139.
73. August 16, 1152. León? Pub. A. Paz y Melia, ed. *Series de los mas importantes documentos
del archivo y biblioteca del Duque de Medinaceli; 1, Serie Histórica, años 860–1814* (Madrid, 1951), pp.
3–5. This grant of a *fuero* by the Countess María, wife of Pons de Cabrera, to the men of Castro
Galvón is dated incorrectly to 1156 by its editor. It is confirmed by many of the court. At least
part of the process took place at León but the curial confirmations could not have.

an anti-Muslim offensive was muted by initial uncertainty about Frederick Barbarossa's intentions.

Within Iberia, Portugal had failed to improve on the border gained five years earlier at the fall of Lisbon. In Navarra the new king needed time to consolidate his rule. The count of Aragón-Barcelona was of some indirect help. A revolt in Valencia against ibn Mardanish in 1152 protested that *taifa* king's close collaboration with Christian rulers. The chronology is unclear but Ramon Berenguer either had or would intervene to prop up the former's regime.[74] At the much same time, the count was rounding out his new frontier near Tortosa with a successful siege of the castle of Miravet.[75] Such activities fell short of an initiative that would preoccupy major Muslim forces. On June 22, 1152, the pope had despatched a bull extending full crusading privileges to all who would join the Barcelonan in such an effort but that ruler made no commitments.[76]

Moreover, Alfonso VII needed to consider his reaction to the developing dynastic union of Aragón-Barcelona. He surely had intelligence that the past April, when Ramon's young bride lay in labor near Barcelona, the latter had his wife will the whole of the kingdom of Aragón to him if neither she nor the child survived.[77] Petronila did recover and outlived her husband. Whether the child survived, and therefore whether the dynastic union would outlive its originators, is unclear.[78] In either event, the king of León had to reconsider his policy toward the expedient of 1137 that had now endured for fifteen years. For these reasons 1153 and 1154 were to be the first years in a decade that the king did not mount a major offensive against al-Andalus. Instead, he set about the repair of his political and dynastic position in Iberia and Europe. Giving up hopes of substantial aid from Aragón-Barcelona, Alfonso effected a major rapprochement with Navarra.

The Leonese monarch's agent in this delicate matter may have been his own son, Sancho, who was at Nájera on the frontier in January 1153. The king had moved south to Toledo and there *Infante* Sancho joined him in February (D779–82). Negotiations had gone well for the court moved north for a rendezvous. In Soria on June 2 Alfonso knighted the young Sancho VI and be-

74. Huici Miranda, *Historia*, 3:138–39.

75. Antonio Ubieto Arteta, *Historia. Formación*, p. 226.

76. ACA, Bulas, Carpeta 1, no. 14.

77. April 4, 1152. ACA, Cancillería, RB IV, Carpeta 38, no. 250. What purports to be that will survives in a document that is certainly not an original and may be a later "improvement" of its terms.

78. The facts of birth of the ultimate heir, Alfonso II, and of the couple's other male children, are entangled in a welter of documents that still need further evaluation. See Antonio Ubieto Arteta, *Historia. Creación*, pp. 177–86.

trothed to him his daughter Sancha (D783–88).[79] Doubtless there were games and feasting to celebrate the young monarch's coming of age and a treaty of alliance as well. Sancho of Navarra is again cited in Alfonso's diplomas as a vassal, a practice which had been dropped after the mysterious initiatives of Sancho the preceding summer. The court then processed through the realm to Carrión, where the marriage took place in July (D789–93).

After the nuptials, the newlyweds then returned to that Navarra. In October and November the king moved through Burgos to Soria (D794–808). Probably from that town, Alfonso dispatched his daughter, Constanza, to be married to Louis VII of France, who had divorced his first wife, Eleanor of Aquitaine (D807–8). This union, as well as Sancha's, was part of the realignment of the dynasty.

Among these initiatives, the Leonese monarch had taken another step toward creating the conditions for the division of 1157. Doubtless it was forced on him by the party of *Infante* Fernando in the face of the growing importance of his older brother Sancho. From May 1153 a variety of private documents cite Fernando as reigning in Galicia and one even in Galicia and León.[80] Since Fernando had not yet been knighted, the exact import of such a change is difficult to gauge. There is no evidence that he had begun, like Sancho, to boast his own court. Nor is there any sign of the existence of a formal appanage such as the latter enjoyed. Before the death of Alfonso, we have but a single diploma, of 1155, issued by Fernando indicating that he possessed real jurisdiction rather than merely formal title. Nevertheless, another concession had been made to a growing rivalry of the two *infantes* and their supporters. Necessary or not, the cumulative results eventually were to prove disastrous. In December Alfonso retired to Medina del Campo (D809–11).

The diplomatic initiatives of the king of León-Castilla during 1153 reacted against the interests of Aragón-Barcelona. Most patently, the recognition of Sancho VI of Navarra consummated in his knighting by, and the marriage to the daughter of, the Leonese marked a radical departure from the oft-contemplated partition of Navarra. Then, too, the marriage of Constanza

79. May 1, 1153. San Vicente de Palacios. AHN, Clero, Carpeta 527, no. 6; Códices, 976B, fol. 14r; pub. Loscertales de García de Valdeavellano, *Tumbos*, 2:40. This grant of Count Fernando de Traba to Sobrado is clearly the model for the "improved" grant in the royal diploma of April 20 (D785). The confirmation of the *Infante* Fernando may indicate the presence of the court.

80. 1153. AHN, Códices, 114B, fol. 398r. May 29, 1153. AHN, Clero, Carpeta 1.126, no. 6, perhaps an original. June 26, 1153. AHN, Clero, Carpeta 1.616, nos. 18 and 19, both copies, and no. 13, another copy dated August 28, 1153; pub. Marcos G. Martínez, "El convento benedictino de Villanueva de Oscos," *BIEA* 8 (1954): 283–84. October 21, 1153. Pub. Francisco Antón, *Monasterios medievales de la provincia de Valladolid*, 2nd ed. (Valladolid, 1942), pp. 260–62. This latter cites León and Galicia.

to the king of France rather than a groom from Barcelona constituted further drift from the close association marked by the Leonese's own marriage to Ramon's sister. Under such circumstances Ramon's campaigns in the peninsula against the Muslims were limited. A siege of the stronghold of Sigena was successful in 1153 and bolstered his position on the lower Ebro.[81] At the same, time he strengthened his direct authority in that river valley. The maritime republic of Genoa had overstrained its resources and found it necessary to liquidate some of its more ambitious ventures to reduce its debts. As a result on November 15, 1153, Ramon was able to repurchase the third of Tortosa they had held since its reconquest for 16,640 gold coins of various origin.[82]

Probably about then the Genoese liquidated their holdings in Leonese Almería, where they had maintained a sort of condominium. There is no known record of such a sale to León, but before 1157 Genoa had withdrawn from that outpost and they would have attempted to salvage something from their assets.

The ruler of Aragón-Barcelona rested content. When a new pope, Anastasius IV, appealed for a major effort against the Muslims in September 1153, the cry fell on deaf ears.[83] Given the changing orientation of León-Castilla, Ramon was inclined to more modest steps. In 1152 a new bishop, Pedro de Tarroja, brother of Bishop Guillermo of Barcelona, was installed in the critical see of Zaragoza. The same year had seen the selection of the Aragonese Martín de Bergua to strategic Tarazona. The attitude of such prelates to the maintenance of the Aragón-Barcelona union was crucial and their accession undercut support for his over mighty neighbor on the middle Ebro.

In 1154 Ramon Berenguer successfully pursued the same policy. Anastasius IV reorganized the structure of the Iberian church, extending the metropolitan authority of the archbishopric of Tarragona to include the suffragan sees of Pamplona, Calahorra, Tarazona, and Zaragoza.[84] The new definition of that ecclesiastical province meant a major increase of influence for the Barcelonan at the expense of Navarra and León. If it also ordered the archbishop of Tarragona, along with those of Compostela and Braga, to recognize the primatial rights of Toledo, the result was yet a considerable net gain.[85] The

---

81. July 24, 1153. A private document published by Antonio Durán Gudiol, ed., *Colección diplomática de la catedral de Huesca*, vol. 1 (Zaragoza, 1965), pp. 220–21, mentioned the siege as still in progress. November 30, 1153. Another private document published by Jaime Santacana Tort, *El monasterio de Poblet, 1151–1181* (Barcelona, 1974), p. 457, speaks of its conquest as a accomplished fact.
82. ACA, Cancillería, RB IV, Carpeta 39, no. 266; pub. Imperiale, *Codice*, 1:291–95.
83. Goñi Gaztambide, *Historia*, p. 87.
84. March 25, 1154. Kehr, "Papsturkunden," 2:336–39.
85. April 8, 1154. Pub. Mansilla, *Documentación*, pp. 113–14.

rights of a primate were shadowy at best and usually suspect in Rome. In contrast, the rights of a metropolitan had rather more substance in the canon law that was rapidly taking shape in the twelfth century.

In the spring Ramon continued his successes north of the Pyrenees. In April he traveled north to Canfranc, in old Aragón on the border of Béarn, where he was recognized by the notables of that viscounty as the guardian of the young Gaston V, whose mother had just died.[86] The trans-Pyrenaen counties of Béarn and Bigorre had a long association with Aragón and his recognition signaled that it had survived the change of dynasty there.

In the same year, Count Armengol VI of Urgel (1102–1154) died. Urgel was a principality second only to Barcelona itself in that Iberian complex that we have come to designate as Catalunya. Not until the fourteenth century did it pass into the hands of the counts of Barcelona. In the first half of the twelfth century Armengol VI was not only a great Catalan prince but, by virtue of his father's marriage to the daughter of Pedro Ansúrez, a major Leonese noble holding the districts of Valladolid, Cabezón, and even Calatrava for a time. He was a leading figure of the court of Alfonso VII, and had taken an active part in the latter's campaigns against Córdoba in 1146 and Almería in 1147. At the same time, Armengol participated actively in the affairs of Aragón-Barcelona, sometimes mediating between Ramon and Alfonso. In 1149 Armengol helped at the siege of Lérida and was awarded a third of its territory. Consequently, his death had major implications for the relations of León-Castilla and Aragón-Barcelona.[87] The Barcelonan moved to draw the new count into his own orbit and was successful initially. Armengol would marry his daughter by Petronila of Aragón, Dulce, sister of the future Alfonso II of Aragón (1162–1196). The count also aided his brother-in-law in political and military ventures in both the Midi and the region of Valencia. Finally, however, like his father, Armengol VII was drawn into the Leonese orbit and became a major figure in the court of Fernando II of León (1157–1188).

The papal action in 1154, extending the jurisdiction of the archbishop of Tarragona and supporting the primatial authority of Toledo, was more than a simple rationalization of ecclesial structures. Doubtless it was a response to a more general request from Alfonso VII to foster the peace and concord in the

---

86. ACA, Cancillería, RB IV, Carpeta 39, no. 268.
87. Derek Lomax, "Catalanes en el imperio leonés," *Toletum* 17 (1983–84): 201–16, is a good recent treatment of this aspect of the relationship. He follows the *Crónica de San Juan de la Peña* rather than Prudencio de Sandoval in placing Armengol's death in 1154 instead of 1153. At the time of his death the count was likely at the court of Alfonso. He confirmed no less than seven royal charters between January and April of that year. Thereafter he disappeared from the record except for a single, forged royal charter of July.

peninsula that would allow the marshaling of greater resources for an Iberian crusade. The Leonese plea likely provoked an approach by Ramon Berenguer with a smaller focus designed to advance the relative position of his realm. Another part of the project was the dispatch of a special legate to Iberia in the person of Cardinal Hyacinth so that papal influence might be brought to bear directly.

Well before his arrival, Alfonso VII had begun to prepare for this long-sought end. In January 1154 the king was in Salamanca together with Queen Rica, *Infantes* Sancho and Fernando, and seventeen of the twenty archbishops and bishops of his realm. Only the bishops of Coria, probably still at Rome, where an earlier pope had detained him, and the new bishops of Zaragoza and Tarazona failed to attend. Also part of this extraordinary curial assemblage were eight counts of the realm and as many other great magnates. Its *acta* have not survived and we know it from royal diplomas and a few other documents (D813–17). From Salamanca the king proceeded to Toledo where he remained into June.

Again the sole source of information are charters, often related to the re-population of an area still a frontier. Doubtless the selection of supply bases for future advance into Muslim lands was discussed. The importance attached to this dimly understood journey to the south is underlined by the fact that two thirds of the prelates at Salamanca accompanied the court (D818–32).[88] The bolstering the valley of the upper Tajo, one thinks, was designed to protect winter and spring wheat crops from Muslim cavalry sweeps. Preparations for a major campaign in al-Andalus in 1155 could hardly be kept secret and preventive raids to destroy provisions for an army of such magnitude were to be expected. Only in July did the royal court return north to Segovia to rendezvous with the papal legate.

The itinerary and timing of the legation of Cardinal Hyacinth has been much confused by nineteenth-century historians, some of whom have him at a council in Valladolid a year too early. Wider consideration makes it clear that on March 25, 1154, the legate was still in Rome, and by March 31, he had just arrived in Narbonne.[89] He appears in Segovia in July (D833–36). The king was accompanied by no less than seventeen prelates of the realm. Clearly the business was important, but the charters tell us only that there Archbishop

---

88. April 21, 1154. Colmenar de Oreja. Pub. Juan Antonio Llorente, ed., *Noticias históricas de las tres provincias vascongados, Alava, Guipúzcoa, y Alava*, 4 vols. (Madrid, 1806–8), 4:118–53. This is a *fuero* given to the men of Molina by Count Manrique de Lara incorrectly dated to 1152 and confirmed by Alfonso VII.

89. Kehr, "Papsturkunden," 22:336 and 341.

Pelayo of Compostela confirmed as "elect." By the time he reached Burgos in mid-August he confirmed simply as archbishop, having been consecrated by the legate in Segovia no doubt.

Cardinal Hyacinth then traveled west, and by November 4 he was in the Benedictine monastery of Tibães not far from Braga, where he took the church of Santa Cruz of Coimbra under papal protection.[90] We may assume that he also conferred both with the archbishop of Braga and with King Afonso on the coming crusade in the peninsula. The Portuguese had that year made another unsuccessful attempt to take Alcácer do Sal.[91] The cardinal then moved north to Túy where he extended papal patronage to the church of Santa María de Refoios in Limia.[92] Then he proceeded to Santiago de Compostela to confer over the ecclesiastical politics of Galicia, to meet a most exalted pilgrim, Louis VII of France, and to celebrate the Christmas liturgy.

The tale of Louis VII's visit to Santiago de Compostela in 1154 was told first by Lucas de Túy, roughly eighty-five years after the event.[93] It was subsequently copied almost verbatim by Rodrigo Jiménez de Rada.[94] At that remove, the stress was placed on the personal and ceremonial aspects of the visit. The French king, we are told, had been half-convinced by mischief-makers in his kingdom that his new Leonese bride was a natural, rather than a legitimate, daughter of Alfonso VII. To get at the truth, Louis decided to visit Iberia personally. There is nothing inherently unlikely in the tale, but it lacks explicit political context. The latter was the effort of Alfonso VII to involve the king of the French in a peninsular crusade. On such an assumption, the opponents of the marriage were not simply malicious but were opposed to any further policy of crusading by their sovereign. On the other hand, the Leonese monarch's plans for such an effort had elicited papal support. He was busy laying the logistical groundwork. Since Constanza was indeed legitimate, it would be simple to discredit his detractors on that score. He, therefore, welcomed the visit as an opportunity to press his arguments for French assistance and to stress the advanced state of preparations. Nonetheless, the visit raises problems.

On the evidence of French sources, it must have taken place between

90. November 4, 1154. Tibaes. Pub. Erdmann, "Papsturkunden," pp. 219–22.

91. Serrão, *História*, p. 100.

92. November 15, 1154. Túy. Pub. Erdmann, "Papsturkunden," pp. 222–25. November 15, 1154. Túy. AHN, Códices, 976B, fol. 32r, pub. Loscertales de García de Valdeavellano, *Tumbos*, 2:80. This private charter also records his presence there.

93. *Chronicon Mundi ab Origine Mundi usque ad Eram MCCLXXIV.* In *Hispanie Illustratae*, ed. Andreas Schottus, vol. 4, pp. 1–116. (Frankfurt, 1608), pp. 104–5.

94. *De Rebus Hispaniae*, ed. Emma Falque Rey (Turnholt, 1987), p. 230.

October and January, since both before and after the king can be placed in the south of France.[95] The urgency of the affair can be seen in the determination to visit at a season when traversing the Pyrenees is hardly congenial. Very probably Louis came by way of Roncesvalles since he was joined by Sancho VI of Navarra. At Burgos, the royal visitor was received by Alfonso VII with great ceremony. Now we know that Alfonso VII and his family were at Burgos in late August but neither Louis VII nor Sancho of Navarra then were (D838–43). Unfortunately, for the next three months the charter record largely fails. The only entirely trustworthy diploma places Alfonso and his court at Ayllón, southwest of San Esteban de Gormaz, in the latter days of September (D846). It is possible that Alfonso was traveling east to meet Louis at Zaragoza or even Tudela, but he may have merely been passing the time in hunting while awaiting the latter's arrival.

Once the two kings had met in Burgos, the narrative source tells us, they proceeded on the pilgrimage to Santiago de Compostela. Of this journey there is not a trace in the copious local documentation of Galicia of the time. Subsequent to the pilgrimage, Louis traveled south to Toledo where he was feted grandly by Alfonso. In addition, the two were joined by Ramon Berenguer IV who affirmed to the French king that Constanza was indeed the child of his deceased sister, Berengaria. Finally, Louis departed content for France.

There is charter evidence for the presence of Alfonso VII and his court at Toledo for two weeks in early November. They furnish no corroboration, however, of the presence of Louis VII, of Sancho VI, or of Ramon. Since the dating formulas of contemporary royal diplomas often make mention of important current events, the absence is striking. Conceivably those rulers had not yet arrived when the particular charters were drafted but it seems just as likely that the French visit to Toledo was a literary invention (D847–53). At any rate, Alfonso later returned to León to winter (D854–57).

Alfonso VII's hopes were high as the new year began. His planned major offensive against Islam had the blessing of the pope and a papal legate, Cardinal Hyacinth, to rally aid. It is unlikely that the king expected substantial assistance from beyond the Pyrenees. The chance to parade his friendship with Louis of France had been helpful in terms of prestige, but Louis had just returned home and major expeditions required more preparation than time then allowed. Moreover, Henry Plantagenet, count of Anjou and Normandy since 1151, had married Eleanor of Aquitaine in 1152 and just now,

---

95. Achille Luchaire, *Études sur les Actes de Louis VII* (Paris, 1885), p. 65. Marcelin Defourneaux, "Louis VII et les souverains espagnols. L'énigme du pséudo-Alphonse," *EDMP* 6 (1956): 647–61, reviewed the known sources.

after the death of Stephen I, had been crowned king of England in December. Louis VII was to be busy with matters English for the rest of his reign.

In Italy, Pope Anastasius IV had died the preceding year and the new English pope, Hadrian IV, had much to occupy him. The German emperor, Frederick Barbarossa, was to descend into Italy to receive the imperial crown at Hadrian's hands. The imperial presence was almost always as much a worry as a help to the papal court in the Middle Ages. Roger II of Sicily had died in 1154 and the accession of his son, William I, saw the south in an uproar. By year's end Hadrian was allied with the Byzantine emperor Manuel I and the rebel barons of the south as all three beset the harried Norman monarch. While the Iberian offensive might have the papal blessing, Rome was too busy closer to home to be of material aid.

There remained the possibility of uniting once again, as in 1147, the forces of the Christian principalities of the peninsula for a coordinated assault on Iberian Islam. Here Cardinal Hyacinth could play a major role and a great national council was scheduled for Valladolid. After January 20, 1155, Alfonso VII proceeded there from Carrión de los Condes. The importance of the coming council was evident in that at Carrión, sixteen archbishops and bishops of the realm were already present(862–63). The council lasted from at least January 25 to February 4. Thirty-two canons have survived. The very first of them extends to the Christian crusader in the peninsula the same indulgences gained by an expedition to the Holy Land. While on crusade, the crusader's person and his goods are protected by the anathema of the church. In addition, canons eighteen and thirty-two, respectively, proclaim the Peace of God and the Truce of God. The acts cite the presence of the legate, two archbishops, and nineteen bishops who participated in the fashioning of these canons that must have given Alfonso VII everything he anticipated.[96] Royal diplomas reveal the presence of yet another three bishops, who may have arrived too late for formal inclusion in the text of the acts. In addition, Cardinal Hyacinth indited a circular letter to all of the archbishops, bishops, abbots, the Templars, and the Hospitallers of Iberia summoning them to participate in the coming expedition.[97]

Most documents deal with the settlement of disputes between bishops and abbots, between the bishops themselves, and between the primate of Toledo and the archbishops of Braga and Compostela over recognition of the

---

96. Pub. Carl Erdmann, *Das Papsttum und Portugal in ersten Jahrhundert der portugiesischen Geschichte* (Berlin, 1928), from a contemporary copy in the cathedral archive of Túy.

97. Mansilla, *Documentación*, pp. 116–17. The letter is not dated but surely belongs in this context.

former's authority. These things were, of course, the very stuff of the emerging hierarchical structure of the western church in the twelfth century and of its adjudication by Rome through the system of legates. Nevertheless, the settlement of such disputes was important, clearing the way for greater ecclesial participation in the crusade. Some ecclesial business dealt yet more directly with the affair of Andalucía. The canons were witnessed by a bishop of Almería. A royal charter of June of this year would be confirmed by a bishop of Baeza. Neither prelate had been previously in evidence, and we can fairly conclude that the council took the necessary steps to restore or bolster the hierarchy in those portions under Christian rule. The major port city of Almería and the strategic base of Baeza were the obvious candidates. The council evidently expected permanent Christian possession of a major portion of Andalucía.

We can also fairly deduce that the other Christian principalities were expected to be involved in the forthcoming campaign. Portuguese bishops, from Oporto, Coimbra, Lamego, and Viseu, are cited in the acts, although the bishop of Lisbon and the archbishop of Braga were not. Bishop Lop of Pamplona was present to signal the aid of Navarra. The bishop of Zaragoza was absent, although those of Calahorra and of Tarazona were there. Surely representation from Aragón-Barcelona had been solicited and its absence boded ill for its participation.

Ordinary royal business took on particular importance, given the council's context and purpose. Charters were acts of royal largesse calculated to move their recipients to greater conformity to the royal desires. The king also confirmed at least one private document drawn up at the council (D864–70).[98] Preparations completed, Alfonso VII moved south to Toledo by mid-March (D871–77).

Cardinal Hyacinth traveled east, to Nájera in the Rioja by March 3, to Logroño by March 5, and to Estella by March 8. He continued negotiating the outstanding problems of the church as his letters illustrate. One reveals that he was accompanied by the archbishop of Compostela, the bishops of Orense, Calahorra, and Tarazona, from the realms of Alfonso VII, and by Bishop Gilbert of Lisbon from Portugal and by Bishops Guillermo of Barcelona and Dodón of Huesca from that of Ramon Berenguer.[99] Unfortunately

---

98. AHN, Clero, Carpeta 1.325D, no. 9. It is a copy of an agreement between the bishop of Lugo and a private individual.

99. The full range of these letters exceeds our present interests and will be examined later. March 3, 1155. Nájera. Pub. Mansilla, *Documentación*, pp. 114–15. March 5–6, 1155. Logroño. Pub. Teresa Abajo Martín, ed., *Documentación de la catedral de Palencia* (Palencia, 1986), pp. 115–18. March 8, 1155. Estella. Pub. Juan de Alamo, ed., *Colección diplomática de San Salvador de Oña,*

for Alfonso VII, the legate's good offices seem to have been frustrated. In a letter from Nájera the cardinal informed the archbishop of Toledo that the archbishop of Braga was suspended for refusal to make his obedience to Toledo. Apparently negotiations had broken down. A bull of Hadrian IV to the primate of Toledo in June announced the papal intention to interdict all of Portugal if Afonso Henriques did not restore Bishop John of Coimbra to his see.[100] That unlucky bishop had signed the acts at Valladolid and may have exceeded his authority in negotiations there. The dispute portends the absence of the Portuguese cooperation in 1155. In April the legate proceeded to Lérida, where he held a small council at which the archbishop of Tarragona and the bishops of Vich, Barcelona, Lérida, and Zaragoza were present.[101] This was most of the hierarchy of the kingdom and the cardinal probably urged cooperation in the crusade.

While Alfonso lay at Toledo awaiting the aid contracted at Valladolid, his son Sancho journeyed northwest to Soria to raise supplies (D873, 875, 881). But when Alfonso VII was setting up the siege of Andújar in mid-June, Sancho was with him (D882). It is possible that Sancho returned north in July again, but relevant charters are not trustworthy (D884, 888). Also the only known charter of Fernando II issued during the life of his father places the former in Compostela at the end of July (D885). Possibly the junior heir was making a formal demonstration of his new authority in that region.

By mid-August the royal host had returned to Toledo (D886–87). The expedition had captured both Andújar and Pedroche. Andújar, the better known, lies fifty kilometers west of Baeza and twenty-five kilometers east of Montoro on the Guadalquivir. Pedroche is in the upper valley of the Guadiana, south of Almadén and west of Calatrava La Vieja. The Leonese monarch had been consolidating his position in the upper reaches of both rivers. With his limited resources this was the maximum that he could achieve that summer. Nevertheless, his objectives illustrate the expected permanence of the reconquest of eastern al-Andalus.

Alfonso remained in the Toledo region through August and into October (D889–91, 894–95).[102] Aside from provision of the ordinary government, it seems probable that he was once again making preparations for a campaign

---

2 vols. (Madrid, 1950), 1:263–64. June 22, 1155. Toulouse. Pub. Kehr, "Papsturkunden," 2:395–96. This last makes reference to the bishops present at Nájera.

100. Erdmann, "Papsturkunden," p. 40, cited the letter.

101. Kehr, "Papsturkunden," 2:389–92.

102. October, 1155. Toledo. Pub. Martín, *Orígenes*, pp. 174–75. This private grant of Count Pedro Alfónsez of Asturias was probably made at court. It is redated from 1125.

in the succeeding year. Later charters also reveal that before September 11 royal forces in Andalucía had captured Santa Eufemia. The reduction of this fortified place south of Almadén strengthened yet more Alfonso's hold on the upper Guadiana.

The charters of the future Sancho III in September raise questions both of history and chancery practice. On September 28 two of them place the young king and much of Alfonso VII's court at Calahorra (D892–93). Neither is an original, and I regard both as suspect, but there are few early charters of Sancho that survive and their diplomatic is quite varied.

Alfonso and his entire court did come northeast at the end of October for a long stay at Burgos (D896–907). On November 11, 1155, probably there, a male heir was born to Sancho III and Blanca, the future Alfonso VIII of Castilla.[103] The occasion was a happy one and the festivities prolonged, but the birth raised the most serious of political questions. Until this point, the evidence suggests that the future Fernando II was regarded as a possible heir of Sancho III. Now that Sancho's son would preempt him, some suitable alternative future had to be elaborated. Since the latter already had at least titular claim on León and Galicia, the time had come to work out the particulars of a division of lands between the two royal scions. The politics of that division of the realm of León-Castilla into two kingdoms, later autonomous for more than seventy years, was fashioned at Burgos in the fall of 1155. The court remained there until December, and the documents demonstrate that eighteen bishops of the realm attended as well as virtually all of the great secular notables.

After mid-December the court moved to Palencia, where it spent Christmas, lingering until January 10, 1156 (D909–10, 918). The season was replete with festivities. In all likelihood the new *infante*, Alfonso, was christened there. But we know for sure that on Christmas day, Alfonso VII armed his younger son, Fernando, knight; that is, Fernando officially attained the estate of manhood and was capable of rule without council of regency or tutelage. The conditions for a dynastic division of the kingdom of León-Castilla were now complete, and only the person of Alfonso VII himself stayed their execution.

During 1155, Alfonso VII had obtained no assistance from Navarra or

---

103. Julio González, *Reino*, 1:144. November 11, 1155? Ayllón. AHN, Clero, Carpeta 378, no. 5. This is a thirteenth-century copy of a private sale by García García and his wife to Count Manrique and his wife. It was witnessed by members of the court including the future Sancho III and the future Fernando II but not by Alfonso VII. The dating formula is defective as to day but the diplomatic style argues a date about November 1155.

Aragón-Barcelona, and he was not to see the reentry of either into the struggle against Islam during the brief remainder of his lifetime. In 1156 Ramon Berenguer was occupied with the fortunes of his house in the Midi. There, on January 15, at Montpellier he welcomed Bishop Lop of Pamplona who had had a falling out with Sancho of Navarra.[104] The Barcelonan's hospitality to the exile could reignite the hostilities between the two that had been almost constant since 1137. Perhaps the count had already moved to renew the treaty of 1151 with Alfonso VII for the joint partition of Navarra. In May 1156 bishops Guillermo of Barcelona and Pedro of Zaragoza met at Lérida and signed a renewal of the treaty providing for just that. It included the marriage of Sancha, daughter of Alfonso, with a son of Ramon (D931).[105] Since Sancha was then wife of Sancho VI of Navarra, León was planning an open break. By the fall of the year, Sancha had returned to her father's kingdom and thereafter was regularly associated with him and her siblings in the intitulation of charters as "Queen of Navarra."

Sancho of Navarra, far from adopting a defensive posture, pursued plans of his own. While Ramon was still in the north, he seized Fontellas, seventy kilometers north of Zaragoza. That position imperiled Ramon's communication with that metropolis, up to whose walls Sancho raided later in the year.[106] Both princes thus occupied, Alfonso VII could expect nothing from either. Meanwhile, he was anxious to launch the campaign. By February he was in Toledo, where he remained through March (D919–28). Presumably the king awaited the gathering of the host. From April until June, the charter record is very bad (D929–35).[107] In mid-June Alfonso had not begun the campaign but is at Maqueda northwest of Toledo (D935). Then, in late June, king and court were back north at Segovia, and the reason for the delay becomes clear. The document was issued after the feast of Saint John the Baptist on June 24 as the Leonese monarch lay ill there (D935–37).

This notice of Alfonso's illness gives no indication of its gravity, but it

104. ACA, Cancillería, RB IV, Carpeta 39, no. 297.

105. Neither bride nor bridegroom is named but González, *Reino*, 1:780, rightly assumes that Alfonso's daughter Sancha by Queen Berengaria is meant. Antonio Ubieto Arteta, "De nuevo sobre el nacimiento de Alfonso II de Aragón," *EEMCA* 6 (1956): 205–6, redated the treaty to 1157 on the basis of the itinerary of Count Ramon. In fact the text does not indicate the physical presence of any of the principals and Alfonso VII could not have been there in May 1156 or 1157.

106. August 1156. Pub. Lacarra, "Documentos," 3:633–34. December 1156. Pub. Pascual Galindo Romeo, *Posesiones de San Sabino de Lavedán en Zaragoza* (Madrid, 1923), p. 20.

107. May 3, 1156. Zamora. ASI, no. 299; Códices, 81, ff. 35r-37r; pub. ibid., pp. 150–51, who called the first of these an original. Alfonso VII is supposed to have confirmed this exchange of properties between San Isidoro and his courtier Abril. This forgery is obviously dependent (D932). May 14, 1156. AHN, Clero, Carpeta 3.563, no. 11. This donation of Bishop Suero of Coria to the monastery of Oya seems to have been done at court.

was sufficient to cancel the summer's campaign. We can suspect that the weakness it produced, or a possible recurrence, resulted in the king's death scarcely more than a year later. The illness is likely attributable to chronic overexertion and exhaustion. Although Alfonso was but fifty-one he had lived the previous thirty years in the saddle and the demands of that life inevitably took their toll.

The king and court moved slowly north, although we cannot gauge at what pace for the charters are mostly unreliable. The last of them indicates a further problem. The king's daughter, Constanza, is cited in the intitulation. She had returned from France, her marriage to Louis VII over (D938–42). Henceforth she is routinely cited in them as "Queen of the Franks." Her failing was to have borne to Louis two daughters when he urgently needed a male heir.[108] Ecclesiastical politics might require that Louis of France delay marriage to Adele of Champagne until 1160, but the Leónese marriage alliance was over. In associating his daughter with himself and continuing to recognize her as queen of the Franks, Alfonso VII doubtless soothed her injured vanity and promoted solidarity in the dynasty, but there is about it a note of desperation. If any lingering hopes of aid from beyond the Pyrenees remained, the return of his soon-to-be-repudiated daughter finally extinguished them.

In August his daughter-in-law, Blanca of Navarra, died and her body was transported to Nájera for burial. Most of the court accompanied it, but Alfonso did not (D945).[109] Again circumstances argue his serious, continuing illness. In late fall the Leonese monarch began slowly to move farther north. In November he passed through Atienza, Peñafiel, and finally reached Palencia where he spent the rest of the year. Taken together, the documents of the year's end indicate the meeting of a great council of the realm at which almost all of the prelates and secular magnates were present (D943–44, 946–957). These in themselves supply information of what transpired only incidentally; that is, the newly elected bishops Pedro of Burgos and Pedro of Oviedo confirm some of them. But surely the assembled notables were anxious to determine the state of the royal health and to make some preliminary political soundings if the end of the thirty-year reign was, in fact, imminent. As for the king, he had already fixed the outlines of a succession settlement in the prior winter but the promotion of its acceptance continued. Then, too, the ordinary business of the realm perhaps needed more attention than usual if Alfonso had been really incapacitated.

108. Marcel Pacaut, *Louis VII et son royaume* (Paris, 1964), pp. 36–37.
109. Blanca died on August 12. Diego de Colmenares, *Historia de la insigne ciudad de Segovia*, 2 vols. 1637 (Segovia, 1969–70), 1:279, saw her tomb and epitaph there.

Above all, there was the matter of the aborted campaign. The royal diplomas bear witness to reverses that it might have averted. The recently conquered positions in the eastern Guadiana basin at Pedroche and Santa Eufemia disappear from the dating formulas. In 1156 the Almohad Emir Abd al-Mūmin had dispatched his son, ibn Sᶜaīd, as governor of Andalucía, and the position of that North African empire was materially strengthened. The last Almoravid stronghold at Granada surrendered and the Portuguese Algarve and western and central Andalucía were now united under the Africans. The upper Guadiana basin had been cleared of Leonese garrisons and the most advanced Christian position on the Guadalquivir, Montoro, had fallen. Its commander, the former royal *alférez* Nuño Pérez, disappeared from the diplomas and a sizable Leonese defeat is probable.[110] Elementary military foresight would expect an assault against the most isolated Leonese position remaining in the south, Almería, from nearby Granada. Doubtless preliminary plans were formulated at Palencia for that contingency.

How long into 1157 the court remained at Palencia is difficult to judge. Royal diplomas from late January to early February yield but one place of issue. Their confirmation by almost all of the prelates of the realm does suggest that talks continued (D959–62). By April the king had reached Toledo (D963–71). Apparently in May, he struck south into Andalucía.[111] The feast of Pentecost on May 19 may have been the date for the assemblage of the royal host. But for the last three months of Alfonso's reign the charter record is useless and we depend on literary testimony (D972–75).

For the campaign of 1157, Alfonso VII disposed of few of the allies of 1147. There is no mention of the Genoese and their fleet in 1157 and sea control, with its consequent ability to resupply troops operating along that coast, belonged to the Muslims. Ramon Berenguer was absent. In 1157 he came no farther south than Tortosa.[112] Sancho of Navarra and the count of Mont-

---

110. Ambrosio Huici Miranda, "Un nuevo manuscrito de al-Bayan al-Mugrib: Datos inéditos y aclaraciones sobre los ultimos años del reinado de Alfonso VII, el Emperador," *Al-Andalus* 24 (1959): 63–84, dates most of these events to 1155. I believe that the charters are more reliable than the literary evidence.

111. May 1157. Pub. Hernández, *Cartularios*, pp. 116–17. This regulation of the cathedral chapter of Toledo by Archbishop Juan was confirmed by the bishops Celebruno of Sigüenza and Pedro of Orense. Had he then been in the city Alfonso VII would have confirmed. May 1157. Pub. F. Javier Peña Pérez, ed., *Documentación del monasterio de San Juan de Burgos, 1091–1400* (Burgos, 1983), pp. 37–38. This purported private donation to that monastery is confirmed by the future Sancho III who was with his father in the south. Ubieto Arteta, "Navarra-Aragón," p. 74, believed erroneously that Alfonso and his sons met in May 1157 with Ramon Berenguer in Lérida. He based that idea on an undated text.

112. May 26, 1157. Tortosa. Augustí Altisent, ed., *Diplomatari de Santa Maria de Poblet*, vol. 1: 960–1177 (Barcelona, 1993), pp. 168–69.

pellier were occupied at home. A pale echo of earlier days was the attack of
Afonso Henriques on Alcácer do Sal beyond the Tajo, carried out jointly with
a crusading fleet enroute to the Holy Land under the count of Flanders, but
the city held out. The sole active ally of Alfonso VII in his campaign was the
Muslim emir of Valencia-Murcia, ibn Mardanish. The alliance was important,
nonetheless, for it meant that the eastern and northern flanks of the route of
march were in friendly hands.

If the expedition set out from Toledo about May 19, 1157, it might have
arrived outside Almería by the first of July. The distance, no less than 500
kilometers, lay through pacified territories up to Úbeda. From there, for 200
kilometers, the southern and western flanks of the Leonese force were open
to ambush by Muslim forces based on Jaén or Granada. But an alert commander and a disciplined marching order could obviate much of that danger,
although the necessary precautions would slow progress of the column. The
real enemies on the march were already familiar from 1147, geography, heat,
and lack of water. It was a grueling march even for experienced campaigners.
Alfonso's army probably consisted of about 600 cavalry and perhaps 1,400 infantry and support personnel. Such an army would have been quite adequate
to a campaign in the field, given the usual tactics and opponents of the period.
To conduct countersiege operations of any size and duration it must be reinforced on the spot, perhaps to as much as twice that number. Of course,
no accounts give the details of the march and few furnish any of operations
around Almería. Both Lucas de Túy and Rodrigo Jiménez de Rada wrote
roughly eighty years after the event and then devoted but a few lines to
it.[113] The Moroccan ibn Idhari wrote slightly later but his sources were more
ample. Modern accounts of the campaign are based on his work.[114]

The march of the Leonese army was apparently uncontested and the
physical difficulties were managed. But it had arrived too late. The Muslim
governor of al-Andalus had prepared his assault through the winter and was
earlier in the field. By June, the siege of the city had begun and the town
itself succumbed quickly while the defenders retreated to the *alcazar*. The
Christian garrison was small, and the port was a sizable town; not the 30,000
population that is alleged for 1147, but still on the order of 10,000 to 15,000.
Although there had probably been some attempt during the previous ten

113. Lucas de Túy. "Chronicon," p. 105. Rodrigo Jiménez de Rada, *De Rebus Hispaniae*, ed. Emma Falque Rey (Turnholt, 1987), pp. 232–33.
114. Tapía Garrido, *Historia*, 3:22–23, whose acceptance even of the figures of the chroni-cler is less than critical, and Ambrosio Huici Miranda, "Un nuevo manuscrito de 'al-Bayan al-Mugrib': Datos inéditos y aclaraciones sobre los ultimos años del reinado de Alfonso VIi, el Emperaodr," *Al-andalus* 24 (1959),: 75–80,and *Historia*, 3:142–46. My account of the campaign largely follows Huici Miranda.

years to recruit a population of Christian Mozarabs for the town, especially after the departure of the Genoese contingent, Muslims may still have formed the majority, and it would have been difficult to hold the walls of the town under those circumstances.

On their arrival, the Leonese found it necessary to conduct a counter-siege of the Almohad forces now ensconced in the town itself. Relief of the *alcazar* was impossible until they were defeated. The only practical way to attack was from the narrow strand along the beach and immediately to the north and south. But in 1147, the sea at their rear had been secured by a friendly fleet and supplies could be had from it. Now the waters offshore were controlled by a Almohad squadron whose activities must be watched at all times. Supplies must have been all but unobtainable. Such a position was difficult at best; and a serious reverse could imperil the survival of the entire force.

Alfonso VII was joined before Almería by ibn Mardanish of Valencia so that a siege was not impossible. We have no real idea of number, probably less than the 6,000 so roundly asserted. Some of the Muslim inhabitants of the vicinity were willing to help against the unpopular North Africans and more aid was recruited from the remaining Mozarab population. We have no information as to the actual mechanics of the countersiege. In some fashion, the potential for outright disaster was not only avoided but the Muslim commanders became sufficiently concerned by Christian progress to send urgent appeals for assistance all the way to Morocco. But if the Muslim commanders were nervous about Leonese prospects, Alfonso VII was not deceived. In the face of a stubborn defense, his own situation became daily more desperate. At the end of July he began a withdrawal northwest. His ally, ibn Mardanish, set out separately for Murcia. The success of such a disengagement and withdrawal through difficult country, given an undefeated enemy, speaks to the caliber of the army and of its commanders.

Moving northwest, probably to Guadix, Alfonso made a feint at Granada, hoping to draw off the Muslim forces at Almería. By this time, however, his army would have been reduced by attrition and losses in the field to less than 400 cavalry and 1,000 infantry and support troops at best, grossly inadequate for a serious attempt on a major city. Only complete surprise could have achieved anything and that was hardly possible. It is also likely that the king was ill, although there is no assertion in the sources that he had been wounded. Most likely the strain, deprivation, and exhaustion of travel and camp life, unavoidable even for the great, had so weakened the king that the illness of the preceding year recurred.

The royal court and some portion of the army journeyed from Almería to Guadix, perhaps briefly towards Granada, then to Baeza, and from there through the pass of Despeñaperros. At the hamlet of Almuradiel, on August 21, 1157, Alfonso VII died at the age of fifty-two, after a reign of thirty-one years.

The unhappy and contentious aftermath began at once. Rodrigo Jiménez de Rada tells us that Fernando II, fearing to be bilked of his inheritance by his brother, at once rode north to León. The implication is that he even deserted his father's body. Sancho III, who had remained in upper Andalucía with a portion of the army, now came north to Almuradiel. He and Archbishop Juan of Toledo escorted the body of Alfonso to Toledo where, it was buried in the cathedral.[115] Division of the realm reported by a thirteenth-century chronicle gave to Sancho III Toledo and the lands south of the Guadarramas, Avila, Segovia and the surrounding trans-Duero region, Castilla La Vieja and the *meseta* north of the Duero as far west as Sahagún, and Asturias de Santillana. Fernando II received León, Galicia, Toro, Zamora, and the trans-Duero about Salamanca.[116] Presumably "León" was understood by then to include Asturias de Oviedo. The description is rough in any event, but the actual holdings of the two were soon to be determined by power rather than by testament.

There are no known documents for events of late August and early September. What we have reflected in the *De Rebus Hispaniae* are the poor opinions of everything Leonese, generated by more than seventy years of hostility between the separate kingdoms of León and Castilla, and inherited by the archbishop of Toledo, confidant of the kings of Castilla. Muslim sources report that the garrison of Almería negotiated its surrender at the end of August or the beginning of September, probably when news reached it of the death of Alfonso, although its position was desperate in any case. It was allowed to take ship north to the lands of ibn Mardanish, from which it returned home.

Perhaps even before that surrender, the evacuation of the garrisons and Christian populations of the remainder of upper Andalucía took place. The major towns of Baeza and Ubeda were reintegrated into Muslim al-Andalus and they and their environs became part of the Iberian provinces of the North African empire of the Almohads. It would be another seventy years before the definitive Christian reconquest of upper Andalucía took place. The conceptual basis and the institutional structure of the kingdom of León-Castilla proved to be too fragile to withstand the dynastic crisis and therefore neither of its successor realms were able to maintain these recent dramatic projections of its power.

115. *De Rebus Hispaniae*, pp. 232–33.
116. Luis Charlo Brea, ed., *Cronica latina de los reyes de Castilla* (Cádiz, 1984), p. 8.

5

King, Dynasty, and Court

IN THE TWELFTH CENTURY in León-Castilla the king, within the dynasty, was much more the substance than the symbol of the kingdom. From the time when Fernando I of Castilla married Sancha of León and defeated and killed his brother-in-law, Vermudo III, at Tamarón in 1037, the essential cohesion of the kingdom had been a product of the politics of family. On the death of Fernando I in 1065, the mere existence of three adult sons had made the division of the realm the political path of least resistance. In 1072 the resolution of the struggle within the family by assassination and coup d'état led immediately to the reunion of the realm under Alfonso VI.

Nonetheless, it would be idle to look for a conscious theory or legal statement concerning succession to the throne, for none existed. Certainly there was a sturdy prejudice in favor of male succession, and Alfonso VI (1065–1109) spent a forty-four-year reign in pursuit of a son. Denied one, he undertook to marry his oldest daughter and heir, Urraca, to her cousin, Alfonso I of Aragón (1104–1134). Yet Urraca (1109–1126), notwithstanding papal annulment of her marriage, invasion by her former spouse, and continual rebellion on behalf of her own son, in fact ruled the kingdom of León-Castilla for seventeen years until her death. During her lifetime, the only successful political challenge to her authority came from her own half sister, Teresa, who dramatically and permanently altered the course of Iberian history by wresting part of the realm away from Urraca. For nineteen years Teresa of Portugal (1109–1128) ruled the new kingdom that was to result from her own dynastic claim despite the death of her husband, Count Henry of Burgundy, in 1112, until being driven into exile by her own son and successor, Afonso Henriques I (1128–1185).

When Alfonso VII succeeded his mother in 1126, his first task was to restore the kingdom by reclaiming the lands wrested away from her by Alfonso I of Aragón. That effort dominated the politics of the period from 1127 to

1134. At the same time, the former had to put down rebellion behind which lay the dynastic claims of the Lara family. Count Pedro González de Lara had been consort and lover of his mother Urraca and the union had given the new king a half brother, in Fernando Pérez, and a half sister, Elvira Pérez. It is significant that their surnames were proper to the dynasty. That problem proved to be manageable, in the first instance by the exile and finally by the death in turn of the Lara counts, Pedro and then Rodrigo González. Fortunately the king's cousin, Count Alfonso Jordan of Toulouse, was content with his own status in the Midi. While he occasionally visited Iberia, he never asserted his own rights there and seems to have supported Alfonso VII in family and general politics. But no more than his mother, could the latter restore the lost unity of the realm by subduing or subverting his aunt Teresa or his cousin Afonso Henriques, and Portugal went its own way. Finally, of course, on the death of Alfonso VII, León-Castilla was again divided among its male heirs.

Because of the dominance of the dynastic understanding of the realm, of what precisely the kingdom consisted is problematic. When we call it the kingdom of León-Castilla we are, in fact, defining it in terms of that which the successes of its rulers caused it to become. Surely narrative should follow the event, but we must not call such description analysis. It is arguable that Fernando I seems not to have called his realm anything at all, at least in his documents. While his charters have not been edited, neither in their intitulation nor in their confirmation does he appear to have styled himself other than simply "rex" or "princeps."[1]

The division of the realm after Fernando's death, perhaps, led Alfonso VI to specify that he was "king of the Leonese," but his reunion of the realm in 1072 and consequent entry on a much larger stage led him to a more radical formulation of his dignity. Confrontation in 1076 with a reforming papacy tentatively asserting its suzerainty over Iberia resulted in the adoption thenceforth by Alfonso's chancery of the title of "emperor of all Spain."[2] Much the same title continued to be used by his daughter and successor, Urraca. That

1. See Pilar Blanco Lozano, ed., *Colección diplomática de Fernando I, 1037–1065* (León, 1987). However useful, this collection is a mere printing rather than an edition. Of that minority of twenty-one among seventy-eight charters in which the king is cited as ruling either León or Castilla, or both, at least nine are forgeries and none of them are original.

2. See Bernard F. Reilly, *The Kingdom of León-Castilla under King Alfonso VI, 1065–1109* (Princeton, 1988), pp. 101–4 and 136–37. Or more particularly, see my "The Chancery of Alfonso VI of León-Castile (1065–1109)," in Bernard F. Reilly, ed., *Santiago, Saint-Denis, and Saint Peter: The Reception of the Roman Liturgy in León-Castile in 1080*, pp. 1–40 (New York, 1985). The prehistory of the use of the imperial title and its political meaning has been repeatedly and heatedly argued, largely without an adequate examination of the documents.

queen experimented briefly with "imperatrix," and thereafter contented herself with the more comfortable but equally sweeping "queen of all Spain."[3]

In turn, Alfonso VII adopted the title of "emperor of all Spain." Clearly the habitual use of this style asserted a hegemony over other political powers in the Iberian peninsula. Its exact theoretical content cannot be further specified. Its practical content, in chancery usage reflecting the royal attitude surely, was expressed in the dating formula of royal documents from 1135. As it was almost uniformly drawn, the emperor ruled in "Toledo, León, Zaragoza, Nájera, Castilla, and Galicia." When the real area of imperial rule expanded, as in 1147, the formula was lengthened to include "Baeza and Almería." Chancery practice thus succinctly stated how far the writ of the dynasty actually ran, and so specified the current, constituent parts of the kingdom. Following the death of Alfonso VII, his sons and successors ordinarily described themselves respectively as "king of León and Galicia" and as "king of Castilla and Toledo."

The authority of the crown, as distinct from its power, was asserted in the same fashion. The dating formulas after late 1149 usually list the "count of Barcelona" and the "king of Navarra" as imperial vassals, when they had actually done homage and were not in rebellion. Muslim princes, such as Saif al-Dawla, ibn Gāniya, and ibn Mardanish, are sometimes listed as vassals when they were so behaving. Doubtless, all parties would have differed over the nature of that authority, and it would be fruitless to attempt to delimit it constitutionally. They assuredly did not. It neither inhibited Alfonso's periodic plots to absorb Navarra outright nor did it preclude him from listing Zaragoza as a constituent part of his realm, although it was precisely for that territory that the count of Barcelona had done him homage.

Nevertheless, Navarra and Barcelona seem to have been included in the intellectual content of "all Spain" in a way in which Portugal was not. Although the county of Portugal had been an integral portion of the realm as late as 1109 and Teresa, his aunt, and Afonso Henriques, his cousin, were every bit as much members of the dynasty's core as was Alfonso VII himself, Portugal is never so listed nor was its prince named as vassal. The attitude seems to be pragmatic. Despite a few attempts, Alfonso had only once, briefly in 1137, been able to project his power to the west and to force his cousin to do homage. Similarly, if princes of the Midi sometimes did homage to Alfonso, as in 1134–1135, that did not lead to their appearance in documentary and

---

3. See Bernard F. Reilly, *The Kingdom of León-Castilla under Queen Urraca, 1109–1126* (Princeton, 1982), pp. 205–11.

official assertions of his authority. They did not come, thereby, under the umbrella of the "empire of all Spain" anymore than did Portugal or al-Andalus.

Within the territories that did, at least with the exception of Zaragoza, Alfonso VII ruled as had his predecessors back through Fernando I "Deo gratia"; that is, although practically speaking it was mediated through the dynasty, the ultimate theoretical ground of the royal authority was divine grace. That formula was a constant of the intitulation of the royal diplomas. This source of royal legitimacy was hallowed by the church of the realm both in its ritual and in its obedience. On Pentecost of 1135 Alfonso VII was crowned "emperor" in the cathedral of Santa María in León. Rites for the well-being of the king on his going forth to battle and on his return from the same and on his entrance into his royal city were traditional in the Mozárabic liturgy.[4] The acceptance of this ultimate religious basis of political authority was general in all the reaches of society in the western world of the time.

Above all, that authority was exercised through the person of the king. What the modern misses in this society is an administrative network for the systematic implementation of the royal authority. Instead, what existed was the direct application of royal power to major problems by means of peripatetic kingship. The king was in constant motion about the realm. Whether conducting war, mediating ecclesiastical disputes, or dispensing justice, the royal presence and charisma were indispensable. That necessity placed an enormous physical strain on any monarch. By the time of Alfonso VII, the kingdom had come to consist of more than 225,000 square kilometers, roughly the size of England, Scotland, and Wales combined. News traversed it in a matter of weeks on the average. Armies, the royal court, and ordinary traffic moved about it at the average rate of twenty-five kilometers a day if ox-drawn carts were employed, or perhaps as swiftly as fifty kilometers per day if only pack animals transported the baggage. The very size of the realm made it unwieldy and impossible to govern in any modern sense.

To some extent the other members of the royal family were pressed into service as surrogates for the king. That was not a new device, and it had proved dangerous in the past. Under Alfonso VI, Count Raymond of Burgundy, married to Urraca, had been a sort of viceroy for Galicia, Portugal, and the Leonese Extremadura. To reduce his power, Count Henry of Burgundy, married to Urraca's half sister, Teresa, had subsequently been so constituted for Portugal. But this step had led on the king's death to the permanent separation of Portugal from the realm. Surely the more cautious experiments with this device by Alfonso VII had that development in mind.

---

4. Marius Férotin, ed., *Le Liber Ordinum* (Paris, 1904), col. 149–56.

The major figure of the dynasty, after the king himself, was his sister, *Infanta* Sancha.[5] She was roughly ten years senior to Alfonso, had shared the vicissitudes of his childhood and minority, and eventually outlived him. She was never to marry and it is difficult to see in that fact other than a refusal to allow it, first by her mother loath to raise up yet more challengers to her rule and then by her brother out of similar motive. Nevertheless by the mere fact of her birth Sancha enjoyed real political and economic power. As early as May 1119 she was in possession of fisc lands, an *infantaticum*, in central León that permitted her to maintain her own court and exercise an individual jurisdiction (D8, 11–12).[6] Sancha's charter of 1124 shows her tenant of the fortress of Grajal, south of Sahagún, and competent to alienate so important a monastery as San Miguel de Escalada to Burgundian Cluny (D26).

Sancha's tenancy of Grajal continued throughout the reign of her brother for in 1157 she was still so cited.[7] Other documents indicate that in 1128 she also held Olmedo, and in 1129 Medina de Rioseco. The first of these important towns lay south of the Duero below Valladolid and the second north of the latter.[8] In 1157 she was still tenant of Medina.[9] From 1128 she held power farther west about Zamora, making a grant of property there to that see (D76). In 1131 she made two grants to the French monastery of Marcigny of properties in that territory (D139–40).[10] Two decades later Sancha still held property in the area (D698).

From 1130 until the end of the reign, she had extensive holdings in the Bierzo, that critical gateway between the heart of the realm and Galicia, around Villafranca del Bierzo, Ponferrada, Villabuena, and Carracedo. At least by 1151, another nexus of her authority lay in Asturias, near Gozón on the Biscayan coast northwest of Gijón, former stronghold of the perpetual rebel, Gonzalo Peláez. With these García Calles would also include an *infantaticum* in Galicia but the evidence for this latter is very slim.[11]

5. The *Chronica Adefonsi Imperatoris*, ed. Antonio Maya Sánchez and Juan Gil, in *Chronica Hispana Saeculi XII*, pp. 109–296 (Turnholt, 1990), p. 155, closely associates both *Infanta* Sancha and Queen Berengaria with Alfonso VII and his decisions.

6. Luisa García Calles, *Doña Sancha* (León, 1972), p. 20. This is the only modern account. It must be used carefully for the author's use of documents was uncritical and others have come to light since she wrote.

7. Pub. José Antonio Fernández Flórez, ed., *Colección diplomática del monasterio de Sahagún, 1110–1199*, vol. 4 (León, 1991), pp. 266–67. Possibly an original.

8. 1128. Pub. María Luisa Ledesma Rubio, ed., *Cartulario de San Millán de La Cogolla, 1076–1200* (Zaragoza, 1989), p. 244. AHN, Clero, Carpeta 895, no. 5; pub. Fernández Flórez, *Colección*, 4:120–21, called this copy an original.

9. May 8, 1157. Pub. Carlos de Ayala Martínez, ed., *Libro de Privilegios de la Orden de San Juan de Jerusalén en Castilla y León, siglos XII–XV* (Madrid, 1994), pp. 234–35.

10. García Calles did not know these two charters and overlooks this center of Sancha's power.

11. *Doña Sancha*, pp. 116–17, 119–20, and 120–21, respectively.

That author also argued another *infantaticum* about the Castilian monastery of Covarrubias since she joined with its abbot to grant a *fuero* to the villagers there in 1148. But the document will not stand scrutiny (D584). García Calles found another *infantaticum* in León and vicinity but more than one of the documents upon which the assumption is founded are unreliable (D576, 592).[12] Certainly Sancha held many scattered properties, from Toledo to Alba de Tormes to the upper Rioja, for which no larger jurisdictional unit may be safely argued. More generally, the influence wielded by Alfonso's sister is illustrated by the seventy-six surviving charters she issued.

The significance of this record is highlighted by the fact that Alfonso VII's two queens seem never to have issued any charters in their own names. They were invariably listed in the intitulation of royal documents, a courtesy due their rank as consorts, as Sancha was only when she had actual claims to the property being conveyed. Marrying into the dynasty did not confer the same rights as being born into it. Clearly the munificence of Sancha was a factor to be considered, second only to that of the king himself, by the prelates, nobles, and townsmen of the kingdom.

The regularity with which the king's sister confirmed her brother's documents, 14 percent of the time, also demonstrates that Sancha was a court figure. When we recall the peripatetic nature of the court, her greater age, and that many documents were issued on the road or on the frontier, that figure is yet more impressive. Finally, the stature of Sancha was emphasized when she was granted the title of "queen" to succeed that of *infanta*, likely at the Christmas court of 1147–1148.[13]

Sancha exercised another traditional role as guardian of her brother's female children. Indeed, her court must have had much the appearance of a nursery. Prominent among her charges was Constanza, daughter by Queen Berengaria, born sometime before 1142, since she was of marriageable age in 1154 and shortly thereafter bore Louis VII of France two daughters. Constanza first reliably appears in public, confirming the charters of her aunt in 1151, and is seen only in that capacity until 1153, shortly before her nuptials (D698, 802).[14]

Alfonso's sister may also have been the guardian of her namesake, al-

12. Ibid., pp. 113–16.
13. Sancha first employed the title in D574, and subsequently used it almost invariably in her own diplomas. Notaries of private documents appear to have continued to use her familiar title.
14. Earlier charters in which she is associated with her father as co-grantor are unreliable. They were inspired by chancery practice of 1156–1157 when she was so associated after the failure of her marriage and her return from France.

though there is no hard evidence for such. Alfonso's daughter, Sancha, was born to him by Berengaria about 1141 to judge from the timing of her subsequent marriage. She makes no appearance in documents until the latter event but her rearing in her aunt's nursery would have been natural.

Another of Sancha's charges was Urraca, natural daughter of Alfonso by the Asturian noblewoman Guntroda Pérez. This duty began somewhere after the former's birth about 1133 and continued until Urraca's marriage to García Ramírez of Navarra in the spring of 1144.[15] Sancha may have functioned as guardian later to the offspring of that marriage.

Finally, there is a mysterious "Pedro Rex" who appears in a series of six documents between 1140 and 1149, usually in association with the *infanta*. In that of September 1146 he is identified as "grandson of King García." That is an impossibility in terms of the Iberian dynasties of the time. But were he rather a "nephew" of García Ramírez, and *nepos* is sometimes so used, then perhaps we have the relative of a sometime ally raised at court and informal hostage for the latter's behavior by the emphasis on the child's ability to inherit in his own right (D377, 533, 553, 574, 623).[16]

At some point, the coterie of retainers that always surrounded Sancha was formed into a proper curia. This is reflected imperfectly in her charters, which have not been edited. It would be too much to say that she had her own chancery. Until 1148 when she began to be entitled "queen," her documents appear to have been drawn up by whatever cleric was convenient, often from the church that was the beneficiary. After that date, one Gudesteo, calling himself scribe or notary of the queen, prepared most of them. The only other officer regularly evident in her service was Nicholas Peláez. From 1140 until the end of the reign, he appears in her charters as her majordomo. He was in charge of ordering and provisioning her household, coordinating and overseeing the work of the *merinos* of the properties of the *infantaticum*. That function is indicated in the charter of November 12, 1142, where Pedro Yañez is noted as "under his direction" (D443). *Merinos* of the queen, distinct from those of the crown proper, are noted in three other of her charters.

To avert confusion, the existence of another *infanta* Sancha during this period should be mentioned. She was the daughter of Alfonso VI by his fourth queen, Elizabeth, born between 1101 and 1105. She was subsequently married to the Lara count, Rodrigo González, during the reign of her half sister, Queen Urraca. A date between 1115 and 1125 is likely. She was not

15. García Calles, *Doña Sancha*, pp. 33 and 39–40.
16. The confirmation of documents by a very young potential heir is unusual but not unknown. Since Pedro does not figure anywhere after 1149, one supposes his death at an early age.

prominent in the reign of Alfonso VII, probably sharing the checkered fortunes of the Lara family between 1126 and and 1135. By the latter date, she was likely dead for Count Rodrigo then remarried.[17]

The *infanta* Elvira Alfónsez, half sister to Urraca and aunt of Alfonso, played a more modest but not unimportant dynastic role during his reign. Elvira was a natural daughter of Alfonso VI by a noble woman of the Bierzo, Jimena Muñoz, and may have been born about 1087.[18] No more than in the case of her sister, Teresa of Portugal, did any stigma of illegitimacy prevent her participation in the active life of the dynasty. Initially, that took the traditional form of a marriage with the powerful Count Raymond IV of Toulouse from which union the future Count Alfonso Jordan of Toulouse was born in the Holy Land in 1103.[19] After Raymond's death in 1105, Elvira returned to Iberia, and by July of 1117 she had remarried. Her spouse was the Leonese noble Fernando Fernández, prominent in the court of Queen Urraca. On that date, the pair granted a small monastery in the territory of Lugo to Cluny. Four years later, Fernando made another grant to one Pedro Braólez of a property in the territory of León.[20] Fernando, sometimes called "count," played a brief part in the court of Alfonso VII but died before 1133. At that date, Elvira and her three children by him granted a property in the territory of León to the canons of that cathedral (D177).

The *infanta* did not again remarry. Over the years she issued nine known charters, a modest record compared with the activity of her niece, Sancha. Nevertheless, they show Elvira alienating properties in León, Astorga, the Bierzo, and Galicia. Unfortunately, we do not know which were part of the dynastic fisc (i.e., an *infantaticum*) and which part of her marriage settlement. Also, while they do show her surrounded by a sizable entourage, they do not identify either a notary of her own or a majordomo. Nor is there sufficient evidence that her residence at her nephew's court was habitual. In the thirty-

17. Benito Sánchez Alonso, ed., *Crónica del Obispo Don Pelayo* (Madrid, 1924), p. 86. Pelayo not only identified her mother but mentioned her subsequent marriage. May 10, 1125. Pub. Luciano Serrano, ed., *Cartulario del monasterio de Vega con documentos de San Pelayo y Vega de Oviedo* (Madrid, 1927), pp. 46–48. This joint charter issued by Queen Urraca and Count Rodrigo cites Elvira as his wife. September 5, 1135. Pub. Manuel Mañueco Villalobos and José Zurita Nieto, eds., *Documentos de la Iglesia Colegial de Santa María la Mayor de Valladolid*, 2 vols. (Valladolid, 1917–20), 1:170–77. This is a *carta de arras* between the count and his new wife, Estefania.

18. Reilly, *Alfonso VI*, pp. 192–93.

19. José María Canal Sánchez-Pagín, "La Infanta Doña Elvira, hija de Alfonso VI y de Gimena Muñoz a la luz de los diplomas," *AL* 33 (1979): 271–87, gives the only major treatment of her. He had, however, less than a complete acquaintance with all of the relevant documents. More recently he dealt with the person of her mother in "Jimena Muñoz, amiga de Alfonso VI," *AEM* 21 (1991): 11–40, and also revised major portions of his conclusions about her daughter.

20. July 8, 1117. Pub. Canal Sánchez-Pagín, "Jimena Muñoz," pp. 37–38. February 25, 1121. AD León, Gradefes, no. 19.

one years of his reign, she confirmed but eight of Alfonso's charters. But if she did not reside at court Elvira had a role to play in the administration of dynastic lands. From 1137 until 1153, documents of the Bierzan monastery of San Pedro de Montes cite her as tenant of Ribeira de Sil in the Bierzo along the *camino de Santiago*.[21] In addition, from 1130 private documents of the Hospitalers, the Leonese monasteries of Sahagún, Gradefes, and the cathedral cite her as the tenant of the Leonese villages of Bolanos de Campos, Castrogonzalo, and Castroverde de Campos, seventy kilometers south of León.[22]

There was also another daughter of Alfonso VI named Elvira, the child of his wife Elizabeth. Born between 1100 and 1104, she was wed before 1120 to Roger II of Sicily and died on that island without returning to the peninsula. She played no part, therefore, in the day-to-day fortunes of the dynasty.[23]

Among the daughters of Alfonso VII, the major figure in the governance of the kingdom was Urraca, daughter of Guntroda Pérez.[24] Born about 1132, she was just canonical age at her marriage to García Ramírez in 1144. She returned to the realm on his death in 1150. A princess of the blood and former queen of Navarra, she was naturally surrounded by a court, but we cannot identify any of its members, for of the three charters attributed to her, with her father, two are forgeries and the third lacks the list of those who confirmed (D801, 872, 910). Nor did she figure regularly in her father's court, for only six diplomas of other members of the dynasty are confirmed by her. Her role lay in the supervision of the major province of Asturias de Oviedo from early 1153. The first royal document to cite Urraca in that role was that of her aunt and former guardian, Queen Sancha, but private documents commence a bit earlier (D802).[25] In that capacity she appears from the first as "queen" although the title might relate to her former marriage. Still, one is reminded of the subsequent position of Asturias in the dynasty and kingdom as the *appanage* of the heir apparent. In the later medieval period the "prince

21. October 24, 1137, and June 6, 1153. Pub. Augusto Quintana Prieto, ed., *Tumbo viejo de San Pedro de Montes* (León, 1971), pp. 248–49 and 279–80.

22. June 3, 1130. Pub. Ayala Martínez, *Libro*, pp. 176–77, the first. The latest citation is May 9, 1157. Pub. José María Fernández Catón, ed., *Colección documental del archivo de la catedral de León, 1109–1187*, vol. 5 (León, 1990), pp. 302–3, who calls it an original. Earlier royal documents that cite her in these tenancies are unreliable.

23. Reilly, *Urraca*, pp. 296–97, and Canal Sánchez-Pagín, "Doña Elvira," p. 275, although he erroneously associated some of the early diplomas of Elvira, daughter of Jimena Muñoz, with her.

24. F. Javier Fernández Conde, "La Reina Urraca 'La Asturiana,'" *AM* 2 (1975): 65–94, is the only modern account of her life. Her tomb was opened in the late nineteenth century, and Francisco Simon y Nieto, "Nuevos datos históricos acerca del sepulchro de la reina Doña Urraca en la catedral de Palencia," *BRAH* 30 (1897): 379–99, reported the results.

25. June 27, 1153. AHN, Clero, Carpeta 1.616, nos. 18 and 19; pub. Marcos G. Martínez, "El convento benedictino de Villanueva de Oscos," *BIEA* 8 (1954): 283–84.

of Asturias" will have much the same connotation as the "prince of Wales" in England. This somewhat isolated area needed to be tied more closely to the developing realm and that was Urraca's role.

By contrast, the role of Alfonso's daughter by Queen Berengaria, *Infanta* Sancha, was modest. In 1153 she, too, became briefly a queen of Navarra when she was married to Sancho VI, son of García Ramírez. Earlier she is invisible in the documents. Presumably she had just come of canonically marriageable age. Only after her repudiation, or recall, when relations between the two kingdoms cooled, did she begin to appear. From November 1156 until the end of the reign, young Sancha was regularly cited with her brothers and sister in the intitulation of royal diplomas, as "queen of Navarra." No known charters of Sancha survive, nor is she mentioned in any documents of the period as the holder of a tenancy or *infantaticum*. She did not even confirm those royal charters in which she was cited. The *infanta* was pledged in marriage to the son of Ramon Berengar IV from 1156, so a larger role for her at home was perhaps precluded by that prospect.

From the beginning of his reign then, the personal governance of Alfonso VII as he perambulated through his sprawling kingdom was reinforced in his absence by his sister Sancha who held key positions in the territory of León itself and on its western fringes about Zamora and in the Bierzo. She also held a major tenancy in Asturias de Oviedo once the rebellion of Gonzalo Peláez there was suppressed. After 1150, the major responsibility for that fringe territory was vested in the king's daughter, Urraca. Sancha's authority in the Bierzo was bolstered by the tenancy of Alfonso's aunt, Elvira, as well.

Late in the reign, by reason of internal dynastic developments as well as the necessities of government, the king's son, Sancho, was entrusted with an appanage consisting of La Rioja, the region of Castilla La Vieja immediately west of that province, and the Sorian highlands. The latter probably included Tarazona, Calatayud, and certainly Agreda. It is unlikely that his control reached west to Burgos or Palencia. Sancho's authority extended to negotiations with his neighbors, the king of Navarra who became his father-in-law, and the ruler of Aragón-Barcelona, his uncle. Such negotiations were subject to the approval of his father as were the former's alienations from the fisc. Sancho was vested with this authority after his knighting in 1152. The grant represented a political adjustment internal to the dynasty, but it became a factor in the closer government of the realm all the same.

Thirty-one charters of Sancho III are known from the period before his father's death and demonstrate his participation in the largesse that was so essential a part of the government. Unfortunately, at least nine of those are forgeries and only three have any claim to be originals. Nevertheless, it is clear that Sancho had his own court. He had a majordomo, or rather three individuals who served serially in that capacity. All were great magnates; Martín Muñoz, Guter Fernández, and Gómez González, in that order. Unlike the courts of his aunts and sisters he also had his own *alférez*, the magnates Gonzalo Rodríguez and then Gómez González. Finally, he also had his own scribe, Martín, and perhaps a modest chancery. Some of his documents show Martín acting at the behest of Nicolás, archdeacon of Palencia and "royal chancellor." Frequently, however, his court must have been only nominally distinct from the curia of his father, in which Sancho was usually present, confirming almost all his father's charters. Moreover, Sancho's own charters were invariably issued with the stated consent of his father.

In late 1155 the king's second son, Fernando, was knighted and a similar arrangement was instituted in the far west. Again dynastic necessities played their part. The dignity of an adult male heir had to be satisfied and celebrated. Nonetheless, Galicia was a relatively remote province, difficult of approach from the heart of the kingdom and with a periodically dangerous neighbor to the south in Portugal. A representative of the dynasty there at least occasionally was useful in moderating the politics of its nobility and overseeing the integrity of its fisc lands. But this particular arrangement was superseded so quickly on the death of Alfonso VII that there is little evidence of its functioning. We have not a single intact charter of Fernando before 1158.

Fernando had his own majordomo, Vela Gutiérrez, from the time of his knighting. From the same time he also could boast his own *alférez*, Menendo de Bragança (D918). But both are known only through the charters of Alfonso VII, which they confirm in nine instances before the end of the reign. The young king also had a chancellor if we can accept the private document that marks this latter's only known appearance.[26] Like his brother, Fernando had his court. However, since he, too, was so often in attendance on his father, it saw little independent functioning.

The center of the governance of the kingdom of León-Castilla was the royal curia but it is difficult to describe exactly what the term curia meant in the mid-twelfth century. Certainly it did not figure very largely in anyone's consciousness. In about 1,000 private documents of the era, that term did not appear even once. In roughly the same number of royal documents, it turns up only fourteen times, and six of those are forged or interpolated. Moreover, two of the remaining six instances are charters of *Infanta* Sancha,

26. March 29, 1126. Pub. Fernández Catón, *Colección*, 5:288–89, who calls it an original.

which follow the norms of private diplomas rather the royal chancery. There the phraseology is applied to private individuals said to be "in the curia of the *infanta*." Such terminology can either be merely descriptive or might conceivably be meant in the institutional sense.[27] In the earliest usage of the royal chancery itself in June 1135, the term is quite clearly used in a general and descriptive sense rather than in an institutional one (D206). In other employment of it by the chancery, the meaning is ambiguous, although a case might be made for an institutional connotation in its usage in the treaty of February 1140, with Aragón-Barcelona (D371).

In all probability, we strain to see an emerging legal institution where contemporaries saw only an obvious fact. Important actions were taken in the king's court and the personal, political, legal and social aspects of that body were rarely distinct. That confusion continued in good measure as long as monarchy itself in the western world.

The royal curia consisted in the first instance of the king, his queen, and other adult members of the blood. The latter extended to aunts and sisters, as well as to sons and daughters. Surely it would have extended as well to uncles if Alfonso VII had had such, but it did not extend to cousins. There would have been too many for comfort. We cannot gauge the extent of the political influence exercised by any of the dynastic participants. Under the monarchy, all political acts were acts of the king by very definition. But, as the several members of the dynasty held real, local political authority, we can judge that they possessed real, if unquantifiable power, at its center as well.

So far as the acts of the king in curia found written expression, they are recorded by the royal chancery, the one undoubted institution of the government. If not strictly a department of government in the modern sense, the chancery of León-Castilla can lay fair claim to being the oldest institution of royal, central government, after the office of king itself. A subordinate, monarchical organization of specialized function with at least one subordinate and one superior office, it dates from the reign of Alfonso VI.[28] That

27. July 15, 1144. Pub. Francisco Javier Fernández Conde, Isabel Torrente Fernández, and Guadalupe de la Noval Menéndez, *El monasterio de San Pelayo de Oviedo*, vol. 1 (Oviedo, 1978), pp. 35–39 append. April 29, 1147. Pub. García Calles, *Doña Sancha*, pp. 145–46. Evelyn S. Proctor, *Curia and Cortes in León and Castile, 1072–1295* (Cambridge, 1980), pp. 7–43, contains a useful, short description of the royal curia for the period 1072–1157. However, care must be taken since most of the critical work on the royal diplomas of the period has begun only since.

28. His diplomas, like his son's, have not been edited. For the present see Reilly, "Chancery," pp. 243–61. A wider context can be partially supplied by Augustín Millares Carlo, "La cancillería real en León y Castilla hasta finales del reinado de Fernando III," *AHDE* 3 (1926): 227–306, although this early study needs revision. Manuel Lucas Alvarez, *El reino de León en La Alta Edad Media*, vol. 8, *Las cancellerías reales astur-leonesa (718–1072)* (León, 1995) and *El reino de León en La Alta Edad Media*, vol. 5, *Las cancillerías reales (1109–1230)* (León, 1993), provides invaluable help.

institution continued to function through the reign of Urraca into that of Alfonso VII.[29]

In the latter's reign, the chancery was very stable. Initially it drew on the traditions and even some of the personnel of Urraca's chancery. The chief officer was the royal chancellor. That title, employed only occasionally under Urraca, became standard for the Alfonsine chancery early in 1131 (D127).[30] At least three of the officers of Alfonso's chancery had been canons of the cathedral of Santiago de Compostela, including Chancellor Bernard who held that post into 1133. Early in 1135 the position passed to Berenguer, former canon of the church of Toledo, who held it until royal favor propelled him into the see of Salamanca in 1135. By mid-1135, Berenguer had been suceeded as chancellor by a "magister Hugonis" who remained in the post until mid-1151. We do not know the antecedents of Hugo, but he may have been a canon of the see of Salamanca.[31]

His successor was Juan Fernández, associated from his first appearance as scribe under Hugo in December 1149 as a canon of Santiago de Compostela as well (D627). There was an interlude, after the disappearance of Hugo, when Juan bore the title of "notarius" and we can suspect that Hugo still lived but was incapacitated by illness. At the beginning of 1154, Juan began

29. Cristina Monterde Albiac, ed., *Diplomatario de la Reina Urraca de Castilla y León, (1109–1126)* (Zaragoza, 1996), has collected all of her charters known to me. Her chancery and charters lack definitive studies, however. For the reign of Urraca it should be supplemented by Reilly, *Urraca*, pp. 205–11, and Lucas Alvarez, *Reino*, 5:33–160.

30. There are some earlier citations but none of them are originals. "Notary" seems at first to have done duty with much the same implications of office. Three quarters of a century ago Peter Rassow, "Die Urkunden Kaiser Alfonso VII von Spanien," *AU* 10 (1928): 327–468, and 11 (1930): 66–137, did a pioneering study on the basis of photographs and printed texts of some 372 royal charters then available to him. The work was so remarkably detailed and precise that it has become the authority down to the present. However, we now know roughly 869 charters of Alfonso himself and another 106 contemporary ones of other members of the dynasty. Consequently, revision is in order. Some of it has been undertaken in Bernard F. Reilly, "The Chancery of Alfonso VII of León-Castilla: The Period 1126–1135 Reconsidered," *Speculum* 51 (1971): 243–61. What I said then needs to be revised occasionally in terms of what is adduced in this work. Also see Lucas Alvarez, *Reino*, 5:160–314.

31. His name is not Iberian nor common in Iberia. March 4, 1121. Pub. Antonio Suárez de Alarcón, *Relaciones genealógicas de la casa de los Marquesas de Trocifal* (Madrid, 1656), p. 8 append. This is a private document confirmed by one Hugo archdeacon of the see of León. January 21, 1133. Pub. José Luis Martín, Luis Miguel Villar García, Florencio Marcos Rodríguez, and Marciano Sánchez Rodríguez, eds., *Documentos de los archivos catedralicio y diocesano de Salamanca, siglos XII-XIII* (Salamanca, 1977), pp. 89–90. This is a private donation of one Hugo archdeacon to the church of Salamanca. Date and association would make this last Hugo the leading contender but the evidence is obviously slim. At this point, I would correct my own previous conclusions, "Chancery," pp. 259–60. The royal confirmation of July 20, 1135, must be re-dated to 1137 for reasons of diplomatic (D296). Moreover, that of January 3, 1136, is not an original and may be false. The scribe is otherwise unknown and it unclear why he should be employed. See other royal charters of the same date (D240–41). March 14, 1151 (D695). This royal grant to the monastery of San Isidro de Dueñas has the last reliable reference to Hugo as chancellor.

to style himself canon of both the see of Toledo and of Compostela as well as imperial chancellor. He continued in the latter office until March 1156 (D818, 928). By July, he had been succeeded by Pedro González, who continued as chancellor to the end of the reign. Of Pedro we know only that he boasted the title of "magister" and that the charters produced under him blossomed with a fulsome rhetoric of classical overtones.[32]

Ordinarily it has been asserted that the chancellorship of León-Castilla belonged of right to the archbishop of Santiago de Compostela, having been granted to Archbishop Diego Gelmírez by Alfonso VII. As we have seen, the influence of Santiago de Compostela on the composition of the chancery was pronounced, but that church had to contend with the growing importance of the restored primate of Toledo. The royal charters that confer the office in perpetuity on the former are flawed (D390, 411).[33] In any event, the king took the initiative in ecclesiastical affairs generally, and one wonders whether the presumed claim of either see meant more than that they had to provide canonries for favored royal clerks.

The subordinate of the chancellor was the scribe. Ordinarily there seems to have been but one, although in the period before 1134 there may sometimes have been two or more. Nonmembers of the chancery were sometimes recruited to draft a particular document. The two most prominent scribes of the early period were Ciprián Pérez and Pelayo Arias, who served in that order and who drafted eighteen and twenty-nine charters, respectively. Both were connected with the church of Santiago.[34] Usually a scribe could expect to succeed to the chancellorship, as happened to both Berenguer of Toledo and Juan Fernández. It did not occur in the case of Gerald, scribe under Master Hugo between 1135 and 1148 and by far the most productive of the royal scribes. We know nothing of his origins but his name, like that of his superior, points to a French derivation. Apparently he died before Hugo.[35] During the last half dozen years of the reign, under Juan Fernández and then Pedro González, one Adrian was the major scribe. From mid-1155, he began to style himself canon and archdeacon of Compostela.

During the first half of 1135, one "Guillelmus de Ponte" appeared in

32. Lucas Alvarez, *Reino*, 5:194 and 312, makes him a canon of Santiago de Compostela but cites only the questionable charter of April 13, 1157, which does not mention him (D968). Two royal charters of the last year of the reign cite one Fernando Palea (Peláez?) as imperial chancellor but both have their difficulties (D938,959).

33. Emma Falque Rey, ed., *Historia Compostellana* (Turnholt, 1988), p. 409.

34. Reilly, "Chancery," pp. 249–50, and 252–54.

35. He is cited in one charter as "vice-chancellor" (D467). This is one of the very few times during the reign that such a term appears. One Alfonso was so styled in some of the early royal charters(50, 53, 81). The sense seems to be of a temporary substitution rather than an office as such.

twelve charters as scribe under the chancellor and bishop-elect Berenguer but did not reappear subsequently. Similarly, in the fall of 1137 one "Eustachius Carnotensis" drafted another dozen diplomas as scribe under Master Hugo. Both perhaps were educated transients, temporarily at court and pressed into service to meet some emergency.[36] It may also be noted that the chanceries Queen Sancha and of *Infans* Sancho were distinct in their operations and diplomatic usage and did not borrow or lend personnel from or to the royal chancery.

By traditional standards, the chancery of Alfonso VII was a busy place. The measure can only be comparative, of course, but for the reign of his great-grandfather, Fernando I (1037–1065), some 124 extant documents are known, an average of 4.5 per year. His grandfather, Alfonso VI (1065–1109), has left us 268, or 6 per year. From his Urraca (1109–1126), just 142 survive, or 8 per year. Alfonso's chancery proper produced 869 surviving documents during the years between 1126 and 1157, roughly 28 per year. A reasonable comparison would be with Louis VI (1108–1137) of France. The recent splendid edition of his documents numbers some 457 items including forgeries. That is a chancery output of slightly less than 16 per year. It might be noted that Louis styled himself "Rex Francorum" and that the dating formula never lists the constituent parts of his realm. The place as well as the date of issue is given, the title of chancellor is employed regularly, but there is no list of confirmants.[37]

Alfonso VII's documents fall into several types by content. Some 673, slightly under 80 percent, of them are donations of real property. Another thirty-three are confirmations of such property granted in the past by the king's predecessors, or sometimes by himself. Eighteen of the documents are exchanges of real property, and five of them sales. If we combine these types, then approximately 85 percent of the business of the royal chancery dealt with the transfer of land through the instrument of royal charters. That is a sobering reminder to the modern of the real foundations of government, wealth, and of society in this period.

The remaining 15 percent of chancery documents are composed of seventy *fueros* (i.e., grants of local law or privilege). There are eighteen *agnitiones*, or records of judicial decisions. There are twelve treaties or pacts but since these latter result from the common action of distinct powers they are not chancery documents, strictly speaking, and there is no separate chancery form for them.

Finally, there are eighteen "mandates," that is, documents that inform a

36. Lucas Alvarez, *Reino*, 5:195, suggests that Eustachius derived from Carnota in Galicia but Chartres seems more likely.
37. Jean Dufour, ed., *Recueil des actes de Louis VI, roi de France, 1108-1137*, 4 vols. (Paris, 1992).

particular individual or group of individuals of a royal decision. They take the letter form. This type must have comprised by far the greatest number of documents to issue from the chancery, for all other sorts of document must have required one or more of these to implement and make it effective. In one happy instance in 1136 we can see that a particular royal act has generated no less than six (D267–73). But unlike the charter of conveyance, the *mandatum* was unlikely to be treasured by an age accustomed to the oral transaction of even the most crucial business.

One form of document was routinely employed for donations, sales, and exchanges of property, and some confirmations of past grants, especially when the latter were combined with new grants, and even for *fueros*. What we can fairly call the charter form was written in a caroline script from which Visigothic elements had almost entirely disappeared. It was preceded by a drawn chrismon and concluded by a drawn royal seal or *signum*, although it has been argued cogently that a pendant seal was at least occasionally employed from the year 1146, the irregularity of that practice continues to be puzzling. Fifty-nine arguably original documents of Alfonso VII survive from this period and only eight of them bear traces of having been sealed.[38] The royal *signum*, on the other hand, was an invariable part of a the charter form.

The form of the invocation and the *arenga* vary and the latter is sometimes omitted entirely. The intitulation might vary with political conditions. Almost without exception, Alfonso is titled "emperor of Spain" and his wife is invariably associated with him. Male children are cited beginning with Sancho in 1146, Fernando from 1149, and in the last year of the reign his daughters Constanza and Sancha. The dating formula always employs the Spanish Era and gives place of issue irregularly before 1135. After that time, the failure of a place to appear in a copy results, one thinks, from the inability of the copyist to read the original exactly. The date is followed, from 1135, by the recital of the major territories of the realm and the order is "Toledo, León, Zaragoza, Nájera, Castilla, and Galicia." From 1147, other major acquisitions are added as the fortunes of war dictate. The dating formula sometimes also includes the year of the empire, dating from Pentecost of 1135, major events such as a royal marriage or knighting, and a citation of the count of Barcelona, the king of Navarra, and sometimes Muslim princes as vassals when they had in fact done homage. The whole is subscribed by the scribe or notary. While notarial *signa* are common in contemporary private usage, the only royal notary who employed one was Gerald. The chancellor did not subscribe ordinarily.

---

38. Richard A. Fletcher, "Diplomatic and the Cid revisited: the seals and mandates of Alfonso VII," *JMH* 2 (1976): 305–38. The problem is magnified when it appears that two different seals can be identified. I have not inspected the examples.

The document is confirmed by Alfonso himself, often by his sister, Sancha, only quite occasionally by his wife, but almost invariably by his sons once they begin to be cited in the intitulation, and in the last year of the reign by his daughters Constanza and Sancha. Others who confirm are the royal majordomo and *alférez*, some bishops of the realm then at court, and some counts and magnates then at court. Occasionally other nobles, tenants, and minor office holders confirm in matters that touch them in some capacity.

The procedure for royal confirmations was quite variable. Sometimes a new charter was drawn incorporating additional grants or simply reaffirming old ones. Or the confirmation might be made directly on the parchment of the old royal charter wherever space allowed. So, too, when the king was confirming a contemporary grant by a subject to another of his subjects, he might do so directly at the bottom of their charter. In all but the first instance, the royal confirmation might consist simply of the royal formula of confirmation, *signum*, and sometimes the date, and the notarial subscription. No others ordinarily subscribe although even then there are exceptions.[39]

The *agnitio* was the official record of a settlement of a dispute at law and might or might not be a chancery product proper, even when done in the king's name. If done outside of the chancery, the form seems to have been fairly standard. Usually it begins with the date in the Spanish Era followed by the phrase "orta intentio fuit" and might be confirmed simply by the two parties. Later in the reign, chancery practice seems increasingly to have utilized the full charter form to record such settlements.

If we can fairly conclude that the actual production of the chancery exceeds, by a factor of ten at least and more likely by a factor of forty, the number of documents that have survived, then some important conclusions follow. The presumption is warranted of a minimum of two clerical assistants to the scribe whose work would be the production of the less formal documents such as mandates and letters proper that accompanied charters, and care for the incidentals of the writing process such as procuring supplies of both ink and parchment. The former might even be made by them but it is doubtful that the processing of hides into vellum was their undertaking. That was a job for the butcher. Given the demand for parchment that such a volume of documents produced, it is probable that butchers in the neighborhood of favorite royal haunts such as the city of León or of the village of Sahagún were regular chancery suppliers.

The itinerant nature of the royal court would have further swelled the

---

39. Although it needs to be supplemented, Luis Sánchez Belda, "Notas de diplomática. La confirmación de documentos por los reyes de Occidente español," *RABM* 19 (1953): 85–116, is still the essential introduction.

personnel attached to the chancery. It is reasonable to believe that the chancellor, the scribe, and the two clerks were each attended by a body servant for the making and breaking camp, setting up shelter for their betters, either preparing or foraging for their food, and driving the carts or mules that transported the lot. One cart was required to carry the supplies of parchment, quills, and ink as well as their own personal possessions and those of their masters. Was there a chancery tent as such? It seems likely, and it would have required a cart of its own. If we believe that regular carters rather than the body servants drove the carts, kept them in repair, and looked after the oxen that drew them as well as the animals that the chancellor and the scribe certainly rode, then the royal chancery was a little department of some ten folk arranged in a rough hierarchy. It might have been at least half again larger if the servants or carters were accompanied by their wives.

Over and above the busy clerks of chancery, the royal curia was also composed of the persons of the majordomo and the *alférez*. One says "persons" rather than officials, because contemporary evidence does not indicate the existence of a department under their direction. The royal charters show them as constantly in the entourage of the king and their absence from the confirmants to such charters is to be regarded, in the first instance, as evidence of the incompleteness of the copy. After the first few years of the reign, such persons ordinarily display considerable stability in their posts. In the latter twenty-seven years of the reign, there are in each post but five men, who serve consecutively.

These, however, are great nobles of the realm. If they are not surrounded by a staff, it is yet impossible to imagine them without a household. As with the king, that sometimes meant their wives, when they were not precluded from travel by pregnancy or the departure of the court on campaign, and just as irregularly by children more than six years of age but not yet adults of fourteen. For the great man himself, we can presume a squire, a groom, and at least two body-servants, perhaps a chaplain, a minimum of two carts for his effects and two carters to see to them, but probably not a separate cook. Both majordomo and *alférez* then would have swelled the numbers of the curia by something on the order of another ten persons apiece.

Confirmations to the royal charters also establish that the number of counts present at court varied between three and nine, with five being a rough average. These, too, were drawn from the great lineages of the realm and cannot be thought to have attended alone. For great festivals and councils, they would have been accompanied by their wives and children of suitable age. Even on the more arduous trips and campaigns they would have had their own body-servants, squires, grooms, carts, and carters. Each count then can be roughly gauged to have added a minimum of seven and a maximum twelve more persons to the royal entourage.

Similarly the charters show that the number of bishops at court varied from a low of four and a high of eighteen, with an average of approximately six. Since the prelates also were great magnates of the realm their suite again must have included body-servants, squires, and grooms, but also secretaries and attendant priests as well as additional carts for their clerical and secular gear. A safe estimate might be that each of them added a dozen persons to the royal curia.

One must presume the presence at all times of a royal bodyguard, the core and elite corps of the royal army, and the only portion of that army continuously in being. This corps consisted of a group of forty to sixty mounted warriors, each supported by a squire and groom. Even given the generally pacific character of the realm in this period, such a force was prudent to provide the minimum level of security to the king as he moved about. Taking an average level of strength as fifty, this military force of some 150 male adults adds in turn another fifty carts and carters to the curia.

If, as is quite probable, the combined eleven counts and bishops had there own small military entourage, say five knights of their household apiece, then the full military element of the court would be swollen by yet another 165 persons and better than 300.

For all this melange the king, eldest male and leader of the dynasty but *pater patria* as well, must continuously provide as he himself was reciprocally provided for. Most pressing, the court must be continuously victualed and watered. It was a huge concentration of individuals, for the times, whose numbers exceeded the ability of all but the largest towns of the realm to provide for it. Surely as it ground across the landscape, provisions and animals were collected from estates of the royal fisc, the larders of unfortunate magnates, bishops, and abbots in its path, and any of the small farmers who boasted a surplus from which they could be parted by purchase, confiscation, or simple theft. Very likely this process, and such advance planning of it as could be done, was under the direction of the royal majordomo and the royal *merinos* through whose districts the curia was to pass.

The size of this royal court made it imperative that at least a three- or four-day supply of provisions actually traveled with it. That meant a herd of cattle, sheep, and goats, a walking larder, of about 100 head at any time and four herders. A minimal supply of dry provisions would require no less than sixty two-wheeled carts to transport them and another sixty carters.

Except when the court was on campaign, water was a more manageable problem. The need to water the livestock regularly, 400 head of oxen, 600 horses and mules, and another 100 head of cattle, sheep, and goats, determined the route of the curia. It followed the existing watercourses, and in the dry lands of the central *meseta*, that meant the major ones for the smaller streams were wont to dry up during the summer months and no well could provide for such needs.[40] Even so, it is necessary to hypothesize another five carts and carters for miscellaneous water needs. Wine was another matter. To supply what must have been a peripatetic curia of approximately 600 people in peacetime with a stingy liter of wine per day, a precarious five-day supply would have required twelve hogsheads. If one hogshead was the carrying capacity of a two-wheel cart, another twelve carts and carters must be added to the ménage.

But the responsibilities of the king went beyond the provision of mere victuals. He probably had to supply the cooks, a dozen perhaps, along with an assistant apiece and, of course, the cook wagons, for at least the greater part of the company. For his immediate entourage two or three tents and tent carts at least. The great ones of the court likely had their own. Lesser folk made do with more informal shelter. And beyond food and shelter, entertainment of some sort was required. In the great society of the day, that meant hunting, and so dogs and their handlers, and falcons and theirs. Spiritual nurture as well demanded at least one cart that was, in fact, a portable altar. Such a large company of warriors and mounted persons would further have needed, even in peacetime, the company of a minimum of two smiths for the repair of armor, weapons, utensils, and some shoeing. For them and assistants, we must add another three carts.

Sensible extrapolation from what can be discerned in the royal charters suggests then an average size of 600 persons for the royal curia proper in its peaceful perambulations. That probably would have given it, at the time, a larger population than all but about two dozen of the towns of the kingdom. Such considerations underline the impossibility of most of them to host its stay and suggest that, even in the largest towns, most of the curia must have found accommodations outside the town proper. The royal court was in itself a sort of traveling town and one of the largest markets of the realm. Wholly aside from organized royal provision, through the majordomo, we must envision the coming and going about it of a wide assortment of farmers,

---

40. A horse requires something like thirty-two liters of water per day to stay in good condition. See Stephen Morillo, *Warfare under the Anglo-Norman Kings, 1088–1135* (Woodbridge, Great Britain, 1994), p. 125.

butchers, bakers, clothiers, hostlers, vintners, musicians, and such. In addition, the movement of such a formidable assemblage attracted to it a further, informal company of merchants, adventurers, pilgrims, and other itinerants for the protection against the hazards of the road that it offered when it traveled in their chosen direction. In addition, a company so largely male and relatively so affluent, can be presumed to have attracted a community of ladies of easy virtue, some regular and others casual, together with their hangers-on. The court was, then, a most potent symbol of the power and the glory of the king. Its advent was a disaster for some and a bonanza for others, but no one was able to disregard or ignore it as it ground through the countryside. It was a proclamation of government in motion.

Happily, the chancery practice of the time gives us a map of its annual itinerary. In deep winter the court settled down for the Christmas season. Most often, a full ten times, Alfonso chose the central region about the royal city of León and the royal monastery of Sahagún not far to the southeast. The importance of both Palencia and Burgos is reflected in the wintering in each of the court no less than five times. Necessities of the Muslim frontier moved the court to winter at Salamanca twice and at Toledo some three times. By way of contrast, we can be sure of the court having spent Christmas in Galicia at Santiago de Compostela only once.

Military needs drew the court south to the great frontier redoubt and staging point of Toledo in no fewer than seventeen summers. That journey from León was about 400 kilometers, or better than twelve days of travel each way by the shortest possible route, which was rarely available under the then conditions of transport. The volatile politics of the eastern frontier required journeys to Burgos and beyond in no less than fourteen traveling seasons, over and above the five winter stays there. Of course, Burgos is hardly more than 200 kilometers from León over largely flat lands. Still, a journey there could easily eat up a week each way. On the other hand, the distance from León to Santiago de Compostela is again 400 kilometers or more by the only practical routes, over truly backbreaking terrain. The politics of that region and the adjoining Portuguese frontier summoned the court there five different times.

Along the way the roster of places where the court stopped long enough to indite a charter furnishes the most comprehensive list of the major towns in the second quarter of the twelfth century. Some, like Astorga, Zamora, Salamanca, Avila, Segovia, Valladolid, Palencia, Nájera, Oviedo, and even Carrión de los Condes, were substantial enough to host the royal curia for days and sometimes weeks and to draw its attention in their own right. A score of others were merely way stations on the route to someplace more vital. But peripatetic kingship brought all into a brief but direct contact with that power that increasingly affected their futures. Even in the humbler countryside through which it rumbled and that it denuded, that visible power excited an awe and a dread that furnished the underpinning of a governmental authority otherwise pitifully weak in instruments to match its theoretical jurisdiction.

6

Curia, Council, and Countship

THE DYNASTY, embedded in the royal curia, was the major instrument of government in León-Castilla during the first half of the twelfth century. Its procession throughout the territories of the realm was the chief method of that government. That must never be forgotten by moderns, because it is so alien to our mental processes. Nevertheless, Alfonso's kingdom was an imperial realm and such peripatetic, dynastic government could not suffice entirely to meet its needs. A variety of other devices and practices supplemented and supported it.

Chief among these was that conceptually elusive practice whose manifestation can only be called by the unsatisfactory names of a "general curia" or a "general council."[1] Now the essence of the peripatetic curia was that it took the authority of the crown to the various locales of the realm and that it thereby applied that power directly to their problems. But there were concerns that involved the entire realm. Not so many, certainly, as confront a modern government, but some nonetheless for whose consideration the realm must travel to the crown, wherever the latter might be found.

This governmental device later blossomed everywhere in western Europe into the institution of the parliament. One hesitates to call it an institution in the middle of the twelfth century but it had clearly become a regular instrument of government in León-Castilla.[2] Contemporaries, too, were unsure as to the proper designation and import of the increasingly frequent practice. For example, only eighteen royal charters inform us in their dating formulas of the holding of a council, and half of those notices come in documents that are unreliable. Moreover, even the royal chancery was uncertain as to how to

---

1. For its development and manifestations during the reign of his mother and predecessor, see Bernard F. Reilly, *The Kingdom of León-Castilla under Queen Urraca, 1109–1126* (Princeton, 1982), pp. 253–59.

2. A brief but useful introduction to the wider problem of origins can be found in Antonio Marongiu, *Medieval Parliaments*, trans. S. J. Woolf (London, 1968).

"name the beast." Its terminology alternated between "council" and "general council." The same hesitation over proper terminology was reflected as well in contemporary narrative accounts.

Royal charters explicitly designate only five councils during the entire reign of Alfonso VII, an average of one every six years. Here, the record obviously lags behind the event. I propose a practical measurement based on the real distinction of the general council from the royal curia, its size. One must resort to such a device to describe adequately the contemporary reality, for there was no legal distinction.

The kingdom during the reign of Alfonso VII apparently boasted a maximum of nine counts at any one time. If one identifies as a general council any meeting during which a royal charter was confirmed by so many as seven counts, more than two thirds, a total of nine general councils results; that is, a general council almost every three years. But the kingdom also contained a maximum of twenty-three bishoprics. Two of those were, however, the sees of Baeza and Almería included in the realm only very late in the reign. Another, Coria, was erected after its reconquest in 1142, and its bishop spent most of his time thereafter in Rome seeking support. Yet three more, Zaragoza, Tarazona, and Calahorra, lay in an area whose control was often contested with Aragón and Navarra. At most times then, the realm consisted of seventeen "working" bishops available for royal consultation. If one defines a general council as any meeting during which a royal charter was confirmed by at least twelve bishops, more than two thirds, no fewer than sixteen general councils appear to have been held. That is roughly one every two years.

But this is likely still a minimum number. It suffers, inevitably, from lacunae in the record of charters. In addition, were it possible to calculate the numbers of vacancies and illnesses among the counts and bishops that reduced the number actually available to royal summons at any given time, the resulting record of general councils would climb yet again. My estimate is that there was at least one general council held each year, during the Christmas season broadly defined, and in at least half of the years of the reign, another held about the Easter season or when campaigning ended in early fall.

It is no exaggeration to say that during the reign of Alfonso VII the "general council," as distinct from the peripatetic royal curia, had become a regular practice and a constituent part of the government. But because it yet had developed no formally-defined structure of its own, no proper officers, and little or no customary procedures, it created little proper record. We follow its existence in casual notations of chancery scribes and, above all, in some extended descriptions of individual councils contained in the contemporary *Historia Compostellana* and the somewhat later *Chronica Adefonsi Imperatoris*.

The description of the Council of Palencia of 1129, given in the *Historia Compostellana*, informs us that the king invited to it bishops, abbots, counts, princes, and magnates to counsel him how to remedy the evils grown up in the land over the preceding two decades. Such summons were written, on the testimony of the same source in regard to the Council of Carrión the following year, but no text of such an invitation is known. On the former occasion, at least Archbishop Gelmírez responded to the invitation and it is likely that responses were expected. The text refers alternately to the meeting as a "council" and a "general council."

In Palencia the archbishop met privately with the king and a few of the latter's advisers and set a particular agenda. Then Gelmírez met with the other bishops to communicate the king's wishes. The next day the archbishop again conferred with the king who apparently found the response of the bishops satisfactory. There is no further mention of the counts, nobles, or abbots, and the inference is that their participation was largely passive. On the evidence of the charters, the participation of abbots in court matters was slight but that was not true of the counts and the great nobility.

The council opened with a mass and a sermon and its *acta* were issued by Archbishop Raymond of Toledo as primate and resident papal legate who associates the Emperor Alfonso with him in concert with the lesser persons said to have subscribed. Unfortunately, the *Compostellana* does not give a list of them. The council closed with the chanting of the customary "Te Deum laudamus."

Much of this procedure gives the impression that what had transpired was simply an ecclesiastical council, but the *acta* make it clear that it was a council of the realm. In fact, the age would not have understood the modern dichotomy. The king was a figure at once religious and secular. The prelates of the realm were certainly magnates as well. The *acta* of the council make clear the intimate relationship. Counterfeiters will be excommunicated by the bishops and blinded by the king. No one shall consort with the adulterous or the incestuous. Magnates of the land are not to despoil their subjects without legal judgment. Churches are not to be given to laymen as fiefs nor to be administered by them. No one shall collect tolls on the roads except where it had been done in the time of Alfonso VI.[3] Many topics were addressed, but the chief matter carefully ignored in this account because of its delicacy was the marriage of the king to Berengaria of Aragón and thus the direction of the dynasty. So critical was its resolution that the council was in session for nearly three weeks and, ultimately, the fate of the marriage and its consangui-

3. Emma Falque Rey, ed., *HC* (Turnholt, 1988), pp. 428–31.

nuity was referred to the papacy. Obviously, questions central to the future of the dynasty itself were matters on which a "general council" was consulted.

The Council of Carrión of February 1130 was a direct sequel to Palencia, and we have an account of it from the same source. Again there is notice of the royal summons; this time, the presiding officer was a legate despatched from Rome, Cardinal Humbert. A preconciliar meeting with Archbishop Gelmírez set the agenda and procedure. It is clear from the circumstances and the outcome that the legitimization of Alfonso VII's marriage was the major business of the council and that the support of the Roman pope had been obtained previously. That goal secured, some of the clerical opposition paid the price for their earlier audacity. The bishops of León, Oviedo, and Salamanca, along with the abbot of the Galician monastery of Samos were deposed. The official *acta* of the council have not survived.[4]

The narrative of the Council of León of late May and June 1135, derives from the *Chronica Adefonsi Imperatoris*.[5] The council is presented as lasting three days, but other evidence makes it clear that its business and festivities lasted at least three times that long. The *Chronica* identifies Queen Berengaria and *Infanta* Sancha as participants along with King García of Navarra, and a host of others. The first day, in the cathedral of León, the council treated of the spiritual needs of the faithful. On the second day, again in the cathedral, the archbishops, bishops, abbots, nobles, and people witnessed the coronation of Alfonso as "emperor," the chanting of the "Te Deum laudamus," the blessing of Alfonso, and then hailed him as emperor. The ceremonies closed with mass. On a third day, this time in the royal palace, the health of the "kingdom of all Spain" was addressed and the emperor issued a series of decrees that are described very generally. Annual campaigns against the Muslims were enjoined on the Christian inhabitants of Toledo and Extremadura. The official *acta* of the council have not survived.

One more narrative account of a "general council" during the reign of Alfonso VII survives and the *Historia Compostellana* again provides it.[6] It was held at Burgos in the fall of 1136 and one of its items of business was the judgment of the conflict between Archbishop Gelmírez and his opponents in Compostela and his cathedral chapter.

The presiding officer of the council was a papal legate, Cardinal Guido. Over and above the designation of the ordinary clerical members, other par-

---

4. Ibid., pp. 439–44.
5. Antonio Maya Sánchez and Juan Gil, eds., *CAI*, in *Chronica Hispana: Saeculi XII*, pp. 109–296, (Turnholt, 1990), pp. 182–84.
6. Falque Rey, *HC*, pp. 513–16.

ticipants are described as "counts and knights" and the action is described as taking three days. Since the emperor and the cardinal-legate were deeply involved in the conspiracy against the archbishop, the author gives us much detail on the politics of the council. No *acta* survive but numerous of the legate's letters regarding other business transacted there do.

From what has been said here, it is clear that the "general council" of Alfonso's reign dealt with what ordinarily we would call legislation. Just as obvious is the fact that it functioned as a sort of supreme court for the resolution of disputes of the highest order. It often was a constitutional assembly in which the fundamental dynastic rules of the kingdom were refined and applied. Finally, it was an executive body in which were set in motion the mechanics of foreign policy, war, and finance and provision to office both in the secular and the religious structures of the realm. The council does none of this without the king, of course, and everything is done in his name and nominally through his will alone. Still, year after year, councils meet regularly and that fact tells as much about the dynamic of government in the mid-twelfth century as does the rhetoric of monarchy. With the king and the curia, like the king and the curia, the general council of the realm was a symbol, an epiphany, a celebration, and an event in the life of the realm. To attempt to dissociate those elements into modern categories is to lose the essential res.

It must be noted, however, that the great officers of the royal government were responsible not to it but to the person of the king. The majordomo was the very heart of the peripatetic curia, seeing to the coordination of its disparate elements as it traveled about the countryside, but there is almost no evidence of a staff subordinate to him, although other individuals sporadically served as assistants.[7] Of the other household posts, most easily discernable are the royal chaplains. At the outset of the reign Muño, bishop of Mondoñedo and former canon of Santiago de Compostela, was chaplain for less than a year (D39, 45, 122). He was succeeded April of 1127 by Arias González, canon and cardinal of Compostela, who may have held that post until February 1130 when he became bishop of León (D63, 93).[8] By spring of

7. (D532) This original was granted to Martín Díaz, "sub-majordomo." This is the only citation of such a post for the entire reign. The majordomo must have had aides, or body-servants who served as such, but this is the only evidence that such service could generate a distinct office. (D440) This charter to the same individual with the same title and deriving from the same monastic archive is a forgery. (D474) This charter is confirmed by Núño Pérez "sub manu Didaci Munionis maiordomus imperatoris." (D534) This charter is confirmed by Pelayo Curvo as majordomo "in loco comitis Poncii."

8. For his promotion see Bernard F. Reilly, "On Getting to Be a Bishop in León-Castile: The 'Emperor' Alfonso VII and the Post-Gregorian Church," *Studies in Medieval and Renaissance History* 1 (1978): 49–50.

1131, another canon and cardinal of Compostela, Martín Pérez, had become royal chaplain. He continued in the post even after he succeeded his brother, Diego, as bishop of Orense in 1132 and certainly until the fall of 1133 (D129, 179).[9] By May of 1135 Bishop Bernard of Sigüenza was chaplain and continued so until May 1146 (D215, 528).

After 1146, there are no known citations known of a royal chaplain. This may be due to lacunae in the documents or to a simple change in chancery practice. I suspect, however, that it results from the title having become ceremonially attached to archbishop of Santiago de Compostela. The surviving documents of the royal grant in perpetuity of both chancellorship and chaplaincy to the archbishops of that see are flawed but likely refer to a real act, although misdated (D390, 411). In such case, the religious needs of the king and curia could have been easily met by one of those royal clerics occasionally noted in the charters or by one of the bishops or their clerics in attendance there.

There are notices of a royal doctor, one "Hugo medicus," although the charters in which he appears are flawed (D470,496,781). Nevertheless his existence seems ensured by the variety of the sources and a royal physician might be presumed in any event. Hugo was also styled "magister" and so joins another scattering of persons so designated at court (D227, 229, 419). The royal chancellor, Hugo, was also styled *magister* but it would be unwise to read too much into the usage. Notices exist as well of a royal cook (D93, 669), a juggler (D250), a porter (D444, 608), and a butler (D610).

Surely, someone coordinated the activities of the *curia*, especially as it was in motion ordinarily. Just as certainly, the majordomo did not do it all himself. He was one of the great magnates. Rodrigo Vermúdez who served from late fall of 1127 until late fall of 1130 was the brother of Count Suero Vermúdez, Leonese magnate and descendant of the older dynasty of León-Castilla (D72).[10] Lop López, majordomo from early 1131 to early 1135, was a Riojan magnate important in the realm from the annexation in 1076 of that territory (D125, 199).[11] The next in office was Guter Fernández, head of the lineage of Castro, who served from early 1135 until the fall of 1138 (D196, 326). Diego Muñoz then became majordomo and continued so until Christmas 1144. Diego boasted the lineage of the Ansúrez of Saldaña and Carrión (D330,

---

9. See Reilly, "Getting to Be a Bishop," p. 51.

10. December 17, 1130. Pub. José Antonio Fernández Flórez, ed., *Colección diplomática del monsterio de Sahagún, 1110–1199*, vol. 4 (León, 1991), pp. 130–31, who calls this private donation an original but the orthography makes that impossible. For Rodrigo, Reilly, *Urraca*, pp. 219–20, and Carlos Estepa Díez, *Estructura social de la ciudad de León, siglos XI–XIII* (León, 1977), pp. 283–85.

11. Reilly, *Urraca*, pp. 213–14.

491).[12] From the new year until the end of the reign the dignity was held by Count Pons de Cabrera, of the family of the Catalan viscounts of Gerona and Ager.[13] Finally, it appears likely that the independent prince and magnate, Count Armengol VI of Urgel (1092–1154), was majordomo for a short time in April and May 1146 (D426, 520, 522, 525–26).[14] Not all of the charters that cite him are beyond suspicion but they are widely enough scattered and sufficiently numerous to make the case. The action remains mysterious, for Count Pons held the post before and after this brief period and the politics of the court seem tranquil at the time. A great campaign against Andalucía was then in prospect, so perhaps it was a war measure soon reconsidered.

The position of royal *alférez* also appears to have lacked any kind of supporting staff. This is more understandable, since the duties of its holder were narrower. He was essentially commander of the royal bodyguard. If that body numbered forty to sixty horse with their personal retainers, their direction was feasible for one man and his body-servants. Ad hoc command arrangements could be made when the bodyguard swelled into an army in wartime.

Early in the reign tenure in that post was volatile. From late in the reign of Urraca until mid-1126 the Riojan magnate later majordomo Lop López held it (D17, 49). From late 1126 until fall 1127 he was succeeded by the Castilian magnate García García de Aza (D56, 72).[15] After García for a most troubled year the Lara count, Rodrigo González, served.[16] Then for another year the Asturian magnate Pedro Alfónsez occupied the post (D108).[17] Afterward, into mid-1131 the *alférez* was Rodrigo Fernández, brother of Guter and scion of the house of Castro (D122).[18] Briefly, in the summer of 1131, it passed

12. Julio González, *El reino de Castilla en la época de Alfonso VIII*, 3 vols. (Madrid, 1960), 1:352–53.

13. January 23, 1145. Pub. Francisco Antón, *Monasterios medievales en la provincia de Valladolid*, 2nd ed. (Valladolid, 1942), pp. 254–55, a private document. June 1, 1157. AD Astorga, Carpeta 1, no. 12. Another private document. Recent publications devoted to the count are Ernesto Fernández-Xesta y Vázquez, *Un magnate catalán en la corte de Alfonso VII* (Madrid, 1991), and Simon Barton, "Two Catalan Magnates in the Courts of the Kings of León-Castile: The Careers of Ponce de Cabrera and Ponce de Minerva Re-examined," *JMH* 18 (1992): 233–66.

14. April 16, 1146. Pub. Teresa Abajo Martín, ed., *Documentación de la catedral de Palencia* (Palencia, 1986), pp. 95–97, a private document. He is cited as *alférez* in a private document of Eslonza, October 29, 1134. AHN, Clero, Carpeta 961, nos. 19 and 20, pub. Jesus Muñoz y Romero, ed., *Manual de paleografía diplomática española de los siglos XII al XVII*, 2nd ed. (Madrid, 1917), p. 376, as an original but it is false. The majordomo is given as Diego Muñoz four years too early.

15. See González, *Reino*, 1:293–94.

16. March 21, 1128. Pub. Guillermo Castán Lanaspa and Javier Castán Lanaspa, eds., *Documentos del monasterio de Santa María de Trianos, siglos XII–XIII* (Salamanca, 1992), pp. 16–17, a private document. February 16, 1129. Pub. Fernández Flórez, *Colección*, 4:118–20, a private document.

17. June 10, 1130. Pub. Fernández Flórez, *Colección*, 4:124–26, as an original private document.

18. June 4, 1131. Ibid., 4:135–37, a private document.

to one Pedro García (D130, 133). He was replaced by the count in Asturias de Oviedo, Gonzalo Peláez, for about five months (D131, 137, 146) and the latter was replaced in 1132 and 1133 by the Astorgan magnate, Ramiro Froílaz (D142, 179).[19] Then, for better than two years, that post was regained by the house of Lara in the person of Manrique, later count (D188, 289). Once more in 1137 it reverted to the house of Astorga and Diego Froílaz, brother of Ramiro, served into mid-1140 (D298, 387).[20] The Catalan Pons de Minerva, unrelated to domestic lineage was chosen in 1140 and served to December of 1144 (D392, 491).[21] Afterward the house of Lara regained that sensitive post for the next ten years. It was held by Nuño Pérez, brother of Count Manrique (D498, 868).[22] For the final two and one-half years of the reign that dignity passed to Gonzalo de Marañon, this a relatively obscure district on the headwaters of the upper Duero, but Gonzalo was of the Castilian lineage of the Aza (D871, 966).[23]

Almost as prominent in the royal curia as the majordomo and the *alférez* were the counts. Fortunately, to illustrate the character of the comital dignity during the reign of Alfonso VII no fewer than twenty-seven different individuals are known.[24] Three of them, however, constitute a special category; that is, Count Alfonso Jordan, although a member of the royal dynasty and sometimes important in its affairs, was count in Toulouse and the nature of his dignity is to be understood in relation to it.

Virtually as independent in its evolution was the countship in the Basque territory of Alava. From the time of the annexation of neighboring La Rioja by Alfonso VI Alava came into ever more frequent relationship with León-Castilla. Then, with the rise of Aragonese power under Alfonso I from 1109 until 1134, Alava gravitated into its orbit. After his death, the middle Ebro saw the reemergence of a truncated kingdom of Navarra and the reassertion of Leonese authority. From then until the death of Alfonso VII the counts of Alava figured sometimes in the Navarrese kingdom and at others in the Leonese. Effectively, the counts in Alava were independent princes and their countship also developed independently.

19. Julio González, *Repoblación de Castilla la Nueva*, 2 vols. (Madrid, 1975–76), 2:38.
20. Reilly, *Urraca*, p. 293.
21. March 22, 1145. Pub. Fernández Flórez, *Colección*, 4:187–89, who called it an an original private document. It is not reliable.
22. For the relationship, Francisco J. Hernández, ed., *Los cartularios de Toledo* (Madrid, 1985), pp. 99–100, a private document.
23. González, *Reino*, 1:298–99.
24. There are three other individuals identified as counts, each in one of the royal diplomas of the reign. Otherwise unknown, they likely are the product of scribal error or worse. Count Fernando Gómez (D442),Count Fernando Díaz (D544), and Count Juan (D953).

Count Latro Jiménez of Alava confirmed some twenty of the diplomas of Alfonso VII and of the future Sancho III and, significantly, almost all of these were issued on the northeast frontier, at Nájera, Calahorra, or at Burgos. The last of his reliable confirmations occurred on July 23, 1155, at Nájera in a diploma of the future Sancho III then overseeing the affairs of the northeast (D884).[25] By July of the following year Latro had been succeeded by his son, Count Vela Latrónez, who confirmed fourteen Leonese royal diplomas, the first in 1156 and the last in 1157 (D940, 970).

Three other counts of the period must be separately considered as well. Count Bertrán of Risnel had been introduced into the Leonese kingdom by Alfonso I of Aragón, whose cousin he was. He played an important role in the area of Burgos and he often acted in concert with the Lara counts and eventually shared their disgrace, but his elevation to the countship had been bestowed elsewhere and constituted a given that Alfonso VII inherited from the reign of his mother. Nevertheless, he confirmed a dozen of that king's 159 charters issued between 1127 and 1133 (D63, 166). While he obviously was not resident at court his comital dignity was recognized there.

Count Armengol VI of Urgel, too, bore a comital title that derived from his princely status elsewhere. Since 1102 he had been ruler of that independent Pyrenean county and his lineage continued there into the fourteenth century, often playing a major role in the emergence of Catalunya and Aragón. But he was closely related to Leonese affairs as well. His mother was the daughter of Count Pedro Ansúrez, and that magnate became his guardian when his father died in battle with the Muslims at Mollerusa in 1102. The young Armengol was about two years old and presumably was raised in León by the Ansúrez.[26] Armengol does not appear in the royal diplomas before 1134 and then his confirmations are sporadic. Then beginning in spring 1146 until his death in 1155, the count of Urgel confirmed 94 of the 343 known royal charters (D247, 862). This time span coincides with the period of Alfonso VII's major campaigns against Andalucía. The correspondence suggests that the central role of the count in León-Castilla was military. Such was Urgel's role in Aragón-Barcelona where the counts of that ruder, upland territory figured prominently in military affairs and often commanded its armies. In any event, although in part derived from another society, the comital dignity of Armengol was accepted in León-Castilla and he was a curial figure from 1146.

Count Pons de Cabrera is slightly different. He too was a Catalán, the son

---

25. For Count Latro see Gregorio de Balparda y las Herrarias, *Historia crítica de de Vizcaya y de sus fueros*, 2 vols. (Madrid, 1924, and Bilbao, 1933–34), 2:335.

26. Reilly, *Urraca*, pp. 36, 280, and 295.

of Viscount Giralt Pons II of Gerona and Ager and a possibly Leonese wife, born about the beginning of the century.[27] Perhaps in the entourage of Berengaria in 1127, he migrated to León. He sporadically confirmed royal charters from 1131 until, in the fall of 1142, he first confirmed as "count." Henceforth he was almost constantly at court. Of the 543 known royal charters of that period Pons confirmed 376, making him the most curial of all the counts (D443, 966).

Obviously in Pons's case the comital dignity was Leonese in origin for he could at best have perhaps claimed for himself a vicecomital rank based on his family origin. That Alfonso VII could have bestowed it on him despite his Catalan origins illustrates clearly his freedom to confer that dignity on whomever he wished. On the other hand, once the comital rank had been bestowed on one member of a great lineage, it would appear virtually impossible for the crown to withhold it thereafter from some member of that family, although it need not pass from father to son. The León-Castilla of Alfonso VII knew comital families.

The Laras are perhaps the most instructive case. Count Pedro González and Count Rodrigo González held that dignity when Alfonso VII acceded, and we have already seen the strife between the brothers and the king that led to the flight and death of the first in 1130 and, later, the permanent exile of the second. Both were sons of Count Gonzalo Nuñez de Lara. Despite this enmity, on August 21, 1145, Alfonso raised Pedro's son, Manrique, to the countship (D502). The elevation came long after his father's death in 1130 but perhaps followed closely on news of his uncle's death reaching the court. The Lara family required a current bearer of an honor that it had come to regard as proper to it. Manrique had been *alférez* in the mid-1130s and continued to be a curial figure. In the period between August 1145 and the end of the reign he confirmed 266 of the known 484 royal diplomas (D502, 966).

Less stormy but influential was the Galician lineage of the Trastámara. The guardian of his youth, Count Pedro Froílaz de Traba, died before Alfonso's accession but Pedro's son, Count Fernando Pérez, was usually present at court after 1134 and confirmed over 200 charters (D85, 862). On his death in 1155 his son, Gonzalo Fernández who had figured in the charters from 1147 immediately began to confirm them as count. (D869,966) The Trastámara boasted another count in the person of Rodrigo Pérez, son of Count Pedro Froílaz who only began regularly to confirm royal diplomas from 1152 (D740, 951). Countship in the family went back at least four generations to Count Froila Vermúdez (D. 1091), father to Pedro Froílaz.[28]

---

27. Barton, "Two Catalan Magnates," p. 236.
28. Antonio López Ferreiro, *Historia de la Santa Apostólica Metropolitana Iglesia de Santiago de Compostela*, 11 vols. (Santiago de Compostela, 1898–1911), 3:322.

In the Bierzo and Astorga, Froila Díaz held the dignity of count from the reign of Alfonso VI until about 1119. His son, Ramiro Froílaz, figured early in the charters of Alfonso VII but held comital title from mid-1138 (D320, 958). Why the title was withheld from the son for almost two decades is unknown.

In the district about the royal city of León, Count Martín Alfónsez appeared often in the documents of Alfonso VI but did not survive into the reign of Urraca. One of his sons, Rodrigo Martínez, regularly confirmed that queen's charters and those of the early reign of her son, although without the comital title. From 1129 Rodrigo appeared as count and continued as such to his death at the unsuccessful siege of Coria in 1138 (D101, 317). Almost immediately thereafter his brother, Osorio Martínez who first appeared in the charters in 1129, confirmed as count and would to the end of the reign (D320, 966).[29] Why it should have taken the family a decade to reclaim the countship is not known but may be explained by its very prominence in a region so sensitive for the dynasty.

In the northwest of Leonese territory was the lineage represented by Suero Vermúdez. Count already in the reigns of Alfonso VI and Urraca, he waited on Alfonso VII with some regularity, confirming 43 out of the 252 known diplomas of the reign till early 1137. Very likely his advanced age made following the court difficult (D39, 286).[30] He also had had a brother, Guter Vermúdez, who bore the comital title and who just survived into the early years of Alfonso VII's reign (D39, 94).[31] Neither appears to have had a son who survived them but Suero had a nephew, Pedro.[32] He had been *alférez* but became count only after the Almería campaign of 1147, in which he participated. From that time forward he confirmed about one in every four of the royal diplomas (D567, 966). The award of the comital title to Count Pedro may be seen as vindication of the family claim or as a possible reward for valuable service at Almería. Most likely it was a combination of the two.

In neighboring Asturias de Oviedo Count Gonzalo Peláez was of obscure lineage. He grew in influence during the reign of Urraca and in the early 1130s, forced Alfonso VII to grant him the comital dignity. That proved

29. For noble lineages in this central portion of the realm Pascual Martínez Sopena, *La Tierra de Campos Occidental: Poblamiento, poder, y comunidad del siglo X al XII* (Valladolid, 1985), is often very helpful. I was unable to use Simon Barton's *The Aristocracy in Twelfth-Century León and Castile* (New York, 1997) before completing this book.

30. Antonio Floriano Cumbreño, *Estudios de historia de Asturias* (Oviedo, 1962), p. 150, made him the son of Vermudo Ovéquez, who never appeared as a count. Estepa Díez, *Estructura*, pp. 275–77, agreed and made him grandson as well of an Asturian count, Pelayo Froilaz.

31. Both are confirmed by him simply as "Count Guter." He was the only count by that name of the reign. Guter was dead by 1130. See Richard A. Fletcher, *Saint James's Catapult: The Life and Times of Diego Gelmirez of Santiago de Compostela* (Oxford, 1984), p. 41.

32. Floriano Cumbreño, *Estudios*, p. 171.

a Pyrrhic victory and the king, Count Suero Vermúdez, and Pedro Alfónsez combined to bring him down, and he ended in exile. His experience illustrates again the authority of the crown to create countships when and for whom it chose.

The easternmost Castilian territories about Oca and in the Bureba were the home of Count Gómez Gonzalez and his lineage. He figured prominently in the reign of Alfonso VI and had ambitions to be royal consort during that of Urraca until his death in 1111 at the battle of Candespina. His son, Rodrigo Gómez, confirmed a few of the documents of that queen from 1119 and appeared early at the court of Alfonso VII. Rodrigo was accused of complicity in the rebellion of Count Gonzalo Peláez, nevertheless, in 1131 he already appears as count. After 1146 Count Rodrigo disappeared from the court (D135, 540). He had three sons each of whom advanced to the comital dignity but none of them before 1157.[33]

The early fortunes of the lineage of the Haros in La Rioja further demonstrate the mutability of countship. Count Jimeno López held Nájera under Navarrese auspices until the annexation of the Rioja by Alfonso VI when he lost it to the Ordoñez. His son, Diego López, recovered it, then lost it again when the territory passed to Aragón. Diego never bore the title of count. But Pedro López, presumably his uncle, was prominent in the charters of Urraca and early in the reign of her son appeared as count until 1135 (D71,219).[34] By this latter date, Alfonso VII had recovered La Rioja and Diego's son, Lop Díaz, appeared at court and thereafter confirmed a 104 of the 782 royal charters as count (D210, 966).[35]

Some lesser lineages of Galicia round out the list. Count Rodrigo Vélaz, associated with the district of Lemos-Sarria, confirmed a fair number of Urraca's charters and figured in her son's until 1143. He was likely the son of Count Vela Ovéquez of the same territory who confirmed charters of Alfonso VI (D39, 357).[36] The son of Count Rodrigo, Alvaro Rodríguez, did not immediately accede to his father's title but may have done so toward the end of Alfonso's reign. The evidence is ambiguous (D872, 956, 958).[37]

Count Muño Peláez dominated the territories about Monteroso in central Galicia during the reign of Urraca and he confirmed as count in ten of her son's charters. He was not a curial figure in any sense (D39,438).[38] Finally

33. Julio González, *Reino*, 1:336–37.
34. For his role during Urraca's reign see Reilly, *Urraca*, p. 219 and passim.
35. Julio González, *Reino*, 1:300–302.
36. Reilly, *Urraca*, p. 290 and passim.
37. Damián Yáñez Neira, "Aproximación al abadologio de Santa María de Meira," *Compostellanum* 33 (1988): 535.
38. Reilly, *Urraca*, pp. 289–90.

there is Count Gómez Nuñez of the district of Toroño in the south of Gali-cia. Count Gómez, too, had been of some importance in Urraca's reign and confirmed 26 of 334 Alfonsine diplomas to December of 1138. He was not a curial figure (D72, 331).[39] Caught between the conflicting rivalries of the kings of León and Portugal for the border district in which his tenancy lay, he finally retired in disgrace to become a monk at Cluny. He appears to have had no successor in the comital office.

Very early in the reign there appears also to have been a Count Muño González. He confirmed no royal documents, but is cited in 1126 and 1127 in three private documents, sometimes as tenant in Mayorga.[40] He seems to have been a member of the minor Leonese nobility during the reign of Urraca.[41]

On the basis of this survey, the first conclusion that can be drawn about the nature of countship during the first half of the twelfth century is that the crown had wide latitude in bestowing it. That the king could create comi-tal families seems beyond doubt. Once created, however, such families could subsequently hardly be denied the comital dignity. This is not a matter of law and to ask whether or not the countship was hereditary, in that sense, is anachronistic. Clearly, custom dictated the continuance of such an honor in a lineage once some member of the family had achieved it. It could be with-drawn from an individual who was guilty of an egregious offense, but the ex-pectation was that some other member of the family would accede to it. The crown might delay such action for years or even for decades but eventually the expectation prevailed. While the ordinary presumption was that the title passed from father to son, there is no compelling evidence for primogeniture. Countship could be passed from brother to brother, from uncle to nephew, and could even be held simultaneously by two members of the same family.

It is also clear that, while most of the counts were fairly continuously at court, residence was not incumbent. The degree of one's influence and the royal favor one enjoyed was proportionate to presence at court, and pro-longed absence from court might raise the question of loyalty. Independent princes such as counts Latro and Vela of Alava might attend only when their interests dictated and their titles continued to be recognized. Except for these latter, then, the issue arises whether the countship was a purely curial distinc-tion and whether the county was a political or administrative jurisdiction. The question is at least as obscure in this period as in most others.

---

39. Ibid., p. 291.
40. July 19, 1126. AHN, Clero, Carpeta 961, nos. 9, 10. July 31, 1126. Pub. Fernández Flórez, *Colección*, 4:102–3. 1127. Cited Luis Fernández Martín, "Registro de escrituras del monasterio de San Salvaldor de Celorio, 1070–1567," *BIEA* 78 (1973): 46.
41. Reilly, *Urraca*, p. 302.

To begin, the countship could be invested with a temporary, territorial military authority. Overwhelmingly attested among such cases are the tenancies held by the Lara count, Manrique, at Baeza in Andalucía and earlier in Toledo. Almost 150 royal charters list Count Manrique as holding Baeza between the fall of that city in late 1147 and 1157 (D564, 971). His tenancy of Toledo, attested by twenty-eight documents, began in mid-1144 even before he was raised to the countship and may have continued into the reign of Sancho III (D480, 486, 622).[42]

There may have been a military dimension in other Manrique tenancies that are not so well documented. Avila is the best attested, where he is given as tenant in no fewer than five documents between late 1144 and the end of 1151 (D486, 521).[43] Two royal charters of 1144 have Manrique holding Madrid (D485, 487). He is also cited as holding Atienza in two documents widely separated in time.[44] Three further documents make the count tenant in Medina, probably Medina del Campo, Segovia, and Extremadura, this latter probably the eastern trans-Duero region (D527, 586).[45] Taken together, these holdings suggest a consolidation of control along key military routes to the south at just the time when royal campaigns were intensifying.

That the original essence of tenancy was military, in any case, is beyond doubt. The tenant was a castellan, commander of a garrison, irrespective of whatever else he might be. Given the almost constant presence of Count Manrique at court and the widely scattered character of his tenancies, however, it is obvious that day-to-day command must have been delegated for extended periods. So, too, must have been ordinary civil authority of legal and police nature for most of these tenancies were in towns that had their own local authorities.

Only three precious royal charters that survive illustrate the overriding authority of the tenant in all matters and his control over the very estates of the royal fisc within his jurisdiction. These charters, drawn by Manrique's

42. A scattering of private documents also cite him at Toledo. April 23, 1148. Pub. Antón, *Monasterios*, pp. 256–57. This is confirmed by Alfonso VII and cites Manrique in Toledo but it is questionable. Annaia Rodríguez is incorrectly given as royal merino in Carrión and Saldaña. February 12, 1148. Pub. Antón, *Monasterios*, p. 256. A document closely related to that of April 23, 1148, cited just above. July 1149. Pub. Hernández, *Cartularios*, p. 67. November 12, 1157. Pub Fernández Flórez, *Colección*, 4:268–69, who calls it an original. Script and orthography make it a copy.

43. Private documents. March 21, 1146. López Ferreiro, *Historia*, 4:41–42, Appendix. It is confirmed by Alfonso VII but is false. May 29, 1146. Pub. Angel Barrios García, ed., *Documentación medieval de la catedral de Avila* (Salamanca, 1981), pp. 7–8, calling it an original. December 31, 1151. Ibid., pp. 8–9, calling it an original but I make it a thirteenth-century copy.

44. 1156. AHN, Clero, Carpeta 1.647, no. 13. A private document of Aguilar de Campoó.

45. 1148. Pub. Luis-Miguel Villar García, ed., *Documentación medieval de la catedral de Segovia, 1115–1300* (Salamanca, 1990), pp. 92–93. It is a private document.

chancellor but in the king's name, alienate royal properties in eastern Andalucía in 1156 in favor of a variety of individuals. They are confirmed not only by Count Manrique and his wife, Ermesinda, as *señors* of Baeza under the king but also by the lesser authorities of the town (D914–16). Since at the time the only secular boundaries in the modern sense were those of real property, it is entirely likely that the tenant's jurisdiction coincided with the local extent of royal property. All things considered, before 1157 tenancy in León-Castilla before 1157 might be military, judicial, or legal in function, but it was above all fiscal in content. The tenancy should be understood first as a grant of income.

The tenancy of Toledo had previously been held for four years until 1136 by Manrique's uncle, Count Rodrigo González (D153, 165, 192).[46] The circumstances of his accession to the tenancy and his later loss of it are described in the *Chronica Adefonsi Imperatoris*, which emphasizes the military aspect.[47] A private document of February 3, 1133, also cites him as tenant in Segovia.[48] Private documents also indicate that he held a tenancy in 1137 at Aguilar de Campoó.[49] He was exiled not long after. Much earlier Count Rodrigo González had held another tenancy of which he was deprived following his rebellion in 1130. This consisted of a variety of places in Asturias de Santillana that may have originally been primarily military when Queen Urraca was attempting to limit the power in Castilla of Alfonso of Aragón. The count passed into the reign of her son with these holdings intact. Between 1126 and 1128 he confirmed no less than eight diplomas as count in Asturias, and a private document extends that tenure until the late fall of 1129 (D49, 90).[50] In all save one of these royal charters he confirmed as Count Rodrigo González "de" Asturias. In one only he confirmed as "Count . . . Campol et superiores Asturias (obtinente?)" and that charter is a forgery and may be safely disregarded (D50).

The fundamental question turns on the interpretation of chancery usage. I believe that the terminology is employed to identify Rodrigo González rather than a territorial countship in Asturias de Santillana. It does not imply that Asturias de Santillana was a "county" in any legal or political sense.

46. January 3, 1136. Pub. Julio A. Pérez Celada, ed., *Documentación del monasterio de San Zoil de Carrión, 1047–1300* (Palencia, 1986), pp. 51–53, a private document. March 31, 1136. Pub. Fernández Flórez, *Colección*, 4:151–52, another private document.

47. Maya Sánchez and Gil, eds., *CAI*, pp. 161, 166, and 172.

48. Pub. Villar García, *Documentación*, pp. 59–60.

49. March 1, 1137. AD León, Gradefes, no. 38. April 1, 1137. Pub. José María Fernández Catón, ed., *Catálogo del archivo del monasterio de San Pedro de las Dueñas* (León, 1977), pp. 21–22.

50. November 26, 1129. Pub. Juan de Alamo, ed., *Colección diplomática de San Salvador de Oña*, 2 vols. (Madrid, 1950), 1:193–94, a private document, the latest in date, and probably an original.

However, this argument must be made largely by inference from better-documented areas, since private documents largely mirror the ambiguity of the royal ones. Occasionally, they do give a better sense of the fluidity of such designations as well as more exact descriptions of the count's varied holdings. One of 1127 cites him as "dominating" in Asturias and Aguilar de Campoó, one of 1129 as "imperante" in Asturias, Aguilar, Petras Negras, and Liébana, and another of 1137 as count in "Castella et Aquilare."[51]

The countship of his brother, Count Pedro González, before his rebellion, presents a simpler problem. He, too, brought his title into the reign of Queen Urraca's son and may have confirmed as many as twenty-two of the latter's charters between mid-1126 and early 1129, although some were confirmed only as "Count Pedro" and there was also a Count Pedro López (D49, 101). In all, save one that is clearly a forgery, Count Pedro González is designated "de Lara." Only there does he confirm as count "partem Castelle cum Lara obtinente." The citations of private diplomas are similarly uncluttered. He is count of Lara, except for one that specifies his tenure as well in Dueñas and Tariego (de Cerrato).[52]

Allied politically to the brothers was Count Bertrán de Risnel. He is cited three times in 1127 as holding the strategic town of Burgos. His position was originally due to an agreement in 1117 between Queen Urraca and Alfonso I of Aragón and was probably continuous down to his involvement in the revolt of the Laras.[53]

The tenures of the Osorio counts, to the degree that they were more than purely fiscal, were related rather to the internal security of the realm. Even before he was raised to the countship in 1129, Rodrigo Martínez held the supremely sensitive tenancy of the royal palace in the city of León, usually styled in the documents the "towers of León," from mid-1126 until shortly before his death in 1138. He was so cited in no less than eight royal documents and forty-three private ones (D46).[54] In 1134 Rodrigo appeared as tenant of

51. May 23, 1127. AHN, Clero, Carpeta 1.740, no. 18. April 24, 1129. Pub. Francisco de Berganza, *Antigüedades de España*, 2 vols. (Madrid, 1719–1721), 2:455. April 1, 1137. Pub. José María Fernández Catón, ed., *Catálogo del archivo del monasterio de San Pedro de las Dueñas* (León, 1977), pp. 21–22, calling it an original. On the basis of script and orthography I judge it a copy of the thirteenth century.
52. May 23, 1127. AHN, Clero, Carpeta 1.740, no. 18.
53. July 16, 1127. Pub. Fernández Flórez, *Colección*, 4:114–15, who calls it an original. October 8, 1127. Pub. José Manuel Garrido Garrido, ed., *Documentación de la catedral de Burgos, 804–1183* (Burgos, 1983), pp. 191–92. The confirmation by Bertran of this private document concerning the church of Burgos is evidence of his tenure.
54. May 6, 1138. Pub. José María Fernández Catón, ed., *Colección documental del archivo de la catedral de León, 1109–1187*, vol. 5 (León, 1990), pp. 188–89, calling this private document an original.

Mayorga, sixty kilometers south of León on a main route from Valladolid, but the citation is suspect.[55] In two royal and thirteen private documents between 1126 and 1133, he was given as holding Aguilar, probably Aguilar de Campos twenty kilometers southeast of Mayorga.[56] In three other private documents of 1136 and 1137 he was cited as the tenant of "Campos," possibly Villalón de Campos a few kilometers southeast of Mayorga, although there are a host of places in the area with some combination of Campos in their name.[57] Five citations from private diplomas would place him as tenant also in Vecilla de Valderaduey and Villalobos in the same general area and even in Grajal, somewhat farther north.[58] Farther from the center of the realm the count held the major fortress of Zamora between spring 1130 and sometime in 1135.[59] One private document makes him tenant of Medina de Rioseco and Atienza in 1135, though it must be regarded with some reserve.[60] There is also slight evidence for a tenancy of the count in Calahorra which I distrust.[61]

After the death of Count Rodrigo at Coria, a fair number of these tenancies were held by his brother, Count Osorio Martínez, although probably not the key tenancy in the city of León.[62] Two royal and three private documents make him tenant of Mayorga even before he was made count (D103, 378). Another three have him tenant in Aguilar de Campos from mid-1139 to early 1141.[63] Yet another three have him succeeding his brother from the fall of 1138 to that of 1140 in Villalón de Campos (D320).[64] One royal and five

55. June 14, 1134. AHN, Clero, Carpeta 824, no. 17.

56. July 19, 1126. AHN, Clero, Carpeta 961, no. 10, an original, is the first. May 7, 1133. AD León, Gradefes, nos. 32 and 33, is the last. Both are private documents.

57. January 3, 1136. Pub. Pérez Celada, *Documentación*, pp. 51–53, the first. October 30, 1137. Ibid., pp. 53–54, the last.

58. Martínez Sopena, *Tierra*, p. 373. But see also, February 15, 1130. Pub. Carlos de Ayala Martínez, ed., *Libro de privilegios de la Orden de San Juan de Jerusalén en Castilla y León, siglos XII–XV* (Madrid, 1994), pp. 173–74. February 1136. Ibid., pp. 181–82. July 8, 1136. Ibid., pp. 182–83.

59. June 3, 1130. Pub. Ayala Martínez, *Libro*, pp. 176–77, the first. 1135. AC Zamora, Legajo 16, no, 19; pub. José Luis Martín, ed., *Documentos zamoranos, vol. 1, Documentos del archivo catedralicio de Zamora, Primera Parte: 1128–1261* (Salamanca, 1982), pp. 12–13, a private document, the last.

60. July 1135. Pub. Toribio Mingüella y Arnedo, *Historia de la diócesis Sigüenza y de sus obispos*, vol. 1 (Madrid, 1910), pp. 355–56, who called it an original. It is a donation of the bishop to his canons and such documents were often interpolated. Some of the language of this one seems anachronistic.

61. 1137. Pub. Ildefonso Rodríguez de Lama, ed., *Colección diplomática medieval de La Rioja: Documentos, 923–1168*, vol. 2 (Logroño, 1976), p. 176, a private document. 1140. AHN, Códices, 105B, ff. 158r-159r. The document is false or badly dated. By this time, the count was dead. Both are private documents.

62. February 1, 1141. AHN, Códices, 994B, fol. 6r-v; pub. Carlos Merchán Fernández, *Sobre los orígenes del regimen señorial en Castilla* (Malaga, 1982), pp. 272–73. This charter of the count and his wife would be the only warrant for it.

63. May 26, 1139. AD León, Gradefes, no. 43, the first. February 1, 1141. See note 62.

64. October 18, 1140. Pub. Pérez Celada, *Documentación*, pp. 54–55, a private document, the last.

private documents show him eventually following his brother in the tenancy of Vecilla de Valderaduey from 1151 until 1157.[65] Four private and one royal documents also cite him in Villalobos between 1147 and mid-1151 (D709).[66] No less than nine private and two royal documents list him as tenant in Melgar (Melgar de Abajo?), twenty kilometers northeast of Mayorga from late 1130 until early 1141 (D402).[67] Another six private documents and one royal one put the castle of Malgrado near Benavente in his hands between mid-1129 and late 1140.[68] Three private diplomas cite him as tenant in Villamayor del Condado, fourteen kilometers northeast of León, from mid-1130 until the spring 1136.[69] A series of single notices make him tenant in Liébana in 1141, Cotanes, forty kilometers southeast of Benavante, in 1155, and Luna (possibly the castle thirty kilometers northwest of León) in 1157. All must be regarded with some reserve.[70]

The tenancies of Count Pons de Cabrera display a markedly military aspect. A half dozen each of royal and private documents between the fall of 1147 and fall of 1153 place him in control of the outpost of Almería in Andalucía (D564).[71] There the military character is obvious but that same element should not be ignored in his tenancy of Zamora, cited in nine royal and fourteen private documents from the spring of 1142 until 1157 (D370).[72] With the capture in that year of Coria, the military problem in the Leonese Extremadura was certainly alleviated, but it would be long before it was eliminated. The same must be said of his tenancy in Salamanca, listed in three royal and four private documents between 1143 and the fall of 1156.[73] His juris-

65. March 1, 1151. AD León, Gradefes, no. 64; pub. Aurelio Calvo, *El monasterio de Grade-fes* (León, 1936), p. 307, the first. May 9, 1157. Pub. Fernández Catón, *Colección*, 5:302–3, the last. Both are private documents.
66. 1147. Pub. Ayala Martínez, *Libro*, pp. 206–7, the first.
67. November 28, 1130. Pub. Fernández Flórez, *Colección*, 4:128–30, a private document, the first.
68. August 7, 1129. AD León, Gradefes, no. 26. November 27, 1140. Pub. Fernández Flórez, *Colección*, 4:176–77. Both are private documents.
69. June 3, 1130. Pub. Ayala Martínez, *Libro*, pp. 176–77, the first. May 20, 1136. Ibid., pp. 200–201, the last.
70. February 1, 1141. AHN, Códices, 994B, fol 6r-v; BN, Manuscritos, 3.147, fol. 415r-v, dated only to 1140; pub. Merchán Fernández, *Orígenes*, pp. 272–73. November 20, 1155. Pub. Fernández Flórez, *Colección*, 4:260–61. May 9, 1157. Ibid., 5:302–3.
71. October 21, 1153. Pub. Antón, *Monasterios*, pp. 260–62, a private document.
72. April 5, 1142. Pub. Fernández Flórez, *Colección*, 4:178–79, a private document. May 9, 1157. Pub. Fernández Flórez, *Colección*, 4:178–79, a private document. May 9, 1157. Pub. Fernández Catón, *Colección*, 5:302–3, a private document, the last.
73. 1143. Pub. Ayala Martínez, *Libro*, p. 201, a private document, the first. September 30, 1156. Pub. José Luis Martín, Luis-Miguel Villar García, Florencio Marcos Rodríguez, and Marciano Sánchez Rodríguez, eds., *Documentos de los archivos catedralicio y diocesano de Salamanca, siglos XII–XIII* (Salamanca, 1977), pp. 105–6, the last, a private document.

diction there included Cepeda, some seventy kilometers south-southwest in 1156 (D954). A tenancy in Toro, east of Zamora, attested from late in 1152 until late in 1156, was intimately related with the latter and likely granted him at the same time.[74] A private document of 1138 that cites the Pons as holding Morales (Morales de Toro) should also be associated with these tenures.[75] Apparently he held Sanabria some 100 kilometers northwest of Zamora even earlier. He is cited so in two royal and six private documents from the spring of 1132 until the end of 1156. That frontier authority, however, was probably directed against the Portuguese.[76] Two other private documents within this period that cite Pons as holding "Cabrera" should be understood to refer to the district of La Cabrera in the Bierzo north of Sanabria and assimilated to the latter.[77]

In two other tenancies, the note of internal security was dominant. From early 1147 until the end of the reign, five private documents place Count Pons de Cabrera in the castle of Malgrado near Benavente, earlier held by Count Osorio Martínez.[78] Another three private documents cite him in Melgar (Melgar de Abajo?), some sixty kilometers northeast of Benavente, from the spring of 1146 until the fall of 1154.[79] The tenancy of a Melgar had also been held earlier by Count Osorio, although the relationship is not clear since both a Melgar de Abajo and a Melgar de Arriba exist. Count Pons also had two more holdings in this general area, although neither of these had appeared specifically as tenancies of Count Osorio. One royal and five private documents cite the former in Villalpando, twenty-seven kilometers southeast of Benavente, from the spring of 1146 until 1157.[80] One royal and one private document cite him in Villafáfila, eighteen kilometers west of Villalpando, from late 1151 until mid-1156 (D709).[81] A single private document of 1128 cites Pons in the tenancy of the castle of Ulver. This would be his earliest appearance anywhere

74. November, 1152. AC Zamora, Tumbo Blanco, fol. 125v-26r, a private document, the first. November 2, 1156. Pub. Ayala Martínez, *Libro*, pp. 226–27, a private document, the last.

75. Augusto Quintana Prieto, ed., *Tumbo viejo de San Pedro de Montes* (León, 1971), pp. 252–53.

76. March 31, 1132. AHN, Clero, Carpeta 3.563, no. 5, a private document. December 3, 1156. Pub. Ayala Martínez, *Libro*, pp. 229–30, a private document, the last.

77. May 13, 1138. Pub. Quintana Prieto, *Tumbo*, pp. 252–53. June 20, 1146. Ibid., pp. 262–63.

78. February 10, 1147. Pub. Ayala Martínez, *Libro*, pp. 205–6, the first. May 9, 1157. Pub. Fernández Catón, *Colección*, 5:302–3, the last.

79. May 11, 1146. Pub. Fernández Flórez, *Colección*, 4:194–95, the first. October 10, 1154. Pub. Luciano Serrano, *Cartulario del monasterio de Vega con documentos de San Pelayo y Vega de Oviedo* (Madrid, 1927), pp. 73–75, the last.

80. June 6, 1146. Pub. Fernández Flórez, *Colección*, 4:195–96, a private document called original by the editor but I think it a copy, the first. May 9, 1157. Ibid., 5:302–3, the last.

81. July 19, 1156. Pub. Angel Rodríguez González, *El tumbo del monasterio de San Martín de Castañeda* (León, 1973), pp. 70–71, a private document.

in the kingdom, if it were to be accepted. In fifteen documents both before and after, however, that castle is cited as the tenancy of Ramiro Froílaz and this exception is a copy marked by what seems to me precocious language.[82]

The major tenancy of Count Ramiro Froílaz, however, was Astorga. No fewer than fourteen royal and nineteen private documents list him so between the summer of 1131 and 1157.[83] The tenancy probably consisted in both the *terra* and the city of Astorga itself where, like Count Froila Díaz, his father before him, Ramiro shared power with the bishop. His tenancies also stretched west into the district of the Bierzo that he is cited as holding in eight private documents between the beginning of the reign and the spring of 1153.[84] More particular holdings lay more westerly, between the tenancies of Count Pons de Cabrera to the south and of *Infanta* Sancha to the north. Fifteen private documents list Ramiro as tenant of the castle of Ulver in the western Bierzo over the entire course of the reign.[85] Farther along the River Sil in the Valdeorras, his holdings approached those of the bishop of Orense, whose loyalties wavered between Alfonso VII and Afonso of Portugal.[86] Two private documents put him at Puebla de Trives south and west of the Sil.[87] Two royal and two more private documents put Ramiro at Castro Caldelas, barely fifty kilometers upstream from the city of Orense (D181, 737). There is a scattering of other citations of locales in this general area difficult to identify.

Count Ramiro was also cited some twenty times after 1142 as tenant in Aguilar and the derivation of the documents makes it certain that the area in question is northeast or east of the city of León.[88] If Aguilar de Campoó is meant then a predominantly fiscal tenancy there is indicated. Reinforcing such an otherwise unlikely identification are two private documents citing Count Ramiro as tenant in 1153 and 1154 in Boñar forty kilometers north of

82. October 27, 1128. Quintana Prieto, *Tumbo*, pp. 239–40.

83. August 25, 1131. Cited Raimondo Rodríguez, ed., *Catálogo de documentos del monasterios de Santa María de Otero de las Dueñas* (León, 1948), p. 68, a private document. June 8, 1157. Pub. Augusto Quintana Prieto, "Los monasterios de Poibueno y San Martín de Montes," *AL* 22 (1968): 118–20. There is another copy of this private document in BN, Manuscritos, 4.357, fol. 200r.

84. March 20, 1126. AHN, Sección de Microfilmas, Caja 1.182, rollo 7.851, Astorga, Seminario, Registro de Escrituras, fol. 121r-v, the first. May 29, 1153. AHN, Clero, Carpeta 1.126, no. 6, the last.

85. March 6, 1126. Pub. Quintana Prieto, *Tumbo*, pp. 230–31, the first. March 23, 1156. Ibid., pp. 285–86, the last.

86. May 18, 1156. Pub. Quintana Prieto, *Tumbo*, pp. 231–32, the first. July 6, 1149. Ibid., pp. 267–68, the last.

87. June 24, 1140. AHN, Sección de Microfilmas, Caja 1.185, rollo 7.872, Astorga, Seminario, Registro de Escrituras, fol. 399r-v. August 26, 1145. AHN, Clero, Carpeta 526, no. 12.

88. March 2, 1142. AD León, Gradefes, no. 52, a private document, the first. February 13, 1157. Pub. Fernández Flórez, *Colección*, 4:266–67, a private document, the last.

León.[89] Additionally, six private documents making him tenant in the valley of the River Esla between 1144 and 1157 should also be adduced.[90]

North of the territories of Count Ramiro Froílaz were those of Count Suero Vermúdez, who had held them from the reign of Queen Urraca.[91] Six royal and five private documents cite him as tenant of the castle of Luna in the far northwest of the territory of León between 1126 and early 1131.[92] Two private documents also list him as the tenant in 1136 of Tineo in Asturias about forty kilometers to the west of Oviedo.[93] These two tenancies controlled a major pass over the Cantabrians between León and Oviedo. The latter of the two documents also cited Suero as count "in Asturias" and Vadabia as well.

Successor in these tenancies was Suero's nephew, Count Pedro Alfónsez. Nine private documents, beginning before he had been made count, cite Pedro as holding Tineo from mid-1146 until early 1155.[94] Thirteen other private documents list him in Oviedo itself from 1145 until 1157.[95] He was tenant in Vadabia from mid-1147 until at least the beginning of 1155, according to six private documents.[96] A single royal document cites Pedro as count of Asturias but the intent was probably to identify (D716). It is worth recalling that in none of the thirty-six royal diplomas that the Asturian rebel, Gonzalo Peláez, confirmed as count did the royal chancery ever cite him with any tenancy, much less that of Asturias. A half dozen private documents so cite him, but again the reference should likely be understood as descriptive rather than territorial.[97]

In the westernmost extremity of the realm, Fernando Pérez de Traba was almost invariably cited in the royal diplomas as "de Galicia," but there is not

89. December 22, 1153. AD León,Gradefes, no. 69. May 14, 1156. AD León, Gradefes, no. 79.

90. December 28, 1144. AD León, Gradefes, no. 56, the first. May 3, 1157. AD León, Gradefes, no. 81, the last.

91. Reilly, *Urraca*, pp. 293–95.

92. May 23, 1126. Pub. María Concepción Casado Lobado, ed., *Colección diplomática del monasterio de Carrizo*, 2 vols. (León, 1983), 1:29–30, a private document, the first. March 27, 1131. Pub. Fernández Flórez, *Colección*, 4:132–34, a private document, the last.

93. May 13, 1136. Pub. Pedro Floriano Llorente, ed., *Colección diplomática del monasterio de San Vicente de Oviedo* (Oviedo, 1968), pp. 308–9. May 21, 1136. Pub. Santos García Larragueta, ed., *Colección de la catedral de Oviedo* (Oviedo, 1962), pp. 386–88.

94. September 1, 1146. Pub. Antonio Floriano Cumbreño, ed., *El monasterio de Cornellana* (Oviedo, 1949), pp. 35–36, the first. January 21, 1155. Pub. Tomas Múñoz y Romero, ed., *Colección de fueros y cartas pueblas* (Madrid, 1847), pp. 162–63, the last.

95. April 18, 1145. Pub. Antonio Floriano Cumbreño, ed., *Colección diplomática del monasterio de Belmonte* (Oviedo, 1960), pp. 84–87, the first. April 1, 1157. Ibid., pp. 131–34, the last.

96. July 10, 1147. AD León, Santa María de Otero de las Dueñas, no. 231, the first. January 21, 1155. Pub. Muñoz y Romero, *Fueros*, pp. 162–63.

97. June 1, 1128. Pub. García Larragueta, *Colección*, p. 375, the first. April 22, 1132. Floriano Llorente, *Colección*, pp. 290–92, the last.

the slightest doubt that the chancery was simply properly identifying him. The clearest fact about the countship in the twelfth century in León-Castilla is that there was no county of Galicia. Three royal documents identify him as "de Traba" but none are reliable (D235, 390, 411). One cites him in 1151 holding the territory of Bubal, only fifteen kilometers north of Orense in Galicia (D710). A private document has him holding Solis in western Asturias south of Avilés in 1152.[98] Two more private documents make him tenant in Trastámara between 1142 and 1145.[99] A single royal charter of 1146 identified him as tenant in Sarria and Monforte de Lemos but in light of evidence below it seems unlikely (D528). But a fortunate marriage seems to have brought the strongpoint of Monterroso, forty-five kilometers southwest of Lugo, into his hands. Lupa, his sister, married its tenant, Count Muño Peláez, and from early 1138 until 1153 five private documents cite Fernando there.[100] As a result of the count's earlier marriage to Teresa of Portugal, he may have held Ginzo de Limia south of Orense in what was Portuguese dominated territory in 1131 but the citation is flawed.[101]

His son, Count Gonzalo Fernández, appears in the same relatively modest fashion. Two private documents cite him as tenant in Traba toward the end of the reign.[102] The same two also make him tenant of Aranga some forty kilometers east of La Coruña. About the same time yet another two make him tenant of Trastámara.[103]

Count Rodrigo Pérez, brother of Count Fernando and uncle of Count Gonzalo, is little different. Five royal documents between late 1127 and early 1131 cite him "de Traba" (D72, 125). One royal document of 1129 makes him tenant of the castle of Luparia (Lobeira?), but it is a forgery (D110). He did, however, succeed his brother in the tenancy of Monterroso from early 1155

98. October 29, 1152. Pub. Serrano, *Cartulario de Vega*, pp. 162–63. Its form is irregular, although the editor calls it an original which it assuredly is not on the grounds of orthography alone.

99. December 3, 1142. Pub. César Vaamonde Lores, ed., *Colección de documentos históricos*, vol. 1 (La Coruña, 1915), pp. 108–9. January 31, 1145. AHN, Códices, 1.047B, fol. 4 r-v.

100. Reilly, *Urraca*, pp. 289–90. January 4, 1138. AHN, Microfilmas, Astorga, Seminario, Registro de escrituras, ff. 466v-467r, the first. 1153. AHN, Clero, Carpeta 1.509, no. 19; pub. Ermelindo Portela Silva, *La colonización cisterciense en Galicia, 1142-1260* (Santiago de Compostela, 1981), p. 158, the last.

101. October 27, 1131. Pub. José Luis Martín, *Orígenes de la orden militar de Santiago* (Barcelona, 1974), pp. 172–74. This private donation lists Bishop Pelayo of Túy and Bishop Martín of Orense, both slightly too early.

102. February 12, 1156. Pub. Pilar Loscertales de García de Valdeavellano, ed., *Tumbos del monasterio de Sobrado de los Monjes*, 2 vols. (Madrid, 1976), 2:145. June 1, 1157. Ibid., 1:196–97.

103. December 18, 1155. AHN, Clero, Carpeta 1.510, no. 1; another copy in Códices, 15B, ff. 82v-83r, dated to December 15. January 12, 1156. Pub. Loscertales de García de Valdeavellano, *Tumbos*, 2:331–32. This last may be a forgery since it lists the deceased Archbishop Pelayo of Santiago de Compostela as still living.

until 1157, as four private documents attest.[104] The striking fact here is that, even if citations of all family members are credited, holdings from the crown of this great lineage are but a handful of obscure places in the extreme north-west. Traba and Trastámara owe their fame to the subsequent influence of that house rather than to any importance of their own, then or now. Despite the prominence of the counts of that family in the curia that pride of place could not be translated into rewarding or responsible royal tenancies.

Even in Galicia, other counts held tenancies that constricted the power of the house, although there are indications the latter lineage expanded at their expense during the reign. In eastern Galicia south of Lugo, some fifteen royal and three private documents cite Count Rodrigo Vélaz in Sarria, thirty kilometers south of Lugo, from early in the reign until the fall of 1143.[105] Two royal and four private documents also list him as tenant of Monteforte de Lemos, thirty kilometers south of Sarria, during the same period.[106] One private document makes him tenant in 1137 of Larín just northeast of the latter town.[107] In three more private documents he is tenant in Rabadé, fifteen kilo-meters northwest of Lugo, from late 1127 perhaps until as late as 1137.[108]

His son, Alvaro Rodríguez, did not become count on Rodrigo's death, which occurred shortly before June 22, 1144. At that time, the same document listed his son as holding the "honor" of Sobrado.[109] Eighteen months later he was cited in another private document as tenant in Ribadeo.[110] He was not cited again until mid-1153 when a private document makes him ten-ant in Sarria.[111] Twice in 1155 Alvaro was cited in private documents as tenant in Montenegro.[112] However, the latter of the two cites one Vela as tenant in Sarria and in Monforte de Lemos. Possibly this was a brother. In none of these documents was Alvaro titled count and he may not have attained that

---

104. January 31, 1155. AHN, Clero, Carpeta 1.325D, no. 9, the first. June 1, 1157. Pub. Loscertales de García de Valdeavellano, *Tumbos*, 1:196–97, the last.

105. September 7, 1127. AHN, Códices, 1.044B, ff. 76v-77r, a private document, the first. September 28, 1143. Pub. Manuel Lucas Alvarez, *El tumbo de San Julián de Samos, siglos VIII–XII* (Santigo de Compostela, 1986), p. 275, a private document, the last reliable one. The royal documents style the count as "de" or "in Sarria" but the private one styles him "tenant."

106. September 7, 1127. AHN, Códices, 1.044B, ff. 76v-77r, a private document, the first. September 28, 1143. Pub. Lucas Alvarez, *Tumbo*, p. 275, a private document, the last reliable one.

107. September 5, 1137. AHN, Clero, Carpeta 1.325C, no. 25.

108. September 7, 1127. See note 106, the first. December 25, 1137. AHN, Códices, 1.044B, ff. 51v-52r. This last cites Bishop Muño in Mondoñedo!

109. Pub. Martín, *Orígenes*, p. 181.

110. Pub. Floriano Cumbreño, *Colección*, pp. 88–90.

111. June 27, 1153. AHN, Clero, Carpeta 1.616, nos. 18, 19, and no. 13, dated to August 28; pub. Marcos G. Martínez, "El convento benedictino de Villanueva de Oscos," *BIEA* 8 (1954): 283–84. It reads "in Suarone."

112. January 31, 1155. AHN, Clero, Carpeta 1.325D, no. 9. December 18, 1155. AHN, Clero, Carpeta 1.510, no. 1; a copy in Códices, 15B, ff. 82v-83r, dated to December 15.

dignity until the reign of Fernando II. As early as May 25, 1150, Alvaro was
the recipient of a donation in which it appears that he had already married *Infanta* Sancha, daughter of Teresa of Portugal and Count Fernando Pérez.[113]
Possibly the marriage allowed the latter lineage to co-opt the holdings of the
lesser family, as they had those of the counts of Monterroso, and may have
had the effect of delaying Alvaro's accession to the comital dignity.

The tenancy about the border episcopate of Túy, held by Count Gómez
Nuñez from the reign of Urraca until about 1138, was not subsequently
awarded to anyone of comital status.

Noteworthy also is the paucity of tenancies of the famous Count Armengol VI. One royal and four private documents cite him as holding Valladolid
between 1147 and 1153. However, both the royal document and one of the
private ones are unreliable. Only for 1152–1153 is his tenancy there assured
(D570).[114] Five private documents indicate that for roughly the same period
he held the tenancy of Cabezón just to the north (D570).[115] It is to be noted
that both locations lay in the center of the possessions of the lineage of the
Ansuréz, and it would have been difficult indeed to deny to Armengol the
prerogatives of his grandfather. Otherwise he is cited in two private documents as holding a half of the tenancy of Cea, 100 kilometers to the north,
from early 1150 until June 1152.[116] The post is best understood as a purely fiscal concession. There is one private document that would indicate his tenancy
in newly reconquered Calatrava in 1148 but it is suspect.[117]

Finally, there are a number of counts and tenancies in the east that should
be considered. First among these is Rodrigo Gómez, who succeeded to the
position of Count Rodrigo González. From 1131 until 1146, some fifteen
private documents cite him as count in Asturias de Santillana.[118] Moreover,
three royal documents and seven private ones mention him as count in Castilla between 1141 and 1146. This is old Castilla northeast of Burgos.[119] Again

113. May 25, 1150. AHN, Clero, Carpeta 1.126, no. 4.

114. April 1152. AHN, Clero, Carpeta 1.647, no. 9, a private document, the first reliable one.
September 13, 1153. AHN, Clero, Carpeta 1.740, no. 20, a private document, the last reliable one.

115. October 21, 1153. BN, Manuscritos, 13.093, fol. 124r-v; pub. Antón, *Monasterios*, pp.
260–62. This latter is suspect, however, and the latest date may be September 13, 1153.

116. March 27, 1150. Pub. Fernández Flórez, *Colección*, 4:222–23. June 23, 1152. AD León,
Gradefes, no. 67.

117. April 23, 1148. BN, Manuscritos, 13.093, fol. 124r-v; pub. Antón, *Monasterios*, pp. 256–
57.

118. December 3, 1131. Pub. F. Javier Peña Peréz, ed., *Documentación del monasterio de San
Juan de Burgos: 1091–1400* (Burgos, 1983), pp. 13–14, the first. September 19, 1146. Pub. Isabel
Oceja Gonzalo, ed., *Documentación del monasterio de San Salvador de Oña: 1032–1284* (Burgos,
1983), pp. 47–48, the last.

119. February 1, 1141. AHN, Códices, 994B, fol. 6r-v; BN, mss, 3.147, fol. 415r-v, the latter

it is less than clear if either Asturias de Santillana or this old Castilla were counties in the territorial sense. All evidence considered, I think not. It is preferable to take the citations in a descriptive sense, in analogy with the four private documents between 1131 and 1144 that cite him as count in the Bureba, the district around Briviesca to the northeast of Burgos.[120] So, too, another private document of 1129 cites him as holding Briviesca, some eighteen kilometers north-northeast of Belorado, in the Bureba before he had been made count.[121] There is the royal document of 1138 that cites him as tenant of Belorado itself (D320). A private document of 1144 mentions him as tenant in Ciresa (Cereza de Riotirón?), ten kilometers north northeast of Belorado.[122] In 1129 before he had become count Rodrigo held the tenancies of Cervera (Cervera de Pisuerga?), some eighty kilometers northwest of Burgos and Mudave (Mudá?) ten kilometers northeast of the former.[123] Two royal charters of 1137 cited him as tenant of Salamanca (D285–86).

After the death of Count Rodrigo in about 1146, he was succeeded in old Castilla by Count Lop Díaz from 1148 until 1156. Five royal and one private documents cite him (D586).[124] Yet farther east, but in an adjoining territory, two royal and seven private documents cite him as tenant of Nájera between early 1139 and 1157.[125]

The Basque Count Latro was an independent prince who figured in the diplomas only sporadically and then in two, widely separated periods. The first of these, 1136 until 1138, occurred when that monarch's influence was at its zenith in the valley of the Ebro. The second period, 1151 until 1157, also marked a time when Alfonso's influence there was strong, as Sancho VI of Navarra (1150–1194) struggled to maintain his father's realm. During the first period our subject was cited merely as Count Latro. During the second period, in six royal charters between 1151 and 1156, he was cited as Count Latro "de Navarra" (D685, 842). Clearly this chancery usage is merely descriptive for the same charters recognize Sancho VI as "king of Navarra" and the latter confirms two of their number (D685, 791). One royal charter of May

---

dated to 1140; pub. Merchán Fernández, *Orígenes*, pp. 272–73, a private document, the first. September 19, 1146. See n. 118.

120. June 1, 1131. Pub. Oceja Gonzalo, *Documentación*, pp. 41–42, the first. January 21, 1144. Pub. Alamo, *Colección*, 1:221–22, the last.

121. November 16, 1129. Pub Alamo, *Colección*, 1:193–94.

122. 1144. Pub. María Luisa Ledesma Rubio, ed., *Cartulario de San Millán de La Cogolla, 1076–1200* (Zaragoza, 1989), p. 268.

123. Pub. Fernández Flórez, *Colección*, 4:121–22.

124. 1156. Pub. Ledesma Rubio, *Cartulario*, p. 282, a private document, the last.

125. January 1139. BN, Manuscritos, 5.790, fol. 166v, a private document, the first reliable one. 1157. Pub. Ledesma Rubio, *Cartulario*, p. 283, a private document, the last.

1148 styled him Latro "count in Alava and in Estivalez" (D586). A royal charter of the future Sancho III dated to July 23, 1155, cited him as count of the
Alavese (D884). Both of these latter two are problematic, however. A private
document of 1138 cites him as tenant in Viguera, twenty kilometers south-
southwest of Logroño, but it, too, is suspect.[126] In contemporary charters
of the king of Navarra, Count Latro is cited four times as tenant in Alava
and once in Guipúzcoa during the years 1135 and 1136.[127] But between 1139
and 1150, seven royal documents of Navarra cite him only as tenant in the
little town of Aibar, forty kilometers south-southeast of Pamplona, and in
the castle of Leguin, fifteen kilometers east of Pamplona.[128]

Until the end of 1157 there is no citation of his son and successor, Vela Latrónez, in the charters of the kings of Navarra. In five charters of Alfonso VII,
Vela is cited as count "de Navarra," as his father had been. The first of these
is also confirmed by Sancho VI of Navarra, and the latter continued to be
routinely recognized as king of Navarra in the dating formulas of the charters
of Alfonso VII (D945, 971). Two private documents cite Vela as "dominans"
in Murillo (el Fruto?), fifty kilometers southeast of Pamplona, in Resa, and
in Grañón, fourteen kilometers east of Belorado, in 1156.[129] Another private
document of February 10, 1156, cites him as tenant in Artajona, thirty kilometers south of Pamplona.[130] Still one more private document of July 26,
1157, cites him as tenant in Salinas.[131]

When all of this evidence is taken into account, it appears that counts
were likely to be given tenancies that were held by their fathers or other family
members before them and, sometimes, were confirmed in tenancies that they
themselves had held before they had been raised to the countship. Often the
tenancies received were in areas in which the family had long held personal
property of its own. Such authorities would tend to reinforce one another
but also to blur the distinctions between one and the other.

---

126. AHN, Clero, Carpeta 1.030, nos. 17, 18; Códices, 105B, ff. 156r-157v; pub. Rodríguez
de Lama, *Colección*, 2:182–83. It also cites Count Lop as tenant in Alava.

127. 1135. Pub. José María Lacarra, ed., *Colección documental de Irache* (Zaragoza, 1965),
pp. 144–46. March 1136. Pub. José María Jimeno Jurio, ed., *Documentos medievales Artajoneses*
(Pamplona, 1968), p. 205.

128. 1139. Pub. José María Lacarra, ed., "Documentos para el estudio de la reconquista y
repoblación del valle del Ebro," *EEMCA* 2 (1946): 544–45, who believed it an original. It is not
and it may be false. Jimeno Aznárez is cited as tenant in Estella, but Lop Jiménez held that honor
until at least December 16 of that year. 1150. Pub. José Antonio Munita Loínaz, ed., *Libro Becerro
del monasterio de Sta. María de La Oliva (Navarra): Colección documental, 1132-1500* (San Sebastián,
1984), pp. 40–41, the last.

129. 1156. Pub. Rodríguez de Lama, *Colección*, 2:263–64. 1156. Ibid., pp. 215–16.

130. Pub. Jimeno Jurio, *Documentos*, p. 217.

131. Pub. Agustín Ubieto Arteta, *Cartularios (I, II, y III) de Santo Domingo de la Calzada*
(Zaragoza, 1978), pp. 36–37.

The comital tenancies held of the crown retained their military trappings but, in most cases, were probably chiefly valuable for the revenues attached to them. This is especially evident in relation to that handful of comital personages whose tenancies were widely scattered through the realm, while they themselves continued to be essentially curial figures. In such cases, they would have retained the ultimate responsibility for the conduct of affairs in their tenancy, but its day to day exercise lay in the hands of subordinates. Such a state of affairs exaggerated even more the primarily fiscal importance of the tenancy to its possessor. If the evidence reveals that countship was alive and well as a curial, political, and fiscal institution, it also makes clear that object of its jurisdiction in the realm was more restricted and particular than ordinarily believed. In fact, the territorial county appears to have had no political or administrative existence except where it was an independent political entity in its own right.

7

Castellans, *Merinos*, and Local Government

IN LEÓN-CASTILLA during the first half of the twelfth century there were large areas in which no regular authority at all held sway. In places the essential authority was that of a churchman or noble. Some areas were subject to the writ of an urban municipal officer. In yet others, the nominal agents of the crown were the primary authority. Of course, in theory, all of these persons exercised an authority delegated by the crown in some manner at some time in the past. Nevertheless, only the most naive historian would assume that these several authorities stood in any systematic relation to one another. At any given moment, their mutual relations were determined more by the rituals of diplomacy than by the rules of government. Even more than in our own age, threat of physical violence, pressures of economic sanctions, and charisma of personality determined the direction of life and society. If the king was the ultimate referee of locally unresolvable differences, that fact was due more to his having let to the several local authorities, on long-term leasehold, the various levers of power than to his having established those autochthonous entities. No more could he abolish them. Indeed, the king was, through his agents on the scene, merely one of the players save for those rare occasions when the curia itself hove into view.

At most times and for most purposes, the crown was a local power by virtue of the activities of its castellans and of its *merinos*. These individuals were ordinarily quite unsupervised. That flowed from the absence of any bureaucratic hierarchy between themselves and the curia to monitor their activities and the fact that the information concerning such activity and response to it moved at best at a rate of a sound horse, forty or forty-five kilometers a day. If the despatch of any considerable number of persons was required, the rate of response would was even slower, since the necessity of a baggage train roughly halved the rate of travel. Practical isolation of local agents magnified their independence.

Following the influence of the crown, as mediated through those worthies, is difficult first by reason of their obscurity. To begin with the castellans, a canvas of some 2,000 royal and private documents of the period yields 102 names of persons cited as tenants, beyond those counts already considered. Of this modest harvest a rough half, fifty-two, are cited in but one document and another eleven are cited in just two documents. Therefore, little can be demonstrated about duration of tenures or the social position of most incumbents. What can be asserted confidently is that they are, overwhelmingly, local figures and not curial ones, as were the counts; that is, fifty-seven of them are known only from their citation in private documents. Another thirty-one are cited in but one or two royal documents. While they may have held royal commissions, most castellans saw the king only when the curia moved into their locale or at least took up matters of local concern.

More can be known and some generalizations ventured about a third of all castellans. Some of them are curial personages of stature. First among these is the Catalan Pons de Minerva. Pons may have been born in the Minervois in the south of France and traveled to León, as a later tradition attests, in the marriage cortege of Berengaria.[1] From 1140 to 1145 he was royal *alférez* (i.e., he enjoyed the fullest confidence of the crown). From 1140 until 1157 he confirmed 141 out of the 600 charters. Such a number indicates his ordinary residence at court but that he was of secondary rank and his confirmation was more often than not unsought.

His major tenancy nevertheless indicated that he continued to enjoy the full confidence of the king. From the spring of 1148 until almost the end of the reign, ten royal documents cite him as the tenant of the "towers of León," the royal fortress-palace that dominated the north gate of the city (D590, 864). It was a most sensitive post. To this tenancy must be added another not cited in royal documents. From 1144 until 1157, fifteen private documents cite him in the important town of Mayorga on the route to Palencia and to Valladolid.[2] Three private documents also indicate that his tenancy at Mayorga either extended to, or was joined with, the relatively nearby hamlets of Villalba de Loma and Gatón de Campos.[3] Finally, there are two further private documents that make him tenant of the hamlet of Cea, ten kilometers north

---

1. See Simon Barton, "Two Catalan Magnates in the Courts of the Kings of León-Castile: The Careers of Ponce de Cabrera and Ponce de Minerva Re-examined," *JMH* 28 (1992): 248–66.

2. January 23, 1144. Pub. José Antonio Fernández Flórez, ed., *Colección diplomática del monasterio de Sahagún, 1110–1199*, vol. 4 (León, 1991), pp. 184–85, the first. May 3, 1157. AD León, Gradefes, no. 81, the last.

3. January 8, 1150. Pub. Fernández Flórez, *Colección*, 4:225–27. November 20, 1155. Ibid., pp. 260–61. February 1, 1156. AD León, Gradefes, no. 78.

of Sahagún, from 1152 until 1156. There was a royal castle at Cea.[4] The usual presence of Pons de Minerva in the royal court would have made it necessary to exercise his tenancy through intermediaries just as did the curial counts. Like them, he held ultimate responsibility for what transpired there, but not day-to-day control. Just so, that would have made fiscal reward his chief concern.

From 1145 to 1155 Nuño Pérez de Lara was *alférez*. Like Pons, Nuño was never raised to the countship during the reign of Alfonso VII, only attaining that honor subsequently. But this Lara scion was also a curial figure and confirmed roughly half of the 560 surviving royal charters issued after the time when he first joined the royal court in 1142 (D443, 963). From late 1154 until mid-1156 thirty-seven royal charters cite him tenant of the crucial military post of Montoro on the Guadalquivir, only forty kilometers east of Córdoba (D855, 939). Notwithstanding its importance, Nuño was a tenant in absentia throughout his tenure, as charter confirmations demonstrate. He he did disappear from the diplomas from the spring of 1156 until January 1157, however, and his personal defense of Montoro and capture on its fall may be assumed. Two private diplomas indicate that Nuño also held the minor tenancy of Aguilar de Campoó between 1146 and 1148.[5] Another private document cites him as tenant in 1156 of the tiny place of Avia (Abia de las Torres?), eighteen kilometers northeast of Carrión de los Condes.[6]

The Castilian magnate García García de Aza was another curial figure and tenant who did not attain the comital dignity. Later testimony makes him the son of Count García Ordoñez and of Eva Pérez de Traba. His mother subsequently wed the Lara Count Pedro González. On that reading, he would have been related to three of the greatest lineages of the realm.[7] He played no part in the court of Urraca but after 1126 emerged as *alférez* of her son and a court figure until 1129. He may have been involved in the eclipse of the Laras, for he does not again confirm royal diplomas regularity until 1145 (D49, 98, 963). In charters, he is styled "de Aza," but the usage is descriptive. Only two documents, one royal of 1155 but unreliable and the other private

---

4. June 23, 1152. AD León, Gradefes, no. 67. He is cited here as sharing the tenancy with Count Armengol de Urgel. June 28, 1156. Pub. Fernández Flórez, *Colección*, 4:261–62.

5. April 27, 1146. AHN, Microfilmas, Astorga, Seminario, Registro de Escrituras, Caja 1.792, Rollo 7.856, no. 21. 1148. AHN, Códices, 994B, between ff. 83–84; pub. Ramón Menéndez Pidal, ed., *Documentos lingüísticos de España* (Madrid, 1966), pp. 198–99. The latter cites him as co-tenant with one "Alvaro," presumably his brother Alvar Pérez.

6. 1156. Pub. Julio A. Pérez Celada, ed., *Documentación del monasterio de San Zoil de Carrión, 1047–1300* (Palencia, 1986), pp. 61–63.

7. Julio González, *El reino de Castilla en la época de Alfonso VIII*, 3 vols. (Madrid, 1960), 1:293–94.

of 1148, actually cite him as tenant there (D879).[8] One royal and one private diploma in 1146, cite him as tenant of half of Zamora, another practice which highlights the fiscal character of these posts (D518).[9] A private document of March 24, 1146, makes him "merino" of half of Avila but it is peculiar.[10] Finally, a private document of April 1137 cites García as "alcalde" of Toro and vicar there of Lop López.[11]

Lop López, usually called "de Carrión" in the royal charters, was a curial figure and royal tenant. His family derived from La Rioja, and his own career began in the reign of Urraca. He had been her majordomo and then *alférez* in the court of her son before 1126. Later he was majordomo to Alfonso VII from 1131 until 1135. Between 1126 and 1140 he confirmed 109 of the 328 known royal charters. After that time, he was much less frequently at court, perhaps due to advancing age, confirming only 14 of the last 485 charters, the latest of 1151 (D722).

The Riojan seems to have been styled "de Carrión" in the royal charters not because he was tenant there, but rather to distinguish him from a contemporary Aragonese magnate of the same name. The latter had been Alfonso I's tenant in a variety of places and after 1134 held other tenancies on the frontier. It is likely that he was acceptable to Alfonso VII, to Ramiro II of Aragón, and after 1137 to Ramon Berenguer IV alike.[12]

Lop López de Carrión, on the other hand, appeared in one royal and four private documents between 1136 and 1146 as tenant in Toro on the middle Duero (D370).[13] Between 1133 and 1150 ten private documents cite him as tenant in the castle town of Cea above Sahagún and in the neighboring hamlet of Ceione.[14] Three private documents cite Lop in the castle of San

8. October 1, 1148. Cited Luciano Serrano, "Los Armíldez de Toledo y el monasterio de Tórtoles," *BRAH* 103 (1933): 46–47, a private document.

9. January 1, 1146. AC Zamora, *Tumbo Negro*, fol. 11r-v, the private one.

10. Pub. Antonio López Ferreiro, *Historia de la Santa Apostólica Metropolitana Iglesia de Santiago de Compostela*, 11 vols. (Santiago de Compostela, 1898–1911), 4:41–42, append., who dated it to March 21.

11. Pub. Fernández Flórez, *Colección*, 4:158–59.

12. Antonio Ubieto Arteta, *Historia de Aragón. La formación territorial* (Zaragoza, 1981), p. 131, cited him as tenant at El Castellar in 1098. On January 20, 1135, he was already tenant of Zaragoza. Pub. Luis Rubio, ed., *Documentos del Pilar* (Zaragoza, 1971), p. 18. He continued there as late as September 1142. Ibid., p. 33. Other private documents cite him as tenant in Calatayud and Daroca. He appears to have held the whole of the "tierra de Zaragoza" during a most delicate period politically.

13. May 27, 1136. ACZamora, *Tumbo Blanco*, ff. 124v-25r, a private document. April 1137. Pub. Fernández Flórez, *Colección*, 4:158–59, another. December 25, 1145. AD León, Gradefes, no. 59, another. January 1, 1146. AC Zamora, *Tumbo Negro*, fol. 11r-v, a final citation.

14. February 7, 1133. Pub. Fernández Flórez, *Colección*, 4:143–44, the first. March 27, 1150. Ibid., pp. 222–23, the last. This latter has him holding but half of Cea with the other half in the hands of Count Armengol. There is a problem with the date since it was not Monday.

Román between 1147 and 1150. Of the many places about León so named San
Román de los Oteros, roughly thirty kilometers west of Sahagún, is the most
likely candidate.[15] His curial career is instructive. Clearly he enjoyed the confidence at different times of both Alfonso VII and of Urraca. He held high
and sensitive posts in the curia and later important tenancies in the heartlands
about the royal city of León. Some, like Toro and Cea, were not disdained by
counts of the realm such as Pons de Cabrera at Toro and Armengol at Cea.
Still, Lop himself never was awarded the countship. He had to be content
with the revenues and royal recognition.

In the Gallegan magnate Fernando Yáñez we have a noncurial tenant
about whom we know a good deal. Fernando had figured modestly in the
reign of Queen Urraca. During that of her son, he confirmed roughly 100 of
the over 900 royal diplomas (D72, 819). That might seem to qualify him as a
curial figure of minor stature but those diplomas are curiously uniform as to
the place of issuance. Most of them were issued in the south of the peninsula
and during the campaigning season. Together with the nature of his major
tenancy, it suggests that Fernando was a military figure rather than a curial
one. In no less than twenty-seven charters between 1148 and 1154 Fenando is
cited as the tenant of Montoro, as he is in two private charters (D571, 664,
819).[16] This was that Leonese Andalucian advance-post later held by Nuñez
Pérez. After February 1154 Fernando disappears from royal charters.[17]

Earlier documents cite Fernando as holding tenancies in his native Galicia. A royal charter of 1129 cites him in "San Pelayo de Lado," in the extreme
south of Galicia, which would be possible although the charter itself is false
(D110). Two private documents of 1136 and 1145 cite him as holding respectively, Ginzo de Limia, south of Orense near the Portuguese border, and the
territory of Toroño, about Túy.[18]

Subsequently, Fernando was cited in other military tenancies. Three
royal charters between 1143 and 1149 place him in the key river crossing at
Talavera de la Reina on the Tajo west of Toledo (D454, 486, 601). In addition,
two royal and one private documents cite him in 1146 and 1153, respectively,

15. January 12, 1147. Pub. Fernández Flórez, *Colección*, 4:199–200. May 13, 1148. Ibid., pp.
207–8. May 3, 1150. Ibid., pp. 223–24.
16. Two later diplomas of 1156 that so cite him are false. 1150. Pub. Fernández Flórez, *Colección*, 4:228–29, a private one. February 1154. AD León, Santa María de los Oteros, no. 233,
another.
17. Luis Sánchez Belda, ed., *CAI* (Madrid, 1950), p. 230, cited a donation of Fernando to
the cathedral of Túy dated August 24, 1154, and regarded it as a probable "death-bed testament."
18. June 8, 1136. AHN, Clero, Carpeta 1.565, no. 9. April 19, 1145. Pub. *ES*, 22:269–70. The
latter is suspect, however, because he holds it so late with a Count Domingo Gómez.

as tenant of Maqueda, the fortress town equidistant northwest of Toledo and northeast of Talavera de la Reina (D522, 526).[19]

Fernando's son, Pelayo Curvo, replaced him as tenant in his Galician holdings when Fernando took up these southern tenancies. Pelayo was cited in three royal charters of 1149 to 1152 as holding the territory about Túy (D616–17, 759). In addition, two private charters cite him as the tenant of Toroño in 1152 and 1155. That territory was largely coterminous with the diocese of Túy.[20] Like his father, Pelayo was no curial figure. In the entire reign, he confirmed but fifty-two royal charters and those before 1155 he does so almost exclusively in the company of his father. From 1155 he confirmed but 16 of the 112 royal charters. Here, unlike his father, he seems to have done so largely at solemn court occasions in the north of the realm. Pelayo appears, then, as a royal tenant in a northern border district where he resided regularly. It is notable that he was able to succeed to some of the tenancies of his father even so.

The most prominent example of the possibility of a brilliant curial career without ever holding comital rank is furnished by Guter Fernández de Castro. Majordomo under Urraca, he held the same post under Alfonso VII. He was entrusted with the early education of the future Sancho III and subsequently became his majordomo. Guter did not appear at the court often until 1134, but from that year until 1157 he confirmed no fewer than 497 of the 807 known royal charters. Therefore, though his tenancies were in the sensitive east of the realm, his supervision of them was indirect. The most critical was Calahorra, that fortress-rock above the Ebro just north of Navarrese Tudela. Two royal charters cite him as tenant there in 1140 and 1146, respectively (D396, 534). However, no fewer than eight private documents from early 1139 until 1151 cite Martín Fernández as tenant or vicar of Calahorra under Guter Fernández.[21] This is probably a cousin related to Guter through the house of the Ansúrez. The names of such vicars are not infrequently cited in the documents but seldom do we know so much about them. Probably they were most often relatives by blood or marriage.

The frontier character of most of Guter's tenancies is evidenced as well in that of Rueda de Jalón. At least in 1148 and 1149, he held that fortress thirty-

19. Pub. José Luis Martín, *Orígenes de la orden militar de Santiago* (Barcelona, 1974), p. 191, a private document.

20. November 1152. Pub. Pascual Galindo Romeo, *Túy en la Baja Edad Media* (Madrid, 1950), pp. ix–x, append. September 13, 1155. AHN, Clero, Carpeta 1.794, no. 13.

21. April 1, 1139. Pub. Ildefonso Rodríguez de Lama, ed., *Colección diplomática medieval de La Rioja: Documentos, 923–1168*, vol. 2 (Logroño, 1976), p. 187, the first. 1151. Ibid., pp. 228–29, the last.

five kilometers west of Zaragoza according to one royal and two private charters (D625).[22] Guter is also cited holding Soria, farther west, from 1140 into 1150 in seven royal and one private documents (D370,645). Three royal charters cite him as "de Castilla" between 1155 and 1157 (D893, 945, 970). Two private charters of 1147 style him "princeps Castilla."[23] The substance of these general references probably lies in his tenancy in a variety of strongpoints within the modern province of Castilla La Vieja. Four royal documents name him tenant in his family's traditional stronghold of Castrojeriz in 1140, 1154, and 1155 (D370, 841, 858, 879).[24] Two royal and three private documents cite him tenant in the fortress of Amaya, fifty kilometers northwest of Burgos, between 1148 and 1156 (D841, 878).[25] Three other private documents make him tenant respectively in Villagarcía (probably Villagarcía de Campos), Monzón north of Palencia, and Carrión de los Condes in 1154 and 1156.[26] In each of these locations, he shares the tenancy with another. Again that fact argues a predominantly fiscal interest, which must have loomed large in his other holdings as well, despite their more obvious military significance.

Rodrigo Fernández had a curial career like that of his older brother, but more modest. He played a minor role in the reign of Urraca and he was *alférez* under Alfonso VII in 1130–1131. Like his brother, he did not become a regular curial figure until 1134. From then until his disappearance from the record in 1144, Rodrigo confirmed 120 of the 280 known royal diplomas of that period (D188, 468).[27] Like his brother, Rodrigo was never raised to the comital dignity. The old enmity of their house for the Laras, which went back at least to the reign of Urraca, may have led the latter lineage to oppose such status for them.[28] In two royal charters of 1139 and 1143, Rodrigo is cited as tenant of the key frontier stronghold of Toledo (D357, 454). There he replaced the Lara Count Rodrigo González.[29] Rodrigo Fernández was, in turn, replaced by the

22. February 12, 1148. Pub. Francisco Antón, *Monasterios medievales de la provincia de Valladolid*, 2nd ed. (Valladolid, 1942), p. 256. April 23, 1148. Ibid., pp. 256–57.
23. April 28, 1147. Pub. F. Javier Peña Pérez, ed., *Documentación del monasterio de San Juan de Burgos: 1091–1400* (Burgos, 1983), pp. 29–30. April 28, 1147. Ibid., pp. 31–32.
24. All of these documents have defects but their cumulative testimony may be reliable.
25. Both royal documents are unreliable in other respects. 1148. AHN, Códices, 994B, between ff. 83–84; pub. Menéndez Pidal, *Documentos*, pp. 198–99. April 23, 1148. Pub. Anton, *Monasterios*, pp. 256–57. 1156. AHN, Clero, Carpeta 1.647, no. 13.
26. February 21, 1154. Pub. Fernández Flórez, *Colección*, 4:253–54. September 19, 1154. BN, Manuscritos, 705, fol. 21r-v. 1156. Pub. Pérez Celada, *Documentación*, pp. 61–63.
27. There are another four confirmations to charters in 1146, 1147, and 1148, but all of these latter are unreliable.
28. Bernard F. Reilly, *The Kingdom of León-Castilla under Queen Urraca, 1109–1126* (Princeton, 1983), pp. 137–38.
29. Antonio Maya Sánchez and Juan Gil, eds., *CAI*, in *Chronica Hispana: Saeculi XII*, pp. 109–296 (Turnholt, 1990), p. 172.

Lara Count Manrique. Three royal diplomas cite the former, respectively, as tenant in Salamanca in 1140, Avila in 1142, and Astudillo in 1143, but all are less than reliable (D386, 441, 450). One royal and two private documents make him tenant in the hamlet of Valderas, sixty kilometers south of León, between 1129 and 1150, although their dependability is open to question (D97).[30]

A third member of the family, Martín Fernández, was vicar for Guter Fernández in Calahorra between 1139 and 1151. He was not a curial figure for he confirmed but thirty-one diplomas during the entire reign (D90, 666). Of those, ten fell in 1146 and 1147 when Alfonso VII was campaigning in Andalucía and Almería. The record confirms what we should have expected: Martín was a working castellan at Calahorra and joined the crown for major campaigns or when the curia was in the eastern portion of the realm. For a brief time in the immediate aftermath of the Almería campaign, he appears to have been tenant in that isolated port city. A royal diploma of February 15, 1149, so cited him (D606). If he was, however, it must have been as vicar of Count Pons de Cabrera, who was then himself tenant. Otherwise, royal charters ordinarily style him "de Fita," probably by way of identification. He may well have been the son of that Fernando García of Fita granted the village by Urraca in 1119 and thus a cousin of Alfonso VII.[31]

There is a handful of other tenants, none of them curial, about whom we can know a bit more than a name and a tenancy. Vela Gutiérrez was likely a middling noble of the Bierzo. Between 1149 and 1157 he confirmed twenty-nine royal charters although he is cited as tenant in none (D597,966). Three private documents of the Bierzan monastery of San Pedro de Montes cite him as tenant in Cabrera between 1149 and 1154.[32] A final notice from the documents of the church Lugo cites him in 1155 as "princeps de Sarria," indicating a somewhat greater stature attained by then.[33] This last was confirmed by Alfonso VII although it was not a product of his chancery.

Vela was the recipient of a royal donation on May 14, 1149, for services performed in the fighting in Andalucía (D618). He is known from a variety of his own documents as well. On June 29, 1141, he donated to Pedro Alfónsez, later count, some territories at Lapedo in Asturias.[34] In a document dated,

---

30. June 14, 1134. AHN, Clero, Carpeta 824, no. 17. December 31, 1150. Pub. Pilar Loscertales de García de Valdeavellano, ed., *Tumbos del monasterio de Sobrado de los Monjes*, 2 vols. (Madrid, 1976), 2:197–78.

31. Reilly, *Urraca*, pp. 221–22.

32. 1149. Pub. Augusto Quintana Prieto, ed., *Tumbo viejo de San Pedro de Montes* (León, 1971), pp. 269–70. June 30, 1150. Ibid., p. 275. August 20, 1154. Ibid., pp. 280–81.

33. January 31, 1155. AHN, Clero, Carpeta 1.325D, no. 9.

34. AHN, Clero, Carpeta 1.066, no. 21; pub. Antonio Floriano Cumbreño, ed., *Colección diplomática del monasterio de Belmonte* (Oviedo, 1960), pp. 74–75.

erroneously, to April 6, 1150, he and his wife, Sancha daughter of Count Pons de Cabrera, donated the villages of Nogales, Bobeda, and Quintanilla, all in the territory of León, to one Aldoara Pérez.[35] In another document of December 31, 1156, Count Ramiro Froílaz and his wife join Sancha Pons and her husband Vela Gutiérrez in a donation of property in the city of León to the monastery of Vega.[36]

Obviously, Vela was able to marry well and became associated with Counts Pons de Cabrera and Ramiro Froílaz, both of them with tenancies adjoining his. Or perhaps the association came first, and the marriage subsequently. He went on to become count himself and royal majordomo during the reign of Fernando II. Despite this seeming wealth of documents, we cannot judge the role of his own family in Vela's rise. He is routinely associated with the lineage of the Osorios. Possibly he was the son of that Elvira, daughter of Count Osorio, who wed Guter Rodríguez.[37]

Two other minor castellans were associated with Count Ramiro Froílaz. One is Pelayo Captivo whom five private documents mention as sharing the tenancy of Astorga with the count between 1148 and 1156.[38] Such sharing was a financial arrangement although the two may have been political allies as well. The second is Fernando Peláez, cited holding the castle of Ulver in the Bierzo between 1133 and 1155 in six private diplomas. In the latter three of these, it is made clear that Fernando holds the castle for the count and, in the last, that he has made Salvador Peláez, probably a brother, his vicar.[39] In this case, the practice of the continuing sub-delegation of tenancies is clearly illustrated. In all likelihood, finances were primary to the several parties.

Pedro González, not to be confused with the Lara count, is cited variously in six private documents between 1146 and 1156 as tenant in Asturias, Liébana, and Aguilar (Aguilar de Campoó).[40] He was obviously a magnate of

35. BN, Manuscritos, 3.147, ff. 403r-404v and 422v-23r; pub. Angel Manrique, *Cisterciensium seu Verius Ecclesiasticorum Annalium a Condito Cistercio*, 4 vols. (Lyons, 1642–59), 2:175. The document is false or at least interpolated. It cites *Infante* Sancho as already ruling in Castilla and *Infante* Fernando in Galicia.

36. AHN, Clero, Carpeta 3.427, no. 16; pub. Luciano Serrano, ed., *Cartulario del monasterio de Vega con documentos de San Pelayo y Vega de Oviedo* (Madrid, 1927), pp. 76–77.

37. María Damién Yáñez Neira, "Abadologio del monasterio leonés de Santa María de Nogales," *AL* 38 (1984): 215. González, *Reino*, 1:325, n. 300. Less believably, Mercedes Durany Castrillo, *La región del Bierzo en los siglos centrales de la Edad Media: 1070-1250* (Santiago de Compostela, 1989), p. 229.

38. April 18, 1148. BN, Manuscritos, 4.357, fol. 208v, the first. September 26, 1156. Pub. Quintana Prieto, *Tumbo*, p. 289, the last.

39. July 2, 1133. Pub. Quintana Prieto, *Tumbo*, pp. 244–45, the first. April 24, 1139. Ibid., pp. 253–54, the first that mentions his subordination there to Count Ramiro. October 8, 1155. Ibid., p. 284, the last.

40. September 19, 1146. Pub. Isabel Oceja Gonzalo, ed., *Documentación del monasterio de*

some importance in Asturias de Santillana, but he figures in only two royal documents. He is cited as tenant there in Alfonso VII's charter of October 12, 1153 (D806). In the charter of *Infanta* Sancha of March 29, 1155, he appears as the tenant of Cabezón de Liébana (D878). Pedro was involved, sometimes with his wife, in a variety of real estate transfers that demonstrate his private stature in the general area of his tenancy. In 1145 he sold land in the district of Villaverde, in 1146 he and his wife donated a church in Castilla La Vieja to the monastery of Oña, in 1150 he sold off a parcel in the vicinity of Cea, and in 1151 purchased land about Aguilar itself.[41] While surviving documents are not usually so plentiful it is safe to surmise that even modest tenants of the crown were men of property in their own right, as Pedro González obviously was.

An earlier tenant in Aguilar de Campoó was Guter Sebastiánez. Three private documents of 1135 to 1137 cite him as such, in the first two jointly with one Rodrigo Sebastiánez, probably his brother.[42] In 1133 Alfonso VII made a grant of a village to Guter for "good service," so that we can assume that the tenancy as well was by way of reward to a once minor figure in his retinue. The only evidence for the presence of the two brothers at court, however, is their confirmation to a much earlier Alfonsine document of 1122, which has its problems (D14, 166).

A better known early tenant whose subsequent fortunes took a different turn was Pedro Díaz de Valle. His confirmations to four royal charters between 1120 and 1127 identify him as "in" or "de Valle" (D11, 37, 44, 60). In 1126 a private document cited him as tenant of the "towers" of León and of Toledo.[43] He was one of the rebels involved in the revolt of the Laras in 1130 and subsequently deprived of his honors. He was sufficiently important in that affair to have merited identification in the *Chronica Adefonsi Imperatoris*. Although his name was common enough to make tracing his property and family difficult, it is clear that he is the same individual.

Pelayo Pérez "de Frómista?" is another castellan whose full identity is complicated because the name is common. A private document of 1130 cited

---

San Salvador de Oña: 1032–1284 (Burgos, 1983), pp. 47–48. This is a donation of Pedro and his wife to that monastery. March 13, 1148. Pub. Mateo Escagedo Salmón, ed., *Colección diplomática de la insigne y real iglesia colegial de Santillana*, 2 vols. (Santoña, 1927), 1:43–45. 1151. Cited Luis Fernández Martín, ed., "Registro de escrituras del monasterio de San Salvador de Celorio," *BIEA* 27 (1973): 52. November 23, 1153. Ibid., pp. 54–55. 1154. Pub. Juan de Alamo, ed., *Colección diplomática de San Salvador de Oña*, 2 vols. (Madrid, 1950), 1:260–61. March 1, 1156. Pub. Luis Sánchez Belda, ed., *Cartulario de Santo Toribio de Liébana* (Madrid, 1948), p. 130.

41. May 18, 1145. Pub. Fernández Flórez, *Colección*, 4:190–91. September 19, 1146. Oceja Gonzalo, *Documentación*, pp. 47–48. March 27, 1150. Pub. Fernández Flórez, *Colección*, 4:222–23. 1151. Fernández Martín, "Registro," p. 52.

42. 1135. Cited Fernández Martín, "Registro," p. 48. 1136. Ibid. 1137. Ibid.

43. July 19, 1126. AHN, Clero, Carpeta 961, nos. 9 and 10.

one Pelayo Pérez as tenant of Tiedra, west of Valladolid.[44] Little over a year later Alfonso VII granted property to Pelayo Pérez "de Val de Fande" for his service, one of them in "Tevuela" (D127). We may well have here the instance of a castellan whose faithful service led the crown eventually to grant him in outright ownership the very fisc property in which he had previously been tenant. Two decades later, the king granted three more charters for good service to a Pelayo Pérez, identified in two of them as "de Frómista" (D655, 663, 880). About the same time, Alfonso granted a charter to another individual of a shop in Toledo "opposite the house of Pelayo Pérez de Frómista" (D851). The question arises whether or not that castellan had continued to render loyal service and had prospered quite considerably as a result.

Fernando Menéndez was cited in two of *Infanta* Sancha's charters of 1131 as tenant of Zamora as vicar of Count Rodrigo Martínez (D139–40). Then, in 1136 and 1137, he was cited in three private documents simply as tenant there.[45] Because the name is not at all common there is good reason to believe he is the same person who held both Zamora and Toro under Queen Urraca in 1117.[46] If so, Fernando must have been influential indeed to hold such an important tenancy for twenty years or better. Subsequently, he disappears from the documents. Could he have been of sufficient stature to have been, in 1145, that Fernando Menéndez who made a grant of a castle near Braga to the Templars in his name and that of his wife, the Portuguese *Infanta* Sancha?[47] The castellan's name suggests Galician or Portuguese ancestry and he may have found the emerging kingdom of Portugal more congenial when Leonese influence became pronounced in Zamora with the advent of Count Pons de Cabrera after 1142.

Another castellan of probable Galician ancestry was Menendo Bofin. In 1123 he was the first of Alfonso's known majordomos, but he was not a court figure long. Between 1123 and 1156 he confirmed but 61 of 969 royal charters and many of these were particularly associated with the city of Toledo (D17, 912). Menendo may have been a Galician who emigrated there after it passed into the hands of the *infante* in 1117. He long figured in its fortunes, and royal diplomas cited him in 1123 as alcalde of Madrid and in 1139 as castellan in Maqueda and Santa Eulalia (D18, 357).[48] A private document of 1145 gave him

44. Pub. Carlos Ayala Martínez, ed., *Libro de privilegios de la Ordende San Juan de Jerusalén en Castilla y León, siglos XII–XV* (Madrid, 1994), pp. 174–75.

45. May 27, 1136. AC Zamora, *Tumbo Blanco*, ff. 124v-125r. February 21, 1137. Archivo de la Hacienda de Zamora, Carpeta 1, no. 1. April 1137. Pub. Fernández Flórez, *Colección*, 4:158–59.

46. Reilly, *Urraca*, p. 125.

47. June 10, 1145. Marquis D'Albon, ed., *Cartulaire général de l'Ordre du Temple, 1119–1150* (Paris, 1913), pp. 230–31.

48. Francisco J. Hernández, ed., *Los Cartularios de Toledo* (Madrid, 1985), p. 720, has a

as castellan in Tordesillas.[49] Although he obviously retained the confidence of the king, his residence on the frontier makes his life difficult to follow. In 1129 Alfonso VII apparently granted some property in Talavera de la Reina to he and his wife, "Hermea Duci," although the charter has problems (D98). Before his public career, there is a private diploma of 1118 in which he and perhaps an earlier wife, María Armillo, join with Martín González and his wife, Elvira, in a grant to the Hospitalers of properties in the northwest.[50]

Also associated with the new lands to the south of the Guadarrama is Martín Muñoz called "de Escalona" in the nine royal charters that he confirmed between 1149 and 1151 (D611, 699). The usage is descriptive. The only tenancies that he held seem to have been north of the central sierra in Villagarcía de Campos in 1146 and in Cuéllar in 1148 according to three private diplomas, if indeed this is the same person.[51]

On the eastern border there is a group of castellans whose allegiance as well as whose identity is sometimes in question. For our consideration, they must be noted in documents of Alfonso, but it is possible to wonder whether the king has chosen the castellan or whether he has simply recognized the local predominance of an Aragonese magnate whose power made his displacement impossible. Pedro Jiménez's tenancy illustrates the point. Of Riojan extraction, he was cited in 1127 as holder of Perelada in a private diploma that also cited Alfonso I of Aragón as king, but just two years later in the same tenancy in another that cited Alfonso VII as king.[52] Pedro may have suffered some eclipse in the stormy times that followed, but between 1147 and 1156 he reappeared now as tenant of the much more important town of Logroño in seven charters of Alfonso VII and of the latter's son, Sancho (D544, 945).

Farther south along the Ebro at Calahorra, the tenancy was rather more contested. In two private documents of 1132 and 1134 Fortún López is cited as one of the tenants of that town under Alfonso I.[53] The record then fails until, from 1139 to 1151, Guter Fernández was tenant for Alfonso VII. Fortún López

---

handy guide to those documents of the cathedral chartularies in which he appears but calls him "Melendo Bofin." One expects that further research in the cathedral archives would produce yet more notices.

49. December 25, 1145. AD León, Gradefes, no. 59.

50. May 16, 1118. Ayala Martínez, *Libro*, pp. 154–66. The dating formula lists Pelayo for Diego in the see of León and Jimeno, a year prematurely, in Burgos however.

51. June 6, 1146. Pub. Fernández Flórez, *Colección*, 4:195–96, in Villagarcía. February 12, 1148. Pub. Antón, *Monasterios*, p. 256. April 23, 1148. Ibid., pp. 256–57. Both of these latter in Cuéllar.

52. Gonzalez, *Reino*, 1:317, for the family. March 15, 1127. Pub. Alamao, *Colección*, 1:191–93. November 16, 1129. Ibid., pp. 193–94.

53. November 27, 1132. Pub. Rodríguez de Lama, *Colección*, 2:164–65. August 16, 1134. Ibid., pp. 167–68.

was eclipsed. Then, between 1152 and 1157 he reappeared, confirming seven charters of the future Sancho III (D727, 970). While they do not specifically cite Fortún as tenant in Calahorra, three private diplomas between 1152 and 1154 do, and the last of these associates his son, Lop, with him in that post.[54]

Yet farther south, at Borovia east of Soria, one Gonzalo Rodríguez is cited as tenant between 1147 and 1156 in three royal documents and one private one (D550, 841, 913).[55] Until 1157 the writ of Alfonso VII ran that far east.

To the north on a major route over the sierra to Tarazona a Portale is cited in two royal documents and three private ones of 1156 and 1157 as tenant in strategic Agreda, and in the latter three with one García Zabata as his vicar (D940, 964).[56] These individuals are otherwise unknown in Leonese diplomas and their names betray Aragonese origins. All the private diplomas also make the pair tenants in Cervera (Cervera del Río Alhama twenty kilometers north of Agreda?) and Tutelón (the name is presently unknown) as well.

At Tarazona itself, Fortún Aznárez was tenant in 1132 under Alfonso I.[57] Five private documents from 1136 until 1149 cite him as still tenant under Alfonso VII and a charter of the future Sancho III cited him there in 1155 (D881).[58] The remarkable durability of Fortún may be due in part to the fact that Bishop Michael of Tarazona (1119–1150) was his brother.[59]

Fifty kilometers southeast of Tarazona lay the fortress of Rueda de Jalón, surrendered to the Leonese by the heir of the Huddid dynasty of Zaragoza in 1131. Very little is known about its tenancy but García Gómez is cited there in three royal and one private diplomas between 1148 and 1155. However, two of the royal charters have their problems (D346, 817, 879). The single private diploma of 1148 is suspect for its too early mention of Bishop Pedro of Sigüenza.[60]

In 1157 two charters of the future Sancho III and one private diploma of 1156 cite "Atorelia" tenant in Rueda (D964, 970).[61] The name is almost un-

54. July 6, 1152. Pub. Rodríguez de Lama, *Colección*, pp. 236–37, the first. December 3, 1154. Pub. ibid., p. 247, the last.

55. 1156. Pub. María Luisa Ledesma Rubio, ed., *Cartulario de San Millán de La Cogolla, 1076–1200* (Zaragoza, 1989), p. 282, a private diploma.

56. 1156. Pub. Cristina Monterde Albiac, ed., *Colección diplomática del monasterio de Fitero: 1140–1210* (Zaragoza, 1978), pp. 415–16. 1156. Ibid., p. 438. 1157. Ibid., pp. 405–6. All private documents.

57. March 1132. Logroño. Pub. José Angel Lema Pueyo, ed., *Colección diplomática de Alfonso I de Aragón y Pamplona, 1104–1134* (San Sebastián, 1990), pp. 392–93.

58. October 28, 1136. Pub. José María Lacarra, ed., "Documentos para el estudio de la reconquista y repoblación del valle del Ebro," *EEMCA* 3 (1947–48), p. 587, the first. 1149. Pub. Antonio Ubieto Arteta, ed., *Cartulario de Santa Cruz de la Serós* (Valencia, 1966), pp. 55–56, the last.

59. 1146. Albon, *Cartulaire*, p. 246, a private document.

60. October 1, 1148. Cited Serrano, "Armíldez," pp. 46–47.

61. January 1156. Pub. Rubio, *Documentos*, p. 61.

known in Leonese documents but a charter of Sancho identifies him as "de Aragón" (D875).[62] He seems to have been transferred to Rueda from Zaragoza, which three private diplomas cite him as having held in 1153–1154.[63] He was the brother-in-law of Jimeno Galíndez, and his successor as tenant under Alfonso I of Sos, Cabañas, Cella, and Alagón.[64]

Zaragoza, then largest city of the peninsula north of Toledo, had been held from 1146 until 1152 by García Ortiz, according to nine private diplomas.[65] García was Aragonese.[66] Before 1146 the city had been the tenancy of the Riojan magnate, Lop López, from 1135 into 1142, an arrangement acceptable to whomever exercised the predominant influence there.[67] These conditions make it probable that Alfonso VII's control in Zaragoza was always more aspiration than reality.

There are, finally, a small group of castellans whose names are identical with the names of *merinos* of the period. That may be mere coincidence, of course, but it would be important if we could find therein a sometime career path from the latter dignity to the former.

Diego Fernández is one such, but the name is quite common. He is cited in four private documents of the same monastery as castellan of Ribeira in the Bierzo between 1144 and 1149.[68] Someone of identical name is cited in 1148 as tenant of Cea east of León but it seems unlikely that a local figure would have been rewarded with such a distant post.[69] In 1147 a Diego Fernández is cited as tenant in "Çeresinos" (Cerecinos del Carrizal?).[70] If the identity of the village could be established the likelihood that this is the same man would be enhanced. Finally, there is a *merino* of the same name although not the same districts in the 1150s. I would reject the latter identification, since it bears the handicap of predicating a descent from the status of tenant to that of *merino*.

---

62. Also May 1128. Pub. Lema Pueyo, *Colección*, pp. 196–97. Ato Orelia made a donation to García Sánchez at the request of Alfonso of Aragón.

63. October 25, 1153. Pub. Rubio, *Documentos*, p. 55. 1154. Pub. María Luisa Ledesma Rubio, ed., "Colección diplomática de Grisén, siglos XII y XIII," *EEMCA* 10 (1975): 701. The latter calls him "count."

64. Clay Stalls, *Possessing the Land: Aragón's Expansion into Islam's Ebro Frontier under Alfonso the Battler, 1104–1134* (New York, 1995), pp. 134, 150.

65. December 1146. AHN, Códices, 595B, fol. 33r; pub. Albon, *Cartulaire*, p. 261, the first reliable one. July 1152. Pub. Rubio, *Documentos*, pp. 52–53, the last. January 1136. Pub. Lacarra, "Documentos," 2:542–43, is badly dated at the least.

66. Ubieto Arteta, *Historia. Formación*, p. 231.

67. January 20, 1135. Pub. Rubio, *Documentos*, p. 18, cited him "per mane de rege de Castelle." September 1142. Ibid., p. 33, cited him in a private document that also cited Ramon Berenguer.

68. March 9, 1144. Pub. Quintana Prieto, *Tumbo*, pp. 260–61, the first. March 3, 1149. Pub. ibid., p. 266, the last.

69. February 7, 1148. Pub. Serrano, *Cartulario de Vega*, pp. 61–62.

70. February 10, 1147. Pub. Ayala Martínez, *Libro*, pp. 205–6.

The same conclusion is indicated in the case of Martín Díaz. A royal document of 1143 of uncertain reliability cites him as tenant in Pajares de Campos (D453). A private document of 1145 names him tenant in San Roman (San Román de los Oteros?) and Villalli (?).[71] A Martín Díaz is cited as *merino* in Carrión de los Condes in a private diploma of 1152 and in two royal charters of 1154 (D833–34).[72] In this instance, the locales involved seem sufficiently close to make a case for the same individual, but the stumbling block is the priority in time of his tenancy.

A third such coincidence occurs with Fernando Rodríguez cited in a royal document of 1147 as tenant in Astudillo, thirty kilometers northeast of Palencia (D554). That charter has its problems, but four private documents in 1152 and 1153 also cite him as tenant in Dueñas, fifteen kilometers south of Palencia, and one of them adds Cuéllar, seventy kilometers south of that city and across the Duero.[73] There is a Fernando Rodríguez named as *merino* at Toro in a private document of 1135 and of Saldaña and Carrión in 1151.[74] One cannot entirely rule out that this is the same person but the likelihood is against it.

Similar ambiguity shadows a fourth instance. Fernando Gutiérrez was *merino* in the city of León in 1132 and after. There is also a Fernando Gutiérrez who is cited in three private documents of the Bierzo of 1156 and 1157 as tenant in Ribeira and in Palacios, respectively.[75] This latter and his wife, Marina Gutiérriz, also bought property in the territory of Astorga in 1145.[76] He was also the recipient of two royal grants for military service (D567, 670). While the chronological sequence is logical, the distinct identities of the two individuals seems well established.

The one clear example of a *merino* become tenant, and even greater, is Pedro Balzán. The name is peculiar by Iberian standards and so the identification is likely secure. Two private documents of 1156 and 1157 cite him as tenant in Cepeda jointly with Alvar Pérez and then in Astorga jointly with Count Ramiro Froílaz.[77] But Pedro was also *merino* and then *merino mayor*

71. December 25, 1145. AD León, Gradefes, no. 59.
72. December 23, 1152. Pub. Fernández Flórez, *Colección*, 4:247–48.
73. April, 1152. AHN, Clero, Carpeta 1.647, no. 9, the first. July 23, 1153. Pub. Antón, *Monasterios*, pp. 259–60, adds Cuéllar. October 21, 1153. Ibid., pp. 260–62, the last.
74. September 1135. Pub. Fernández Flórez, *Colección*, 4:146. July 23, 1151. Pub. Antón, *Monasterios*, pp. 257–58, but it is false.
75. June 19, 156. Pub. Quintana Prieto, *Tumbo*, pp. 287–88. July 16, 1156. Ibid., pp. 288–89. Both give him as tenant in Ribeira. June 1, 1157. AD Astorga, Carpeta 1, no. 12, cites him in Palacios.
76. María Concepción Casado Lobato, ed., *Colección diplomático del monasterio de Carrizo*, 2 vols. (León, 1983), 1:33–34.
77. April 29, 1156. AD Astorga, Carpeta 1, no. 10. June 8, 1157. Pub. Augusto Quintana

for León, Luna, and Coyanza between 1153 and the end of the reign, as will be noted. In 1162 he became majordomo of Fernando II of León.[78] Perhaps we could understand better this exceptional history if we knew more of the man's antecedents. For now he appears as a solitary example of what might be possible given great good fortune. All told, there is no convincing evidence that the responsibility of *merino* regularly led to elevation to the rank of tenant during the reign of Alfonso VII or earlier.

What the historian can say about the position and the persons of the *merino* in León-Castilla during this epoch is at once more impoverished and, in other respects, richer than the foregoing remarks about castellans. First, they are slightly fewer. The identical 2,000 documents that furnished us with 102 of the former yield ninety-eight of the latter. Of that total number, fifty-seven are known to us from but a single citation and another thirteen from but two. That is, slightly over 30 percent of them furnish more than the barest materials to establish either their identity or their function.

They are only rarely curial figures. A full sixty-two of them are known to us only from private diplomas of the period. Another twenty-six appear in just one or sometimes two royal documents. Like most castellans, they were local figures whose contact with the crown that they served was, on the whole, sporadic and circumstancial.

Nevertheless, a certain few of them are better known to us than all but a handful of castellans, because we know both their predecessors and their successors. Because the *merino* is often a civic figure a few major cities will furnish a series of such individuals, which will allow at least some rudimentary generalizations about tenure in and access to such positions. For that reason, the investigation here is better centered initially on the locale rather than the person. The royal city of León is the ideal place with which to begin because its prominence has left the fullest and longest list of *merinos*.

The first is Isidoro Nebzánez who held the post in 1128–1129 on the evidence of eight private documents. He also appeared in two royal charters of 1129, but they are both unreliable (D102, 105). He may have served in that capacity from the latter part of the reign of Urraca.[79] Isidoro and his brothers are known Leonese of minor rank.[80]

Prieto, "Los monasterios de Poibueno y San Martín de Montes," *AL* 22 (1968): 118–20. Another copy unknown to the author is BN, Manuscritos, 4.357, fol. 200r.

78. Carlos Estepa Diéz, *Estructura social de la ciudad de León, siglos XI–XIII* (León, 1977), pp. 297–98.

79. May 4, 1128. AHN, Clero, Carpeta 961, no. 12; pub. Vicente Vignau, ed., *Cartulario del monasterio de Eslonza* (Madrid, 1885), pp. 97–98, the first reliable one. May 17, 1129. Pub. José María Fernández Catón, ed., *Colección documental del archivo de la catedral de León, 1109–1187*, vol. 5 (León, 1990), pp. 137–38, the last. February 23, 1123. AD León, Gradefes, no. 20, so cites

By the middle of 1129 he had been succeeded by Albertino who was then *merino* in the royal city until early 1132 according to a dozen private diplomas.[81] Albertino is well known. He was father of Bishop Juan Albertínez of León (1139–1181). His name is certainly not Leonese, but he was resident in the city in 1122 when he was involved with a sale of property there.[82] In 1130 he and his wife, Estefanía, participated with a Radulfo in the purchase of a vineyard.[83] A dozen years later *Infanta* Sancha, daughter of Teresa of Portugal, bestowed a property in the district of León on Albertino and his second wife, María Jiménez.[84] Finally, in 1146 Alfonso VII granted him and María Jiménez another vineyard in that territory (D515).

On the evidence of his son's elevation to the episcopacy, we might conclude that Albertino was more than simply *merino* to the king in his royal city. But the *Historia Compostellana* describes him acting as agent for Alfonso in dealings with the lordly archbishop of Compostela in 1129 and again in 1134 or 1135.[85] These are the events that will finally lead to the conspiracy against Archbishop Gelmírez in which the king himself, and doubtless Albertino, was involved, the attempt at the assassination of the archbishop, and the latter's eventual trial and acquittal at the Council of Burgos in 1136. In other words, this *merino* enjoyed the fullest confidence of the crown.

Although he will return to the post, by the spring of 1133 Albertino had been replaced in the royal city by Fernando Gutiérrez. Between April 1133 and October 1137 some ten royal charters and twenty private diplomas cite Fernando (D170, 301). His family seems to have been Leonese, although it had property in Asturias as well. Estepa Díez knows Fernando and his brother, Alvaro Gutiérrez, although he accepts an unreliable document of 1140 that made Fernando a count and gave him a wife named María Pérez.[86] A better guide, although not entirely reliable, is the 1145 Alfonsine charter to Fernando and his wife, María Ovéquez, of property in Asturias (D508).

During the period in which Fernando Gutiérrez was *merino* of León, there are also five private diplomas that cite him as holding that position in

him and I make it an original. June 30, 1124. AC León, no. 1.386; ibid., pp. 119–20, cites a Nuño González as *merino* but it is a copy.

80. Estepa Díez, *Estructura*, pp. 286–88.

81. July 19, 1129. María Encarnación Martín López, ed., *Patrimonio cultural de San Isidoro de León. Serie documental.* Vol. 1, Parte 1, *Documentos de los siglos X–XIII* (León, 1995), pp. 47–48, the first. February 19, 1132. Pub. Fernández Catón, *Colección*, 5:153–54, the last.

82. Estepa Díez, *Estructura*, pp. 181–82.

83. January 26, 1130. Pub. Fernández Catón, *Colección*, 5:144–46.

84. March 23, 1142. Ibid., 5:207–8.

85. Emma Falque Rey, ed., *HC* (Turnholt, 1988), pp. 432,438–39, and 489–92.

86. *Estructura*, pp. 285–86, 448.

Asturias de Oviedo as well. The relevant royal documents never did. Noticing this and other analagous cases, Estepa Diéz was led to speculate whether the post of *merino* for León could include that of both the city proper and the territory as well as other towns and territories. Leaving the general question of pairing to other instances it may be said here that it is doubtful at least in as regards Fernando Gutiérrez. One of these diplomas is likely false.[87] The four other diplomas are all from a single source and all rather obviously related.[88] I believe that it is at least possible that the copyist mistook the name of Fernando Muñoz, *merino* in Asturias in the period 1141–1142, for that of Fernando Gutiérrez.

Two further caveats are in order. The more general is that one should not look for territorial boundaries internal to the realm in this period for they do not exist in any fixed, political sense. The *merino*, like the count, controlled a number of royal properties whose limits were defined in the law of property and whose boundaries were neither contiguous nor public in the modern sense. The second consideration is that during this time span, Asturias de Oviedo was the scene of armed struggle between Count Gonzalo Peláez and royal partisans and it is likely that there was no functioning *merino*.

For a brief period in the winter and spring of 1138 Albertino seems to have become *merino* in León for the second time. Two private diplomas so cite him.[89] Then he was replaced by Juan Peláez cited in five private diplomas between 1139 and 1141.[90] Estepa Diéz knows Juan only as *merino*, and I do not find him in other documents of León and vicinity that suggests that he was not a native. He seems earlier to have been *merino* in Zamora and will subsequently hold that post in Villafáfila, which suggests a mobility and even a certain professionalization of the position.

Juan Peláez may have been succeeded in 1141 for a brief period by Pedro Peláez de Manzaneda (Manzaneda de Torio?), according to two private diplomas. However, the first cites him as *merino* of the queen. It seems that she had

87. June 14, 1134. AHN, Clero, Carpeta 824, no. 17. It cites Fernando as *villicus* in León, Coyanza, and Asturias, but also Count Rodrigo Martínez as tenant of Mayorga when his brother, Osorio, actually held that town.

88. November 17, 1134. Pub. Pedro Floriano Llorente, ed., *Colección diplomática del monasterio de San Vicente de Oviedo* (Oviedo, 1968), pp. 303–4, cites him as "Iudex in Asturiis." May 12, 1136. Ibid., pp. 307–8, cites him as "presidente Asturiis et Legioni." December 31, 1136. Ibid., pp. 309–11, cites him as "maiorino in Asturias." April 13, 1137. Ibid., pp. 311–12, cites him as "in Asturiis economi." The editor calls all of these diplomas originals, but I think, on the basis of orthography, that they are copies of a century later.

89. February 8, 1138. Pub. Fernández Catón, *Colección*, 5:185–87. May 6, 1138. Ibid., 5:188–89.

90. December 30, 1139. AD León, Gradefes, no. 44, the first. February 28, 1141. AD León, Gradefes, no. 49, the last.

her own officer there.[91] The common patronymic, joined to the immediacy of their terms, makes it possible that they were brothers. Estepa Díez knows no such *merino* but Pedro was also often associated with *Infanta* Sancha.

In any event, in 1141–1142 eight private documents cite Pedro Manga as *merino* (D453).[92] Estepa Díez knows him only as *merino* but likely he was native to the contry about León. There is a private sale of 1134 in which he figures and Alfonso VII made him a grant in 1148. Neither document is entirely reliable and both derive from the archive of the monastery of Santa María de Carbajal, originally about five kilometers north of the city. Quite possibly the family did have its seat in that general area (D579).[93] At the turn of the decade, Pedro again became *merino* in León and in the meantime served in that capacity in Coyanza. At León, Albertino returned as *merino* one final time. Five private diplomas cite him as such between the spring of 1143 and the fall of 1144.[94]

Annaia Rodríguez succeeded Albertino. The former was probably a native of central León for all of the known documents involving him personally are drawn from the archive of the monastery of Sahagún. There is a royal charter of 1131 but it is clearly unreliable in some respects. There is a sale in 1145 to Annaia and his wife, Sancha Menéndez. Finally, there is his own *carta de arras* of 1147 to his new wife, Urraca Téllez (D136).[95] With Annaia we encounter a new phenomenon. He is cited in no fewer than fourteen royal charters as *merino* in León between 1145 and 1147, but in another two as *merino* in Carrión de los Condes, and still another as *merino* in Carrión and in Saldaña. In addition, in four more he is cited as *merino* in both León and Carrión de los Condes (D499, 512–13, 564). Seventeen private diplomas over the period 1145 to 1148 yield much the same mixture. But one of 1145 calls Annaia *merino mayor* of León, Carrión, and Saldaña; another of 1146 calls him *merino* of León, Carrión, Saldaña, and Cea; and that of 1147 calls him *merino mayor* of the emperor.[96]

91. May 21, 1141. Pub. María Amparo Valcarce, ed., *El dominio de la real colegiata de S. Isidoro de León hasta 1189* (León, 1985), pp. 145–46. December 29, 1141. Pub. Fernández Catón, *Colección*, 5:200–1.

92. March 21, 1141. Pub. Serrano, *Cartulario de Vega*, pp. 55–56, the first. April 16, 1142. Pub. Martín López, *Patrimonio*, p. 60, is the last. A private diploma cites him as vicar in León for the empress but it is unreliable. May 9, 1146. Pub. Floriano Llorente, *Colección*, pp. 350–51. It cites a Bernard as then bishop of Astorga.

93. June 14, 1134. AHN, Clero, Carpeta 824, no. 17.

94. May 17, 1143. AD León, Gradefes, no. 55, the first. October 30, 1144. Pub. Fernández Catón, *Colección*, 5:230–31, the last.

95. May 18, 1145. Pub. Fernández Flórez, *Colección*, 4:190–91. April 30, 1147. Ibid., 200–1.

96. January 23, 1145. Pub. Antón, *Monasterios*, p. 254. September 6, 1146. Pub. Fernández Flórez, *Colección*, 4:196–97. April 30, 1147. Ibid., pp. 200–201.

Clearly then *merinos* were sometimes called on to administer royal property in fairly widely scattered locations. The practice raises two possibilities. First; that this post was evolving like that of the countship toward an essentially fiscal grant with the day-to-day responsibilities in the hands of a vicar, and second, that the administration of the fisc proper was beginning to develop a hierarchy of officials with a *merino mayor* supervising a number of subordinate *merinos*. While the choice cannot be made with complete confidence, it appears to me that the second is the more likely. At least for the most crucial and developed portion of the fisc in the region between the royal city itself, the Cantabrians to the north, the Carrión River to the east, and Coyanza to the south some such closer supervision was being sought and has left other faint but discernable traces in the documents.

In León itself Pedro Manga returned to the post one final time. Between the late winter of 1149 and the fall of 1150 four private diplomas cite him as *merino*.[97] However, from as early as January of 1150 he may have served under Martín Nebzánez, brother of Isidoro Nebzánez who earlier held that post. From 1129 a sale by Martín to the cathedral of León of property in the vicinity survives.[98] Royal charters list him as *merino* in Campos, Coyanza, Luna, and Asturias off and on from 1139 up to 1151. Only in 1151–1152 is he cited in five as *merino* in León (D709,776). In three private diplomas of 1131–1132, however, Martín is cited as *merino* in León during the time that the post was held by Albertino. While the diplomatic of private documents has not been systematically examined for this period it seems cavalier to disregard all three. On the face of them, they have few other problems and they come from two different sources.[99] It is preferable to see Martín as subordinate to Albertino although the latter was never cited specifically as *merino mayor*.

On the other hand, another six private diplomas indicate that in the period 1139 to 1140 Martín had himself become something like *merino mayor*, although that title is not accorded him explicitly. He is variously styled "merino in León," "villicus in León," "villicus regis," and the last cites him as "merino regis," while simultaneously citing Juan Peláez as "merino in León."[100] Then, from January of 1150 until June of 1153, Martín Nebzánez is cited in nineteen private diplomas as *merino* in León, or simply as *merino*

---

97. March 13, 1149. Pub. José Luis Martín, "La orden militar de San Marcos de León," *León y su historia* 4 (1977): 50–51, the first. November 9, 1150. AD León, Gradefes, no. 62, the last.
98. Pub. Fernández Catón, *Colección*, 5:132–33, 140–41.
99. May 15, 1131. Ibid., 5:151–52. April 29, 1132. Ibid., 155–56. The editor styles both of these originals but I believe them copies. July 13, 1132. AHN, Clero, Carpeta 824, no. 16.
100. 1139. AD León, Gradefes, no. 42, the first. May 27, 1140. AD León, Gradefes, no. 47, the last.

in documents closely associated with León, and in one of them as *merino* in Luna, and in three others as *merino* in León and Coyanza.[101]

The general tendency of the private diplomas then is to reinforce that the impression given by the royal charters; that is, that from 1140 at least down until the middle of 1153 Martín Nebzánez held the post of *merino mayor* for royal properties stretching from Luna through León south to Coyanza. While he is not specifically accorded that title in either, it is clear that others held the post of *merino* in some of those places simultaneously and under his jurisdiction. The alternative to this conclusion would be an unwarranted disregard of the documents.

Sometime in 1153 a Rodrigo González succeeded Martín as *merino mayor* in León and held it into 1154. Four royal charters cite him as *merino*, but of six private charters one cites him also as *merino mayor*.[102] Since his name is fairly common it is not possible to venture more about Rodrigo.

During the latter part of his tenure, one Pedro Balzán probably served as *merino* for León under him. Three reliable royal charters of 1155 so cite Pedro and private documents do so from spring 1153 into 1157. But from the late winter of 1155 three of them also mention Pedro as *merino* in Luna and in Coyanza.[103] While the title is not specifically employed, these latter indicate that Pedro was *merino mayor* as well from 1155.

After León, Burgos was the most populous and largest city of the realm north of the Guadarramas. Unfortunately, the survival rate of private documents there in our period is low. However, the visiblity of its *merinos* in royal charters is high. The first is Miguel Féliz who appears in ninety royal charters between 1133 and 1150. Nevertheless, only for a more limited span between the winter of 1135 and 1146 is his tenure assured.[104] His patronymic is so un-

101. January 28, 1150. Pub. Fernández Catón, *Colección*, 5:253, the first. 1151. AHN, Clero, Carpeta 825, no. 3, cites him as *villicus* in Luna and names one Pelagio Rubio as his subordinate. March 1, 1151. AD León, Gradefes, no. 64; pub. Aurelio Calvo, *El monasterio de Gradefes* (León, 1936), p. 307, cites him as "imperial vicar in León and Coyanza." June 1, 1153. AD León, Santa María de Otero, no. 232, cites him as "merino in León and Coyanza." June 20, 1153. AD León, Gradefes, no. 74, the last, cites him in the same way.

102. August 12, 1153. Pub. Fernández Catón, *Colección*, 5:277–78, the earliest reliable private document. February 28, 1154. AHN, Clero, Carpeta 825, no. 5, a private document, the last. December 22, 1153. AD León, Gradefes, no. 69, a private document cites him as *merinomaior*.

103. April 1, 1153. AD León, Gradefes, no. 70, a private document, the earliest reliable. August 15, 1157. Pub. Fernández Catón, *Colección*, 5:308–9, a private document, the last. February 20, 1155. Pub. Floriano Cumbreño, *Colección*, pp. 127–29, "villicus in Luna et in Legione." November 22, 1155. Pub. Casado Lobato, *Colección*, 1:35–36, "villicus in Luna." 1156. Pub. Fernández Flórez, *Colección*, 4:262–65, "in Legione et Coianca."

104. February 1, 1135. Pub. Luciano Serrano, *El obispado de Burgos y Castilla primitiva desde el siglo V al XIII*, 3 vols. (Madrid, 1935), 3:170–71, the first reliable one. August 19, 1146. Pub. Peter Rassow, "Die Urkunden Kaiser Alfonso VII von Spanien," *AU* 11 (1930): 97–98, is the last trustworthy one. For him as for the other *merinos* at Burgos during the period, my findings are paral-

usual that we can believe that he was the son of Felix, also *merino* in the area in the latter 1090s during the reign of Alfonso VI.[105]

From 1135 until 1142 Miguel Féliz was regularly at court confirming 79 of the 344 known royal charters. After the latter date, he confirmed but four more charters in the next four years so that his presence in Burgos may have become more critical. But beginning in 1142 and sporadically until 1149 another *merino* appears for Burgos in the person of García Rodríguez. García may have replaced Miguel for a time but four of the nine royal charters in which the former appears are suspect and the charter of 1146, in which Miguel appeared is certainly an original (D441, 447, 557, 581, 601). Perhaps García was subordinate to Miguel although the latter is not cited as *merino mayor*. The hint that he might have been are citations of Miguel as *merino* in Castilla and in Nájera in three private documents.[106]

After García's tenure, however understood, in the month of March, 1149 a Pedro Micháelez is cited in three royal charters as *merino* in Burgos (D611, 613–14). He was likely the son of Miguel Féliz and may have had a longer tenure. By March 1150 perhaps, by February 1152 surely, he had been replaced by Alfonso Muñoz whose career there is illustrated by five royal charters of that year (D643, 730, 776).

For our period the last recorded *merino* in Burgos was Diego Fernández. Between the summer of 1154 and the late winter of 1157 he was cited in some ten royal charters. In just one of them Diego was styled *merino mayor* but unfortunately it is less than entirely reliable (D839, 879, 962).[107]

The record of the royal *merinos* at Burgos is instructive because it begins only tardily in Alfonso VII's reign. While recognizing the paucity of private documents one must still realize that their scarcity reflects the political history of the region. Castilla La Vieja had been separated from the parent kingdom during the reign of Sancho II (1065–1072). Then it had been under Aragonese control from 1110 until 1127. Even after that, the region had remained under the control of the Lara house and their ally, Count Bertrán, perhaps until the

---

leled largely by those of Ignacio Alvarez Borge, *Monarquía feudal y organización territorial; Alfoces y Merindades en Castilla, siglos X–XIV* (Madrid, 1993), pp. 151–57, although he does not consider the possibility of the simultaneous existence of a *merino* subordinate to a *merino maior*. I would also be cautious about asserting the coincidence of the latter's jurisdiction with anything like the boundaries of the former county of Castilla, even if the latter had existed in any formal fashion.

105. September 30, 1098. Pub. Marius Férotin, ed., *Recueil des chartes de l'abbaye de Silos* (Paris, 1897), pp. 33–34, for example.

106. 1138. Pub. Rodríguez de Lama, *Colección*, 2:182–83, "in Nájera." January 1139. BN, Manuscritos, 5.790, fol. 166v, "in all Castilla." 1140. AHN, Códices, 105B, ff. 158r-159r, "in Nájera."

107. The twelfth-century offices in Burgos and its district are discussed in some length in Carlos Estepa Díez, Teófilo F. Ruiz, Juan A. Bonachia Hernando, and Hilario Casado Alonso, *Burgos en la Edad Media* (Madrid, 1984), pp. 84–85.

fall of Count Rodrigo González in 1135. The royal fisc in the region must have suffered. As a result, there seems to have been only a tentative experimentation with the possibility of more elaborate supervision of dynastic properties. If the post of *merino mayor* was instituted, it may have consisted largely in a responsibility as well for equally scattered royal lands in La Rioja and the mountains between the latter and Burgos, as at Belorado and Bureba for which there are a few notices of *merinos*, once control of that territory was regained.

Approximately midway between Burgos and León, in the plain of the Carrión River lay two moderately important towns, Carrión de los Condes and Saldaña. The two were the center of a bloc of royal fisc lands important enough to have had one *merino* almost continuously for the entire reign. This was Diego Muñoz of Saldaña. He had been royal majordomo from 1138 to 1144. In 1126 his adherence to the cause of Alfonso VII was sufficiently important to be noted in the *Chronica Adefonsi Imperatoris*.[108] His father, Muño Díaz had been *merino* for the same lands in the reign of both Alfonso VI and his daughter Urraca.[109] Diego's son, Boso, will succeed him in the position. Diego's family, a branch of the Ansúrez, held lands of its own in the district and used them to endow the monasteries of San Pelayo de Valdavia near Saldaña and San Zoil in Carrión.[110] Alfonso VII added to the families holdings thereabouts in 1137 and again in 1142 with donations to Diego and his wife, Urraca Téllez (D288, 435). The special status of the man is evident in that he was occasionally castellan in one location while not ceasing to be *merino* in others. At the end of his career he was tenant in all of Saldaña and shared half of Carrión with Guter Fernández. By then Diego was probably no longer *merino* in either but in 1138 and 1140 he had shared the tenancies of Cea and Ceione with Lop López.[111] In 1130, he may have shared the tenancy of Melgar (Melgar de Abajo?) with Count Osorio Martínez.[112]

Between the spring of 1130 and the fall of 1155 no less than seventy-two royal charters and forty private diplomas cite Diego as *merino* in Carrión, Saldaña, or both (D118, 891). In addition, the private diplomas sometimes cite him as *merino* in Frómista, twenty kilometers southeast of Carrión, and Abia de las Torres, the same distance northeast, and of Cabezón, a few kilometers

---

108. Maya Sánchez and Gil, *CAI*, pp. 151–52.

109. Reilly, *Urraca*, pp. 39 and 345.

110. October 1, 1132. Pub. Antón, *Monasterios*, pp. 298–99. January 17, 1152. Ibid., pp. 299–301. Both are for San Pelayo and have their defects. 1156. Pub. Pérez Celada, *Documentación*, pp. 61–63, for San Zoil.

111. November 30, 1138. Pub. Fernández Flórez, *Colección*, 4:163–44. November 27, 1140. Ibid., 4:176–77.

112. November 28, 1130. Ibid., 4:128–30.

north of Valladolid.[113] They thus suggest a wider supervision of dynastic property in the district about Carrión and Saldaña and sometimes even beyond. The total data would indicate the post of *merino mayor*. Documents occasionally cite him as such. This occurs once in a royal charter, although not a very reliable one, and six times in private diplomas (D570).[114]

There is one further complication. In the royal charters citing Diego as *merino* there is a gap between the end of 1139 and the beginning of 1148 (D354, 578). In the private diplomas the hiatus lasts only from early 1144 to early 1148.[115] A partial explanation may be that it is during 1147 and 1148 that Diego most frequently confirms royal charters. Moreover, between 1145 and and 1148 Annaia Rodríguez, whom we have already seen as *merino* then in León, is cited in six royal charters, although only two of them inspire full confidence, and four private diplomas as *merino* in Carrión and Saldaña.[116] Presumably, for whatever reason, the authority of the *merino mayor* of León was temporarily extended that eastern district as well.

During the later portion of his tenure, Diego seems to have had a subordinate at Carrión itself. Two royal charters and one private document name a Martín Díaz as *merino* there in 1152 and 1154 (D833–34).[117] Diego either died or became seriously incapacitated in 1156. His donation of that year to the monastery of San Zoil in Carrión suggests a will. His son, Boso, mentioned in it, emerges in midyear as himself *merino* in Carrión and Saldaña and continued in that post into 1157 according to four private diplomas.[118]

North of these three blocks of *fisc* properties lay the territory of Asturias de Oviedo. It was virtually beyond royal control until the fall of the rebel Gonzalo Peláez and few notices of *merinos* have survived. Private documents

113. March 27, 1131. Ibid., 4:132–34, in Cea. May 22, 1137. AHN, Ordenes militares, Carpeta 574, no. 5; BN, Manuscritos, 714, fol. 142v, in Frómista and Abia de las Torres. December 1, 1139. Pub. Luciano Serrano, ed., *Colección diplomática de San Salvador de El Moral* (Madrid, 1906), pp. 52–53, in Cabezón.

114. December 20, 1131. Pub. L. Díez Canseco, "Fuero de San Pedro de las Dueñas (León)," *AHDE* 2 (1925): 463–64. April 1, 1137. Partially pub. José Luis Fernández Catón, ed., *Catálogo del archivo del monasterio de San Pedro de las Dueñas* (León, 1977), pp. 21–22. May 22, 1137. AHN, Ord. Mil., Carpeta 574, no. 5. This diploma also lists one Pedro Cídez as *merino* in Frómista. October 18, 1140. Pub. Pérez Celada, *Documentación*, pp. 54–55. January 26, 1150. Pub. Fernández Flórez, *Colección*, 4:220–21. September 22, 1150. AD León, Santa María de Otero, no. 232.

115. January 21, 1144. Pub. José Luis Martín, ed., *Documentos zamoranos*, vol. 1, *Documentos del archivo catedralicio de Zamora, Primera Parte; 1128-1261* (Salamanca, 1982), pp. 10-11. February 1, 1148. Pub. Fernández Flórez, *Colección*, 4:203–4.

116. January 23, 1145. Pub. Antón, *Monasterios*, p. 254, a private diploma, the earliest reliable. April 23, 1148. Ibid., pp. 256–57, a private document, the latest.

117. December 23, 1152. Pub. Fernández Flórez, *Colección*, 4:247–48.

118. 1156. Ibid., 4:262–65. June 28, 1156. Ibid., 4:261–62, calls him *merinomaior*. February 13, 1157. Ibid., 4:266–67. May 30, 1157. AHN, Clero, Carpeta 963, no. 18; pub. Vignau, *Cartulario*, pp. 143–44.

between 1134 and 1137 indicate that the *merino* of León, Fernando Gutiérrez, had jurisdiction there as well.[119] That arrangement apparently sufficed for the Leonese *merino*, Martín Nebzánez, functioned in the same capacity in 1140 (D367, 383). Juan Peláez who had served at León under Martín was also noted once in 1142 as "merino in Oviedo."[120] But by late 1141 and 1142 a Fernando Muñoz, not associated with León, appeared as *merino* in Asturias.[121]

In 1143 Gonzalo Vermúdez first appears and will hold the post down until 1153 at least. He is cited in nine royal charters and twenty-eight private diplomas (D799).[122] At the same time, it is clear that there were other *merinos* in Asturias. A private diploma of 1141 cites one Pedro Gutiérrez as the "queen's merino." Given the timing, only some property of Queen Berengaria can have been meant.[123] On the other hand, Muño García was associated with *Infanta* Sancha in the forged *fuero* to the town of Avilés in January of 1155 as her *merino* in Gozón and earlier in 1154 in the same capacity (D826, 861). He had also been listed in 1148 and 1149 simply as *merino* in Asturias.[124] At that point he may have been a subordinate of Gonzalo Vermúdez or already *merino* to the *infanta*, which data the scribe simply chose to omit. We simply do not know.

One Diego Cídez was also cited in the falsified *fuero* of Avilés in 1155 as *merino* in Oviedo. Pedro Peláez appeared in in a private document of 1151 as *merino* in Gijón and in a royal charter of 1152 as *merino* of Queen Sancha in Gijón (D769).[125] Finally, in 1157 Gonzalo Vermúdez reappears once more but this time apparently as castellan for Sancha in Gozón.[126]

East of León and west of Carrión and Saldaña, the plains of the Rivers Valderaduey and Cea held a series of modest towns where royal properties were organized rather differently. There are scattered notices of a number of *merinos* in Cea and nearby Ceione. But just ten kilometers to the south of the former lay the royal pantheon and monastery of Sahagún to which, presumably, most of the royal fisc lands of the district had long been alienated. The abbot had his own *merinos* to see to them. Another ten kilometers south of the monastery lay the royal fortress and center of Grajal. There the fisc lands

---

119. November 17, 1134. Pub. Floriano Llorente, *Colección*, pp. 303–4. May 12, 1136. Ibid., pp. 307–8. December 31, 1136. Ibid., pp. 309–11. April 13, 1137. Ibid., pp. 311–12.

120. March 1142. Ibid., pp. 328–29, a private document.

121. November, 1141. Ibid., pp. 326–28, "merino regis." But in the two subsequent private documents he is otherwise titled. March 1142. Ibid., pp. 328–29, "iudex regis." April 1142. Ibid., pp. 329–31, "dominating Asturias." These might indicate a tenancy.

122. March 11, 1143. Ibid., pp. 333–35, a private diploma, the first.

123. Ibid., pp. 72–73.

124. March 1148. Ibid., pp. 364–66. April 1148. Ibid., pp. 366–67. May 7, 1148. Ibid., pp. 368–69. February 2, 1149. Ibid., pp. 373–74.

125. August, 1151. Ibid., pp. 383–84.

126. May 1157. Ibid, pp. 406–7.

were part of an *infantaticum* of the Alfonso's sister, Sancha, who oversaw them through the instrument of her own proper *merinos*.

West of the royal city in the valley of the Orbigo River lay a land of even smaller hamlets. A few notices of *merinos* from the royal castle at Luna in the north have survived but that specific area was often under the control of the *merino* at León. Places farther to the south have left no notices that I have encountered. Still, the smaller the institution, the less likely its documents to survive, and we must not imagine the region entirely bereft either of royal properties or royal supervision. Probably, however, it was too humble to have created much in the way of structures.

Yet farther west, beyond the Montes de León in the Bierzo again, the supervision of the crown seems to have rested largely upon the *merinos* of the *infantaticum* of *Infanta* Sancha. Beyond that, in Galicia proper, little can be said for this period. Part of the difficulty can be traced to a difference of the notarial tradition. The dating formulae of private documents there only infrequently include the citation of those holding local posts, which practice is so rewarding for the local historian in the Leonese territories. Still, it is difficult to believe that the dynasty had ever possessed very rich resources in that isolated province.

Yet more to the southwest of León was the episcopal city of Astorga. Most of its medieval documents were destroyed by French troops occupying the city during the Napoleonic Wars, and one must piece together what one can from surviving early-modern copies. But as in most of the cities of the north of the peninsula, the secular jurisdiction of its bishop and the cathedral properties were probably extensive. Four private diplomas furnish citations of six individuals who were *merinos* there between 1141 and 1150. More than likely, most royal properties there had long been alienated into the episcopal fisc and there was precious little for royal *merinos* to oversee.

One hundred and thirty kilometers south of the royal city was the important town of Zamora on the old Roman silver road from Mérida and Badajoz. Until the fall of Toledo to Alfonso VI in 1085 it had always been a frontier town. It had had no bishopric in antiquity, a checkered existence in the ninth and tenth Centuries, to put it positively, and until 1120 was simply the ordinary residence of the bishop of Salamanca whose titular see had been reestablished only in 1102.[127] That circumstance, along with the usual proliferation of the royal fisc common along the frontier, suggests that there would have been work to occupy royal *merinos*. Nonetheless, the names of but seven

---

127. Bernard F. Reilly, *The Kingdom of León-Castilla under King Alfonso VI, 1065–1109* (Princeton, 1988), p. 312.

of them survive from the period between 1127 and 1151, five of them in but single notices and all of them from private diplomas.

Two particularly rich diplomas tell us that Juan Peláez and Salvador González were *merinos* there in 1133 while Count Rodrigo Martínez held the tenancy and continued to share it still in the fall of 1138 after the count's death the preceding summer.[128] The only other multiple notices tell us that Martín Annáiz was *merino* between 1148 and 1151 during the tenancy of Count Pons de Cabrera.[129] From 1135 until 1156 Zamora's sister fortress just thirty kilometers to the west on the Duero River at Toro furnishes but three names of *merinos* gleaned from three private diplomas.

The old southeast of the kingdom displays the same paucity of evidence as the old southwest. Only at Palencia, well up the Pisuerga from the Duero, can one find as many as five individuals cited as *merinos* in four different documents, none of them royal charters. By way of contrast with what must have then been at least the third largest city of the kingdom north of the Duero, the little village of Villafáfila, only twenty kilometers south of Benavente, boasts as many as four surviving names.

Even more marked is the difference in the lands across the Duero stretching down to the Tajo River in the second quarter of the twelfth century. The area was only fifty years removed from being either Muslim territory subject to some *taifa* kinglet or a land of war between them and the kings of León-Castilla. On its southern and western fringes, it still was into the 1140s. A new population from the Christian north was flowing irresistably into it, encouraged by the crown, but one has still the sense of very large spaces beyond any authority or even simple ownership.[130] Inevitably, those institutions proven farther north would be transferred into it but in different proportions corresponding to the exigencies of a new age and a new environment. Except for the newly great archbishopric of Toledo the episcopal role would be perhaps the least changed of these traditional instruments. Independent monasteries would be fewer and rather more urban and the new religious orders would come to be more typical. Towns, too, would have a larger place.

Of those institutions just now under consideration, the extent to which countship and castellany were features of the society north of the Duero may already be noticeable. They were surely not unknown south of it but were

---

128. November 22, 1133. AC Zamora, *Tumbo Negro*, ff. 17v-18r. October 14, 1138. AHN, Clero, Carpeta 3.563, no. 8.

129. August 25, 1148. AC Zamora, *Tumbo Blanco*, ff. 121v-122r. January 2, 1150. Pub. Martín, *Documentos zamoranos*, pp. 12–13. May 13, 1151. Ibid., pp. 13–15.

130. Still the most imaginative and suggestive attempt to portray the emergence of society in these lands as a "process" is Angel Barrios García, *Estructuras agrarias y de poder en Castilla: El ejemplo de Avila, 1085–1320* (Salamanca, 1983).

certainly fewer there and perhaps more extensive simply because they were fewer. In some degree, this impression may again be a function of the poverty of our sources. The preservation of records is a late feature of an increasingly stable society and that is particularly true of private, nonroyal documents. Ecclesiastical documents, whether episcopal or monastic, are no more than a handful before 1150 and secular, urban ones belong rather to the thirteenth century almost without exception.

It is in this context that we should accept that even of so great a town as Salamanca there is only a single private diploma of 1133 that preserves the names of one judge, who may be a *merino* since the terms are sometimes interchangeable, and three *sayones* to assist him there.[131] For Toledo itself there is but one *merino*, and he from a single private document of 1141, for the entire period.[132] It must also be pointed out that royal charters identify only a single *merino* of 1138 in the entire area between the Duero and Tajo Rivers and this Pedro Muñoz is cited for Ayllón, Atienza, and Medinaceli in the northeast (D320–22). The conclusion is inescapable that the royal fisc more irregularly organized south of the Duero.

As we have seen, local agents of the crown were drawn from different gradations of society. Castellans among themselves might range in dignity from Guter Fernández and Nuño Pérez who were count in everything but title to modest nobles who are scarcely knowable in other than their royal dignity. *Merinos* were, on the average, more humble still. A few might be among the great of the realm, figuring in royal and court affairs, and recipients of royal largesse. But where we can glimpse something of their family they seem clearly non-noble, even though men of property and sometimes with a family history of royal service such as the Nebzánez of León or the Féliz of Burgos.

With the obvious exceptions, neither castellans nor *merinos* were curial figures like the counts. Ordinarily they resided in their jurisdictions and participated in local life. We cannot trace there a regular subordination of *merino* to castellan in the exercise of their several responsibilities. Sometimes our sources speak of a *merino* acting "sub manu" of a castellan or of the former as "vicar" of the latter but this is unusual and may well indicate that the same individual has the care, at once, of the royal property in the district and that of the count or castellan.

Indeed the documents seem to indicate a difference of personage and with it a difference of emphasis in function rather than a bureaucratic rela-

---

131. José Luis Martín, Luis Miguel Villar García, Florencio Marcos Rodríguez, and Marciano Sánchez Rodríguez, eds., *Documentos de los archivos catedralicio y diocesano de Salamanca, siglos XII–XIII* (Salamanca, 1977), pp. 89–90.

132. AC Toledo, V.11.B.1.10; part. pub. Hernández, *Cartularios*, p. 46.

tionship. Where the latter seems to be implied it runs between *merino* and *merino mayor* rather than between *merino* and castellan. The latter exercised a primarily military jurisdiction though the control of property and justice were associated with it in some degree. The former exercised a jurisdiction directed toward the custody of royal estates though this in turn could not be entirely divorced from the administration of justice nor the occasional service of military needs. Contemporaries would have been more resigned than we to the confusion and contention that such overlapping functions regularly produced.

That is to say, of course, where they did overlap. There is no need to assume that a castellan existed in every jurisdiction of a *merino* and scarcely better warrant to presume a *merino* necessary to every tenancy. For both are best understood precisely as jurisdictions related to dynastic properties, not as territorial divisions and subdivisions. If jurisdictions were granted over private properties, rather than in and over public territories as we are wont to conceive it, then their relevance one to the other may be entirely circumstancial. Physical proximity, where it existed, would inevitably lead to practical accommodation but not necessarily to an institutional framework.

In fact, it clearly appears that a tentative institutional frame was rather developing during the reign, at least in areas of more complex and extensive dynastic holdings, toward the subordination of lesser *merinos* to a *merino mayor*. The failure of contemporary royal documents to register the development seems to me to stem from the conservative instinct of the royal chancery. But private scribes could and did see, and put a tongue to, a growing change that made a practical difference in what they must needs record.

But the most sensitive and nuanced study of this development to date still, it appears to me, to place too great and too early an emphasis on the territorial frame.[133] At some point subsequent to 1157 what we should term a civil, territorial organization is going to emerge of which the *merindad* will be the unit and groups of *merindades* will be subordinated to *merinos mayores*. But still in the first half of the twelfth century the conception of such possible territorial regularities has yet to be grasped. *Merinos* are everywhere, *merinos mayores* are beginning to be instituted, but *merindades* are nowhere to be found.

133. Alvarez Borge, *Monarquía*, pp. 40, 45, and then by extension, pp. 99–145. I have not found in documents I trust a usage of the terminology of *alfoz*, *territorium*, *aldea*, or *barrio*, the sense of a more than descriptive denotation rather than a legal or political one. Nevertheless, the author frames the questions and points the directions in a more constructive fashion than has been done in any earlier study. See, for example, Atanasio Sinués Ruiz, *El merino* (Zaragoza, 1954).

8

King and Realm

IN THE SECOND QUARTER of the twelfth century the kingdom of León-Castilla remained what it had always been, an agricultural society. The subjects of Alfonso VII were overwhelmingly more concerned with the state of the weather, the readiness of the soil for planting, and the promise of the harvest than with the health of the kingdom or that of the king himself. When the monarch and his court appeared in their vicinity it was an event, a celebration, a danger, but ordinarily he was safely somewhere else. Local potentates, the castellan, the *merino*, the abbot, the bishop, were much more central to their lives and their fortunes.

Of all possible royal initiatives, that which touched them most directly was war. Moreover, war was endemic. Of the thirty-one years of the reign of Alfonso VII, only seven were marked by the absence of a major campaign in which the monarch personally participated. And in at least three of those, major campaigns were organized but had to be abandoned because of other emergencies. Fortunately for the population of the realm, with brief and modest exceptions, all of these wars were fought on the borders of the realm or within the territories of adjoining kingdoms.

True, their king was a warrior by birth and by office. All kingship in the west of Europe had been for the past 600 years and would continue to be for the next 600. That dangerous calling was part of the mystique of, and most of the justification for, a king's authority. He was the greatest warrior of the land, theoretically, and thus its natural ruler and its divinely ordained protector. In the end, at every moment of his reign, that was the essential ground on which he was judged.

Yet the kingdom of León-Castilla was not at war for twenty-four of the years between 1126 and 1157 simply because Alfonso was destined by office to the warrior life. The inescapable fact was that in 1126 the entire peninsula had been in turmoil for better than a century. The collapse of the caliphate of Córdoba and the abrupt end of Islamic hegemony in Iberia had left the question of its political organization radically unsettled. In the Christian north, the principalities of León-Castilla, Aragón, Navarra, Barcelona, and Portugal, were emerging and disputing with one another the reach of their geography as well as the form of their political life. As a result, Alfonso VII would campaign against Aragón in 1127, 1128, 1131, 1132, and 1134. He would campaign against Portugal in 1127, 1134, 1137, and 1141. Navarra was the opponent in 1136, 1137, and 1140. Only in 1130 against the Lara family and in 1132 and 1133 against revolt in Asturias were his campaigns launched against an internal foe.

After 1134 when the political evolution of the north, partly as a result of his own diplomacy, began to respond to a more irenic logic, the major direction of his campaigns was south, against the Islamic powers of Iberia and North Africa. In 1133, 1137, 1138, 1139, 1142, 1143, 1144, 1146, 1147, 1148, 1150, 1151, 1152, 1155, and 1157, Alfonso made major attacks on the crumbling empire in Andalucía of the Almoravids, and finally on the growing new empire there of North African Almohads. In the end, his efforts in that arena cost him his life.

Inescapably, the dynamic of his times and the rationale of his being combined to make the overriding necessity of his rule the military one.[1] Ironically, for most of this period there was no army in being. The warrior king was surrounded by warriors, his bodyguard directed by his *alférez*. We should imagine their number at about fifty effectives, mounted warriors as befitted the king's and their own rank. Each of them was supported by at least a squire and a groom so that the extended royal guard consisted of at least 150 men with some military training. They constituted the core and the elite force of the royal army when that latter was called into being.

But, as we have seen, the king was ordinarily attended at court by something like five counts, by perhaps another five magnates of similar power and wealth, and at least five bishops of the realm. Now all of these were military figures, directly or indirectly. Because they would not have presumed an individual equality to the king but also because they would certainly not have scanted his or their own honor, it is probable that each would have had their own military entourage. If we assume five mounted warriors apiece including their own persons, a total of more than seventy-five attendants meant an additional armed force immediately available to the king of 225 men. It is not adventurous, then, to suppose that the crown could almost without effort put into the field roughly 400 men, a third of them certainly mounted. It

---

1. James F. Powers, *A Society Organized for War* (Berkeley, Calif., 1988), is the best guide to the technical aspects of much of what follows. Derek W. Lomax, *The Reconquest of Spain* (London, 1978), is a briefer but broader coverage.

was hardly an army, even by the standards of the day, but it was more than enough to deal with domestic discord, overawe all but the most determined rebellions, or even to do a bit of raiding against neighboring princes as opportunity and inclination offered.[2]

All had to be continuously supported. The upkeep of the royal bodyguard proper must have constituted one of the major charges against the royal fisc. It was part of the meaning of the king "living of his own." As for the ordinary upkeep of the others, that must have been a good part of the raison d'être of countship, of tenancy, and even of episcopacy. But major campaigns on an almost yearly basis were another matter and demanded to be separately financed.

Apart from the revenues produced by the fisc, the most essential support specifically for the army was the *fossatum*, the duty of every freeborn male subject to render military service. Even more important, since the service of every male subject was by no means desirable, was the *fossatera*, payment due in lieu of personal military service. We have only rare insight into the mechanics of its collection, but doubtless that was the duty of each bishop, abbot, count, tenant, and *merino*, who eventually were accountable to the *alférez* in the matter.

The ubiquity of the *fossatum* and *fossatera* is witnessed in the royal documents. Almost one in ten mentions them, usually to exempt the grantee from their burden, although only twenty-three of the total eighty-one date after 1144. The demands of the war in Andalucía made further exemptions inopportune. In terms of the surviving evidence and concerning the frequency with which the exemption was sought, it seems to have made little difference whether the grantee was a religious institution, a lay magnate, or a group of townsmen. The very language of the exemption was, in chancery usage, a formula contained in a grant of *coto*, general immunity from royal jurisdiction. Such an exemption could be partial and, in that respect, may often have been simply an attempt to regularize and standardize some royal income (D198).[3]

The grant of immunity did not so much allow the mighty and their property to escape war dues as it changed the machinery of war finance. The right to exact *fossatum* or *fossatera* passed rather to a bishop of Sigüenza, to a bishop of Osma, and even once to an abbot of Cluny (D320–21, 432, 817).

2. J. O. Prestwich, "The Military Household of the Norman Kings," *EHR*, 96 (1981): 1–35, has used a different type of source to delineate the military nature and potential of the *familia regis* before and during the time of Henry I and Stephen who were contemporaries of Alfonso VII. Nevertheless, the reality of the king's personal warriors is remarkably similar. Analogous conditions give rise to analogous solutions.

3. A single *solidus* paid annually at Michaelmass and four days of work satisfies a variety of military obligations of the men of Villalbilla near Burgos.

Iberian bishops were be diligent in its assessment for they would need their
share of these resources to offset or supplement their own military obligations to the crown. Indeed, a remarkable series of diplomas of Bishop Juan
of León have survived that show him turning *fossatera* into an annual obligation of four solidi per man to be paid to him on the feast of All Saints by
his vassals in a variety of villages.[4] Bishop Bernard of Zamora had somewhat
earlier exempted the men of the village of Fresno from *fossatum* and *fossatera*
in return for annual payment in money and kind.[5]

When he granted a *fuero* to the men of Noceda in 1149, Abbot Pedro
of the Bierzan monastery of San Pedro de Montes safeguarded his right to
collect war dues.[6] When Count Manrique and Countess Ermesinda alienated
the village of Cobeta in 1153 they carefully specified the military duties of its
inhabitants.[7] The right to collect *fossatera* passed with the sale of property and
doubtless helped to determine its price.[8] It seems, then, royal *merinos* collected war levies only from estates of the fisc and from such lordless men as
lived in proximity to them. The magnates, clerical and lay, were expected to
furnish the bulk of the mounted army of the realm and the towns the largest
portion of its footmen.

The theoretical potential of the kingdom might be estimated at something like 1,750 heavy cavalry and another 3,500 squires and grooms necessary
to their effective operation. That would be the force provided if the king,
the nine counts of the realm, another eight magnates of comital resources
although not title, and seventeen bishops each contributed a troop of fifty
mounted warriors. Of course, no such force was ever mobilized. Some of it
had to be permanently in reserve near the various frontiers of the kingdom.
Some of it was too distant from the theaters of action to be useful very often.
Wars were fought, when possible, with troops drawn from the regions closest
to the scene of conflict. We may also be sure that, as always, fair numbers
found good reasons that made it impossible to serve. This reluctance was far
from unwelcome since their *fossatera* could be used to hire more eager warriors. With all of this in mind, it does seem that the crown might regularly be

---

4. December 30, 1156. Pub. José María Fernández Catón, ed., *Colección documental del archivo de la catedral de León, 1109-1187*, vol. 5 (León, 1990), pp. 293–95. January 1, 1157. Ibid., pp.
295–96. May 3, 1157. Ibid., pp. 300–302.
5. January 1, 1146. AC Zamora, *Tumbo Negro*, fol. 11r-v. For a general statement of the
routine obligations such provisions were designed to offset see Luciano Serrano, *El obispado de
Burgos y Castilla primitiva desde el siglo V al XIII*, 3 vols. (Madrid, 1935), 2:13–14.
6. 1149. Pub. Augusto Quintana Prieto, ed., *Tumbo Viejo de San Pedro de Montes* (León,
1971), pp. 269–70.
7. December 5, 1153. Pub. Toribio Minguella y Arnedo, *Historia de la diócesis de Sigüenza y
de sus obispos*, vol. 1 (Madrid, 1910), pp. 390–91.
8. December 22, 1153. AD León, Gradefes, no. 69.

able to raise a force of 700 horse with the other 1,400 or so persons necessary to their service.

These same factors would have been even more true for the foot contingents furnished, for the most part, by the towns. By nature they were less mobile. Northern campaigns could theoretically call on the militia service of the major towns; León, Compostela, Burgos, Palencia, Oviedo, and Astorga. The first three of these probably owned a population of 3,000 persons apiece, Palencia perhaps 2,000, and the latter two about 1,500 each.[9] Of the resultant 14,000 total one calculates roughly 3,500 adult males of whom about 40 percent, or 1,600, might have been available at any one time. But not all of those could be called out, for local security and order would have kept on the order of a quarter of them at home. Moreover, it ordinarily was impractical to use the militia of Compostela or Oviedo for campaigns in the Rioja or that of Burgos or Palencia for campaigns in Galicia. In short, the foot contingent for campaigns north of the Duero probably never exceeded about 600.

South of the Duero more numerous foot were available, largely due to the very large population of Toledo itself. If one credits it with 25,000 people, Salamanca and Segovia with 2,000, Avila with 1,000, and Valladolid and Zamora at the extreme range of utility with about 1,500 each, a total urban population of 35,000 is reached. From the resulting 8,500 adult males, a pool of 3,400 foot soldiers existed. Even with the reservations necessary for distance and local defense, royal armies operating along the line of the Tajo, in La Mancha, or Andalucía proper, must often have counted 1,000 to 2,000 infantry.

Numbers are always problematic before the nineteenth century established the necessity of counting everything and everyone. However, these appear to be quite congruent with estimated sizes elsewhere in Europe.[10] They also correspond well to occasional peninsular evidence. Alfonso was criticized for bringing but 400 horse and 1,000 foot against Almería in 1147. The same source informs us that Count Ramon Berenguer furnished fifty-three horse there.[11] One looks very much like the ordinary royal army and the other the typical operational troop that a magnate might provide.

9. Medieval population figures are the matter of much dispute. In general, I believe that the approach of Josiah Cox Russell, *Medieval Regions and Their Cities* (Bloomington, 1972) and *Twelfth Century Studies* (New York, 1978), is among the more useful. I have supplemented his general framework with the more traditional method of estimating the occupied geographical area of walled towns north of the Duero. See Bernard F. Reilly, *The Kingdom of León-Castilla under King Alfonso VI, 1065–1109* (Princeton, 1988), pp. 151–60, for the conclusions that have been adjusted here for the intervening fifty years of development.

10. Philippe Contamine, *La guerre au Moyen Age* (Paris, 1980), pp. 118–40.

11. Caffaro, *De Captione Almerie et Tortuose*, ed. Antonio Ubieto Arteta (Valencia, 1973), pp. 27, 24.

The *Chronica Adefonsi Imperatoris* tells us that Alfonso VII assembled 700 horse in 1128 for the campaign about Almazán against the Aragonese.[12] In 1111 during the reign of Urraca Alfonso of Aragón disposed of 770 cavalry and 2,000 foot at the battle of Viadangos.[13] Forty years earlier Sancho II of Castilla led an army of 300 horse to dispossess his brother García of the latter's kingdom of Galicia and that number seemed unremarkable to the *Crónica Nájerense* in the latter twelfth century.[14] In 1129 a Leonese scouting party of fifty horse encountered an Almoravid army returning from a raid and, reinforced to 300, then gave battle with success.[15]

An army of the largest size, a royal expeditionary force into Andalucía, might number 2,000 mounted men and 1,500 foot. But even presuming such a number does not fully flesh out the logistical problem. Each soldier requires roughly a kilo or more of food per day and that meant that practically he could carry food for only ten days. He also required a liter of drinking water at the absolute minimum. If each mounted warrior were minimally supplied with four horses; for combat, for his assistants, and for baggage, that estimate alone produces livestock numbering 2,800 head, each of which needed fourteen kilos of fodder and thirty-two liters of water daily to remain effective.[16] Base requirements for such an expedition then were 3,500 kilos of food and 3,500 liters of water per day for the troops and 39,200 kilos of fodder and 89,600 liters of water for the livestock.

Such statistics determined the routes of advance and retreat. An army of that dimension and composition had to follow watercourses of some size and to move through terrain that could be grazed and systematically plundered for food. It could depart from them only for quite short periods of time before it began to deteriorate rapidly as a fighting force. The ordinary attrition

12. Antonio Maya Sánchez and Juan Gil, eds., *CAI*, in *Chronica Hispana Saeculi XII*, pp. 109–296 (Turnholt, 1990), p. 156.

13. Bernard F. Reilly, *The Kingdom of León-Castilla under Queen Urraca, 1109–1126* (Princeton, 1982), pp. 274–77.

14. Antonio Ubieto Arteta, ed. (Zaragoza, 1985), p. 110.

15. Ambrosio Huici Miranda, "Contribución al estudio de la dinastía almorávides: el gobierno de Tashfin ben Ali ben Yusuf en al-Andalus," in *Études d'orientalisme dédiés à la mémoire de Lévi-Provençal*, vol. 2 (Paris, 1962), pp. 607–8.

16. Only slowly have historians begun to come to grips with the basic logistics of warfare and the insight they can furnish as to the possibilities and probabilities of what are ordinarily badly reported campaigns. John W. Nesbit, "The Rate of March of Crusading Armies in Europe," *Traditio* 19 (1963): 167–81, was an early study. Bernard Bachrach, "The Angevin Strategy of Castle Building in the Reign of Fulk Nerra, 987–1040," *AHR* 88 (1983): 533–60, another. Albert C. Leighton, *Transport and Communication in Early Medieval Europe, A.D. 500–1100* (New York, 1972), has particular relevance. More recently the works of military historians have put more emphasis on the inescapable logistics. John Keegan, *A History of Warfare* (New York, 1994). Geoffrey Parker, *The Military Revolution* (Cambridge, 1988). Stephen Morillo, *Warfare under the Anglo-Norman Kings, 1066–1135* (Woodbridge, Great Britain, 1994).

among the men due to major sprains, broken bones, exhaustion, heatstroke, diarrhea, dysentery, and desertion were magnified rapidly if supplies failed. These brute necessities meant that the scouts for opposing forces knew where to look for the enemy. They must be in the vicinity of adequate streams and the larger villages.

But the army's needs were part of its appalling effectiveness. Without fighting a single battle or wielding a single weapon, the appetites of its men and livestock were a terrible engine of destruction in territory through which it passed. In an age when few farming populations lived far from the edge of hunger, the very passage of such a force during the growing or harvest seasons meant disaster. When the simple operations of its subsistence were augmented by a desire for spoil and a deliberate destruction of what could not be carried off, common to most armies operating in foreign territory especially when the native population is felt to be of alien character, the results spelled poverty, famine, and disease for the district for months and years after the army had moved off.

Such facts are spelled out graphically in the *Chronica Adefonsi Imperatoris*. Surely the passage of such armies, both Christian and Muslim, over the territories lying between the Tajo and Guadalquivir rivers for almost two centuries between the fall of Toledo in 1085 and the fall of Sevilla in 1248 was the most potent factor in the decline of both the area of cultivation and the gross population in that region from its height under the caliphate. On the other hand, in the north smaller armies, shorter distances and campaigning seasons, and some greater rapport even between enemies limited this destructive process materially.

In measuring this effect, we must keep in mind that the army required yet more support. While no regular provision could be made for needs so immense, by standards then current, as those of the livestock, no prudent commander relied simply on foraging to supply his men. Water carts, probably two-wheeled and accommodating a hogshead apiece, must have accompanied the army in such number as to furnish it drinking and cooking water for a minimum of three days. And since slowing the advance of the force to the fifteen kilometers daily possible for ox-drawn carts was unavoidable, surely more carts were found to transport wine and dry provisions. Yet more carts were essential for blacksmiths and their gear, for priests and theirs, for cooks and theirs, for the tents of the mighty, for the paraphenalia of the chancery, and of course for the wheelwrights and carpenters needed to repair those same carts, for they broke down with great regularity. All of these added yet more mouths, human and animal, to the daily requirements. We need to presume as well that the meat larder traveled with the army in herds of cattle and sheep and that these, too, had to be watered in all but the most dire circumstances. Finally, there would have been that miscellany of family, adventurers, vagrants, entrepreneurs, prostitutes, casual travelers, and thieves, that any army attracts even under the most difficult conditions.

For all but these last, the crown had to make provision. *Fossatera* paid by those who preferred to stay at home purchased the food and the carts to carry it, the animals to draw them, weapons for those who had nothing suitable, wine and beef and mutton to cheer them occasionally, and stipends for mercenary people such as cooks, carpenters, and blacksmiths. Advances may be presumed necessary for soldiers with special skills and perhaps a general distribution if the hazard or the unpopularity of the campaign advised it.[17]

In the time Alfonso VI, such costs were defrayed in good measure by *parias* paid earlier by the prospective victims. Great sums had been realized from the *taifa* princelings who had succeeded to the fallen caliphate but the subjection of Islamic Iberia by the North African Almoravids after 1090 had eliminated that source.[18] Only briefly, on their collapse after 1144, did new *taifas* appear from whom funds could be extorted by threat of attack and then be converted into the resources for new attacks. Most such *parias* went to the prince of Aragón-Barcelona.

Like all medieval campaigns, those of Alfonso VII were partially self-financing. They attracted warriors from all stations in life by their prospect of rich booty if successful. The crown, too, looked to such rewards when they were to be had although we have just two contemporary references to the royal *quinto*, or fifth, and one appears in a seriously flawed charter.[19] This voluntary participation reinforced the army but did not create one. Beyond specific revenues gleaned from *fossata* and *fossatera* then, the finance of military operations blends with the general problem of crown resources.

Second to military operations, the prerogative of the crown that touched his subjects most broadly was the regulation of the currency. If it ever had had a wide exercise, the period of a "natural" economy was definitely over. Some 2,000 documents reveal only seventeen transactions that record the exchange

---

17. Powers, *Society*, pp. 162–87, has a most instructive account of "Spoils and Compensations" even if drawn from the materials of a somewhat later period.

18. Reilly, *Alfonso VI*, pp. 210–13 especially, for early *parias*. Bernard F. Reilly, *The Contest of Christian and Muslim Spain, 1031–1157* (Cambridge, 1992), pp. 217–18, for the situation at mid-century. For the dismay of contemporary Muslim princes then and their offers to renew the *parias* see Maya Sánchez and Gil, *CAI*, pp. 166–69.

19. Other forms of military dues seem not to have been very important to judge by their infrequent appearance in the documents. *Anubda*, or castle guard, is mentioned in only fourteen royal charters and a full ten of those come from sources less than reliable. *Apellido*, the duty of response to a local attack, finds place in but eight with three of those unreliable. *Castillería*, contribution to the repair or upkeep of a castle, is cited but three times. Three references to the *lid campal* occur only in untrustworthy documents despite Powers, *Society*, p. 149.

of goods for goods. Moreover, thirteen of those examples are contained in the documents of two monasteries, San Vicente and Belmonte, in Asturias de Oviedo, a backward province.

In the royal diplomas the conservative tendency of the chancery is evident in the use of a classical and Carolingian terminology in the penal clauses. The gold libra comprises 154 (25 percent) of all such usages. The solidus is employed for another 17 percent, the silver mark 8 percent, the gold talent 1 percent, and the humble denarius another 1 percent. More revealing, however, is the employment of the term *morabetino* in a full 48 percent of such documents. The *morabetino* was a real gold coin minted in Andalucía or North Africa from Almoravid times. It is a strong indication of the increasing liquidity of the economy, especially when careful consideration reveals that rather better than two thirds come after 1145.

Whether or not the *morabetino* is being used as a money of account, the changing terminology reflects the economy at large. The Muslim coin never achieved a monopoly of usage in royal documents but its predominance after 1145 indicates the renewed flow of gold coins from the south into León-Castilla resulting from increasingly successful Christian military expeditions. Both as *parias* and as simple loot, Muslim wealth was effecting a major alteration in the northern economy and in the way in which wealth itself was being conceptualized. Even the chancery could not ignore such things entirely. In September of 1146 Alfonso VII had promised to pay the Genoese some 10,000 *morabetinos* within thirty days of the signing of the treaty for the Almería expedition. He also pledged the payment of yet another 10,000 the following Easter.

Private notaries prove to be still more conservative and classical than the chancery. Most of the notices derive from actual sales although penal clauses are far from unknown. The solidus was utilized in 289 (37 percent) of the 775 citations. The terminology also employed the gold libra (22 percent), the gold talent (4 percent), the silver mark (3 percent), and the denarius (3 percent). *Morabetinos* figured in 244 (32 percent).

The royal coinage consisted only of the billon penny, the denarius of a silver-copper alloy. Alfonso VII had inherited from his predecessors a network of mints, located in León, Sahagún, Palencia, Segovia, Toledo, Salamanca, Zamora, Oviedo, Lugo, and Santiago de Compostela, in which it was struck.[20] Alfonso had a sense of their utility for at Burgos and Nájera he either established or reformed mints. Burgos had a mint under Alfonso of Aragón

20. Except that the existence of a mint at Oviedo has since passed from speculation to an established fact and one at Salamanca has come to light, I find no reason to modify the conclusions that I first described twenty-two years ago. Reilly, *Urraca*, pp. 271–74.

and Alfonso VII's charter mentioning a mint came soon after its reconquest (D87). At Nájera we have but the mute testimony of a coin.[21]

The policy of the king was of a piece with that of his predecessors. The operation of the mint was entrusted to the bishop of the city. For such care the bishop was allotted some portion, at Burgos a tenth, of the royal profits from its operation. More or less routine reconfirmations of the possessions of an episcopal see such as those in 1126 to Salamanca, in 1132 and 1135 to Zamora, in 1135 to León, to Toledo in 1137, and to Palencia in 1146 demonstrate the same share (D39, 151, 215, 218, 287, 512).[22] On the other hand, the 1137 grant to Bishop Berenguer of Salamanca, former royal chancellor, allotted him a third (D301). More than simply a reward for a royal favorite, we should also see it as a special aid for a diocese that had been struggling since its refoundation about 1102, whose bishop until 1120 had usually been resident in Zamora, and whose occupancy since that time had been bitterly contested until the king installed Berenguer in 1135. In the latter year a third was awarded to Segovia and then reduced to a fourth a year later (D201, 247).

A precious charter to the bishop of Palencia in 1140 adds an important detail about the working of a mint and the relationship of bishop and king. Alfonso then altered the practice of his predecessors of making a gift of vestments to the bishop whenever the physical character of the coin was changed and stipulated henceforth a compensation of 500 *morabetinos* (D363). In this we may perhaps see the earliest recognition of that wider responsibility of the crown when altering the coinage of the realm which will later crystalize as the thirteenth-century practice of the *moneda forera*.[23]

Of course, the coinage of the crown was not the only currency in circulation. We have noted the ubiquity of the *morabetino*, if as a money of account, and some of these transactions must have employed the coin itself. The issue of Melgueil, the tiny bishopric on the south French coast below Montpellier, was specified twenty-two times in private documents as the real coin in which *morabetinos* were to be paid and in thirteen as that in which solidi

21. The coin is cited in Octavio Gil Farrés, *Historia de la moneda española*, 2nd ed. (Madrid, 1976), p. 322. This latter is the best current survey. Fernando Alvarez Burgos, Vicente Ramón Benedito, and Vicente Ramón Pérez, eds., *Catálogo general de la moneda medieval hispano-cristiana desde el siglo IX al XVI* (Madrid, 1980), pp. 8–15, illustrate a wide variety of these pennies from the reign of Fernando I through that of Alfonso VII. For our period one may supplement Gil Farrés with James J. Todesca, "The Monetary History of Castile-Leon (ca. 1100–1300) in Light of the Bourgey Hoard," *American Numismatic Society Museum Notes* 33 (1988): 129–203.

22. The routine treatment of the mint at Salamanca, coming at the very beginning of the reign, argues that it dates from the preceding reign although there is no other evidence for its prior existence.

23. Joseph F. O'Callaghan, *The Cortes of Castile-León, 1188–1350* (Philadelphia, 1989), pp. 133–35.

were to be rendered. Even Alfonso VII's promised 10,000 *morabetinos* to the Genoese in 1146 were stipulated to be the coin of Melgueil (D533).[24] No less than thirty private documents specify solidi are to be paid in the denarii of Aragonese Jaca.[25]

Another source of income visible in the documents was the *portaticum* or tax on travelers and goods. Its collection at key points of the realm was already fairly well organized.[26] Of Alfonso's charters, sixty-seven refer to it. Twenty-seven are grants of exemption. The remainder, however, refer to its collection at points where traffic entered the kingdom; Toledo and Talavera de la Reina in the south, Túy in the far west, Gozón and Oviedo in the north, and Logroño and Calahorra in the east. But the toll was organized internally as well, being levied at every major town and many of the smaller ones, river crossings, and mountain passes. The inference is that it was more a levy on local than on long-distance trade.

It is reasonably clear that the bishops were the crown officers primarily responsible for its collection. Surviving documents record royal grants of a tenth share to thirteen, of the regularly constituted seventeen, bishoprics. Six monasteries, at least, were also so empowered, and one document records a grant to an individual. Typically, the revenue from the toll was granted in the same document that bestowed a tenth as well of income from local royal property that might include mints, markets, baths, mills, saltworks, and even agricultural rents.

Nor were such grants necessarily limited to the episcopal city or its immediate environs. Those of Toledo included Talavera de la Reina in 1142, Madrid in 1145, and in 1147 Calatrava La Vieja (D442, 504, 545). Salamanca was confirmed in its own tolls in 1126, and in 1144 and 1149 those of Alba de Tormes (D39, 484, 621). Sigüenza had its share at home from 1124, but in 1138 the tolls of Medinaceli, Atienza, Almazán, Berlanga, and some lesser places were granted (D91, 320). Palencia held the usual tenth of tolls there in 1146, increased in 1154 to an unprecedented one-half share (D512, 820).

With one exception, the remaining bishoprics of the central *meseta*; Avila, Burgos, León, Osma, and Segovia are known to have held a share of

24. Peter Spufford, *Money and its Use in Medieval Europe* (Cambridge, 1988), pp. 191–92, for the coinage of the bishops of Maguelonne. If anything, he apppears to have understated its employment in Iberia.

25. Santiago Aguade Nieto, *De la sociedad arcaica a la sociedad campesina en la Asturias medieval* (Madrid, 1988), pp. 299–300, has called attention to the employ of the coins of Jaca and Melqueil in that northern province. Probably it was a phenomenon due to both the Compostela pilgrimage and small boat trade in the Bay of Biscay. See also, Jean Gautier-Dalché, "L'histoire monétaire de l'Espagne septentrionale et centrale du XI au XII siècle," *AEM* 6 (1969): 43–95.

26. Reilly, *Urraca*, pp. 270–71.

the *portaticum*. Coria, newly reclaimed from the Muslim in 1142, was given an exceptional one-third share (D437). Astorga alone seems to have lacked this form of royal largesse. No fewer than sixteen royal charters to Astorga survive, and only six other sees boast records of greater royal generosity. Yet even in 1131 when Alfonso confirmed to Astorga the freedoms and properties held since his grandfather's time, no mention of the toll appears.

This surprising omission may have a parallel in Galicia. There, only the tiny episcopate of Túy appears to have a share in the *portaticum* (D436). It does not appear in the twenty-four royal charters to Santiago de Compostela, in the dozen to Orense, the scant three of Mondoñedo, or the single charter to Lugo. Finally, there is no record of the toll in the four charters to Oviedo.

Although chance cannot be entirely ruled out, the coincidence makes one wonder if there were not, perhaps, some particular configuration of episcopal rights in these ancient dioceses of the realm that made the crown unwilling to concede them this additional privilege. In Asturias the king granted instead a tenth of the *portaticum* at Oviedo itself and a fifth of that at Gozón to the monastery of San Pelayo (D509, 548). In a document less than entirely reliable, Alfonso even granted a half share in the toll of Olloniego, probably at the old Roman bridge seven kilometers south of Oviedo, and another sixth share in that village proper to his former mistress, Guntroda Pérez, and the monastery of Vega that she then headed (D837). A tenth share both at Logroño on the bridge over the Ebro and at Nájera itself was let to the monastery of Santa María la Real and to its mother house at Cluny in 1135 (D229, 602, 607). Twenty years later, the *infante*, Sancho, let a tenth share of the toll at Arnedo, fifteen kilometers southwest of Calahorra, to the bishop of the latter city (D892). In 1136 the bishop of Osma had been given a tenth at San Esteban de Gormaz (D240).

In the heartland of the realm, tolls were sometimes let to monasteries. In 1140 San Salvador at Villacete southeast of León claimed the toll at Bustillo del Páramo, on the latter river twenty-five kilometers southwest of the royal city (D370). In 1136 Sahagún was given the *portaticum* and the village of Villalil and in 1152 that monastery had possessed a share of the tolls in the village of Sahagún from the time of Alfonso VI (D245, 775). The only mention of tolls in a private diploma cites the archbishop of Toledo freely alienating part of his share to his canons (D312).

Related to the *portaticum* was the *mercatum*, or market tax. Unfortunately, the documents do not yield a very full picture of the levy or its importance. There are fairly frequent references to markets, but it is clear in only four royal charters that a tax is involved. Two refer to Burgos, and a tenth of the impost was granted to its bishop together with the grant of a mint in 1128. In 1136 such an impost was granted to the abbot of Sahagún along with the village of Villalil, in which the market was held, and the *portaticum* there as well. Finally, in 1140 a tenth of the *mercatum* along with other royal income in his town was granted to the bishop of Calahorra (D396).

Two other notices of similar royal actions may properly be joined with these four. In 1124 Alfonso had already bestowed a tenth of the *alcabala* of Sigüenza on its bishop and of that of Talavera de la Reina on the archbishop of Toledo. Both grants were part of the bestowal of the *portaticum*. The *alcabala* can be taken as the equivalent of the *mercatum* in those parts of the realm where Arabic was a major language. Again the *alcabala* can be so understood when in 1138 the archbishop of Toledo granted half of his share at Talavera to the endowment of his canons.[27] In the only other clear reference to a market tax, an abbot of Sahagún agreed in 1150 that the levy would be held by the cellarer of the monastery, who would annually, on the Feast of the Circumcision, pay the abbot fifty *aurii* and another ten to the senior monks for the privilege.[28]

The last in what may be termed "public levies" is the *petitum* or grant-in-aid. It has been argued that in the latter half of the twelfth century the strain placed on royal finances by the renewed *reconquista* and the expansion of the Almohad North African empire into Andalucía resulted in the genesis of this special form of fund-raising which would have a long subsequent history.[29] The problem here is that such a levy would have overlapped with the extant, healthy imposts of the *fossata* and *fossatera*. A possible distinction might be that the latter were levies on individuals, while the *petitum* was directed toward corporate entities such as towns and clergy.

At any rate, evidence for such a development during the reign of Alfonso VII is slim. Granted, that is always true of origins. But interpretation is compounded by the documentary prevalence of such terms as *pectum* and *posta*, which refer to seignorial levies, in an age in which orthography is irregular and documentary transmission variable. One must allow both for scribal

27. 1138. Part pub. Francisco J. Hernández, *Los cartularios de Toledo* (Madrid, 1985), pp. 43–44.

28. 1150. Pub. José Antonio Fernández Flórez, ed., *Colección diplomática del monasterio de Sahagún, 1110–1199*, vol. 4 (León, 1991), pp. 228–29.

29. Luis G. de Valdeavellano, *Historia de las instituciones españolas* (Madrid, 1968), p. 610. For general reference this work remains the standard resource. Also Claudio Sánchez Albornoz, "Notas para el estudio del 'Petitum,'" in *Homenaje a Don Ramón Carande*, vol. 2 (Madrid, 1963), pp. 383–418. Reprinted in *Viejos y nuevos estudios sobre las instituciones medievales españolas*, vol. 2 (Madrid, 1976), pp. 929–967. Using slightly less evidence the author puts the case for its emergence rather more strongly than I should.

confusion and for subsequent "improvement" of the document. Possible references to the *petitum* then are few. The earliest is in a royal charter to the Toledan monastery of San Servando in 1136, which confirmed its exemption from a variety of imposts including "nec pro appetitu" (D239). In the same year Alfonso granted an exemption to the clergy of Salamanca from, among other levies, "omni offertione sive petitione" (D249). In 1149 there is a grant to Salamanca of a tenth share in royal income there, including "de peticionibus" (D621). Finally, an exemption of 1153 to the Asturian monastery of Corias includes "neque dare tributum vel petitum" (D801). Based on these, the most adventurous conclusion would be that certain traces of a new terminology for the old *fossatera* were beginning to appear. Such changes in terminology not infrequently signal an emerging but still inchoate new conceptualization of a former practice.[30]

A special form of income that falls somewhere between a public and a private impost was that derived from the Jewish and Muslim communities. In a kingdom officially Christian, practitioners of other faiths were aliens by definition, although their presence was ordinarily tolerated and unofficially valued. Some Jewish communities dated to Roman times. A Muslim population in the form of slaves began to grow from almost the very inception of Christian realms, dependent on warfare for their existence. But the extraordinarily successful aggression of León-Castilla after 1050 brought new communities of free Muslims and Jews into the realm. The relations with such peoples were regulated by royal *fueros* usually issued on or soon after the conquest.[31]

Both communities preserved the right to the public practice of their faith, to live in accord with their own religious and customary law, and to their property and their lives at the price of becoming royal wards. In return, free adult males and their households were subject to a capitation tax, collected for the crown ordinarily by their respective Jewish or Muslim leaders. The form of this revenue was already traditional, but its substance must have been growing very rapidly. Nevertheless, I have found but one documentary

30. Hilda Grassotti, "Sobre una concesión de Alfonso VII a la iglesia salmantina," *CHE* 49–50 (1969): 331, argued that just such a shift of conceptualization was illustrated in the diploma of April 12, 1136.

31. The negotiations at Toledo on its fall in 1085 represent a classic case. For a quick review, see Reilly, *Alfonso VI*, pp. 171–72. For more comprehensive treatment, see Pilar León Tello, *Judios de Toledo*, vol. 1 (Madrid, 1979), Justiniano Rodríguez Fernández, *Las juderías de la provincia de León* (León, 1976), or Yitzak Baer, *Historia de los judios en la España cristiana*, trans. José Luis Lacave (Madrid, 1981) is a much updated and annotated edition of the classic Yitzak Baer, *Die Juden im Christiliche Spanien*, vol. 1 (Berlin, 1929). The Muslim communities are less well served. A series of studies, James M. Powell, ed., *Muslims under Latin Rule, 1100–1300* (Princeton, 1990), constitutes a start on what needs to be done.

reference to it. In 1144 the king granted to the bishop of Avila a tenth of that levy there that "the Jews annually render to the crown" (D486). The alienation of this income was evidently quite unusual and, since ordinary records of its payment would have been kept within the subject communities, the paucity of evidence is perhaps not startling. Nevertheless it makes assessment of its relative value impossible.

Income from the administration of justice must have been more important than most levies. The exemptions in hundreds of charters illustrate its ordinary enforcement and collection by *merinos* and *sayones* even while it is being given away. The penal clauses of virtually all royal charters highlight the expectation that revenue will result from the enforcement of the law. Those clauses often allot a portion of fines for infringement to the beneficiary. Grants of more than simple property often indicate that the grantee, usually a bishop, is entitled to a tenth of the royal income from justice. Probably it was also the ordinary remuneration for agents acting as justiciars on the dynastic lands. In this respect the latter arrangement would have been largely indistinguishable from tax farming and would have precluded the need for a royal officialdom to oversee it.

Finally, there is a scattering of miscellaneous incomes that appear even less prominently. Saltworks and even mines crop up occasionally (D320).[32] The context infrequently permits a judgment of whether they are simply dynastic property let out or whether they are private property, but subject to the royal taxing power after the precedent of Roman law and practice.

For none of these revenues of the crown can we form an estimate of the quantitative returns. It is impractical to attempt to gauge even the proportion of the royal income they furnished, as against that of dynastic lands proper. One suspects that, except for the specifically military levies of *fossata* and *fossatera*, the income of the royal estates furnished the bulk of the ordinary income. Further, we cannot go. Nor is it possible to gauge the income, in kind and coin, derived from the fisc lands. Their extent remains a mystery but they were in no danger of exhaustion. The bulk of royal documents preserved are acts of their alienation and the annual rate of issue of such records increased sixfold between the reigns of Fernando I and Alfonso VII. Still, this speaks as much to the rate of documentary survival as to any putative deple-

---

32. Reyna Pastor de Togneri, "La sal en Castilla y León," *CHE* 37–38 (1963): 70–72, has argued that Alfonso VII introduced a new policy regarding the revenue from saltworks. I find the argument exaggerated. It also relied on the so-called *Ordenamiento de Nájera* which her mentor, Sánchez-Albornoz, believed he had proved to have been redacted during the reign of Alfonso VII.

tion of fisc. Since custom provided that all land conquered from the Muslims passed into it accretions likely proceeded much faster than dispersals in an age of great conquests.

On the other hand, it is clear that conquered Muslims, Mozarabs, and Jews retained much of their lands unless they chose to desert them and flee. Such deserted lands automatically fell to the crown but only began to produce revenue when they were repopulated and the latter most often involved their alienation to bishops, abbots, magnates, and townsmen, who had a particular interest in one or the other region.

The reconquests from Aragón in the northeast were another matter entirely. The Christian populations of Castilla La Vieja and the Rioja reclaimed in 1127 and 1135 could not be routinely despoiled unless actively engaged in support of Aragón. Even then, individuals might forfeit their lands but, as in the case of the internal rebels of 1130, other members of the family soon successfully asserted their right to them.

The survey already done in connection with the examination of the *infantaticum*, the countship, tenancy, and the *merino*, illustrate where the major blocs of crown lands were located. They continued to be clustered in the same regions as they had been for the past century.[33] They were concentrated above all in the territory of León from the Cantabrians south to the Duero and from the Pisuerga River in the east up into the mountains of the Bierzo in the west. Asturias de Oviedo furnished a lesser group but one surely augmented after the fall Gonzalo Peláez in the 1130s and the reclamation of former royal estates. The collapse of Aragón in 1134 allowed the retrieval of royal lands between the Pisuerga and the Ebro Rivers, but the thinness of royal *merinos* and tenants there suggests an incomplete one. There were royal estates in Galicia, of course, but the lack of significant numbers of identifiable royal *merinos* indicates their relative paucity. Above all, the same deficiency in the new conquests to the south of the Duero illustrates the brute fact that royal lands became exploitable only as repopulation proceeded, under largely nonroyal direction, a process that continued well into the next century.

Royal estates provided all of the ordinary seignorial revenues to their master. Proportions of produce from grains to wines and oil, livestock for consumption and transportation, rents from mills, ovens, winepress, and baths, and labor to maintain and construct local royal residences, facilities, and roads, all were the due of ownership. The king was an ordinary *señor* in

33. For a brief survey of their distribution in the preceding reign see Reilly, *Urraca*, pp. 260–65.

that sense. But the bulk of the charters indicate the extent to which he was an extraordinary proprietor who could purchase loyalty and service out of the vastness of his property. This partial devolution of the dynastic patrimony may properly be regarded as the condition of its successful management and that of the kingdom itself.

The general pattern of that management can be discerned in the proportional distribution of charters by grantee. Of approximately 1,000 documents, roughly two thirds were grants to religious institutions, slightly more than a quarter to various individuals, and the remainder to groups of townsmen. These figures are skewed somewhat, of course, for the first and third of these were tenacious of their privileges but individuals were generally less likely to preserve their diplomas. Indeed the latter come to us, ordinarily, because the property concerned subsequently passed to a religious group. Notwithstanding, the figures highlight the role of church and urban elites in the management of the kingdom.

A reminder that we are considering the second quarter of the twelfth century lies in the fact that slightly more than half of the ecclesiastical grants went to monasteries. The monastery of Sahagún was recipient of no fewer than twenty grants, more than all but five of the archbishoprics and bishoprics of the realm. Of the latter, Santiago de Compostela preserves twenty-four diplomas, Toledo twenty, Segovia twenty-five, Zamora twenty-four, and Sigüenza twenty-one.

The democratic, egalitarian, and secular proclivities of the past century have accustomed moderns to view such royal largesse as frivolous at best and destructive of the power of the crown at worst. Quite probably, the opposite is true. Given the physical and social constraints of the age, such devolution of control provided oversight and direction at the local level strictly impossible for the crown itself. Moreover, it produced additional resources for the crown by providing a path along which a portion of the primary production that it oversaw and encouraged found its way into royal hands. The clearest instance of this is the church. Bishops particularly were regularly endowed with tenths of the mints, tolls, justice, and market taxes in their locales but also with that from baths, ovens, mills, and agricultural dues as well. Now it is possible to see such acts as simply reducing the royal revenues, but it is also possible to see them as a long-term farm, which makes bishops collectors of those very revenues on behalf of the crown. If so, that would help to explain the near absence of a royal administrative machinery. The need was obviated by the ability of the church to provide an extant and alternative network. If the documents do not make explicit such a working relationship, they do lend themselves to such an interpretation, and occasionally we do see bishops acting as if they had such responsibilities.

Unfortunately we do not possess episcopal *gestas* from the period other than the *Historia Compostellana*.[34] The relationship between bishop and king displayed in that text was in some degree exceptional since Archbishop Diego Gelmírez had once been Alfonso's guardian and tutor and Santiago de Compostela itself was unique among the churches of Iberia. Nonetheless, that shrine-see and its ambitious prelates were subject to the vicissitudes then attendant on the relationship between bishop and crown and, indeed, some factors may be illustrated better as its history throws them into high relief. From the outset Alfonso made financial demands on the see of the Apostle. These are presented by the author of the *Historia*, even as he complains bitterly of them, as inspired by the king's military necessities on the Portuguese border. The archbishop finally gave way in 1127 after long and hard bargaining and furnished the king with 1,000 silver marks. During the course of negotiations, Alfonso consulted regularly with the enemies of the archbishop within the cathedral chapter and their allies in the city who made alternative offers for his support, invoked the mediation between himself and the archbishop of Count Fernando Pérez de Traba, promised the eventual burial both of himself and his sister Sancha at Compostela, pledged a variety of properties, and the royal chaplaincy and chancery to the see, and issued a charter confirming the right of the canons to the free election of their archbishop, forswearing the right of the crown to administer its properties during a vacancy.[35]

Archbishop Diego emerged fairly well from this confrontation. But the matter was hardly concluded. Enemies of Gelmírez continued dissatisfied, offering the king the opportunity to bring more pressure. The otherwise obscure affair of Chancellor Bernard, canon of the Compostela, who passed into the royal court as a result of those negotiations and his subsequent falling-out with the archbishop should be understood in this context. The archbishop had had to make concessions to his chapter, and Bernard may have been its leader. The choice of the latter as chancellor kept the king in touch with the disaffected party at Compostela. While Bernard's departure from Compos-

---

34. Although some portions at least of a vita of Archbishop Bernard of Toledo (1086–1125) survive and the entire text may eventually be found among the imperfectly known manuscripts of the cathedral chapter there. See Bernard F. Reilly, "Rodrigo Giménez de Rada's Portrait of Alfonso VI of León-Castile in the 'De Rebus Hispaniae': Historical Methodology in the Thirteenth Century," in *Estudios en Homenaje a Don Claudio Sánchez Albornoz en sus 90 años*, vol. 3 (Buenos Aires, 1985), pp. 87–97.

35. Emma Falque Rey, ed., *HC* (Turnholt, 1988), pp. 395–418. The author devotes the final ten chapters of Book Two of the work to these negotiations and their resolution.

tela was initially welcome to Diego, the canon's proximity to the crown was bound to become intolerable.

The king reopened negotiations in 1129. In secret meeting, his major-domo, Rodrigo Vermúdez, and his sometime *merino* at León, Albertino, extracted from the prelate a promise to pay the crown 100 silver marks annually, although in the future, when his finances should have improved, the king promised to repay the entire sum.[36]

Alarmed by his continuing vulnerability, Gelmírez made efforts to placate his cathedral chapter. Nevertheless, his enemies continued to plot with Chancellor Bernard. Finally the archbishop acted to remove him from the chancellorship in 1133, but Alfonso supported Bernard, again negotiating with the prelate through the invaluable Albertino and the Galician magnate, Fernando Yáñez. But Gelmírez prevailed and Bernard had to resign his dignities. Alfonso now turned on his former chancellor and imprisoned him and despoiled him of his possessions. Doubtless some of these properties held from the see, for the archbishop protested violently and there were disturbances in the city. The archbishop now enlisted the aid of Rome and in a meeting in the city of León with the Cardinal-legate Guido in 1134 the king agreed that Bernard should be freed and his property returned.[37] However the momentary triumph was expensive. Not only was Bernard not restored to the royal chancellorship but that dignity passed to the archrival of Compostela in the peninsular church, Toledo. Its former canon, Berenguer, assumed that post. Worse, within another year Alfonso had managed the election of Berenguer to the see of Salamanca, a suffragan of Compostela.

Nor was the king finished in his pursuit of the wealth of the Galician see. Alfonso conspired with the anti-Gelmírez faction at Compostela who now promised him some 3,000 silver marks if he would assist in the deposition of the archbishop. The king agreed and sought out the Cardinal-legate Guido for advice as to how to bring Rome to countenance the action. A delegation was despatched to Italy but the conspirators in Compostela lost control of their own followers, who rose against the elderly prelate in August 1136, pursued him into the cathedral itself, and attempted unsuccessfully to kill him there. That too-precipitate action was hastily disavowed by all parties. At the Council of Burgos in the fall of 1136 Gelmírez was received with honor and his attackers condemned. The archbishop had managed to present his own case at Rome and at Cluny and both powers wrote in his support. Of course,

36. Ibid., pp. 438–39.
37. Ibid., pp. 489–94.

he was vindicated, but Gelmírez still felt it necessary to pledge to the crown an annual payment of 400 silver marks for the support of its armies and to make, in addition, a gift of 300 *morabetinos* to the legate.[38]

Nor was the archbishop permanently free from the pressure of the king's search for funds. In a fit of generosity following his triumph over Portugal in 1137, the Leonese visited Compostela and remitted the annual subsidy. He also plundered the goods of the prelate's enemies. But by the following summer, Alfonso had regretted his generosity and resumed his demands. Our exasperated author compares him to Crassus, the legendary greedy Roman. The archbishop apparently considered a confrontation, even the excommunication of Alfonso, his own exile, and an appeal to Rome. In the end, he decided that another payment of 300 silver marks was preferable. The story ends here because the death of the elderly prelate followed in early 1140 and his biographer broke off his account.[39]

One can regard this tale as simply a discrete set of events. Alfonso needed funds and the see of Santiago was uniquely wealthy. Its victimization therefore was unique. There is no record of demand for funds from any other episcopal see. But there is no such record of their contemporary history either. More, if the see of Compostela was singularly wealthy, it was also singularly positioned to resist royal initiatives. The church of Saint James was internationally famous and influential. Archbishop Gelmírez was the senior prelate of the peninsula and had been a papal legate, an advisor of the crown, and the young king's guardian and tutor. If the prelate had his enemies the king in 1127, it must be remembered, was scarcely twenty-two and soon would be forced to defend his marriage from the charge of consanguinity, until 1134 faced the formidable Alfonso of Aragón as an active foe, was beset by internal revolt of the house of Lara and of Gonzalo Peláez of Asturias, and had to repel attacks from both Portugal and Navarra.

In other words, was Alfonso VII in his need simply choosing a target of opportunity or had the archbishop opted to challenge his young sovereign by refusing the latter the customary royal due? It is entirely possible that the king was merely reasserting, or perhaps defending, the crown's right to an annual money payment from each of the realm's bishoprics and abbeys in support of the royal army. The see of Santiago de Compostela became the object of crown attention not gratuitously or incidentally but because it had chosen to lead a clerical opposition and was uniquely fitted for that role. If Gelmírez

38. Ibid., pp. 504–16.
39. Ibid., pp. 519–29.

could be reduced to obedience no other prelate or abbot could hope to resist. The much maligned *tercias reales* of the thirteenth century, officially formulated with papal permission in 1236 in preparation for the siege of Muslim Sevilla, may have had longer precedent than heretofore supposed.[40]

Whether or not major clerical institutions had such an annual financial obligation to the crown, it is clear that bishops at least were responsible for supplying finances and troops to a campaign when requested. In 1127 and again in 1137 the *Historia Compostellana* describes royal requests that Archbishop Diego Gelmírez mobilize the militia of the city and the barons of Galicia. In 1127 that prelate himself accompanied the king on campaign. This was not a novel practice, for our source described that process during the civil wars of Urraca's reign and includes royal letters of summons in its text.[41]

Less direct testimony indicates that Alfonso expected, as did every contemporary western European monarch, that his bishops would both furnish him troops for and accompany him to his wars. Seven campaigns south of the Duero River between 1139 and 1157 furnish royal diplomas whose confirmation lists indicate some of those present. There were seven bishops at the siege of Oreja in 1139, another seven at the siege of Coria in 1142, ten at Córdoba in 1146, again seven at Almería in 1147, but two at Córdoba in 1150, perhaps only one at Jaén in 1152, and seven at Almería in 1157. Two further aspects are worthy of notice. First, there is a high degree of correlation between the number of bishops present and the success of the royal offensive. Second, the bishops present usually came from those sees closest to the theater of operations. In southern campaigns the archbishop of Toledo and the bishops of Segovia and Palencia were present in five of the seven, the bishop of Osma at four, and the bishops of Avila and Sigüenza at three. At the siege of Córdoba in 1146 Bishop Pedro Domínguez of Burgos met his death, and contemporaries did not find that remarkable.

For the campaigns in Galicia in 1127, 1137, and 1141, the evidence holds no surprises. Logistics dictated that wars in that far province be fought largely with local troops. In 1127 there is no documentary evidence for an episcopal contingent, although we know from the *Historia Compostellana* that Gelmírez was there. At the great victory over Afonso Henriques in 1137 the Galician bishops of Lugo, Túy, and Orense, were joined by those of Burgos, Palencia, and Segovia. At Alfonso VII's resounding defeat in 1141 only those three Galician bishops appear.

---

40. O'Callaghan, *Cortes*, pp. 132–33.
41. Reilly, *Urraca*, pp. 271–72, for an analysis of the obligation.

For the eastern frontier the data is similar. Against Aragón in 1127 at
Támara three bishops appear, at the siege of Castrojeriz in 1131 none. In the
shows of strength in the Rioja in 1134 and 1135, there are three in the first and
four in the second. Only in 1137 when his campaign against Navarra reduced
that principality to permanent subordinate status did the Leonese monarch
muster as many as nine bishops in the episcopal contingent. Bishoprics of the
area, Burgos, Osma, and Calahorra were represented in three of the five instances and were primarily summoned.

Analysis of the evidence for the military obligation of the counts produces analogous results. Proportionally, given that their total numbers are
roughly but half that of the total number of bishops, they are better represented, averaging a little better than five over the same campaigns. One might
also speculate that their resources were thinner than those of the bishops, for
at places such as Córdoba in 1150 and Jaén in 1152, where they were present in
good numbers and the bishops almost not at all, the royal army was notably
unsuccessful.

In Galicia, the counts serving tend to be of that region. Aside from that,
however, the counts seem to have been more mobile. Like the great crown
tenants generally, they appear available to the king no matter where the campaign is to be waged. By the last two decades of the reign, most of them, like
the Galicians Count Fernando Pérez and the magnate Fernando Yáñez, the
Lara Count Manrique and his brother Nuño Pérez, and, of course, the Catalan Counts Armengol of Urgel and Pons de Cabrera, if not quite mercenaries
do seem to have become something on the order of professional soldiers
rather than warrior nobles.

A question remains to be asked. By the fifth decade of the twelfth century the kingdom of León-Castilla had developed a structure more complex
than that of a dynastic monarchy surviving on the resources of the family fisc,
military charisma, and religious sanction. The management of dynastic lands
was beginning to be organized beyond the individual estate and its *merino* on
the somewhat halting basis of the *infantaticum* and the *merino maior*. Beyond
the fisc itself, a variety of functions and revenues were being invested in the
bishops and a handful of great abbots of the realm who could be summoned
to court, to war, and very probably to an accounting for the royal portion
of those revenues. While the outlines of the tenancy are less clear, it appears
that something of the same sort was occurring with that institution and its
associated great magnates. To ask then whether the conceptual framework
supporting this development was feudal is perfectly proper. Given the course
of the historiography of the peninsula in our own century, it is unavoidable.

For Spanish medievalists the existence or character of Iberian feudalism has been the battlefield on which the argument for the survival of peninsular practices and institutions against those imported from beyond the Pyrenees has been fought. Even if that prickly particularism no longer concerns us its fruits have been important. Following the lead of her *magister* Sánchez-Albornoz, Hilda Grassotti devoted a lifetime to the painstaking chronicling of feudal terminology in the documentary record of León-Castilla and the conclusions that can be drawn from it.[42] We can hardly do better than to follow the same methodology for the more restricted period of Alfonso VII for which her sources were scant.

The central term "vassal" is found in the dating formula of royal charters after 1148, where it is routinely applied to the count of Barcelona and king of Navarra and sometimes to Muslim princes such as Saif al-Dawla, ibn Gāniya, and ibn Mardanish. The king of Portugal is never so listed. The *Chronica Adefonsi Imperatoris* lists magnates of the south of France, including Count Alfonso of Toulouse and Count William of Montpellier, as vassals. About the same time, Count Latro of Alava, Lop Díaz of Haro, and Pedro Taresa of Aragón all did homage to Alfonso VII.[43]

At a less exalted level, some dozen royal grants are to individuals who are called "meo fideli vassallo." The earliest was awarded to Count Lop Díaz in 1136 and the latest to Count Pons de Cabrera in 1153 (D243, 808). In every one the property is conveyed in hereditary right. In nine some form of the phrase "pro servitio" is employed to justify the award. Nevertheless the latter phrase is not limited to individuals explicitly designated "vassal." It appears no fewer than ninety-nine times in the royal charters.[44]

Analagous terms are employed in a handful of charters. Twice in the 1150s, an individual is styled simply "meo fideli," and once the phrase "pro servitio" appears, while in both the property is conveyed specifically in hereditary right (D702, 779). In the treaty of July 4, 1137, with Afonso Henriques the latter is styled "amicus eius et fidelis." Finally, in a charter of 1130 the bishop of Palencia is called "fidelissimo meo" in a grant in hereditary right (D118). In 1147 Pelayo Calvo is styled "meo homini" in a grant "pro servitio" and in hereditary right (D568). In 1149 Vela Gutiérrez is called "militi meo" in another grant "pro servitio" and in hereditary right (D618).

---

42. *Las instituciones feudo-vasalláticas en León y Castilla*, 2 vols. (Spoleto, 1969). This work resumed a host of her earlier studies.

43. Hilda Grassotti, "Homenaje de García Ramírez a Alfonso VII," *CHE* 37–38 (1963): 63–66.

44. For the phrase in a wider context, Grassotti, *Instituciones*, 2:483–552.

Of precarial tenures the documents say just as little and then they are seemingly never joined to a person designated precisely as a vassal. The traditional term, *prestimoniam*, appears but twice in reliable royal documents. In 1136 *Infanta* Elvira employed it in a grant to the canons of León, and in 1150 her brother Alfonso used the term in another to one John Achui. Both documents have been called originals, but in neither is the precarial element well defined (D259, 669). Two related designations, *benfectoria* and *behetría*, never appear in any reliable royal document.

The more contemporary term *honor* is employed in a dozen royal documents but not consistently in the precarial sense. The "miles" Vela Gutiérrez mentioned just above was awarded his hereditary property "cum toto eius honore!" Most often, the term seems almost a synonym for "hereditate," although it may be that it designated a precarial jurisdiction joined to hereditary real property. A survey of private diplomas yields similar results. Not surprisingly, given the non-noble status of most of the participants, the term *vassus* appears but twice and the term *fideles* just once in the 1,000 documents. That is just sufficient to illustrate that vassalage was not exclusively a royal relationship. *Prestimoniam* is a little bit more visible with eighteen appearances. In at least seven of these, the text is sufficiently clear to demonstrate that it is a precarial tenure that is meant. *Beneficium* appears just twice, and each time it is clear that a precarial tenure is meant. *Behetría* appears four times, always as precarial tenure.

From this broad canvas it is clear that a familiarity with the terminology ordinarily designated as feudal exists. It even becomes slightly more prevalent in the 1140s and 1150s. Nonetheless, the evidence is inadequate to predicate a society in which real property is held predominantly in precarial tenure. In fact, the opposite seems to be true.

Only at the very highest level is there clear evidence that conditional tenure held as the result of *homage* exists. For example, in 1137 Afonso Henriques pledges that he will defend Alfonso VII against all enemies, including his own *hominibus*, that if he fails to do so he will return the *honorem* held, and that if he fails in this *iuramentum* he will become a perjurer and a traitor (D293).[45] In 1140 the count of Barcelona agreed to do such homage to Alfonso VII, for the lands to be taken from García Ramírez, as Sancho Ramí-

45. That *honor* is not identified. Curiously a document of *Infanta* Sancha (D461) cites the Portuguese as tenant of Astorga and Fernando Captivo and Pelayo Captivo as undertenants. Another royal document (D567) cites García Ramírez of Navarra as tenant of territory in that western district. It may be that symbolic transfer of real property not previously held by the vassal as independent prince was necessary to the full integrity of the feudal contract.

rez I and Pedro I of Aragón had done for the same territories to Alfonso VII's grandfather (D371).[46] Again in 1151 at Tudején, the count of Barcelona agreed to do such homage to Alfonso VII, for the lands now projected to be taken from Sancho VI of Navarra. This time, given the death of the Alfonso VII, the count also agrees that he will hold his portion of Navarra and the kingdom of Aragón, all that *honorem*, from *Infante* Sancho and, given the latter's death, from *Infante* Fernando (D683). Of course, we do not have the original text of any of these documents, but they do not give evidence of having been reworked later.

Reliable documents introduce us to a world where the heir to the throne, Sancho, was knighted in 1152 and subsequently entrusted with an appanage (D731). In 1153 Sancho VI of Navarra was knighted by Alfonso VII, signed a treaty with him whose text we lack, and then married his daughter (D788). At Christmas in 1155 the king knighted *Infante* Fernando, who would hold an appanage in the west (D918). At the marriage of García Ramírez of Navarra to Urraca of León in 1144, the *Chronica Adefonsi Imperatoris* describes what can hardly be seen as other than a tournament.[47]

In such a world it would be natural to assume that lesser folk, bishops, counts, and tenants generally, held their "honors" or jurisdictions from the crown by reason of homage, that these were fiefs in the feudal sense. The difficulty with such an assumption is that there is no documentary proof of it. No surviving text records the oath for such a transaction.[48]

Nevertheless, it is quite clear that the king could revoke tenancies. Some of these actions are vividly described in the *Chronica Adefonsi Imperatoris* in the cases of Pedro Díaz del Valle, Count Pedro de Lara, and Count Rodrigo de Lara. Less spectacular and likely less punitive revocations are implicit in the changing holders of tenancies described above. The abilities of the king in this regard extended even to the church as the former incumbents of the bishoprics of León, Salamanca, and Oviedo and the abbot of Samos could testify in 1130. What is presently impossible to resolve is the legal basis on which such acts rested. In the first, perhaps simply the traditional public law of treason was invoked. In the second, the ordinary dynastic prerogative of

46. Antonio Ubieto Arteta, "Navarra-Aragón y la idea imperial de Alfonso VII de Castilla," *EEMCA* 6 (1956): 76–82, found two different kinds of feudalism, one before and the other subsequent to Alfonso's coronation as emperor in May 1135. I regard his analysis as more subtle than the documents and events upon which he bases it.

47. Maya Sánchez and Gil, *CAI*, pp. 191–94.

48. Ironically the oath of Archbishop Maurice of Braga to the then Bishop Gelmírez of Compostela by which the former agrees to hold half of the possessions of Compostela in northern Portugal "in prestimonium sive feudum" survives. Falque Rey, *HC*, p. 128.

the crown over the realm may have sufficed. In the third, quite possibly some convenient canon was plead or reinterpreted. Given the lack typical in the age of formal legal distinctions, that such actions were conceived, at least in part, in feudal terms is quite probable. We simply do not know.[49]

But so long as he had control, irrespective of its justification, over the secular and clerical tenancies of the realm, Alfonso possessed the sinews of war. Under whatever guise, the major tenants of the kingdom were held responsible for fleshing out the royal army and, with a few exceptions, clearly did so. The alienation of resources was a means of their effective management even if it entailed a partial loss of direct revenue. With that in mind, it is unnecessary to posit any extraordinary and developing crisis in royal finance. The spread of feudal ideas, without a consequent development of precarial tenure, therefore did not deprive the crown of military services because it could not reward them in coin. The argument for the prevalence already of the later institution of *las soldadas* rests on no solid contemporary evidence. To cite sources that say that the king had to raise money to compensate his troops does not speak to the instrumentality by which that was accomplished.[50]

That it was accomplished is written in the achievements of the reign. While it is obvious that Alfonso VII did not realize, permanently, that annexation of La Mancha, Almería, and eastern Andalucía he doubtless planned, it is misleading to write the history of the reign simply in those terms. Perhaps it would have been beyond the strength of any twelfth-century kingdom to project its power over such distance and over so largely hostile a population permanently. It certainly proved impossible when that population found an ally in a vibrant new North African empire. The resources of León-Castilla did not so much fail, as they were simply overmatched.

At the same time, behind that shield of frontier warfare, the hold of the kingdom on the lands between the Duero and the Guadarramas was being consolidated. There, and in the valley of the Tajo in Castilla La Nueva between the Guadarramas and the mountains of Toledo, a new society was taking root in farms and villages, monasteries, and towns. It was a world

49. Appeals to the text of the *Fuero Juzgo*, or *Liber Judiciorum*, on the part of earlier historians are touching acts of faith where the twelfth century is concerned. I have not found in trustworthy royal or private documents of the reign a single reference to it. By way of contrast Roger Collins, "Sicut Lex Gothorum continet," *EHR* 100 (1985): 489–512, has illustrated the extent to which legal practice still incorporated the procedures of the Visigothic code in the ninth and tenth centuries. Given the conservatism of ordinary judicial practice it is likely as well that those practices did not change greatly, although their original source became more and more obscured in the conciousness of succeeding ages.

50. Grassotti, *Instituciones*, 2:723–895.

that had barely more than a skeletal existence at the beginning of the reign.[51] When that new community matured, it would furnish more than adequate power to accomplish not only what Alfonso VII had earlier had in mind but also that of which he may scarcely have dreamed.

51. The essential guides to the gradual nature of the process are to be found in Angel Barrios García, *Estructuras agrarias y de poder en Castilla. El ejemplo de Avila, 1085–1320* (Salamanca, 1983), and Julio González, *Repoblación de Castilla la Nueva*, 2 vols. (Madrid, 1973).

9

The Church of the Realm

THE MOST UBIQUITOUS INSTITUTION in medieval Europe, after the farm, was the Christian church. Long essential to the rural order of things, it predated the realm itself. In the eyes of the ordinary person, it was the incarnation of the eternal and the definition of the necessary. If or when one thought about such things, the church was likely to be conceived both as quintessentially local and yet as coterminous with the civilized world. Present in the village, the church rather encompassed counties and principalities and kingdoms. Notwithstanding this traditional understanding, the church in twelfth-century Europe was everywhere undergoing massive and even violent restructuring.

In Iberia, as elsewhere, this change was due in part to what is most often called the Gregorian Reform. That movement of renewal was expressed in moral, in educational, even in financial terms, but all of these coalesced steadily in the elaboration of an institutional structure designed to carry them to fruition. Although it was to be realized in an international hierarchy culminating in a papal monarchy just then aborning, a college of cardinals partially constructed, and a canon law on the verge of achieving classic expression, the intentions that were collaborating in its erection were particular and provincial as well as ecumenical. But increasingly, the Roman church was asserting its mission to oversee, coordinate, and control. Everywhere in Europe, the questions produced by the revival and realization of that claim became the stuff of clerical ideals and of clerical ambitions.

A second factor that everywhere drastically affected the restructuring of the institutional church was the simultaneous recasting, perhaps invention, of the medieval kingdom in which it partly inhered. Alfonso VII, after all, was the contemporary of Henry I of England (1100–1135), Louis VII of France (1137–1180), the Holy Roman Emperor Conrad III (1137–1152), and Roger II of Sicily and south Italy (1137–1154). All these men would have declared themselves partisans of church reform, but they had royal necessities and priorities that they insisted must determine its course and timing, even its outcome in some degree.

In Iberia both factors combined with yet another set of circumstances, reflected only more palely elsewhere. England had its Celtic Fringe, the Empire its *Drang nach Osten*, and France, alas, its Plantagenets. Christian Iberia had its *reconquista*. From the renewed vigor of that process in the late eleventh century two questions arose. Since the *reconquista* was uncovering the Christian classical and Visigothic past, how far were the claims of either to be honored against the imperious necessities of the present? Often that past was not an archaeological remnant but was still enshrined in a Mozarabic church that had survived four centuries of Muslim overlordship. What claims had it on the liberators?

The second of these questions remains incompletely investigated, for church historians of the peninsula have hardly begun to formulate the query. Nevertheless, the matter already had been determined, in its large outlines, during the reign of Alfonso VI. The Council of Burgos in 1080 initiated the suppression of the Mozarabic rite in favor of the Roman one. Functioning Mozarabic bishops were to be swept aside, as at Valencia, Coimbra, and perhaps Toledo, and Latin ones installed.[1] If there was active opposition to this resolution of the problem it has not left much impression in the documents or in the chronicles.

In 1116 during the reign of Urraca, a bishop of Granada is said to have attended her council in Sahagún.[2] But Granada was beyond the high-water mark of the *reconquista* for almost another four centuries. What is known for the reign of her son is that in June 1150 a royal charter made reference to a bishop of Denia, in January 1155 a Bishop B. of Almería confirmed the canons of the Council of Valladolid, and that spring a Bishop Pedro of Baeza confirmed a charter of the king (D665, 882).[3] These notices are too laconic to reveal in the latter cases whether an indigenous Mozarabic bishop has been

---

1. Javier Fernández Conde, ed., *Historia de la iglesia en España*, vol. 2 (Madrid, 1982), is part of the most recent attempt to provide a modern account. The series is dominated by older scholarship and even older assumptions. For the beginnings of a new approach see Bernard F. Reilly, *The Kingdom of León-Castilla under King Alfonso VI, 1065–1109* (Princeton, 1988), pp. 136–48, and 169–84. Recently Esther Pascua Echegaray, "Hacía la formación política de la monarquía medieval. Las relaciones entre la monarquía y la iglesia castellano-leonesa en el reinado de Alfonso VII," *Hispania* 172 (1989): 397–441, attempted a survey but drew on a too limited documentary base and with an insufficient familiarity with the literature.

2. Bernard F. Reilly, *The Kingdom of León-Castilla under Queen Urraca, 1109–1126* (Princeton, 1982), pp. 114–15. At that time I was more skeptical than I am now.

3. January 1155. Carl Erdmann, *Das Papsttum und Portugal in ersten Jahrhundert der portugiesischen Geschichte* (Berlin, 1928), pp. 55–58. In his careful fashion, Julio González, *Repoblación de Castilla la Nueva*, 2 vols. (Madrid, 1975–76), 2:71–74, has traced the survival of a vestigial Mozarabic church at Toledo.

recognized or a new Latin bishopric erected, and the subsequent loss of both towns in 1157 returned the matter to obscurity.

The claims of tradition and the imperatives of the present had also begun to find some resolution during the reign of Alfonso VI. The primacy of the Toledo was restored under the former French Cluniac Bernard of Sauvetat, who became archbishop. The collaboration of the king and primate over the next quarter of a century saw the restoration of bishoprics on the then frontiers of the kingdom at Osma and Salamanca and the installation of former French Cluniac monks as bishops in many north Iberian sees. Cooperation continued between Archbishop Bernard and Queen Urraca and resulted in the restoration of the sees of Avila, Segovia, and Sigüenza. The policy of the crown aimed at the creation of an ecclesiastical province under Toledo and coterminous with the realm. That policy foundered on complexities sprung from the earlier history of the *reconquista*.

Among the most important bishoprics of the realm, Oviedo and Burgos had no warrant in antiquity but were products of the emergence of the kingdom. The status of León itself rested on the thinnest of claims. Alfonso VI would have legitimated them as suffragan sees of Toledo but the resistance of local prelates to that southern upstart had combined with the prerogatives of Rome to prevent such a resolution. Before Alfonso's death all three had been recognized by the papacy as sees in immediate dependence on itself and so free of Toledo's control.

In the west further difficulties were implicit in two developments. Alfonso had been unable to forestall the recognition by Rome of a restored ecclesiastical province of Braga. That see had as good warrant in antiquity as Toledo to the dignity. Moreover, it had title to all of the sees of Galicia and Astorga on the central *meseta* as suffragans. In Galicia these complications were compounded yet again by the remarkable blossoming of the shrine-church of the apostle Saint James the Great at Compostela in the period. That church had secured from Rome the transfer of the classical see at Iria Flavia, once suffragan of Braga, to itself and then a papal grant of dependence immediately on Rome and hence independence of both Braga and Toledo.

Success in the Rioja in 1076 brought within the purview of Alfonso VI bishoprics at Calahorra, Tarazona, and Zaragoza. All had a tradition in antiquity and, it may be, Mozarabic substance as well. The latter two lay within the *taifa* of Zaragoza. The first as "bishop of Nájera," was at the center of Leonese power in the Rioja. All three had formed part of the province of Tarragona during the Visigothic period. In 1076 there was no metropolitan in Muslim Tarragona, but Barcelona and the papacy were shortly to restore one.

During the reign of Urraca the seizure by Alfonso I of Aragón of the Rioja and much of Castilla resulted in his control of Calahorra and Burgos. His conquest of Zaragoza in 1118 and Tarazona in 1120 brought those churches into his orbit. Only Alfonso VII's reconquest of Castilla early in his reign and Aragonese collapse after Fraga in 1134 returned ecclesiastical decisions there to the Leonese monarch.

In the west the de facto independence of Portugal under Teresa challenged Urraca's claim to direct church affairs south of the Miño River and in the Galician border sees of Túy and Orense. Those ambiguities she bequeathed to her son. But the most spectacular of her legacies to him was the archbishopric of Santiago de Compostela. Diego Gelmírez, the great churchman, had persuaded Pope Calixtus II in 1120 to transfer to his shrine and bishopric the ancient metropolitan rights of Mérida and to further endow it with suffragan bishops at Salamanca and Coimbra. Since the pope had also made him legate for the province of Braga, the new archbishop had levers with which to humble Compostela's former metropolitan and to recruit another suffragan at Avila.[4] Late in the reign Diego even sought the primacy in the peninsula. On the evidence of the *Historia Compostellana*, Alfonso joined with his mother even before his accession to reprove such excess.[5] Royal policy continued to regard the consolidation of the prerogatives of Toledo, its chosen ecclesiastical instrument, as the fundament of all church reform in the peninsula.

At Toledo, the great royal counsellor of the last two reigns died on April 3, 1125.[6] Given the then relationship of the king and his mother and

4. Reilly, *Urraca*, pp. 234–46. Richard A. Fletcher, *St. James's Catapult: The Life and Times of Diego Gelmírez of Santiago de Compostela* (Oxford, 1984), pp. 202–12, adds much valuable detail to what is an extraordinary tale to begin.

5. Emma Falque Rey, ed. (Turnholt, 1988), p. 372.

6. The date of his death has been sufficiently controverted to be worth attention. The early chroniclers are hopelessly confused. Ambrosio Huici Miranda, ed., "Annales Toledanos I," *Las crónicas latinas de la reconquista*, 2 vols. (Valencia, 1913), 1:345, placed it in 1128. Rodrigo Jiménez de Rada, *De Rebus Hispaniae*, ed. Emma Falque Rey (Turnholt, 1987), p. 255, gave a list of dates impossible to reconcile. Later historians reflected his confusion. Fidel Fita, "San Miguel de Escalada: Documento apócrifo del siglo XII, autenticos del XIII," *BRAH* 32 (1898): 28, began the modern debate by setting Bernard's death in April 1124 and challenging *Infanta* Sancha's grant of San Miguel to Cluny (D26). He was followed by Marcelin Defourneaux, *Les Français en Espagne au XI et XII siècles* (Paris, 1949), p. 43, and even by Juan Francisco Rivera Recio, *La iglesia de Toledo en el siglo XII* (Rome, 1966), p. 193. But Peter Rassow, "La Cofradia de Belchite," *AHDE* 3 (1926), p. 210, n. 25, pointed out that the year of Bernard's death must be 1125. As Rassow observed, the first documentary reference to Raymond as archbishop dates to July 21, 1125, and is false (D33). The charter of Alfonso VII misdated to February 10, 1125, must be corrected to 1129 since Berengaria appears as queen and Rodrigo Vermúdez as majordomo (D100).

Moreover, the supposedly dead Bernard confirmed a private document of June 3, 1124, BN, Manuscritos, 720, fol. 294r-v, and he was cited in a private document of Palencia of Au-the former's particular competence south of the Duero, the choice of a new archbishop was his.[7] He picked Raymond, bishop of El Burgo de Osma, a suffragan of Toledo. The new archbishop was a south French Cluniac brought to Iberia and installed first in the cathedral chapter at Toledo, then in Osma, by Archbishop Bernard.[8] That Raymond was acceptable to Alfonso is evident, for the prelate confirmed roughly 30 percent of all royal charters issued during his pontificate. He was constantly in the royal presence and the most trusted of counsellors (D34, 750).[9]

At Osma Raymond was replaced by Bertrán, another Bernardine import and former archdeacon of Toledo.[10] The first notice of his episcopate dates to the spring of 1128, for until 1127 his diocese lay in territory controlled by Aragón. He was also acceptable to Alfonso but, the bishop of a small, remote see, Bertrán confirmed only 33 of the 320 royal charters issued during his episcopate (D85, 375).[11]

From his succession, the king had to defend the prerogatives of Toledo. Bishop Jerome of Salamanca had died on June 30, 1120, possibly about the time of the papal bull raising Compostela to an archepiscopate and awarding it Salamanca as a suffragan reached the peninsula.[12] But the issue raised was wider than the latter prize. Jerome had been bishop of Salamanca and Avila, both of which had antique warrant, and had resided at Zamora ordinarily. Archbishop Gelmírez moved promptly to install one Gerald as bishop

---

gust 8, 1124, pub. Teresa Abajo Martín, ed., *Documentación de la catedral de Palencia* (Palencia, 1986), pp. 68–71. He confirmed Alfonso VII's charter to Sigüenza of November 1, 1124 (D27), and was cited in another private document of November 5, 1124, pub. Luciano Serrano, ed., *Colección diplomática de San Salvador de El Moral* (Madrid, 1906), pp. 31–34. On February 20, 1125, Bernard confirmed still another private document, BN, Manuscritos, 18.387, fol. 252r, and finally another private document cited him as archbishop of Toledo on March 26, 1125, pub. José Antonio Fernández Flórez, ed., *Colección diplomática del monasterio de Sahagún, 1110–1199*, vol. 4 (León, 1991), pp. 92–94. A thorough search done merely with this object in mind would uncover still further citations. Ludwig Vones, *Die "Historia Compostellana" und die Kirchenpolitik des Nordwestspanischen Raumes, 1170–1130* (Cologne, 1980), pp. 551–52, suffers from a less than full acquaintance with the documents. If the Toledan tradition is itself unsure about the actual date of Bernard's demise that is likely because he was buried at Sahagún. Ambrosio de Morales, *Viaje a los reinos de León, y Galicia, y principado de Asturias*, ed. Enrique Flórez, 1765 (Oviedo, 1977), p. 37.

7. November 30, 1125. AHN, Códices, 987B, fol. 109r-v; BN, Manuscritos, 13.022, fol. 20r-v; pub. Fidel Fita, "Dos bulas inéditas de Honorio II," *BRAH* 7 (1885): 414–23. The papal letters specifically mention the young Alfonso but not his mother.

8. Reilly, *Alfonso VI*, pp. 263–64.

9. Antonio Ubieto Arteta, ed., *Listas episcopales medievales*, 2 vols. (Zaragoza, 1988), 2:386, gives his death as August 19, 1152.

10. S. Ruiz, "Beltran," *DHGE* 7:955–56, sketched his career.

11. Ubieto Arteta, *Listas*, 2:270, cites him as dead by October 1, 1140.

12. Fidel Fita, "Variedades: Bernardo de Perigord, arcediano de Toledo y obispo de Zamora," *BRAH* 14 (1889): 459, n. 6.

at Salamanca and was initially successful. Gerald was consecrated at Rome. But the queen objected, and by 1123 a new bishop, Muño, was consecrated by Archbishop Bernard of Toledo, even if he subsequently had to swear obedience to Compostela.[13]

Although he lacked specific authority for it, Gelmírez had also resurrected the diocese of Avila and, then or later, the papal bull was falsified to make it his suffragan. His creature, Bishop Sancho, was consecrated by Diego in 1121 and maintained himself with papal support over the objections of Urraca and Archbishop Bernard. Toledo meanwhile consecrated another of its archdeacons, Bernard of Perigord, as bishop of Zamora. At this, Braga's suffragan, the bishop of Astorga, objected that Zamora and its territories lay within his diocese. A council in Valladolid in 1124 settled the matter temporarily with the decree that Bernard of Zamora should hold his office for life and that afterward the territory should revert to Astorga.[14] In the meantime, Bishop Bernard confirmed 15 percent of royal charters issued during his episcopate which indicates strong royal support if not that he was a curial bishop (D18, 621).[15]

At the outset, Alfonso's support for Toledo had been tempered while he sought recognition of the legitimacy of his marriage to Berengaria. At the Council of Carrión in 1130, he finally secured it but at considerable cost. Bishops Diego of León, Muño of Salamanca, and Pelayo of Oviedo were deposed for having opposed the royal match. At Salamanca Alfonso Pérez and at León Arias González, both former canons of Compostela, became bishops, although Raymond of Toledo insisted on consecrating the latter. For that impertinence, the primate drew papal rebuke and Arias most probably had to make satisfaction with a trip to Rome. At Oviedo, Bishop Pelayo was replaced by a native of Asturias, Alfonso, about whom little is known. Presumably he, too, was consecrated by Archbishop Raymond and he was subsequently denounced to Rome by Archbishop Gelmírez.[16] That lordly prelate had had much of his own way but the matter of the consecrations made it clear that the king would see to the resurgence of Toledo.

In the interim the relationships of the crown and the archbishops of

13. Reilly, *Urraca*, pp. 243–44.
14. Reilly, *Urraca*, pp. 245–46, and 184.
15. Ubieto Arteta, *Listas*, 2:433, has him dead by March 1149 but unfortunately often depends on incomplete and old notices.
16. Bernard F. Reilly, "On Getting to Be a Bishop in León-Castilla: The 'Emperor' Alfonso VII and the Post-Gregorian Church," *Studies in Medieval and Renaissance History* 1 (1978): 48–51. Also Richard A. Fletcher, *The Episcopate of the Kingdom of León in the Twelfth Century* (Oxford, 1978), pp. 73–74.

Compostela and Braga figured in the selection of no less than three bishops in two or three years. Astorga was the most crucial. The see was suffragan of Braga, on the clear testimony of antiquity, but that metropolitan was far away, more than 200 kilometers as the crow flies and over rugged country. On the other hand, it was but forty kilometers by an easy road from León. Politics had collaborated with geography to ensure that from its restoration in the ninth century it was in the "gift" of the king of León. So it continued to be in the twelfth century, although bishops selected in León continued dutifully to make their canonical obedience to the archbishop of Braga.[17]

Former Bishop Alo died after March of 1131 and had been succeeded by Robert before mid-July.[18] Little is known of his antecedents, although the case has been made that he was a local figure for a Robert had appeared with some frequency in the cathedral chapter at Astorga.[19] At any rate, the Toledan archbishop is likely to have consecrated him and he was welcome at the court of Alfonso VII though not a court figure.

The bishoprics of Túy and Orense stood in exactly inverse relationship to those at Braga and León. Both suffragans to Braga, they lay in the contested lower Miño basin. They were not much more than 70 and 100 kilometers, respectively, from Braga and more than 200 from León over rough country. In these circumstances, Alfonso VII found the ambitions of Archbishop Gelmírez to annex the suffragans of Braga complementary to his own.

Former Bishop Diego of Orense had been a canon of Compostela whose last notice is in a royal donation of May 1132 to the cathedral of Orense (D148). He was succeeded by Martín Pérez whom the *Historia Compostellana* knew well. Martín had been a canon of Compostela, brother to the late bishop of Orense, and royal chaplain.[20] He first appears in a royal donation of early 1132 and finally in one of 1156. He confirmed 14 percent of the royal charters of the time which is a remarkable performance for a bishop from the fringes of the realm (D165, 957).

About the same time Bishop Alfonso of Túy died. He was succeeded by Pelayo Menéndez, a local figure from a family with ties to the Trastámara. Pelayo would long move in the sphere of Braga and Portugal. There is a dispute about the date of Alfonso's demise and Pelayo's succession, but spring or summer of 1132 seems likely. The new bishop was consecrated by

17. Fletcher, *Episcopate*, pp. 45–46.
18. March 31, 1131. Pub. Enrique Flórez, *ES* 16 (1787, Madrid): 200. July 13, 1131. Pub. Alexandre Bruel, ed., *Recueil des chartes de l'Abbaye de Cluny*, 6 vols. (Paris, 1876–1903), 5:376–77. Both are private documents.
19. Augusto Quintana Prieto, *El obispado de Astorga en el siglo XII* (Astorga, 1985), pp. 173–97, who furnishes a detailed if somewhat old-fashioned history of this prelate as of the others.
20. Fletcher, *Episcopate*, p. 49. Reilly, "On Getting to Be a Bishop," pp. 45–46, 51.

the archbishop of Braga and not before 1136 did he confirm a document of the Leonese king.[21] His presence in the royal curia is slight.

These concessions to necessity duly negotiated, Alfonso VII returned to a single-minded assault on the position of the archbishop of Compostela. Opportunity was provided in 1133 by the death of Gelmírez's creature, Bishop Sancho at Avila. What followed is supplied by the *Historia Compostellana*. Bishop Pedro of Segovia presided at the funeral of Sancho and, probably, at the election of Jimeno (Iñigo), brother of the deceased and archdeacon of Avila. The latter wrote to Gelmírez stressing the unanimity of his election and the crown's approval. The *concejo* of Avila also wrote to the same effect and asked Jimeno's early consecration. Finally the text supplies an abrupt letter of the king to the archbishop directing Jimeno's consecration. Gelmírez complied on July 25, 1133, the feast of Saint James the Great, in concert with the bishops of Túy, Lugo, Mondoñedo, and Orense. Jimeno then swore obedience to the Compostelan as his canonical metropolitan.[22]

To follow what had transpired it is necessary to note the names of both bishops. Sancho and Iñigo are Castilian rather than Leonese and Avila itself was fated to become a Castilian town despite its geographical location west of the expected southern drift of repopulation. Probably in 1121 Gelmírez had made common cause with the local Castilian element but the crown outbid him in 1133, and a local candidate chose a tie to the king instead. Jimeno proved acceptable to the king, 13 percent of whose charters he confirmed and whom he outlived (D196, 966).

For Compostela the direction of affairs at Avila was bad, but worse was to come. At Salamanca his successful candidate of 1130, Bishop Alfonso Pérez, died while returning from the Council of Rheims in late 1131. Then Bishop Muño, who had been deposed at Carrión in 1130 and had fled to Portugal, returned. He seems to have appealed to Bernard of Clairvaux, Peter the Venerable of Cluny, and the papacy itself for recognition but without success. The king's opportunity came at the Council of León in the spring of 1135 when a delegation from the chapter at Salamanca asked the king to approve their choice of one Peter, likely Gelmírez's candidate, as bishop. But a disappointed faction at Salamanca asked the king to quash the election, and Alfonso chose

21. Fletcher, *Episcopate*, p. 51, who opts for 1131. But Bishop Alfonso confirmed a royal charter in January 1132 (D143). Flórez, *ES* 22:79, knew a private document of July 30, 1131, that cited Pelayo as already bishop. There is a private document of October 27, 1131, that does so but it is probably false. Pub. José Luis Martín, *Orígenes de la orden militar de Santiago* (Barcelona, 1974), pp. 172–74. The first reliable appearance of Bishop Pelayo was on July 25, 1133, at a consecration of the bishop of Avila in Santiago de Compostela. Falque Rey, *HC*, p. 480.

22. Falque Rey, *HC*, pp. 476–81. The documents of the cathedral of Avila which might have shed more light on local figures involved were largely destroyed in an early modern fire.

to do so. With the aid of the papal legate, Cardinal Guido, he then browbeat the canons present at León into electing Berenguer and sent the latter to Salamanca in the company of Archbishop Raymond of Toledo, Bishop Pedro of Segovia, and Bishop Bernard of Zamora to have the election ratified there.

In mid-August 1135, Berenguer styled himself both as imperial chancellor and bishop-elect of Salamanca, and in January 1136 Alfonso granted a charter to the church of Salamanca and Bishop Berenguer (D225, 241). The *Historia Compostellana* preserves a priceless series of letters. Berenguer, the clergy of Salamanca, the king, and the archbishop of Toledo all wrote to Gelmírez describing the process and asking his consecration of Berenguer. Marginally proper, they describe in detail events that must already have been familiar to the Compostelan and the authorities the crown had mustered against him. The archbishop accepted the coup and consecrated Berenguer, whose oath of obedience is preserved.[23]

While the structure of his province remained untouched and his new suffragans carefully swore formal obedience, Gelmírez would have had no illusions as to where their real loyalties lay. The crown and Toledo had made Avila and Salamanca props to their own purposes, so long as the new incumbents should live. At the same time, Alfonso was already plotting with significant elements in the Compostelan's own cathedral chapter to secure his deposition. The attempt failed at the Council of Burgos in 1136, in part because of a failed attack on Diego's life, which discredited and forced the disavowal by the crown of the conspirators. Rome, too, must have had doubts about the wisdom of allowing the imperious Leonese king to reduce the entire church of his realm to a monolith, subservient to the crown and the primate of Toledo. It chose to support Gelmírez in 1136.

Two other bishoprics were filled in 1135. Bishop Pedro III of the sleepy hill town of Lugo appeared in so few royal documents that we cannot date his demise.[24] His successor, Guy, appears first participating in consecration of Berenguer of Salamanca in 1135.[25] It seems he was of French extraction and

23. Falque Rey, *HC*, pp. 481–82 and 499–502. Reilly, "Getting to Be a Bishop," pp. 53–55. Fletcher, *Saint James's Catapult*, pp. 284–90. There are some ambiguities that remain and are reflected in the differences between the latter two accounts. Most important, I believe that the charter record speaks convincingly to Berenguer having been elected at the Council of León of 1135 rather than that of 1134. I have also found Count Pedro López to have been castellan only at Toro, according to the documents although it is possible that his sometimes jurisdiction reached as far south as Salamanca about 1130 or 1131.

24. April 19, 1133. Pub. José María Fernández Catón, ed., *Colección documental del archivo de la catedral de León, 1109–1187*, vol. 5 (León, 1990), pp. 159–62, the testament of Bishop Arias of León is his last appearance.

25. Falque Rey, *HC*, p. 502.

had been prior of the cathedral chapter at Lugo.[26] He figures only sporadically in the royal diplomas. Possibly Alfonso VII's pressing concerns at the time advised leaving the selection at Lugo to local forces.

Bishop Arias González of León had died soon after presiding at Alfonso's imperial coronation (D218).[27] Arias had been a canon of Santiago de Compostela as was his sucessor, Pedro Anáiaz. But, in the circumstances of 1135, we must think he was a member of the faction opposed to Gelmírez. Pedro's accession to León went unmentioned in the *Historia Compostellana* except for its inclusion of a letter of Pope Innocent II warning Gelmírez against consecrating a bishop immediately dependent on the Holy See.[28] Pedro is cited as bishop-elect in the fall of 1135 and as late as the following spring.[29] He may finally have been consecrated by the cardinal-legate Guido.

Nevertheless, there was still room for maneuver in the complicated currents of the time, and the archbishop of Compostela was never loath to do so. The see of the important city of Zaragoza had fallen vacant and the debility of the crown of Aragón offered Alfonso VII maximum opportunity in that old objective of Leonese ambitions.[30] Sometime in early 1136, a Bishop William was elected at Zaragoza. His name is not Iberian, but French influence had been strong at Zaragoza since 1118 and perhaps he was a canon. By October he was at the council of Burgos.[31] Probably as a part of the settlement worked out there, William was consecrated by Gelmírez, presumably with the blessing of both king and legate since the see lay in the province of of Tarragona.[32]

The prelate of Compostela may have been able to use the embarrassment of king and legate in yet another respect. The canon of Santiago and bishop of

26. Fletcher, *Episcopate*, p. 66.

27. Antonio Maya Sánchez and Juan Gil, eds., *CAI*, in *Chronica Hispana: Saeculi XII*, pp. 109–296 (Turnholt, 1990), pp. 182–83.

28. Falque Rey, *HC*, p. 503.

29. October 28, 1135. Pub. Fernández Flórez, ed., *Colección*, pp. 147–48. March 31, 1136. Ibid., pp. 151–52. Private documents. Reilly, "Getting to Be a Bishop," p. 56, and Fletcher, *Episcopate*, p. 70, who sees Pedro rather differently.

30. November 13, 1135. Pub. Luis Rubio, ed., *Documentos del Pilar* (Zaragoza, 1971), p. 21, who called the private document original. It is the last notice of Bishop García de Majones. Ubieto Arteta, *Listas*, 2:439, would prolong his life to July 16, 1136, on the basis of an old necrology of Montearagón.

31. November 26, 1135 (D232), is his first appearance in an Alfonsine diploma but it is unreliable and his predecessor was still alive. August 24, 1136. Pub. José María Lacarra, ed., "Documentos para el estudio de la reconquista y repoblación del valle del Ebro," *EEMCA* 3 (1947–48): 586, a private document is the first reliable notice. The editor dated it to July 3, but the feast of Saint Bartholomew, mentioned in the dating formula, is August 24. He also dated the Alfonsine diploma above to 1136. Ibid., pp. 588–89. October 4, 1136 (D264), is the only trustworthy royal diploma in which he appears. Ubieto Arteta, *Listas*, 2:439, followed Lacarra's incorrect dating of both documents.

32. Falque Rey, *HC*, p. 517.

Galician Mondoñedo, Muno Alfónsez, had apparently died on June 26, 1136.[33] He was succeeded by the former abbot of the nearby monastery of Lorenzana. A local figure, Pelayo was not the king's man. He confirmed few royal charters, his church received no royal donations, and he was ultimately deposed at the Council of Valladolid in 1155. One sees the hand of the king in that. Pelayo is invisible until 1138 when he confirmed a royal document (D317).[34]

Archbishop Paio Mendes of Braga had also attended the Council of Burgos along with Bishop Bernard of Coimbra. Paio may have accepted the obedience of Pelayo of Mondoñedo there as part of a quid pro quo. The longtime bishop and former canon of Compostela, Bishop Hugh of Oporto died sometime between 1134 and 1136.[35] His successor, João Peculiar, first appears as bishop-elect of Oporto in a council document at Burgos. He was probably elected and perhaps consecrated there (D264). Joao had been *magister scholarum* at Coimbra, then chief residence of Afonso Henriques. He was the candidate of that Portuguese prince, of the bishop of Coimbra and of the archbishop of Braga. The archbishop of Braga may have accepted Gelmírez's candidate at Mondoñedo while the archbishop of Compostela resigned himself to the loss of his former influence at Oporto.[36]

Both Alfonso VII and Diego Gelmírez were, as it eventuated, giving up rather more than they intended. Northern Portugal was slipping away. Moderns miss the significance of the development for we assume the independence of Portugal with the infallibility of hindsight. For contemporaries, the de facto separation of Portugal under renegades from the Leonese dynasty was less than thirty years old. The geography was difficult but the land had been part of the Leonese realm before and there was little reason to assume its permanent loss.

On July 4, 1137, Alfonso VII scored a remarkable victory over his first cousin who was forced to recognize that he was a vassal of the Leonese. Archbishop Paio Mendes of Braga witnessed that document and then rode north with the king to Santiago de Compostela where he confirmed a royal charter (D293–94). It was the last time that he would do so. Before the end of October, Archbishop Paio was dead and had been succeeded at Braga by

33. Flórez, *ES*, 18:133–34, from an old calendar. There is a private document of July 12, 1137, to a Compostelan monastery that gives "M" as bishop of Mondoñedo. AHN, Códices, 1047B, ff. 6v–7r; pub. Santiago Montero Díaz, ed., "La colección diplomática de San Martín de Jubia," *Boletín de la Universidad de Santiago de Compostela* 7 (1935): 81, who rendered it as "Martinus," for which there is no warrant.

34. Fletcher, *Episcopate*, p. 63, saw Pelayo as the monastery of Lorenzana's man.

35. Fortunato de Almeida, *História da Igreja em Portugal*, new ed., vol. 1 (Oporto, 1967), p. 275.

36. Almeida, *História*, 1:275.

Joao Peculiar. Moreover, Joao arranged to be replaced at Oporto by his own nephew, Pedro. In canon law the metropolitan of Braga might long continue to face north toward his traditional suffragans in Galicia but a new Braga was taking shape notwithstanding. Archbishop Joao now had suffragans to the south at Oporto and Coimbra and in the High Middle Ages his metropolitanate was to extend ever more southward as would the emerging realm that it came to complement. On the other hand, Braga's traditional claim to a suffragan at Astorga grew ever more faint. Bishop Robert died some time in February 1138 and by March another local man, Jimeno Eriz, had been elected. Jimeno derived from a family long if distantly associated with the crown, his father had been royal *merino* and he himself was a member of the cathedral chapter at Astorga.[37] The royal court was then in the vicinity and the election may have taken place at court. We can be sure that he was regarded as a safe man if not a curial figure.

The following year saw the influence of the crown and the primate of Toledo over the episcopate of the kingdom continue and grow. At Palencia, Bishop Pedro I died and was replaced by Bishop Pedro II. The former had been archdeacon of Toledo and the latter had been archdeacon of Segovia and nephew of Bishop Pedro of Segovia, another Toledan canon. The new bishop of Segovia was perhaps the brother of Bishop Bernard of Sigüenza, another Toledan, as well.[38] The same year saw the death of Bishop Pedro Anáiaz of León.[39] Juan Albertínez was bishop-elect there as early as March 22, 1140.[40] Juan was son of the royal *merino*, Albertino, long a trusted crown servant. The bishop had an episcopate of over forty years. He confirmed almost a third of royal charters in his period and can fairly be called a curial bishop.[41] But León was a see dependent on Rome, its bishop could not be canonically consecrated by another without papal dispensation, and for two years Juan remained mere bishop-elect. His cause, and the ambitions of Alfonso VII, became tangled in other matters that made them suspect in Rome.[42]

37. Quintana Prieto, *Obispado*, pp. 199–224, who provides a detailed biography, puts his death before February 27, 1138. Pedro Rodríguez López, *Episcopologio asturicense*, 2 vols. (Astorga, 1907), p. 192, cited a document of April 29, 1138, in which he appeared.

38. María de la Soterraña Martín Postigo, "Alfonso I el Batallador y Segovia," *Estudios Segovianos* 19 (1967): 34. Rivera Recio, *Iglesia*, p. 268.

39. December 30, 1139. AD León, Gradefes, no. 44, a private document cites him as deceased. Manuel Risco, *ES* 35 (1786): 192, cited a document of July 24, 1139, in which his successor already appeared as elect. It was probably misdated.

40. Pub. Fernández Flórez, *Colección*, 4:171–72, who calls it an original. I think it a copy of the next century.

41. Fletcher, *Episcopate*, pp. 70–71. Also, Bernard F. Reilly, "The Court Bishops of Alfonso VII of León-Castilla, 1147–1157," *Medieval Studies*, 36 (1974): 67–78.

42. Reilly, "Getting to Be a Bishop," p. 58.

The first of those grew from the death of Bishop Jimeno of Burgos in October 1139. That see was very important to the king and notice of a new incumbent already came in November. Pedro Domínguez confirmed as bishop-elect (D358).[43] Pedro was an old servant of the crown, rewarded by Alfonso for faithful service in 1127 when that city deserted Aragón for Leonese allegiance (D63). Burgos was a hub of Leonese power in the east, and the reliability of its bishop was critical. Tradition was the enemy of royal design, however, for that see was canonically the descendant of ancient Oca, which hill-town episcopate had been a suffragan of Tarragona. Alfonso VI forty years earlier had influenced Pope Urban II to make Burgos temporarily independent of its metropolitan, then in Muslim hands, and directly dependent on the Holy See. But in the preceding decade, the drive of the count of Barcelona for the liberation of the city of Tarragona and the restoration of its metropolitan had met more success and reopened the question of Burgos' status.[44]

The king moved immediately upon Pedro's election to request Rome to allow him to be consecrated in Iberia, presumably by the primate of Toledo. Royal policy was eventually to succeed in having Burgos made a suffragan of Toledo but in May 1140 Pope Innocent II wrote to deny the request and Bishop Pedro may have had to go to Rome. The latter does not appear as bishop rather than bishop-elect in a reliable document until February 1141.[45] The royal initiatives at León and now at Burgos must have acted to make Rome wary and shortly an even more inflammatory example of royal ambitions came to the pontiff's attention.

On April 6, 1140, Archbishop Diego Gelmírez of Santiago de Compostela died full of years and honors. Alfonso could not fail to try to bring that metropolitan see, so often the rival of the chosen crown instrument of Toledo, under secure control. Before the king was aware of his death, however, the cathedral chapter had proceeded to the election of its dean, Pedro Elias.[46] In Salamanca in June, a delegation from Galicia waited on the king, in all likelihood to request his assent to the election (D382–83). But the king refused their choice and disregarded his own pledge of 1128 for a free election by the canons. Instead, he nominated his former chancellor, Bishop Beren-

43. Luciano Serrano, *El obispado de Burgos y Castilla primitiva desde el siglo V al XIII*, 3 vols. (Madrid, 1935), 1:424, cites a calendario of the cathedral for Jimeno's death on October 14, 1139. Reilly, "Getting to Be a Bishop," pp. 58–59.
44. Reilly, *Alfonso VI*, p. 264. Fernández Conde, *Historia*, 2-1:314–16.
45. Reilly, "Getting to Be a Bishop," pp. 58–59.
46. August 1, 1140. ARG, Documentos pontificios, no. 66. This private document cites Pedro already as archbishop.

guer of Salamanca. It is doubtful that the Compostelans resisted the king to his face, and Berenguer may have been elected there under duress, although further negotiation appears more likely. Not until November is there a trustworthy citation of the Salamancan as archbishop.[47]

Meanwhile, the chapter had sent its candidate off to seek Rome's recognition, and Innocent II gave it. By June 1141 Pedro Elias returned to Iberia and the king had to recognize him but subsequently decided to appeal. Berenguer was despatched to Rome in the fall, and the support of Peter the Venerable of Cluny and of Bernard of Clairvaux was enlisted in his behalf. But the papacy was not to be moved on this particular issue, although it may earlier have accepted Alfonso's candidates at León and Burgos in an attempt to placate that monarch. At the Council of Valladolid in 1143, in the presence of the papal legate, Cardinal Guido, the bishops of León and Burgos, Bishop Berenguer of Salamanca, and Archbishop Pedro Elias all participated. Alfonso had been bilked again in his ambitions in the northwest, but the contest had been such that it is likely the new archbishop was sensitive to royal desires.

The monarch was also busy extricating himself from an embarrassing situation in another exempt see. Bishop Alfonso of Oviedo died in early 1142. The still-living former bishop, Pelayo, attempted to regain that dignity and is recognized in four private documents between March 1142 and March 1143.[48] In June 1143 a private document cites Froila García, archdeacon of the cathedral of Oviedo, as administrator of the see.[49] At Valladolid in the fall a new bishop, Martín, was chosen. He is identified as a native of Santiago de Compostela and in 1156 was translated to that shrine-church as archbishop.[50] The evidence indicates that the new bishop of Oviedo was on more familiar terms with the king than any of his predecessors. He confirmed 17 percent of current royal charters. Since the king visited Oviedo but once in that twenty-three-year span, it is hard to avoid the conclusion that Martín was and remained a curial figure (D479, 930).

Episcopal successions in the province of Toledo were simpler. At Osma, Bishop Bertrán is last seen on May 14, 1140, confirming a royal charter at Berlanga. That same month a private document cites Bishop Stephen at Osma

47. Reilly, "Getting to Be a Bishop," pp. 59–61, is the account followed here for the most part. Richard A. Fletcher, "Archbishops of Santiago de Compostela between 1140 and 1173: A New Chronology," *Compostellanum* 17 (1972): 45–61, has added new testimony to supplement what I had earlier developed.

48. Reilly, "Getting to Be a Bishop," pp. 52, 61. Pelayo lived until January 28, 1153, according to an old calendar of the cathedral. Risco, *ES* 38 (1793): 109.

49. Pub. Santos García Larragueta, ed., *Colección de documentos de la catedral de Oviedo* (Oviedo, 1962), pp. 392–95.

50. Reilly, "Getting to Be a Bishop," p. 61.

(D375).[51] If Bertrán died at court his successor may have been chosen there. In any event, royal influence may be presumed.

A year before the Council of Valladolid Alfonso VII had reconquered Muslim Coria on the southwestern edge of the Duero basin. There he installed there Bishop Navarro, a former canon of Segovia and probably one of those Navarrese who formed a good part of Segovia's population (D437).[52] Coria eventually became a suffragan of Compostela but for the present it was safely within the fold of Toledo.

At Astorga on May 8, 1141, Bishop Jimeno Eriz died and by September 22 his successor had been chosen. Very little is known of the brief episcopate of the latter, usually called "Amadeus," but his most recent biographer suggests he should properly be styled "Ameus."[53] He had been archdeacon of Astorga. At the Council of Valladolid the cardinal-legate Guido ruled against him in a territorial dispute with Orense. By the end of December 1143 or shortly thereafter the bishop was dead.

His successor in the see, Bishop Arnold, is well documented. His swift promotion, he is functioning as bishop by the end of February of 1144, argues his election at court. Quintana Prieto is content to make him a cleric of the diocese of Gerona who came to León in the suite of Queen Berengaria and who subsequently was the author of the *Chronica Adefonsi Imperatoris*.[54] Unfortunately, none of the documentation of Gerona that he cites furnishes anything but a common name. Arnold's putative authorship rests on no more than his being mentioned in that peculiar chronicle, assembled out of a variety of different accounts, and his undoubted participation in the Almerian campaign of 1146–1147. Nevertheless, there is no doubt that he was the royal choice. There is no previous trace of him at Astorga and his name is hardly Leonese. He confirmed about 13 percent of all royal diplomas issued during his pontificate, followed the court of Alfonso so constantly that his modern biographer calls him "cortesano," was emissary of the king to the counts of Barcelona and Montpellier in 1146, and served his sovereign in the campaign of Almería. Still, he was careful to make his obedience to the metropolitan of Braga whose suffragan he remained.[55]

When Bishop Pedro Domínguez of Burgos died during the siege of

51. May 25, 1140. Pub. F. Javier Peña Pérez, ed., *Documentación del monasterio de San Juan de Burgos, 1091–1400* (Burgos, 1983), pp. 23–24.

52. Fletcher, *Episcopate*, pp. 31–32.

53. Quintana Prieto, *Obispado*, pp. 225–47. The point is worth noting because "Amadeo" would suggest an extra-peninsular origin and "Ameus" is simply peculiar.

54. *Obispado*, pp. 249–300.

55. Fletcher, *Episcopate*, pp. 46–47.

Córdoba in June, the choice of his replacement seems to have been uncompli-
cated. By September a Bishop-elect Victor already confirmed a royal charter
(D533).[56] His is another extrapeninsular name, and we do not know his antecedents. Over the next ten years he would confirm no less than 23 percent of
all royal diplomas. Certainly he was a curial figure. The modern historian of
the see speculated that he may have been consecrated in France by Pope Eugenius III.[57] If true, that would have been tactful of the crown.

In the Rioja, Bishop Sancho of Calahorra died in 1146. A private document informs us that Bishop Rodrigo de Cascante had been consecrated to
that see by May 1147, probably at Tarragona by his proper metropolitan.[58] We
know no more of Bishop Rodrigo. In 1147, when Alfonso VII sought the aid
of Ramon Berenguer in the coming campaign at Almería, the Leonese could
hardly object to Rodrigo's being consecrated at Tarragona. In any event, the
new bishop was quickly drawn into the orbit of the Leonese court. Over the
remainder of the reign, Rodrigo confirms about 17 percent of all royal diplomas despite the frontier character of his diocese.

Also on the eastern frontier, at the end of 1147 Osma was vacant again,
Bishop Stephen having died. His successor was Juan Téllez, former archdeacon of Segovia and a safe choice from the standpoint of Toledo and the
court (D562).[59] Subsequently, Juan spent most of his time at court, confirming
89 of the roughly 400 royal diplomas between 1148 and 1157 (D578, 970).

Another of Toledo's suffragan sees was filled about this time, for Bishop
Pedro of Palencia apparently lost his life in the Almería campaign (D562). The
new incumbent was a brother or half brother of Queen Berengaria and son
of Count Ramon Berenguer of Barcelona and Countess Dulce of Provence.
Bishop Ramon appears as bishop-elect first in 1148 (D578).[60] Subsequent
charters of Alfonso VII reveal him constantly at court.

The same year saw the death of Bishop Pedro of Segovia. At the end of
April 1148 Pope Eugenius III had sent him back to Alfonso VII from France
bearing a golden rose, the traditional sign of particular papal favor. The king
received this token, for the final reliable notice of Bishop Pedro is his confir-

---

56. Maya Sánchez and Gil, *CAI*, p. 246.

57. Serrano, *Obispado*, 2:38.

58. Ubieto Arteta, *Listas*, 1:83, gives Sancho as dead by November 11, 1146. May 18, 1147.
Pub. Ildefonso Rodríguez de Lama, ed., *Colección diplomática medieval de La Rioja: Documentos,
923–1168*, vol. 2 (Logroño, 1976), p. 217.

59. Ubieto Arteta, *Listas*, p. 270, says that Juan had been consecrated by January 11, 1148.
Julio González, *El reino de Castilla en la época de Alfonso VIII*, 3 vols. (Madrid, 1960), 1:412, for
his archdiaconate at Segovia.

60. Derek W. Lomax, "Don Ramón, Bishop of Palencia (1148–1184)," in *Homenaje a Jaime
Vicens Vives* (Barcelona, 1965), pp. 279–91, and Reilly, "Getting to Be a Bishop," pp. 40–41 and 63.

mation of a charter in May (D590).[61] Bishop Juan appears in a royal charter in March, 1149 (D614). We know nothing more of him except that within four years Juan will have become archbishop of Toledo and primate of Iberia. Royal favor seems safe to presume and a Toledan background probable.[62]

This round of transitions in the province of Toledo continued in 1149 with the death of Bishop Bernard of Zamora. Bishop Stephen had succeded him by January 2, 1150 (D621, 633). The new bishop remains an obscure figure and not until 1153 does he begin to play the part at court that we should expect of an heir of Bishop Bernard. This absence has to be related to the agreement of 1123, approved by the papacy, providing that the see of Zamora should be quashed at Bernard's death and its territories returned to Astorga. It has been asserted that Stephen was hastily consecrated by the archbishop of Toledo so as to present both Rome and Astorga with a fait accompli. The bishop of Astorga did appeal to Rome, although without success.[63] Such a maneuver posits full royal confidence in Stephen, who must bear the brunt of such audacity.

The controversy at Zamora came at an unfortunate time. Its initiation coincided closely with the death of Archbishop Pedro Elías of Compostela on November 8, 1149, and the king now had the opportunity to reverse the verdict of 1140–1142. He immediately nominated his former candidate, Bishop Berenguer of Salamanca. We do not hear of any local opposition this time, and Berenguer set off for Rome and consecration in 1150 but died on the return journey. In 1151 Alfonso nominated Bishop Bernard of Sigüenza who too was duly elected (D701). Now Bernard traveled to Rome, but the journey was exhausting at his age. He returned only to die in Compostela on April 26, 1152.[64]

On receiving this news the king must have been at his wits end and possibly half-convinced that Saint James himself opposed his placing a nominee in the shrine-see. Alfonso now accepted another local man for archbishop. Pelayo Caamundo, former archdeacon of Santiago and native of the city, was elected at the royal court in 1153, probably by members of the cathedral chapter. He proceeded to Rome, was recognized, and had returned to Iberia and the court by mid-1154 (D833).[65]

61. April 27, 1148. Pub. Demetrio Mansilla, ed., *La documentación pontificia hasta Inocencio III, 965–1216* (Rome, 1955), pp. 94–96.
62. Manuel Alonso Alonso, "Notas sobre los traductores toledanos Domingo Gonsalvo and Juan Hispano," *Al-Andalus* 8 (1943): 155–88, attempted to identify him with the latter but the argument seems tenuous.
63. Rivera Recio, *Iglesia*, p. 310. The episcopal appeal is recorded in a later papal letter of Innocent III for such matters were regularly re-appealed. Enrique Flórez, *ES* 14, 2nd ed. (1786): 363–64.
64. Fletcher, "Archbishops," pp. 49–50.
65. Ibid., pp. 51–52.

Such maneuvers demanded other adjustments. The translation of Bishop Berenguer to Santiago was accompanied by that of Bishop Navarro from Coria to Salamanca (D700).[66] In turn, the translation of Bishop Bernard to Santiago was accompanied by his replacement at Sigüenza by a Bishop Pedro. The new bishop was a native of Leucate near Narbonne, nephew of the former bishop Bernard, and prior at Sigüenza, credentials that recommended him to the crown. Pedro appears in charters in 1152 and was frequently at court until his death four years later (D727, 749).[67]

Then, on August 20, 1152, while Alfonso VII was in Andalucía, Archbishop Raymond of Toledo died after an episcopate of sixteen years at Osma and twenty-seven at Toledo. When the king returned in September he translated Bishop Juan from Segovia to Toledo. By February 23, 1153, the latter had visited Rome and received the approbation of Pope Eugenius.[68] As a result, the see of Segovia had been vacated, of course, and was filled by a Vincent whose past is unknown. He was agreeable to the crown. From his first appearance in January 1154 Bishop Vincent confirms better than a third of all charters down to 1157 (D813, 971).

Meanwhile, Astorga had fallen vacant. Our last reliable notice of Bishop Arnold there occurs in August 1152, but it is possible he lived into early November (D757, 768). He was replaced by Pedro Cristiano, former abbot of the Cistercian monastery of San Martín de Castañeda, good friend of Alfonso VII, and member of a noble house of the region. Pedro appears as bishop-elect in January 1153.[69] During the same period, Bishop Guido of Lugo died. Another monk, Juan, formerly abbot of the Benedictine Galician monastery of Samos, became bishop after him. He managed to be a friend both of Alfonso VII and of his metropolitan, Joao Peculiar of Braga, by whom he was consecrated. Our first notice of Bishop Juan is March 1152.[70]

Change of a more controversial nature took place in February 1155 at the Council of Valladolid. Bishop Pelayo of Mondoñedo was deposed there but

---

66. May 17, 1150. Part pub. Francisco Hernndez, *Los cartularios de Toledo* (Madrid, 1985), p. 74, is the last notice of Berenguer.

67. Toribio Minguella y Arnedo, *Historia de la diócesis de Sigüenza y de sus obispos*, vol. I (Madrid, 1910), p. 96. Reilly, "Court Bishops," pp. 75–76.

68. Juan Franciso Rivera Recio, *Los arzobispos de Toledo en la baja Edad Media* (Toledo, 1969), pp. 17–20. Angel González Palencia, *El Arzobispo D. Raimundo de Toledo* (Barcelona, 1942), is still useful.

69. Fletcher, *Episcopate*, p. 47. January 25, 1153. Pub. Augusto Quintana Prieto, ed., *Tumbo viejo de San Pedro de Montes* (León, 1971), p. 278.

70. Fletcher, *Episcopate*, pp. 66–67. Fidel Fita, "Concilios nacionales de Salamanca en 1154 y de Valladolid en 1155," *BRAH* 24 (1894): 461, n. 2, placed the death of Guido between April 22 and July 6, 1152 without citing his source. The latest mention known to me is February, 1152. AD Astorga, Registro de Escrituras, fol. 470v. A private document of March 12, 1152, cites Juan as then bishop. AHN, Códices, 1.044B, fol. 37r-v.

the notice of it in the dating formula of a royal charter is laconic. The confirmation list of another charter of that date names his successor, Bishop Pedro Gudestéiz as bishop-elect (D869, 868). Possibly Bishop Pelayo's transgression lay in having been the candidate of Diego Gelmírez in 1136, and the king finally found a pretext to rid himself of the prelate. His replacement, prior of a house of Augustinian canons at Sar, tutor of the future Fernando II, was agreeable to, and probably the candidate of, the crown.[71]

Perhaps also at Valladolid, the see of Coria was filled. From 1151 when Bishop Navarro had been translated to Salamanca no bishop of Coria appears. Only in 1155 do we find there Bishop Suero, formerly abbot of the monastery of Nogales in the region of Astorga. The poverty of the see makes it likely that he was chosen by the king and the archbishop of Toledo. No one else would have been interested (D887).[72]

During the remaining two and a half years of the reign, no fewer than six more episcopal appointments were made, but none of them produced significant disputes. At Sigüenza, Bishop Pedro was reported dead by May 20, 1156, although his last charter confirmation was the December 1155 (D907). His successor Celebruno, a Frenchman and former archdeacon of Toledo, first appears in the following November (D948).[73] Ten years later he was translated to Toledo.

In the see of Burgos, Bishop Victor is last seen in a royal diploma of October 1156 (D946). His successor, Pedro Pérez, confirmed another as bishop-elect the following January (D960).[74] Nothing is known of Pedro's past. While Alfonso VII was always sensitive to who held Burgos and the see remained dependent on Rome, no one objected to Pedro's promotion.

Astorga was another sensitive episcopate because of its continuing relationship to Braga. Bishop Pedro Cristiano died, probably at court, on or about November 2, 1156 (D948).[75] His successor, Bishop Fernando, was likely elected there. He first appears in a private document of December 29, 1156. His antecedents are unknown, but he early made his obedience to the archbishop of Braga.[76]

The church of Compostela had been the center of most disputes over the past two decades but even it changed hands without controversy on the

71. Fletcher, *Episcopate*, pp. 63–64.
72. Ibid., pp. 32–33.
73. Minguella y Arnedo, *Historia*, p. 107. Ubieto Arteta, *Listas*, 2:356, dates Celebruno first confirmation to January 22, 1156, but this royal diploma must be redated to 1157 (D960).
74. Ubieto Arteta, *Listas*, 1:70, cited a private document dated only to 1156.
75. Qintana Prieto, *Obispado*, p. 355, dates it on the very day that Pedro confirmed a royal charter in Atienza.
76. Ibid., p. 363, cites a private document of December 29. Fletcher, *Episcopate*, p. 46, n. 1.

death of Archbishop Pelayo Caamundo in 1155. Bishop Martín of Oviedo was translated to it. The change was effected by April 1156, probably at court. That summer he traveled to Rome and was recognized.[77] The opening in the church of Oviedo was filled by Pedro, Benedictine abbot of the monastery of San Vicente. The choice of a monk rather than a member of the cathedral chapter suggests that royal influence was operative. Our first reliable notice of Pedro as bishop-elect is in a royal charter of January 1157. The next spring, he went to Rome to be consecrated and returned with the direct dependence of his see on Rome confirmed by Pope Hadrian IV (D960).[78]

Finally, Bishop Martín of Orense died, as he had lived, at court in December 1156 or January 1157. The close ties between the crown and that see, established with his promotion, were maintained with the election at court of Pedro Seguini before the end of January (D952–53, 957, 959).[79]

In the valley of the Ebro at Tarazona the bishop was Miguel Aznárez. He had been installed at the reconquest of the city in 1119 and was the brother of the Aragonese noble and longtime royal tenant there, Fortún Aznárez.[80] After Fraga, no one disturbed either brother and he confirmed diplomas of Alfonso VII only when the latter was in the region. Miguel did accompany García Ramírez on the campaign in Andalucía in 1150 and its exertions may have cost both their lives (D664, 671, 675, 679).[81] The Aragonese Martín de Bergua succeeded in 1151 or 1152 and was likely the choice of Ramon Berenguer, since Bergua is in the territory of Huesca. Toward the end of Alfonso's reign, however, Martín did confirm four Leonese charters (D860, 951, 956, 960).[82]

At Zaragoza, the Aragonese García de Majóns was bishop when Alfonso VII entered the city in 1134. García confirmed eight of that king's diplomas in the following year and attended the imperial coronation in León in May 1135. His last citation is November 13, 1135. He was succeeded very briefly by Bishop William, Alfonso's choice, consecrated at the Council of Burgos in

77. Fletcher, "Archbishops," pp. 52–53, supplies the basic information. His account can be made slightly more precise, however. December 18, 1155. AHN, Clero, Carpeta 1.510, no. 1, a private diploma cites Archbishop Pelayo as dead. April 26, 1156 (D930). Martín confirmed as elect.

78. Fletcher, *Episcopate*, p. 75. May 1157. Pub. Pedro Floriano Llorente, ed., *Colección diplomática del monasterio de San Vicente de Oviedo* (Oviedo, 1968), pp. 406–7, a private document relates that Bishop Pedro had left for Rome.

79. Fletcher, *Episcopate*, p. 49.

80. Ubieto Arteta, *Listas*, 2:372. José María Lacarra, "La restauración ecclesiástica en las tierras conquistadas por Alfonso el Batallador, 1118–1134," *RPH* 4 (1947): 268, conjectured that he was French but see Marquis D'Albon, ed., *Cartulaire général de l'Ordre du Temple, 1119–1150* (Paris, 1913), p. 246. A private donation dated only to 1146.

81. Ubieto Arteta, *Listas*, 2:372, erroneously put his death on February 16, 1150.

82. Ibid., 2:372, cites July 28, 1152, as his first appearance.

1136. His few citations, before his disappearance after October 1136, include two of the latter's diplomas (D230, 264).[83] The office now went to Bernard, probably that archdeacon of Zaragoza who had appeared with Bishop García at Alfonso's court in 1135. His first reliable citation comes in 1137.[84] Bishop Bernard was likely a Bearnese who came to Zaragoza in 1118 or shortly thereafter. He never became a Leonese court figure and, except for three diplomas all issued at Almazán in 1138, never appeared in that king's company after his consecration (D320–22). When Bernard died in the first half of 1152, he was followed by a nominee of Ramon Berenguer. Bishop Pedro de Torroja, installed by June 28, 1152, was the brother of Guillermo de Torroja, bishop of Barcelona.[85] Bishop Pedro never appeared in a charter of Alfonso VII.

Careful royal selection of individual bishops, an option the king pursued vigorously, could effect much. Once installed, those bishops could severally be dealt with as the royal administrators and lieutenants that they undoubtedly were. Yet the coordination of episcopal actions and the resolution of their ambitions and disputes domestically remained the sphere of the church council. But the question of the nature of such councils during this period remains. By and large, church historians have continued to assume that the church council in this period was that identifiable, separate, and independent institution of which later canon law would dream. The reality was more ambiguous.

To be sure, monarchs did not confuse bishops, or even abbots, with the other dignitaries of their realm. They were, however, regarded as just that, dignitaries of the realm as well as of the church. The crown simply assumed the direction and jurisdiction over them that it had possessed immemorially. The language of prelate and monarch alike testify to a routine expectation of the exercise of royal authority in matters we should regard as properly ecclesiastical.[86] As the selection and actions of individual bishops was carefully overseen their joint actions were even more closely controlled. Notwithstanding, the most recent, extended study of the subject defines the council in a fashion that can only be regarded as anachronistic. Rejecting the term "national councils," it argues for councils "whose distinctive note is that they were convoked, presided over, and controlled by a papal legate."[87] Describing them as

83. November 13, 1135. Pub. Rubio, *Documentos*, p. 21, a private document. October 28, 1136. Pub. Lacarra, "Documentos," *EEMCA* (1947–1948): 340–41, a private document is last.

84. November 1137. Pub. Ubieto Arteta, *Documentos*, pp. 136–37. In *Listas*, 2:439, he overlooked his own citation.

85. Ubieto Arteta, *Listas*, 2:439. The relationship of Pedro and Giuillermo is given in Joachim Miret y Sans, "Le roi Louis VII et le Comte de Barcelone," *Moyen Age* 25 (1912): 295.

86. Andrés E. Mañaricua, "Provisión de obispos en la Alta Edad Media española," *Estudios de Deusto* 14 (1966): 61–92, has made a valuable and extended study of the language of early texts. Reilly, *Alfonso VI*, p. 98. Reilly, *Urraca*, pp. 225–50.

87. Antonio García y García, "Concilios y sínodos en el ordenamiento jurídico del reino

"legatine" councils, the author then treats nine councils of the realm under Alfonso VII. One must be disregarded, for the author accepts a date of 1127 for 1117, despite the attendance of Bishops Paschal of Burgos and Jerome of Salamanca, both deceased by the later date.[88] Of the remaining eight, I regard as constituitive the presence of the king rather than that of the legate. Moreover, at the Council of León in 1135 there was no legate present. At Palencia in 1129 the legate was Archbishop Raymond of Toledo, more realistically seen as agent of the king than of the pope.

Now precisely, a greater attention to form and propriety sets the second half of the twelfth century off from preceding ages. In that sense, one can speak of the success of ecclesiastical reform. But substance was a different matter. With that in mind, it should be noted that the initiative for each of these councils, so far as we can tell, lay with the crown rather than the papacy. Nonetheless, the success of the reform papacy is again to be measured in the fact that abbots, bishops, and even kings began to employ Rome's claim to an appellate jurisdiction as a weapon to achieve domestic aims otherwise unattainable. Yet the church history of the peninsula in the twelfth century, and long after, is testimony to their several unwillingnesses to accept the judgment of the papacy as final unless it coincided with their own desires.

It is also instructive to look at the few surviving *acta*. At Palencia in 1129, the text is promulgated by Archbishop Raymond as archbishop, primate, and papal legate together with the bishops in attendance, the Emperor Alfonso present and approving. The canons are designed for the health of "the holy church and the entire realm." Seven of those eighteen canons deal with what we should style secular matters, from the punishment of counterfeiters to the safety of oxen.[89] One could argue fairly that mixed legislation assumes a mixed legislature.

At Valladolid in 1143 the *acta* are promulgated by the Cardinal-legate Guido together with the archbishops, bishops, and abbots and with many others "in the presence of the Emperor Alfonso." The twenty-four canons, it might be observed, represent a clearer concentration on purely ecclesiastical matter although two condemn arson and the harassment of farmers and merchants as well as monks and pilgrims.[90]

If the Council of León in the spring of 1135 were accepted as a council, and its chronicler so calls it, then we have a report on its *acta* rather than

---

de León," in *El reino de León en la Alta Edad Media*, vol. 1, *Cortes, concilios y fueros*, pp. 353–494 (León, 1988), p. 364.

88. Ibid, pp. 425–26. The author knows the text from Fidel Fita, "Concilio nacional de Burgos (18 de febrero de 1127)," *BRAH* 48 (1906): 387–407. See also Reilly, *Urraca*, pp. 119–22.

89. Falque Rey, *HC*, pp. 429–30.

90. Carl Erdmann, ed., "Papsturkunden in Portugal," *AGWG* 20 (1927): 198–203.

their text. The language employed indicates a largely undifferentiated concern with the health of church and realm, although they were addressed on
separate days.[91]

The *acta*, then, are not terribly helpful in specifying the nature of the
body that enacted them. García y García wavers between making the presence
of a papal legate definitive and simply following the language of the chronicler or even that of a royal document. The character of those in attendance
at a council complicates the problem. The language of contemporaries suggests that they were councils of the realm, but the presence now and again
of prelates from the realm of Aragón or of Portugal did not prompt different
language or a different focus. They were clearly not provincial councils in the
ecclesiastical sense. They might be claimed to have been primatial councils,
for the archbishop of Toledo seems always to be present, but they were never
so styled. All the data testify that they were convoked by the king on his own
initiative, for his own purposes, and held in his presence. They are, in short,
royal councils, composed of all those who owe obedience to the king, whom
he sees fit to summon, and who dare not absent themselves.

They differ little from the ordinary royal curia and not at all from a *curia
generalis*. A look at the itinerary of the curia, when chancery practice after
1135 routinely records the place of issue of charters, indicates that, practically
speaking, a council of the metropolitan province of Toledo was always attendant on the king, and it is doubtful that the practice was an innovation. Confirmations of the archbishop of Toledo and the bishops of Segovia, Palencia,
and Sigüenza indicate that these prelates were continuously in the royal entourage if they were not in Rome or dead or dying. The record of the bishops
of Astorga is harder to judge. For one thing, the rapid alternation in its bishops creates a problem, as does the relative closeness of the see to stops on the
royal itinerary such as León, Sahagún, and Zamora. But from the accession of
Bishop Arnold in 1144 he, and his successor Pedro Cristiano, were more often
at court than in Astorga. Zamora presents the same problem, since that episcopal city also figured in the royal itinerary. Notwithstanding, it is safe to say
the Bishop Bernard spent extended periods with the court two or three times
each year and, after a hiatus between 1150 and mid-1153, so did his successor
Bishop Stephen. The see of Osma, too, lay proximate to the royal itinerary
along the eastern frontier. But its bishops were available for royal purposes,
at Burgos, Palencia, or Nájera, two or three times a year and not infrequently
at Segovia or Toledo.

91. Maya Sánchez and Gil, *CAI*, pp. 182–84.

The canonically exempt sees of the heartland of the realm were as well represented at court as those of the Toledo province. The bishops of León rivaled the archbishops of Toledo in their continuous attendance. Those of Burgos were fortunate that their episcopal city was so often on the royal itinerary, for they could then be at once in residence and at court, but from 1146 Bishop Victor seems to be in the company of the king three or four times a year at places far from his own city. Oviedo was beyond the Cantabrians and seldom visited by the king. But from 1143, Bishop Martín, too, was found in the royal presence at least twice a year and when he became archbishop at Compostela he seems to have continued the practice. The latter would have found there two of his nominal suffragans in the company of their more usual patrons, the archbishop of Toledo and the king. These were the bishops of Salamanca and Avila, whose sheep were more likely to see their shepherd when the curia was passing through their episcopal city than at any other time. Even distant Orense, from the period of Bishop Martín, was regularly represented at court by its prelate.

Summing up, the king of León-Castilla traveled constantly in the presence of a cadre of bishops drawn from the most important sees of his realm. They graced his court, illustrated his authority, and supplied him counsel. Even if they acted in concert on matters technically ecclesiastical, they could not escape, probably could not conceive the desireability of escaping, the context that routinely shaped the texture of their careers and lives. Bishops everywhere seem to have so far adopted the style of the royal curia that the Third Lateran Council in 1179 had to legislate that archbishops and bishops on canonical visitations must limit their retinue to forty to fifty horsemen and to twenty to thirty horsemen, respectively. In Iberia as elsewhere, one presumes that meant these prelates, when not with the crown, traveled in their personal curia of a almost hundred persons.[92]

By contrast, the Roman Papacy was an alien presence. However revered it might be in the purely religious sense, its authority and agents were still a novelty and an intrusion. Yet it was a novelty impossible to ignore. Therefore, it was a power to be carefully controlled and managed. But the history of the period demonstrates how difficult that could be. During the reign of Alfonso VI, the reform papacy had secured the supression of the Mozarabic Rite only at the cost of considerable exertion, and even then with some connivance by the crown.[93] In that of Urraca, to her dismay, the papacy had

92. Josiah Cox Russell, *Twelfth Century Studies* (New York, 1978), p. 45.
93. Reilly, *Alfonso VI*, pp. 97–112.

raised the see of Santiago de Compostela to metropolitan status and thereby thrown the canonical relationships of the Iberian provinces into turmoil for a century.[94] Alfonso VII was aware of the need to conduct business with this new power carefully.

Above all, appeals to Rome had to be screened and managed. In 1130, once the validity of the king's marriage to Berengaria had been questioned, resort to Rome could not be prevented. The Council of Carrión, with its deposition of three bishops, however, could be and was employed to illustrate the cost of such an initiative if one lost. In its aftermath, the consecration of the new Bishop Alfonso of Oviedo in Iberia, probably by Archbishop Raymond of Toledo, was reported to Rome by Archbishop Gelmírez, his creature Bishop Arías of León, and Bishop Pedro of Lugo.[95] That sort of audacity surely exacerbated Alfonso VII's continuing vendetta with Gelmírez.

Nevertheless, if blatant resort to Rome in opposition to the royal will could be prevented or punished, more subtle fashions of circumventing one's primate, one's metropolitan, or even one's king could not be. By this time the tradition of the episcopal *ad limina* visit to the Holy See had been successfully reinvigorated by the reform party, and the crown could not easily block such practice, although it could sometimes discourage it. The visit to Rome was almost always accompanied by the solicitation from the papacy of a guarantee of the episcopal possessions and rights of the visitor.[96] Since those rights and possessions included those held, or claimed to be held, from king, metropolitan, or against fellow bishop, monasteries in the diocese, and noblemen of the district, the seeming innocent request for a papal guarantee could in fact mask the initiation of a plea.

Although the crown was hardly misled by such tactics, they were difficult to oppose outright. Sometimes it must have been positively convenient to appear neutral in such matters, when two subordinates were at odds over advantages important to themselves but indifferent to the crown. Thus resolution by Rome of boundary disputes between the archbishop of Toledo and the bishop of Segovia in 1130 or between the bishops of Burgos and of Osma in 1136 was probably preferable to arbitration by the king. Even so, a body of

---

94. Reilly, *Urraca*, pp. 241–43.

95. Falque Rey, *HC*, pp. 468–69.

96. We still lack an edition of papal letters to León-Castilla of the sort that Carl Erdmann provided for Portugal and Paul Kehr provided for Catalonia, Navarra, and Aragón. Demetrio Mansilla has provided a useful catalog of some materials but a glance at the contents of any cathedral archive illustrates immediately how much has yet to be done. Hernández, *Cartularios*, pp. 495–511, for the "Documentos pontificios" is a good example. In the absence of such an edition most present observations must be recognized as subject to at least modest subsequent revision.

precedent for papal jurisdiction in a variety of matters was being constructed thereby that would be increasingly difficult either to manage or deny in the future.

Then, too, the crown had its own reasons for sometimes seeking the approval of Rome. One of the oldest recognized juridical rights of the Roman bishops was that of approval for the translation of a bishop from one see to another. Alfonso VII sought such approval no fewer than four times for the archepiscopate of Compostela alone and twice for the archepiscopate of Toledo. In these instances, and in other lesser ones, only once was his candidate rejected. When the validity of his marriage was argued at Rome in 1129, the decision was favorable, and when he sought the inclusion of Iberia as an acceptable sphere of concentration for the Second Crusade in 1147, Rome also obliged. Royal and papal interests were more often than not compatible and, even when the merits of the case were evenly balanced from the Roman viewpoint, the king could usually outbid his domestic opposition. Alfonso was fortunate, too, in that he enjoyed a continuity in his realm that the popes lacked in theirs. Between 1126 and 1157 there was but one king in León-Castilla but there were seven different bishops of Rome. Moreover, the longest ruling of these popes, Innocent II (1130–1143), was for years seriously hampered by a rival anti-pope, Anacletus II (1130–1138). Innocent needed to be wary of decisions that would drive the disappointed into the camp of his rival. Under such circumstances, Rome was rather more amenable than it might otherwise have been.

Everywhere in western Europe, however, the preferred vehicle of papal jurisdiction was the papal legate. Already it had something like a century of precedent behind it in Iberia and its full history there is still imperfectly known.[97] Not surprisingly, the crown preferred a resident prelate be granted legatine authority such as Archbishops Bernard of Toledo and Diego Gelmírez had enjoyed in their heydays. But Rome had grown wary of the resident legate. Archbishop Bernard of Toledo enjoyed the peninsular legateship for almost two decades, although he lost a significant portion in 1115. Archbishop Gelmírez was legate for the ecclesiastical province of Braga from 1120 until 1124, but after that time none of his efforts to reclaim it were successful.[98] Archbishop Raymond of Toledo seems to have held the post for a brief time in 1129 but not thereafter, as Rome resorted to sending its cardinals as legates.

Alfonso VII declined to dispute that decision. On occasion, he actively

97. Gerhard Säbekow, *Die päpstliche Legationen nach Spanien und Portugal bis zum Ausgang des XII Jahrhunderts* (Berlin, 1931), although useful, needs to be thoroughly reworked.
98. Fletcher, *St. James's Catapult*, pp. 211–15.

sought legates from Rome. They were frequently in the peninsula and generally were amenable to royal desires. There is no record of his conflict with one. At Carrión in 1130, a legate had concurred in the deposition of no fewer than three sitting bishops. At Valladolid in 1155, Alfonso secured the legatine blessing for a crusade in the peninsula. At Burgos in 1136, the papacy had to intervene against its own legate, who had become party to the royal plot to deprive the archbishop of Santiago de Compostela of his office.

In matters relating to the peninsular church, even the papacy supported royal desires up to a point. Certainly, it upheld the primatial right's of Toledo over its neighboring metropolitans of Tarragona, Santiago de Compostela, and Braga.[99] Yet although both Alfonso and the primate pursued such support vigorously, the primacy was canonically a weak reed for any practical purpose. A primate had the right to a formal declaration of obedience on the part of his metropolitans, and even Braga was finally moved to make one in 1150.[100] He had the right to summon a council, which his subordinates were obliged to attend. Portuguese and Aragonese bishops and archbishops sometimes did attend such councils of the realm, as at Burgos in 1136 and Valladolid in 1155, although the presence at each of a papal legate obscures the operative authority. In any event, in such a setting the bishops could be brought face to face with the person of the king, whose desires were difficult to withstand.

Beyond those two prerogatives the authority of the primate becomes very shadowy indeed. Roman reformers had no interest in adding a potent, intermediate power between them and the local church. The crown and Toledo hoped the primatial authority might be made a useful disciplinary instrument in the Iberian church but it did not so develop. Nor did Alfonso find the papacy more helpful in bolstering Toledo's metropolitan jurisdiction. Archbishop Bernard had succeeded in the time of Alfonso VI in having the independent sees of León and Oviedo incorporated into his province only to see them subsequently escape.[101] At the very beginning of his episcopate Archbishop Raymond also secured their subjection but within five years both sees had regained their independence.[102] Eventually Toledo would have its way but Alfonso VII was not to live to see it. The see of Burgos would also be drawn into that net later in the Middle Ages, but for the present, lesser

99. Rivera Recio, *Iglesia*, pp. 315–44. Hernández, *Cartularios*, pp. 497–511, cites a long list of papal bulls issued during the reign and addressed to securing recognition for Toledo's primatial jurisdiction.

100. Hernández, *Cartularios*, p. 74.

101. Reilly, *Alfonso VI*, pp. 272, 300, 335.

102. Hernández, *Cartularios*, pp. 495–96. At the Council of Carrión in 1130 both newly named bishops canonically had to be consecrated at Rome.

concessions had to be accepted. When Pope Anastasius IV formally defined Tarragona's suffragans in 1154, Burgos was not included although Zaragoza, Tarazona, and Calahorra were.[103] The papacy was, at most, willing to tolerate Alfonso's control of episcopal selection to the sees of León, Oviedo, and Burgos, and the king had to settle for that.

Closer to Toledo, the sees of Salamanca, Avila, and Zamora were eventually to be lost to Santiago de Compostela. Alfonso was able to place his candidates in them during his lifetime but not to persuade the papacy to remove them from the jurisdiction of Compostela. He was able to prevent the enforcement of the papal decision of 1123 for the suppression of the see of Zamora at the death of Bishop Bernard in 1149 but unable to forestall its being acknowledged a suffragan of Braga in 1153.[104] Nor was he able to detach Astorga from Braga, although the former lay but half a day's ride from his royal city.

In the far west, literally nothing could be made out of the confusion resulting from Calixtus II's decision of 1120 to make Santiago de Compostela a metropolitan see at the expense of Muslim-held Mérida. At that time, Coimbra and Salamanca had been designated as its suffragans and Gelmírez claimed Avila as well. But Compostela remained surrounded by the Galician suffragans of Braga; Lugo, Mondoñedo, Orense, and Túy, which it sought to dominate. This was to fight the king's fight as well, once Portugal became finally independent after 1143. Alfonso did seek, sometimes with success, to place his own candidates in Compostela and Orense and to tolerate the succession of local figures elsewhere in the northwest.

In the east there was no such rivalry to exploit. Only so long as Aragón was crippled by the disaster of Fraga could Alfonso hope to place his own men in the sees of Zaragoza, Tarazona, and Calahorra. Once Ramon Berenguer IV had made good his bid for a new Aragón-Barcelona after 1137, both the territory and the sees were lost to Tarragona and the Barcelonan.

All in all, if the second quarter of the twelfth century was visibly a time of increased contact between Rome and Iberia and the influence of the former was everywhere on the rise, the king and curia remained by far the more important force shaping the operation the secular church of the realm. With few exceptions, bishops were the king's men and the episcopate was the key institutional element. The sort of government and energy that flowed into local dioceses was directly related to those men chosen by the crown. This tradi-

103. Fernández Conde, *Historia*, 2–1:317–18.
104. Ibid., 2–2:620.

tional practice was, assuredly, not a novelty in the reign of Alfonso VII but only more clearly visible. It interacted with the rise of the cathedral chapter, as a subordinate structure, and indirectly fostered its growth. While the practice of some sort of common life among the clergy of the bishop's *familia* was not an entirely new practice, it was one seized on by the Gregorian Reform. The ideal was to create a community about the bishop that would be celibate, educated, protected by their common life from the grosser forms of vice, and that would perform in his church the continuous, corporate, liturgical worship of God that had come to mark Benedictine monasticism, but in a cathedral setting.

Attempts to create such communities had begun already during the reign of Fernando I (1037–1065) and intensified under his successors, as the flow of monks from the reformed monasteries of southern France into the episcopates of Iberia became commonplace.[105] Although the development of cathedral chapters was a general phenomenon and responded to common ideals, everywhere the increasing integration of the episcopate into the royal curia was creating conditions that favored the rise of the cathedral chapter as a key institution for the realization of local aims.

To become a bishop during the reign of Alfonso VII was to become a member of the royal court, traveling with the king almost continuously, and spending large amounts of time traveling to and from the court if not actually resident. Given the difficulties of travel, even brief trips to court became major absences from one's cathedral. Such absences of the bishop insensibly promoted the rise of the practical authority of the cathedral chapter and its dean or prior. The day-to-day administration of the bishop's church, of the diocese at large, and of the property of the diocese fell to its execution almost by default.[106]

Further momentum was given by the all too prevalent practice of royal choice of a curial figure for the bishopric, a person initially a stranger to his new diocese. The potential was then always present for the chapter to become the vehicle of local ambitions and interests, as against those of the crown and the crown's prelate. The cathedral chapter first took shape as the institutional, ecclesiastical expression of the ideals and purposes of the local nobility and of the bourgeois of the cathedral towns.

---

105. Unfortunately the movement has few historians and most of those marked by an unimaginative, canonistic approach to a growth that was rowdy and opportunistic.

106. The same development is visible everywhere. Compare Everett U. Crosby, "The Organization of the English Episcopate under Henry I," *Studies in Medieval and Renaissance History* 4 (1967): 40–41.

The reform movement, inheriting a fairly inchoate tradition regarding episcopal selection, initially sought to vest this local church interest with the power to choose the bishop. That instinct finally found central expression in the canons of the Second Lateran Council of 1139, although it had earlier achieved practical adoption in a wide variety of places.[107] Alfonso VII could agree in principle to episcopal election by cathedral chapter, which right he formally guaranteed to the church of Santiago de Compostela in 1128 (D85). In 1135 he was careful to point out that the canons of Salamanca had elected Berenguer their bishop. Nonetheless the history of the reign illustrates that the understanding and the practice of the law was sufficiently elastic to satisfy royal purposes.

That being so, and given the absence of the bishops for extended periods, the cathedral chapter sought practical independence from these non-native prelates more quickly than would otherwise have occurred. In the first half of the twelfth century, the cathedral chapters of León-Castilla began to insist on a formal division of the goods and income of the cathedral. Having achieved an economic base, they subsequently then moved to secure the right of election of their own officers, usually subject to the bishop's confirmation, the right to co-opt to membership in the chapter, and eventually even to strike their own seal. The chronology and dynamic of this movement that ended by producing the second most important executive authority of the secular church in the peninsula has hardly begun to be studied.[108] The rise of the cathedral chapter has been somewhat better chronicled elsewhere in western Europe, but the forcing role of the crown's activities has gone largely unrecognized due to the inability to trace the daily whereabouts of bishops.[109]

Along with the rise of the cathedral chapter in the secular church everywhere in western and central Europe, the first half of the twelfth century saw as well a marked change in the relative importance of the secular church and

107. Robert L. Benson, *The Bishop-elect* (Princeton, 1968), pp. 23–45, contains probably the clearest and best commentary on canonical thinking about the episcopal election. Demetrio Mansilla, *Iglesia castellano-leonesa y curia romana en los tiempos del rey San Fernando* (Madrid, 1945), p. 154, comments realistically and succinctly on its practical effect then and later.

108. Insofar as it exists, José Luis Martín, "Cabildos catedralicios del occidente español hasta mediados del siglo XIII," in *Homenaje a Fray Justo Pérez de Urbel* (Silos, 1977), pp. 125–36, surveyed the literature and sketched the development on the basis of it. The individual studies not only suffer from their isolation and a failure to appreciate the dynamic but also from an inability thoroughly to critique the documents, all of which were subject to subsequent interpolation that falsifies the chronology.

109. England has been particularly studied. Dom David Knowles, *The Monastic Order in England* (Cambridge, 1941), pp. 140–41. M. Brett, *The English Church under Henry I* (Oxford, 1975), pp. 190–96. Most particularly and recently see, Everett U. Crosby, *Bishop and Chapter in Twelfth-Century England* (New York, 1994).

the monastic church. Hadrian IV (1154–1159) was be the last of the popes drawn from monastic ranks for a long time. The future would belong to the secular clergy trained in canon law. Bishops increasingly would be drawn from the secular, university-trained clergy who had served a stint in royal service. Nevertheless, the influence of the monastic church would remain strong at the popular level for centuries yet and, in the first half of the twelfth century, it still furnished very considerable figures and numbers to the episcopate in Iberia and in western Europe.[110]

Meanwhile, the monastic church itself was undergoing remarkable transformations and the tempo of that process, too, was mediated in good measure by the crown. Generally speaking, we are less well informed of the individual mechanics of that movement than we are of the selection of bishops and of the rise of cathedral chapters.[111] In Iberia the primary tools for gauging the direction of development are the royal diplomas. Roughly a third of all surviving charters are grants to religious houses. This largesse was a major instrument though which royal influence was effected. Its distribution is instructive, although one must bear in mind that the character and affiliation of smaller monastic houses is not always easy to determine.

That said, it is evident that traditional Benedictine monasticism continued to be alive, well, and well patronized. Two thirds of Alfonso VII's grants to monastic institutions went to such independent establishments. With some sixty-four houses sharing 203 benefactions, the average house thus received roughly two royal grants during a reign of some thirty-one years. Of course, not all monasteries, even of the traditional type, were equally favored. Seven great monasteries; Antealtares in Galicia, Sahagún in León, Silos and Arlanza in the south of Castilla La Vieja, Oña and San Millán in the north of that region, and Santa María de Nájera in the Rioja, shared among them a full eighty-six grants. These favored houses bloomed under a royal patronage that bestowed an average of slightly better than a dozen grants on each. They had been, as well, the established favorites of the dynasty since the time of Fernando I.

Nevertheless, this traditionalism of the dynasty was not unrelieved. Almost as old as the dynasty itself was its special relationship with Cluny. One aspect of that relationship involved the gradual affiliation of certain penin-

110. Constance B. Bouchard, "The Geographical, Social and Ecclesiastical Origins of the Bishops of Auxerre and Sens in the Central Middle Ages," *Church History* 46 (1977): 287, furnishes some handy figures for France and England.
111. Antonio Linage Conde, *Los orígines del monacato benedictino en la peninsula Iberica*, 3 vols. (León, 1973), ends just where it would have begun to make a contribution to our period. Older scholarship is less critical, more particular, and of only incidental use.

sular monastic houses with the great Burgundian abbey brought about by the royal charter.[112] Alfonso VI had begun that practice with the transfer of seven peninsular monasteries to the Cluniacs. Urraca had added one more. Alfonso VII added another but failed, ultimately, in his attempt to add yet two further houses to the Burgundian abbey's network.[113] In addition to the transfer of the abbeys there were the five donations made both to Cluny by Alfonso, and twenty-four made to the affiliated monasteries of Sahagún and Santa María de Nájera by the same monarch.

The case of Sahagún is instructive for the interplay of royal and papal power in the sphere of monastic reform. The convent of San Facundo and Primitivo at Sahagún had been a favorite of the founder of the dynasty, Fernando I. Alfonso VI had made it the pantheon of a series of his wives.[114] A royal palace adjoined it and in 1080 the monk of Cluny, Bernard, who went on to become the first archbishop of Toledo after its reconquest in 1085, had been installed as its abbot. Despite that, the monastery continued its independence and was taken under direct papal protection in the time of Queen Urraca.[115]

It is curious, therefore, that Alfonso VII should have imagined that it would be possible to convey that monastery to the control of Cluny without a contest. Yet that is precisely what the king enacted on September 7, 1132 (D153).[116] What followed is not entirely clear except that the monastery appealed to Rome and its dependence on the Holy See was finally upheld. Cluny never made good its claim and instead of Sahagún paying an annual *cens* to the Burgundian house, it continued to be one of those thirty Iberian churches that paid directly to Rome.[117] It is perhaps significant that the anonymous chronicle of Sahagún has nothing to say of the reign of Alfonso VII.

The Leonese monarch continued his efforts to strengthen the position of Cluniac Benedictinism in his realm when on July 29, 1142, almost exactly ten years later, he conveyed the Castilian monastery of San Pedro de Cardeña to the Burgundian house (D432). The grant was made in the presence

112. Charles Julian Bishko, "Fernando I and the Origins of the Leonese-Castilian Alliance with Cluny," in *Studies in Medieval Spanish Frontier History*,: 491–515 (London, 1980). First pub. in Spanish in *CHE* 47–48 (1968): 31–135, and 49–50 (1969): 50–116, is the fundamental study. Peter Segl, *Königtum und Klosterreform in Spanien* (Kallmünz, 1974), concentrates more closely on the technical aspects.
113. Segl, *Königtum*, pp. 50–116.
114. Reilly, *Alfonso VI*, p. 190, n. 8.
115. Reilly, *Urraca*, p. 113.
116. The charter is not a chancery product but was probably done by a notary of the abbey of Cluny. The circumstances surrounding its issue give no easy rationalization for the step. See also Segl, *Königtum*, pp. 93–102.
117. I. S. Robinson, *The Papacy, 1073–1198: Continuity and Innovation* (Cambridge, 1990), pp. 270–73.

of Abbot Peter the Venerable of Cluny and was specifically addressed to the settlement of financial obligations owed by the kingdom to the Burgundian abbey.[118] This matter should have been simpler, for Rome had no prior claim on Cardeña. Nevertheless, the monks there appealed to the papacy and a long dispute followed. Despite strenuous efforts, Alfonso was bested again and the Castilian house passed under the control of Rome, another Iberian house that paid a *cens* to the papacy.

In addition to bolstering the position of Cluny and thereby furthering reformed and organized monasticism in the peninsula, Alfonso took other similar initiatives whose extent is not fully appreciated. If it had not been for the recent rediscovery in an English archive of a late medieval chartulary of the crusading order of Saint John of the Hospital of Jerusalem, we should still have a much impoverished notion of the spread of that order in Iberia during the reign of Alfonso VII.[119] It now appears the royal family made no fewer than twenty grants to the Hospitallers, which is remarkable in that it was a foreign order of fairly recent origin. Five of them were made in June 1140 alone when the Grand Master Raymond was at the court of Alfonso VII.

Templar materials boast no such happy find, and we still see but two recorded grants to that order during the entire reign. It seems likely, on the basis of analogy, however, that royal encouragement of the Templars was more substantial than currently appears.

Crown support for the new "white monks" of Citeaux is better known.[120] The endowment of new foundations or the encouragement of the adhesion to the Cistercians of older Benedictine houses in the peninsula led to a full fifteen such priories in the kingdom before 1157. The total number of royal grants to the Cistercians is forty-two or an average of roughly three per house.

The order of Prémontré was later still in making its Iberian appearance. Still, by 1157 there were three houses in León-Castilla and they had been the object of eight royal donations.

Collegiate churches, nonepiscopal but with a resident body of clergy living a regular life according to a constitution of more or less formal nature, had a relatively low profile. The church of Valladolid is the best known of them in this period. They had no current structure beyond the individual house, but a later age would see some of them formed into a more general

118. Segl, *Königtum*, pp. 102–10.
119. Carlos Ayala Martínez, ed., *Libro de Privilegios de la Orden de San Juan de Jerusalén en Castilla y León, siglos XII–XV* (Madrid, 1994).
120. Maur Cocheril, "L'implantation des abbayes cisterciennes dans la péninsule ibérique," *AEM* 1 (1964): 217–87, is the handiest authoritative introduction.

framework called the Augustinian Order. Some fourteen royal grants went to six such houses during the reign.

As near as one can tell at present, the crown at least was familiar with twelve houses of nuns. They were the recipients of some twenty-two grants from various members of the dynasty.

Royal grants to monasteries outside Iberia were rare, but not unknown. Aside from the five grants to Cluny there are two to the Cluniac house of Marcigny-sur-Loire, three to the nuns of Fontevrault near Poitiers, and one each to Clairvaux, to St. Denis, to St. Victor of Marseilles, to St. Ruf of Avignon, to St. Ginés (Arles?), and to San Angeli in Apulia.

Wherever one looks then in the second quarter of the twelfth century, the crown is the most important single factor in the institutional life of the church. Alfonso VII oversaw its geographical expansion along with that of the realm. He controlled its machinery and the selection of its key personnel. Through the largesse flowing from his fisc, he largely determined the vigor and manipulated the ambitions of its several components. In equal measure, the king was largely responsible for both its virtues and for its shortcomings. They both mirrored the growing sophistication and the brutal necessities of his own curia.

He had to respond, of course, in some measure to the new definitions of responsibility and respectability stirring in his own realm and in western Europe generally. Nor was he hostile to them insofar as they left his own real powers largely untouched. Moreover, those same powers allowed him to mediate with good success between the rising organizational power of the papacy and the generally respectful and docile churches of his own kingdom. At the same time Alfonso particularly favored the reform and reorganization of the regular clergy. Most probably he saw their growing incorporation into the larger systems of Cluny, Clairvaux, Prémontré, the Hospital, and the Templars, as a rationalization and simplification of his own task of the control and utilization of their resources.

Under Alfonso VII the church of León-Castilla became less isolated and more European. At the same time, it became more sophisticated in its institutional processes and more complex in its structures. Its growth, like that of the realm in which it inhered, was managed successfully and major crises were avoided, if sometimes narrowly. Overall royal control was maintained but no breach with the international church was allowed to develop. In ecclesiastical affairs, as elsewhere, Alfonso VII continued, orchestrated, and elaborated the policies of his dynasty now traditional from the days of Fernando I, as the opportunities of a new era permitted.

IO

The Towns of the Realm

MEDIEVAL TOWNS are ordinarily treated under three aspects: their demographic and physical development, their economic growth, and their legal and institutional evolution. The primary theme of this work and the nature of the sources available dictate a concentration on the last of these areas, but some preliminary remarks are in order concerning the first two.

In León-Castilla at the beginning of the second quarter of the twelfth century the total urban population of the realm constituted but a tiny fraction, probably little more than 2.5 percent, of the total population of perhaps two million. Even that diminutive figure most likely represented more than double the number of townspeople of a half century earlier. The towns were growing, to be sure, but in such of them as had ever boasted Roman walls, the circuit of the latter was still more than adequate to their needs.

Indeed, apart from the erection of individual dwellings, which left little trace that has endured down to our own times, the most remarkable construction then under way in them was ecclesiastical. In 1126 the towns are still best described as primarily religious centers in which a cathedral, an episcopal palace, the residences of canons, and a variety of monastic churches and monasteries dominated the physical landscape, supported the bulk of the economic activity, and supplied most administrative structures. Even where the bishop was not the outright *señor* of the town, the church was its largest single property holder, the episcopal courts were likely to be the busiest, and the bishop administered a major share of royal rights within and without its walls.

In some measure, the towns were already centers of exchange but the volume is impossible to judge. Explicit reference to markets is sporadic in the documents, although they must have existed everywhere.[1] As already noted,

---

1. Luis G. de Valdeavellano, *El mercado en León y Castilla durante la Edad Media*, 2nd ed. (Seville, 1975), is still the best general guide. Miguel-Angel Ladero Quesada, *Las ferias de Cas-*

the exchange of goods for goods was very rare. Coins from the south of France, Aragón, and the Muslim south were in frequent use, and no fewer than a dozen royal mints provided the necessary additional medium of exchange. The crown exploited bishops and abbots to collect tolls on overland trade as it passed through their bailiwicks. For the most part, however, we remain unaware of the substance of this trade as well as its quantity. In the greatest city of the realm, Toledo, we can presume on the continuance from the Muslim period of the export of manufactured steels and leathers both to the south and to the north. That city was also the major entrepôt for the goods of Andalucía, for it long retained its relationships with the more advanced societies of the south. We do know as well that some wheat of the northern *meseta* moved yet farther north over the Cantabrians to Asturias and that sea salt came south in return. Notwithstanding, by far the greatest artery of trade was the *camino de Santiago*, which ran east and west from Santiago de Compostela through León and Burgos to the Pyrenaen passes of Roncesvalles and Somport.

Surely goods also traveled that route but the major feature of its trade was purveyancing. The thousands who trudged along it each year must be victualed, housed, and occasionally horsed and clothed to boot. Certainly hundreds of tiny markets operated over its entire length supplying the humble goods of the countryside to that never-failing, seasonal stream of humanity. In like manner, the major economic activity of the entire kingdom, agriculture, found in purveyancing to the towns within practical reach a modest and occasional participation in something like a market. Still, that activity must be understood as a local rather than even a regional trade, for ordinarily agricultural goods were too bulky for economic transport of more than ten miles or so in a region so desperately poor in suitable watercourses as are the two *mesetas* of León-Castilla.[2] The first reliable notices of extended, regional fairs come at the very end of the reign.

Both church and trade probably did more to stimulate the gradual

---

tilla, siglos XII a XV (Madrid, 1994), supplies a brief update of one particular aspect of the market phenomenon.

2. Most attempts at explicitly economic history have concentrated on the later period for obvious reasons. Jean Gautier Dalché, *Historia urbana de León y Castilla en la Edad Media, siglos IX–XIII* (Madrid, 1979), is one recent attempt at a general survey. Among even the major towns only León has so far found in Carlos Estepa Díez, *Estructura social de la ciudad de León, siglos IX–XIII* (León, 1977), someone who has essayed a general history. Yet both authors depend primarily on materials from the late twelfth and thirteenth centuries. Summary descriptions for the earlier periods and guides to the periodical literature may be found in Bernard F. Reilly, *The Kingdom of León-Castilla under King Alfonso VI, 1065–1109* (Princeton, 1988) and *The Kingdom of León-Castilla under Queen Urraca, 1109–1126* (Princeton, 1982).

growth of towns than did the crown. The latter remained a peripatetic, predominantly rural institution whose direct contact with the towns was inter-
mittent, if fairly regular by season. León itself was the royal city but by no
means a royal capital. Like Burgos, Toledo, and Zamora, among the major
cities, it contained a royal palace or castle that was the center of local crown
administration but ordinarily of little more import. Castellans there were
scarcely more significant in the overall scheme of royal government than their
opposite numbers in rural palaces or castles such as Grajal, Sahagún, or even
tiny Cea. In but one respect the crown was essential to urban development.
When the latter became sufficiently pronounced to bring pressure on the
local status quo, the explicit action of the crown was necessary to legitimize
the necessary changes.

Such restructuring was authorized by means of a royal charter that subsequently has been styled a *fuero*. In the age of Alfonso VII the terminology,
and the conception itself, was rather more flexible. It can be said that every
community had a *fuero* and that, paradoxically, none did. At least the latter
is true as later legists and historians understood the term and as they defined
the instrument of its creation. The usage of the royal chancery of the age of
Fernando I, Alfonso VI, Urraca, and Alfonso VII made no provision for the
fuero as a documentary type. Of the roughly 2,000 royal and private documents of the period of Alfonso VII employed in this study, the Latin word
foro or *forum*, from which the Castilian *fuero* is derived, appears in sixty-eight
royal diplomas and in thirty-seven private ones. In forty-two of the former
and in thirty-five of the latter, the usage of the word is so general that the
meaning abstracted amounts to little more than the equivalent of "custom"
or "usage." In fact, such an equivalence is not infrequently explicitly made in
the documents themselves.

In this sense, every person, every property, every district, and every institution had a *fuero*. Persons purchasing property might thereby extend their
fuero to the new property. Conversely, the purchase or gift of property might
bring the new owner under the *fuero* of the district in which it lay, or the *fuero*
of the bishop or abbot who bestowed it, or of a *fuero* already held by the men
who held property in the same area. In the ordinary language of the time,
then, every extant person, property, area, or institution already had its *fuero*,
which consisted in a mixture of legal rights, economic obligations, property
rights, and customary procedures.

The alteration of such status came, usually by royal action but also occasionally by that of bishop, abbot, or noble, by way of a documentary grant
that bestowed a new status in some measure. The operative document con-

tinued to take the form of a charter of donation. There is little evidence of an awareness on the part of the actors that a novel legal or administrative process was being utilized.[3]

That is hardly surprising if we reflect that a good portion of the content of such acts is traditional. Quite often, some exemption is included, from *fossatum* or the *fossatara*, more rarely from the *portaticum*. Frequently, too, the royal permission is granted exclusively to a given group of the right to settle in a given locale, to repopulate it.[4] Or again, a specific locale or properties are exempted from royal legal jurisdiction, that is; a legal *coto* is awarded. Of whatever particular sort then, the essence of these charters is to create or alter a special status or jurisdiction. At least for the latter two instances, the authorization of a separate juridical person to administer the new status conferred is implied where it is not explicitly stated. Unless that juridical person is an officer of the church or a private individual, invariably it takes the form of what the documents style a "council," or *concejo* in Spanish. The much discussed problem of the distinction between the rural and the urban *concejo* thus becomes a question of structure and magnitude rather than essence. They exercised the same basic, delegated authority on behalf of two different social entities.

In documents utilized here, the *concejo* appears explicitly in 128. Great towns such as Toledo, León, Burgos, Nájera, Segovia, and Santiago de Compostela boast them, but so do tiny hamlets whose very location is now difficult to pinpoint. As an institution, the *concejo* was already ubiquitous.[5]

In the private documents, the most prominent function of the *concejo* is that of official witness for the transfer of local property or the ownership of the same. In sixty-one of eighty mentions of the former in private documents, that is the only discernable feature. If such a function seems nugatory, one should reflect on the potential for such a practice in itself to create a court in which local land law is adjudicated. But a sufficient number of private documents testify to the fact that the *concejo* was then recognized as a juridical person capable of owning property in its own right. Already in 1126 the *concejo* of tiny Lillo could dispute its rights over a portion of a village with the

3. This partial and practical character of the *fueros* had already been pointed out by by their earliest modern student. Eduardo de Hinojosa y Navaros, "Origen del regimen municipal en León y Castilla." In *Obras*, ed. Alfonso García-Gallo, vol. 3, pp. 271–317 (Madrid, 1974), pp. 292–93. Initially pub. in *La administración: Revista internacional de administración, derecho, economía, hacienda y política* 28 (1896): 417–38. Unfortunately it is still often being ignored.

4. Quite properly then the first real attempt to come to grips with this subject reflected this aspect in its title. Tomas Muñoz y Romero, ed., *Colección de fueros y cartas pueblas* (Madrid, 1847).

5. María del Carmen Carlé, *Del concejo medieval castellano-leones* (Buenos Aires, 1968), still the only comprehensive treatment of the subject, is limited by the thinness of the documentary materials then available to her.

mighty abbey of Sahagún and that quarrel could reach all the way to Rome.[6] No fewer than six documents testify to the *concejo*'s ability to alienate the property that it possessed by donation or sale.[7] Two others portray neighboring *concejos* jointly delimiting their respective jurisdictions.[8] Certain private documents reveal a bit more but they are best considered in another relation.

Royal documents are somewhat fuller. Nevertheless, almost a quarter, eleven of forty-eight, refer solely to the *concejo* in the role of witness to property transactions. Twenty-seven concern the *concejo* as property holder, confer the boundaries of its jurisdiction, and grant it certain exemptions, or the right to populate within certain territories, or a combination of the four. Of the remainder, the most significant notices for the present purposes are six of 1136 that take the form of royal *mandata*, forbidding the *concejos* of Avila, Toledo, Madrid, Segovia, Sepúlveda, Iscar, Fresno, and Pedraza to interfere with certain royal exemptions granted to the clergy of the realm (D268–73). A seventh such of 1150 is directed to the *concejos* of Atienza, Medinaceli, Ayllón, and Almazán (D660). Important here is the royal recognition of an ordinarily wide-ranging jurisdiction possessed by the *concejos* of these towns. Lacking is mention of the agency or officers through which that normal jurisdiction is exercised.

In its most antique and simple form, the *concejo* may often have been simply the totality of the property-owning inhabitants of a given village acting jointly. Even in Alfonso's period, the documents sporadically explicitly equate the *concejo* with a collection of individuals given by name or as the "boni homines" of the district. Nevertheless, to provide effect to its collective will, some sort of officers must have been necessary from the first. More, at some point those officers collectively must themselves have come to constitute the *concejo*, now understood as an institution. That this last stage has clearly arrived is reflected in the documents of our period, for it is accepted as ordinary in their language. Unfortunately, we remain largely ignorant of the processes of its development and of the details of its customary operation.[9]

---

6. December 7, 1126. Pub. José Antonio Fernández Flórez, ed., *Colección diplomática del monasterio de Sahagún, 1110–1199*, vol. 4 (León, 1991), pp. 108–9.

7. Usually to neighboring ecclesiastical institutions, although that may be a function of the church's superior ability to protect its records. See July 22, 1148, pub. Juan Loperráez Corvalón, *Descripción histórica del obispado de Osma*, 3 vols. (Madrid, 1788), 3:24–25, or 1151, pub. Ildefonso Rodríguez de Lama, ed., *Colección diplomática de La Rioja: Documentos, 923–1168*, vol. 2 (Logroño, 1976), pp. 228–29.

8. 1155. Pub. María Luisa Ledesma Rubio, ed., *Cartulario de San Millán de La Cogolla, 1076–1200* (Zaragoza, 1989), pp. 279–80. 1155. Ibid., pp. 281–82.

9. Magdalena Rodríguez Gil, "Notas para una teoría general de la vertebración jurídica de los concejos en la Alta Edad Media," in *Concejos y ciudades en la Edad Media hispánica*, pp. 321–

Although we deal here with a generalized institution that probably followed a similar evolution everywhere in the realm, its exact particulars in any given place or time depended greatly on local conditions and accidents of royal politics. For that reason, it seems to me that individual surveys of conditions discernable in the major towns will be more useful than an attempt to construct a general model. The order followed here is be that employed in my survey of the towns during the reign of Urraca, both for the way in which that simplifies the narration and in which it illuminates the historical progression.

The primatial city of Toledo was, from its reconquest in 1085, demographically both the largest city of the kingdom and the most complex in its human composition. Into the city, already composed of separate communities of Muslims, Jews, and Mozarabs, flowed quite considerable numbers of Galicians, Leonese, Castilians, and even French.[10] Each of these religious or ethnic communities hoped to continue to enjoy its own life subject, to its own *fuero*, and the crown wished to satisfy that expectation in the degree possible.

The surrender capitulation guaranteed to the Muslim population the continuing right to live subject to their religious law and judges (i.e., their own *fuero*), though no text survives. Most certainly the same provision was made for the Jewish population, although again we have no text. Less sweeping provision, probably, was made for the Mozarabs, and there is a partial indication of the terms in Alfonso VII's confirmation of them in 1155 (D877). *Fueros* were also granted to Castilians and Franks, but Galicians and Leonese may simply have been included in the former of these for some modicum of simplicity.[11] To this absolute minimum of five jurisdictions must be added those of the crown and of the archbishop. This state of affairs certainly continued through the reign of Urraca. A variety of officials are attested for one or the other of these communities but no city government, or *concejo*, is in evidence.[12]

During the reign of Alfonso VII, the situation was partially simplified, probably at the royal initiative. His purported charter dated November 16, 1118, was addressed to "all of the citizens of Toledo, Castilians, Mozarabs,

---

45. (León, 1990), outlines this problem and its bibliography in good detail while illustrating the present scholarly inability to come to grips with it convincingly. Useful immediate background for the consideration of the *concejo* and its bibliography in this period is contained in the chapter on the towns in Reilly, *Urraca*, pp. 314–51.

10. Julio González, *Repoblación de Castilla La Nueva*, 2 vols. (Madrid, 1975–76), 2:67–138, marshals the evidence of their numbers and new situations in both the city and its adjoining territories.

11. Alfonso García-Gallo, "Los fueros de Toledo," *AHDE* 45 (1975): 341–488, is the essential study.

12. Reilly, *Urraca*, pp. 316–19.

and Franks" and was evidently designed to substitute a single *fuero*, in good measure of Mozarab character, although Franks were allowed resort to their peculiar *fuero* if they so wished, for all Christian inhabitants of the city (D5). Clearly this document was produced later in the century, most probably in Mozarab circles to bolster their position, but it testifies to an already established tradition of unified city government.[13] One should see its remote model in the more limited Alfonsine grant of 1137 already addressed to the "Mozarabs, Castilians, and Franks" of the town (D286). On the other hand, the Alfonsine confirmation of the *fuero* of the Mozarabs in 1155, mentioned above, was addressed to "the entire concejo of Toledo," which had clearly come into being by then.

This increasing simplification and centralization of the municipal government, at least in so far as it concerned the Christian population, likely occasioned the issuance on April 24, 1136, of a special charter to the Franks of Toledo that guaranteed them their own *merino* and their own *sayon* within their *barrio* proper (D250). There is no mention of any municipal *concejo* in the document, but the charter suggests a necessary palliative, given the institution of one. Less than two months later, the king found it useful to reaffirm the particular *fuero* of the church of Toledo, its personnel, and its possessions, perhaps for the same reason (D255). Notwithstanding, in January 1144 the archbishop himself and the *zalmedina* of Talavera de la Reina submitted a dispute before the *concejo* of Toledo.[14] In 1154 the royal settlement of a dispute recognized the legal standing of its *concejo* (D812). Still, however, in March 1155, allowance was being made that disputes within the lands of Toledo might be judged according to the *fuero* of the Castilians.[15]

Yet even after this partial consolidation a considerable tangle of jurisdictions remained. The military one was technically in the hands of a count; early in the reign of Count Rodrigo González de Lara, from 1144 by his nephew, Count Manrique de Lara. But the import of the countship was largely financial and the actual head of Toledo's troops in the field were often Rodrigo Fernández de Castro, the Galician Muño Alfonsez, and later Guter Ermíldez, all of whom the *Chronica Adefonsi Imperatoris* is likely to style "princeps Toletanae militiae" or "alcalde Toleti" indifferently. As the same source makes clear, their appointment came at the hands of the king. With scarcely more

---

13. García-Gallo, "Fueros," pp. 359–62, believed that the document was produced before 1174, largely on the basis of its content. My own feeling is that the orthography, "Adephonsus rex" or "Aldephonsus Raymundiz" for the almost invariable "Adefonsus" argues a date still closer to the end of the century.

14. Francisco J. Hernández, ed., *Los cartularios de Toledo* (Madrid, 1985), p. 52.

15. Ibid., pp. 103–4.

qualification the same assertion may be ventured about the archepiscopal dignity whose religious jurisdiction pervaded the city and the *terra* of Toledo.

Judges or leaders of the resident communities of Muslims and Jews were guaranteed by their *fueros* to be of their own faith, although they were of necessity royal appointees. These were communities directly dependent on the crown. Notwithstanding, it is likely that those societies themselves informally nominated the men whom Alfonso then authorized to lead them.

The new, loosely unified community of the Christians of the city had their own officials. *Alcalde, alvazil,* and *zalmedina.* They appear as confirmants of almost all royal diplomas issued in the city in the 1150s when the king was constantly in Toledo. Clearly they are men of substance and importance. But we have no compelling evidence of how they were chosen. One thinks that they were royal appointees from men nominated by the archbishop, the royal tenant, the "princeps militiae," or other royal appointees, past or present. In short, co-option into the establishment would be a fair description of the likely process.[16] Did they themselves constitute the corporation of the *concejo*? Again one thinks such a state of affairs likely, but the documents are silent.

The reach of the municipal government into the surrounding countryside is impossible to reduce to orderly description. A town such as Talavera de la Reina had its own *zalmedina* and *alcalde* (D89). Doubtless it had its own *concejo* as well. Madrid and Maqueda did (D399, 748). So did smaller places such as Escalona and Santa Olalla.[17] In 1150 and 1156 the king conceded *fueros* to the new settlers in San Miguel and Ocaña (D60, 926). Again this state of affairs was already an established order.[18] If we are not able to follow it in any detail doubtless the powers of that era understood their respective rights sufficiently well to defend them vigorously in the face of challenge.

The world south of the Sierra de Guadarrama was still a frontier district, of course. Even this northern portion of the old *taifa* of Toledo continued to be the object of serious attempts to reclaim it by the Almoravid emirs of North Africa first and then by their Almohad successors. If that threat did not altogether eliminate friction, it did put a premium on the collaboration of local and royal powers. North of the Guadarrama and below the River Duero lay another world whose slow repopulation was one of the quiet triumphs

16. The offices were already traditional from the preceding reign at the least. Reilly, *Urraca*, pp. 316–19.

17. Hernández, *Cartularios*, p. 98. Nevertheless the *fueros* of January 4, 1130 to Escalona, pub. García-Gallo, "Fueros," pp. 464–65, cannot be of that early date. The otherwise careful study of Antonio Malalana Ureña, *Escalona medieval, 1083–1400* (Cubierta, 1987), pp. 104–10, is too trusting in this regard.

18. Reilly, *Urraca*, p. 319.

of the reign.[19] Originally been made possible by the reconquest of Toledo, it had continued since to be pressed forward behind the cover of that embattled redoubt.

One of the two leading towns of this sprawling area was the once classical city and bishopric of Salamanca. Its definitive recovery as a Christian center began with its repopulation under Count Raymond of Burgundy in the reign of Alfonso VI. During the reign of Urraca, it was an area contested by that queen and her half sister Teresa of Portugal. As a result, the development of Salamanca remains obscure indeed, until Alfonso VII installed his former chancellor, Bishop Berenguer, there in 1135 and then partially secured its southwestern flank with the reconquest of Coria in 1142. The bishop of Salamanca had actually resided in Zamora up until 1120, and subsequently the former's episcopacy had been disputed until the succession of Berenguer. Fully reliable documents of any sort begin only with the reign of Alfonso VII, underlining the achievement of a secure order. The 1140s also saw the beginning of the construction of a major Romanesque cathedral and a new system of walls to replace the derelict Roman wall.[20]

The town's population was simpler in composition than that of Toledo. It had never been a Muslim center and so that element consisted of but a few domestic slaves. Similarly, there was little to the barren spot on the River Tormes at this time to attract any Jewish population of note. French adventurers, merchants, and warriors were there but never enough to merit their own *fuero*. The bulk of the settlers were Portuguese, Galicians, Leonese, and Castilians and a good number of Mozarabs, refugees from the world of Islam.[21]

As in any episcopal city, the jurisdiction of the bishop bulked large. There is some reason to suspect that early on Salamanca was, indeed, an episcopal *señorio* and that at his accession in 1126 Alfonso VII found it advisable to restore episcopal control in the city and its territories (D39). Nevertheless, just as Raymond of Burgundy apparently controlled both town and

19. The detailed history of this process is just beginning to be written. Angel Barrios García, *Estructuras agrarias y de poder en Castilla: El ejemplo de Avila, 1085–1320* (Salamanca, 1983). Luis Miguel Villar García, *La Extremadura castellano-leonesa: Guerreros, clérigos y campesinos, 711–1252* (Valladolid, 1986). María Trinidad Gacto Fernández, *Estructura de la población de la Extremadura leonesa en los siglos XII y XIII* (Salamanca, 1977). The latter is based entirely on the *fueros* of Salamanca, Ledesma, Alba de Tormes, and Zamora and constitutes a useful analysis and resume of their contents. However, since the actual text of none of these is earlier than the thirteenth century, the synthetic picture that emerges is difficult to attribute to any given time before then.
20. Manuel González García, *Salamanca: La repoblación y la ciudad en la Baja Edad Media* (Salamanca, 1988), pp. 41 and 55.
21. González García, *Salamanca*, p. 17.

countryside earlier, Pons de Cabrera was tenant there for the king from 1144 until late 1156. In 1135 the letter of Archbishop Raymond of Toledo to Archbishop Diego Gelmírez of Santiago de Compostela that informed the latter of the election of Bishop Berenguer stated that the new bishop-elect has been honorably received in Salamanca by the electors and the "entire Salamancan *concejo.*"[22] Near the end of the reign, in 1156, the Frenchman Martin and his sister Melina donated property to the cathedral and the act was witnessed by the *concejo* and an *iudex* and two *sayones* were cited in the dating protocol.[23] The form of government in the municipality seems then to be quite unexceptionable. There is the text of a *fuero* extant, but it is late and difficult if not impossible to employ to illustrate conditions for the time of Alfonso VII.[24]

Twenty kilometers southeast of Salamanca was the hamlet of Alba de Tormes. In 1140 it appears to have had a *fuero* and *concejo* of its own, but the documentation that supports the attribution is late and its form and substance have clearly been reworked (D387).

Roughly ninety kilometers southeast of Salamanca, the town of Avila had a history closely linked to the former during this period. Avila, too, had been a bishopric during the classical age. When Alfonso VI restored Salamanca, its first bishop, Jerome, became administrator of Avila as well. The two districts shared much the same vicissitudes in the reign of Urraca, and Avila only begins to emerge into clearer view with Alfonso VII's imposition of Bishop Jimeno there in 1133.[25] A new Romanesque cathedral was begun, and an imposing new set of walls that still dominate the surrounding countryside. The latter are usually assigned to the period of Alfonso VI, specifically to his son-in-law Count Raymond of Burgundy, but it is difficult to imagine how the massive resources necessary for that project could have been secured so early. The position of Avila at the foot of the long, low pass of Arrebatacapas leading up from the Tajo plain perhaps made essential some preliminary work on them to provide against the possibility of a Muslim reconquest of Toledo.

Given the royal support and long episcopate of Bishop Jimeno (1133–1158), that prelate probably played a strong role in the government of the

22. Emma Falque Rey, ed., *HC* (Turnholt, 1988), p. 500.

23. September 3, 1156. Pub. José Luis Martín, Luis Miguel Villar García, Florencio Marcos Rodríguez, and Marciano Sánchez Rodríguez, eds., *Documentos de los archivos cathedralicio y diocesano de Salamanca, siglos XII–XIII* (Salamanca, 1977), pp. 105–6. January 21, 1133. Ibid., pp. 89–90, a private document already cited an *iudex* and three *sayones* by name but no *concejo* appeared.

24. Reilly, *Urraca*, p. 320, n. 21.

25. The documentary record for Avila is even more impoverished than that of Salamanca, due perhaps to an early modern fire that struck the cathedral archives. Of late what can be done has been undertaken by Barrios García, *Estructuras*, and Angel Barrios García, ed., *Documentación medieval de la catedral de Avila* (Salamanca, 1981). See also, Reilly, *Urraca*, pp. 319–20.

town. Royal control proper was represented by the tenancy of Count Manrique de Lara that lasted from at least 1144 until 1151 and quite possibly until
the end of the reign. Municipal government per se would have been somewhat simpler to structure, for the population was even more homogeneous
than at Salamanca. Only slaves constituted a Muslim element and while later
Avila was to have a significant Jewish community it was unlikely to have
arrived so early. The Mozarabs were well represented and the number of Castilians seems to have been large in proportion to other groups from north of
the Duero. Despite the early participation of Count Raymond of Burgundy
in the affairs of the town the French element was insignificant.

A *concejo* of clergy and laity is first recorded in the *Historia Compostellana*
when it despatched a letter to Archbishop Diego Gelmírez informing him of
the selection of Jimeno as bishop in 1133.[26] In 1136 the *concejo* of Avila was one
of those notified by Alfonso VII not to interfere with exemptions granted to
the clergy of the realm. A private diploma of 1146 purports to be a grant of
Bishop Jimeno and the *concejo* of a church of Avila to the cathedral of Santiago de Compostela. It was confirmed by two *alcaldes* and an *iudex*. In other
words, the structure revealed comports well with what exists elsewhere at the
time. Unfortunately this last document is not entirely trustworthy (D520).[27]
There are references to a *fuero* of Avila reputedly bestowed by Alfonso VI but
it is lost and its content is problematic.[28]

The town of Zamora on the north bank of the Duero sixty kilometers
north of Salamanca, was closely associated with that town and Avila during
the first two decades of the twelfth century. Zamora had been a frontier town
up until the early reign of Alfonso VI. It was the logical place from which
the new Bishop Jerome of Salamanca could safely oversee the halting development of both diocese. When he died in mid-1120, the affairs of all three
towns were thrown into confusion. Zamora was particularly threatened because it had no claim to a bishopric from classical days but had grown accustomed to having its own prelate during Jerome's long residence. The problem
was solved when Archbishop Bernard of Toledo established his friend and
countryman, Bernard of Perigord (1121–1149), in the see, which was to secure
permanent existence despite squabbles over the next century with the see of
Astorga from whose territories it had been carved.

26. Falque Rey, *HC*, p. 476.
27. May 29, 1146. Pub. Barrios García, *Documentos*, pp. 7–8, is a seemingly reliable private
document that cited an *iudex* and four *alcaldes* by name. December 31, 1151. Ibid., pp. 8–9, is
another private document that cited an *iudex* and eight *alcaldes* by name.
28. For a brief statement of current opinion on it see James F. Powers, "The Creative Interaction between Portuguese and Leonese Municipal Military Law, 1055 to 1279," *Speculum* 62
(1987): 63.

Of course, Zamora had considerable strategic importance for the kingdom well before the bishopric was domesticated there. It was a royal town to which immigration was encouraged and that had begun to find political organization, some would say as early as Fernando I, but certainly in the time of Alfonso VI and Count Raymond of Burgundy. That attention continued into the reign of Urraca, although the town sat at just that geographical point where her interests, those of Queen Teresa of Portugal, and those of her son collided.[29] Its population was quite mixed. The Mozarab contingent was substantial, proximity made Galicians, Asturians, and Leonese settlers numerous, a French contingent resulted from Count Raymond's early influence, and there was a Jewish community as well.[30]

Separate municipal government in Zamora is difficult to delineate. There was a *concejo* as early as 1142 when it witnessed a royal grant to its bishop (D428). That act placed the future settlers of the deserted village of Fradejas under the exclusive jurisdiction of the bishop. In witnessing it the *concejo* perhaps assented to the tacit exclusion of its own authority there. Not quite four years later, the bishop himself granted a *fuero* to the settlers of Fresno de la Ribera without any reference to a *concejo*, even though he agreed to rule them according to the terms of the *fuero* of Zamora.[31] When during the last year of his reign Alfonso VII granted the *fuero* of the canons of Palencia to the canons of Zamora it is impossible to tell if he was shielding them from the authority of their bishop or of the *concejo* (D965).

In 1153 Alfonso granted a *fuero* to the *concejo* of Toro, another fortress-town on the north bank of the river upstream from Zamora and frequently joined to it for political and military purposes (D784). It may be that the military significance of both inhibited the growth of a civil government. We are well supplied with information about royal power. Count Rodrigo Martínez was tenant of Zamora from at least 1131 to 1135. After him, Count Pons de Cabrera combined that tenancy with the one at Toro from 1141 until 1157. We know the names of seven royal *merinos* of Zamora in this period, so that royal property must have been considerable.

To the east of Zamora and just north of the pass of Somosierra leading over the Guadarramas to Madrid is the tiny town of Sepúlveda. It had been an advance post of the realm during the reign of Alfonso VI, but with the

29. Reilly, *Urraca*, pp. 297–98 and 320–22. Since I wrote that volume some materials for research have become more available. José Luis Martín, ed., *Documentos zamoranos*, vol. 1, *Documentos del archivo catedralicio de Zamora, Primera Parte: 1128–1261* (Salamanca, 1982).
30. Salvador de Moxó, *Repoblación y sociedad en la España cristiana medieval* (Madrid, 1979), pp. 212–13. Amando Represa Rodríguez, "Genesis y evolución urbana de la Zamora medieval," *Hispania* 122 (1972): 527–29.
31. January 1, 1146. AC Zamora, Tumbo Negro, fol. 11r-v.

conquest of Toledo its military importance ended. There was a royal tenant there when Urraca and Alfonso of Aragón were contesting the district, but we hear of none for the reign of her son. My reservations about the wisdom of describing the government of the town on the basis of its famous *fuero* are as strong now, as they were when I first discussed it fifteen years ago.[32]

In a private document of 1129, when the writ of Alfonso of Aragón still ran, its *concejo* appears in the role of witness to a property transaction, along with Ordoño Pérez as tenant, and a *judex* and a *sayon*.[33] This *concejo* also was one of those advised in 1136 by Alfonso VII to respect exemptions granted to the clergy of the realm (D271). Obviously, it had some real authority recognized by the crown and, probably, the customary municipal officers. In 1143 Alfonso VII granted the *fuero* of Sepúlveda to the town of Roa, fifty miles north on the Duero River. The text, which vouches for the existence of a *concejo*, exists only in an eighteenth-century copy and otherwise does not advance the argument (D462).

Segovia, fifty kilometers southwest of Sepúlveda, owed its importance in the late eleventh century to its position at the foot of another pass through the Guadarramas, Navacerrada. But it had also been the site in antiquity of a bishopric that was restored in 1120 by Queen Urraca. When its military significance eroded after the conquest of Toledo, the town had an alternative basis of growth. During the reign of Urraca the control of Segovia had been contested with Aragón. Local powers, organized into a *concejo*, were able to exercise a considerable degree of independence.[34] At that time, the population had been fairly homogeneous with the Mozarab element, usual for the trans-Duero, bolstered by immigration from Castilla. During Alfonso VII's reign it became more complex with the addition of newcomers from León and Galicia.[35]

The reintroduction of the bishopric checked the freedom of action of the *concejo*. But the royal charter that supposedly defined the boundaries of the diocese and referred to it as an "honor" is a forgery. Moreover, two reliable royal charters make reference to the agreement of the *concejo* in the transfer of a certain territory (D247, 358). Although there was a royal castle in Segovia, the record of crown tenants is slight. In 1133 Count Rodrigo González was cited in a private document. In 1148 Rodrigo's nephew, Count Manrique, was so cited in a private document.[36] The context suggests that the Laras held a

32. Reilly, *Urraca*, pp. 322–24.
33. 1129. Pub. Ledesma Rubio, *Cartulario*, p. 245.
34. Reilly, *Urraca*, pp. 325–26.
35. Amando Represa Rodríguez, "La 'tierra' medieval de Segovia," *Estudios Segovianos* 21 (1969): 228.
36. February 3, 1133. Pub. Luis-Miguel Villar García, ed., *Documentación medieval de la catedral de Segovia, 1115–1300* (Salamanca, 1900), pp. 59–60. 1148. Ibid., pp. 92–93.

general responsibility for the oversight of the eastern trans-Duero and that their direct supervision at any one place was correspondingly diluted. All in all, the visibility of the *concejo* is not great during Alfonso VII's reign although it was one of those *concejos* admonished in 1136 to respect the royal exemption of the clergy. In 1137 the *concejo* of the tiny village of San Felices, described in a private document as "in the territory of Palencia," witnessed a property transfer.[37]

The royal letters of admonition just mentioned above also went to the *concejos* of Iscar, fifty-five kilometers northwest of Segovia, Fresno de la Fuente, seventy kilometers northeast of Segovia, and Pedraza, thirty kilometers northeast. In 1121 a *concejo* had already appeared at Medina del Campo, eighty kilometers northwest.[38] At Soria a *concejo* was visible in private documents in 1127 and again in 1148.[39] The important strongpoints of Almazán on the Duero, thirty kilometers south of Soria, and Ayllón, eighty kilometers southwest of Soria, also had *concejos* addressed by Alfonso VII in 1136 (D685). Yet farther south of Almazán, in the critical gap between the Sierra de Guadarrama and the Sierra de Albarracín, lay Medinaceli and Atienza. The former had some dubious claim to the possession of a *concejo* already in the time of Alfonso VI, but by 1129 a private document illustrates the existence of one there as well as an *iudex* and a *sayon* and by 1146 a royal document confirmed the former, at least by implication (D527).[40] A *concejo* in Atienza was the object of a royal document of the same year, but it is false (D589). Both towns had been long closely related to the jurisdiction of the bishop of Sigüenza, with whose town they formed a defensive complex in that strategic corridor.[41] A more southeasterly gap, leading into the south of Aragón was filled by the village of Molina whose *concejo* joined in 1153 with Count Manrique de Lara in ceding Villar de Cobeta, twenty-five kilometers to its west, jointly to the church of Sigüenza and the monasteries of Silos, Arlanza, and Oña.[42]

All of these towns, including Sigüenza, were diminutive and the hill region surrounding them still had a Muslim population. At this time, the latter also had relatively easy communication with free Muslim communities to the

37. October 30, 1137. Pub. Julio A. Pérez Celada, ed., *Documentación del monasterio de San Zoil de Carrión, 1047–1300* (Palencia, 1986), pp. 53–54.

38. December 23, 1121. Pub. Carlos Ayala Martínez, ed., *Libro de Privilegios de la Orden de San Juan de Jerusalén en Castilla y León, siglos XII–XV* (Madrid, 1994), pp. 157–58.

39. 1127. Pub. Rodríguez de Lama, *Colección*, 2:150–51. July 26, 1148. Pub. Loperráez Corvalón, *Descripción*, 3:24–25.

40. Reilly, *Urraca*, pp. 326–27. 1129. Pub. Ledesma Rubio, *Cartulario*, p. 245.

41. Reilly, *Urraca*, pp. 177–80 and 326.

42. December 5, 1153. Pub. Toribio Minguella y Arnedo, *Historia de la diócesis de Sigüenza y de sus obispos*, vol. 1 (Madrid, 1910), pp. 390–91, from what he called an original still bearing its pendant seal.

east in Valencian territories and to the south about Cuenca. Therefore, a close defensive association of the small Christian communities of the district was natural and continued, as is made clear by the first of these royal charters of 1146, which also establishes that Sigüenza also had its *concejo*, together with an *iudex* and *sayon*, and that there was appeal from its judgments to the king himself. Nevertheless the town council was subject, however uneasily, to the bishop for the town was an episcopal *senorio*.[43] In 1150 Alfonso VII wrote to the *concejos* of Almazán, Ayllón, Medinaceli, and Atienza and admonished them to respect the exemptions of the clergy of Sigüenza (D660).[44] The latter also had a small Jewish community that had survived the transition from Muslim to Christian rule, whose presence added yet another element of complexity.

Municipal institutions of some type were common then in the developing lands south of the Duero during the reign of Alfonso VII. Their presence is another illustration of the way in which the institutions of the older world to the north were transferred to the new one coming into being.

Just north of the Duero on the Pisuerga River and south of Palencia was the old señorial town of Valladolid, originally a foundation of the great Leonese noble Pedro Ansúrez in the times of Alfonso VI. Although not an episcopal, town its location guaranteed it a substantial future and its prominent collegial church would finally be raised to episcopal status in the early modern period. From 1095 it boasted a *concejo* along with a comital *merino* and *sayon*. Royal authority found its way as well to the growing town before, and more strongly after, the death of Pedro in 1117 or 1118.[45] The royal tenancy of the town was held by Count Armengol VI of Urgel, the grandson of Pedro Ansúrez, during the last third of Alfonso VII's reign. In 1155 the king made a grant of land to the *concejo* there and in the following year, at the same time as he confirmed all the privileges of the town's collegiate church, conceded to the council the right to an annual fair on August 15, the feast of the Assumption of the Virgin (D874, 919).

Farther up the Pisuerga the town of Palencia dated from classical antiquity and boasted a bishopric, which was restored early in the eleventh century. Before the reconquest of Toledo Alfonso VI briefly considered having it erected into the metropolitan see of the realm.[46] Ties to the crown remained

43. Julio González, *Repoblación*, 2:25.
44. December 15, 1156 (D955). This royal grant also contains a reference to the *concejo* of Atienza. Almost twenty years earlier, when the king granted the bishop of Sigüenza the right to repopulate the deserted village of Aragosa he also directed that the settlers were to have the right to chose one among the *fueros* of these four towns for their own. September 20, 1143 (D456).
45. Reilly, *Urraca*, pp. 344–46.
46. Reilly, *Alfonso VI*, pp. 140–41.

close and assured its continuing growth.[47] Given its geographical position and history, it is unsurprising that Palencia had a sizeable Mozarab and Castilian population. A Muslim or Jewish population is not in evidence. Perhaps from its refounding, the town had been an episcopal *señorio*, a phenomenon not uncommon north of the Duero.[48] That would account for the absence of a royal tenant, even in such an important and wealthy center. It may also explain the apparent absence of any contemporary reference to a *concejo* there since episcopal government of the towns ordinarily was more restrictive precisely in that it was more local. In the sweeping confirmation of the privileges of the see of Palencia given by Alfonso VII in 1155, no *concejo* was called to witness (D862). By contrast, in the same year the *concejos* of the two hamlets of Palenzuela and Baltanás to its northeast and east, respectively, required royal adjudication of their proper jurisdictions, if the document can be believed (D879).

Northeast of Palencia on the Arlanzón, a tributary of the Pisuerga, lay the town of Burgos founded in the late ninth century. It had no classical antecedents. It was growing into a major town of 2,500 or 3,000 people by the mid-twelfth century and had an even more brilliant future before it. Part of that was due to its location on the pilgrimage route to Compostela, where the latter debouched onto the plains of Castilla. The same phenomenon assured it substantial minorities of Franks and Jews. Alfonso VI enhanced its importance by securing the translation to it of the ancient bishopric of Oca and both he and his grandson were careful to secure that see's independence of the Catalan metropolitan at Tarragona. Due to Burgos's strategic position vis-à-vis the kingdom of Aragón, the town became a favored royal residence and often hosted meetings of the *curia regis*.[49] During the reign of Urraca the town was usually in the hands of Aragón. In April 1127 her son Alfonso VII reclaimed it permanently but the contest of the preceding twenty-five years must have worked to enhance the bargaining position of the local populace with every wider authority.

The customs of the town had been recognized already by Alfonso VI and used as a model for similar institutions in some smaller hamlets of the

47. Amando Represa Rodríguez, "Palencia: Breve análisis de su formación urbana durante los siglos XI–XIII," *En la España Medieval* 1 (1980): 385–97.

48. Reilly, *Urraca*, pp. 343–44. Since the time when I wrote the latter the work of research in the archive of the cathedral has been greatly facilitated by the publication of Teresa Abajo Martín, ed., *Documentación de la catedral de Palencia* (Palencia, 1986).

49. Carlos Estepa Diéz, Teofilo F. Ruiz, Juan A. Bonachia Hernando, and Hilario Casado Alonso, *Burgos en la Edad Media* (Madrid, 1984), is a useful if not entirely satisfactory account of a town whose history deserves more attention. Luciano Serrano, *El obispado de Burgos y Castilla primitiva desde el siglo V al XIII*, 3 vols. (Madrid, 1935), is still the standard though it would profit from a new edition. For our purposes, see also Reilly, *Alfonso VI*, pp. 97–100, and *Urraca*, pp. 328–30.

countryside. Urraca too had recognized some limitations on the royal power within the city.[50] Nevertheless a powerful royal castle overlooked the town and, although there seems never to have been a royal tenant per se after 1130, one of the most important of the royal *merinos* looked to the fisc lands not only in the city but in surrounding Castilla. If not the city's *señor*, the bishop of Burgos was a major player in local politics both in his own right and as a royal favorite.

In 1129 a private document illustrates the *concejo* there exercising the traditional function of witness.[51] In 1128 Alfonso VII recognized the *concejo*, conferring on "omnibus in Burgos" a series of exemptions from duties owed the crown (D89). In 1152 the king granted the *concejo* the privilege of exemption from direct responsibility for murders committed in its territories (D736).

Doubtless this familiar, if difficult to specify, state of affairs was replicated from Burgos up into the mountainous area to the east of it. Royal diplomas tell of *concejos* at Santo Domingo de la Calzada on the pilgrim road from Logroño to Burgos in 1137 and at nearby Corporales in 1138 (D279, 324). From 1147 there may be another to mention in Pancorvo farther north along the road from Vitoria to Burgos, although certainly the diploma is flawed (D550). On the same road, the *concejo* at Briviesca was supposedly granted a *fuero* by Alfonso VII in 1123 but the diploma, as we have it, is false (D20).

In the foothills to the southeast of Burgos lay the famous monastery of Santo Domingo de Silos. In the spring of 1135 Alfonso VII granted a *fuero* governing the relations of its abbot and the men of the adjoining hamlet of San Sebastián on the model of that which governed the relationship of the men of the town of Sahagún and the monastery of that name. Although the text probably derives from the thirteenth century and provisions may have been added, the very fact of the action indicates that San Sebastián had its *concejo* (D210). A few kilometers north was Lara de los Infantes, the *fueros* of which town Alfonso had confirmed only three weeks earlier. The text derives from a *vidimus* of Sancho IV in 1289 and has surely been embroidered somewhat, but we can probably accept Lara as having a *concejo* and even the *alcalde* and *judex* (D207). Twenty kilometers farther southeast of the latter was Salas de Los Infantes where a private document of 1156 mentions an existing *concejo*.[52]

50. Reilly, *Urraca*, pp. 328–29.
51. December 23, 1129. Pub. José Manuel Garrido Garrido, ed., *Documentación de la catedral de Burgos, 804–1183* (Burgos, 1983), pp. 198–99.
52. July 1, 1156. Luciano Serrano, ed., *Cartulario de San Pedro de Arlanza* (Madrid, 1925), pp. 210–11.

This common, one may say customary, existence of a village *concejo* in the eastern foothills of the realm extended as well out onto the *meseta* west of Burgos. In 1136 in diminutive Lodoso, a dozen kilometers northwest, the town council witnessed a property transfer.[53] From Los Balbases, some thirty-five kilometers southwest of Burgos, a *fuero* granted by Alfonso VII in 1135 to its *concejo* survives in a sixteenth-century copy of a *vidimus* of Fernando III of Castilla. It has been embellished somewhat, but its *concejo* likely dated to our period (D221). Not ten kilometers north of Palencia at Husillos, in a private document of 1154, Abbot Raymond of Santa María de Husillos sold property to the town's council.[54] A scarce ten kilometers northwest of Los Balbases is the hill town and fortress of Castrojeriz. Apparently the town had had some sort of *fuero* from the time of Alfonso VI, but the text is most peculiar.[55] We know almost nothing more of it except that at least from 1140 until the end of the reign, Guter Fernández de Castro was royal tenant. West of Castrojeriz was Frómista, where in 1137 a private document cited a town *concejo* as well as one of the collegiate church of San Martín. The town had a royal *merino* and *sayon*, and fell under Diego Muñoz, as *merino mayor*. Nevertheless, sandwiched between the royal authority and that of the prior of San Martín, the town council obviously had some independent standing.[56] Another thirty-five kilometers west of Frómista a private document of 1147 was witnessed by the council of tiny San Román de la Cuba.[57]

One of the two most famous town governments of the preceding reign was that of Sahagún. The town was blessed in its position on the pilgrimage road to Compostela, by the nearby royal palace, and by the royal monastery of Sahagún. While its population was probably never much more than 1,000 souls, it was likely more wealthy than other towns of similar size but less opportunity and there was a fair admixture of Franks and Jews there. Nevertheless, we know the town because of the greatness of the monastery that endured down to the time of the French invasion under Bonaparte, the documents that it preserved, and the products of its *scriptorium*.

Sahagún was a señorial town under the abbot. The civil war between Urraca and Alfonso of Aragón gave at least a portion of the burghers of the town a chance to attempt to modify their condition. They, as well as simi-

---

53. October 17, 1136. Pub. F. Javier Peña Pérez, ed., *Documentación del monasterio de San Juan de Burgos, 1091–1400* (Burgos, 1983), pp. 19–20.
54. September 19, 1154. BN, Manuscritos, 705, fol. 21r-v.
55. Bernard F. Reilly, "The Chancery of Alfonso VI of León-Castile (1065–1109)," in *Santiago, Saint-Denis, and Saint Peter*, pp. 1–40, ed. Bernard F. Reilly (New York, 1985), p. 17.
56. AHN, Ord. Mil., Carpeta 574, no. 5; BN, Manuscritos, 714, fol. 142v, a note only.
57. April 30, 1147. Pub. Fernández Flórez, *Colección*, 4:200–1.

lar factions in Carrión de los Condes, Castrojériz, and Burgos, allied with Alfonso against the queen between 1111 and 1117. They fashioned themselves some sort of *fuero*, against which the biographer of the abbot railed but which he did not describe, and acted in effect as a *concejo*. The term itself was never used in any surviving source or reliable document of the period. Given the circumstances, the actions of the townsmen must have been limited to what the Aragonese military commander would tolerate.[58]

When Urraca came to terms with her former husband, the burghers of Sahagún had to submit, especially since the queen had also enlisted the support of the pope. We hear no more of them and, given the bitterness of the immediate past, it is difficult to imagine that the queen or abbot would have allowed them a *concejo* of any sort. The young Alfonso in 1119 purportedly issued a charter to the monastery which referred to a *concejo*, but the document cannot be trusted.[59]

But even the lordly abbot of Sahagún could not resist totally the evolving institutional structure of town life. In 1126 the very pope directed the mediation of a dispute between a *concejo* of the insignificant town of Puebla de Lillo high in the Cantabrians and the great abbey.[60] Ten years later, the Leonese monarch settled a dispute between the abbey and a noble woman over the town of Villavicencio. The place was partitioned among the claimants, but in the process, Alfonso recognized the *concejo* of the village (D238). In 1152 the abbot found himself involved in a lawsuit against the *concejo* of the town of Grajal de Campos, just ten kilometers south. Some of the men of the town had destroyed a dam serving a mill of the abbey. The abbot came off well in the settlement, but nevertheless he had been forced to accept a *concejo* as an equal, at least for the purposes of litigation.

A week later, Alfonso addressed the problem of the relations between the monastery and the inhabitants of Sahagún directly. This new *fuero* was issued to the men of the village jointly by the monarch and the abbot, but clearly the former took the initiative to remedy an impossible situation. The provisions of it largely favor the monks, but a *concejo* is nonetheless recognized. Moreover, there are to be two *merinos*, one Castilian and one Frenchman, who own homes in Sahagún, who are residents of the village and vassals of the abbot, and who will be installed "by the hand of the abbot and the authority of the

58. Reilly, *Urraca*, pp. 101–24 and 346–49. Ana María Barrero García, "Los fueros de Sahagún," *AHDE* 42 (1972): 385–597, is still the most detailed documentary study although so restricted in context as to be less than entirely satisfactory.

59. Ibid, p. 348.

50. December 7, 1126. Pub. Fernández Flórez, *Colección*, 4:108–9.

61. Reilly, *Urraca*, pp. 300–304 and 330–32.

concejo" (D776). The arrangement is the essentially pragmatic one typical of the age.

The royal city of León was a sometime residence of the court, site of a royal castle, of another dynastic pantheon, of a bishopric, and a major city of the pilgrimage road. Its population of Leonese, Mozarabs, Franks, and Jews must have approximated 3,000 by mid-century. It boasted a royal tenant in the "towers of León" drawn from among the most important magnates of the realm. It had a royal *merino*, usually an important citizen of the town, who was also ordinarily a *merino mayor* for the lands between the Cantabrians and the town of Coyanza. This state of affairs continued that typical in the reign of Urraca.[61] The authority of the bishop there was large, especially as he had the ear of the king. Under these circumstances, the role of a separate municipal government must have been quite constricted, although never completely nugatory. The city has been credited with a famous *fuero* granted to it by Alfonso V in 1017. However, the oldest purported texts of that document come to us from better than a century and a quarter later and have already been combined, reorganized, and interpolated for purposes that remain obscure despite extended scholarly argument.[62]

Our best guide to the existing state of affairs at León during the reign of Alfonso VII is a private grant of its *fuero* in 1152 to the town of Castrocalbón sixty kilometers southwest.[63] The grant was made by Countess María Fernández de Traba, wife of the Pons de Cabrera, who adapted the then *fuero* of León to the needs of a proprietarial town. Allowing for the obvious changes, we see a *concejo* with the right to receive a portion of certain fines and to regulate trade within the town and its market, and which functions together with judges and *merinos*. All residents have one *fuero* and the *concejo* meets at least once a year, on the first day of Lent in the chapel of the church of San Salvador, to set prices and measures for the coming year. The "iudices" of Castrocalbón will be "electi," but it does not say by whom although we should likely presume the proprietor in consultation with the chief figures of the town. In any event, "elected" cannot be given its limited modern democratic meaning in the period.[64]

62. The case was made by Alfonso García Gallo, "El fuero de León," *AHDE* 39 (1965): 5–171. It was the subject of a furious if incomplete rebuttal by Claudio Sánchez-Albornoz, "El fuero de León," *León y su historia* 2 (1973): 11–60. Further refinement of the argument seems to me to wait on a careful codicological and paleographical analysis of the structure of the *Liber Testamentorum* of Oviedo and of the *Liber Fidei* of Braga in which the two variants are contained.

63. August 16, 1152. I have not seen the document itself. A. Paz y Melia, ed., *Series de los más importantes documentos del archivo y biblioteca del Duque de Medinaceli*, vol. 1, *Serie histórica, años 860–1814* (Madrid, 1951), pp. 3–5, published it without critical comment.

64. The text is remarkably close to the latter portions of the *fureo* of León as that docu-

The totality of evidence suggests that the situation in León was, in fact, analogous to that in contemporary Toledo. At the turn of the century, there had been individual *fueros* for Franks and a separate *concejo* for them is documented as late as 1122.[65] Almost certainly the Jews had their own, as did various religious bodies, and even neighborhoods, or *barrios*. These gave way gradually to a single *concejo*, whose few appearances during the reign of Alfonso VII are documented by Estepa Diéz.[66] In 1132, however, a separate *concejo* of the *infantado* of San Pelayo still existed.[67]

The council of the city had its counterparts in the wider territory surrounding it. In 1130 the lordly Hospitallers submitted to the witness by the *concejo* of Valderas, almost sixty kilometers south of the city, to a property transfer to it as the same order also did in 1147 to that of the *concejo* of San Félix, one of the many of that name, in similar circumstances.[68] On a more domestic note, the *concejo* of San Roman de la Cuba, in what would be the modern province of Palencia, witnessed in 1147 the *carta de arras* between Annaia Rodríguez and his beloved Urraca Téllez. The properties were transferred according to the *fuero*, read usage, of León.[69] Sometimes one can mark the continuing existence of a *concejo* over two decades or better, as in the case of Villacete, only ten kilometers southeast of León, which was exercising its authority in 1157 much as it had in 1135.[70] Finally, in 1153 Alfonso VII granted to the hamlet of Villa Zelame, fifteen kilometers southeast of León, the *fuero* of neighboring Mansilla de las Mulas including a *concejo* with some criminal jurisdiction (D792).

Asturias de Oviedo had been the historical nucleus of the kingdom but was increasingly a backwater in twelfth century. It is the only portion of the realm for which there is evidence of trade being conducted in kind rather than in coin, for example. At the beginning of the century Bishop Pelayo (1100–

ment appears in the Oviedo version. García Gallo, "Fuero de León," p. 148, hypothesized that both were derived from a third variant of the original text produced by a Leonese canon about 1126. Bishop Pelayo is held to have added the early materials attributed to Alfonso V (999–1028), which the version of the Countess María does not know. One need not accept all of García Gallo's very close critique and, in fact, he does not suggest why a third version should have been needed just about then. It seems possible that the centralizing tendency noticeable in the text derives from a new *fuero* of Queen Urraca or of Alfonso VII about that date.

65. December 13, 1122. Pub. José María Fernández Catón, ed., *Colección documental del archivo de la catedralde de León, 1109–1187*, vol. 5 (León, 1990), pp. 104–5. A private document.

66. *Estructura*, pp. 456–58.

67. February 19, 1132. Pub. Fernández Cáton, *Colección*, 5:153–54, A private document.

68. February 10, 1130. Pub. Ayala Martínez, *Libro*, pp. 173–74. February 10, 1147. Ibid., pp. 205–6. Both private documents.

69. April 30, 1147. Pub. Fernández Flórez, *Colección*, 4:200–201.

70. September 1135. Pub. Ibid., 4:146. February 13, 1157. Ibid., 266–67. Both private documents.

1130) had labored mightily, if not always honestly, to secure for its cathedral some portion of the growing pilgrimage traffic to Compostela. That added a French element to the perhaps 2,000 inhabitants of the city by 1150.[71] Oviedo was a royal town and, after a troubled time during the hegemony and outright revolt of Count Gonzalo Peláez during the 1130's, ultimately became the seat of an *infantaticum* vested in the king's natural daughter, Urraca. The authority of its bishop was also important in the city. Nevertheless, there is good evidence for the operation of a municipal government there, including some separate institutions for the French element, from the reign of Queen Urraca.[72] But the purported *fuero* of 1145 granted to the inhabitants of the city by Alfonso VII cannot be taken as a reliable guide (D505).

Private documents in the collection of the monastery of San Vicente inform us of the existence as well of *concejos* in the seaport of Gozón, thirty kilometers north of Oviedo, in 1136 and 1146 and in the village of Laviana, twenty-seven kilometers southeast of Oviedo, in 1137.[73] Gozón was the center of an *infantaticum* under the control of Alfonso's sister Sancha from at least 1151. The famous *fuero* of Alfonso VII of 1155 to the seaport of Avilés, 12 kilometers southwest of Gozón, has long been recognized as a forgery (D861).

In the Roman period, Astorga had been the seat of a bishopric and a moderately important town, one of the few in the northwest of the peninsula. But from the ninth century, it had fallen more and more under the shadow of the refounded León and its new bishopric. In 1150 it may have had as many as 1,500 inhabitants and Frankish and Jewish communities, thanks to its location on the pilgrimage road.[74] Astorga boasted a formidable wall and a royal castle, whose usual tenant in this period was Count Ramiro Froílaz. The authority of its bishops was enhanced by the fact that he was usually designated by the king himself.

While we lack notices for the reign of Alfonso VII, it is unimaginable that a town of its size and importance lacked a *concejo* and the usual municipal officials omnipresent elsewhere. Even in the hill country to its west, the chartulary of the monastery of San Pedro de Montes illustrates the function-

71. Oviedo could benefit from a thorough, modern history. Santos García Larragueta, *Sancta Ovetensis* (Madrid, 1962), is hardly more than a sketch.
72. Reilly, *Urraca*, pp. 341–43.
73. December 31, 1136. Pub. Pedro Floriano Llorente, ed., *Colección diplomática del monasterio de San Vicente de Oviedo* (Oviedo, 1968), pp. 309–11. July 5, 1146. Ibid., pp. 351–53. September 1137. Ibid., pp. 312–13.
74. Valentín Cabero Diéguez, *Evolución y estructura urbana de Astorga* (León, 1973), treated mainly the modern development of the town. Reilly, *Urraca*, pp. 332–33. All accounts of the medieval city face the lacunae created by the wholesale destruction of local documents consequent on its siege and conquest in the Napleonic Wars.

ing of municipal councils in more than a score of tiny hamlets, even if only a limited number of such places can be positively identified. Corporales, forty kilometers southwest of Astorga, had one in 1126, Truchas, eight kilometers to the south of the latter, had one in 1138, so did Sigüeya, eighteen kilometers northwest of Corporales, in 1137, and in the same year, only fifty-five kilometers east from Orense in the valley of the Sil, the little hamlet of Casayo boasted one as well.[75] At Villafranca del Bierzo in 1152 the Queen Sancha, sister of the king, agreed to make a donation to allow the construction of an bakeoven at the request of the town's *concejo* (D756).

In Galicia proper, the old hill town of Lugo was a *señorial* municipality, the preserve of the oldest, continuously existing bishopric of the kingdom. The bishop and his cathedral chapter had governed the city and its surrounding countryside since at least the time of Alfonso VI. The same king established one of the mints of the realm there. By the twelfth century its population had risen to perhaps 2,000 souls, including a community of Franks, for it too benefited from its location on the pilgrimage road. Nonetheless, it was an upland, landlocked town. During the early reign of Queen Urraca, its bishop had to be replaced for treasonous activity, but no royal tenant was installed, then or later nor was there a royal castle in the city.[76]

Episcopal rule in Lugo seems to have been paternalistic but firm. The documents of the town have not been systematically edited and those still in the cathedral archive are difficult of access. There does not appear to be any record of a *concejo*.[77] Almost at the very end of the reign, in 1155 perhaps, there seems to have been a communal rising against the bishop's authority but neither the date or the details are entirely clear. The bishop's *merino* was killed and the prelate himself fled the city. The dispute subsequently came to the attention not only of Fernando II of León (1157–1188) but also to that of Pope Calixtus III (1168–1179) and a *concejo* ultimately was recognized.[78]

At the end of the pilgrim road was Santiago de Compostela. The reputed discovery there of the relics of Santiago gradually had created a town around them, caused the transfer there of the classical bishopric of Iria Flavia and then the elevation of that see to archepiscopal status, and had shaded the other bishoprics of Galicia. The town was the most important, populous, and

75. March 6, 1126. Pub. Augusto Quintana Prieto, ed., *Tumbo viejo de San Pedro de Montes* (Léon, 1971), pp. 230–31. May 13, 1138. Ibid., pp. 252–53. November 20, 1137. Ibid., pp. 250–51. November 1, 1137. Ibid., pp. 249–50.
76. Reilly, *Urraca*, pp. 333–35.
77. Carlé, *Concejo*, p. 269. However, I am not sure that she had access to all the documents.
78. Antolín López Peláez, *El señorío temporal de los obispos de Lugo*, 2 vols. (La Coruña, 1897), pp. 110–20, is still the authoritative treatment.

wealthy of the region with perhaps as many as 3,000 souls in 1150. The absence
of a royal residence or tenant bothered it not at all. Typically for the region it
was an episcopal *señorio*. Nevertheless it had its municipal council subordinate
to the bishop, perhaps from 1095. During the reign of Urraca, a communal
uprising succeeded briefly in subjecting the bishop to their authority in 1116–
1117. Although they failed in that revolutionary endeavor a *concejo* survived the
violence but we are ignorant of its constitution.[79] Some such group, or members of it, entered into negotiations with Alfonso VII almost from the beginning of his reign. While all particulars are not made clear, that they intended
to make themselves masters of the city with royal assistance is obvious. At the
time a *concejo* would have been the only possible vehicle for such a program.

The attempted coup of 1135–1136, like the earlier one, degenerated into a
near-fatal assault on the person of Archbishop Diego Gelmírez, which effectively cost it any straightforward royal support. But the king neither lost
interest nor entirely disavowed his late allies. The next-to-last chapter of our
source for the matter contains the text of a royal letter to the cathedral chapter and the burghers of Compostela ordering them to remain faithful to their
archbishop. But the very fact of the letter's having been written points up
both the continuing potential of the group and the royal recognition of it.
We may confidently accept that behind the "canonicorum conventui et omnibus eiusdem ville burgensibus" addressed stood a still persisting *concejo*.[80]

The death of Archbishop Gelmírez in the spring of 1140 led the author
of his biography to break off the narrative in late 1139. Moreover, the documents of the see have been thoroughly mined for the history of the church
but only incidentally for the history of the city over which it presided. As
a result, little can be said about the municipal government of Compostela
over the next seventeen years. We can be sure, however, that the extraordinarily troubled history of the archbishopric in that period, during which six
different incumbents, or claimants, succeeded one another, would have contributed to the enhancing of the authority of the *concejo*.

When Peter the Venerable of Cluny wrote to Pope Innocent II in support of the royal candidate in 1142 that Bishop-elect Berenguer had been
chosen by the "clergy and people" of Compostela one perhaps can see the
royal allies of 1135–1136 in their usual role.[81] The latter lost influence no doubt
when the royal candidate finally failed to secure papal support. Nevertheless,

79. Reilly, *Urraca*, pp. 335–38.
80. Falque Rey, *HC*, p. 529.
81. Bernard F. Reilly, "On Getting to Be a Bishop in León-Castile: The 'Emperor' Alfonso
VII and the Post-Gregorian Church," *Studies in Medieval and Renaissance History* 1 (1978): 60–61.

four of the six archbishops of the period were royal candidates and surely Alfonso's regular supporters in the city saw their personal and organizational power wax rather than wane over the long run.

Away from the pilgrimage road, that province was more purely rural and agricultural than any other portion of the realm perhaps. Doubtless even small *aldeas*, here as elsewhere in this society, had their *concejos* but one would be hardpressed to write their history. Bishoprics inspired the occasional use of civic terminology for what was in reality scarcely more than an episcopal enclave. Even then, one's confidence in, and ability to see, the historical reality behind the language varies considerably.

As a bishopric, Mondoñedo was hard-pressed to remain distinct severally from a chaplaincy of the house of Trastámara, the abbacy of the monastery of Lorenzana, a canonry of Santiago de Compostela, or a curial plum.[82] The town, fifteen kilometers inland from the Bay of Biscay in the extreme northwest of the peninsula, was less prepossessing then than now. Only most recently has anyone ventured to take in hand a survey of the documents of the church.[83] Under such circumstances one hesitates even to speak of the town as an "episcopal *señorio.*"

Southwest of Galicia was the bishopric of Túy. During the reign of Urraca and the early days of Alfonso VII, it was more often a part of Portugal than of León-Castilla.[84] When its bishop was functioning as part of the latter, however, he was recognized as *señor* of the town. That had happened as early as 1095 when Count Raymond of Burgundy was the royal vicar for Galicia. It was reinforced under Urraca, and in 1142 Alfonso reaffirmed episcopal authority in the town and its environs and turned over the royal fortress there to the prelate. There is no record of a royal tenant in the town (D436).[85]

Under the circumstances, the bishop of Túy must have been as much a petty king as a royal *señor*, although his freedom would have been tempered by the rival designs of the sovereigns of Portugal and León-Castilla. The town itself was even more diminutive then than now. Its location, near the mouth of the Miño River, thirty kilometers from the Atlantic, made it a local fishing port and some pilgrim traffic from the south passed through it on the way north to Santiago de Compostela. It is more the context of the times than any evidence that suggests that Túy probably had a *concejo* subordinate to its

82. Richard A. Fletcher, *The Episcopate of the Kingdom of León in the Twelfth Century* (Oxford, 1978), pp. 61–63.

83. Enrique Cal Pardo, *Catálogo de los documentos escritos en pergamino del archivo de la catedral de Mondoñedo* (Lugo, 1990). What new information may come to light is still an open question.

84. Fletcher, *Episcopate*, pp. 50–51.

85. Reilly, *Urraca*, pp. 339–40.

bishop. It seems unlikely that the burghers of the town should have been of such numbers or wealth as to represent a serious impediment to the episcopal will. More may appear if the documents of the cathedral there find an editor.[86]

Seventy kilometers upstream from Túy on the Miño River as the crow flies lay the episcopal city of Orense. Like its sister downstream, it had been the object of rivalry between Urraca and Teresa of Portugal but the hold of León-Castilla over it grew under Alfonso VII. The town was an episcopal *señorio*, recognized by both crowns at least from 1122, and in 1131 Alfonso VII reaffirmed the authority of the bishop and his chapter there (D129).[87] For almost a quarter of a century after 1133 the bishop of Orense was the former chaplain of the king. The existence of a *concejo* is probable on the analogy of other places of like nature, however it is not demonstrable presently. The documents of the cathedral are rich but unpublished.[88] Orense itself is isolated. The town lies in a fairly extensive agricultural river bottom on which it depended and of which it was the natural center of exchange. But travel either upstream or downstream to any distance is difficult and in other directions must have depended on mule trains if there was trade at all beyond the town's environs, largely considered. It is improbable then that the burghers of such a town, with perhaps a total population of 500, developed the wealth or influence necessary to modify the authority of their bishop seriously. Another episcopal regime, ordinarily paternal in operation and with some collaboration from the *concejo*, is the most likely state of affairs.

At the other end of the kingdom lay the territory of La Rioja, along the middle course of the Ebro River from Miranda del Ebro south to Zaragoza. At the beginning of the eleventh century when the caliphate of Córdoba was in full dissolution, this fertile land with its largely Muslim population became the object of a long contest between the Christian kingdom of Navarra and the emerging *taifa* kingdom of Zaragoza. By 1054 the frontier between the two had been fixed at the river town and fortress-citadel of Calahorra. There it remained through the collapse of the kingdom of Navarra in 1076, which

86. When I visited the town some twenty-five years ago in search of royal documents the cathedral archive seemed promising in materials but not easy of access and largely unorganized.

87. Fletcher, *Episcopate*, pp. 48–49. Reilly, *Urraca*, pp. 340–41.

88. The former archivist, Emilio Duro Peña, ed., *Catálogo de los documentos privados en pergaminos de la catedral de Orense, 888–1554* (Orense, 1973) and "Catálogo de documentos reales del archivo de la catedral de Orense, 884–1520," in *Miscelánea de textos medievales*, vol. 1 (Barcelona, 1972), pp. 9–145, performed an invaluable service in preparing the ground but thus far no one has taken up the challenge of editing the documents. On my last visit there, ten years ago, the documents were still difficult but not impossible of access. At that time my interest was primarily with the royal documents so I have little idea of what the private ones might furnish although Duro Peña listed only six such before 1160.

allowed its lands west of the river to be absorbed by León-Castilla and those to the east by the kingdom of Aragón.

After the death of Alfonso VI, Aragón was able to extend its control over the western half of La Rioja as well. In addition, on the decline of the kingdom of the Huddid at Zaragoza it overran first that city itself in 1118 and then Tudela and Tarazona in 1119. The whole of these lands then remained in the hands of Aragón until 1134, when near chaos in that kingdom allowed Alfonso VII to occupy the whole of La Rioja west of the Ebro down to and including Zaragoza. The resurgence of Navarra after 1135 and the emergence of a new, hybrid Aragón-Barcelona under Ramon Berenguer gradually forced the surrender of Tudela to the first and Zaragoza and Tarazona to the second, although both monarchs became Leonese vassals. Most of the west bank of the river thereafter remained part of the Leonese kingdom.

Perhaps because of their strategic importance to whomever held them at any given moment and, after 1118, their crucial status as Christian strongholds in a countryside largely Muslim, the towns of the territory had a particularly vigorous municipal tradition. Indeed Carlé began her pioneering consideration of municipal institutions in León-Castilla with these towns.[89]

Tiny Miranda de Ebro owed its slight importance totally to its place on a branch of the pilgrim road where the latter crossed the river. Its population of a few hundred at best included some Franks due to that fact. There is a text of a *fuero* asserted to have been given to the town by Alfonso VI in 1099 and there may have been some such action, but we have no reliable guide to its details. The document, as we have it, derives from a *vidimus* of Fernando IV of 1298 in the municipal archive, and a strong argument has been made that the present text is based on a forgery from a diploma of Sancho III of 1157.[90] At the very least, it is obvious that it is a conflation of three originally distinct documents, by a scribe unacquainted with chancery norms, and some later additions.

One of these three documents is a diploma of Alfonso VI dated to January 1099. Another is a diploma of Alfonso VII and Queen Berengaria without date. Yet another is a diploma of Sancho III of Castilla of November 11, 1157. There is as well a confirmation by Alfonso VIII of Castilla of December 1177. Obviously, the substantial content is dated at one's peril. That is especially true since during the entire period from 1112 until 1134 the town was con-

89. *Concejo*, pp. 37–42.
90. Reilly, *Alfonso VI*, pp. 292–93. Francisco Cantera Burgos, ed., *Fuero de Miranda de Ebro* (Madrid, 1945) is the critical edition. Gonzalo Martínez Díez, "Fueros locales en el territorio de la provincia de Santander," *AHDE* 46 (1976): 59–62. But see also Ana María Barrero García, "La política foral de Alfonso VI," in *Estudios sobre Alfonso VI y la reconquista de Toledo*, pp. 115–156 (Toledo, 1987), pp. 141–42.

trolled by the king of Aragón who may or may not have honored any previous Leonese arrangements. For what it is worth then, the *fuero* shows a *concejo*, with an *alcalde*, a *merino*, and a *sayon* as officers. The portion attributed directly to Sancho III concedes to the former the right of choosing the latter annually. If accepted, it would mark the first reliable grant of the privilege of election.

Roughly sixty kilometers southeast of Miranda lies another and more important crossing of the Ebro at Logroño. Despite its somewhat greater importance and size, it lacked a bishopric, that font of power and wealth. It too boasted a famous *fuero* whose text is long and complex and exists only in seventeenth-century paper copies (D586). In its present form it is an amalgam of four documents combined and embellished with scant care for chancery norms. The first, which furnishes the basic framework, is that of Alfonso VI and his wife Berta and is dated to 1095. The second, which adds some additional exemptions to the list, is that of Alfonso VII, strangely calling himself "king emperor." It is dated to May 1146, but 1148 is proper for the dating protocol cites Almería (D586). On November 11, 1157, Sancho III of Castilla further modified and confirmed it. The final modification came at the hands of Sancho VI of Navarra in 1168.

This is a text much and carelessly reworked. Only with trepidation might one deduce from it what the functioning parameters of municipal government were in Logroño during the reign of Alfonso VII. From the confirmation of Alfonso VII it appears that from 1148 the town was a royal tenancy held by the Riojan noble Pedro Jiménez with *alcalde*, *merino*, *sayon*, and judges subject to him. Only in the confirmation of Sancho III is it specified that the *alcalde* shall be chosen annually and by the hands of the "bonos homines" (i.e., *concejo*, and the *señor*, Pedro Jiménez, jointly).

Twenty-five kilometers west of Logroño was the former royal city of the Navarrese kings and subsequent nerve center of the Leonese La Rioja, the town of Nájera. From it, the pilgrim road to Santiago wound up into the Sierra de la Demanda and then down into Burgos. As always, such a favored position meant a precocious development, but Nájera had its own appeal to pilgrims as well. A marvelous image of the Virgin associated with the eleventh-century triumph of its Navarrese kings over the Muslim inhabitants of Calahorra was enshrined in its major monastery, Santa María la Real. Alfonso VI authorized the transfer of the monastery to Cluny and both he and his son continued to endow the foundation richly. The Cluniac prior of Santa María de la Real was a significant power in the municipal life of the town and held a tenth of the tolls of Logroño and Nájera from 1135 (D228).

Nájera had not been a bishopric in antiquity. That advantage had been held by Calahorra, sitting on its rock forty-five kilometers downstream from Logroño. But at some point well after the Muslim conquest, Calahorra's bishops had found it comfortable to move north into emerging Christian territory. The matter has not been sufficiently investigated.[91] In the late eleventh century they were sometimes resident in the monastery of San Martín in Albelda de Iregua, ten kilometers south of Logroño, but after 1076 when La Rioja passed into the realm of Alfonso VI they began to style themselves "bishops of Nájera." After the death of Alfonso VI and the passage of the territory into the hands of Alfonso I of Aragón, the incumbent Sancho of Funes adopted the style of "bishop of Calahorra" once more. But with the reversion of the land into Leonese hands in 1134 a new bishop, Rodrigo de Cascante, employed the title of "bishop of Nájera" yet again, and there is some evidence that he was so addressed even by the Cardinal Guido, papal legate at the Council of Valladolid, in 1155. Although there seems never to have been an episcopal palace in Nájera, and Santa María la Real would have found it an awkward companion, it is impossible to imagine that the bishop could have been totally without power in the town.

The town was a crucial royal tenancy with a royal palace.[92] Count García Ordóñez held the town from 1080 until his death at Uclés in 1108.[93] For virtually all of the reign of Alfonso I, the tenant was the great Aragonese noble, Fortún García Cajal. After the Leonese recovery of La Rioja Count Lop Díaz of the house of Haro was tenant between 1139 and 1157.

Benefiting from the pilgrim traffic, the monastery-shrine, and the royal palace, the population of Nájera probably numbered some 1,000 persons and included a community of Franks and another of Jews.[94] The town boasts the inevitable *fuero*, purportedly issued by Alfonso VI in 1076 and confirmed by Alfonso VII in 1136 (D252). This text also exists only in early modern paper copies and suggests considerable emendation simply by virtue of its length and complexity. The intitulation of Alfonso VI employs a style unknown to the eleventh-century royal chancery.[95] For what it is worth, the text asserts the existence of a *concejo*, *alcaldes*, and *sayones*, with the right of the council to choose two of the latter annually.

More authority rests with a private document of 1126 that cites the *con-*

91. M. Alamo, "Diocese de Calahorra et de la Calzada," *DHGE* 11 (1949), cols. 275–95, is the best extended and modern treatment of a most complex subject.

92. Reilly, *Urraca*, p. 269.

93. Reilly, *Alfonso VI*, pp. 146–47 and passim.

94. Francisco Javier García Turza, "Morfología de la ciudad de Nájera en la Edad Media," in *III semana de estudios medievales*, pp. 63–88 (Logroño, 1993), is a useful introduction.

95. Reilly, "Chancery," pp. 6–11.

cejo, an *alcalde*, a municipal *merino* as well as a *merino* of Santa María la Real, and two municipal *sayones*.[96] Another private document of 1153 also cites the *concejo* of Nájera as well as those of those of four small towns of the surrounding district, testifying to the ordinary status of such institutions.[97] Finally, in 1154 Sancho III confirmed the possessones of the *concejo* there in a most concise and austere charter (D842).

The old bishopric of Calahorra was settled in prehistoric times and became a late Roman town and bishopric. When he retook it from the Muslims, King García Sánchez III supposedly granted it a *fuero* in 1046. On July 10, 1076, when the town had passed into Leonese control Alfonso VI confirmed that document.[98] In 1129 when Calahorra was under Aragonese domination, a private document proves it a *señorial* town and mentions a *sayon* but implies that the bishop was not then resident.[99] Three years later, another private document carries the same implication but also cites a *concejo* and an *alcalde*.[100] In 1140, under Leonese control again, another private document mentions the bishop, Guter Fernández as royal tenant and his kinsman, Martín Fernández, as *alcalde*. The tenancy of these two can be demonstrated at least until 1151. This document also mentions a *sayon* and a "conventus ecclesie Beate Marie."[101] In 1142 a private document repeats this information and cites no less than four *alcaldes de concejo*.[102]

Calahorra lay only forty kilometers up the Ebro from Navarrese Tudela whose relations with León before 1147, and frequently after, were markedly tense. The government of the town likely had a distinctly military tenor and its bishop, if he was in residence, would have seen his authority diminished thereby. The same factors would have militated against the civil authority of the *concejo*.

Relations of the bishopric with the crown of León are confusing. Royal diplomas to it are often unreliable (D396, 497, 613, 727). Only in 1155 do we get two that inspire confidence. In one, Sancho III gave the bishop permission to build a bridge over the Ebro at Miranda de Ebro and to collect the royal *portaticum* there. In the other, Sancho granted a tenth of the *portaticum* at Arnedo, fourteen kilometers southwest of Calahorra (D884, 892). Then, in

96. April 21, 1126. Pub. Rodríguez de Lama, *Colección*, 2:149.
97. 1153. Pub. Margarita Cantera Montenegro, ed., *Colección documental de Santa María la Real de Nájera, Tomo I, siglos XII–XV* (San Sebastián, 1991), p. 84.
98. BN, Manuscritos, 9.194, ff. 147r-49v; RAH, Colección Salazar, O-8, fol. 83v. These are paper excerpts of the seventeenth century.
99. May 5, 1129. Pub. Rodríguez de Lama, *Colección*, 2:159–60.
100. November 27, 1132. Ibid., pp. 164–5. The addendum to the document is suspect.
101. February 26, 1140. Ibid., p. 196.
102. March 1, 1142. Ibid., p. 201. 1151. Ibid., pp. 228–29, also mentions a *concejo*.

1157, Sancho III granted the church of Calahorra the *fueros* of the church of Burgos (D971). The municipal *concejo* is not cited. By then the tenancy had passed to the Aragonese Fortún López and his son Lop López.[103] A fair inference is that the crown now was bolstering the church there against the new non-Leonese tenants, something he could not do for the *concejo*.

Another 120 kilometers down the Ebro sat the most populous city, after Toledo, of the Christian north, Zaragoza. It was long an object of Leonese ambition, but its Muslim population had yielded instead to Aragón. Only for a brief time, after the defeat at Fraga in 1134, was it under the control of León. Until the end of his reign, the Alfonsine chancery listed Zaragoza among the major possessions of the crown, but from the betrothal of Ramon Berenguer and *Infanta* Petronila in 1137 and the abdication in the latter's favor of her father, Ramiro II, the absorption of the city by Aragón-Barcelona was inevitable. Alfonso's concession of it to Ramon in vassalage that year merely gave legal form to the dictates of power. For seven years after 1135, however, the tenancy of the Riojan magnate and Leonese ally, Lop López, in Zaragoza gave León a foothold. The episcopate of Bishop Bernard had a like effect, since that prelate was chosen by Alfonso. But Lop was succeeded in 1146 by the Aragonese García Ortiz as tenant and Bernard by the Aragonese Bishop Pedro de Torroja in 1152 and the last remnants of Leonese hegemony went aglimmering.

Two diplomas of Alfonso VII to Zaragoza in 1134 and 1135 give no sign of a *concejo* there (D190, 227). But private documents between 1135 and 1141 testify to the existence of a *fuero* of Zaragoza in the broad sense of that term. The first also cites one Sancho Fortúnez as *zalmedina*, or market judge.[104] The earliest reference to a *concejo* comes in a private document of 1143, but one thinks that the assimilation to customary north-Iberian municipal practices in Zaragoza preceded that date.[105]

The foregoing survey illustrates that municipal institutions had emerged virtually everywhere in the north of Iberia by the end of the reign of Alfonso VII. They are not peculiar to the greater towns, but rather it appears virtually every village had them and that they were routinely extended to new settlements. The municipality had taken on a legal personage that allowed it to own and alienate property, to witness private property transfers within its own circumscriptions, and at least to monitor the actions of local officials

103. December 3, 1154. Ibid., p. 247.

104. April 28, 1135. Pub. Luis Rubio, ed., *Documentos del Pilar* (Zaragoza, 1971), p. 19. March 2, 1141. Ibid., p. 30.

105. ACA, Cancillería, Pergaminos, RB IV, Carpeta 4, no. 156.

against the background of a custom of which it was itself the custodian. Individuals could ordinarily claim the right to be judged solely in terms of that local custom but could also appeal from such determinations to the royal power that was its ultimate legitimation.

Slighter evidence indicates that some localities were already recognized in law to be entitled to have local *alcaldes*, *iudices*, *sayones*, and *merinos* chosen from among members of their own legal community. Still slimmer evidence points to the occasional annual choice by the municipal *concejo* of some of these local officials. Where a narrative source is available, as at Sahagún or Santiago de Compostela, there is convincing testimony that the choice of its own officials was an objective recognized and sought by urban communities. Against such a background it seems obvious that the grants of *fuero* (i.e., distinctive legal personality) that emerge as the prerogative and initiative of the crown must as often as not have resulted from the petition, purchase, or pressure of the urban community itself.

Nevertheless, the evidence does not support that overt violence or revolution was the ordinary road to municipal status or autonomy. Rather it seems more accurate to hypothesize an ordinary human interaction in which the choice of officials in the towns, as elsewhere, was made by the king, bishop, or lay *señor* in more or less informal consultation with the community simply because that was usually the most effective way to secure cooperation and obedience. Such a process always has its own politics, of course, and some people were rewarded by its operation as others were victimized by it. When the politics of the larger world, invasion or civil war as well as clashes between crown and churchman or noble, intruded on this urban microcosm, its own balance could be violently altered in one direction or the other. In the twelfth and thirteenth centuries that direction seems ordinarily to have been toward greater municipal autonomy. With the exceptions already recorded, however, that movement appears to have been incremental and on the whole peaceful during the reign of Alfonso VII.

Alfonso VII: An Appraisal

THE HISTORY OF ALFONSO VII is primarily the history of the public man. While the source materials for a history have multiplied roughly by a factor of ten from the period of his grandfather or even his mother, these materials reflect events, officials, offices, institutions, and practices. Personalities are almost never directly addressed in them. At best these latter can sometimes be deduced or intuited from the former. With that in mind, we can proceed to assess the king of León-Castilla and his achievements during the thirty-two years of his reign in the twelfth century.

While not possessed of the truly remarkable physical stamina of his grandfather, who died in his seventy-second year, Alfonso VII was blessed with a strong constitution. Although he died at fifty-two, he had spent virtually his entire life on the road and in camp if not in battle itself. Based on the itineraries traced in the preceding chapters and the geography of his swollen kingdom, I estimate that the king spent, on the average, a minimum of four months per year simply in travel. That is, four months on horseback, in the open and exposed to the weather. That is in addition, of course, to the time he spent in temporary quarters, themselves varying in character from the relative comfort of a monastery or a permanent royal estate house to the primitive accommodations of the overnight or forward camp in a battle zone. Surely the accumulating disabilities and infirmities of years so spent were what killed him in 1157. On balance, one may say that he stood up well to the contemporary stresses of kingship.

In dynastic and familial terms, Alfonso was more fortunate by far than his grandfather. His first marriage to Berengaria of Barcelona endured for the twenty-two years from 1127 until that queen's death in 1149, and his second marriage to the Polish noblewoman, Rica, in 1152 lasted until his own death in 1157. Berengaria's health must have been excellent and she solved almost immediately for him the problem that had plagued his grandfather down to the last hours of the latter's death. Despite the dangers then attendant on childbirth, his first queen gave birth to no fewer than the five sons and two daughters of whom we have notice. Although Ramón, Alfonso, and García failed to survive their father, Sancho and Fernando did. The crises contingent on the absence of a male heir were thus missing from the experience and reign of the grandson.

Indeed, the survival of two potential male heirs and the prospect of a second royal marriage that might produce yet more resulted in much jostling in the year 1152 and after. Queen Rica supplied the king with two more children. One was curiously named Fernando, perhaps because his failure to survive was foreseen from the first, and the other was named Sancha. She was quickly betrothed to the heir of Aragón-Barcelona, the future Alfonso II. The queen herself left León-Castilla after her husband's death and also subsequently married into the house of Barcelona, in the person of the count of Provence.[1]

One could deduct from this that the king was a correct husband, although not necessarily that he was a good husband. At the very least, he did not subject the dynasty and the realm to the sort of public marital scandals perpetrated by more than one later peninsular king. The one irregular union he is known to have enjoyed was with an Asturian noblewoman, Guntroda Pérez. As so often in dynastic liaisons of the period, the motivation seems to have been political. In any event, there is no evidence that it endangered the unity of the dynasty and its sole known product, his natural daughter, Urraca, became an honored and important member of the royal family.

Alfonso maintained that harmony within the dynasty that was the first necessity of monarchical government. His sister, Sancha, was a major figure in the politics of the kingdom and his aunt, Elvira, a not unimportant one. His natural daughter, Urraca, also became an important prop of his government in the Asturias of her birth. Does this argue mutual affection or simply common interests? A bit of both, I should think.[2]

But the material illustrates the difficulty of such conclusions about the personal characteristics of the king. He was an active opponent and rival of his cousin, Afonso Henriques of Portugal, as he was of his stepfather, Alfonso I of Aragón. He was, it seems, an inveterate foe of another stepfather, Count Pedro González de Lara, and there seems little doubt that he deliberately

1. Maria Dembińska, "A Polish Princess-Empress of Spain and Countess of Provence in the Twelfth Century," in *Frauen in Spatantike und Fruhmittelalter*, ed. Werner Affeldt, pp. 283–90 (Sigmaringen, 1990), pp. 287–88.

2. His chronicler comments upon the king's propensity for consulting his wife and sister. Antonio Maya Sánchez and Juan Gil, eds., *CAI*, in *Chronica Hispana: Saeculi XII*, pp. 109–296 (Turnholt, 1990), p. 155.

relegated his half brother and half sister by the count's marriage to Urraca to near total obscurity. On the other hand, his cousin Alfonso Jordan and he cooperated well. Again it is not adventurous to argue that both political and personal feeling came into play: they do with most of us. In the sole comment in the entire chronicle that has the ring of simple reporting rather than literary composition, we are told that Alfonso tried literally to throttle the rebel Count Rodrigo González de Lara, and both fell from their horses, when the king found the count insolent during negotiations.[3]

Turning rather to the testimony of policies pursued by Alfonso as king of León-Castilla, we conclude that perhaps the best phrase to describe his reign is "largely traditional." In the east he began the drive to reclaim the Castilian and Riojan territories lost to Aragón during the reign of his mother immediately on his accession. Most of the former he succeeded in repossessing by a mixture of military and diplomatic measures between 1127 and 1131. La Rioja had to wait until the death of Alfonso I at Fraga in 1134 radically disrupted the kingdom of Aragón.

That near collapse created an absolutely novel state of affairs in the eastern peninsula. It seemed initially to open up the possibility of the realization of the old Leonese ambition to possess the great city of Zaragoza. But when the true dimensions of the military and diplomatic difficulties of such a task made themselves evident in the years between 1134 and 1137, Alfonso opted for an alternative. He resorted to the umbrella of empire and vassalage as a device to maintain some claim there at much less cost in time and resources. Hindsight reveals that his decision opened the way to the emergence of another major Christian kingdom in the peninsula, Aragón-Barcelona. At the time, the consolidation of Catalunya itself about the county of Barcelona was only just beginning and to foresee that such a process would continue and prosper and that Barcelona would simultaneously maintain its foothold in Aragón proper for any length of time would have required a seer rather than a monarch.

Alfonso's acceptance of the fait accompli of the betrothal of Petronila and Ramon Berenguer in 1137 continued his alliance with Barcelona, struck with his own marriage to Berengaria in 1127. The policy had its uses. One does not know quite what to make of the sporadic projects of Alfonso and Ramon to partition Navarra. Success would have brought only marginal gain to either and also a new frontier common to the allies, difficult for either to defend against the other. Perhaps these proposals are best seen as gambits

---

3. Ibid., pp. 160–61.

that forced first García Ramírez IV and then Sancho VI into vassalage and cooperation, even to the point of intermarriage with the Leonese monarchy, at little real cost to the latter.

The explanation for the relative modesty of Alfonso's eastern policy after 1135 lies elsewhere. To free his hands for the consolidation of his rule and the reclamation of Castilla, he had reversed his mother's policy of hostility toward his aunt, Teresa of Portugal, immediately in 1126. But the old claims of the dynasty in that western territory were hard to resist. In any event, Portuguese affairs tended to be inseparable from those of southern Galicia. Increasing tensions between Teresa and her son, Afonso Henriques, beckoned in 1127 and 1128 and apparently convinced the Leonese king that his control could be extended as far south as Braga. Given the diminutive size of the emerging kingdom of Portugal at that time, such a feat would have reincorporated it almost fully in its parent kingdom.

But geography and the determination of Afonso Henriques were to prove that aim unrealizable. The mountainous character of the country where the interior *meseta* of the peninsula dips down toward the coastal strip that constitutes the essence of Portugal was an insuperable barrier to the military logistics of the time. The only feasible approach was from Galicia in the north, and that territory itself was difficult to reach from the heartland of the Leonese kingdom. To these obstacles were conjoined the active opposition of the Portuguese ruler as he consolidated his power at home after the victory over his mother and her Galician allies at São Mamede in 1128.

Afonso of Portugal even essayed an alliance with García Ramírez of Navarra in 1136–1137 against their over mighty neighbor. The Leonese monarch was able to meet and defeat both, and his Portuguese cousin was forced to do homage. But that challenge probably cost the former the direct control of Zaragoza. Moreover, the Portuguese monarch had no intention of accepting his reverse of 1137 as final. He began in 1140 openly to style himself as king rather than *infante* and to encroach on southern Galicia. When Alfonso VII attempted a military riposte in 1141 his defeat at Arcos de Valedevez led him to abandon hope of reclaiming direct control in Portugal. Two years later, he sealed that change by the recognition of his cousin's kingship in 1143 in the aftermath of the Council of Valladolid. Some sort of vassalage was arranged, but it never became substantial enough to warrant the Leonese chancery to cite the monarch of Portugal in the dating formulas of royal diplomas.

This gradual recognition between 1136 and 1143 of the need to temper the traditional Leonese ambition of dominance in Christian Iberia grew out of increasing demands and opportunities consequent on the pursuit of yet another traditional aim of that monarchy. Its waging of the *reconquista* against Islam in the peninsula had been largely dormant during the reign of Urraca. For the first years of her son's rule, while he was consolidating his power internally and reestablishing the dominant position of León vis-a-vis its Christian neighbors, that neglect of the *reconquista* had perforce continued. The muted complaint of Alfonso's own chronicler indicates that such inaction was felt to be unsatisfactory.[4]

After 1133, the king took up the traditional role of his office as leader of the *reconquista*. That task was progressively to absorb his energies and resources and dictated the new diplomatic stance toward his Christian neighbors. From Colmenar de Oreja in the valley of the Tajo in 1139, to Coria on the western plain of the Duero valley in 1142, to the conquest of far Almería in 1147 and in the futile attempt at the reconquest of which city in 1157 he was to find his death, this role conditioned if not determined most of Alfonso VII's other activities. Therefore, his execution of it must be one of the prime measures in any estimate of the significance of his reign. Such an estimate will always labor under the shade of the roll up of his conquests in Almería and in eastern Andalucía in 1156–1157 by the new Almohad power that culminated in the death of the Leonese monarch. Such a result moved the leading English historian of the *reconquista* to characterize the results of Alfonso's activities as ephemeral.[5] That conclusion requires considerable qualification.

First, Alfonso established an excellent record as military leader and general. His ability to raise armies year after year, to commit them on the riskiest of campaigns, and to realize the ends of most of those expeditions is incontestable. His career was marked by a long and impressive string of victories. We know of one clear defeat, that at the hands of the Portuguese in 1141 from which he had to be extricated by diplomacy. We also know of five failed sieges, one at Coria in 1138 and the others at Córdoba in 1150, Jaén in 1151, Guadix in 1152, and finally, that of Almería in 1157. But sieges are notoriously difficult operations and it must be noted that in all of the foregoing he was able to hold his army together and withdraw in good order. He never knew such a disaster as had his grandfather at Zalaca in 1086.

On a wider stage, clearly he attempted a task beyond the practical strength of the resources that he could marshall. That is, Alfonso undertook the conquest of the central and upper basin of the Guadalquivir and its eastern extension to the coast at Almería. That a permanent annexation was intended is implicit in the recognition, or foundation, of Christian bishoprics at Baeza

4. Ibid., p. 204.
5. Derek W. Lomax, *The Reconquest of Spain* (London, 1978), pp. 86–93.

and Almería. That sprawling area, perhaps with a majority of Muslim inhabitants, must be governed and exploited by a tiny minority of Christian soldiers and settlers drawn from the north. Daunting in itself, that settlement would then have to have been defended against the major Muslim communities of the lower Guadalquivir in concert with, or as subjects of, a North African empire of formidable power in its own right.

The daring of the undertaking strikes one as epic even now. Certainly Alfonso did not lack imagination or ambition. One can realize as well the contemporary ambiguities and uncertainties. The power of the Almoravid empire was in full decline. The rise of the Almohad empire was far from assured. Something like simple chaos might have resulted from the contest of the two across the straits. Nevertheless, it was surely an extreme gamble and was likely recognized as such at the time, even given the piecemeal information obtainable concerning events internal to the world of Islam. The task set was very nearly beyond the greater powers of a kingdom of Castilla in the thirteenth and fourteenth centuries. The practicalities were not really decided until the victory on the Río Salado in 1340.

Even so, it needs to be understood that Alfonso VII did not expect to have to effect that result with the unaided resources of León-Castilla itself. The failure of his grand military design resulted in good measure from the failure of his grand diplomatic design.

The offensive against Upper Andalucía took place within the context of the Second Crusade in Europe and there can be little doubt that Alfonso both hoped and worked for an infusion of aid from beyond the Pyrenees. The extension of the offensive to the coast at Almería resulted, according to both his and the Genoese chroniclers, from the initiative of the latter.[6] While the king responded to the overtures of the Genoese, he also worked successfully to involve Aragón-Barcelona, Navarra, Portugal, and the papacy. Seen within that context, the successes of Alfonso VII were anything but ephemeral. They resulted in the permanent extension of Portugal south from the Mondego to the Tajo. They resulted in a similar extension of Aragón-Barcelona south and west to Tortosa and Lérida. His gamble on more general European aid, save for some fortuitous assistance at these three places, failed. His Iberian allies pursued their own concerns for consolidating these conquests. The collapse of the Genoese economy led to their near withdrawal from Iberian affairs until the next century. Ideally, all should have been in some measure anticipated and provided against.

---

6. Maya Sánchez and Gil, *CAI*, pp. 246–47. Caffaro, *De Captione Almerie et Tortuose*, ed. Antonio Ubieto Arteta (Valencia, 1973), 22–22.

Even so, the full assessment of Alfonso VII's conduct of the *reconquista* requires further consideration. In 1135, fifty years after his grandfather's capture of Toledo, that city still stood as the southernmost redoubt of the realm. Simply to retain his forebear's great achievement required what one might call a forward defense; that is, irrespective of such additional territories as they might secure, more than two decades of continuous ravaging and destruction in the Muslim lands to the south had a value in itself. On the one hand, it promoted the continuing flow of Christian Mozarabs to the north, weakening the adversary and strengthening León-Castilla. On the other, by the creation of something on the order of a no-man's-land in Extremadura and La Mancha it made increasingly difficult a future major Muslim attempt on Toledo and the basin of the Tajo.[7] While not the prime aim of his policy, surely these benefits could not have been totally absent from the king's calculations or those of his subjects and the half century after his death proved their value.

One final benefit of this forcing of the zone of conflict deep into Andalucía was that it permitted behind it a flow of settlers from the north of the realm toward the south. This was a slow process and even fifty years after Alfonso VI's seizure of Toledo, the lands between the Duero and the Guadarramas were far from fully occupied. The settled territories in the diocese of Avila, for example, only slowly expanded from the areas close to the Duero about Olmedo south to Arévalo, reached Avila even later, and then tentatively probed beyond the Guadarramas by the end of the reign of Alfonso VII.[8] What was true of Avila was also typical of the region generally, especially in its western reaches, subject, up until 1142, to raids from places as near as Coria. Before 1157, a survey of place names through the entire region indicates the halting nature of progress south with none known in the areas southwest of Salamanca, for example.[9]

Yet more dependent on the respite afforded by Leonese armies operating in Andalucía were the new settlements being established in the middle and upper basin of the Tajo. This repopulation had begun in the time of Alfonso VI but had been limited largely to the north bank of that river and even there was halting and had been reversed in some measure during the turmoil of Urraca's reign. Under Alfonso VII, it resumed and gradually filled

7. It could not, of course, prevent the fairly constant raids from places such as Medellín, Trujillo, and Cáceres mentioned as routine by the Muslim geographer of the mid-twelfth century. Al-Idrisi, *Description de l'Afrique et de l'Espagne*, trans. Rheinhart Dozy (Paris, 1866), pp. 226–27.
8. Angel Barrios García, *Estructuras agrarias y de poder en Castilla: El ejemplo de Avila, 1085–1320* (Salamanca, 1983), illustrates in some detail how gradual that progress could be.
9. Luis-Miguel Villar García, *La Extremadura castellano-leonesa: Guerreros, clérigos, y campesinos, 711–1252* (Valladolid, 1986), p. 124.

in the deserted lands from Colmenar de Oreja, northeast of Toledo, to Mora, to its southeast, and to Santa Olalla, to its northwest. Good portions of this were accomplished by immigrants from the south, Mozarabs.[10] The latter also caused the population of Toledo itself to grow once more. Finally, most vulnerable of all were the advanced hamlets situated towards Muslim Cuenca in the east such as Alcocer, Uclés, and Huete and even on the verges of La Mancha at Consuegra and Belmonte.[11]

It is not too much to say that the creation of Castilla La Nueva was accomplished during these years that also saw the final consolidation of the *meseta* south of the Duero. One should be cautious, I believe, about positing a conscious royal policy of territorial repopulation. Much of it was accomplished through simply validating what humble instruments, nobles, churchmen, and the peasants themselves initiated and carried to completion. Quite as much must have resulted from the ordinary operation of the royal largesse, the royal desire for building up the income of the fisc, and particular decisions that sprang from just as particular military necessities. Nevertheless, the tempo, the magnitude, and the perdurance of that process, all was directly dependent on the armies of León that contained the forces of Islam to the lands of al-Andalus during the quarter of a century before 1157.

In a consideration of the internal government of the realm, it is well to keep in mind the limitations imposed by the contemporary conception of human society. That conception was profoundly conservative. It looked to the king to preserve an already extant, fundamentally moral, and essentially changeless order. Where the traditional order had broken down, royal action was expected to restore it. Where individuals or groups acted in defiance of the norms of that order, royal action was expected to repress and punish them. Innovation could result from such activity, accidentally and out of sheer practical necessity, of course, for any real restoration of the past happily is beyond human ability. Nonetheless, it would be a mistake to look for a conscious, progressive redesign of political or social institutions. Such an idea is modern, and it is profoundly anachronistic to employ it as a measure of successful or adequate kingship in the medieval period.

With that in mind, what we must describe belongs rather to the order of household and estate management than to the order of government as moderns conceive it. Royal government continued to be peripatetic in character

10. Salvador de Moxó, *Repoblación y sociedad en la España cristiana medieval* (Madrid, 1979), pp. 219–20, 240–43.

11. Ricardo Izquierdo Benito, *Castilla-La Mancha en la Edad Media* (Madrid, 1985), pp. 64–65. Julio González, "Repoblación de las tierras de Cuenca," *AEM* 12 (1982): 184–88.

and method. Major court dignities remained unchanged. The use of the term "chancellor" for the head of the royal writing office became customary, but it would be difficult to detect a corresponding change in chancery organization that accompanied the new terminology.

The language of royal documents does reflect a changing perception of the nature of the kingdom. From 1126 Alfonso VII was entitled "Imperator Totius Hispanie" in the fashion that his grandfather had made usual. After 1135 and the imperial coronation of that spring, it became usual for the dating formula to specify the constituent parts of the realm; "Toledo, León, Zaragoza, Nájera, Castilla, and Galicia" at first and without fail. "Baeza and Almeria, Santa Eufemia, and Pedroche" were added as they were conquered. In this it would seem that the sense of the territoriality of the realm was gaining as against its personification in the dynasty. This change coincides roughly with the appearance in the chancery of Hugo as chancellor and Gerald as scribe, but one hesitates to ascribe the conceptual change either to their persons or their probable French backgrounds. The politically altered configuration of the realm was the more likely stimulus.

From 1149 the rulers of neighboring realms are added to the dating formula when they had actually done homage but this conforming of language to the existing state of affairs was tardy. The princes of Aragón-Barcelona and Navarra had begun to do homage years earlier, as had Saif al-Dawla and ibn Gāniya. Yet the routine conservatism of the court was being challenged somewhat by the extraordinary circumstances of the kingdom after 1147. Too much should not be made of the coincidence of these formulaic novelties and the appearance as chancellor of Juan Fernández.

On balance the traditional processes and mechanisms of the curia remained. As we have seen, the chancery forms were unaltered although the rise of the towns produced a legal personality hardly well contained within the royal charter format. The regular convocation of expanded royal councils continued to mark the government of imperial León-Castilla, as it had during the reigns of Alfonso VI and Urraca, but no effort to distinguish them from strictly ecclesiastical councils can be detected, although the contemporary reform movement in the church was heigtening the distinction between things lay and clerical, generally. Neither can one yet detect any movement toward a conceptual or operational distinction between a curia and a *cortes*.

Given the tasks that the crown perceived as proper to it, occasional intervention in local affairs sufficed, if perhaps only barely. The resort to regional supervision by some member of the dynasty, or by a curial dignitary such as count or castellan, was already a traditional device made incumbent by the swollen size of the realm resulting from the past and present political and military prowess of the dynasty. Primarily a measure for the management of the royal fisc, it was only secondarily a measure to govern the realm. Nevertheless, it is possible to descry some royal innovation at the local level precisely in regard to the royal fisc. The gradual and hesitating employment of a new official, the *merino mayor*, to provide additional oversight to the more concentrated and productive blocs of fisc land carried the seed of a future, public territorial division, the *merindad*. But this was an improvement in dynastic property management rather than an intention to build a new public order. All the same, it was a progressive change if a modest one.

Most of what we would be inclined to call local development was beyond the ability and probably the interest of the crown to direct. It appears that town institutions, for example, arose similarly from similar needs and circumstances, although the tempo certainly varied from place to place. The crown by no means had an urban policy, but its participation in town growth answered and channeled local initiative. As I see it, the *fuero* was an instrument to legitimate local needs. The crown was happy to foster such development, probably for purposes of enhancing, in turn, its revenue and the organization and the defense of the countryside. When burghers came into conflict with other local forces, bishops or nobles, clearly the king was willing to respond to the overtures of the highest bidder and to use his unquestioned authority to preserve or restore the peace. To see in any of this a conscious royal policy to support town growth to check noble or episcopal power is to advance leagues beyond what present evidence will support.

The same must be said concerning the rising power of the nobility. In a smaller arena, they were engaged in the same development and consolidation of dynastic property and authority as was the king. Recently it has been argued that in so doing they were cannibalizing an older public and royal order.[12] Perhaps that is true elsewhere. In León-Castilla my researches suggest such a public order simply did not exist after the Islamic invasion of the eighth century and very possibly not before. In the period directly under discussion here, both crown and nobility thought primarily in terms of property rather than territory in the administrative sense. Both would have understood thoroughly what the other was about and would not have dreamed of objecting to it on principle.

Of course, when dynastic claims or even influence conflicted with those of the magnates, the reaction was prompt and the struggle real. Alfonso VII was quick to respond to what he perceived as lèse-majesté in the various in-

---

12. Pierre Bonnassie, *From Slavery to Feudalism in Southwestern Europe* (Cambridge, 1991). The author was attempting to broaden the application of the thesis he advanced in *Cataluña mil años atrás: siglos X–XI* (Barcelona, 1988). It may apply to Catalonia.

stances involving Pedro González de Lara, his brother Rodrigo, and Gonzalo Peláez of Asturias. But from the information that we possess, it appears that his ire was directed at individuals rather than at lineages or at the rights of the nobility in the abstract. The means and the attitude adopted by Alfonso were demonstrably effective for his time and, once his accession was assured, the royal power was unchallenged domestically.

Aside from matters military the contemporary arena in which change and development were most marked was the Christian church both within and without the peninsula. Even there, however, the most revolutionary changes were justified in the name of "reform" and an appeal to a primal, ancient order. While Alfonso VII could not have been unaware of the ferment in the most central organ of society, once again he seems to have done little more than to defend the traditional policy and prerogatives of the crown; that is, he maintained the preeminence of the primatial see of Toledo within the kingdom of León-Castilla and within Iberia, generally. He also exercised forcefully and generally successfully the royal right to designate all of the bishops of the León-Castilla, made use of them as royal officers in their cities and dioceses, and called on them for both funds and military service as the need arose.

Occasionally, his stance caused rebuke from Rome, but papal thunders were directed rather at his hapless instruments than at the king himself. If the contemporary papacy had had stronger incumbents and fewer troubles itself, one suspects that Alfonso would have experienced more difficulties. But the king was not doctrinaire in his religious policies. He was willing to let papal legates circulate freely in the realm. He expected to be consulted by them, to have his preferences respected, and to be able to suborn them if need be. No doubt, he limited the travel of his bishops to Rome as potentially troublesome. Nevertheless he allowed appeal to Rome when his clerics quarreled among themselves and no royal interest was touched directly. He himself sometimes appealed to Rome when it was, and his wishes were respected there more often than not.

Obviously, he continued the traditional dynastic patronage of the Benedictines of Cluny, although on a somewhat reduced scale. Toward the end of his reign, he and his family seem to have seen no contradiction in simultaneously undertaking the patronage of the monks of Citeaux as well. Recent discoveries have brought to light the surprisingly generous treatment accorded to the new order of Hospitalers by the crown.[13] One thinks that it

---

13. Carlos Ayala Martínez, ed., *Libro de Privilegios de la Orden de San Juan de Jerusalén en Castilla y León, siglos XII–XV* (Madrid, 1994). Before its appearance, the Hospitallers seemed to be very modest players indeed during the second quarter of the twelfth century in the peninsula.

was probably matched by similar generosity to the Templars, although the belief remains just that in the absence of a comparable discovery. On balance there appears to have been no real policy to favor one religious order over the other, such as marked royal actions in regard to the episcopacy. All orders were welcomed as producers of wealth, promoters of new settlement, as, guarantors, generally of a more regular order in the countryside, and, of course, as practitioners and purveyors of sanctity.

In short, Alfonso VII was the very embodiment of the medieval king. Doubtless he was pious, although his piety found reflection in no single monument or foundation. He fully understood that the Christian church had ends of its own that were more properly the interest of clerics than of even a crowned layman. He respected those ends and tolerated the ecclesiastical politics that effected and rationalized them. At the same time, the church's particular organization, discipline, and resources made it an invaluable and unique part of the realm and he expected churchmen to recognize their resultant responsibilities to the crown. Bishops particularly were his companions, his advisors, his assistants, and his subordinates. It had always been so.

Beyond the glacial expansion southward of the peasant Christian community of the northern peninsula, the other fundamental change, common to the reigns of his great-grandfather, his grandfather, and his mother, as well as to his own, was the cultural and institutional reorientation of that community to the western European world to the north. In relation to the latter, the dispute dearly beloved of Hispanic historiography concerning the fact and desirability of leaders whose conscious policy was "afrancesado" approaches the frivolous. It presumed that they pursued such an idea and that they possessed the resources to realize it. Both presumptions rested on a radical overestimate of the power of the medieval monarchy.

The reorientation of Iberian Christendom away from the peninsular south and Africa and toward trans-Pyrrenaen Europe resulted from currents much broader and deeper than any controlled, or indeed controllable, by the crowned heads of the Christian peninsular monarchies. Most fundamental among these was the cult of Santiago and the pilgrimage it spawned that each year brought tens of thousands of western Europeans into the peninsula. The crown had not produced the cult, certainly never controlled it, and only sporadically patronized it. Yet year after year, the pilgrimage continued to flood the largely passive, agricultural society of northern Iberia with strangers from the north; with their persons, their styles, and eventually with their ideologies and their art. The alteration of the host society was profound and obvious, but the agents of the reception, although they might include the crown, were

massively broader and deeper than the latter. They were to be found throughout all of peninsular society.

So it was, too, with the enlivening current of trade, to the degree that this
factor can be separated from the pilgrimage phenomenon. To a real if lesser
extent, the activities of the merchants of the Midi, of Genoa, and of Pisa were
overshadowing those of the merchants of Córdoba, Sevilla, Valencia, and Almería. True, the crown might at one time or another cooperate with these new
entrepreneurs for generally limited and political ends, but the broad initiative came from without and found its most enduring and significant response
at much more humble levels than the royal one. In the eleventh and twelfth
centuries the crown of León-Castilla recognized trade by franchising it with
local fairs, taxing it with tolls, and exempting it from those same tolls. The
sum of these does not come to a trade policy much less an economic policy.
They represented, conceptually, no more than fiscal or political opportunism.
This was as true of Alfonso VII as it had been of his dynastic forebears.

The final major agent of change in Iberian society of the period was the
reform movement within the western Christian church. That movement was
a self-conscious one with a definite ideological content, and it took particular
institutional and organizational shapes. As such, it was susceptible to being
easily recognized by the crown and to some extent influenced by it. Here, too,
however, the essential initiatives and definitions were crafted in France and
Rome. In Iberia from the founder of the dynasty, Fernando I, taste, wisdom,
or conviction had led to the gradual acceptance of the new religious establishment. Alfonso VII was no exception to that already traditional stance. The
decision entailed, although certainly its full implications for the future were
not realized, the partial subordination of the Iberian Christian church within
a hierarchy culminating in the Roman papacy, the establishment within the
former of new institutional forms such as the cathedral chapter and the religious order, and the regulation of the new whole by a systematized canon law.

Taken together, these changes meant the obliteration or the reduction
to vestigial remains of the Mozarabic church in the peninsula. Alfonso VII
inherited this stance, refined it somewhat, cooperated where he could, and
resisted where it pinched. His attitude toward church affairs comes as close
to constituting a crown policy, in the modern, self-conscious sense, as can be
found in the reign. Yet here again, the monarchy was but a single if influential agent among the contemporary hundreds of indigenous ones that were
collaborating in the refashioning of the Iberian church.

The king's relationships with contemporary neighboring and foreign
monarchs and powers must be evaluated against a similar understanding of

the circumstances and possibilities of the time. Surely to speak of "foreign policy" in the twelfth century is anachronistic. Directing a dynasty rather than a kingdom, not to say a "state," monarchs of the period seldom possessed the resources to make themselves dangerous to their neighbors. Only when they could position themselves at the head of plundering expeditions, such as the *reconquista*, the Norman Conquest, or the Crusades, could something like modern warfare over distance result.

In Iberia itself, there are glimmers of something more ambitious in the brief attempt of Portugal and Navarra to ally against León-Castilla in 1137. Alfonso VII himself may have been the first of his dynasty to realize the significance of the new power coalescing around the county of Barcelona at the beginning of the century, and he drew it into alliance against the Aragón of his stepfather Alfonso I by his marriage with Berengaria in 1127. Yet at the same time he certainly realized the importance of that prestigious marriage to set off his own regal position from the too-numerous claimants to the throne of León-Castilla surrounding him.

After the collapse of the kingdom of Aragón following on the disaster at Fraga, the reemergence of the kingdom of Navarra was followed by a series of projects hatched by Alfonso VII and Ramon Berenguer IV to dismember it. Even that design, however, proved beyond their joint capabilities, and the dynastic expedient of intermarriage was adopted by Alfonso VII to frame the relationship of the two monarchies. There can be no doubt that the conceptual framework of the *reconquista* was utilized by the Leonese monarch from 1144 to mobilize the combined forces of León-Castilla, Portugal, Aragón-Barcelona, and Navarra against the failing Almoravid empire in al-Andalus. Yet after the brilliant successes of 1147–1148, the localized dynamics of the participants made it impossible to maintain such a coalition even with the considerable assistance of religious enthusiasm.

In those initial successes, Alfonso VII labored to involve wider European participation. He succeeded in enlisting the prestige of the Roman papacy, and the Iberian enterprise was formally recognized as a crusade. Under such a banner, he was able to enlist Genoa and Montpellier to reinforce the efforts of the properly Iberian powers against the Muslims. In subsequent years, he persisted in utilizing papal support to encourage participation by the English and French monarchies, although without success.

At our remove in time, it is impossible to estimate the relative strengths of the welter of religious enthusiasm, simple desire for plunder, dynastic gamesmanship, and utopian schemes of empire that combined in such an endeavor. Nevertheless, it would be naive to see in Alfonso's choice of the

Polish princess Rica as a new bride in 1152 a "German" or "imperial" policy, although the consent of Conrad III and then Frederick Barbarossa had to be sought. The principal motivation of that union is to be sought in dynastic prestige within León-Castilla rather than in geopolitical strategy in Europe. With the marriage of *Infanta* Constanza to Louis VII of France in 1154, the political element, as such, was doubtless stronger. Notwithstanding, we can be sure that it took the form of suasion to enlist the French monarchical house for the purposes of crusade in Iberia rather than a project for an enduring alliance of the two crowns. To see in it a "French policy" is again to project modern predilections on medieval concerns. Moreover, we can be sure that, just as Louis VII needed a fertile bride for dynastic purposes, Alfonso VII was sensitive to that enhancement of his family's domestic prestige predictably consequent on the French marriage.

All of these considerations make the description of the reign of Alfonso VII of León-Castilla as traditional the most apt. To see him as a strong, energetic king, quick to seize on the opportunities offered by the chance of warfare, the weakness of peninsular rivals, or the more general currents of European affairs is accurate. He was, as well, capable of adapting and modifying, within modest limits, contemporary dynastic institutions and practices to deal with the strains resulting from the monarchy's own successes or from profounder social trends only dimly apprehended. By and large, however, his rule displays a constant reliance on those established conceptions and proved practices that had sustained his dynasty for the three preceding generations. If that means that Alfonso VII was an actor and innovator solely within strictly constrained compass, by no means does it make him either unusual or of lesser merit among his crowned contemporaries. It may even prove him wise.

In any event, the criteria on which we should evaluate Alfonso VII would have seemed incomprehensible or utopian to that king. For us, the division of his kingdom on his death in 1157 is tragic and the ultimate condemnation of a traditionalism unable to redefine itself. That conclusion is itself a function of our own ideal of the state as an indivisible sovereignty, however. Alfonso regretted that necessity as subversive of the ideal unity of the dynasty but as one of dynastic politics' inevitable risks. And dynastic politics was the only sort of politics that existed.

If we follow the explanation of that division given by Rodrigo Jiménez de Rada in the following century, we again see in it the failure of the crown to restrain if not eliminate the power of the nobility and its capacity for mischief. That is, if the chronicler was not reading back the spectacular rivalry of the Castro and the Lara lineages of the latter part of the century into the events of 1152–1153.[14] Here, once more, we assume as ideal the egalitarian modern state to which the very idea of a hereditary nobility is offensive. Alfonso VII, on the other hand, would have been most sensitive to any infringement of the proper prerogative of the crown, while nevertheless regarding the preferences and advice of his magnates as natural components in the determination of such problems.

Very likely, he himself saw the division of the realm as the inevitable outcome of the brute facts of births and marriages within the dynasty. From the vantage of our own century we impatiently await the crown to get on with the consolidation of the nation-state. To such an intellectual ideal, the division of the realm of 1157 was a tragic step backward. Alfonso VII, too, would have felt, one thinks, some little frustration at that same division in the dynasty. Yet he would have been astonished that we should hold him responsible for it.

14. Rodrigo Jiménez de Rada, *De Rebus Hispaniae*, ed. Emma Falque Rey (Turnholt, 1987), p. 229.

An Annotated Guide to the Documents of Alfonso VII and His Dynasty, 1107–1157

THE LIST BELOW includes the documents not only of the king but also of the *infantes* of the dynasty. It does not include those of Queen Urraca, a collection of which has recently been published, nor those of Urraca's documents in which her son was associated with her. Adequate reference to the latter can be found in my earlier work. Nor does it include royal confirmations to private documents unless these are dated. Others have been noted in the study itself when relevant.

Citations here are only to the most recently published scholarly text of documents. Where the document is unpublished, the archival data are supplied. Where the archival data are incomplete in the best printed text, the necessary additional information is given.

Ordinary citations consist of the date, place (when supplied), grantor, grantee, published text, and comments as necessary.

1. August 16, 1107. Toledo. Alfonso VII, Rica, *infantes* Sancho and Fernando. Monastery of Caabeiro. AHN, Códices, 1,439B, ff. 2r–3r. Patently false.
2. November 27, 1116. Villabañez. Alfonso VII. Monastery of Santa María de Duero. Miguel C. Vivancos Gómez, ed., *Documen tación del monasterio de Santo Domingo de Silos, 954–1254* (Burgos, 1988), pp. 38–39. Also, BN, Manuscritos, 3.546, ff. 123r–124r.
3. December 9, 1117. Alfonso VII. Pedro Martínez. José Antonio Fernández Flórez, ed., *Colección diplomática del monasterio de Sahagún, Vol. 4; 1110–1199* (León, 1991), 4:51–52.
4. September 20, 1118. Segovia. Alfonso VII. Count Gómez Nuñez. Joao Pedro Ribeiro, *Dissertações chronologicas e criticas sobre a História e jurisprudencia ecclesiastica e civil de Portugal*, 5 vols. (Lisbon, 1856–96), 2:108. A note and dating formula only.
5. November 16, 1118. Alfonso VII. Men of Toledo. Alfonso García Gallo,

"Los fueros de Toledo," *AHDE* 45 (1975): 341–488, who rightly sees it as a later synthesis of earlier acts.

6. November 20, 1118. Alfonso VII. Cathedral of Toledo. José Antonio García Luján, ed., *Privilegios reales de la catedral de Toledo, 1086–1462,* 2 vols. (Toledo, 1982), 2:33–34.

7. November 28, 1118. Alfonso VII. Monastery of San Clemente de Toledo. Andrés Merino, *Escuela paleografía* (Madrid, 1780), pp. 14–15. Later interpolations and mistakes.

8. May 6, 1119. *Infanta* Sancha. Randulfo de Baheus. Luisa García Calles, *Doña Sancha* (León, 1972), who called it an original. Its Caroline script precludes that. AHN, Clero, Carpeta 3,427, no. 8.

9. September 26, 1119. Simancas. Alfonso VII. Monastery of San Julián de Moraime. Manuel Lucas Alvarez, "El monasterio de San Julián en Galicia," in *Homenaje a Don Augustín Millares Carlo* (Gran Canaries, 1975), pp. 626–28, who believed it an original. The script and usage preclude that.

10. October 8, 1119. Alfonso VII. Monastery of Sahagún. Fernández Flórez, *Colección,* 5:58–59, calls no. 22 an original.

11. September 27, 1120. *Infanta* Sancha. Gonzalo Alvarez. García Calles, *Doña Sancha,* pp. 130–31. AHN, Clero, Carpeta 961, no. 7.

12. September 1, 1121. *Infanta* Sancha. Monastery of San Pedro de las Dueñas. José María Fernández Catón, "Documentos leoneses en escritura visigótica," *AL* 27 (1973): 224–26. An original.

13. March 22, 1122. Alfonso VII. Monasterio of San Martín de Pinario. *Colección diplomática de Galicia,* 2 vols. (Santiago de Compostela, 1901–03), 1:230–32. ARG, Documentos reales, no. 2. An original.

14. July 1, 1122. Alfonso VII. Pedro García. Pedro Floriano Llorente, ed., *Colección diplomática del monasterio de San Vicente de Oviedo* (Oviedo,1968), pp. 260–61. Certainly dated too early and perhaps a falsification based on an originally private grant.

15. 1123. Alfonso VII. Cathedral of Segovia. Luis-Miguel Villar García, ed., *Documentación medieval de la catedral de Segovia, 1115–1300* (Salamanca, 1990), pp. 53–54.

16. May 26, 1123. Arbas. Alfonso VII. Monastery of Santa María de Arbas. Vicente García Lobo and José Manuel García Lobo, *Santa María de Arbas. Catálogo de su archivo y apuntes para su historia* (Madrid, 1980), p. 49. Some paraphrasing and a notice only.

17. October 29, 1123. Alfonso VII. Cathedral of Osma. AHN, Códices, 946B, fol. 55r–v. Francisco J. Hernández, ed., *Los cartularios de Toledo* (Madrid, 1985), pp. 26–27, published the dating formula and the confirmants only.

18. November 29, 1123. Alfonso VII. Cathedral of Toledo. García Luján, *Privilegios*, 2:35–37.

19. December 11, 1123. Segovia. Alfonso VII. Pedro Vélaz. Juan de Alamo, ed., *Colección diplomática de San Salvador de Oña*, 2 vols. (Madrid, 1950), 1:188–89. The diplomatic marks it as false. Moreover, Lop López was not royal majordomo in 1123.

20. December 26, 1123. Burgos. Alfonso VII. Concejo of Briviesca. Felix Sagrado Fernández, *Briviesca antigua y medieval*, 2nd ed. (Madrid, 1979), pp. 239–43. The text is contained in a *vidimus* of Fernando IV of July 2, 1299, and is anachronistic as we have it.

21. April 6, 1124. Alfonso VII. Concejo of Santa Olalla. García Gallo, "Fueros," p. 463. A fragment only.

22. April 8, 1124. Compostela. Alfonso VII. Monastery of San Payo de Antealtares. AHN, Clero, Carpeta 518, no. 7. A confirmation of the charter of Alfonso VI to the same, dated May 28, 1098.

23. May 31, 1124. Alfonso VII. Cathedral of Santiago de Compostela. Antonio López Ferreiro, *Historia de la Santa Apostólica Metropolitana Iglesia de Santiago de Compostela*, 11 vols. (Santiago de Compostela, 1898–1911), 4:7–9 appendix. Also BN, Manuscritos, 7.472, fol. 41 r–v.

24. May 31, 1124. Alfonso VII. Muño Tacón. AC Compostela, copy of Tumbo A, fol. 110r–v.

25. June 22, 1124. Alfonso VII. Cathedral of Astorga. AHN, Códices, 1.195B, fol. 72r–v; 1.197B, ff. 132v–155v (the pagination skips); BN, Manuscritos, 712, ff. 106r–7r; 9.194, ff. 105r–6r; Acad. Hist., Colección Salazar, O–24, ff. 38r–40r; Catedrales de España, Astorga, 9-25-1-C-2, ff. 38v–40r and 45r–47r. Clearly false.

26. June 23, 1124. *Infanta* Sancha. Monastery of Cluny. Alexandre Bruel, ed., *Recueil des chartes de l'Abbaye de Cluny*, 6 vols. (Paris, 1876–1903), 5:327–28, who called it an original. In fact it is a copy in Caroline script of the late twelfth century. Also BN, Manuscritos, 720, ff. 283v–284v; Acad. Hist., Colección Salazar, O–17, ff. 786v–787v.

27. November 1, 1124. Alfonso VII. Cathedral of Sigüenza. Toribio Minguella y Arnedo, ed., *Historia de la diócesis de Sigüenza y de sus obispos*, vol. 1 (Madrid, 1910), pp. 349–50. Also BN, Manuscritos, 13.073, ff. 165r–166v.

28. January 19, 1125. Alfonso VII. Cathedral of Toledo. García Luján, *Privilegios*, 2:38–40, incorrectly dated to January 25. False.

29. March 23, 1125. Toro. Alfonso VII. Hospitallers. Carlos Ayala Martínez, ed., *Libro de Privilegios de la Orden de San Juan de Jerusalén en Castilla y León, siglos XII–XV* (Madrid, 1994), pp. 160–61.

30. April 1, 1125. Alfonso VII. Velasco Ramirez. Arturo Vázquez Núñez. "Documentos históricos," *BCMOrense* 3 (1905), p. 343. AHP Orense, Pergaminos, Celanova, no. 2. False. Those who confirm are mutually incompatible.

31. June 1, 1125. Alfonso VII. Cathedral of Mondoñedo. Enrique Flórez, *ES*, 27 vols. (Madrid, 1747–72), 18:344–5. Enrique Cal Pardo, ed., *Catálogo de los documentos escritos en pergamino del archivo de la catedral de Mondoñedo* (Lugo, 1990), pp. 18 and 126. Also BN, Manuscritos, 5.928, ff. 32v–33r.

32. June 26, 1125. *Infanta* Elvira. Hospitallers. Ayala Martínez, *Liber*, pp. 161–62.

33. July 21, 1125. Alfonso VII. Monastery of Silos. Vivancos Gomez, *Documentación*, pp. 45–47. False. Interpolation of Urraca's diploma of identical date.

34. September 11, 1125. Alfonso VII. Monastery of San Pedro de las Dueñas. AD León, Fondo San Pedro de las Dueñas, nos. 9–10.

35. 1126. Alfonso VII. Cathedral of Avila. Angel Barrios García, ed., *Documentación medieval de la catedral de Avila* (Salamanca, 1981). This copy lacks a date but from Alfonso's intitulation, it must precede the death of Urraca in March.

36. 1126. Alfonso VII. Cathedral of Segovia. Antonio Ubieto Arteta, ed., *Colección diplomática de Cuellar* (Segovia, 1961), p. 15, cites an undated thirteenth-century copy there.

37. March 9, 1126. Sahagún. Alfonso VII. Pedro Muñoz. AHN, Códices, 1.002B, ff. 12v–13r.

38. April 1, 1126. Alfonso VII. Monastery of Silos. Vivancos Gómez, *Documentación*, pp. 52–53.

39. April 13, 1126. Zamora. Alfonso VII. Cathedral of Salamanca. José Luis Martín, Luis-Miguel Villar García, Florencio Marcos Rodríguez, Marciano Sánchez Rodríguez, eds., *Documentos de los archivos catedralicio y diocesano de Salamanca, siglos IX al XII* (Salamanca, 1977), pp. 88–89.

40. April 14, 1126. Alfonso VII. Monastery of San Tomas of Zamora. AC Zamora, Tumbo Negro, fol. 19r–v; Tumbo Blanco, ff. 67v–68r.

41. June 18, 1126. Alfonso VII. Monastery of Silos. Vivancos Gómez, *Documentación*, pp. 56–58. Also BN, Manuscritos, 3.546, ff. 127r–v. False. Confirmed by the deceased Archbishop Bernard of Toledo and Bishop Paschal of Burgos, also deceased.

42. June 18, 1126. Alfonso VII. Monastery of Silos. Ibid., 57–59. Possibly false since it shares the general diplomatic of no. 41.

43. June 18, 1126. Alfonso VII. Monastery of Silos. Ibid., pp. 59–61. False for same reason as no. 41 above.

44. July 18, 1126. Alfonso VII. Rodrigo Vermúdez. María Encarnación Martín López, ed., *Patrimonio cultural de San Isidoro de León. Serie documental.* Vol. 1, Parte 1, *Documentos de los siglos X–XIII* (León, 1995), pp. 44–45, who cites it as an original. It is not. The royal notary Ciprian Peréz used the Visigothic rather than the Caroline script of the document. The editor also cites it as document no. 745 of the archivo but it is no. 744.

45. July 18, 1126. León. Alfonso VII. Pedro Ovéquez. AC Orense, Monacales, no. 245. Emilio Duro Peña, ed., "Catálogo de documentos reales del archivo de la catedral de Orense, 844–1520," in *Miscelánea de textos medievales*, vol. 1 (Barcelona, 1972), p. 77, called it an original. It is not, for the same reason as no. 44.

46. July 18, 1126. Alfonso VII. Cathedral of León. José Luis Fernández Catón, ed., *Colección documental del archivo de la catedral de León, 1109–1187*, Vol. 5 (León, 1979), pp. 125–27, who calls it an original. It is not for the same reason as nos. 44 and 45 above.

47. July 21, 1126. León. Alfonso VII. Monastery of Cornellana. Antonio Floriano Cumbreño, ed., *El monasterio de Cornellana* (Oviedo, 1949), pp. 26–27. An original of notary Ciprian Pérez in the Visigothic script.

48. July 23, 1126. Alfonso VII. Council of Oviedo of 1115. See Francisco Fernández Conde, *El Libro de Testamentos de la Catedral de Oviedo* (Rome, 1971), pp. 39–41. There was no such council.

49. July 29, 1126. Palencia. Alfonso VII. Hospitallers. Ayala Martínez, *Liber*, pp. 163–64. Defective dating formula.

50. August 4, 1126. Sahagún. Alfonso VII. Sahagún. Fernández Flórez, *Colección*, 4:103–6, who redates it from the 1129 of the document and calls it an original. At best it is a heavily interpolated copy.

51. September 7, 1126. *Infanta* Sancha. Monasterio of San Pedro de las Dueñas. José María Fernández Catón, ed., *Catálogo del archivo del monasterio de San Pedro de las Dueñas* (León, 1977), pp. 20–21. A fragment only.

52. October 12, 1126. Alfonso VII. Pedro Peregrino. Luis Vázquez de Parga, José María Lacarra, and Juan Uría Ríu. *Las peregrinaciones a Santiago de Compostela*, 3 vols. (Madrid, 1948–1949), pp. 15–16. Also AC Compostela, copy Tumbo A, fol. 111r–v.

53. November 5, 1126. Alfonso VII. Monastery of Sahagún. Fernández Flórez, *Colección*, 4:107–8. False. The diplomatic is that of a private document.

54. November 17, 1126. Alfonso VII. Monastery of San Antolín de Toques. Archive of the University of Santiago de Compostela, Documentos, no. 13. Partially legible fourteenth-century copy.

55. November 18, 1126. Alfonso VII. Monastery of Eslonza. AHN, Clero,

Carpeta 961, no. 11. Miguel Bravo, "Monasterio de Eslonza; adiciones al cartulario de Eslonza de V. Vignau," *AL* 2 (1948): 102–3.

56. December 12, 1126. Alfonso VII. Pedro de Fania and Eldara Crescónez, ux. Fernández Flórez, *Colección*, 4:109, who calls it an original. That is unlikely since there is no notary given.

57. 1127. Alfonso VII. Alvaro Gutierrez. Fernández Catón, *Colección*, 5:128, who calls it an original. That is unlikely since no day or month is given.

58. 1127. Alfonso VII. Cathedral of Sigüenza. Minguella y Arnedo, *Historia*, 1:351–52. Also BN, Manuscritos, 13.073, ff. 218r–219r.

59. March 28, 1127. Alfonso VII. Countess Inés and convent of Fontrevaud. Luciano Serrano, ed., *Cartulario del monasterio de Vega con documentos de San Pelayo y Vega de Oveido* (Madrid, 1927), p. 44.

60. April 2, 1127. León. Alfonso VII. Monastery of Sahagún. Fernández Flórez, *Colección*, 4:110–11. An original.

61. April 12, 1127. *Infanta* Sancha. Pedro Braólez and Jimena Pérez ux. García Calles, *Doña Sancha*, pp. 132–33.

62. April 17, 1127. Alfonso VII. Jimeno Eriz. BN, Manuscritos, 4.357, fol. 132v. A partial paraphrase in Spanish.

63. April 30, 1127. Burgos. Alfonso VII. Domingo de Vazalamio and Pedro Domínguez. Luciano Serrano, *El obispado de Burgos y Castilla primitiva desde el siglo V al XIII*, 3 vols. (Madrid, 1935), p. 159, who called it an original. Also BN, Manuscritos, 720, ff. 230v–231v; 6.683, fol. 3r–v; and 13.093, 2r–v, all date to 1122.

64. May 1, 1127. Alfonso VII. Men of Saldaña, Cea, Carrión, Valle de Anoza, Valle de Cisneros, and Valle de Moratinos. Fernández Flórez, *Colección*, 4:111–12. Likely false. Dating formula of private document.

65. May 1, 1127. Alfonso VII. Martín Pelaez. Ibid., pp. 113–14, who calls it an original. More likely it is false. The date has been altered. Both the royal majordomo and the *alférez* are wrong for the date.

66. May 13, 1127. Alfonso VII and Berengaria. Cathedral of Segovia. Villar García, *Documentacion*, pp. 54–56, who dates it to 1124 and calls it an original. False. Berengaria was not yet queen on either date and there are other manifest errors.

67. June 26, 1127. Salamanca. Alfonso VII. Sancho González and García González. Vázquez Núñez, "Documentos," 1:393–96. False. There is no way to reconcile the various figures who confirm.

68. August 8, 1127. Alfonso VII. Domingo Fernández. Francisco de Berganza, *Antigüedades de España*, 2 vols. (Madrid, 1719–21), 2:455, who called it original. The diplomatic is too peculiar to admit that.

69. August 9, 1127. Alfonso VII. Cathedral of Burgos. José Manuel Garrido Garrido, ed., *Documentación de la catedral de Burgos, 804–1183* (Burgos, 1983), pp. 190–91.

70. August 26, 1127. *Infanta* Sancha. Convent of San Pelayo de León. María Amparo Valcarce, *El dominio de la real colegiata de S. Isidoro de León hasta 1189* (León, 1985), pp. 101–2. Possibly an original.

71. November 1127. Alfonso VII, Count Pedro González de Lara, and Countess Eva. Men of Tardajos. Alfredo Herrera Nogal, *El concejo de la villa de Tardajos: Fueros e historia* (Burgos, 1980), pp. 25–39.

72. November 13, 1127. Alfonso VII. Cathedral of Santiago de Compostela. López Ferreiro, *Historia*, 4:12–13 append.

73. November 13, 1127. Alfonso VII. Cathedral of Santiago de Compostela. Ibid., 4:13–14.

74. November 13, 1127. Alfonso VII. Cathedral of Santigo de Compostela. Ibid., 4:14–15.

75. November 22, 1127. Saldaña. Alfonso VII and Berengaria. Salvador Fernández. BN, Manuscritos, 4.357, ff. 126v–127r. A notice only.

76. 1128. *Infanta* Sancha. Monastery of San Tomas of Zamora. García Calles, *Doña Sancha*, p. 134, who calls it an original. The lack of a notary or *signum* makes that doubtful. Also, AC Zamora, Tumbo Negro, fol. 9r–v; BN, Manuscritos, 714, fol. 166v.

77. January 5, 1128. Tardajos. Alfonso VII and Berengaria. Cathedral of León. Fernández Catón, *Colección*, 5:95–98.

78. January 9, 1128. Alfonso VII and Berengaria. Urraca Vermudez. Amparo Valcarce, *Dominio*, pp. 100–101, but dated erroneously to 1124.

79. January 27, 1128. Alfonso VII and Berengaria. Monastery of San Tomas of Zamora. AC Zamora, Tumbo Negro, ff. 9v–10r; BN, Manuscritos, 714, fol. 155r–v, dated January 30, 1124, and fol. 167r, dated March 29, 1125.

80. January 29, 1128. Alfonso VII. Cathedral chapter of Zamora. BN, Manuscritos, 714, fol. 167r. An excerpt only dated erroneously to 1125.

81. February 28, 1128. Valdevice. Alfonso VII. Monastery of Pedroso. Cal Pardo, *Catálogo*, p. 112, who calls it an original. The diplomatic would suggest a date in 1126 if it is accepted at all.

82. March 26, 1128. Alfonso VII and Berengaria. Count Suero. Floriano Cumbreño, *Cornellana*, pp. 28–29, with a bad date. AHN, Clero, Carpeta 1.591, no. 20. A likely original.

83. April 14, 1128. Alfonso VII and Berengaria. Cathedral of Palencia. Pedro Fernando de Pulgar, *Historia secular y ecclésiastica de la ciudad de Palencia*, vol. 1 (Madrid, 1680). The diplomatic is irregular.

84. May 22, 1128. Maqueda. Alfonso VII and Berengaria. Cathedral chapter of Toledo. García Luján, *Privilegios*, 2:42–44. The original is displayed in the Museo de Santa Cruz in Toledo.

85. May 26, 1128. Segovia. Alfonso VII and Berengaria. Cathedral of Santiago de Compostela. José María Fernández Catón, "El llamado Tumbo Colorado y otros códices de la iglesia compostelana: Ensayo de reconstrucción," *AL* 44 (1990): 139–40. Also, AC Compostela, copy Tumbo A, fol. 107v–109v, dated to 1124, and ff. 112v–3r, dated to 1128; Tumbo B, ff. 52v–53r, dated to 1124.

86. July 4, 1128. Alfonso VII and Berengaria. Paredes de Nava. Justiniano Rodríguez Fernández, *Palencia: Panorámica foral de la provincia* (Palencia, 1981), pp. 228–34.

87. July 8, 1128. Burgos. Alfonso VII and Berengaria. Cathedral of Burgos. Serrano, *Obispado* 3:161–62, from the original. Also BN, Manuscritos, 6.683, fol. 4r–5r; 9.194, fol. 16r–v; 13.093, fol. 56r.

88. July 10, 1128. Palencia. Alfonso VII and Berengaria. Cathedral of Mondoñedo and Count Rodrigo Vélaz. Flórez, *ES* 18:345–49. AHN, Clero, Carpeta 1.185, no. 8; BN, Manuscritos, 5.928, ff. 33r–36r. Cal Pardo, *Catálogo*, p. 17, cited a copy there dated to 1124 which he believed to be an original but is simply false.

89. July 12, 1128. Burgos. Alfonso VII and Berengaria. Concejo of Burgos. Tomas Múñoz y Romero, ed., *Colección de fueros y cartas pueblas* (Madrid, 1847), p. 266, with the erroneous date of 1124. See Juan Antonio Bonachia Hernando and Julio Antonio Pardos Martínez, eds., *Catálogo documental del archivo Municipal de Burgos: Sección Histórica,, 931–1515*, 2 vols. (Salamanca, 1983), pp. 50–51.

90. July 12, 1128. Alfonso VII and Berengaria. Cathedral of Burgos. Serrano, *Obispado*, 3:163–66, from what he called the original. Also BN, Manuscritos, 13.093, fol. 56r; Acad. Hist. Colección Salazar, O-16, ff. 522v–523r, dated to 1124.

91. July 13, 1128. Burgos. Alfonso VII and Berengaria. Cathedral of Sigüenza. Minguella y Arnedo, *Historia*, pp. 348–49, with erroneous date of 1124.

92. August 23, 1128. Alfonso VII and Berengaria. Cathedral of Zamora. AC Zamora, Tumbo Negro, fol. 15v.

93. October 15, 1128. Alfonso VII and Berengaria. Cathedral of León. Fernández Catón, *Colección*, 5:129–30, calling it an original.

94. December 20, 1128. León. Alfonso VII and Berengaria. Monastery of San Salvador de Cinis. AHN, Clero, Carpeta 494, no. 12; Microfilmas, Santiago de Compostela, Biblioteca del Seminario, Rollo 5.380; Acad. Hist.,

Colección Sobreira, 9-21-6-117, "Colección diplomática del siglo XII" (unpaginated). The charter is dated to 1133 but 1128 is necessary in view of those who confirm.

95. 1129. Alfonso VII. Cathedral de Oviedo. Ciriaco Miguel Vigil, *Asturias monumental, epigráfica, y diplomática*, 2 vols. (Oviedo, 1887), 1:89. A notice.

96. January 6, 1129. Alfonso VII. Monastery of Santa María Ferraria de Palliares and Countess Guntroda Rodríguez. AHN, Clero, Carpeta 1.082, no. 8; BN, Manuscritos, 18.387, fol. 304r–v. The document's date of 1109 must be changed to 1129 if it is to be accepted at all.

97. February 2, 1129. Alfonso VII and Berengaria. Men of Castrotoraf. José Luis Martín, *Orígines de la orden militar de Santiago* (Barcelona, 1974), pp. 175–76. Also Acad. Hist., Colección Salazar, Appendix, Legajos B, no. 39,dated to February 10. Unreliable. Dating formula is that of private document. Count Pons of Cabrera is too soon as castellan of Zamora.

98. February 4, 1129. Alfonso VII and Berengaria. Menendo Bofín. Ayala Martínez, *Liber*, pp. 169–70. Unreliable. The diplomatic is thoroughly confused.

99. February 6, 1129. Alfonso VII and Berengaria. Monastery of Saint-Victor of Marseille. Martin Guerard, ed., *Cartulaire de l'Abbaye de Saint-Victor de Marseille*, 2 vols. (Paris, 1857), 2:190–91.

100. February 10, 1129. Alfonso VII and Berengaria. Cathedral of Toledo. García Luján, *Privilegios*, 2:40–42, who dates it erroneously to 1125. See Hernández, *Cartularios*, pp. 33–34.

101. March 25, 1129. Alfonso VII and Berengaria. Cathedral of Santiago de Compostela. Emma Falque Rey, ed., *Historia Compostelana* (Turnholt, 1988), pp. 428–32. AC Compostela, Tumbo A, ff. 40v–41r; copy Tumbo A, fol. 113v–115v; Acad. Hist., Colección Salazar, O-22, fol. 265r.

102. March 29, 1129. Alfonso VII and Berengaria. Martín Ciprianez. Fernández Flórez, *Colección*, 5:146–48. False. The date is wrong for those who confirm and the diplomatic is that of a private document.

103. April 27, 1129. *Infanta* Elvira. Hospitallers. Ayala Martínez, *Liber*, pp. 170–72.

104. May 1, 1129. Alfonso VII and Berengaria. Gómez Cídez and Elo Galíndez, ux. Julio A. Pérez Celada, ed., *Documentación del monastery de San Zoil de Carrión, 1047–1300* (Palencia, 1986), pp. 46–47. An original.

105. May 15, 1129. Alfonso VII and Berengaria. Cathedral of León. Fernández Catón, *Colección*, 5:134–37, who calls it an original. Neither the notary nor the diplomatic are of the royal chancery.

106. June 6, 1129. Alfonso VII and Berengaria. Monastery of San Pedro de

Montes. Augusto Quintana Prieto, ed., *Tumbo viejo de San Pedro de Montes* (León, 1971), pp. 241–42.

107. June 22, 1129. Alfonso VII. Monastery of Santa Marta de Tera. Augusto Quintana Prieto, *El obispado de Astorga en el siglo XII* (Astorga, 1985), pp. 675–76. Diplomatic indicates that it is false.

108. July 4, 1129. Alfonso VII and Berengaria. Cathedral of Astorga. BN, Manuscritos, 712, ff. 88r–89r; 6.683, fol. 6r–v; 9.194, fol. 107r, dated July 8; 13.093, fol. 69r–v; Acad. Hist., Colección Salazar, O-22, fol. 155r, dated July 4. Prudencio de Sandoval, *Historia de los reyes de Castilla y León*, 2 vols. (Pamplona, 1634), 2:144v, cited it under date of June 7, 1129, and Peter Rassow, "Die Urkunden Kaiser Alfonso VII von Spanien," *AU* 10 (1928): 327–468, and 11 (1930), pp. 66–137; 10:420, followed him.

109. July 5, 1129. Alfonso VII. Men of El Pónton and Mariandres. Cited by Juan Ignacio Ruiz de la Peña, "El coto de Leitariegos," *AM* 3 (1979): 181, n. 7, cited this but it is actually the work of Alfonso XI.

110. July 8, 1129. Alfonso VII. Monastery of San Salvador de Lérez. AHN, Clero, Carpeta 1.786, no. 13. False. Seal is wrong, majordomo is wrong.

111. July 8, 1129. Alfonso VII. Monastery of San Juan de Poyo. AHN, Clero, Carpeta 1,861, no. 17. False. Clearly related to 110.

112. November 19, 1129. Alfonso VII and Berengaria. Monastery of San Zoil de Carrión. Pérez Celada, *Documentación*, pp. 47–49.

113. 1130. Alfonso VII and Berengaria. Cathedral of Segovia. Villar García, *Documentación*, pp. 58–59.

114. 1130. Alfonso VII. Men of Belver. Cited Ursicino Alvarez Martínez, *Historia general, civil y ecclesiástica de la provincia de Zamora* (Madrid, 1965), p. 163.

115. February 7, 1130. Carrión. Alfonso VII. Cathedral of Sigüenza. Mingüella y Arnedo, *Historia*, 1:352–54. Also BN, Manuscritos, 13073, ff. 220r–221v.

116. February 22, 1130. Alfonso VII and Berengaria. Cathedral of Santiago de Compostela. López Ferreiro, *Historia*, 4:20 Appendix.

117. March 22, 1130. Alfonso VII and Berengaria. García Pérez and Teresa Pérez, ux. Aurelio Calvo, *El monasterio de Gradefes* (León, 1936), pp. 164–65, who redated it from 1140.

118. April 23, 1130. Alfonso VII and Berengaria. Cathedral of Palencia. Teresa Abajo Martín, ed., *Documentación de la catedral de Palencia.* (Palencia, 1986), pp. 75–76, incorrectly dated to April 24. Also Acad. Hist., Catedrales de España, Palencia, 9-25-1-C-6, ff. 37r–38r.

119. May 15, 1130. *Infanta* Sancha. Monastery of Sahagún. Fernández Flórez, *Colección*, 4:122–24, who calls it an original. On paleographic grounds I suspect it to be a copy of later in the century.

120. June 13, 1130. Alfonso VII. Monastery of Sahagún. Ibid., 4:127–28. False. The diplomatic is not of this date.

121. June 27, 1130. Alfonso VII and Berengaria. Monastery of Oya. AHN, Clero, Carpeta 1.794, no. 2; Códices, 60B, fol. 2r. Forgery modeled on charter of June 27, 1137, to same monastery.

122. August 26, 1130. Asturias. Alfonso VII. Cathedral of Burgos. Serrano, *Obispado*, 3:168–69. Also BN, Manuscritos, 720, ff. 247v–248r, dated August 29, 1127; Acad. Hist., Colección Salazar, O-17, fol. 721r–v, dated August 25, 1131. Suspect. Any date leaves the absence of the citation of Berengaria unexplained.

123. October 25, 1130. Alfonso VII. Men of Avia. Cited Rodríguez Fernández, *Palencia*, p.234.

124. December 21, 1130. Alfonso VII and Berengaria. Monastery of Arlanza. Luciano Serrano, ed., *Cartulario de San Pedro de Arlanza* (Madrid, 1925), pp. 174–76. Unreliable. Alfonso is entitled "rex Castelle."

125. March 18, 1131. Alfonso VII and Berengaria. Cathedral of Santiago de Compostela. López Ferreiro, *Historia*, 4:16–18. Appendix. An original.

126. March 23, 1131. Astorga. Alfonso VII and Berengaria. Cathedral of Astorga. BN, Manuscritos, 712, fol. 89r–v; 6.683, fol. 9r–v; 9.194, fol. 108r; 13.093, fol. 72r; Acad. Hist., Colección Salazar, O-22, fol. 156r. All copies are dated 1130 but the diplomatic requires 1131 if it is to be accepted.

127. April 14-May 15, 1131. Alfonso VII and Berengaria. Pelayo Pérez. Rassow, "Urkunden," 11:71. An original whose date is partially obscured.

128. April 25, 1131. Alfonso VII. Gonzalo Muñoz and Juliana, ux. Fernández Flórez, *Colección*, 4:134–35. A rough copy.

129. May 15, 1131. Palencia. Alfonso VII and Berengaria. Cathedral of Orense. Muñoz y Romero, *Colección*, pp. 501–2. An original. Also Acad. Hist., Catedrales de España, Santiago de Compostela y Orense, 9-25-1-C-9, ff. 48v–54r, in *vidimus* of 1430.

130. May 29, 1131. Alfonso VII and Berengaria. Monastery of San Vicente, Oviedo. Floriano Llorente, *Colección*, pp. 288–89. A rough copy, perhaps better dated to June 28, 1131, on the basis of the *alférez* cited.

131. July 1, 1131. Alfonso VII. Pedro García and Aldonza, ux. Ibid., pp. 289–90, perhaps better dated to December 29, 1131, on the basis of the *alférez* cited.

132. August 28, 1131. Castrojeriz. Alfonso VII and Berengaria. Pedro González. María Luisa Ledesma Rubio, ed., *Cartulario de San Millán de La Cogolla, 1076-1200* (Zaragoza, 1989), p. 262. Luciano Serrano, ed., *Cartulario de San Millán de La Cogolla* (Madrid, 1930), p. 309, published the same charter, calling it an original, with the impossible date of September 1, 1137.

133. September 28, 1131. Castrojeriz. Alfonso VII and Berengaria. Pedro Muñoz de Carneta. AHN, Códices, 1.002B, fol. 5r; Acad. Hist., Colección Salazar, O-8, fol. 68r.

134. October 23, 1131. León. Alfonso VII and *Infanta* Sancha. Monastery of San Isidoro. Amparo Valcarce, *Dominio*, pp. 102–3, who calls it an original. It is not. The style of Alfonso's *signum* is later and he is called "rex."

135. November 18, 1131. Alfonso VII and Berengaria. Monastery of Sahagún. Fernández Flórez, *Colección*, 4:137–38.

136. November 20, 1131. León. Alfonso VII and Berengaria. Annaia Rodríguez. Ibid., 140–41, correctly styling it false.

137. November 22, 1131. León. Alfonso VII and Berengaria. Cristóforo Yañez and Ceti, ux. Fernández Catón, *Colección*, 5:152–53, who calls it an original.

138. December 3, 1131. Alfonso VII and Berengaria. Cathedral of Astorga. Quintana Prieto, *Obispado*, p. 671. Also BN, Manuscritos, 712, fol. 85r–v; 6.683, fol. 8r–v; 9.194, fol. 109r; Acad. Hist., Colección Salazar, O-22, fol. 156r. All copies are dated to 1130 but the year must be 1131 if it is to be accepted.

139. December 20, 1131. *Infanta* Sancha. Monastery of Marcigny. Jean Richard, ed., *Le cartulaire de Marcigny sur Loire, 1048–1144* (Dijon, 1957), pp. 180–82.

140. December 20, 1131. *Infanta* Sancha. Monastery of Marcigny. Ibid., 182–83.

141. 1132. Alfonso VII. Monastery of Oña. Juan de Alamo, ed., *Colección diplomática de San Salvdor de Oña*, 2 vols. (Madrid, 1950), 1:197–98. A notice only.

142. 1132. Alfonso VII. Monastery of Eslonza. Vicente Vignau, ed., *Cartulario del monasterio de Eslonza* (Madrid, 1885), pp. 19–20.

143. January 6, 1132. Alfonso VII and Berengaria. Cathedral of Santiago de Compostela. AC Compostela, copy Tumbo A, ff. 11v–18r; Tumbo C, pt. 2, fol. 202r.

144. January 29, 1132. Alfonso VII, Berengaria, Sancho rex, and Fernando rex. Monasterio of San Vicente. BN, Manuscritos, 834, ff. 157r–58r. False. Neither Sancho nor Fernando were made king in Berengaria's lifetime.

145. February 1, 1132. Alfonso VII and Berengaria. Muño Tacón. Guillermo Castán Lanaspa, ed., *Documentos del monasterio de Villaverde de Sandoval, siglos XII–XV* (Salamanca, 1981), p. 42. An original.

146. March 8, 1132. Alfonso VII. Monastery of Sahagún. Fernández Flórez, *Colección*, 4:142–43, calls it an original. I take it for a later copy both on paleographic grounds and because Berengaria does not appear in the intitulation.

147. May 18, 1132. Toledo. Alfonso VII, Berengaria, Sancho rex, and Fernando rex. Aifia Avenzadoch and Aleazar frater. AHN, Ord. mil., Carpeta 417, no. 4. False. There is no date on which some of the persons cited were contemporaries.

148. May 28, 1132. Carrión. Alfonso VII and Berengaria. Cathedral of Orense. *ES* 17:250–52. AC Orense, Reales, no. 12; Acad. Hist., Catedrales de España, Santiago de Compostela y Orense, 9-25-1-C-9, ff. 20r–23r.

149. May 29, 1132. Alfonso VII and Berengaria. Alvar Gutiérrez. Floriano Llorente, *Colección*, pp. 292–94. Unreliable copy. The bishop of León and the royal *alférez* are given incorrectly.

150. August 18, 1132. Oviedo. Alfonso VII and Berengaria. Monastery of San Martín de Anes. Santos García Larragueta, ed., *Colección de documentos de la catedral de Oviedo* (Oviedo, 1962), pp. 381–82.

151. September 2, 1132. Oviedo. Alfonso VII and Berengaria. Cathedral of Zamora. AC Zamora, Tumbo Negro, fol. 20r–v.

152. September 6, 1132. Oviedo. Alfonso VII and Berengaria. María Froílaz. Fernández Catón, *Colección*, 5:156–57.

153. September 7, 1132. Alfonso VII, Berengaria, and *Infanta* Sancha. Monastery of Cluny. Alexandre Bruel, ed., *Recueil des chartes de de l'Abbaye de Cluny*, 6 vols. (Paris, 1876–1903), 5:391, who called it an original. It is certainly not a product of the Leonese chancery.

154. September 29, 1132. Alfonso VII. Men of village of San Pedro de las Dueñas. Cited Vicente Vignau, ed., *Indice de los documentos de la monasterio de Sahagún* (Madrid, 1874), p. 27.

155. October 13, 1132. Alfonso VII. Cathedral of León. Fernández Catón, *Colección*, 5:157–59, who calls it an original. It is probably false. Among other things, Alfonso is styled "rex."

156. 1133. Alfonso VII. Monastery of Oña. Isabel Oceja Gonzalo, ed., *Documentación del monasterio de San Salvador de Oña, 1032–1284* (Burgos, 1983), pp. 43–44. Unreliable. Alfonso listed alone and as "rex."

157. 1133. Alfonso VII. Monastery of Oña. Alamo, *Colección*, 1:205. A notice only.

158. January 2, 1133. Alfonso VII and Berengaria. Monastery of Oña. Ibid., 1:198–99. A late, rough copy.

159. January 10, 1133. Alfonso VII. Monastery of Oña. Ibid., 1:201–2. Unreliable. Alfonso listed alone and as "rex."

160. January 10, 1133. Oña. Alfonso VII. Alvaro presbyter. Ledesma Rubio, *Cartulario*, p. 247.

161. January 10, 1133. Alfonso VII. Monastery of Oña. Alamo, *Colección*, 1:199–201. Unreliable. Diplomatic is irregular.

162. January 11, 1133. Alfonso VII and Berengaria. Monastery of Oña. Ibid.,
1:203–4. Unreliable. Diplomatic is irregular.

163. January 18, 1133. Sahagún. Alfonso VII and Berengaria. Cathedral of
Orense. Manuel Castro y Sueiro, ed., "Documentos del archivo catedral
de Orense," *BCM Orense*, 2 vols. (Orense, 1922–1923), 1:430–31.

164. January 25, 1133. Alfonso VII and Berengaria. Alvito Muñoz and Pelayo
Muñoz, frater. Guillermo Castán Lanaspa and Javier Castán Lanaspa, eds.,
Documentos del monasterio de Santa María de Trianos, siglos XII–XIII (Salamanca, 1992) p. 18, who call it an original and misdate it to 1128. Water has
blurred the date but it is rather a contemporary copy in my judgment.

165. February 3, 1133. Segovia. Alfonso VII. Monastery of Santa María de
Sacramenia. Villar García, *Documentación*, pp. 59–60. Alfonso confirms a
grant of Bishop Pedro of Segovia.

166. March 1, 1133. Alfonso VII and Berengaria. Guter Sebastianez. Serrano,
Cartulario de Vega, pp. 51–52, calling it an original.

167. March 29, 1133. Carrión. Alfonso VII and Berengaria. Monastery of
Vega. Ibid., pp. 50–51.

168. April 1, 1133. Palencia. Alfonso VII and Berengaria. Cathedral of Santiago de Compostela. Falque Rey, *HC*, pp. 470–71.

169. April 11, 1133. Avila. Alfonso VII and Berengaria. Cathedral of Orense.
Castro y Sueiro, "Documentos," pp. 451–53.

170. April 19, 1133. Alfonso VII, Berengaria, *Infanta* Sancha, and *Infanta*
Elvira. Cathedral chapter of León. Fernández Catón, *Colección*, 5:159–62.
Confirm charter of Bishop Arias of León.

171. April 27, 1133. Alfonso VII and *Infanta* Sancha. Pedro Domínguez and
Christina Flaíñez, ux. Martín López, *Patrimonio*, p. 151.

172. May 5, 1133. Alfonso VII and Berengaria. Men of Guadalajara. Muñoz y
Romero, *Fueros*, pp. 507–11. Text is Spanish copy.

173. May 13, 1133. Toledo. Alfonso VII and Berengaria. Cathedral of Orense.
Castro y Sueiro, "Documentos," pp. 454–55.

174. June 17, 1133. Haro. Alfonso VII and Berengaria. Church of Santo Domingo de la Calzada. Augustín Ubieto Arteta, ed., *Cartularios (I, II, y III)
de Santo Domingo de la Calzada* (Zaragoza, 1978), pp. 15–16. False. Irrecon-
ciliable diplomatic elements.

175. August 1133. Alfonso VII and Berengaria. Suero Ordoñez. García Larragueta, *Colección*, pp. 382–83. Confirm grant of Bishop Alfonso of Oviedo.

176. September 2, 1133. León. Alfonso VII, Berengaria, Sancho, and Fernando. Vicente García Lobo and José Manuael Garcí Lobos, *Santa María
de Arbas*, p. 52, dated to September 12. Unreliable. Sancho and Fernando
do not appear in intitulations so early.

177. September 8, 1133. *Infanta* Elvira. Cathedral of León. Fernández Catón, *Colección*, 5:164–66, calls it an original.

178. September 13, 1133. Alfonso VII and Berengaria. Monastery of San Vicente. Floriano Llorente, *Colección*, pp. 297–98.

179. September 18, 1133. Alfonso VII and Berengaria. Cathedral of Orense. *Colección diplomática de Galicia*, 2 vols. (Santiago de Compostela (1901–03), 1:28–30.

180. 1134. Alfonso VII and Berengaria. Church of Santo Domingo de la Calzada. Augustín Ubieto Arteta, *Cartularios*, pp. 18–19. False. Closely related to June 17, 1133.

181. January 13, 1134. Alfonso VII. Monastery of Santa María de Monterramo. AHN, Clero, Carpeta 1.481, no. 6. False. Bishops of León, Astorga, Zamora all incorrect.

182. April 20, 1134. Alfonso VII and Berengaria. Monastery of San Martín de Pinario. AHN, Clero, Carpeta 512, no. 12. Jesus Muñoz y Romero, *Manual de Paleografía diplomática española de los siglos XII al XVII*, 2nd ed. (Madrid, 1917), p. 155, published a plate of it. Not a chancery product surely.

183. May 12, 1134. Alfonso VII and Berengaria. Monastery of San Millán de la Cogolla. Ledesma Rubio, *Cartulario*, pp. 247–49 and 251–52, incorrectly dated November 10, 1134. Also BN, Manuscritos, 13.093, fol 79r–v, a notice; Acad. Hist., Colección Salazar, O-22, fol. 160r; O-23, fol. 3r–v, notices dated only to 1134. False. Refers to death of Alfonso I of Aragón and coronation of Alfonso VII both before they occurred, and other mistakes as well.

184. June 1, 1134. Alfonso VII. Pedro Fernández and Urraca Ovequez, ux. Amparo Valcarce, *Dominio*, p. 104, who calls it an original. Unreliable. The majordomo is wrong and Alfonso is styled "rex imperator." Diplomatic generally is irregular.

185. June 10, 1134. Alfonso VII and Berengaria. Men of Villadiego. Amancio Rodríguez López, "Los fueros de Villadiegos inéditos," *BRAH* (1912), 61:431–36.

186. September 30, 1134. Alfonso VII. Knights of Zaragoza. A later confirmation, perhaps in December, of the grant of Ramiro II of Aragón. Antonio Ubieto Arteta, ed., *Documentos de Ramiro II of Aragón* (Zaragoza, 1988), p. 30.

187. November 10, 1134. Alfonso VII and Berengaria. Monastery of San Millán de La Cogolla. BN, Manuscritos, 712, fol. 41v. A notice and paraphrase.

188. November 10, 1134. Alfonso VII and Berengaria. Monastery of San Millán de La Cogolla. Ledesma Rubio, *Cartulario*, pp. 249–51. Unreliable. The underlying document has been interpolated.

189. December 1134. Zaragoza. Alfonso VII. Infanzons and barons of Aragón. Angel Canellas López, ed., *Colección diplomática del concejo de Zaragoza* (Zaragoza, 1972), pp. 92–94. Certainly not a product of the Leonese chancery.

190. December 26, 1134. Alfonso VII. Cathedral of Zaragoza. José María Lacarra, ed., "Documentos para el estudio de la reconquista y repoblación del valle del Ebro," *EEMCA* 2 (1946) pp. 538–39. The diplomatic is unusual for the Leonese chancery.

191. 1135. Alfonso VII and Berengaria. Infanzons of Entrena. Gonzalo Martínez Díez, "Fueros de La Rioja," *AHDE* 49 (1979), pp. 419–20.

192. 1135. Alfonso VII. Monastery of Santa María del Puerto. Margarita Cantera Montenegro, ed., *Colección documental de Santa María La Real de Nájera, Tomo I, siglos X–XIV* (San Sebastián, 1991), pp. 73–75, who dated it to 1137. Text itself is dated to 1112. Unreliable.

193. 1135. Alfonso VII. Monastery of Osera. Rassow, "Urkunden," 10:423. A notice only.

194. 1135. Alfonso VII. Faularichero. Lacarra, "Documentos," 5:555–56. Confirmation of charter of Alfonso I of Aragón dated February 1134.

195. January 1135. Alfonso VII and Berengaria. Monastery of San Millán de La Cogolla. Ledesma Rubio, *Cartulario*, pp. 269–70.

196. February 1135. Alfonso VII and Berengaria. Miguel Mídez. BN, Manuscritos, 13.093, ff. 81r–82r.

197. February 1135. Alfonso VII and Berengaria. Velasco Velasquez. AHN, Ord. Mil., Carpeta 581, no. 4.

198. February 1, 1135. Alfonso VII and Berengaria. Men of Villalbilla. Serrano, *Obispado*, 3:170–71.

199. February 5, 1135. Alfonso VII and Berengaria. Hospital of Ortega. AHN, Clero, Carpeta 180, no. 4; AC Burgos, Vol. 30, fol. 314.

200. March 1135. Alfonso VII and Berengaria. Cathedral of Zamora. AC Zamora, Tumbo Negro, ff. 12v–13r; Tumbo Blanco, fol. 67r–v.

201. March 27, 1135. Alfonso VII and Berengaria. Cathedral of Segovia. Villar García, *Documentación*, pp. 60–61.

202. April, 1135. Alfonso VII and Berengaria. Ermesinda. José Luis Rodríguez de Diego, ed., *El tumbo del monasterio cisterciense de La Espina* (Valladolid, 1982), p. 185. The text itself is dated to 1095!

203. April 24, 1135. Alfonso VII. Cathedral of Astorga. Sandoval, *Historia*, p. 162. A notice.

204. May 1135. Nájera. Alfonso VII and Berengaria. Fortún García. AGN, Documentos, signatura 11.019, Cartulario 3, pt. 2, pp. 205–6.

205. May 1135. Alfonso VII. García Ramírez IV of Navarra. Hilda Grassoti, "Homenaje de García Ramírez a Alfonso VII," *CHE* 37–38 (1963): 63–66.

206. May 1135. León. Alfonso VII and Berengaria. Ramiro García. Ildefonso Rodríguez de Lama, ed., *Colección diplomática de La Rioja: Documentos, 923–1168*, vol. 2 (Logroño, 1976), pp. 169–70.

207. May 3, 1135. Alfonso VII. Men of Lara. Serrano, *Cartulario de Arlanza*, pp. 176–81. Also see Bonachia Hernando and Pardos Martínez, *Catálogo*, p. 50.

208. May 5, 1135. Alfonso VII and Berengaria. Hospital of Rubena. Alamo, *Colección*, 1:207–8. Unreliable. Bishop Michael given for Osma.

209. May 25, 1135. León. Alfonso VII and Berengaria. Monastery of San Payo de Antealtares. AHN, Clero, Carpeta 518, no. 7. Confirmation of concessions of Count Raymond and Urraca of 1098.

210. May 26, 1135. León. Alfonso VII and Berengaria. Men of Santo Domingo de Silos. Vivancos Gómez, *Documentación*, pp. 60–53.

211. May 26, 1135. León. Alfonso VII. Cathedrals of Zaragoza and Sigüenza. Minguella y Arnedo, *Historia*, 1:356–57. Also, BN, Manuscritos, 13.073, fol. 189r–v. Alfonso confirms a pact between the two.

212. May 26, 1135. Alfonso VII and Berengaria. Monastery of Arlanza. Serrano, *Cartulario de Arlanza*, pp. 186–87.

213. May 26, 1135. León. Alfonso VII and Berengaria. Cathedral of Palencia. Abajo Martín, *Documentación*, pp. 76–78.

214. May 29, 1135. Alfonso VII. Count Fernando Pérez and Vermudo Pérez, frater. Pilar Loscertales de García de Valdeavellano, ed., *Tumbos del monasterio de Sobrado de los monjes*, 2 vols. (Madrid, 1976), 2:24–25.

215. May 31, 1135. León. Alfonso VII and Berengaria. Cathedral of Zamora, Tumbo Negro, ff. 19v–20r.

216. June 1135. Toro. Alfonso VII and Berengaria. Cathedral of Sigüenza. Minguella y Arnedo, *Historia*, pp. 354–55. Also, AHN, Clero, Carpeta 3, 591, no. 1; BN, Manuscritos, 13.073, fol. 178r–v.

217. June 1135. Toro. Alfonso VII. Cathedral of Sigüenza. Minguella y Arnedo, *Historia*, p. 350. Also BN, Manuscritos, 13.073, fol. 166.

218. June 2, 1135. Alfonso VII and Berengaria. Cathedral of León. Fernández Catón, *Colección*, 5:171–74, who calls it an original. It is not a chancery product and more likely it is an interpolated copy of a genuine document.

219. June 2, 1135. Alfonso VII and Berengaria. Monastery of San Millán de La Cogolla. Ledesma Rubio, *Cartulario*, p. 253.

220. June 2, 1135. Alfonso VII and Berengaria. Count Rodrigo Martínez. Manuel Mañueco Villalobos and José Zurita Nieto, eds., *Documentos de la*

Iglesia Colegial de Santa María la Mayor de Valladolid, 2 vols. (Valladolid, 1917–20), 1:160–63.

221. June 11, 1135. Alfonso VII and Berengaria. *Concejo* de Los Balbases. Muñoz y Romero, *Fueros*, pp. 514–17. Also, BN, Manuscritos, 5, 741, ff. 18r–20v. Unreliable. Diplomatic is irregular.

222. July 1135. Alfonso VII and Berengaria. Count Rodrígo González, Countess Estefanía Armengol, ux, Count Rodrigo Martínez, and Countess Urraca ux. Mañueco Villalobos and Zurita Nieto, *Documentos*, pp. 164–69.

223. July 1, 1135. Silos. Alfonso VII. Monastery of Silos. Vivancos Gómez, *Documentación*, pp. 65–66. False. The diplomatic is not proper for this period.

224. July 1, 1135. Silos. Alfonso VII. Monastery of Silos. Ibid., pp. 63–65. Also, AHN, Clero, Carpeta 3.404, no. 1; BN, Manuscritos, 3.546, ff. 127r–128v. False. Closely related to no. 223.

225. August 18, 1135. Alfonso VII and Berengaria. Cathedral of Orense. *Colección Galicia*, 1:142–44.

226. September 2, 1135. Toledo. Alfonso VII and Berengaria. Monastery of Osera. Benito F. Alonso, "Monasterio de Santa María de Osera. Privilegio de su fundación," *BCM Orense* 16 (1900): 282–83. AHN, Clero, Carpeta 1.509, nos. 5, 6, 7; Códices, 15B, fol. 74r–v. False. Those who confirm are not contemporaries.

227. September 27, 1135. Pradilla de Ebro. Alfonso VII and Berengaria. Cathedral of Zaragoza. Lacarra, "Documentos," 2:542.

228. November 10, 1135. Nájera. Alfonso VII. Church of Santa María de Nájera. Cantera Montenegro, *Colección*, pp. 65–66.

229. November 10, 1135. Nájera. Alfonso VII and Berengaria. Monastery of Cluny and Church of Santa María de Nájera. Ibid., pp. 64–65.

230. November 25, 1135. Saldaña. Alfonso VII and Berengaria. Hospitallers. Ayala Martínez, *Liber*, pp. 180–81.

231. November 26, 1135. Saldaña. Alfonso VII and Berengaria. Monastery of Santa Eufemia. AHN, Ord. Mil., Cajón 94, nos. 1 and 1 bis.

232. November 26, 1135. Zaragoza. Alfonso VII and Berengaria. Miguel Nuñez. Lacarra, "Documentos," 3:588–89. Unreliable. Among a variety of scribal errors are the place and date of 1136.

233. December 5, 1135. Palencia. Alfonso VII and Berengaria. Monastery of Tojos Outos. Angel Manrique, *Cisterciensium seu Verius Ecclesiasticorum Annalium a Condito Cistercio*, 4 vols. (Lyons, 1642–1659) 2:53–54. AHN, Clero, Carpeta 556, no. 1; Códices, 1.002B, ff. 3r–4r and 32v–33r; Acad. Hist., Colección Salazar, O-8, ff. 67r–68r.

234. December 5, 1135. Palencia. Alfonso VII and Berengaria. Velasco Ramí-

rez. AC Orense, Reales, no. 248. False. The majordomo, *alférez*, and bishop of Mondoñedo are all incorrect.

235. December 5, 1135. Palencia. Alfonso VII, Berengaria, Sancho and Fernando, sons. Cathedral of Palencia. Sandoval, *Historia*, 2:165–66. A notice only. False. Alfonso's sons do not appear in the intitulation at this time.

236. December 5, 1135. Palencia. Alfonso VII and Berengaria. Monastery of Santa María de Monfero. AHN, Códices, 259B, ff. 3r–4r. False. Same errors as no. 235 above.

237. December 30, 1135. Coca. Alfonso VII and Berengaria. Monasteries of Cluny and San Isidro de las Dueñas. BN, Manuscritos, 720, ff. 280r–281r; Acad. Hist., Colección Velasquez, vol. 4, Legajo 4, nos. 1.399 and 1.454.

238. 1136. Alfonso VII. Monastery of Sahagún and María Gómez. Fernández Flórez, *Colección*, 4:155–56. Alfonso mediates a dispute.

239. January 2, 1136. Coca. Alfonso VII and Berengaria. Monasteries of San Servando de Toledo and San Salvador de Peñafiel. Hernández, *Cartularios*, p. 38. Partial publication.

240. January 3, 1136. Coca. Alfonso VII and Berengaria. Cathedral of Osma. Juan Loperráez Corvalón, *Descripción histórica del obispado de Osma*, 3 vols. (Madrid, 1788), 3:15–16.

241. January 3, 1136. Alfonso VII and Berengaria. Cathedral of Salamanca. Martín, Villar García, Marcos Rodríguez, and Sánchez Rodríguez, *Documentos*, pp. 91–92, who called it an original. Diplomatic peculiarities make that unlikely.

242. February 20, 1136. Alfonso VII. Santa Eugenia de Cordevilla. Alamo, *Colección*, 1:210–11. False. Diplomatic atypical.

243. March 9, 1136. Sahagún. Alfonso VII and Berengaria. Monastery of Santa María de Puerto. Cantera Montenegro, *Colección*, pp. 66–68. Also, AHN, Clero, Carpeta 1.030, no. 13.

244. March 15, 1136. *Infanta* Sancha. Cathedral of Pamplona. AC Pamplona, Libro Redondo, ff. 62r–63r; Usún, no. 16.

245. March 21, 1136. Sahagún. Alfonso VII and Berengaria. Monastery of Sahagún. Fernández Flórez, *Colección*, 4:148–50, who calls it an original despite the date being quite clearly wrong.

246. March 30, 1136. León. Alfonso VII and Berengaria. Monastery of Vega. Serrano, *Cartulario de Vega*, pp. 52–53, who called it an original despite dating it to 1135. Paleography marks it as a copy. AD León, Monasterio de Vega, not numbered.

247. April 9, 1136. Zamora. Alfonso VII and Berengaria. Cathedral of Segovia. Villar García, *Documentación*, pp. 62–63, who calls it an original.

248. April 11, 1136. Zamora. Alfonso VII and Berengaria. Cathedral of Sala-

manca. Martín, Villar García, Marcos Rodríguea, and Sánchez Rodríguez, *Documentos*, pp. 83–85. Alfonso confirms the grant of his parents dated June 22, 1102.

249. April 12, 1136. Alfonso VII and Berengaria. Cathedral of Salamanca. Ibid., pp. 93–94. Also, Acad. Hist., Colección Salazar, O-16, fol. 267r–v.

250. April 24, 1136. Burgos. Alfonso VII and Berengaria. Franks of Toledo. García Gallo, "Fueros," pp. 467–68. An original, AMun Toledo, Cajón 10, Legajo 8, no. 3, but in May 1990 it was actually framed and hung on the wall of the directora's office.

251. April 28, 1136. Májera. Alfonso VII. Artisans of the cathedral at Santiago de Compostela. Juan Pérez Millán, ed., *Privilegios reales y viejos documentos de Santiago de Compostela* (Madrid, 1965), no. 1. Alfonso confirms a grant of his grandfather.

252. April 29, 1136. Nájera. Alfonso VII. Inhabitants of Nájera. Rodríguez de Lama, *Colección*, pp. 79–85.

253. May 15, 1136. Vertavillo. Alfonso VII and Berengaria. Monastery of San Isidro de las Dueñas. BN, Manuscritos, 720, ff. 281r–282r; 3.386, fol. 16r–v, dated February 13, 1136; 13.093, fol. 85r–v.

254. June 13, 1136. Paramo. Alfonso VII and Berengaria. Church of Santa Eufemia. AHN, Ord. Mil., Cajón 94, no. 1; BN, Manuscritos, 5.790, ff. 127r–129r.

255. June 18, 1136. Burgos. Alfonso VII and Berengaria. Cathedral of Toledo. García Luján, *Privilegios*, 2:44–46.

256. June 19, 1136. Burgos. Alfonso VII and Berengaria. Hospital of San Juan de Burgos. F. Javier Peña Pérez, ed., *Documentación del monasterio de San Juan de Burgos, 1091–1400* (Burgos, 1983), pp. 17–19.

257. June 30, 1136. Soria. Alfonso VII. Hospital of Santa Cristina de Somport. José Angel Lema Pueyo, ed., *Colección diplomática de Alfonso I de Aragón y Pamplona, 1104–1134* (San Sebastián, 1990), pp. 395–96. The Leonese monarch confirms a grant of his deceased stepfather.

258. August 18, 1136. Burgos. Alfonso VII and Berengaria. Cathedral of Orense. Castro y Sueiro, "Documentos," 1:30–31. Also, AHN, Códices, 1,195B, fol. 765r–v; Acad. Hist., Cathedrales de España, 9–25–1-c-9, ff. 9v–10r. A forgery modeled on authentic grant to Orense of August 18, 1135.

259. August 18, 1136. *Infanta* Elvira, Diego, Fernando, and Teresa, children. Cathedral of León. Fernández Catón, *Colección*, 5:179–81. Probably an original.

260. August 24, 1136. Alagón. Alfonso VII. Juan Caballero. Luis Rubio, ed., *Documentos del Pilar* (Zaragoza, 1971), p. 22. Alfonso confirms a grant of Fortún Aznar, his *merino*.

261. September 1136. Burgos. Alfonso VII. Bishoprics of Burgos, Osma, Sigüenza, and Zaragoza. José Manuel Garrido Garrido, ed., *Documentación de la catedral de Burgos, 804–1183* (Burgos, 1983), pp. 207–8. Alfonso ratifies the decision of the Council of Burgos.

262. September 14, 1136. Nájera. Alfonso VII and Berengaria. Monasteries of Cluny and Santa María de Nájera. Cantera Montenegro, *Colección*, pp. 68–69.

263. October 2, 1136. Burgos. Afonso VII and Berengaria. Cathedral of Astorga. Quintana Prieto, *Obispado*, pp. 678–79. Also, AHN, Códices, 1.197B, ff. 250r–253r; BN, Manuscritos, 712, fol. 87r–v; 6.683, fol. 15r–v; 9.194, fol. 110r–v; 13.093, fol. 84r–v; Acad. Hist., Catedrales de España, Astorga, 9–25–1-C-2, ff. 48r–49v.

264. October 4, 1136. Burgos. Alfonso VII and Berengaria. Cofradia de Belchite. Peter Rassow, "La Cofradía de Belchite," *AHDE* 3 (1926), pp. 200–226.

265. October 25, 1136. Palencia. Alfonso VII and Berengaria. Cathedral of Segovia. Villar García, *Documentación*, pp. 64–65. Very possibly an original.

266. October 27, 1136. Toledo. Alfonso VII and Berengaria. Cathedral of Segovia. Ibid., pp. 66–67. Unreliable because of the given location. Possible copyist's error.

267. October 27, 1136. Palencia. Alfonso VII and Berengaria. Cathedral of Segovia. Ibid., pp. 65–66.

268. October 27, 1136? Alfonso VII. *Concejos* of Segovia, Avila, Toledo, and Madrid. Ibid., pp. 99–100. Alfonso advises them of the grant in no. 267.

269. October 27, 1136? Alfonso VII. *Concejo* of Segovia. Ibid., pp. 100–101. Alfonso advises it of the exemptions of the canons of Segovia.

270. October 27, 1136? Alfonso VII. *Concejo* of Pedraza. Ibid., p. 101. Alfonso advises it of the exemptions of Segovia's canons.

271. October 27, 1136? Alfonso VII. *Concejo* of Sepúlveda. Ibid., p. 102. Alfonso advises it of the exemptions of Segovia's canons.

272. October 27, 1136? Alfonso VII. *Concejo* of Fresno. Ibid., pp. 102–3. Alfonso advises it of the exemptions of Segovia's canons.

273. October 27, 1136? Alfonso VII. *Concejo* of Iscar. Ibid., p. 103. Alfonso advises it of the exemptions of Segovia's canons.

274. October 27, 1136? Alfonso VII. Bishopric of Segovia and Domingo Muñoz. Ibid., pp. 103–4. Alfonso adjudicates their quarrel.

275. December 27, 1136. Alfonso VII. Bishopric of Orense. Acad. Hist., Catedrales de España, Santiago de Compostela and Orense, 9-25-1-C-9, ff. 6v–8v. Alfonso confirms the bull of Innocent II of the above date to Orense.

276. December 28, 1136. Burgos. Alfonso VII and Berengaria. Men of Pineda de la Sierra. Floriano Ballesteros Caballero, *Catálogo de documentos de la villa de Pineda de la Sierra (Burgos)* (Burgos, 1974), p. 71.

277. 1137. Alfonso VII. Gonzalo Menéndez. Antonio Floriano Cumbreño, ed., *El Libro Registro de Corias*, 2 vols. (Oviedo, 1950), 1:117.

278. 1137. Alfonso VII. Bishoprics of Burgos and Calahorra. Ciriaco López de Silanes and Eliseo Saínz Ripa, eds., *Colección diplomática calceatense archivo catedral. Años 1125–1397* (Logroño, 1985), pp. 22–23. Alfonso settles their dispute.

279. 1137. Alfonso VII and Berengaria. Catedral of Calahorra. Agustín Ubieto Arteta, *Cartularios*, pp. 18–19.

280. 1137. Valladolid. Alfonso VII, Berengaria, Sancho and Fernando "regibus." Monastery of Villanova de Oscos. Pedro Floriano Llorente, ed., "Colección diplomática del monasterio de Villanueva de Oscos. Primera serie; años 1136–1200," *BIEA* 102 (1981): 135–36. Also, AHN, Clero, Carpeta 1.616, no. 16; Códices, 227B, fol. 2r–v. Clearly false given the intitulation.

281. 1137. Alfonso VII and Berengaria. Urraca "retruse." Ledesma Rubio, *Cartulario*, pp. 257–58.

282. 1137. Burgos. Alfonso VII and Count Rodrigo Gómez. Monastery of Oña. Alamo, *Colección*, 1:215–17. False. Both Bishop Pedro of Burgos and the royal majordomo are too early.

283. January 30, 1137. Burgos. Alfonso VII and Berengaria. Monasteries of Cluny and Santa María de Nájera. Cantera Montenegro, *Colección*, pp. 69–71. Also AHN, Clero, Carpeta 1.030, no. 15.

284. February 1137. Alfonso VII and Berengaria. Juan Rodríguez. Fernández Flórez, *Colección*, 4:157–58, who calls it an original. It is a copy. It is not in the hand of the scribe Gerald.

285. March 1137. Burgos. Alfonso VII and Berengaria. Guter Fernández and Toda Diáz, ux, Pedro González and Sancha Diáz ux. Emilio Sáez and Carlos Sáez, eds., *El fondo español del Archivo de la Academia de las Ciencias de San Petersburgo* (Alcalá de Henares, 1993), pp. 65–66, who call it an original. Also, BN, Manuscritos, 712, fol. 391v; Acad. Hist., Colección Salazar, O-16, fol. 493v.

286. March 18, 1137. Coyanza? Alfonso VII and Berengaria. Men of Toledo. Juan Francisco Rivera Recio, *Privilegios reales y viejos documentos*, vol. 1 (Madrid, 1963), no. 4. Also, BN, Manuscritos, 712, fol. 10v; 6.683, fol. 28r–v; 13.093, fol. 89r–v; AGS, Patronato real, no. 5.096; AMun Burgos, Sección Histórico, no. 78, badly dated to April 16; AHN, Microfilmas,

Biblioteca Seminario de Santiago de Compostela, Rollo 5.283. It has been called false because the place of issue appears as "Cohenca" and Cuenca was not then in Christian hands. But the diplomatic is impeccable and Coyanza was perhaps the original reading.

287. May 12, 1137. Toledo. Alfonso VII and Berengaria. Canons of Toledo. García Luján, *Privilegios*, 2:46–48.

288. June 1137. Montealegre. Alfonso VII and Berengaria. Diego Muñoz. Fernández Flórez, *Colección*, 4:159–60. Probably an original.

289. June 2, 1137. Palencia. Alfonso VII and Berengaria. Monastery of Silos. Vivancos Gómez, *Documentación*, pp. 67–68.

290. June 26, 1137. Salamanca. Alfonso VII. Monastery of San Pedro de Ramiranes and Alvaro Rubeus. Emilio Duro Peña, "El monasterio de San Pedro de Ramiranes," *AL* 25 (1971): 59–60. A copy of a royal judgment supposedly done in the royal chancery but not confirmed by Alfonso. False. There are a variety of mistakes in the diplomatic.

291. June 26, 1137. Túy. Alfonso VII and Berengaria. Monastery of Oya. AHN, Códices, 60B, fol. 307v.

292. June 27, 1137. Túy. Alfonso VII and Berengaria. Oya. Ermelindo Portela Silva, *La colonización cisterciense en Galicia, 1142–1260* (Santiago de Compostela, 1981), p. 153. Also, AHN, Códices, 60B, fol. 150r. Rassow, "Urkunden," 10:430, called it an original but it is not. The royal *signum* is unique.

293. July 4, 1137. Túy. Alfonso VII. Afonso Henriques. Fernández Flórez, *Colección*, 4:161. Treaty of vassalage.

294. July 17, 1137. Compostela. Alfonso VII and Berengaria. Cathedral of Santiago. López Ferreiro, *Historia*, 4:28–30, Appendix.

295. July 20, 1137. Compostela. Alfonso VII. Monastery of Santa María de Sar. Pérez Millán, *Privilegios*, no. 2. Alfonso confirms the grant of Archbishop Gelmírez. Both are original.

296. July 20, 1137. Compostela. Alfonso VII. Froila Alfónsez and Pedro Muñoz. Manrique, *Cisterciensium*, 2:53. Also, Acad. Hist., Colección Salzar, O-8, fol. 66r–v. Alfonso confirms a private document of December 17, 1134.

297. July 29, 1137. Compostela. Alfonso VII and Berengaria. Monastery of San Payo de Anteáltares. *Colección diplomática Galicia*, 1:433–35.

298. October 3, 1137. Circa Logroño. Alfonso VII and Berengaria. Cathedral of Segovia. Villar García, *Documentación*, pp. 69–70.

299. October 9, 1137. C. Calahorra. Alfonso VII and Berengaria. Monastery of Santa María de Nájera. Cantera Montenegro, *Colección*, pp. 72–73. Also, BN, Manuscritos, 6.683, fol. 30r–v.

300. October 9, 1137. Burgos. Alfonso VII and Berengaria. Monastery of Santa María de Nájera. Ibid., pp. 71–72. Also, BN, Manuscritos, 13.093, fol. 86r. Unreliable on the basis of the royal itinerary.

301. October 20, 1137. c. Calahorra. Alfonso VII and Berengaria. Cathedral of Salamanca. Martín, Villar García, Marcos Rodríguez, and Sánchez Rodríguez, *Documentos*, pp. 94–95. An original.

302. October 29, 1137. Nájera. Alfonso VII and Berengaria. Suero Froílaz. BN, Manuscritos, 712, fol. 139r–v; 8.863, fol. 29r–v; 9.194, fol. 111r; 13.093; fol. 86r. Paraphrase only.

303. November 2, 1137. San Millán. Alfonso VII and Berengaria. Monastery of San Millán. Ledesma Rubio, *Cartulario*, pp. 255–77.

304. November 2, 1137. San Millán. Alfonso VII and Berengaria. Monastery of San Millán. Ibid., pp. 254–55.

305. November 19, 1137. Burgos. Alfonso VII and Berengaria. Monastery of Oña. Alamo, *Colección*, 1:211–13.

306. November 19, 1137. Burgos. Alfonso VII and Berengaria. Monastery of Oña. Isabel Oceja Gonzalo, ed., *Documentación del monasterio de San Salvador de Oña: 1032–1284* (Burgos, 1983), pp. 44–45. Unreliable. The name of the abbot is wrong.

307. November 21, 1137. Burgos. Alfonso VII and Berengaria. Count Rodrigo Gómez. Alamo, *Colección*, 1:214–15.

308. November 23, 1137. Burgos. Alfonso VII. Rodrigo Pérez and Marina Laínez, ux. Rassow, "Urkunden," 10:431. Notice only.

309. December 14, 1137. Segovia. Alfonso VII and Berengaria. Pedro, archdeacon of Segovia. Villar García, *Documentación*, pp. 70–71.

310. December 22, 1137. Salamanca. Alfonso VII and Berengaria. García Pérez and Pedro Alfónsez. AHN, Microfilmas, Astorga, Seminario, Registro de Escrituras, Caja 1.185, Rollo 7.871, fol. 483r–v.

311. 1138. Countess Elvira. Monastery of San Payo de Anteaitares. Antonio Suárez de Alarcón, *Relaciones genealógicas de la cas de los Marqueses de Trocifal* (Madrid, 1656), p. 1, Appendix. Alfonso confirms this grant by his half sister, daughter of Queen Urraca and Count Pedro González.

312. 1138. Alfonso VII. Canons of Toledo. Hernández, *Cartularios*, pp. 43–44. Alfonso confirms the archbishop's new constitution.

313. February 28, 1138. Alfonso VII and Berengaria. Canons of Túy. *ES* 22:260–61. Also AGS, Gracía y Justícia, Legajo 1.672 (Varios), Túy, no. 3. Alfonso confirms the new constitution of the bishop to his chapter.

314. March 7, 1138. León. Alfonso VII, Berengaria, and *Infanta* Sancha. Cathedral of Santiago de Compostela. AC Compostela, copy of Tumbo

A, ff. 118r–119r; Tumbo C, ff. 201v–202r. The charter is dated to 1135 but those who confirm indicate rather 1138. Unreliable.

315. April 20, 1138. Alfonso VII and Berengaria. Leocadia, nun. Rodríguez de Lama, *Colección*, 2:185, who calls it an original. The notary and the royal *alférez* are incorrect. Unreliable.

316. May 9, 1138. Carrión. Alfonso VII and Berengaria. Monastery of Tojos Outos. César Vaamonde Lores, "Santa Marino de Gomáriz," *BCM Orense* 4 (1910): 8–15, 34–42. Likely false. AHN, Códices, 1.002B, fol. 17r, a private donation, records the grant of the same village to the monastery.

317. May 10, 1138. Carrión. Alfonso VII and Berengaria. Monastery of San Cristóbal. AHN, Códices, 1.002B, ff. 6v–7r; ff. 31v–32r. Another forgery closely related to no. 315. Some of those who confirm are mutually exclusive.

318. June 19, 1138. Carrión. Alfonso VII and Berengaria. Rodrígo Vermúdez and Guntroda Cidez, ux. Amparo Valcarce, *Dominio*, pp. 104–5, who calls it an original. It is a forgery. Sancho and Fernando confirm as "rex" among many other errors.

319. July 27, 1138. *Infanta* Sancha. Monastery of San Salvador de Carracedo. Ambrosio de Morales. *Viaje a los reinos de León, y Galicia, y principado de Asturias*, ed. Enrique Flórez. 1765 Reprint (Oviedo, 1977), pp. 168–69. A partial paraphrase.

320. September 14, 1138. Almazán. Alfonso VII. Cathedral of Sigüenza. Minguella y Arnedo, *Historia*, 1:368–69, who dated it to 1139 but the text requires 1138. Also, BN, Manuscritos, 13.073, ff. 196r–198v. Suspicious for the absence of Berengaria from the intitulation.

321. September 16, 1138. Almazán. Alfonso VII. Cathedral of Sigüenza. Ibid., pp. 366–67. Also, BN, Manuscritos, 13.073, ff. 190r–191v. Suspicious for the same reason.

322. September 16, 1138. Almazán. Alfonso VII and Berengaria. Cathedral of Sigüenza. Ibid., pp. 364–65. Also, BN, Manuscritos, 13.073, ff. 181r–183r.

323. October 11, 1138. Burgos. Alfonso VII and Berengaria. Victor, archdeacon of San Vicente de Buezo. Garrido Garrido, *Documentación*. pp. 210–11.

324. October 18, 1138. Villafranca de Oca. Alfonso VII and Berengaria. Hospitallers. Jean Delaville le Roulx, ed., *Cartularie général de l'Ordre des Hospitaliers de Saint-Jean de Jérusalem, 1110-1310*, 4 vols. (Paris, 1894–1900), 1:104–6. Also, AHN, Ord. Mil., Carpeta 577, nos. 19 and 21; BN, Manuscritos, 13.077, fol. 11r–v.

325. October 20, 1138. Carrión. Alfonso VII and Berengaria. Guter Fernán-

dez. Luciano Serrano, ed., *Colección diplomática de San Salvador El Moral* (Madrid, 1906), pp. 39–41, who called it an original.

326. October 24, 1136. Palencia. Alfonso VII and Berengaria. Cathedral of Zamora. AC Zamora, Tumbo Negro, ff. 16v–17r.

327. November 6, 1138. *Infanta* Sancha. Monastery of San Salvador de Carracedo. García Calles, *Doña Sancha*, pp. 137–38.

328. November 6, 1138. Toledo. Alfonso VII and Berengaria. Monastery of San Salvador de Carracedo. Antonio de Yepes, *Corónica general de la Orden de San Benito*, 7 vols. (Irache and Valladolid, 1609–21), 5:450. False. Modeled on no. 327.

329. November 12, 1138. Segovia. Alfonso VII. Monastery of Tojos Outos. AHN, Códices, 1.002B, fol. 8r–v; Acad. Hist., Colección Salazar, O-8, fol. 69r, dated September 12. False. Berengaria missing from intitulation, Alfonso Styled "rex," and other peculiarities.

330. December 11, 1138. Compostela. Alfonso VII and Berengaria. Monastery of Tojos Outos. AHN, Clero, Carpeta 556, no. 3.

331. December 12, 1138. Compostela. Alfonso VII and Berengaria. Monastery of Sobrado. AHN, Clero, Carpeta 526, nos. 8, 9, 12, and 13. Rassow, "Urkunden," 11:79–80, believed that no. 8 was an original. I would take it for a near contemporary copy.

332. December 18, 1138. Compostela. Alfonso VII and Berengaria. Cathedral of Túy. AC Túy, no. 4/2. *ES* 22:261–62. False. Some of those who confirm are not contemporary. Diplomatic is atypical in part.

333. 1139. Alfonso VII. Monastery of San Vicente de Lugo. *ES* 40:227. A notice only.

334. January 21, 1139. Palencia. Alfonso VII and Berengaria. Countess Urraca Fernández, widow of Count Rodrigo Martínez. Mañueco Villalobos and Zurita Nieto, *Documentos*, 1:185–89.

335. February 20, 1139. Palencia. Alfonso VII and Berengaria. Cathedral of Palencia. Abajo Martín, *Documentación*, pp. 78–80. Unreliable. The date is too early for Bishops Pedro of Burgos and Juan of León who confirm.

336. March 26, 1139. Olmedo. Alfonso VII and Berengaria. Cathedral of Segovia. Villar García, *Documentación*, pp. 73–74.

337. 1139. Alfonso VII. *Concejo* de Ayllón. Ibid., p. 100. Alfonso orders the *concejo* to respect the rights given in no. 336.

338. April 5, 1139. Alfonso VII, Berengaria, and Sancho "rex." Monastery of San Salvador El Moral. Serrano, *Colección*, pp. 45–51. Alfonso confirms donation of Guter Fernández and Tota, ux. False. Sancho was not then king, among other errors.

339. April 5, 1139. Alfonso VII, Berengaria, and Sancho "rex." Guter Fernán-

dez and Toda, ux. Serrano, *Colección*, pp. 41–45. Alfonso confirms the grant of Bishop Simon of Burgos False. Among other errors Sancho is not king this early. Companion forgery to no. 338.

340. April 17, 1139. Sahagún. Alfonso VII and Berengaria. Monastery of Oya. AHN, Clero, Carpeta 1.794, no. 4; Códices, 60B, ff. 2r–v and 120r–v. *ES* 22:263–64. False. Those who confirm are mutually exclusive and the diplomatic is atypical.

341. June 24, 1139. Sahagún. Alfonso VII. Monastery of Oya. AHN, Clero, Carpeta 1.794, no. 5. A forgery closely related to no. 339.

342. July 13, 1139. *Infanta* Sancha. Cathedral of León. Fernández Catón, *Colección*, 5:190–92, who calls it an original.

343. July 25, 1139. Colmenar de Oreja. Alfonso VII and Berengaria. Monastery of Osera. AC Orense, Reales, no. 249; AHN, Códices, 1.008B, fol. 3r–v; 15B, fol. 77r–v.

344. August 14, 1139. Toledo. Alfonso VII and Berengaria. Cathedral of Zamora. AC Zamora, Legajo 8, no. 6, a possible original; Tumbo Negro, ff. 10r–11r; BN, Manuscritos, 9.880, fol. 402v, erroneously dated to 1129.

345. August 31, 1139. Colmenar de Oreja. Alfonso VII. Cathedral of Zamora. BN, Manuscritos, 9.880, fol. 408r–v. A notice only.

346. Sept. 1139. Belorado. Alfonso VII. Monastery of San Millán de La Cogolla. Ledesma Rubio, *Cartulario*, p. 260. Clearly false on the grounds of the royal itinerary and diplomatic errors.

347. September 4, 1139. Burgos. Alfonso VII and Berengaria. Cristóbal, monk. AHN, Clero, Carpeta 351, no.3, no. 5, dated to 1142; Códices, 279B, fol. 2r. Julián García Sáinz de Baranda, "El monasterio de monjes bernardos de Santa María de Rioseco," *BIFG* 156 (1961): 635–42. False. Royal itinerary and diplomatic.

348. September 7, 1139. Colmenar de Oreja. Alfonso VII and Berengaria. Pelayo Domínguez and Orodulce, ux. Ayala Martínez, *Liber*, pp. 183–85. Also, BN, Manuscritos, 714, ff. 131r–v and 148r–v; 9.880, fol. 405r.

349. September 12, 1139. Colmenar de Oreja. Alfonso VII and Berengaria. Cathedral of Zamora. AC Zamora, Legajo 8, no. 7, a possible original; Tumbo Negro, fol. 13r–v; BN, Manuscritos, 714, ff. 167v–168r.

350. September 26, 1139. Colmenar de Oreja. Alfonso VII and Berengaria. Gonzalo Vermúdez and Cristina Peláez, ux. *ES* 38:143–44. A notice only.

351. October 18, 1139. Colmenar de Oreja. Alfonso VII and Berengaria. Martín Pérez de Barahona. AHN, Ord. Mil., Carpeta 417, no. 5. Rassow, "Urkunden," 11:80–81, calls it an original but I believe the script marks it as a thirteenth-century copy.

352. October 1139. Colmenar de Oreja. Alfonso VII and Berengaria. Do-

mingo and Clemente, frater. Garrido Garrido, *Documentación*, pp. 213–14. The day is given only as the day the castle fell.

353. October 26, 1139. Toledo. Alfonso VII and Berengaria. Miguel Pérez. Ayala Martínez, *Liber*, pp. 185–86.

354. October 27, 1139. *Infanta* Sancha. Monastery of Sahagún. Fernández Flórez, *Colección*, 4:165–66 who calls it an original.

355. November, 1139. Toledo. Alfonso VII. Amor. Martín, *Orígenes*, pp. 127–28. Unreliable. The royal chancellor and scribe are too early.

356. November 3, 1139. Toledo. Alfonso VII. Inhabitants of Colemenar de Oreja. García Gallo, "Fueros," pp. 469–71. The absence of Berengaria in the intitulation is troubling.

357. November 15, 1139. Maqueda. Alfonso VII and Berengaria. Miguel Cortide de Santa Eulalia and Andrés de Fagege. Rassow, "Urkunden," 11:84–85, as an original.

358. November 30, 1139. Segovia. Alfonso VII and Berengaria. Cathedral of Segovia. Villar García, *Documentación*, pp. 75–77, who calls it an original.

359. 1140. *Infanta* Sancha. Pons de Minerva. García Calles, *Doña Sancha*, p. 140. A notice only.

360. 1140. *Infanta* Sancha. Estefanía Armengol. Ibid., p. 140.

361. January 1140. Burgos. Alfonso VII. Cathedral of Burgos. Bernard Dorado, *Compendio histórico de la ciudad de Salamanca* (Salamanca, 1776). A notice only.

362. January 12, 1140. Castrojeriz. Alfonso VII and Berengaria. Men and women of Salinas de Añana. Santiago López Castillo, ed., *Diplomatario de Salinas de Añana, 1194–1465* (San Sebastián, 1984), pp. 57–59 and 67–73.

363. January 25, 1140. Palencia. Alfonso VII and Berengaria. Cathedral of Palencia. Abajo Martín, *Documentación*, pp. 80–82.

364. January 25, 1140. Palencia. Alfonso VII and Berengaria. Monastery of Husillos. BN, Manuscritos, 705, fol. 20r–v.

365. January 26, 1140. Palencia. Alfonso VII and Berengaria. Cathedral of Burgos. Garrido Garrido, *Documentación*, pp. 214–15.

366. January 27, 1140. Valladolid. Alfonso VII and Berengaria. Cathedral of León. Fernández Catón, *Collección*, 5:193–94.

367. January 28, 1140. Valladolid. Alfonso VII and Berengaria. Monastery of San Martín de Valdepueblo. Ibid., pp. 195–96.

368. January 31, 1140. Valladolid. *Infanta* Sancha. Cathedral of Segovia. Villar García, *Documentación*, pp. 77–78.

369. January 31, 1140. Valladolid. *Infanta* Sancha. Cathedral of Segovia. Ibid., pp. 79–80, who calls it an original. It is a forgery modeled on no. 367. Her nephew Sancho is cited as "rex."

370. February 12, 1140. Alfonso VII. Monastery of San Salvador de Villacete. Fernández Flórez, *Coleccion*, 4:168–69, who calls it an original. False. The diplomatic is not that of the chancery.

371. February 21, 1140. Carrión. Alfonso VII. Count Ramon Berenguer IV of Barcelona. ACA, Cancillería, Ramon Berenguer IV, Carpeta 35, no. 96, with the text dates given as A.D. 1139 but 1140 in the Spanish Era; Carpeta 36, no. 134, with the text dates given as A.D. 1139 but 1141 in the Spanish Era. Francisco M. Rosell, ed., *Liber Feudorum Maior* (Barcelona, 1945), pp. 37–38, published it incorrectly as of 1141.

372. March 16, 1140. Alfonso VII and Berengaria. Martín Pérez. AD León, Gradefes, no. 45.

373. April 24, 1140. Nájera. Alfonso VII and Berengaria. Monastery of Valvanera. Francisco Javier García Turza, ed., *Documentación medieval del monasterio de Valvanera (siglos XII a XIII)* (Zaragoza, 1985), pp. 198–99.

374. May 14, 1140. Atienza. Alfonso VII and Berengaria. Cathedral of Sigüenza. Minguella y Arnedo, *Historia*, pp. 371–72, from what he called the original but the dating formula is defective. Also, BN, Manuscritos, 13.073, ff. 269r–271r.

375. May 14, 1140. Berlanga. Alfonso VII and Berengaria. Guter Fernández and Toda, ux. BN, Manuscritos, 714, fol. 133v; Acad. Hist., Colección Salazar, M-59, fol. 169r.

376. June 9, 1140. Toledo. Alfonso VII. Velasco Arevalo and Juan Sánchez. AHN, Registro de Escrituras, IX, fol. 11r–v; Acad. Hist., Colección Salazar, I-38, ff. 266v–267r, both dated to 1139. Unreliable. The dating formula is defective.

377. June 10, 1140. Medina. *Infanta* Sancha. Hospitallers. Ayala Martínez, *Liber*, pp. 187–90.

378. June 17, 1140. Zamora. Alfonso VII and Berengaria. Hospitallers. Ibid., pp. 191–92.

379. June 24, 1140. Salamanca. Alfonso VII and Berengaria. Hospitallers. Ibid., pp. 193–95. Also, BN, Manuscritos, 714, fol. 139r–v, dated to July 25.

380. June 24, 1140. Salamanca. Alfonso VII and Berengaria. Hospitallers. Ibid., pp. 192–93.

381. June 24, 1140. Segovia. Alfonso VII and Berengaria. Hospitallers. Ibid., pp. 195–96. Scribal error for place?

382. June 26, 1140. Salamanca. Alfonso VII and Berengaria. Hospital of "monte Ranie longe." AC Compostela, Tumbo C, ff. 154v–155r. *Colección diplomática Galicia*, 1:75–76.

383. June 26, 1140. Toledo. Alfonso VII and Berengaria. Monastery of Celanova. AHN, Clero, Carpeta 1.430, no. 17. Scribal error for place?

384. June 27, 1140. Zamora. Alfonso VII and Berengaria. Monastery of Oya. *ES*, 22:264–65. False. Place of issue, citation of Guter Fernández as major-domo.

385. July 1140. Salamanca. Alfonso VII. Cathedral of Zamora. BN, Manuscritos, 714, fol. 162v. Unreliable. Deceased Pedro given as bishop of León.

386. July 1, 1140. Alba de Tormes. Alfonso VII and Berengaria. Cathedral of Santiago de Compostela. López Ferreiro, *Historia*, 4:25–28 Appendix. Also AC Compostela, copy Tumbo A, ff. 122r–123r. False. Capture of Muslim Coria cited two years too early. Sancho and Fernando given as "rex."

387. July 4, 1140. Salamanca. Alfonso VII and Berengaria. *Concejo* of Alba de Tormes. Américo Castro and Federico de Onis, eds., *Fueros leoneses de Zamora, Salamanca, Ledesma, y Alba de Tormes* (Madrid, 1916), pp. 291–92.

388. July 8, 1140. Salamanca. Alfonso VII, Berengaria, Sancho, and Fernando. Bartolomé Yañez Villaamil. Vigil, *Asturias*, 1:343–44. A notice only but in obvious error, given the intitulation.

389. July 29, 1140. Logroño. Alfonso VII and Berengaria. Monastery of San Miguel de Escalada. Serrano, *Obispado*, 3:181–82, who redated the 1133 of the text erroneously to 1141. Also, BN, Manuscritos, 841, fol. 429r–v.

390. August 12, 1140. Alfonso VII and Berengaria. Cathedral of Santiago de Compostela. López Ferreiro, *Historia*, 4:31–32, Appendix. Not a chancery product and likely false.

391. September 9, 1140. Hornillos de Cameros. Alfonso VII and Berengaria. Countess Urraca Fernández. Mañueco Villalobos and Zurito Nieto, *Documentos*, 1:190–93. Also, Acad. Hist., Colección Salazar, O-17, ff. 416v–417r.

392. October 7, 1140. c. Calahorra. Alfonso VII and Berengaria. Cathedral of Sigüenza. Minguella y Arnedo, *Historia*, 1:373–74.

393. October 25, 1140. c. Calahorra. Alfonso VII and Berengaria. Monastery of Fitero. Cristina Monterde Albiac, ed., *Colección diplomática del monasterio de Fitero: 1140–1210* (Zaragoza, 1978), pp. 355–57, from a possible original. Also, BN, Manuscritos, 700, ff. 292r–294r.

394. November 3, 1140. Santo Domingo de La Calzada. Alfonso VII. Bishops of Burgos and Calahorra. Rodríguez de Lama, *Colección*, 2:197. Alfonso adjudicates quarrel of the two. Unreliable. Late mention of Count Rodrigo González.

395. November 12, 1140. Soria. Alfonso VII, Berengaria, sons Sancho and Fernando. Hospital of Val de Muñeca. AHN, Clero, Carpeta 351, no. 4; Códices, 279B, fol. 3r. Julián García Sáinz de Baranda, "El monasterio de monjes bernardinos de Santa María de Rioseco," *BIFG* 156 (1961): 638–39. False on basis of the intitulation.

396. November 30, 1140. Soria. Alfonso VII, Berengaria, and son Sancho. Cathedral of Calahorra. Rodríguez de Lama, *Colección*, 2:198–99. Those who confirm are incompatible at any date.

397. 1141. Alfonso VII and Berengaria. Monastery of San Millán de La Cogolla. Ledesma Rubio, *Cartulario*, p. 263.

398. January 30, 1141. Alfonso VII. Monastery of Santa María de Sacramenia. Diego de Colmenares, *Historia de la insigne ciudad de Segovia*, 2 vols. 1637 Reprint (Segovia, 1969–70), 1:127. Notice only.

399. February 21, 1141. Segovia. Alfonso VII, Berengaria, Bishop Pedro, and cathedral chapter of Segovia. *Concejo* de Calatalifa. Villar García, *Documentación*, pp. 80–81.

400. February 21, 1141. Segovia. Alfonso VII and Berengaria. Pedro Brimón. Ayala Martínez, *Liber*, pp. 196–97.

401. March 3, 1141. Sepúlveda. Alfonso VII, Berengaria, and Sancho, son. Domingo Pérez of Segovia. Villar García, *Documentación*, pp. 81–82. Unreliable. Sancho cited too early.

402. March 5, 1141. *Infanta* Sancha. Hospitallers. Ayala Martínez, *Liber*, pp. 197–98.

403. March 21, 1141. Burgos. Alfonso VII. Monastery of Santo Domingo (de La Calzada?). Rassow, "Urkunden," 10:436. Notice only.

404. March 21, 1141. Burgos. Alfonso VII. Monastery of San Pedro de Arlanza. Serrano, *Cartulario de Arlanza*, pp.189–90. False. Diplomatic atypical.

405. April 1, 1141. Soria. Alfonso VII and Berengaria. Monastery of Valvanera. García Turza, *Documentación*, pp. 199–200.

406. April 18, 1141. Carrión. Alfonso VII and Berengaria. Cathedral of Burgos. Serrano, *Obispado*, 3:179–80.

407. April 27, 1141. Alfonso VII and Berengaria. Cathedral of León. Fernández Catón, *Colección*, 5:203–4, who calls it an original. It is no chancery product and is probably false.

408. May 5, 1141. Zamora. Alfonso VII and Berengaria. Monastery of San Salvador de Celanova. Rassow, "Urkunden," 11:85–86. AHN, Clero, Carpeta 1.430, no. 19, the possible original; Carpeta 1.431, no.11.

409. May 29, 1141. Palencia. Alfonso VII, Berengaria, Sancho and Fernando, sons. Cathedral of Palencia. Abajo Martín, *Documentación*, pp. 82–84. False. Early citation of *infantes* and other diplomatic irregularities.

410. June 3, 1141. Alfonso VII and Berengaria. Countess Estefanía Armengol. Acad. Hist., Colección Salazar, o–18, fol. 207r–v. Unreliable and probably false. Not chancery form.

411. June 6, 1141. Alfonso VII and Berengaria. Cathedral of Santiago de Compostela. Fernández Catón, "Llamado colorado," p. 144. Also AC Compostela, copy Tumbo A, fol. 124r–v; Archivo del Arzobispado de Compostela, Capellanía mayor, no. 20; Acad. Hist., Colección Salazar, Appendices, Legajo B, Carpeta 3, no. 8. Forgery based on August 12, 1140.

412. September 1141. Compostela. Alfonso VII. Monastery of San Martín de Pinario and Pelayo Curvo. López Ferreiro, *Historia*, 4:228, n. 1. Alfonso adjudicates their quarrel. Notice only.

413. September 24, 1141. Compostela. Alfonso VII and Berengaria. Monastery of San Payo de Antealtares. Archivo Universitario, Santiago, Documentos, no. 1.

414. October, 1141. Palencia. Alfonso VII and Berengaria. Martín Fernández. Gregorio Sánchez Doncel, "Historia de Vertavillo," *Publicaciones del Instituto Tello Téllez de Meneses* 4 (1950): 117.

415. October 10, 1141. Palencia. Alfonso VII and Berengaria. Rodrigo Pérez. Angel Rodríguez González, ed., *El tumbo del monasterio de San Martín de Castañeda* (León, 1973), pp. 48–49. Also, BN, Manuscritos, 18.382, ff. 47v–48r. A rough copy at best.

416. November 3, 1141. Nájera. Alfonso VII and Berengaria. Cathedral of Calahorra. Augustín Ubieto Arteta, *Cartularios*, pp. 20–21, calls no. 203 of the archive of the cathedral an original.

417. 1142. Belorado. Alfonso VII and Berengaria. Cathedral of Calahorra. López de Silanes and Sáinz Ripa, *Colección*, pp. 21–22. The dating formula is confused.

418. 1142. Alfonso VII and Berengaria. Inhabitants of San Miguel de Pedroso. Ledesma Rubio, *Cartulario*, pp. 264–65. False. Manrique of Lara is cited as count four years too early.

419. 1142. Alfonso VII. Pons de Minerva. BN, Manuscritos, 834, fol. 172v; Acad. Hist., Colección Salazar, O-16, fol. 331r. Notices only. False. List of those confirming is wildly inaccurate.

420. 1142. Alfonso VII and Berengaria. Hospitallers. Delaville le Roulx, *Cartulaire*, 1:116. Notice only.

421. 1142. Vega de Doña Olimpia. Alfonso VII and Berengaria. Monastery of Eslonza. Vignau, *Cartulario*, pp. 22–23.

422. 1142. Burgos. Alfonso VII. Count Rodrígo Gómez and Countess Elvira, ux, to Monastery of Oña. Alamo, *Colección*, 1:220–21. Alfonso confirms the donation.

423. January, 1142. Alfonso VII, Berengaria, Sancho and Fernando "kings." Juan de Quintanaortuño. Garrido Garrido, *Documentación*, pp. 217–18.

Also, BN, Manuscritos, fol. 164r–v. False. Intitulation listing of Sancho and Fernando among other errors.

424. February 3, 1142. Valladolid. Alfonso VII, Berengaria, and Sancho, son. Cathedral of Palencia and Pedro Rodríguez de Torquemada. Abajo Martín, *Documentación*, pp. 85–86. Unreliable. Sancho is cited too early.

425. May 10, 1142. Coria. Alfonso VII and Berengaria. Cathedral of Burgos. Serrano, *Obispado*, 3:183–84.

426. June 3, 1142. León. Alfonso VII, Berengaria, and sons. Monastery of Santa María de Lapedo. Antonio Floriano Cumbreño, ed., *Colección diplomática del monasterio de Belmonte* (Oviedo, 1960), pp. 76–79. False. Intitulation and other errors in those who confirm.

427. June 3, 1142. León. Alfonso VII, Berengaria, and sons. Monastery of Santa María de Lapedo. Ibid., pp. 80–82. False. Based upon no. 426.

428. June 6, 1142. Coria. Alfonso VII and Berengaria. Cathedral of Zamora. AC Zamora, Tumbo Negro, ff. 12v–13r.

429. June 19, 1142. *Infanta* Elvira, Diego, Fernando, and Teresa, children. AHN, Códices, 1.195B, fol. 402r. Unreliable. Pons de Minerva appears as royal majordomo three years too soon.

430. July 28, 1142. Carrión. Alfonso VII and Berengaria. Monastery of Santa María de Nájera. Cantera Montenegro, *Colección*, pp. 85–86, who redates it to 1152. Also Instituto de Valencia de Don Juan, Fondo antiguo, Signatura A.2.8. Unreliable. Berengaria died in 1149 but those who confirm require a later date.

431. July 28, 1142. Salamanca. Alfonso VII and Berengaria. Cathedral of Avila. Angel Barrios García, ed., *Documentación medieval de la catedral de Avila* (Salamanca, 1981), p. 4, who calls it an original. The orthography makes that doubtful.

432. July 29, 1142. Salamanca. Alfonso VII and Berengaria. Monastery of Cluny. Bruel, *Chartes*, 5:425–26.

433. July 30, 1142. Alfonso VII. Velasco Suárez. AC Orense, Reales, no. 250. False. Sancho and Fernando confirm as "king."

434. August 1142. Carrión. Alfonso VII and Berengaria. Monastery of Cluny. Bruel, *Chartes*, 5:426–27.

435. August 1142. Abía de las Torres. Alfonso VII and Berengaria. Diego Muñoz and Urraca Téllez, ux. Rassow, "Urkunden," 11:87–88, who calls it an original. AHN, Clero, Carpeta 977, no. 7.

436. August 1142. Carrión. Alfonso VII and Berengaria. Cathedral of Túy. *ES*, 22:266–68. AC Túy, nos. 1/5, 1/6, 4/3; Primero Libro Becerro, fol. 145r–v; AGS, Gracia y Justicia, Legajo 1.672 (varios), Túy, no. 2; Acad. Hist., Catedrales de España, Túy, 9–25–1-C-3, f. 6r–8v.

437. August 30, 1142. Burgos. Alfonso VII and Berengaria. Cathedral of Coria. José Luis Martín, ed., *Documentación medieval de la iglesia catedral de Coria* (Salamanca, 1989), pp. 25–26.

438. September 7, 1142. Burgos. Alfonso VII and Berengaria. Men of San Zoil de Carrión. Pérez Celada, *Documentación*, pp. 56–57. An original.

439. September 7, 1142. Burgos. Alfonso VII. Rodrigo Muñoz *el viejo*. Charles Julian Bishko, "Peter the Venerable's Journey to Spain," *Studia Anselmiana* 40 (1956): 173. A citation only.

440. September 18, 1142. c. Toledo. Alfonso VII and Berengaria. Martín Díaz. Vignau, *Cartulario*, pp. 21–22. Unreliable. Sons Sancho, Fernando, and García confirm and Bishop Martín of Oviedo appears a year too soon.

441. September, 27, 1142. Avila. Alfonso VII and Berengaria. Cathedral of Avila. Barrios García, *Documentación*, pp. 4–5. Also, Acad. Hist., Colección Salazar, O-16, fol. 373r–v. Frequent mistakes of copyist.

442. October 27, 1142 Toledo. Alfonso VII and Berengaria. Cathedral of Toledo. Hernández, *Cartularios*, pp. 46–47. Partial publication.

443. November 12, 1142. Villabuena. *Infanta* Sancha. Monastery of Carracedo. José María Fernández Catón, ed., *Catálogo del Archivo Histórico Diocesano de León*, 2 vols. (León, 1978–1979), 2:12–13. A fragment only.

444. 1143? Alfonso VII, Berengaria, Sancho and Fernando, sons. Monastery of San Miguel de Canero. Floriano Cumbreño, *Libro Registro*, 1:112. Undated but patently false.

445. 1143. *Infanta* Sancha. Cathedral of Astorga. AHN, Microfilmas, Astorga, Registro de Escrituras, fol. 101r. Notice only.

446. 1143. *Infanta* Sancha. María Froílaz. García Calles, *Doña Sancha*, pp. 136–37. The text is dated erroneously to 1133.

447. January 22, 1143. Palencia. Alfonso VII and Berengaria. Monastery of San Servando de Toledo. Hernández, *Cartularios*, pp. 48–49, from what he called the original. Partial publication.

448. January 29, 1143. Palencia. *Infanta* Sancha. Cathedral of Toledo. Ibid., pp. 49–50, from what he called the original.

449. January 30, 1143. Palencia. Alfonso VII, Berengaria, and *Infanta* Sancha. Cathedral of Toledo. Fernández Catón, *Colección*, 5:213–16, from what he called the original. That is unlikely since the dating formula is confused.

450. January 31, 1143. Dueñas. Alfonso VII and Berengaria. Church of Santa Eufemia de Cozoles. Maximiliano Castrillo, *Opusculo sobre la historia de la villa de Astudillo* (Burgos, 1877), pp. 188–89. Dating formula is confused.

451. February 15, 1143. Valbuena. Alfonso VII and Berengaria. Countess Estefanía Armengol and the monastery of Santa María de Valbuena. Francisco

Antón, *Monasterios medievales de la provincia de Valladolid*, 2nd ed. (Valladolid, 1942), pp. 9–10. Alfonso confirms the foundation of the countess. A partial publication.

452. April 21, 1143. Toledo. Alfonso VII and Berengaria. Rodrigo Suárez and Acenda Peláez, ux. Julieta Guallart and María del Pilar R. Laguzzi, "Algunos documentos reales leoneses," *CHE* 2 (1944): 367–68.

453. May 5, 1143. Alfonso VII. Men of Pajares de Campos. Fernández Catón, *Colección*, 5:218–22. Very rough copies. Perhaps never a chancery product. Unreliable.

454. August 23, 1143. Toledo. Alfonso VII and Berengaria. Cathedral of Toledo. García Luján, *Privilegios*, 2:51–53.

455. August 25, 1143. Alfonso VII and Berengaria. Cathedral of Santiago de Compostela and monastery of Tojos Outos. AHN, Códices, 1.002B, ff. 13v–14r. Alfonso, Berengaria, and Sancho, son, confirm exchange. Doubtful because of Sancho's appearance.

456. September 20, 1143. Valladolid. Alfonso VII and Berengaria. Cathedral of Sigüenza. Minguella y Arnedo, *Historia*, 1:374–75. Also, BN, Manuscritos, 13.073, ff. 208r–209v.

457. September 23, 1143. Valladolid. Alfonso VII and Berengaria. Juan Raymundez? AHN, Ord. Mil., Carpeta 577, no. 1.

458. October 4, 1143. Zamora. Alfonso VII and Berengaria. Martín Cidez. Joseph Sáenz de Aguirre, ed., *Collectio Maxima Conciliorum Hispaniae*, vol. 5 (Rome, 1755), pp. 54–55. Also, BN, Manuscritos, 712, fol. 363r–v; Acad. Hist., Colección Salazar, O-16, fol. 446r–v; Appendices, Legajo C, Carpeta 2, no. 5; AGS, Registro General de Sellos, Legajo 1.491, Abril, fol. 1. All these late copies are erroneously dated to 1137.

459. October 5, 1143. Zamora. Alfonso VII and Berengaria. Pons de Cabrera. Isabel Alfonso Antón, *La colonización cisterciense en la meseta del Duero* (Zamora, 1986), pp. 294–95. Also, BN, Manuscritos, 3.147, ff. 420v–421r.

460. October 29, 1143. Nájera. Alfonso VII and Berengaria. Monastery of Cluny. Bruel, *Chartes*, 5:428–30, from what he called an original.

461. December 4, 1143. *Infanta* Sancha. Hospital of Foncebadón. BN, Manuscritos, 4.357, fol. 140r. A notice only.

462. December 22, 1143. Castrojeriz. Alfonso VII, Berengaria, and Sancho, son. *Concejo* of Roa. Muñoz y Romero, *Fueros*, pp. 544–45. Appearance of Sancho raises questions.

463. 1144. Alfonso VII and Berengaria. Monastery of San Millán de La Cogolla. Ledesma Rubio, *Cartulario*, pp. 266–67.

464. 1144. Alfonso VII. Monastery of San Millán de La Cogolla and the *con-*

cejo of Belorado. Ibid., p. 268. Alfonso confirms the settlement of their dispute.

465. January 24, 1144. León. Alfonso VII, Berengaria, and Sancho, son. Martín Díaz and Jimena Pérez, ux. Fernández Catón, *Colección*, 5:223–24, who calls it an original. The early appearance of Sancho and of García Rodríguez as *merino* in Burgos make it more likely that it is an interpolated copy.

466. February 25, 1144. Alfonso VII, Berengaria, *Infanta* Sancha, and *Infanta* Elvira. Cathedral of León and monastery of Carbajal. Ibid., pp. 225–28, who calls it an original. It is not for the long-deceased Bernard is given as archbishop of Toledo and *Infanta* Sancha confirms as "regina." At best, it is interpolated.

467. February 29, 1144. Arévalo. Alfonso VII and Berengaria. Monastery of Santa María de Sacramenia. María de la Soterrana Martín Postigo, *Santa María de Cardaba, priorato de Arlanza y granja de Sacramenia* (Valladolid, 1979), pp. 116–17.

468. March 3, 1144. Segovia. Alfonso VII. Cathedrals of Segovia and Palencia. Rassow, "Urkunden," 11:90–91, an original. Alfonso adjudicates a dispute between them.

469. March 26, 1144. Castillo de Muñó. Alfonso VII and Sancho and Fernando, sons. Monastery of Oña. Alamo, *Colección*, 1:224–26. Forgery based on genuine grant of March 26, 1149.

470. April 22, 1144. Zamora. Alfonso VII and Berengaria. Monastery of Santiago de Moreruela. Alfonso Antón, *Colonización*, pp. 295–96. Unreliable. Pons de Cabrera appears as royal majordomo too early.

471. April 25, 1144. Salamanca. Alfonso VII, Berengaria, and Sancho, son. Cathedral of Zamora. AC Zamora, Tumbo Negro, ff. 14v–15r.

472. April 25, 1144. Salamanca. Alfonso VII, Berengaria, and Sancho, son. Cathedral of Salamanca. Martín, Villar García, Marcos Rodríguez, and Sánchez Rodríguez, *Documentos*, pp. 95–96, an original.

473. June 1144. León. Alfonso VII, Berengaria, and Sancho and Fernando, sons. Monastery of San Lorenzo de Caabeiro. Manuel Lucas Alvarez, ed., "La colección diplomática del monasterio de San Lorenzo de Carboeiro," *Compostellanum* 3 (1958): 295–96, who called it an original. I make the script to be later.

474. June 1144. Sahagún. Alfonso VII, Berengaria, *Infanta* Sancha, and Sancho, son. Martín Pérez et ux. Fernández Flórez, *Colección*, 4:185–86. A fragment only.

475. June 1144. Carrión. Alfonso VII, Berengaria, and Sancho, son. Church of Santa María Parva de Jerusalén. Martín, *Orígines*, pp. 182–83.

476. June 1144. Alfonso VII, Berengaria, *Infanta* Sancha, and Sancho and Fernando, sons. Aldonza Fernández and Alvaro Gutiérrez, husband. Francisco Javier Fernández Conde, Isabel Torrente Fernández, and Guadalupe de la Noval Menéndez, eds., *El monasterio de San Pelayo de Oviedo*, vol. 1 (Oviedo, 1978), pp. 33–35, who called it an original. It is false. Among other defects, Sancho and Fernando already confirm as "kings."

477. June 22, 1144. Alfonso VII, Berengaria, and Sancho and Fernando, sons. Unspecified hospital. Vigil, *Asturias*, 1:89. A notice only.

478. June 25, 1144. Carrión. Alfonso VII and Berengaria. Monastery of Tojos Outos. AHN, Códices, 1.002B, fol. 4v. False. The bishop of León and the royal majordomo and *alférez* are all incorrect.

479. June 30, 1144. León. Alfonso VII and Berengaria. Monastery of Santa María de Montederramo. Manrique, *Annales*, 3:248. AHN, Clero, Carpeta 1.481, nos. 6, 7, 8, 9.

480. June 30, 1144. León. Alfonso VII and Berengaria. Monastery of Santa María de Osera. AHN, Clero, Carpeta 518, no. 15, a badly faded original; Códices, 15B, ff. 77v–78v; 1.008B, fol. 4r; AC Orense, Reales, no. 251.

481. July 4, 1144. Alfonso VII and Berengaria. Aldonza Fernández and Alvaro Gutiérrez, husband. García Larragueta, *Colección*, pp. 395–97, who calls it an original. Alfonso agrees to recover her inheritance for the cession to him of half. Unreliable. Son Sancho confirms as "rex."

482. July 8, 1144. León. Alfonso VII. Cathedral of Orense. AC Orense, Reales, no. 19.

483. July 15, 1144. *Infanta* Sancha. Alvaro Gutiérrez and Aldonza Fernández, ux. Fernández Conde, Torrente Fernández, and Menéndez, *Monasterio*, pp. 35–39, calls it an original.

484. August 4, 1144. Salamanca. Alfonso VII, Berengaria, and Sancho, Fernando, and García, sons. Cathedral of Salamanca. Martín, Villar García, Marcos Rodríguez, Sánchez Rodríguez, *Documentos*, pp. 97–98, from the original. Also, BN, Manuscritos, 712, fol. 228r–v; 6.683, ff. 37r–38r; 13.093; ff. 115r–116r; Acad. Hist., Colección Salazar, O-16, fol. 264r–v.

485. October 1144. Toledo. Alfonso VII and Berengaria. Cathedral of Segovia. Villar García, *Documentación*, pp. 83–84, who called it an original.

486. November 1144. Toledo. Alfonso VII and Berengaria. Cathedral of Avila. Barrios García, *Documentación*, pp. 6–7.

487. November 1144. Toledo. Alfonso VII and Berengaria. Anaia González. Juan Antonio Llorente, ed., *Noticias históricas de las tres provincias vascongadas, Alava, Guipúcoa, y Vizcaya*, 4 vols. (Madrid, 1806–8), 4:81–82. Unreliable. The deceased Berenguer is cited as still archbishop of Compostela.

488. November 1144. Toledo. Alfonso VII and Berengaria. Hospitallers. Ayala Martínez, *Liber*, pp. 202–4.

489. December 4, 1144. Segovia. Alfonso VII and Berengaria. Diego Fernández. AHN, Clero, Carpeta 962, no. 15. Rassow, "Urkunden," 11:94–95, regarded it as an original. But I would regard the script as not that of the scribe Gerald.

490. December 4, 1144. Segovia. Alfonso VII and Berengaria. Fernando Peláez. Fernández Flórez, *Colección*, 4:186–87 who calls it an original.

491. December 19, 1144. Valladolid. Alfonso VII, Berengaria, and Sancho, son. Gonzalo de Marañon. Alamo, *Colección*, 1:227–28.

492. December 26, 1144. Alfonso VII and Berengaria. Cathedral of Sigüenza. Minguella y Arnedo, *Historia*, 1:375–77. Alfonso confirms Bishop Bernard's new constitution for his chapter.

493. 1145. Alfonso VII. Monastery of Junta (Xuarros). AC Burgos, Códice 35, fol. 5. Notice only.

494. January 31, 1145. Almazán. Alfonso VII and Berengaria. Cathedral of Santiago de Compostela. López Ferreiro, *Historia*, 4:37–38, Appendix.

495. March 1145. Fresno. Alfonso VII, Berengaria, Sancho and Fernando, sons. Miguel Pérez. Angel Rodríguez González, ed., *El tumbo del monasterio de San Martín de Castañeda* (León, 1973), pp. 49–51. Also, AHN, Clero, Carpeta 1.977, no. 1; BN, Manuscritos, 18.382, ff. 46v–47r.

496. March 21, 1145. Astorga. Alfonso VII and Berengaria. Cathedral of Astorga. AHN, Sección de Osuna, Carpeta 12, nos. 22, 23.

497. April 22, 1145. Sancho III. Cathedral of Calahorra. Rodríguez de Lama, *Colección*, 2:211–12. A clear forgery.

498. May 4, 1145. Toledo. Alfonso VII and Berengaria. Pedro Rodríguez. Rodríguez González, *Tumbo*, pp. 51–52.

499. May 31, 1145. Toledo. Alfonso VII, Berengaria, *Infanta* Sancha. Pedro Leonis. Fernández Catón, *Colección*, 5:234–36.

500. June 15, 1145. Toledo. Alfonso VII, Berengaria, and Sancho, son. Monastery of San Prudencio de Lagunilla. Sandoval, *Historia*, 2:245–46. Notice only.

501. August 17, 1145. Alfonso VII and Berengaria. Pedro Domínguez and Cristina Flaínez, ux. AHN, Clero, Carpeta 825, no. 1. Irregular diplomatic makes it suspect.

502. August 21, 1145. León. Alfonso VII and Berengaria. Cathedral of Orense. Castro y Sueiro, *Documentos*, 1:33–34.

503. September 1145. Alfonso VII. Monastery of Oña. Alamo, *Colección*, 1:233. Notice only. False. Sandoval, *Historia*, p. 246, cited Sancho confirming as "king."

504. September 1, 1145. Frómista. Alfonso VII and Berengaria. Cathedral of Toledo. García Luján, *Privilegios*, 2:54–56.

505. September 2, 1145. Alfonso VII, Berengaria, and Sancho, Fernando, and García, sons. Inhabitants of Oviedo. Llorente, *Noticias*, 4:96–107. Interpolated at the least. Sancho and Fernando confirm as "kings." Other diplomatic peculiarities.

506. September 12, 1145. Burgos. Alfonso VII, Berengaria, and Sancho, Fernando, and García, sons. Monastery of Oña. Alamo, *Colección*, 1:231–32.

507. September 12, 1145. Burgos. Alfonso VII. Monastery of Oña. Ibid., p. 233. A notice only.

508. November 10, 1145. Valladolid. Alfonso VII, Berengaria, *Infanta* Sancha, and Sancho and Fernando, sons. Fernando Gutiérrez, María Ovéquez, ux, and Pedro Gordón, son. Fernández Conde, Torrente Fernández, and Menéndez, *Monasterio*, 1:41–44; two copies with variants the first of which the editors call an original. The atypical character of the diplomatic makes that impossible.

509. November 10, 1145. Valladolid. Alfonso VII, Berengaria, *Infanta* Sancha, and Sancho and Fernando, sons. Monastery of San Pelayo. Ibid, pp. 39–41, calling both copies origina! Neither the script nor the format are typical.

510. November 20, 1145. León. Alfonso VII and Berengaria. Monastery of Celanova. Vázquez Nuñez, "Documentos," pp. 148–51. Also, AHN, Clero, Carpeta 1.430, no. 20; 1.433, no. 3; AGS, Mercedes y Privilegios, Legajo 372, no. 2; Registro General de Sellos, Legajo 1.480, September, fol. 1. False. Berenguer given as archbishop of Compostela and other similar problems.

511. 1146. Avila. Alfonso VII. Monastery of Santa María de Retuerta. Gonzalo Martínez, "Diplomatario de San Cristóbal de Ibeas," *BIFG* 55 (1975): 696. A notice only.

512. January 29, 1146. Carrión. Alfonso VII and Berengaria. Cathedral of Palencia. Abajos Martín, *Documentación*, pp. 93–95.

513. January 29, 1146. Carrión. Alfonso VII and Berengaria. Guter Fernández and Toda, ux. Serrano, *Colección El Moral*, pp. 54–56.

514. February 10, 1146. León. Alfonso VII and Berengaria. María Alfonsez and Pedro Domínguez, husband. Fernández Catón, *Colección*, 5:238–39.

515. February 10, 1146. León. Alfonso VII and Berengaria. Albertino and María Jiménez, ux. Ibid., pp. 236–38, who calls it an original.

516. February 12, 1146. Coyanza. Alfonso VII. Cathedral of Astorga. Quintana Prieto, *Obispado*, pp. 279–80. Also, BN, Manuscritos, 712, ff. 89v–90r; 9.194, fol. 112r–v.

517. February 13, 1146. Coyanza. Alfonso VII and Berengaria. Pons de Minerva. AHN, Clero, Carpeta 1.794, no. 8.

518. February 20, 1146. Alfonso VII. Bishop of Zamora and abbot of Celanova. AC Zamora, Tumbo Negro, fol. 12r. Alfonso adjudicates their dispute.

519. February 25, 1146. Zamora. Alfonso VII and Berengaria. Monastery of Santiago de Moreruela. Alfonso Antón, *Colonización*, pp. 297–98.

520. March 24, 1146. Avila. Alfonso VII and Berengaria. Bishop and *concejo* of Avila and cathedral of Santiago de Compostela. López Ferreiro, *Historia*, 4:41–42, Appendix. False. The date is in error and Sancho confirms as "king."

521. March 30, 1146. Avila. Alfonso VII and Berengaria. María Gómez, Nazareno, García Pérez, and Diego Almadran, sons. Fernández Flórez, *Colección*, 4:192–93, an original.

522. April 29, 1146. Toledo. Alfonso VII and Berengaria. Various inhabitants of Toledo. Hernández, *Cartularios*, pp. 55–56.

523. May 2, 1146. Toledo. Alfonso VII and Berengaria. Various inhabitants of Toledo. Ibid., pp. 56–57, who called it an original.

524. May 2, 1146. Toledo. Alfonso VII and Berengaria. Pedro Girberti, canon of Toledo. Rassow, "Urkunden," 11:96–97. Also, AHN, Ord. Mil., Carpeta 417, no. 6, an original; Acad. Hist., Colección Salazar, I-38, fol. 274r-v.

525. May 2, 1146. Toledo. Alfonso VII and Berengaria. Various inhabitants of Toledo. Hernández, *Cartularios*, pp. 57–58.

526. May 6, 1146. Sezina c. Toledo. Alfonso VII and Berengaria. Juan, archdeacon of Segovia and Arnaldo de Corbín, canon of Toledo. Ibid., pp. 58–59, who calls it an original.

527. May 7, 1146. Almonacid de Toledo. Alfonso VII and Berengaria. Cathedral of Sigüenza. Mingüella y Arnedo, *Historia*, 1:380–81. Also, BN, Manuscritos, 13.073, ff. 214r–216r.

528. May 10, 1146. Almonacid de Toledo. Alfonso VII and Berengaria. Monastery of Samos. Manuel Lucas Alvarez, ed., *El tumbo de San Julián de Samos, siglos VIII–XII* (Santiago de Compostela, 1986), pp. 168–70.

529. May 21, 1146. Córdoba. Alfonso VII. ?. García Calles, *Doña Sancha*, p 42, n.118. A notice only.

530. June 1146. Alfonso VII. Guter Fernández and Toda, ux, and monastery of El Moral. Serrano, *Colección El Moral*, pp. 56–58. Alfonso confirms the grant. False. Sancho confirms as "king."

531. August 16–23, 1146. Toledo. Alfonso VII and Berengaria. María Cídez and Suero Calvez, husband. Suárez de Alarcón, *Relaciones*, p. 16, Appendix. Also, Acad. Hist., Colección Salazar, I-38, fol. 275r–v.

532. August 19, 1146. Toledo. Alfonso VII and Berengaria. Martín Díaz. Rassow, "Urkunden," II:97–98, an original. Also, Acad. Hist., Colección Salazar, O-16, fol. 50IV, dated 1096.

533. September 1146. Alfonso VII. Count Ramon Berenguer IV of Barcelona. Caesare Imperiale di Sant' Angelo, ed., *Codices diplomatico della Republica di Genova*, vol. I (Rome, 1936), pp. 204–17. Two documents following the norms of their respective chanceries. Sáez and Sáez, *Fondo*, pp. 67–70, publish what seems to be a preliminary draft.

534. October 15, 1146. Niencebas. Alfonso VII and Berengaria. Santa María de Niencebas. Monterde Albiac, *Colección*, pp. 360–61.

535. November? 1146. Alfonso VII, Berengaria, Sancho, son. Pedro Ibáñez. Serrano, *Obispado*, 3:123–25. Alfonso confirms grant of his grandfather.

536. November 1146. Burgos. Alfonso VII and Berengaria. Monastery of Oña. Alamo, *Colección*, 1:235–36.

537. November 1146. San Esteban de Gormaz. Alfonso VII and Berengaria. Templars. Marquis D'Albón, ed., *Cartulaire général de l'Ordre du Temple, 1119–1150* (Paris, 1913), pp. 257–58.

538. November 15, 1146. San Esteban de Gormaz. Alfonso VII, Berengaria, and Sancho, son. Cathedral of Toledo. García Luján, *Privilegios*, 2:56–58, a possible original.

539. December 1146. Atienza. Alfonso VII and Berengaria. *Concejo* of Atienza. Juan Loperráez de Corvalón, *Descripción histórica del obispado de Osma*, 3 vols. (Madrid, 1788), 3:23–24. Mingüella y Arnedo, *Historia*, 1:384, dated it to 1149. Also, BN, Manuscritos, 9.194, fol. 205r–v. False. The elements of its diplomatic cannot be reconciled with any one date.

540. December 8, 1146. Arévalo. Alfonso VII, Berengaria, and Sancho, son. Cathedral of Segovia. Villar García, *Documentación*, pp. 84–85, from what he calls an original.

541. January 9, 1147. Calatrava. Alfonso VII and Berengaria. Cathedral of Segovia. Ibid., pp. 86–87.

542. January 20, 1147. *Infanta* Sancha. Monastery of Clairvaux. Rodríguez de Diego, *Tumbo*, pp. 185–87.

543. February 3, 1147. Salamanca. Alfonso VII, Berengaria, and Sancho, son. Cathedral of Astorga. BN, Manuscritos, 712, fol. 90r–v; 6.683, fol. 42r–v; 9.194, fol. 116r; 13.093, fol. 123r–v, dated to 1137; Acad. Hist., Colección Salazar, O-22, fol. 175r; Catedrales de España, Astorga, 9–25–1-C-2, ff. 52v–53r; AMon Silos, Ms. 7, fol. 67r–v.

544. February 10, 1147. Nájera. Alfonso VII, Berengaria, and Sancho, son. Monastery of San Prudencio. López de Silanes and Saínz Ripa, *Colección*,

pp. 23–24. False. Sancho confirmas as "king" and the diplomatic is generally confused.

545. February 13, 1147. Salamanca. Alfonso VII. Cathedral of Toledo. García Luján, *Privilegios*, 2:58–60. Also, BN, Manuscritos, 13.042, ff. 82r–84r. The grant has been interpolated. It does not follow chancery form for this period.

546. February 13, 1147. Salamanca. Alfonso VII, Berengaria, Sancho and Fernando, "kings." Cathedral of Santiago de Compostela. López Ferreiro, *Historia*, 4:43–45, Appendix. False. The intitulation and other mistakes.

547. February 24, 1147. Zamora. Alfonso VII, Berengaria, and Sancho, son. Cathedral of Zamora. AC Zamora, Tumbo Negro, ff. 22v–23r; Tumbo Blanco, ff. 83v–84v.

548. February 28, 1147. Zamora. Alfonso VII, Berengaria, Sancho and Fernando, sons, and *Infanta* Sancha. Monastery of San Pelayo. Fernández Conde and Torrente Fernández, and Menéndez. *Monasterio*, pp. 45–46.

549. March 1, 1147. Zamora. Alfonso VII, Berengaria, and Sancho, son. Monastery of Santo Angel de Ursaria. Pedro Floriano Llorente, ed., "El fondo antiguo de pergaminos del Instituto Valencia de Don Juan: Documentos reales, primera serie, 875–1224," *BRAH* 168 (1971): 466–68. Also, AHN, Clero, Carpeta 3.581, no. 7, possibly the original; Acad. Hist., Colección Salazar, M179, without pagination; AC Zamora, Tumbo Negro, ff. 106r–v and 125r–126r.

550. March 8, 1147. Burgos. Alfonso VII, Berengaria, and Sancho, "king." *Concejo* of Pancorbo. Luciano Serrano, "Fueros y privilegios del concejo de Pancorbo (Burgos)," 10 *AHDE* (1933): 325–27. Unreliable. Intitulation is wrong.

551. March 25, 1147. Segovia. Alfonso VII, Berengaria, and Sancho, son. Cathedral of Segovia. Villar García, *Documentación*, pp. 87–88.

552. April 4, 1147. Alfonso VII. Cathedral of Astorga. Rassow, "Urkunden," 10:444. A notice only.

553. April 29, 1147. *Infanta* Sancha. Monastery of Eslonza. García Calles, *Doña Sancha*, pp. 145–6.

554. May 10, 1147. Salamanca. Alfonso VII and Berengaria. Men of Astudillo. Rodríguez Fernández, *Palencia*, pp. 236–39. Unreliable. Bishop Raymond of Palencia confirms months too early.

555. May 20, 1147. León. Alfonso VII, Berengaria, Sancho, Fernando, and Constancia, children, and *Infanta* Sancha. Domingo Stephánez and Luste Lustez, ux. Amparo Valcarce, *Dominio*, pp. 106–7, who calls it an original. It is false on the basis of the location and the intitulation.

556. May 23, 1147. Toledo. Alfonso VII and Berengaria. Gonzalo Vermúdez. García Larragueta, *Colección*, pp. 399–400, who called it an original.

557. June 4, 1147. Calatrava. Alfonso VII, Berengaria, and Sancho, son. Monastery of Sacramenia. Richard A. Fletcher, "Diplomatic and the Cid Revisited: The Seals and the Mandates of Alfonso VII," *JMH* 2 (1976): 332–33, from what he called the original. Also, AHN, Códices, 104B, fol. 2r–v, dated June 20.

558. June 8, 1147. Alfonso VII, Berengaria, and children. Cathedral of Santiago de Compostela. AD Compostela. Carpeta 5. Almost illegible and likely unreliable.

559. June 9, 1147. c. Calatrava. Alfonso VII, Berengaria, Sancho and Fernando, sons. Cathedral of Orense. *Colección diplomática de Galicia*, 2 vol. (Santiago de Compostela, 1901–1903), 1:145–47. AC Orense, Reales, no. 21.

560. July 11, 1147. Calatrava. Alfonso VII, Berengaria, and Sancho and Fernando, sons. Monastery of Antealtares. Jesús Caro García, "El privilegio de Alfonso VII al monasterio de Antealtares," 7 *CEG* (1952): 153–55. Irregular diplomatic.

561. July 17, 1147. c. Andújar. Alfonso VII, Berengaria, and Sancho and Fernando, sons. Monastery of Caabeiro. AHN, Códices, 1.439B, fol. 5r–v. Interpolated in part.

562. August 18, 1147. Baeza. Alfonso VII, Berengaria, and Sancho and Fernando, sons. Rodrigo de Azagra. Rodríguez de Lama, *Colección*, 2:218–19.

563. September 12, 1147. Burgos. Alfonso VII, Berengaria, and Sancho, Fernando, and García, sons. Monastery of Oña. Alamo, *Colección*, 1:236–38. False. *Infans* García was already dead as were a number of those who confirmed.

564. November 25, 1147. Baeza. Alfonso VII, Berengaria, and Sancho, son. García Pérez. Fernández Flórez, *Colección*, 4:202–3, who calls it an original. It is not on the basis of the irregular format and the bad *signum*.

565. December 1147. Alfonso VII. García García and the cathedral of Burgos. Suárez de Alarcón, *Relaciones*, p. 12, Appendix. A notice only. Alfonso confirmed this donation. But Bishop Pedro of Burgos was already deceased in 1146.

566. December 25, 1147. Toledo. Alfonso VII, Berengaria, and Sancho and Fernando, sons. Monastery of Sar. AD Compostela, Fondo San Martín; Serie Priorato de Sar, Carpeta 14, no. 4.

567. December 26, 1147. Toledo. Alfonso VII, Berengaria, and Sancho and Fernando, sons. Fernando Gutiérrez. BN, Manuscritos, 9.880, ff. 356r–

357r; Acad. Hist., Colección Salazar, Appendix, Legajo B, Carpeta 3, no. 11. Both mistakenly dated to 1148.

568. December 29, 1147. Toledo. Alfonso VII, Berengaria, and Sancho, son. Pelayo Calvo. Hernández, *Cartularios*, p. 62. Partial publication.

569. 1148. Alfonso VII, Berengaria, and Sancho, Fernando, and Constancia, children. Monastery of San Isidoro de León. BN, Manuscritos, 5.790, fol. 122r, a notice only. False. Sancho and Fernando confirm as "kings."

570. 1148. Alfonso VII, Berengaria, and Sancho and Fernando, "kings," Constancia, daughter, and Berta "queen." Monastery of Sahagún. Fernández Flórez, *Colección*, 4:210–17. False on the basis of intitulation alone.

571. January 13, 1148. Alfonso VII, and Sancho and Fernando, "kings." Monastery of San Martín de Pinario. *Colección diplomática*, 1:435–37. Also AHN, Clero, Carpeta 512, no. 14, dated January 8, 1142; ARG, Reales, no. 4. False. Intitulation and much else is wrong.

572. January 13, 1148. Alfonso VII, and Sancho and Fernando, "kings." Monastery of Santa María de Mozonzo. AHN, Clero, Carpeta 511, no. 3; Biblioteca Seminario de Compostela, not numbered. False. Closely related to no. 571 above.

573. February 3, 1148. Segovia. Alfonso VII, Berengaria, and Sancho and Fernando, sons. Countess Urraca Fernández. Mañueco Villalobos and Zurita Nieto, *Documentos*, pp. 444–45.

574. February 16, 1148. Palencia. Queen Sancha. Hospitallers. Ayala Martínez, *Liber*, pp. 207–8.

575. February 17, 1148. Palencia. Alfonso VII, Berengaria, Sancho, Fernando, Constancia, children, and *Infanta* Sancha. Monastery of San Pelayo de León. Amparo Valcarce, *Dominio*, pp. 107–8, who called it an original. Also ASI, Códice 81, ff. 29v–32v. It is false on the basis of the intitulation alone.

576. February 17, 1148. Palencia. Alfonso VII, Berengaria, Sancho, Fernando, and Constancia, children, and *Infanta* Sancha. Cathedral of León. Fernández Catón, *Colección*, 5:241–44, who calls it an original. Also, Acad. Hist., Catedrales de España, León, 9–25–1-C-4, ff. 99r–101r. Another forgery closely related to no. 575.

577. February 23, 1148. Palencia. Alfonso VII, Berengaria, and Sancho and Fernando, sons. Monastery of Carracedo. Fernández Catón, *Catálogo*, 2:12. A fragment only.

578. March 1, 1148. Palencia. Alfonso VII, Berengaria, and Sancho and Fernando, sons. Cathedral of Salamanca. Martín, Villar García, Marcos Rodríguez, and Sánchez Rodríguez, *Documentos*, pp. 98–100, who call it an original. I believe the orthography indicates it to be a copy.

579. March 5, 1148. Alfonso VII, Berengaria, and Sancho and Fernando, sons, and *Infanta* Sancha. Pedro Manga and María Raimúndez, ux. AHN, Clero, Carpeta 825, no. 2. False. Majordomo and notary are incorrect for the period and the diplomatic is atypical.

580. March 12, 1148. Burgos. Alfonso VII, Berengaria, and Sancho, son. Diego Fernández de Buniel. María del Carmen Palacín Gálvez and Luis Martínez García, eds., *Documentación del Hospital del Rey de Burgos (1136–1277)* (Burgos, 1990), pp. 4–5.

581. March 31, 1148. Soria. Alfonso VII, Berengaria, and Sancho, son. Arnaldo Gaeto and Giraldo Esperoner. Rodríguez de Lama, *Colección*, 2:219–20, from a possible original.

582. April 5, 1148. Almazán. Alfonso VII, Berengaria, and Sancho, son. Monastery of Fitero. Monterde Albiac, *Colección*, p. 368.

583. April 6, 1148. Alfonso VII, Berengaria, and Sancho, "king." Count García Fernández, Monastery of San Pedro de Cardeña, and *concejo* of Castrellum de Val. Berganza, *Antigüedades*, 2:456–57. False. Intitulation and dating formula are incorrect.

584. April 19, 1148. Covarrubias. *Infanta* Sancha and Abbot Martín of Covarrubias. Inhabitants of Covarrubias. García Calles, *Doña Sancha*, pp. 149–51, from what she styled the original. Also, BN, Manuscritos, 5.471, ff. 34r–35v. False. Sancho and Fernando confirm as "kings."

585. April 25, 1148. Toledo. Alfonso VII. Monastery of Samos. Lucas Alvarez, *Tumbo*, pp. 474–76. False on the basis of the intitulation and the dating formula.

586. May 1148. Alfonso VII and Berengaria. Inhabitants of Logroño. Muñoz y Romero, *Fueros*, pp. 334–43. Alfonso confirms the *fuero* granted by his grandfather.

587. May 10, 1148. Burgos. Alfonso VII. Monastery of Santa María del Aguilar de Campoó. Sandoval, *Historia*, 2:284–85. An excerpt only. False. The bishops of both Oviedo and Segovia are incorrect.

588. May 10, 1148. Castrojeriz. Alfonso VII and Berengaria. Pedro Díaz. Alamo, *Colección*, pp. 240–45. Unreliable. The diplomatic is atypical and sometimes in error.

589. May 23, 1148. Alfonso VII, Berengaria, and Sancho and Fernando, sons. Monastery of San Payo de Antealtares. AHN, Códices, 258B, ff. 3r–v and 21v–22r. False. The grant is dated to 1144 but the dating formula would require sometime after late 1147. Nevertheless, the diplomatic elements are irreconcilable.

590. May 26, 1148. Toledo. Alfonso VII, Berengaria, and Sancho and Fer-

nando, sons. Martín Peláez and Jimena Ectaz, ux. BN, Manuscritos, 5.790, fol. 111v. An excerpt only.

591. July 8, 1148. Salamanca. Alfonso VII. Hospitallers. Cesáreo Fernández Duro, *Memorias históricas de la ciudad de Zamora*, vol. 1 (Madrid, 1882), p. 338. A notice only.

592. August 30, 1148. *Infanta* Sancha. Churches of *infantaticum* of San Pelayo. Fernández Catón, *Colección*, 5:247–49, who calls it an original. False. Sancho confirms as "king" and Diego Muñoz is wrongly given as *merino* of León.

593. September 1, 1148. *Infanta* Sancha. Templars. García Calles, *Doña Sancha*, p. 44 and n. 126; p. 153. A notice only.

594. November 15, 1148. Alfonso VII. Monastery of Osera. AHN, Clero, Carpeta 1.509, no. 13; Códices, 15B, ff. 78v–79r; 1.008B, fol. 4v; AC Orense, Reales, no. 253. False. Both intitulation and dating formula are erroneous for this date.

595. November 30, 1148. Toledo. Alfonso VII and Sancho "king." Monastery of Valdeiglesias. Miguel Barcelo, "Dos documentos del siglo XIi," in *Miscelánea de textos medievales*, vol. 2 (Barcelona, 1974). False. The diplomatic is atypical and both Sancho and Fernando confirm as "king."

596. December 13, 1148. León. Alfonso VII. Inhabitants of Nueve Villas de Campo. Rodríguez Fernández, *Palencia*, p. 240. A fragment only and that in the vernacular.

597. 1149? Alfonso VII, ..., Sancho and Fernando, sons, and *Infanta* Sancha. Juan de Tolosa. AMon Antealtares, fragment.

598. 1149. Queen Sancha. Various inhabitants of Toledo. Hernández, *Cartularios*, pp. 69–70. Partial publication.

599. 1149. Sancho III. Monastery of Santa María Magdalena de Fuente de la Encina. Julio González, *El reino de Castilla en la época de Alfonso VIII*, 3 vols. (Madrid, 1975–1976), 2:11. Also, BN, Manuscritos, 9.194, fol. 20r. False. Sancho was not yet king.

600. January 6, 1149. Alfonso VII. Bishop of Orense and abbot of Celanova. Miguel Serrano y Sanz, ed., "Documentos del monasterio de Celanova, 975–1164," *Revista de ciencias jurídicas y sociales* 12 (1929): 45–46. AC Orense, Privilegios, 1:30. Alfonso confirms the pact between the two prelates.

601. January 18, 1149. Toledo. Alfonso VII, Berengaria, and Sancho, "king." Cathedral of Osma. BN, Manuscritos, 5.790, fol. 225r. False. Intitulation and irregular dating formula.

602. January 30, 1149. Toledo. Alfonso VII, Berengaria, and Sancho and Fernando, sons. Monastery of Cluny. Cantera Montenegro, *Colección*, pp. 80–81.

603. January 30, 1149. Alfonso VII, Berengaria, and Sancho and Fernando, "kings." Monastery of San Vicente de Pena. BN, Manuscritos, 18.387, fol. 252r–v, dated to 1139; Acad. Hist., Colección Salazar, O-16, fol. 320r–v, dated January 29, 1130; Colección Sobreira, 9-21-6-117, no pagination. False. No assigned date entirely reconciles the various elements.

604. February 8, 1149. Zorita. Alfonso VII. Men of Almoguera. Julio González, "Repoblación de las tierras de Cuenca," *AEM* 12 (1982): 184. A notice only.

605. February 15, 1149. c. Zorita. Alfonso VII, Sancho *rex*, and Fernando, son. Guter and Toda, ux. Serrano, *Colección El Moral*, pp. 58–60. Unreliable. Sancho is shown as already king with own court.

606. February 15, 1149. Madrid. Alfonso VII, Berengaria, and Sancho and Fernando, sons. Pedro *alguacil*. BN, Manuscritos, 13.093, ff. 125r–126v, dated 1148; Acad. Hist., Colección Salazar, Appendix, Legajo A, Carpeta 1, no. 6, also dated 1148. Reference to death of Berengaria makes it problematic and also requires redating.

607. February 27, 1149. Carrión. Sancho III. Monasteries of Santa María de Nájera and Cluny. Cantera Montenegro, *Colección*, 1:81–2. False. Sancho was not yet king and the deceased Bernard is given as archbishop of Toledo.

608. March 8, 1149. León. Alfonso VII. Cathedral of Santiago de Compostela. López Ferreiro, *Historia*, 4:49–50, Appendix.

609. March 10, 1149. León. Alfonso VII, Sancho and Fernando, sons, and *Infanta* Sancha. Miguel Pérez. Floriano Llorente, *Colección*, pp. 374–76.

610. March 15, 1149. Carrión. Alfonso VII, and Sancho and Fernando, sons. Pennasalbas, my butler, and Sancha Alfónsez, ux. Guillermo Castán Lanaspa and Javier Castán Lanaspa, eds., *Documentos del monasterio de Santa María de Trianos, siglos XII–XIII* (Salamanca, 1992), pp. 19–20. It is an original.

611. March 23, 1149. Burgos. Alfonso VII, and Sancho and Fernando, sons. Monastery of San Juan de Burgos. Peña Pérez, *Documentación*, pp. 33–35.

612. March 24, 1149. Burgos. Alfonso VII, and Sancho and Fernando, sons. *Concejo* de Villanueva. García Turza, *Documentación*, pp. 200–201.

613. March 25, 1149. Burgos. Alfonso VII, and Sancho and Fernando, sons. Cathedral of Calahorra. Rodríguez de Lama, *Colección*, 2:224–25. Some interpolation likely.

614. March 26, 1149. Castillo de Muñó. Alfonso VII, and Sancho and Fernando, sons. Monastery of Oña. Alamo, *Colección*, 1:245–48.

615. April 6, 1149. Zamora. Alfonso VII, and Sancho and Fernando, sons. Monastery of Clairvaux. Rodríguez de Diego, *Tumbo*, pp. 187–88.

616. April 23, 1149. Salamanca. Alfonso VII, and Sancho and Fernando, sons. Monastery of Oya. Rassow, "Urkunden," 11:103–5, from the original.

617. April 23, 1149. Salamanca. Alfonso VII, and Sancho and Fernando, sons. Aurelio Velídez. AC Túy, 3/24; Primero Libro Becerro, ff. 37v–38r. A possible original.

618. May 14, 1149. Alba de Tormes. Alfonso VII, and Sancho and Fernando, sons. Vela Gutiérrez. Rassow, "Urkunden," 11:105–6, from the original. Also, BN, Manuscritos, 3.147, fol. 403r–v.

619. May 18, 1149. León. Alfonso VII, Berengaria, and Sancho, Fernando, and Constancia, children. Pedro Domínguez and Cristina, ux. García Lobo and García Lobo, *Santa María de Arbas*, p. 55. False. Intitulation and location.

620. June 27, 1149. Toledo. Alfonso VII. Cathedral of Toledo. Hernández, *Cartularios*, p. 66, partial publication. Unreliable. Sancho confirms as "king."

621. June 27, 1149. Toledo. Alfonso VII, Sancho and Fernando, sons, and *Infanta* Sancha. Cathedral of Salamanca. Martín, Villar García, Marcos Rodríguez, and Sánchez Rodríguez, *Documentos*, pp. 100–101, call it an original. Since no notary appears that is impossible.

622. July, 1149. Alfonso VII and Sancho, king. Cathedral of Toledo. García Luján, *Privilegios*, 2:61–62. False. Diplomatic is atypical for the period.

623. September 15, 1149. Santiago de Compostela. *Infanta* Sancha. Cathedral of Santiago de Compostela. García Calles, *Doña Sancha*, pp. 153–54.

624. October 18, 1149. Toledo. Alfonso VII and Sancho, king. Cathedral of Osma. Loperráez Corvalón, *Descripción*, 3:25–26. Eccentric diplomatic.

625. December 1, 1149. *Infanta* Elvira. Monastery of Sahagún. Fernández Flórez, *Colección*, 4:218–19. Unreliable as to date. Fernando Yañez is cited as tenant of Montoro before it was captured.

626. December 7, 1149. Alfonso VII and Sancho, king, Cathedral of Segovia. Villar García, *Documentación*, p. 93. Unreliable. Eccentric diplomatic.

627. December 15, 1149. Avila. Alfonso VII and Sancho, king. Various inhabitants of Toledo. AHN, Clero, Carpeta 378, no. 2.

628. December 30, 1149. Salamanca. Alfonso VII and Sancho, king. April, "my vassal." Martín López, *Patrimonio*, p. 76.

629. 1150. Alfonso VII. Monastery of Ribas de Sil. Rassow, "Urkunden," 10:447, calls it false. Citation only. Alfonso confirms a grant of King Ordoño.

630. 1150. Toledo. Alfonso VII and Sancho, king. Various inhabitants of San Vicente near Toledo. Martín, *Origenes*, pp. 185–86.

631. 1150. Alfonso VII and Sancho, king. Monastery of Silos. Vivancos Gómez, *Documentación*, pp. 77–78. Very rough copy at best.

632. January 11, 1150. Zamora. Alfonso VII, and Sancho and Fernando, "kings," and *Infanta* Sancha. Cathedral of Astorga. Quintana Prieto, *Obispado*, pp. 680–81. AHN, Códices, 1.197B, ff. 203v–205v; BN, Manuscritos, 712, ff. 90v–91r; 6.683, fol. 44r–v: 9.194, fol. 114r; 13.093, fol. 132r–v and ff. 224v–227r. Acad. Hist., Catedrales de España, Astorga, 9–25–1-C-2, ff. 54r–55r. False. The diplomatic is irregular and Fernando is not styled "king" at this time.

633. January 19, 1150. Palencia. Alfonso VII and Raymond, archbishop of Toledo. Bishops of Astorga and Orense. Pedro Rodríguez López, *Episcopologio asturicense*, 2 vols. (Astorga, 1907), 1:549–50. Also, BN, Manuscritos, 712, ff. 86v–87r; 6.683, fol. 46r–v; 9.194, fol. 113r–v; 13.093, fol. 133r–v; Acad. Hist., Catedrales de España, Astorga, 9–25–1-C-2; ff. 56r–57r; and ff. 197r–198r.

634. January 30, 1150. Burgos. Alfonso VII and Sancho, king. Monastery of San Isidro de Dueñas. BN, Manuscritos, 720, fol. 282v; 6.683, fol. 49r–v; 13.093, fol. 136r–v.

635. February 12, 1150. Burgos. Alfonso VII, Berengaria!, and Sancho, son. Cathedral of Segovia. Villar García, *Documentación*, pp. 93–94, who dates it incorrectly to February 6. False on the basis of the intitulation.

636. February 12, 1150. Burgos. Alfonso VII and Sancho, king. Cathedral of Segovia. Ibid., p. 95, who calls it an original. It is not. Guter Fernández confirms as *alférez*, a post he never held.

637. February, 14–28, 1150. Segovia. Alfonso VII ....? Alvar Pérez. Rassow, "Urkunden," 11:106–7, who calls the fragment an original.

638. February 14, 1150. León. Alfonso VII, and Sancho and Fernando, sons. Monastery of Santa María de Quintanajuar. Alamo, *Colección*, 1:248–49. Also, AHN, Clero, Carpeta 351, nos. 9, 10, 11, 12, 13; Códices, 279B, ff. 7r–8r. False. Location and Fernando confirms as king.

639. February 22, 1150. Peral de Arlanza. Alfonso VII and children. Bishops of Lugo and Oviedo. Francsco Vázquez Saco, "Un diploma de Alfonso VII," *BCM Lugo* 2 (1947): 286–87, from what he called an original. It is not for the text was misdated to 1151.

640. March 1, 1150. Burgos. Alfonso VII. Cathedral of Orense. *Coleccion diplomática*, 1:36–38. AC Orense, Reales, no. 23.

641. March 1, 1150. Burgos. Alfonso VII. Cathedral of Oviedo. Vigil, *Asturias*, 1:89. Notice only.

642. March 1, 1150. Burgos. Alfonso VII and Sancho, king. Monastery of San Cristóbal de Ibeas. Garrido Garrido, *Documentación*, pp. 226–28. Very rough copy, probably interpolated.

643. March 2, 1150. Alfonso VII and Sancho, king. Monastery of Oña. Alamo, *Colección*, 1:249–50. Very rough copy.

644. March 2, 1150? Alfonso VII and Sancho, king. Monastery of Oña. *ES*, 49:339. Another rough copy possibly of this date.

645. March 11, 1150. Carrión? Alfonso VII and Sancho, king. Cathedral of Osma. Loperráez Corvalón, *Descripción*, 3:26–27. Also, AHN, Microfilmas, Osma, Caja 1.132, no. 48, cites Carrión.

646. March 18, 1150. Segovia. Alfonso VII and Sancho, king. Guter Pérez. AHN, Códices, 994B, fol. 14r. Dating formula is defective.

647. March 22, 1150. Toledo. Alfonso VII and Sancho, king. *Concejo* of San Miguel. Rassow, "Urkunden," 11:107–8. Probable original.

648. March 22, 1150. Toledo. Alfonso VII, and Sancho and Fernando, sons. Hospitallers. Ayala Martínez, *Libro*, pp. 209–10. Unreliable. The dating formula is seriously defective.

649. March 22, 1150. Toledo. Alfonso VII and Sancho, king. Focen el Bracadón. Hernández, *Cartularios*, pp. 70–71, partially published.

650. March 22, 1150. Toledo. Alfonso VII and Sancho, king. Inhabitants of Los Alamos south of Toledo. Ibid., pp. 71–72. The dating formula is defective.

651. March 23, 1150. Toledo. Alfonso VII and Sancho, king. Sancho and Pedro, nephews of a canon of Toledo. Ibid., p. 73.

652. March 29, 1150. Alfonso VII and Sancho, king. Guter Pérez de Reinoso. Ayala Martínez, *Libro*, p. 211, improperly dated to April 10.

653. March 30, 1150. Noez. Alfonso VII and Sancho, king. Guter Pérez de Reinoso. Ibid., p. 210.

654. April 6, 1150. Toledo. Alfonso VII and Sancho, king. Rodrigo Muñoz. Martín, *Orígenes*, pp. 184–85.

655. April 8, 1150. Toledo. Alfonso VII and Sancho, king. Pelayo Pérez de Frómista and Pedro Díaz de Marros. AHN, Clero, Carpeta 417, no. 8. Rassow, "Urkunden," 10:450, called it false. Possibly because of a grant of the same places in no. 647 above.

656. April 9, 1150. Toledo. Alfonso VII and Sancho, king. Cathedral of Santiago de Compostela. López Ferreiro, *Historia*, 4:52–66, Appendix. Also, AC Compostela, copy Tumbo A, ff. 127v–129r. False. Part of the literature of the controversial "votos" to the shrine of Santiago.

657. April 19, 1150. Toledo. Alfonso VII, sons, daughters, and kin. Monastery of San Martín de Castañeda. Rodríguez González, *Tumbo*, pp. 52–54. Suspect. Fernando confirms as king.

658. April 20, 1150. Toledo. Alfonso VII and Sancho, king. Cathedral of

Sigüenza. Minguella y Arnedo, *Historia*, 1:385–86. Also, BN, Manuscritos, 13.073, ff. 212r–213r.

659. April 22, 1150. Toledo. Alfonso VII and Sancho, king. Cathedral of Zamora. AC Zamora, Tumbo Negro, fol. 2r–v; BN, Manuscritos, 714, ff. 165r–166r, and 9.880. fol. 407v, both dated April 18; Acad. Hist., Colección Salazar, M-179, fol. 19r–v.

660. April 25, 1150. Toledo. Alfonso VII and Sancho, king. Cathedral of Sigüenza, *concejos* of Medinaceli, Atienza, Almazán, and Ayllón. Minguella y Arnedo, *Historia*, 1:386. Also, BN, Manuscritos, 13.073, ff. 206r–207r.

661. April 29, 1150. *Infanta* Elvira. Monastery of San Pedro de Montes. Augusto Quintana Prieto, ed., *Tumbo viejo de San Pedro de Montes* (León, 1971), pp. 271–73.

662. May 1150. Gauceleto. Alfonso VII, sons, daughters, and kin. Monastery of Santa María de Sar. Archivo universitario de Compostela, Clero, Fondo Blanco Cicerón, no. 125. Poorly preserved and date is incomplete. Fernando confirms as king.

663. May 1, 1150. Daraferza. Alfonso VII, and Sancho and Fernando, sons. Pelayo Pérez. AMon Santo Domingo de Silos de Toledo, Signatura 2/1, a possible original; AHN, Registro de Escrituras, 11, fol. 24, dated April 28. Fernando confirms as king.

664. May 22, 1150. Córdoba. Alfonso VII and Sancho, king. Pedro Alva de San Justo. Hernández, *Cartularios*, pp. 75–76, partial publication.

665. June 3, 1150. Córdoba. Alfonso VII. Pelayo Calvo. Ibid., pp. 76–77, from a possible original. Partial publication.

666. July 23, 1150. Córdoba. Alfonso VII and children. Pelayo Captivo. Muñoz y Romero, *Fueros*, p. 165. Also BN, Manuscritos, 712, fol. 91r; 6.683, fol. 47r–v; 13.093, fol. 134r–v.

667. July 26, 1150. Córdoba. Alfonso VII and Sancho, king. Fernando Pérez. Ledesma Rubio, *Cartulario*, pp. 273–74.

668. August 15, 1150. Jaén. Alfonso VII and Sancho, king. Vermudo Vermúdez. Amparo Valcarce, *Dominio*, pp. 109–10, who calls it an original. It is not. The hand is not that of the notary Juan Fernández.

669. August 15, 1150. Jaén. Alfonso VII. Juan Achui, my cook. Fernández Catón, *Colección*, 5:254–55, who calls it an original.

670. August 23, 1150. Córdoba. Alfonso VII. Fernando Gutiérrez. BN, Manuscritos, 9.880, fol. 357r–v; Acad. Hist., Colección Salazar, Appendix, Legajo B, Carpeta 3, no. 12. Possible bad date.

671. August 23, 1150. Baeza. Alfonso VII, children, and kin. Monastery of Silos. Vivancos Gómez, *Documentación*, pp. 75–76.

672. September 1, 1150. Toledo. Alfonso VII and Fernando, king. Ordoño Sánchez. Ayala Martínez, *Libro*, p. 212. The intitulation is unusual but the diplomatic is otherwise unexceptionable.

673. September 10, 1150. Alfonso VII and Sancho, king. *Concejo* of Maqueda supposedly confirms the agreement of April 9, 1150. See no. 656 above.

674. September 14, 1150? Toledo. Alfonso VII .... fideli militi. Acad. Hist., Colección Salazar, I-38, fol. 310v. A fragment perhaps of this year. Dating formula is irregular and Alfonso confirms as "rex."

675. October 25, 1150. Toledo. Alfonso VII and Sancho, king. Domingo Domínguez. Hernández, *Cartularios*, pp. 77–78, partial publication.

676. October 26, 1150. Toledo. Alfonso VII, and Sancho and Fernando, sons. Domingo Cídez. Ibid., pp. 78–79, who calls it an original. Only Sancho confirms and then as "king."

677. October 27, 1150. Regina Sancha. Monastery of San Isidoro of León. García Calles, *Doña Sancha*, p. 155, who fails to note no. 151, a copy dated to 1149. No. 150 is probably an original.

678. December 3, 1150? .....? .....? AD Compostela, Fondo San Martín, Priorato de Sar, Carpeta 40, no. 10. Fragment of a private document confirmed by Fernando as king.

679. December 13, 1150. Segovia. Alfonso VII, children, and kin. Cathedral of Segovia. Villar García, *Documentación*, pp. 96–97, from what he calls the original. Its orthography makes that dubious.

680. December 28, 1150. Logroño. Alfonso VII, and Sancho and Fernando, sons. Martín and Juan. Julián García Sáinz y Baranda, "El monasterio de monjes bernardos de Santa María de Rioseco," *BIFG* 156 (1961): 640. Also, AHN, Clero, Carpeta 351, nos. 7, 8; Códices, 91B, fol. 1r–v, dated December 28, 1140; 279B, 6r. Unreliable. Its dating formula puts the marriage of Sancho of Castilla and Blanca of Navarra in the past.

681. January 10, 1151. Alfonso VII. Inhabitants of Cerezo. Marino Pérez Avellaneda, *Cerezo de Río Tirón* (Madrid, 1983), pp. 233–34. This heavily interpolated copy is incorrectly dated to 1146.

682. January 21, 1151. Burgos. Alfonso VII, children, and kin. Calvet, "my vassal." Eliseo Sáinz Ripa, ed., *Colección diplomática de las colegiatas de Albelda y Logroño, Tomo 1: 924–1399* (Logroño, 1981), pp. 37–38. A probable original.

683. January 27, 1151. Tudején. Alfonso VII and Sancho, king. Count Ramon Berenguer IV. Francisco M. Rosell, ed., *Liber Feudorum Maior* (Barcelona, 1945), pp. 39–42, with the incorrect date of 1150. The document follows the chancery form of Barcelona.

684. January 30, 1151. Calahorra. Alfonso VII, children and kin. Pons de Minerva. José María Canal Sánchez-Pagín, "Documentos del monasterio

de Carrizo de la Ribera (León) en la Colección Salazar de la Real Academia de Historia," *AL* 32 (1978): 392–93. Also, BN, Manuscritos, 3.147,
ff. 392v–393r; 9.880, ff. 344–45. The dating formula of the copies incorrectly give 1146.

685. January 30, 1151. Calahorra. Alfonso VII, children and kin. Monastery
of Santa María de Cántavos. José Antonio García Luján, ed. *Cartulario del
monasterio de Santa María de Huerta* (Soria, 1981) pp. 3–4.

686. January 31, 1151. Alfonso VII and Sancho, king. Monastery of San Pedro
de Arlanza. Serrano, *Cartulario de Arlanza*, pp. 197–98. Unreliable. Prepared outside the royal chancery at least.

687. February 1, 1151. Calahorra. Alfonso VII, children and kin. Martín Fernández de Calahorra. AC Pamplona, vol. 31, Arca 5. It is an original.

688. February 4, 1151. Nájera. Alfonso VII, Sancho, king, children, and kin.
Monastery of Santa María de Nájera. Cantera Montenegro, *Colección*,
2:231–32.

689. February 10, 1151. Nájera. Alfonso VII, children, and kin. Sancha. Rodríguez de Lama, *Colección*, 2:233.

690. February 12, 1151. Burgos. Alfonso VII and Sancho, king. Monastery of
San Nicolas de Orteja. BN, Manuscritos, 5.790, fol. 169r–v.

691. March 1151. Alfonso VII. Monastery of Fontevraud. Serrano, *Cartulario
de Vega*, pp. 68–69. Also, AHN, Clero, Carpeta 3.427, no. 12. False. The
diplomatic is that of a private document.

692. March 1151. Villafranca. Alfonso VII and Sancho, king. Juan de Ortega
and his nephew, Martín. BN, Manuscritos, 5.790, fol. 170r. A notice only.

693. March 1151. Villafranca. Alfonso VII and Sancho, king. Cristóbal. Ibid.

694. March 12, 1151. Alfonso VII, Sancho and Fernando, kings, Constancia
and Sancha, queens, and *Infanta* Sancha. Monastery of Santa María de
Lapedo. Floriano Cumbreño, *Colección*, pp. 100–107. False. Diplomatic is
thoroughly unreliable.

695. March 14, 1151. Palencia. Alfonso VII, children, and kin. Monasteries
of San Isidro de Dueñas and Cluny. BN, Manuscritos, 720, ff. 279r–280r;
6.683, fol. 51r–v; 13.093, fol. 138r–v.

696. March 14, 1151. Palencia. Alfonso VII. Monastery of Barrantes. *ES*
22:270–72. Also, AC Túy, 3/7; Libro Becerro Primero, ff. 28v–29r. Rough
copy with errors in those who confirm.

697. April 8, 1151. Toledo. Alfonso VII, Rica, and Sancho and Fernando,
sons. Monastery of Sobrado. Loscertales de García de Valdeavellano, *Tumbos*, 2:28–29. Also, AHN, Sellos, Carpeta 1, no. 2; Clero, Carpeta 526, nos.
18 and 19. False. Rica was not yet married to Alfonso.

698. April 10, 1151. *Infanta* Sancha. Cathedral of Zamora. AC Zamora, Tumbo Negro, fol. 2r; BN, Manuscritos, 714, fol. 165v, dated 1150.

699. May 12, 1151. Toledo. Alfonso VII, children, and kin. Monastery of Santa María de Osera. AHN, Códices, 15B, fol. 80v; 1.008B, ff. 4v–5r. Sancho and Fernando confirm as kings.

700. May 12, 1151. Toledo. Alfonso VII, children, and kin. Monastery of Santa María de Osera. AHN, Clero, Carpeta 1.509, no. 16. AC Orense, Reales, no. 255.

701. May 14, 1151. Toledo. Alfonso VII, and Sancho and Fernando, sons. Monastery of San Miguel de Caneles. Portela Silva, *Colonización*, p. 186, from a late copy misdated to 1131. Also, AC Túy, 3/2, a probable original but badly preserved. Sancho and Fernando confirm as kings.

702. July 11, 1151. Jaén. Alfonso VII, and Sancho and Fernando, sons. Abd al-Aziz. AHN, Registro de Escrituras, 9:13; BN, Manuscritos, 6,683, fol. 52r–v; 13.093, fol. 144r–v. Sancho and Fernando confirm as kings.

703. August 4, 1151. Jaén. Alfonso VII, and Sancho and Fernando, sons. Osorio Pérez. Fernndez Catón, *Colección*, 5:261–63, from the original. Sancho and Fernando confirm as kings.

704. August 8, 1151. Sancho III. Monastery of San Pedro de Arlanza. González, *Reino*, 2:13–15, who regards it as unreliable.

705. August 24, 1151. Jaén. Alfonso VII, and Sancho and Fernando, sons. Various inhabitants of Toledo. Hernández, *Cartularios*, pp. 82–83, partial publication.

706. August 24, 1151. Jaén. Alfonso VII, and Sancho and Fernando, sons. Jimeno "scout." Ibid., pp. 81–82, who calls it an original.

707. August 25, 1151. Baeza. Alfonso VII, and Sancho and Fernando, sons. García Pérez and Teresa ux. Aurelio Calvo, *El monasterio de Gradefes* (León, 1936), p. 166. AD León, Gradefes, no. 66, a probable original. Sancho and Fernando confirm as kings.

708. August 27, 1151. Baeza? Alfonso VII, and Sancho and Fernando, sons. Alvaro Rodríguez. Portela Silva, *Colonización*, p. 157. Also, Acad. Hist, Colección Salazar, O-8, fol. 65r with date of August 18. Sancho and Fernando confirm as kings.

709. September 28, 1151. *Infanta* Elvira. Pedro Díaz and Marina Froilaz, ux. Fernández Catón, *Colección*, 5:263–64.

710. October 6, 1151. Toledo. Alfonso VII, and Sancho and Fernando, sons. Fernando Odoarez. Martín, *Orígenes*, pp. 187–88, from the original. Also, Acad. Hist., Colección Salazar, Appendix, Legajo B, Carpeta 9, no. 14. Sancho and Fernando confirm as kings.

711. October 8, 1151. Toledo. Alfonso VII, Berengaria, and Sancho and Fernando, sons. Velasco Pérez. AHN, Códices, 1.197B, ff. 277v–279r. Obvious problem with intitulation. Sancho and Fernando confirm as kings.

712. October 21, 1151. Queen? Sancha. Monastery of Carvajal. García Calles, *Doña Sancha*, p. 156. A citation only.

713. October 27, 1151. Queen Sancha. Monastery of San Isidoro of León. Amparo Valcarce, *Dominio*, pp. 110–11, who calls it an original. Also, ASI, Reales, no. 154.

714. October 27, 1151. Toledo. Alfonso VII, and Sancho and Fernando, sons. Pedro Burrín. AHN, Registro de Escrituras, 9:25. Very rough copy. Sancho confirms as king.

715. November 1151. Alfonso VII. Monastery of San Cristóbal de Ibeas. Gonzalo Martínez, "Diplomatario de San Cristóbal de Ibeas," *BIFG* 55 (1975): 699. False. Alfonso is cited as "rex" as well as general diplomatic problems.

716. November 5, 1151. Toledo. Alfonso VII and Sancho, king. Cathedral of Toledo. Hernández, *Cartularios*, p. 83, partial publication.

717. December 5, 1151. Toledo. Alfonso VII, children, and kin. Monastery of Santa María de Armenteira. AHN, Clero, Carpeta 1.749, no. 3. Sancho and Fernando confirm as kings.

718. December 6, 1151. *Infanta* Elvira. Cathedral of Astorga. BN, Manuscritos, 4.357, fol. 15r. A notice only.

719. December 15, 1151. Toledo. Alfonso VII. Monastery of Santa María de Arbas. García Lobos and García Lobos, *Santa María de Arbas*, p. 56. A notice only.

720. December 18, 1151. Toledo. Alfonso VII, and Sancho and Fernando, kings, and kin. Monastery of San Juan de Corias. Floriano Cumbreño, *Libro Registro*, 1:125–26. The text is wrongly dated to 1150.

721. December 26, 1151. Toledo. Alfonso VII, children, and kin. Monastery of Santa María de Sobrado. Loscertales de García de Valdeavellano, *Tumbos*, 2:79–80.

722. December 27, 1151. Toledo. Alfonso VII, and Sancho and Fernando, sons. Rodrigo Peláez. Ayala Martínez, *Libro*, pp. 215–17. Sancho and Fernando confirm as kings.

723. December 27, 1151. Toledo. Alfonso VII, and Sancho and Fernando, sons. Rodrigo Rodríguez. Ibid., pp. 217–19. False. Archbishop Pedro of Compostela, dead in 1149, confirms.

724. 1152. Alfonso VII, Rica, and Sancho and Fernando, kings, and Constancia and Sancha, queens. Monastery of Santa María de Retuerta. AHN,

Clero, Carpeta 1.647, no. 10; Códices, 994B, ff. 12v–13r; BN, Manuscritos, 841, ff. 362v–363v; 9.194, 22r–23r. False. Intitulation is improper for that date and several of those who confirm are mutually incompatible.

725. 1152. Alfonso VII. Joao, archbishop of Braga. Lucas Alvarez, *Tumbo*, pp. 476–77. Alfonso advises Braga of the election of Bishop Juan of Lugo.

726. January 8, 1152. Alfonso VII, and Sancho and Fernando, kings. Monastery of San Martín de Pinario. *Colección de Galicia*, 1:435–37. Also, AHN, Códices, 258B, ff. 14v–5r. False. The diplomátic is atypical for the date.

727. January 18, 1152. Almazán. Sancho III. Cathedral of Calahorra. González, *Reino*, 2:15–16, who dates it to 1152 despite the 1157 given in all existing copies. False. Those who confirm would be incompatible with either date.

728. January 31, 1152. Toledo. Alfonso VII, children, and kin. Monastery of Santa María de Sotosalbos. María de la Soterrana Martín Postigo, *Santa María de Cardaba, priorato de Arlanza y granja de Sacramenia* (Valladolid, 1979), pp. 121–22, dated improperly to 1151.

729. February 3, 1152. León. Alfonso VII. Cathedral of Astorga. BN, Manuscritos, 4.357, fol. 112r. A notice only. Suspect because of place of issue.

730. February 24, 1152. Valladolid. Alfonso VII, children, and kin. Monastery of Silos. Vivancos Gómez, *Documentación*, pp. 78–79.

731. February 27, 1152. Valladolid. Alfons VII, and Sancho and Fernando, sons. Monastery of San Cristóbal and Pedro Gutiérrez, canon of Burgos. Garrido Garrido, *Documentación*, pp. 229–30. Also, BN, Manuscritos, 6.683, fol. 17r–v. Sancho confirms as king.

732. March 2, 1152. Valladolid. Alfonso VII, and Sancho and Fernando, sons. Monastery of San Payo de Antealtares. ARG, Reales, no. 5, an original but almost illegible. The dating formula reads, "when King Sancho, the emperor's son, was armed there." Sancho and Fernando confirm as kings.

733. March 3, 1152. Valladolid. Alfonso VII, children, and kin. Monastery of Santa María de Carracedo. AC Astorga, Registro de Escrituras, fol. 22r. Dated "quinto nonas Feb." Excerpt only. Sancho and Fernando confirm as kings.

734. March 5, 1152. Valladolid. Alfonso VII, Sancho, king, children, and kin. Monastery of Sahagún. Fernández Flórez, *Colección*, 4:230–33, from the original. Sancho confirms as king.

735. March 5, 1152. Valladolid. Alfonso VII, children, and kin. Monastery of San Isidro de Dueñas. BN, Manuscritos, 720, fol. 283r–v; 6.683, fol. 53r–v; 13.093, fol. 143r–v; Acad. Hist., Colección Salazar, O-17, fol. 786r–v. Sancho confirms as king.

736. March 5, 1152. Valladolid. Alfonso VII, Sancho king, and children. Men

of Burgos. Muñoz y Romero, *Fueros*, p. 268. See also Bonachia Hernando and Pardos Martínez, *Catálogo*, 1:52, and Acad. Hist., Colección Salazar, O-22, ff. 248v–249r.

737. March 7, 1152. Valladolid. Alfonso VII, children, and kin. Monastery of Santa María de Montederramo. Rassow, "Urkunden," ii:110–2, from the original. AHN, Clero, Carpeta 1.481, no. 10; 1.482, no. 12. Sancho confirms as king.

738. March 11, 1152. Valladolid. Alfonso VII, children, and kin. Monastery of San Isidoro de León. Amparo Valcarce, *Dominio*, pp. 111–12, with the erroneous date of February 11, and calling no. 155 the original. I believe that no. 156 may be. Sancho and Fernando confirm as kings.

739. March 14, 1152. Tordesillas. Sancho III. Juan de Quintanaortuño. González, *Reino*, 2:16–18. Perhaps the first authentic and properly dated diploma of Sancho.

740. March 23, 1152. Salamanca. Alfonso VII, children, and kin. Cathedral of Salamanca. Martín, Villar García, Marcos Rodríguez, and Sánchez Rodríguez, *Documentos*, pp. 103–4, from the original. Also, BN, Manuscritos, 6.683, fol. 21r–v, with date of 1154. Sancho and Fernando confirms as kings.

741. March 24, 1152. Salamanca. Alfonso VII, children, and kin. Monastery of San Martín de Castañeda. Rodríguez González, *Tumbo*, pp. 60–61, dated improperly to 1153. Sancho and Fernando confirm as kings.

742. March 25, 1152. Salamanca. Alfonso VII, children, and kin. Monastery of San Martín de Castañeda. Ibid., pp. 58–60, dated improperly to 1153. Also, BN, Manuscritos, 712, fol. 375r; 13.093, fol. 151r–v; 18.382, fol. 46r–v and fol. 61r–v; Acad. Hist., Colección Salazar, O-16, fol. 465r, dated to 1126. Sancho and Fernando confirm as kings.

743. March 25, 1152. Salamanca. Alfonso VII, children, and kin. Monastery of San Martín de Castañeda. Ibid., pp. 55–56, following the text and dating it improperly to January 25, 1153. Also, AHN, Clero, Carpeta 3.563, no. 9; BN, Manuscritos, 18.382, ff. 50v–1r. Sancho and Fernando confirm as kings.

744. April, 1152. Toledo. Alfonso VII, and Sancho and Fernando, kings. Julián Pérez. Martín, *Orígenes*, pp. 188–89. Also, Acad. Hist., Colección Salazar, Appendix, Legajo B, Carpeta 10, no. 98. The date in the text is 1142 but the diplomatic requires 1152.

745. April 12, 1152. Alfonso VII, Rica, and Sancho and Fernando, sons, and Queen Sancha. Pedro Martínez. Amparo Valcarce, *Dominio*, pp. 112–13, who calls it an original but the script makes it a copy at best. Unreliable. The diplomatic would require a date at least two years later.

746. April 30, 1152. Sancho III. Monastery of San Salvador El Moral. González, *Reino*, 2:18–19, who apparently accepts it as an original. False. There is no other evidence for Sancho's having a chancellor at this early date.

747. May 1152. Toledo. Queen Sancha. Cathedral of Sigüenza. García Calles, *Doña Sancha*, pp. 153 and 160–61. The text is dated only to 1152 but Bishop Pedro only appears in that see in the spring. Sancho and Fernando confirm as kings and Constancia as queen. Unreliable.

748. May 1, 1152. Toledo. Alfonso VII, and Sancho and Fernando, sons. *Concejo* of Madrid. Timoteo Domingo Palacio, ed., *Documentos del Archivo General de la Villa de Madrid*, vol. 1 (Madrid, 1889), pp. 13–15. A possible original. Sancho and Fernando confirm as kings.

749. May 20, 1152. Toledo. Alfonso VII, and Sancho and Fernando, sons. Monastery of San Julián de Moraime. *Colección de Galicia*, 1:80–81. Archivo Biblioteca Seminario de Compostela, Fondo San Martín, copy of 1721. Sancho and Fernando confirm as kings.

750. May 27, 1152. Soria. Sancho III. Monastery of San Pedro de Arlanza. González, *Reino*, 2:19–21.

751. July 12, 1152. Queen Sancha. Pedro de Tolosa. Martín, *Orígenes*, p. 189. Sancho and Fernando confirm as kings and Constancia as queen.

752. July 24, 1152. Baeza. Alfonso VII, and Sancho and Fernando, sons. Monastery of San Julián de Quintana de Zepeda. BN, Manuscritos, 9.880, fol. 327r–v, dated to 1155; 13.093, fol. 146v, dated to 1153. Diplomatic requires 1152. Sancho and Fernando confirm as kings.

753. July 29, 1152. *Infanta* Sancha. Arias, archdeacon. García Calles, *Doña Sancha*, p. 48, no. 156, citation only. AHN, Ord. Mil., Carpeta 373, no. 5. Constancia confirms as queen.

754. August? 1152. Júcar. Alfonso VII, and Sancho and Fernando, sons. Martín Ordoñez and Sancha Martínez, ux. Acad. Hist., Colección Salazar, I-38, fol. 310r–v, a fragment. Antonio Pareja Serrada, ed., *Diplomática arriacense* (Guadalajara, 1921), pp. 37–38.

755. August 6, 1152. Toledo. Alfonso VII, children, and kin. Pelayo Pérez. Suárez de Alarcón, *Relaciones*, pp. 13–14, Appendix. Also, AHN, Ord. Mil., Carpeta 417, no. 10; Registro de Escrituras, 9, fol. 29r–v; Acad. Hist., Colección Salazar, I-38, ff. 283v–284v. The text is date to 1153 but the diplomatic indicates 1152.

756. August 28, 1152. Queen Sancha. Pedro Bruno. Fernández Catón, *Colección*, 5:267–68, who calls it an original. Sancho and Fernando confirm as kings and Constancia as queen.

757. August 28, 1152. Queen Sancha. Monastery of Carracedo. García Calles, *Doña Sancha*, pp. 156–57.

758. September 5, 1152. Uclés. Alfonso VII, and Sancho and Fernando, kings. Pelayo Taulatello. Fernández Catón, *Colección*, 5:268–69, who calls it an original.

759. September 9, 1152. Toledo. Alfonso VII, and Sancho and Fernando, kings. Melendo Peláez. AC Túy, 3/5, an original; Primero Libro Becerro, fol. 182v.

760. September 13, 1152. Toledo. Alfonso VII, children, and kin. Cathedral of Zamora. AC Zamora, Tumbo Negro, ff. 2v–3r; Tumbo Blanco, fol. 61r. Sancho and Fernando confirm as kings.

761. September 18, 1152. Toledo. Alfonso VII, and Sancho and Fernando, kings. Pedro Domínguez de Nava. Fernández Catón, *Colección*, 5:269–71, who calls it an original.

762. September 18, 1152. Toledo. Alfonso VII, children, and kin. Monastery of Santa María de Sobrado. Loscertales de García de Valdeavellano, *Tumbos*, 2:71–72, 77–78, and 264–65. Sancho and Fernando confirm as kings.

763. October 4, 1152. San Esteban de Gormaz. Alfonso VII and Sancho, king. Monastery of Santa María de Montesacro. AHN, Microfilmas, Burgos de Osma, Caja 1.132, no. 39; BN, Manuscritos, 6.683, fol. 27r–v; 13.093, ff. 169v–170r. Loperráez Corvalón, *Descripción*, 3:31–32.

764. October 18, 1152. Guadalajara. Alfonso VII, and Sancho and Fernando, kings. Pons de Cabrera. AHN, Ord. Mil., Carpeta 417, no. 10; Registro de Escrituras, 9, fol. 27r–v. Pareja Serreda, *Diplomática*, pp. 99–100. False. Diplomatic elements are incompatible.

765. October 18, 1152. Guadalajara. Alfonso VII, and Sancho and Fernando, kings. Galindo. AHN, Registro de Escrituras, 9: fol. 28r–v.; Acad. Hist., Colección Salazar, I-38, ff. 282v–283r. Ibid., pp. 101–2. False. Shares almost all elements of no. 764 above.

766. October 23, 1152. Soria. Alfonso VII, and Sancho and Fernando, sons. García García. Rassow, "Urkunden," 11:112–13, from the original. AHN, Clero, Carpeta 351, no. 6 and no. 14, the original; Códices, 91B, fol. 44r–v; 279B, fol. 1r. Sancho and Fernando confirm as kings.

767. October 29, 1152. *Infanta* Sancha. Monastery of San Pelayo de Oviedo. Fernández Conde, Torrente Fernández, and Menéndez, *Monasterio*, 1:50–51, who call it an original. Obviously not a chancery product.

768. November 1, 1152. Alfonso VII. Monastery of Santa María de Monfero. Loscertales de García de Valdeavellano, *Tumbos*, 1:176–77. Also AHN, Códices, 259B, fol. 9r–v. Sancho and Fernando confirm as kings. False. The intitulation of Alfonso and his sons is atypical.

769. November 5, 1152. Queen Sancha. Monastery of San Vicente de Oviedo.

Floriano Llorente, *Colección*, pp. 388–90, who calls it an original. Sancho and Fernando confirm as kings and Urraca and Constancia as queens.

770. November, 15, 1152. Agreda. Alfonso VII and Sancho, king. Community of nuns. Rodríguez de Lama, *Colección*, 2:238–39.

771. November 25, 1152. Castrojeriz. Alfonso VII, Rica, and Sancho and Fernando, sons. Cathedral of Burgos. Serrano, *Obispado*, 3:194–95, from the original. Sancho and Fernando confirm as kings.

772. November 29, 1152. Queen Sancha. Cathedral of Palencia. Abajo Martín, *Documentación*, pp. 99–101. Dating formula cites Rica as wife and empress of Alfonso.

773. December 4, 1152. Carrión. Alfonso VII, Rica, children, and kin. Monastery of Santa María de Nájera. Cantera Montenegro, *Colección*, pp. 86–87, from the original. Sancho and Fernando confirm as kings.

774. December 9, 1152. Carrión. Alfonso VII, Rica, children, and kin. Monastery of Celanova. AHN, Clero, Carpeta 1.431, no. 14; Sellos, Carpeta 7, no. 6.

775. December 11, 1152. Grajal. Queen Sancha. Monastery of Sahagún and *concejo* of Grajal. Fernández Flórez, *Colección*, 4:233–42, from what he calls the original. Not a chancery product. Sancha mediates a dispute between the two.

776. December 18, 1152. Sahagún. Alfonso VII. Monastery of Sahagún and burghers of Sahagún. Ibid., 4:242–47, who calls them originals. Since no chancellor or notary appears it is unlikely that they are. Alfonso settles a dispute between the two. Also AHN, Clero, Carpeta 921, no. 24; BN, Manuscritos, 772, ff. 308r–311v.

777. December 26. 1152. Palencia. Alfonso VII, Rica, Sancho and Fernando, sons. Monastery of Santa María de Sobrado. Rassow, "Urkunden," 11:114–15, who called it an original. Also, AHN, Clero, Carpeta 527, nos. 1 and 2; Códices, 976B, 2:11r.

778. 1153. Alfonso VII, Rica, Sancho and Fernando, sons?, and Queen Sancha. Monastery of San Isidoro de León. BN, Manuscritos, 5.790, fol. 122v. An excerpt only.

779. 1153. Toledo. Alfonso VII, Rica, and Sancho and Fernando, sons. Guter Rodríguez. AHN, Registro de Escrituras, 9, fol. 5r–v; BN, Manuscritos, 6.683, fol. 18r–v, dated to 1152; 13.093, 146r–v; Acad. Hist., Colección Salazar, I-38, fol. 263r–v.

780. January 22, 1153. Nájera. Sancho III. Pedro Martínez. Rodríguez de Lama, *Colección*, 2:242–43.

781. January 30, 1153. Alfonso VII, Rica, and Sancho and Fernando, sons.

Cathedral of Toledo. García Luján, *Privilegios*, 2:48–51, with text date of 1142. But see Hernández, *Cartularios*, pp. 84–85, who gives 1152 which is also unacceptable for Rica. Most probably it is simply false.

782. February 10, 1153. Toledo. Alfonso VII, Rica, and Sancho and Fernando, sons. Pedro Apulichen. BN, Manuscritos, 13.093, ff. 41r–42r.

783. April 6, 1153. Queen Sancha. Monastery of San Martín de Castañeda. Rodríguez González, *Tumbo*, pp. 62–63.

784. April 12, 1153. Alfonso VII, Rica, and children. *Concejo* de Toro. AMun-Toro, Libro Becerro, ff. 49v–50r. Antonio Gómez de la Torre, *Corografía de la provincia de Toro* (Madrid, 1802), pp. 64–66. Rough copy.

785. April 20, 1153. Valladolid. Alfonso, Rica, and Sancho and Fernando, sons. Monastery of Santa María de Sobrado. Rassow, "Urkunden," 11:115–16, from what he called an original. AHN, Clero, Carpeta 527, no. 4; Códices, 976B, 2:12v–13r. Suspect for too early citation of Juan Fernández as chancellor.

786. April 28, 1153. Cuéllar. Alfonso VII, Rica, and Sancho and Fernando, sons. Monastery of Santa María de Sacramenia. Rassow, "Urkunden," 11:117–18, an original. Also, AHN, Códices, 104B, fol. 3r.

787. May 15, 1153. c. Medina. Alfonso VII, Berengaria, and Sancho and Fernando, sons. Monastery of San Payo de Antealtares. AHN, Clero, Carpeta 518, nos. 17 and 18; Microfilmas, Biblioteca Seminario de Santiago de Compostela, Rollo 5.380; Acad. Hist., Colección Sobreira, 9-21-6-117, no pagination. False? Citation of Berengaria.

788. June 2, 1153. Soria. Alfonso VII, Rica, and Sancho and Fernando, sons. Monastery of Santa María de Fitero. Monterde Albiac, *Colección*, pp. 381–82.

789. June 17, 1153. Palencia. Sancho III. Clerics of Grañon. González, *Reino*, 2:21–22.

790. June 26, 1153. Segovia. Alfonso VII, Rica, and Sancho and Fernando, sons. Monastery of Santa María de Batres. Hernández, *Cartularios*, pp. 88–89, partial publication.

791. July 20, 1153. Carrión. Sancho III. Monastery of Santa María de Nájera. González, *Reino*, 2:22–3.

792. July 20, 1153. Carrión. Alfonso VII, Rica, and Sancho and Fernando, sons. Men of Villa Zelame. AHN, Clero, Carpeta 825, no. 4.

793. July 23, 1153. Carrión. Sancho III. Diego Sesgúdez. Fernández Flórez, *Colección*, 4:248–49, who calls it an original.

794. July 28, 1153. Sahagún. Alfonso VII, Rica, children, kin, and *Infanta* Sancha. Monastery of San Isidoro de León. Amparo Valcarce, *Dominio*,

pp. 114–15, who calls it an original. The use this late of the tile *infanta* for Sancha makes it suspect.

795. August 1, 1153. Zamora. Alfonso VII, Rica, and Sancho and Fernando, sons, and *Infanta* Sancha. Cathedral of Santiago de Compostela. AC Compostela, Tumbo B, fol. 57r–v; ff. 210v–211r; Tumbo C, fol. 120r–v. Suspect. Again the use of *infanta* for Sancha and also the early appearance of Juan Fernández as "chancellor."

796. August 3, 1153. Zamora. Alfonso VII, Rica, and Sancho and Fernando, sons. Monastery of Moreruela. Rassow, "Urkunden," 11:118–19, an original. Also, AHN, Clero, Carpeta 3.548, nos. 14 and 15; BN, Manuscritos, 3.546, fol. 152r; Acad. Hist., Colección Salazar, O-8; ff. 122v–123r.

797. August 17, 1153. Toro. Alfonso VII, Rica, and Sancho and Fernando, sons. Cathedral of Zamora. AC ZAmora, Tumbo Negro, fol. 4r.

798. August 25, 1153. León. Alfonso VII, Rica, and Sancho and Fernando, sons. Pedro, archpriest. Fernández Catón, *Colección*, 5:278–79.

799. September 6, 1153. Oviedo. Alfonso VII, Rica, and Sancho and Fernando, sons. Pelayo Vermúdez. AHN, Clero, Carpeta 1.646, no. 29.

800. September 14, 1153. Oviedo. Alfonso VII, Rica, and Sancho and Fernando, sons. Monastery of Santa María de Arbas. García Lobo and García Lobo, *Santa María de Arbas*, p. 56. A notice only.

801. September 17, 1153. Alfonso VII, Rica, and Sancho and Fernando, kings, Urraca, queen, *Infanta* Sancha, and my counts. Monastery of Corias. Floriano Cumbreño, *Libro Registro*, 1:201–3. False. Intitulation and general diplomatic.

802. September 22, 1153. Alfonso VII and Queen Sancha. Monastery of San Pelayo de Oviedo. Fernández Conde, Torrente Fernández, and Menéndez, *Monasterio*, pp. 52–53, who call it an original.

803. October 8, 1153. León. Alfonso VII, Rica, and Sancho and Fernando, sons. Monastery of San Pedro de Rocas. Ludwig Vones, "Die Diplome der Könige Alfonso VII von Kastilien-León und Ferdinands II von León für das Kloster San pedro de Rocas (Prov. Orense)," *GAKS* 31 (1984): 158–80, from what he called an original. It is a copy nonetheless for it shows a notarial *signum* for Juan Fernández who never used one.

804. October 9, 1153. León. Alfonso VII, Rica, and Sancho and Fernando, sons, *Infanta* Sancha. Monastery of San Isidoro de León. Amparo Valcarce, *Dominio*, pp. 113–14, from what she calls the original. Also ASI, Reales, nos. 159 and 160.

805. October 12, 1153. Sahagún. Alfonso VII, Rica, and Sancho and Fernando, sons. Cathedral of León. Fernández Catón, *Colección*, 5:280–81,

from what he calls the original. Again it is suspect. It is the only other time when Juan Fernández employs a notarial *signum*.

806. October 12, 1153. Sahagún. Alfonso VII, Rica, and Sancho and Fernando, sons. Monastery of Sahagún. Fernández Flórez, *Colección*, 4:249–53, an original.

807. October 27, 1153. Burgos. Alfonso VII, Rica, and Sancho and Fernando, sons. Cathedral of Lugo. Muñoz y Romero, *Fueros*, pp. 431–32. Also AHN, Microfilmas, Lugo, Rollo 5.851, perhaps an original. AC Lugo, Tumbo Viejo, ff. 17v–18r; Tumbo Nuevo, fol. 172r.

808. November 18, 1153. Soria. Alfonso VII, Rica, and Sancho and Fernando, sons. Count Pons de Cabrera. Martín, *Orígenes*, p. 190, from the original.

809. December 19, 1153. Medina del Campo. Alfonso VII, Rica, and Sancho and Fernando, sons. Monastery of Santa María de Valbuena. Floriano Llorente, "Fondo antiguo," pp. 464–66, from what he calls the original and dated to 1143. The diplomatic requires 1153 but the date has been retouched in the document and this just may have been the first reading.

810. December 19, 1153. Medina del Campo. Alfonso VII, ..., Sancho and Fernando. Cathedral of Palencia. Abajo Martín, *Documentación*, pp. 108–10, so dated although the text reads 1123. Also, Acad. Hist., Colección Salazar, O-17, ff. 245r–246r.

811. December 19, 1153. Medina del Campo. Alfonso VII, Rica, and Sancho and Fernando, sons. Cathedral of Palencia. Ibid., pp. 103–4, dated June 18, 1153 although the text reads 1123.

812. 1154. Toledo. Alfonso VII. Monastery of San Servando de Toledo and Cipriano Domínguez, María, ux, and Nesina, widow of Domingo Ciprianez. Hernández, *Cartularios*, pp. 99–100, partial publication. Alfonso settles dispute between the parties.

813. January 3, 1154. Salamanca. Alfonso VII, Rica, and Sancho and Fernando, sons. Cathedral of Oviedo. García Larragueta, *Colección*, pp. 409–11. Also AC Lugo, Legajo 5; Tumbo Viejo, fol. 18r and fol. 57r–v; Tumbo Nuevo, ff. 172v–173r; BN, Manuscritos, 13.074, ff. 134r–136r; Acad. Hist., Catedrales de España, Lugo, 9–25–1-C-1, ff. 64r–65v.

814. January 6, 1154. Salamanca. Alfonso VII, Rica, and Sancho and Fernando, sons. Cathedral of Astorga. Rodríguez López, *Episcopologio*, 1:554–55

815. January 7, 1154. Salamanca. Alfonso VII, Rica, Sancho and Fernando, kings, and Regina Sancha. Monasterio of Ayo de Nogales. Alfonso Andrés, "Documentos inéditos de Alfonso VII y Alfonso IX de León," *HS* 11 (1958): 403–4, from what he called the original.

816. January 9, 1154. Alfonso VII. Rodrigo González. BN. Manuscritos, 9.880, fol. 339r; 13.093, fol. 146r. The text of this notice is dated to 1124 but only the above date will satisfy. Sancho and Fernando confirm as kings.

817. January 14, 1154. Soria. Sancho III and Blanca. Cathedral of Osma. González, *Reino*, 2:27–28, from what he called the original. Also, Acad. Hist., Colección Salazar, O-4, ff. 21v–22r.

818. January 28, 1154. Avila. Alfonso VII, Rica, and Sancho and Fernando, kings. Cathedral of Segovia. Villar García, *Documentación*, pp. 98–99, dated incorrectly to 1155.

819. February 6, 1154. Toledo. Alfonso VII, Rica, and Sancho and Fernando, kings. Pedro Cruciato. Hernández, *Cartularios*, pp. 89–90, partial publication.

820. March 11, 1154. Toledo. Alfonso VII, Rica, and Sancho and Fernando, kings. Cathedral of Palencia. Abajo Martín, *Documentación*, pp. 104–6.

821. March 11, 1154. Toledo. Sancho III and Blanca. Cathedral of Palencia. AMon Santo Domingo de Silos de Toledo, Signatura 2/2.

822. March 15, 1154. Territory of Lemos. Alfonso VII. Monastery of Santa María de Montederramo. AHN, Clero, Carpeta 1.481, nos. 1 and 2. False. Diplomatic is atypical.

823. March 17, 1154. Toledo. Alfonso VII, Rica, and Sancho and Fernando, kings. Cathedral of Sigüenza. Minguella y Arnedo, *Historia*, 1:391–92. Also, BN, Manuscritos, 13.073, ff. 179r–180r.

824. March 19, 1154. Toledo. Alfonso VII, Rica, and Sancho and Fernando, kings. Cathedral of Sigüenza. Ibid., p. 393. Also, BN, Manuscritos, 13.073, ff. 194r–195v.

825. March 21, 1154. Toledo. Alfonso VII, Rica, and Sancho and Fernando, kings. Cathedral of Segovia. Villar García, *Documentación*, pp. 97–98, from what he calls the original.

826. April, 1154. Guadalajara. Alfonso VII. Pedro Miguélez and Eulalia, ux. Pareja Serrada, *Diplomática*, pp. 330–1. Also, AHN, Registro de Escrituras, 9, fol. 6r–v; BN, Manuscritos, 6.683, fol. 22r–v; 13.093, fol. 152r–v; Acad. Hist., Colección Salazar, I-38, ff. 272r–273v. Unreliable. Pedro is given for Victor, bishop of Burgos.

827. April 6, 1154. Toledo. Alfonso VII, Rica, and Sancho and Fernando, kings. Men of Illescas. Hernández, *Cartularios*, pp. 90–91, from a probable original. Partial publication.

828. April 28, 1154. Toledo. Alfonso VII, Rica, and Sancho and Fernando, kings. Monastery of Santa María de Sobrado. Loscertales de García de Valdeavellano, *Tumbos*, 2:36–37.

829. April 30, 1154. Toledo. Alfonso VII, Rica, and Sancho and Fernando, kings. Cathedral of Salamanca. Martín, Villar García, Marcos Rodríguez, Sánchez Rodríguez, *Documentos*, pp. 104–5.

830. May 23, 1154. Madrid. Alfonso VII, Rica, and Sancho and Fernando, kings. Monastery of San Pedro de las Dueñas. AD León, San Pedro de las Dueñas, nos. 15, fragmentary original, and 16.

831. May 23, 1154. Madrid. Alfonso VII, Rica, and Sancho and Fernando, kings. Monastery of Sahagún. Fernández Flórez, *Colección*, 4:254–56, from the original.

832. June 22, 1154. Madrid. Alfonso VII, Rica, and Sancho and Fernando, kings. García Nafarri. Hernández, *Cartularios*, pp. 91–92. Partial publication.

833. July 2, 1154. Segovia. Sancho III and Blanca. Cathedral of Segovia. Abajo Martín, *Documentación*, pp. 106–8, from what he calls an original. Also, Acad. Hist., Colección Salazar, O-17, ff. 263r–265v.

834. July 2, 1154. Segovia. Alfonso VII, Rica, and Sancho and Fernando, kings. Cathedral of Palencia. Ibid., pp. 118–20, redated from 1125 in text to 1155. Also, Acad. Hist., Colección Salazar, O-17, ff. 256r–257v. Probable forgery modeled on grant of Sancho III above. Cardinal Hyacinth who confirms had left the peninsula by 1155.

835. July 6, 1154. Segovia. Alfonso VII, Rica, and Sancho and Fernando, kings. Monastery of Santa María de Meira. Manrique, *Cistercensium*, 1:456. Also, Acad. Hist., Colección Salazar, O-8, fol. 64v.

836. July 11, 1154. Segovia. Alfonso VII, Rica, and Sancho and Fernando, kings. Cathedral of Toledo. García Luján, *Privilegios*, 2:62–64.

837. July 12, 1154. Astorga. Alfonso VII. Guntroda Pérez. Serrano, *Cartulario de Vega*, pp. 168–69. False. Itinerary, intitulation, dating formula, etc.

838. August 8, 1154. Palencia. Alfonso VII, Rica, and Sancho and Fernando, kings. Nuño Peláez. Ayala Martínez, *Libro*, p. 221.

839. August 18, 1154. Burgos. Alfonso VII, Rica, and Sancho and Fernando, kings. Monastery of San Juan de Burgos. Peña Pérez, *Documentación*, pp. 35–37. Also, BN, Manuscritos, 5.790, ff. 142v–143r.

840. August 18, 1154. Burgos. Alfonso VII, Rica, and Sancho and Fernando, kings. Monastery of San Pedro de Arlanza. Palacín Gálvez and Martínez García, *Documentación*, pp. 6–8.

841. August 23, 1154. Burgos. *Infanta* Sancha. Monastery of San Juan de Burgos. Peña Pérez, *Documentación*, pp. 14–16. Unreliable. Intitulation, date in text is 1132, Gonzalo de Marañon is given as royal *alférez* six months too soon.

842. August 25, 1154. Burgos. Sancho III and Blanca. *Concejo* de Nájera. González, *Reino*, 2:31–32.

843. August 28, 1154. Burgos. Alfonso VII, Rica, and Sancho and Fernando, kings. Monastery of San Pedro de Arlanza. Martín Postigo, *Santa María*, pp. 123–24.

844. September 1, 1154. Alfonso VII, Rica, and and Sancho, son. Monastery of San Pedro de Arlanza. Serrano, *Cartulario de Arlanza*, pp. 206–7. Unreliable. Intitulation, dating formula, Pedro given for Vicente as bishop in Segovia.

845. September 18, 1154. Queen? Sancha. Fernando Ponz. BN, Manuscritos, 4.357, fol. 109v and fol. 141r. Notices only.

846. September 24, 1154. Ayllón. Alfonso VII, Rica, and Sancho and Fernando, kings. Cathedral of Sigüenza. Minguella y Arnedo, *Historia*, pp. 393–94. Also, BN, Manuscritos, 13.073, fol 187r–v.

847. October 18, 1154. Toledo. Sancho III. Monastery of Santa María Magdalena de Fuente de la Encina. González, *Reino*, 2:32–34.

848. October 27, 1154. Alfonso VII and Rica. Pedro Brimón. Martín, *Orígenes*, pp. 191–92, who properly redates the text from 1124. Also, AHN, Ord. Mil., Carpeta 373, no. 6; Códices, 1.045B, ff. 120–121; Acad. Hist., Colección Salazar, Appendix, Legajo B, Carpeta 9, no. 33. False. The diplomatic is that of a private document.

849. November 4, 1154. Toledo. Alfonso VII, Rica, and Sancho and Fernando, kings. Various individuals of the district of Toledo. Ibid., pp. 192–93, from the original. Also, AHN, Registro de Escrituras, 9, fol. 30r–v; Acad. Hist., Colección Salazar, I-38, ff. 284v–285v.

850. November 4, 1154. Toledo. Alfonso VII, Rica, and Sancho and Fernando, kings. Miguel, archdeacon of Málaga. Rassow, "Urkunden," 11:125–26, from the original. Also, AHN, Ord. Mil., Carpeta 417, no. 2; Acad. Hist., Colección Salazar, I-38, fol. 286r–v.

851. November 8, 1154. Toledo. Alfonso VII, Rica, and Sancho and Fernando, kings. Pedro de San Pablo. Hernández, *Cartula-rios*, p. 99. Partial publication.

852. November 8, 1154. Toledo. Alfonso VII, Rica, and Sancho and Fernando, kings. Guter Pérez. AC Orense, Monacales, no. 256, dated incorrectly to 1152.

853. November 19, 1154. Toledo. Alfonso VII, Rica, and Sancho and Fernando, kings. Antolino Portaguerra and Pelayo Pérez. Martín, *Orígines*, pp. 193–94, from the original. Also, Acad. Hist., Colección Salazar, Appendix, Legajo B, Carpeta 10, no. 41.

854. December 20, 1154. Alfonso VII and Rica. Monastery of Poibueno.

Augusto Quintana Prieto, "Los monasterios de Poibueno y San Martín de Montes," *AL* 22 (1968), pp. 117–18. A rough copy at best.

855. December 24, 1154. Alfonso VII, Rica, and Sancho and Fernando, kings. Monastery of Santa María de Sobrado. Loscertales de García de Valdeavellano, *Tumbos*, 2:105. The text is dated to 1155 but the diplomatic necessitates the earlier date.

856. December 30, 1154. Alfonso VII and Berengaria. Cathedral de Astorga. AHN, Códices, 1.195B, fol. 528r–v. False. The diplomatic has mutually incompatible features.

857. 1155. Alfonso VII. Rodrigo de Azagra. AHN, Códices, 595B, fol. 157r. Notice only.

858. 1155. Madrid. Alfonso VII, Rica, and Sancho and Fernando, kings. Gonzalo, *alvazil*. Martín, *Orígines*, pp. 197–98. The date in the text is largely obscured.

859. 1155. Alfonso VII, Rica, and Sancho and Fernando, kings. Rodrigo Rodríguez. Hernández, *Cartularios*, pp. 109–10. Suspect. Diplomatic is reminiscent in part of a private document.

860. 1155. Olite. Sancho III. Men of Olite. José María Jimeno Jurío, ed., *Documentos medievales artajonenses* (Pamplona, 1968), pp. 215–16, from what he called the original.

861. January 1155. Alfonso VII, Rica, and Sancho and Fernando, sons. Men of Avilés. Aureliano Fernández-Guerra, *El fuero de Avilés* (Madrid, 1865), pp. 111–35. False. Various elements of the diplomatic are incompatible.

862. January 15, 1155. Carrión. Alfonso VII and Rica. Cathedral of Palencia. Abajo Martín, *Documentación*, pp. 112–14. Also, Acad. Hist., Catedrales de España, Palencia, 9–25–1-C-6, ff. 35r–36v. Suspect. Intitulation and notarial subscription are unusual.

863. January 20, 1155. Carrión. Alfonso VII, Rica, and Sancho and Fernando, kings. Monastery of Santa María de Armenteira. AHN, Clero, Carpeta 1.749, no. 4. Suspect. Pedro is given as bishop of León rather than Juan.

864. January 25, 1155. Valladolid. Queen Sancha. Monastery of Eslonza. García Calles, *Doña Sancha*, pp. 161–62. Also, AHN, Clero, Carpeta 963, no. 14, a probable original; Acad. Hist., Colección Salazar, O-16, fol. 501r–v.

865. January 25, 1155. Valladolid. Alfonso VII, Rica, and Sancho and Fernando, kings. Monastery of Eslonza. Vignau, *Cartulario*, pp. 27–28. Also, AHN, Clero, Carpeta 963, nos. 12 and 13; Acad. Hist., Colección Salazar, O-18, fol. 299r–v. Forgery based on Sancha's document of the same date.

866. February 1, 1155. Valladolid. Alfonso VII, Rica, and Sancho and Fernando, kings. Monastery of San Zoil de Carrión. Pérez Celada, *Documentación*, pp. 60–61.

867. February 2, 1155. Valladolid. Alfonso VII, Rica, and Sancho and Fernando, kings. Monastery of San Pelayo de Cerrato. Luis Fernández Martín, "Colección diplomática del monasterio de San Pelayo de Cerrato," *HS* 26 (1973): 289–90. Suspect. Dating formula is unusual.

868. February 4, 1155. Valladolid. Alfonso VII, Rica, and Sancho and Fernando, kings, and kin. Monastery of Celanova. Rassow, "Urkunden," 11:130–32, from what he called the original. But AHN, Clero, Carpeta 1.431, no. 1, is unusual in format and cites Queen Sancha as *infanta*.

869. February 4, 1155. Valladolid. Alfonso VII, Rica, and Sancho and Fernando, kings. Monastery of Sahagún. Fernández Flórez, *Colección*, 4:256–58, from what he called the original. I make it a later copy.

870. February 4, 1155. Valladolid. Alfonso VII, Rica, and Sancho and Fernando, kings, and kin. Monastery of Santa Comba de Naves. Váquez Nuñez, *Documentos*, 2:169–71. Also, AHN, Clero, Carpeta 1.506, nos. 1 and 14.

871. February 7, 1155. Tordesillas. Alfonso VII, Rica, and Sancho and Fernando, kings. Cathedral of Santiago de Compostela. López Ferreiro, *Historia*, 4:68–69, Appendix.

872. February 27, 1155. Queen Urraca. Monastery of San Vicente de Oviedo. Floriano Llorente, *Colección*, pp. 399–400. False. Ordoño is given as abbot instead of Pedro and Juan Fernández as "scriptor" raher than chancellor.

873. March, 1155. Soria. Sancho III. Monastery of Santa María de Aguilar de Campoó. Fidel Fita, "Primera legación del Cardinal Jacinto en España. Bulas inéditas de Anastasio IV. Nuevas luces sobre el concilio nacional de Valladolid (1155) y otros datos inéditos," *BRAH* 14 (1889): 532. A confused citation.

874. March 2, 1155. Avila. Alfonso VII, Rica, and Sancho and Fernando, kings. *Concejo* de Valladolid. Mañuecos Villalobos and Zurita Nieto, *Documentos*, pp. 210–15.

875. March 14, 1155. Soria. Sancho III. Monastery of Santo Domingo de Silos. Vivancos Gómez, *Documentación*, pp. 81–82. Also, BN, Manuscritos, 3.546, ff. 129v–130r. Unreliable. Intitulatio and itinerary. Queen Blanca confirms although missing from the intitulation.

876. March 15, 1155. Toledo. Alfonso VII, Rica, and Sancho and Fernando, kings. Various inhabitants of the Toledo district. Hernández, *Cartularios*, pp. 102–3.

877. March 25, 1155. Toledo. Alfonso VII, Rica, and Sancho and Fernando, kings. Mozarabs of Toledo. García Gallo, *Fueros*, pp. 471–72.

878. March 29, 1155. *Infanta* Sancha. Rodrigo Pérez. Fernández Flórez, *Colec-*

ción, 4:258–59, who calls it an original. The usage of the title *infanta* rather than queen makes that unlikely.

879. March 30, 1155. Valladolid. Alfonso VII. Gonzalo de Marañon. Fernández Martín, "Colección," pp. 290–92, who calls it an original and dates it to 1145. False. The diplomatic is wildly atypical and the date untenable.

880. April 4, 1155. Toledo. Alfonso VII, Rica, and Sancho and Fernando, kings. Pelayo Pérez de Frómista. Rassow, "Urkunden," 11:132–33, from the original. Also, AHN, Registro de Escrituras, 9, fol. 32r–v.

881. April 10, 1155. Sancho III. Pedro Sanz. Monterde Albiac, *Colección*, pp. 393–94. Queen Blanca confirms although missing from the intitulation.

882. June 15, 1155. Andújar. Alfonso VII, Rica, and Sancho and Fernando, kings. Abd al-Aziz de Baeza. Rassow, "Urkunden," 11:133–34, from the original.

883. June 18, 1155. Nájera. Sancho III and Blanca. Cathedral of Calahorra. González, *Reino*, 2:37–38.

884. July 23, 1155. Nájera. Sancho III. Cathedral of Calahorra. Rodríguez de Lama, *Colección*, 2:256–57. Day and month supplied by editor. Queen Blanca confirms.

885. July 31, 1155. Santiago de Compostela. Fernando II. Rodrigo Menéndez. AHN, Códices, 417B, fol. 18r–v; 267B, fol. 175r–v.

886. August 11, 1155. Toledo. Alfonso VII, Rica, and Sancho and Fernando, kings. Various inhabitants of the district of Toledo. Hernández, *Cartularios*, pp. 106–7. Partial publication.

887. August 11, 1155. Toledo. Alfonso VII, Rica, and Sancho and Fernando, kings. Monastery of San Servando de Toledo. Ibid., 107–8. Partial publication.

888. August 12, 1155. Burgos. Sancho III. Monastery of San Juan de Ortega. Garrido Garrido, *Documentación*, pp. 243–44, who dates it erroneously to 1157. Unreliable. Queen Blanca does not appear. Nuño Pérez still confirms as royal *alférez*.

889. September 1, 1155. Toledo. Alfonso VII, Rica, and Sancho and Fernando, kings. Pedro Jiménez. Pareja Serrada, *Diplomática*, pp. 109–10. Also, Acad. Hist., Colección Salazar, I-38, ff. 273r–274r; Appendix, Legajo B, Carpeta 3, no. 10.

890. September 6, 1155. Toledo. Alfonso VII, Rica, and Sancho and Fernando, kings. Various inhabitants of the district of Toledo. Martín, *Orígenes*, pp. 194–95, who corrects the date from 1115.

891. September 11, 1155. Toledo. Alfonso VII, Rica, and Sancho and Fernando, kings. Miguel, cardinal of Compostela. López Ferreiro, *Historia*, 4:70–71, Appendix.

892. September 18, 1155. Calahorra. Sancho III and Blanca. Cathedral of Calahorra. Rodríguez de Lama, *Colección*, 2:258–59.

893. September 18, 1155. Calahorra. Sancho III and Blanca. Templars. Ibid.,
pp. 257–58.

894. September 22, 1155. Talavera de la Reina. Alfonso VII, Rica, and Sancho
and Fernando, kings. Domingo Domínguez. BN, Manuscritos, 6.683, fol.
25r–v; 13.093, fol. 159r–v; AGS, Libro de Copias de Documentos, 8, ff.
119v–120v.

895. September 25, 1155. Talavera de la Reina. Alfonso VII, Rica, and Sancho
and Fernando, kings. Suero Díaz. Rassow, "Urkunden," 11:134–35, from
the original. Also, Acad. Hist., Colección Salazar, I-38, ff. 280v–281r.

896. October 28, 1155. Burgos. Alfonso VII, Rica, and Sancho and Fernando,
kings. Monastery of Santa María de Montesacro. BN, Manuscritos, 13.093,
fol. 157r–v.

897. October 28, 1155. Burgos. Alfonso VII, Rica, and Sancho and Fernando,
kings. Monastery of Santo Domingo de Silos. Vivancos Gómez, *Documen-*
tación, pp. 83–84.

898. October 28, 1155. Burgos. Alfonso VII, Rica, and Sancho and Fernando,
kings. Monastery of Santo Domingo de Silos. Ibid., pp. 85–86.

899. October 28, 1155. Burgos. Alfonso VII, Rica, and Sancho and Fernando,
kings. Monastery of Santo Domingo de Silos. Ibid., pp. 80–81.

900. November 1, 1155. Madrid. Alfonso VII, Rica, and Sancho and Fernando, kings. Various inhabitants of the Toledo region. Hernández, *Car-*
tularios, pp. 110–11, dated simply to 1155. Also, Bn, Manuscritos, 13.093, ff.
161r–162v, with the date shown.

901. November 25, 1155. Alfonso VII, Rica, and Sancho and Fernando, kings.
Monastery of Santa María de Nájera. Cantera Montenegro, *Colección*, pp.
90–91.

902. December 6, 1155. Burgos. Alfonso VII, Rica, and Sancho and Fernando,
kings. Cathedral of Burgos. Garrido Garrido, *Documentación*, pp. 235–37.
Also, BN, Manuscritos, 720, ff. 269r–270r; 6.683, fol. 746r–747v.

903. December 7, 1155. Burgos. Alfonso VII. Fernando Téllez. Palacín Gálvez
and Martínez García, *Documentación*, p. 8. A notice only.

904. December 9, 1155. Burgos. Alfonso VII, Rica, and Sancho and Fernando, kings. Monastery of Santa María de Aguilar de Campoó. Rassow,
"Urkunden," 11:136–37. Also, AHN, Clero, Carpeta 1.647, no. 12; 3.436,
nos. 4 and 5; Códices, 994B, ff. 21r–22r; BN, Manuscritos, 841, ff. 320r–
321r; 9.194, fol. 24r–v.

905. December 9, 1155. Burgos. Alfonso VII, Rica, and Sancho and Fernando,

kings. Monastery of Santa María de Carracedo. AC Astorga, Registro de Escrituras, ff. 501v–502r.

906. December 9, 1155. Burgos. Alfonso VII, Rica, and Sancho and Fernando, kings. Monastery of San Pedro de Arlanza. Serrano, *Cartulario de Arlanza*, pp. 209–10.

907. December 16, 1155. Burgos. Alfonso VII, Rica, and Sancho and Fernando, kings. Cathedral of Burgos. Garrido Garrido, *Documentación*, pp. 237–39.

908. December 16, 1155. Arévalo. Alfonso VII and Queen Sancha. Monastery of St. Ruf of Avignon. Fidel Fita, "San Miguel de Escalada. Antiguous fueros y nuevos ilustraciones," *BRAH* 32 (1898): 373–76. Suspect because of supposed place of issue.

909. December 28, 1155. Palencia. Alfonso VII, Rica, and Sancho and Fernando, kings. Monastery of Santa María de Varzana. Manrique, *Cisterciensium*, 1:436. Also, AHN, Clero, Carpeta 1.240, no. 10; Códices, 323B, 2: fol. 196r–v.

910. December 31, 1155. Palencia. Alfonso VII, Urraca "domina," and Sancho and Fernando, kings. Monastery of San Pedro de Vilanova. Enrique Fernández Villamil, *Privilegios reales de Museo de Pontevedra* (Pontevedra, 1942), pp. 82–83, from a text date of 1124 which must be redated as above.

911. December 31, 1155. Molina. Sancho III. Cathedral of Sigüenza. González, *Reino*, 2:45–46. Suspect because of place of issue given.

912. 1156. Alfonso VII, Rica, and Sancho and Fernando, kings. Monastery of San Cristóbal de Ibeas. Gonzalo Martínez, "Diplomatario de San Cristóbal de Ibeas," *BIFG* 55 (1975): 700–701, from what he calls the original. The diplomatic precludes that.

913. 1156. Alfonso VII. Inhabitants of Poza de la Sal and Padrones de Bureba. Alamo, *Colección*, 1:266–67.

914. 1156. Alfonso VII, Rica, and Sancho and Fernando, kings. Pedro García, alcalde de Baeza. Luis Sánchez Belda, "Notas de diplomática. En torneo de tres diplomas de Alfonso VII," *Hispania* 11 (1951): 60–61, from a possible original.

915. 1156. Alfonso VII, Rica, and Sancho and Fernando, kings. Abd al-Aziz Aboalil. Ibid., pp. 59–60. Also, Acad. Hist., Colección Salazar, I-38, ff. 290v–291v.

916. 1156. Alfonso VII, Rica, and Sancho and Fernando, kings. Abd al-Aziz Aboalil. Ibid., pp. 58–59.

917. 1156. Alfonso VII. Monastery of Santa María de Moreruela. Rassow, "Urkunden," 10:465. Notice only.

918. January 10, 1156. Palencia. Alfonso VII, Rica, and Sancho and Fernando,

kings. Monastery of St. Denis. Michael Féliben, *Histoire de l'Abbaye royale de Saint Denys en France* 1706. new ed. (Paris, 1973), pp. 109–10.

919. January 11, 1156. Valladolid. Alfonso VII, Rica, and Sancho and Fernando, kings. *Concejo* de Valladolid. Fernando Pino Rebolledo, ed., *Catálogo de los pergaminos de la Edad Media, 1191–1393. Transcripción y notas críticas* (Valladolid, 1988), pp. 64–70.

920. January 11, 1156. Valladolid. Alfonso VII, Rica, and Sancho and Fernando, kings. Collegiate church of Valladolid. Mañueco Villalobos and Zurita Nieto *Documentos*, 1:217–18.

921. January 18, 1156. Valladolid. Alfonso VII, Rica, and Sancho and Fernando, kings. Monastery of Santa María de Retuerta. Anton, *Monasterios*, pp. 262–63. Text is dated to 1154 but the diplomatic does not accommodate it.

922. February 4, 1156. Madrid. Alfonso VII, Rica, and Sancho and Fernando, kings. Monastery of San Ginés. Hernández, *Cartularios*, pp. 111–12. Partial publication.

923. February 17, 1156. Toledo. Alfonso VII, Rica, and Sancho and Fernando, kings. Pelayo Cabecha. AHN, Ord. Mil., Carpeta 568, no. 2, a possible original. BN, Manuscritos, 714, ff. 131r–132v; 9.880, fol. 403r–v.

924. March 4, 1156. Toledo. Alfonso VII, Rica, and Sancho and Fernando, kings. Various Mozarab inhabitants of Toledo region. Pareja Serrada, *Diplomática*, pp. 114–16.

925. March 9, 1156. Toledo. Alfonso VII, Rica, and Sancho and Fernando, kings. García García. AHN, Clero, Carpeta 3.134, no. 18; BN, Manuscritos, 13.093, ff. 165r–166r.

926. March 24, 1156. Toledo. Alfonso VII, Rica, and Sancho and Fernando, kings. Inhabitants of Ocaña. Pareja Serrada, *Diplomática*, pp. 111–13. Also BN, Manuscritos, 13.073, ff. 169r–170v.

927. March 25, 1156. Toledo. Alfonso VII, Rica, and Sancho and Fernando, kings. Inhabitants of Ocaña. Martín, *Orígenes*, pp. 195–97, who corrected the date from the 1156 of the text.

928. March 30, 1156. Toledo. Alfonso VII, Rica, and Sancho and Fernando, kings. Nuño Pérez. Hernández, *Cartularios*, pp. 113–14. Partial publication.

929. April 22, 1156. Olmedo. Alfonso VII, Rica, and Sancho and Fernando, kings. Monastery of Santa María de Valbuena. Acad. Hist., Colección Salazar, O-18, ff. 195r–196v, dated April 22, 1142; Appendix, Legajo C, Carpeta 2, no. 4, dated September 22, 1147. Bishop Martín of Oviedo who confirms was translated to Compostela only in 1156. The notarial confirmation fits only 1153.

930. April 26, 1156. Queen Sancha. Hospitallers. Ayala Martínez, *Libro*, pp. 224–26.

931. May 1156. Lérida. Alfonso VII, and Sancho and Fernando, kings. Count Ramon Berenguer IV of Barcelona. Rosell, *Liber*, 1:42–43.

932. May 3, 1156. c. Zamora. Alfonso VII, Rica, Sancho and Fernando, kings, and Sancha, sister. Monastery of San Isidoro of León and April. Amparo Valcarce, *Dominio*, pp. 116–17, from what she called the original, and pp. 150–51. Alfonso approves an exchange of property between the parties. A strange mixture of public and private diplomatic. False.

933. May 30, 1156. *Infanta* Sancha. Pons de Minerva and Estefanía Ramírez, ux. Canal Sánchez-Pagín, "Documentos," pp. 390–91. Also, BN, Manuscritos, 3.147, fol. 392r–v; 9.880, ff. 343v–44r. All copies are dated 1140, which is impossible diplomatically. False.

934. June 14, 1156. Sahagún. Alfonso VII. Pons de Minerva and Estefanía Ramírez, ux. María Concepción Casado Lobato, ed., *Colección*, 1:31–33, dated 1141. Also, BN, Manuscritos, 9.880,ff. 336v–337r; Acad. Hist., Colección Salazar, M-76, fol. 373r–v. The diplomatic demands 1156 but it is likely false.

935. June 19, 1156. Maqueda. Alfonso VII, Rica, and Sancho and Fernando, kings. Various inhabitants of the Toledo region. Hernández, *Cartularios*, pp. 114–15. Partial publication.

936. June 25–30, 1156. Palencia. Alfonso VII, Rica, and Sancho and Fernando, kings. Diego Almadrano and Velasquita González, ux. José Luis Martín, "La orden militar de San Marcos de León," *León y su historia* 4 (1977): 53–44. The text date of 1154 must be corrected as above. The day is specified merely as "after the feast of Saint John."

937. June 25–30, 1156. Segovia. Alfonso VII, Rica, and Sancho and Fernando, kings. García Pérez and Teresa, ux. Calvo, *Monasterio*, pp. 308–9. The dating formula again reads "after the feast of Saint John" and also "when the emperor lay there detained by illness."

938. July 1, 1156. Alfonso VII, Sancho and Fernando, kings, with Nuño Pérez and Teresa Fernández, ux. Inhabitants of Castro Benevente. Ayala Martínez, *Libro*, pp. 219–20, dated to 1152. False. Neither date can accomodate all of the diplomatic elements.

939. July 11, 1156. Segovia. Alfonso VII, Rica, and Sancho and Fernando, kings. Abd al-Aziz of Baeza. Acad. Hist., Colección Salazar, I-38, ff. 289v–290r.

940. July 29, 1156. Calahorra. Sancho III. Monastery of Castellón. Monterde Albiac, *Colección*, pp. 401–2, dated to August 2, 1156.

941. July 29, 1156. *Infanta* Sancha. Pons de Minerva. AHN, Ord. Mil., Carpeta 179, no. 19; 373, nos. 4 and 5. False. Improper intitulation and *merino* in León for the period.

942. July 30, 1156. Alfonso VII, Rica, Sancho and Fernando, kings, and Constanza and Blanca (*sic*), queens. Count Pons and Maria, ux. AHN, Clero, Carpeta 948, no. 2. Suspect for irregularity of the diplomatic, especially Blanca as queen of Navarra.

943. August 1156. Alfonso VII, and Sancho and Fernando, kings. Nuño Pérez and Teresa Fernández, ux. BN, Manuscritos, 714, fol. 141r–v, dated to 1152. False. The various diplomatic elements cannot be reconciled for any date.

944. August 20, 1156. Alfonso VII, Sancho and Fernando, kings, and Sancha, queen. Monastery of San Pedro de las Dueñas. Fernández Catón, *Catálogo*, pp. 23–24. Prepared by Sancha's notary rather than the royal chancery. *Merino* for León is erroneous. Suspect.

945. August 30, 1156. Nájera. Sancho III. Monasteries of Santa María de Nájera and Cluny. González, *Reino*, 2:49–50.

946. October 6, 1156. Alfonso VII, Rica, Sancho and Fernando, kings, and Constanza and Sancha, queens. Fernando Rodríguez, and Sancha, ux. BN, Manuscritos, 712, fol. 140r–v; 9.194, fol. 117r; 13.093, 160r–v.

947. November 1156. Alfonso VII, Rica, Sancho and Fernando, kings, and Constanza and Baecia [*sic*] queens. Cathedral of Toledo. García Lujan, *Privilegios*, 2:64–66.

948. November 2, 1156. Atienza. Alfonso VII, Rica, Sancho and Fernando, kings, and Constanza and Sancha, queens. Sancho Yañez and Mayor Guim, ux. AC Compostela, Tumbo B, fol. 222r–v.

949. November 9, 1156. Peñafiel. Alfonso VII, Rica, Sancho and Fernando, kings, and Constanza and Sancha, queens. Cathedral of Mondoñedo. Floriano Llorente, "Fondo," pp. 468–9, dated October 28. Also, AHN, Clero, Carpeta 1.185, no. 9; BN, Manuscritos, 5.928, ff. 37v–38r, dated October 28; Acad. Hist., Catedrales de España, Mondoñedo, 9–25–1-C-3, ff. 16r–19r, dated November 9. Cal Pardo, *Catálogo*, p. 19, gives an excerpt from what he calls an original in the cathedral archive of Mondoñedo, he also dated to October 28. The date should be read as above however.

950. November 12, 1156. Peñafiel. Alfonso VII, Rica, Sancho and Fernando, kings, and Constanza and Sancha, queens. Alfonso and Pelayo Alfónsez, monks. Floriano Llorente, "Colección," pp. 132–34.

951. November 20, 1156. Palencia. Alfonso VII, Rica, Sancho and Fernando, kings, and Constanza and Sancha, queens. Hospitallers. Ayala Martínez, *Libro*, pp. 227–29. Also, BN, Manuscritos, 714, fol. 162r, dated September 20; AGS, Mercedes y Prilegios, Legajo 342, no. 15, dated December 1.

A Count Raymond, otherwise unknown in the realm at this time, confirms.

952. December 1, 1156. Palencia. Alfonso VII, Rica, Sancho and Fernando, kings, and Constanza and Sancha, queens. Juan Martínez. Fernández Catón, *Colección*, 5:291–93, who calls it an original.

953. December 1, 1156. Palencia. Alfonso VII, Rica, and Sancho and Fernando, kings. Cathedral of Túy. *ES*, 22:273–79. Also, AC Túy, 1/7; Libro Becerro Primero, ff. 13r–14v and 191r–192v.

954. December? 1156. Palencia. Alfonso VII, Rica, and Sancho and Fernando, kings. Suero Rodríguez and María Pérez, ux. Martín, "Orden militar," pp. 56–57. Also AHN, Ord. Mil., Carpeta 373, no. 7. The text is dated only by year but the royal chancellor, Pedro, makes December likely.

955. December 15, 1156. Palencia. Alfonso VII, Rica, Sancho and Fernando, kings, and "my daughters." Cathedral of Sigüenza and *concejo* of Atienza. Pareja Serrada, *Diplomática*, pp. 117–18. Also, BN, Manuscritos, 13.073, ff. 224r–225r.

956. December 21, 1156. Valladolid. Alfonso VII, Rica, Sancho and Fernando, kings, and Constanza and Sancha, queens. Monastery of San Pelayo de Cerrato. Fernández Martín, "Colección," pp. 292–94. There are mistakes in the confirmation list and perhaps in the place of issue also.

957. December 29, 1156. Palencia. Alfonso VII, Rica, Sancho and Fernando, kings, and Constanza and Sancha, queens. Mayor Fernández, a nun. AHN, Clero, Carpeta 1.749, no. 5. Virtually unreadable.

958. 1157. c. Río Celete. Alfonso VII, Rica, and Sancho and Fernando, kings. Cathedral of Orense. Castro y Sueiro, "Documentos," 2:38–40. Also, Acad. Hist., Catedrales de España, Orense, 9-25-1-C-9, ff. 10r–13r and 23r–27r.

959. January 18, 1157. Valladolid. Alfonso VII, Rica, Sancho and Fernando, kings, and Constanza and Baetia [*sic*], queens. Hospitallers. Ayala Martínez, *Libro*, pp. 222–24, dates improperly to 1156. The confirmation of Bishop Pedro of Orense makes 1157 preferable.

960. January 22, 1157. Alfonso VII, Rica, Sancho and Fernando, kings, and Constanza and Sancha, queens. Pedro Isidoro. Alamo, *Colección*, 1:265–66, dated to 1156. The confirmation of Pedro as bishop-elect of Burgos and Pedro as bishop-elect of Oviedo make 1157 preferable.

961. February 1, 1157. Alfonso VII, Rica, Sancho and Fernando, kings, and Constanza and Sancha, queens. Ordoño, prior (Hospitallers?). BN, Manuscritos, 714, fol. 126r–v.

962. February 4, 1157. Alfonso VII, Rica, and Sancho and Fernando, kings. Hospital of Burgos. Serrano, *Obispado*, 3:201–2.

963. February 28, 1157. Zamora. Alfonso VII, Rica, Sancho and Fernando, kings, and Constanza and Sancha, queens. Cathedral of Zamora. AC Zamora, Tumbo Negro, ff. 3r–v; AHN, Clero, Carpeta 3.584, no. 14; BN, Manuscritos, 714, ff. 158r–160v; Acad. Hist., Colección Salazar, O-3, ff. 167v–168r.

964. March 1157. Sancho III. Monastery of Santa María de Tulebras. González, *Reino*, 2:51–52.

965. March 10, 1157. Zamora. Alfonso VII, Rica, Sancho and Fernando, kings. Canons of Zamora. AC Zamora, Tumbo Nuevo, fol. 1v; BN, Manuscritos, 714, fol. 165r, a notice only.

966. March 25, 1157. Alba de Tormes. Alfonso VII, Rica, Sancho and Fernando, kings, and Constanza and Sancha, queens. Hospitallers. Ayala Martínez, *Libro*, pp. 230–34. Also BN, Manuscritos, 714, fol. 141v–142r.

967. April 12, 1157. Alfonso VII and Sancho, son. Cathedral of Osma. Loperráez Corvalón, *Descripción*, 3:35–36, from the text dated to December, 1157. Unreliable. Intitulation and other diplomatic features.

968. April 13, 1157. Alfonso VII. Guntroda Pérez. Serrano, *Cartulario de Vega*, pp. 171–72. The confirmation cites Rica, Sancho and Fernando, kings, and Queen Sancha, his sister. The form is strange indeed.

969. April 14, 1157. *Infanta* Elvira. Cathedral of Astorga. BN, Manuscritos, 6.683, fol. 41r–v, dated to 1147; 9.194, fol. 118r, dated to 1157; 13.093, fol. 122r–v, dated to 1147; Acad. Hist., Colección Salazar, O-24, fol. 174r. The mention of Rica in the dating formula requires 1157.

970. April 15, 1157. Toledo. Sancho III. Monastery of Santa María de Castellón. Monterde Albiac, *Colección*, pp. 432–34, from what she called the original. Also, Acad. Hist., Colección Salazar, M39, ff. 86v–87r.

971. April 29, 1157. Toledo. Sancho III. Cathedral of Calahorra. Rodríguez de Lama, *Coleción*, 2:275–77. Also, BN, Manuscritos, 5.741, fol. 34r.

972. April 30, 1157. León. Queen Sancha. Cathedral of Zamora. García Calles, *Doña Sancha*, pp. 163–64. False. Confirmed by Alfonso VII, Sancho and Fernando who were then far to the south.

973. May 29, 1157. Oviedo. Queen Urraca. Monastery of San Pelayo de Oviedo. Fernández Conde, Torrente Fernández, and Menéndez, *Monasterio*, pp. 59–61, who call it an original.

974. July 1157. Sahagún. Alfonso VII and Berengaria. Monastery of Oya. AHN, Códices, 60B, fol. 81r–v. False on the basis of the intitulation.

975. July 30, 1157. Alfonso VII, Rica, Sancho and Fernando, kings, and Constanza and Blanca [*sic*], queens. Monastery of Santa María de Osera. AHN, Clero, Carpeta 1.510, no. 2; Códices, 15B, ff. 76v–77r; 1.008B, fol. 5r–v. Suspect. Intitulation and the deceased Bishop Pedro of Astorga confirms.

Bibliography

PUBLISHED BOOKS

Abajo Martín, Teresa, ed. *Documentación de la catedral de Palencia*. Palencia, 1986.

Aguade Nieto, Santiago. *De la sociedad arcaica a la sociedad campesina en la Asturias medieval*. Madrid, 1988.

Alamo, Juan de, ed. *Colección diplomática de San Salvador de Oña*. 2 vols. Madrid, 1950.

Albon, Marquis D', ed. *Cartulaire général de l'Ordre du Temple, 1119–1150*. Paris, 1913.

Alfonso Antón, Isabel. *La colonización cisterciense en la meseta del Duero*. Zamora, 1986.

Al-Idrisi. *Description de l'Afrique et de l'Espagne*. Trans. Reinhart Dozy. Paris, 1866.

Almeida, Fortunato de. *História da Igreja em Portugal*. New ed. Vol. 1. Oporto, 1967.

Altisent, Augustí, ed. *Diplomatari de Santa Maria de Poblet*. Vol. 1: *960–1177*. Barcelona, 1993.

Alvarez Borge, Ignacio. *Monarquía feudal y organización territorial: Alfoces y Merindades en Castilla, siglos X–XIV*. Madrid, 1993.

Alvarez Burgos, Benedito Fernando, and Vicente Ramón Pérez, eds. *Catálogo general de la moneda medieval hispano-cristiana desde el siglo IX al XVI*. Madrid, 1980.

Alvarez Martínez, Ursicino. *Historia general, civil y eclesiástica de la provincia de Zamora*. Madrid, 1965.

Amari, Michele, ed. *I diplomi arabi del R. Archivio Fiorentini*. Florence, 1863.

Amparo Valcarce, María. *El dominio de la real colegiata de S. Isidoro de León hasta 1189*. León, 1985.

Antón, Francisco. *Monasterios medievales de la provincia de Valladolid*. 2nd ed. Valladolid, 1942.

Argaiz, Gregorio de. *La soledad laureada por San Benito y su hijos en las iglesias de España*. 7 vols. Madrid, 1765.

Arribas Arranz, Filemón. *Paleografía documental hispánica*. 2 vols. Valladolid, 1965.

Ayala Martínez, Carlos, ed. *Libro de Privilegios de la Orden de San Juan de Jerusalén en Castilla y León, siglos XII–XV*. Madrid, 1994.

Azevado, Rui Pinto de, ed. *Documentos Medievais Portugueses*. Vol. 1. Lisbon, 1958.

Baer, Yitzak. *Die Juden im Christlichen Spanien*. Vol. 1. Berlin, 1929.

———. *Historia de los judios en la España cristiana*. Trans. José Luis Lacave. Madrid, 1981.

Ballesteros Caballero, Floriano. *Catálogo de documentos de la villa de Pineda de la Sierra (Burgos)*. Burgos, 1974.

Balparda y las Herrarias, Gregorio de. *Historia crítica de Vizcaya y de sus fueros*. 2 vols. Madrid, 1924 and Bilbao, 1933–34.

Barceló, Miguel. "Dos documentos del siglo XII." In *Miscelanéa de textos medievales*, 9–12. Vol. 2. Barcelona, 1974.

Barrero García, Ana María, ed. "La política foral de Alfonso VI." In *Estudios sobre Alfonso VI y la reconquista de Toledo*, 115–56. Toledo, 1987.

Barrios García, Angel. *Estructuras agrarias y de poder en Castilla: El ejemplo de Avila, 1085–1320.* Salamanca, 1983.

Barrios García, Angel, ed. *Documentación medieval de la catedral de Avila.* Salamanca, 1981.

Benito Ruano, Eloy. "Alfonso Jordan, Conde de Toulouse." In *Estudios sobre Alfonso VI y la reconquista de Toledo*, pp. 83–98. Toledo, 1987.

Benson, Robert L. *The Bishop-elect.* Princeton, 1968.

Berganza, Francisco de. *Antiguedades de Espana.* 2 vols. Madrid, 1719–21.

Berry, Virginia. "The Second Crusade." In *A History of the Crusades*, ed. Kenneth M. Setton, 463–512. Philadelphia, 1955.

Bishko, Charles Julian. "Fernando I and the Origins of the Leonese-Castilian Alliance with Cluny." In *Studies in Medieval Spanish Frontier History*, 491–515. London, 1980. First pub. in Spanish in *CHE* 47–48 (1968): 31–135, and 49–50 (1969): 50–116.

———. "The Spanish and Portuguese Reconquest, 1095–1492." In *A History of the Crusades*, ed. Kenneth M. Setton, 396–456. Vol. 3. Madison, Wisc., 1975.

Blanco Lozano, Pilar, ed. *Colección diplomática de Fernando I, 1037–1065.* León, 1987.

Blocker-Walter, Monica. *Alfons I von Portugal.* Zurich, 1966.

Bonachia Hernando, Juan Antonio, and Julio Antonio Pardos Martínez, eds. *Catálogo documental del Archivo Municipal de Burgos: Sección Histórica, 931–1515.* 2 vols. Salamanca, 1983.

Bonnassie, Pierre. *Cataluña mil años atrás: Siglos X–XI.* Barcelona, 1988.

———. *From Slavery to Feudalism in Southwestern Europe.* Cambridge, 1991.

Bosch Vilá, Jacinto. *Los Almorávides.* 1956. Granada, 1990.

Branco Marques da Silva, Maria Joao Violante. "Portugal no Reino de León. Etapas de uma relaçao, 866–1179." In *El Reino de León en la Alta Edad Media.* Vol. 4, *La Monarquia, 1109–1230*, 533–625. León, 1993.

Brett, M. *The English Church under Henry I.* Oxford, 1975.

Bruel, Alexandre, ed. *Recueil des chartes de l'Abbaye de Cluny.* 6 vols. Paris, 1876–1903.

Buescu, Ana Isabel. "O mito das origens da nacionalidade: O milagre de Ourique." In *A Memória da Naçao*, 49–69. Lisbon, 1991.

Cabero Diéguez, Valentín. *Evolución y estructura urbana de Astorga.* León, 1973.

Caffaro. *De Captione Almerie et Tortuose.* Ed. Antonio Ubieto Arteta. Valencia, 1973

Cal Pardo, Enrique. *Catálogo de los documentos escritos en pergamino del archivo de la catedral de Mondoñedo.* Lugo, 1990.

Calvo, Aurelio. *El monasterio de Gradefes.* León, 1936.

Canellas López, Angel, ed. *Colección diplomática del concejo de Zaragoza.* Zaragoza, 1972.

Cantera Burgos, Francisco, ed. *Fuero de Miranda de Ebro.* Madrid, 1945.

Cantera Montenegro, Margarita, ed. *Colección documental de Santa María La Real de Nájera, Tomo I, siglos X–XIV.* San Sebastián, 1991.

Carlé, María del Carmen. *Del concejo medieval castellano-leones.* Buenos Aires, 1968.

Casado Lobato, María Concepción, ed. *Colección diplomática del monasterio de Carrizo.* 2 vols. León, 1983.

Castán Lanaspa, Guillermo, ed. *Documentos del monasterio de Villaverde de Sandoval, siglos XII–XV*. Salamanca, 1981.

Castán Lanaspa, Guillermo, and Javier Castán Lanaspa, eds. *Documentos del monasterio de Santa María de Trianos, siglos XII–XIII*. Salamanca, 1992.

Castrillo, Maximiliano. *Opusculo sobre la historia de al villa de Astudillo*. Burgos, 1877.

Chalandon, Ferdinand. *Histoire de la domination Normande en Italie et en Sicile*. 2 vols. 1907. New York, 1969.

Charlo Brea, Luis, ed. *Cronica latina de los reyes de Castilla*. Cádiz, 1984.

Cocheril, Maur. *Études sur le monachisme en Espagne au Portugal*. Paris, 1966.

Codera, Francisco. *Decadencia y desaparición de los Almorávides en España*. Zaragoza, 1899.

Colección diplomática de Galicia. 2 vols. Santiago de Compostela, 1901–03.

Colmenares, Diego de. *Historia de la insigne ciudad de Segovia*. 2 vols. 1637. Reprint, Segovia, 1969–70.

Concejos y ciudades en la Edad Media hispánica. León, 1990.

Contamine, Philippe. *La guerre au Moyen Age*. Paris, 1980.

Crosby, Everett U. *Bishop and Chapter in Twelfth-Century England*. New York, 1994.

David, Charles Wendell, ed. *De Expugnatione Lyxbonensi*. New York, 1936.

"De Expugnatione Scalabis." *PMH, Scriptores*. Vol. 1., pp. 93–95. Lisbon, 1856.

Defourneaux, Marcelin. *Les Français en Espagne aux XI et XIII siècles*. Paris, 1949.

Delaville le Roulx, Jean, ed. *Cartulaire général de l'Ordre des Hospitaliers de Saint-Jean de Jerusalem, 1110–1310*. 4 vols. Paris, 1894–1900.

Dembinska, Maria. "A Polish Princess-Empress of Spain and Countess of Provence in the 12th Century." In *Frauen in Spatantike und Fruhmittelalter*, ed. Werner Affeldt, 283–90. Sigmaringen, 1990.

Domingo Palacio, Timoteo, ed. *Documentos del Archivo General de la Villa de Madrid*. Vol. 1. Madrid, 1889.

Dorado, Bernardo. *Compendio histórico de la ciudad de Salamanca*. Salamanca, 1776.

Dufour, Jean, ed. *Recueil des actes de Louis VI, roi de France, 1108–1137*. 4 vols. Paris, 1992.

Durán Gudiol, Antonio, ed. *Colección diplomática de la catedral de Huesca*. Vol. 1. Zaragoza, 1965.

Durany Castrillo, Mercedes. *La región del Bierzo en los siglos centrales de la Edad Media: 1070–1250*. Santiago de Compostela, 1989.

Duro Peña, Emilio, ed. "Catálogo de documentos reales del archivo de la catedral de Orense, 844–1520." In *Miscelánea de textos medievales*, 9–145. Vol. 1, Barcelona, 1972.

———. *Catálogo de los documentos privados en pergamino del archivo de la catedral de Orense, 888–1554*. Orense, 1973.

Erdmann, Carl. *Das Papsttum und Portugal in ersten Jahrhundert der portugiesischen Geschichte*. Berlin, 1928.

Escagedo Salmón, Mateo, ed. *Colección diplomática de la insigne y real iglesia colegial de Santillana*. Santoña, 1927.

Escalona, Romualdo. *Historia del real monasterio de Sahagún*. 1782. Reprint, León, 1982.

Estepa Díez, Carlos. *Estructura social de la ciudad de León, siglos XI–XIII*. León, 1977.

Estepa Díez, Carlos, Teofilo F. Ruiz, Juan A. Bonachia Hernando, and Hilario Casado Alonso. *Burgos en la Edad Media*. Madrid, 1984.

Falque Rey, Emma, ed. *Historia Compostellana*. Turnholt, 1988.

Felibien, Michel. *Histoire de l'abbaye royale de Saint Denys en France*. 1706. Paris, new ed. 1973.

Fernández Catón, José María, ed. *Catálogo del archivo del monasterio de San Pedro de las Dueñas*. León, 1977.

———. *Catálogo del Archivo Histórico Diocesano de León*. 2 vols. León 1978–79.

———. *Colección documental del archivo de la catedral de León, 1109–1187*. Vol. 5. León, 1990.

Fernández Conde, Francisco Javier. *El Libro de Testamentos de la catedral de Oviedo*. Rome, 1971.

Fernández Conde, Francisco Javier, ed. *Historia de la Iglesia en España*. Vol. 2. Madrid, 1982.

Fernández Conde, Francisco Javier, Isabel Torrente Fernández, and Guadalupe de la Noval Menéndez. *El monasterio de San Pelayo de Oviedo*. Vol. 1. Oviedo, 1978.

Fernández de Madrid, Alonso. *Silva palentina*. 3 vols. Palencia, 1932–42.

Fernández Duro, Cesáreo. *Memorias históricas de la ciudad de Zamora*. Vol. 1. Madrid, 1882.

Fernández Flórez, José Antonio, ed. *Colección diplomática del monasterio de Sahagún, 1110–1199*. Vol. 4. León, 1991.

Fernández-Guerra, Aureliano. *El fuero de Avilés*. Madrid, 1865.

Fernández Villamil, Enrique, ed. *Privilegios reales del Museo de Pontevedra*. Pontevedra, 1942.

Fernández-Xesta y Vázquez, Ernesto. *Un magnate catalán en la corte de Alfonso VII*. Madrid, 1991.

Férotin, Marius, ed. *Le Liber Ordinum*. Paris, 1904.

———. *Recueil des chartes de l'abbaye de Silos*. Paris, 1897.

Fletcher, Richard A. *The Episcopate of the Kingdom of León in the Twelfth Century*. Oxford, 1978.

———. *St. James's Catapult: The Life and Times of Diego Gelmirez of Santiago de Compostela*. Oxford, 1984.

Flórez, Enrique. *España Sagrada*. Vols. 1–27. Madrid, 1747–72.

———. *Memórias de las reinas católicas de España*. 2 vols. 1761. Reprint, Madrid, 1964.

Floriano Cumbreño, Antonio C. *Curso general de paleografía y diplomática española*. 2 vols. Oviedo, 1946.

———, *Estudios de historia de Asturias*. Oviedo, 1962.

Floriano Cumbreño, Antonio C., ed. *Colección diplomática del monasterio de Belmonte*. Oviedo, 1960.

———. *El Libro Registro de Corias*. 2 vols. Oviedo, 1950.

———. *El monasterio de Cornellana*. Oviedo, 1949.

Floriano Llorente, Pedro, ed. *Colección diplomática del monasterio de San Vicente de Oviedo*. Oviedo, 1968.

Forey, Alan J. *The Templars in the Corona de Aragón*. London, 1973.

Gacto Fernández, María Trinidad. *Estructura de la población de la Extremadura leonesa en los siglos XII y XIII*. Salamanca, 1977.

Galindo Romeo, Pascual. *Posesiones de San Sabino de Lavedán en Zaragoza*. Madrid, 1923.

————. *Túy en la Baja Edad Media*. Madrid, 1950.

García Calles, Luisa. *Doña Sancha*. León, 1972.

García Larragueta, Santos. *El gran priorado de Navarra de la Orden de San Juan de Jerusalén*. 2 vols. Pamplona, 1957.

————. *Sancta Ovetensis*. Madrid, 1962.

García Larragueta, Santos, ed. *Colección de documentos de la catedral de Oviedo*. Oviedo, 1962.

García Lobo, Vicente, and José Manuel. *Santa María de Arbas: Catálogo de su archivo y apuntes para su historia*. Madrid, 1980.

García Luján, José Antonio, ed. *Cartulario del monasterio de Santa María de Huerta*. Soria, 1981.

————. *Privilegios reales de la catedral de Toledo, 1086–1462*. 2 vols. Toledo, 1982.

García Turza, Francisco Javier. "Morfología de la ciudad de Nájera en la Edad Media." In *III semana de estudios medievales*, pp. 63–88. Logroño, 1993.

García Turza, Francisco Javier, ed. *Documentación medieval del monasterio de Valvanera (siglos XI a XIII)*. Zaragoza, 1985.

García y García, Antonio. "Concilios y sínodos en el ordenamiento jurídico del reino de León." *El reino de León el la Alta Edad Media*. Vol. 1, *Cortes, concilios y fueros*, 353–494. León, 1988.

Garrido Garrido, José Manuel, ed. *Documentación de la catedral de Burgos, 804–1183*. Burgos, 1983.

Gaspar Remiro, Mariano. *Historia de Murcia musulmana*. Zaragoza, 1905.

Gautier Dalché, Jean. *Historia urbana de León y Castilla en la Edad Media, siglos IX–XIII*. Madrid, 1979.

Gil, Juan, ed. "Prefatio de Almeria." In *Chronica Hispana Saeculi XII*, ed. Emma Falque, Juan Gil, and Antonio Maya, 249–67. Turnholt, 1990.

Gíl Farrés, Octavio. *Historia de la moneda española*. 2nd ed. Madrid, 1976.

Gomez de la Torre, Antonio. *Corografía de la provincia de Toro*. Madrid, 1802.

Goñi Gaztambide, José. *Historia de la Bula de la Cruzada en España*. Vitoria, 1958.

Goñi Gaztambide, José, ed. *Catálogo del archivo catedral de Pamplona: Tomo I (829–1500)*. Pamplona, 1965.

González, Julio. *El reino de Castilla en la época de Alfonso VIII*. 3 vols. Madrid, 1960.

————. *Repoblación de Castilla la Nueva*. 2 vols. Madrid, 1975–76.

González, Tomas, ed. *Colección de privilegios, franquezas, exenciones y fueros concedidas a varios pueblos y corporaciones de la corona de Castilla*. Vol. 5. Madrid, 1830.

González García, Manuel. *Salamanca: El repoblación y la ciudad en la Baja Edad Media*. Salamanca, 1988.

González Palencia, Angel. *El Arzobispo D. Raimundo de Toledo*. Barcelona, 1942.

Grassotti, Hilda. *Las instituciones feudo-vasalláticas en León y Castilla*. 2 vols. Spoleto, 1969.

Guerard, Martin, ed. *Cartulaire de l'Abbaye de Saint-Victor de Marseille*. 2 vols. Paris, 1857.

Hernández, Francisco J., ed. *Los cartularios de Toledo*. Madrid, 1985.

Herrera Nogal, Alfredo. *El concejo de la villa de Tardajos: Fueros e historia*. Burgos, 1980.

Hinojosa y Navaros, Eduardo de. "Origen del regimen municipal en León Y Castilla." In *Obras*, vol. 3, ed. Alfonso García-Gallo, 271–317. Madrid, 1974. Initially pub.

in *La administración; Revista internacional de administración, derecho, economía, hacienda y política*. 28 (1896): 417–38.

Huici Miranda, Ambrosio, "Contribución al estudio de la dinastía almorávides: el gobierno de Tasfin ben Ali ben Yusuf en al-Andalus." In *Études d'orientalisme dédiés à la mémoire de Lévi-Provençal*, 605–21. Vol. 2. Paris, 1962.

———. *Historia musulmana de Valencia y su región*. 3 vols. Valencia, 1969–70.

Huici Miranda, Ambrosio, ed. *Las crónicas latinas de la reconquista*. 2 vols. Valencia, 1913.

Hyde, J. K. *Society and Politics in Medieval Italy*. New York, 1973.

Ibn al-Athir. *Annales du Maghreb et de L'Espagne*. Trans. E. Fagnan. Algiers, 1898.

Imperiale de Sant' Angelo, Caesare, ed. *Codice diplomatico della Republica di Genova*. Vol. 1. Rome, 1936.

Izquierdo Benito, Ricardo. *Castilla-La Mancha en la Edad Media*. Madrid, 1985.

Izquierdo Benito, Ricardo, ed. *Privilegios reales otorgados a Toledo durante la Edad Media*. Toledo, 1990.

Jaffé, Philip, and Wilhelm Wattenback, eds. *Regesta Pontificium Romanorum*. Vol. 1. 2nd ed. Leipzig, 1885.

Jiménez de Rada, Rodrigo. *De Rebus Hispaniae*. Ed. Emma Falque Rey. Turnholt, 1987.

Jimeno Jurio, José María. *Documentos medievales Artajoneses*. Pamplona, 1968.

Keegan, John. *A History of Warfare*. New York, 1994.

Knowles, Dom David. *The Monastic Order in England*. Cambridge, 1941.

Kritzeck, James. *Peter the Venerable*. Princeton, 1964.

Lacarra, José María. *Vida de Alfonso el Batallador*. Zaragoza, 1971.

Lacarra, José María, ed. *Colección documental de Irache*. Zaragoza, 1965.

Ladero Quesada, Miguel-Angel. *Las ferias de Castilla, siglos XII a XV*. Madrid, 1994.

Ledesma Rubio, María Luisa, ed. *Cartulario de San Millán de La Cogolla, 1076–1200*. Zaragoza, 1989.

Leighton, Albert C. *Transport and Communication in Early Modern Europe, A.D. 500–1100*. New York, 1972.

Lema Pueyo, José Angel, ed. *Colección diplomática de Alfonso I de Aragón y Pamplona, 1104–1134*. San Sebastián, 1990.

León Tello, Pilar. *Judíos de Toledo*. Vol. 1. Madrid, 1979.

Linage Conde, Antonio. *Los orígines del monacato benedictino en la península Iberica*. 3 vols. León, 1973.

Llorente, Juan Antonio, ed. *Noticias históricas de las tres provincias vascongadas, Alava, Guipúzcoa, y Vizcaya*. 4 vols. Madrid, 1806–08.

Lomax, Derek W. "Don Ramón, Bishop of Palencia (1148–1184)." In *Homenaje a Jaime Vicens Vives*, 279–91. Barcelona, 1965.

———. *The Reconquest of Spain*. London, 1978.

Loperráez Corvalón, Juan. *Descripción histórica del obispado de Osma*. 3 vols. Madrid, 1788.

López Castillo, Santiago, ed. *Diplomatario de Salinas de Añaña, 1194–1465*. San Sebastián, 1984.

López-Ferreiro, Antonio. *Historia de la Santa Apostólica Metropolitana Iglesia de Santiago de Compostela*. 11 vols. Santiago de Compostela, 1898–1911.

Lopéz Pelaéz, Antolín. *El señorio temporal de los obispos de Lugo*. 2 vols. La Coruña, 1897.

López de Silanes, Ciriaco, and Eliseo Sáinz Ripa, eds. *Colección diplomática calceatense archivo catedral; Años 1125–1397.* Logroño, 1985.

Loscertales de García de Valdeavellano, Pilar, ed. *Tumbos del monasterio de Sobrado de los Monjes.* 2 vols. Madrid, 1976.

Lucas Alvarez, Manuel. "El monasterio de San Julián de Moraime en Galicia." In *Homenaje a Don Augustín Millares Carlo,* 605–43. Grand Canaries, 1975.

———. *El reino de León en la Alta Edad Media.* Vol. 5. *Las cancellerías reales (1109–1230).* León, 1993.

———. *El reino de León en la Alta Edad Media.* Vol. 8. *Las cancillerías reales asturleonesas (718–1072).* León, 1995.

Lucas, Alvarez, Manuel, ed. *El tumbo de San Julián de Samos, siglos VIII–XII.* Santiago de Compostela, 1986.

Lucas Alvarez, Manuel, and Pedro Lucas Domínguez, Pedro, eds. *El priorato bendictino de San Vicenzo de Pombeiro y su colección diplomática en la Edad Media.* La Coruña, 1996.

Lucas de Túy, "Chronicon Mundi ab Origine Mundi usque ad Eram MCCLXXIV." In *Hispaniae Illustratae,* ed. Andreas Schottus, 1–116. Vol. 4. Frankfurt, 1608.

Luchaire, Achille. *Études sur les Actes de Louis VII.* Paris, 1885.

Malalana Ureña, Antonio. *Escalona medieval 1083–1400).* Cubierta, 1987.

Manrique, Angel. *Cisterciensium seu Verius Ecclesiasticorum Annalium a Condito Cistercio.* 4 vols. Lyons, 1642–59.

Mansilla, Demetrio. *Iglesia castellano-leonesa y curia romana en los tiempos del rey San Fernando.* Madrid, 1945.

Mansilla, Demetrio, ed. *La documentación pontificia hasta Inocencio III, 965–1216.* Rome, 1955.

Mañueco Villalobos, Manuel, and José Zurita Nieto, eds. *Documentos de la Iglesial Colegial de Santa María la Mayor de Valladolid.* 2 vols. Valladolid, 1917–20.

Marazuela, María Teresa de la Pena, and León Tello, Pilar, eds. *Archivo de los Duques de Frias.* Madrid, 1955.

Marchegay, Paul, and Emile Mabille, eds. "Chronicon Sancti Maxentii Pictavensis." In *Chroniques des églises d'Anjou,* 351–433. Paris, 1869.

Marongiu, Antonio. *Medieval Parliaments.* Trans. S. J. Woolf. London, 1968.

Martín, José Luis. *Orígines de la orden militar de Santiago.* Barcelona, 1974.

———. "Cabildos catedralicios del occidente español hasta mediados del siglo XIII." In *Homenaje a Fray Justo Pérez de Urbel,* 125–36. Vol. 2. Silos, 1977.

Martín, José Luis, ed. *Documentación medieval de la iglesia catedral de Coria.* Salamanca, 1989.

———, *Documentos zamoranos,* Vol. 1. *Documentos del archivo catedralicio de Zamora, Primera Parte; 1128–1261.* Salamanca, 1982.

Martín, José Luis, Luis Miguel Villar García, Florencio Marcos Rodríguez, and Marciano Sánchez Rodríguez, eds. *Documentos de los archivos catedralicio y diocesano de Salamanca, siglos XII–XIII.* Salamanca, 1977.

Martín Duque, Angel J., ed. *Documentación medieval de Leire, siglos IX al XII.* Pamplona, 1983.

Martín López, María Encarnación, ed. *Patrimonio cultural de San Isidoro de León. Serie documental.* Vol. 1, Parte 1, *Documentos de los siglos X–XIII.* León, 1995.

Martín Postigo, María de la Soterrana. *Santa María de Cardaba, priorato de Arlanza y granja de Sacramenia*. Valladolid, 1979.

Martínez Díez, G. *Fueros locales en el territorio de la provincia de Burgos*. Burgos, 1982.

Martínez Sopena, Pascual. *La Tierra de Campos Occidental: Poblamiento, poder, y comunidad del siglo X al XIII*. Valladolid, 1985.

Maya Sánchez, Antonio, and Juan Gil, eds. "Chronica Adefonsi Imperatoris." In *Chronica Hispana: Saeculi XII*, pp. 109–296. Turnholt, 1990.

Menéndez Pidal, Ramón, ed. *Documentos lingüísticos de España*. Madrid, 1966.

Merchán Fernández, Carlos. *Sobre los orígenes del regimen señorial en Castilla*. Malaga, 1982.

Merino, Andrés. *Escuela paleografía*. Madrid, 1780.

Migne, J. P., ed. *Patrologiae Latinae*. 221 vols. Paris, 1844–1864.

Mingüella y Arnedo, Toribio. *Historia de la diócesis de Sigüenza y de sus obispos*. Vol 1. Madrid, 1910.

Monterde Albiac, Cristina, ed. *Colección diplomática del monasterio de Fitero: 1140–1210*. Zaragoza, 1978.

———. *Diplomatario de la Reina Urraca de Castilla y León, 1109–1126*. Zaragoza, 1996.

Morales, Ambrosio de. *Viaje a los reinos de León, y Galicia, y principado de Asturias*. Ed. Enrique Flórez. 1765. Reprint. Oviedo, 1977.

Morillo, Stephen. *Warfare under the Anglo-Norman Kings, 1088–1135*. Woodbridge, Great Britain, 1994.

Moxó, Salvador de. *Repoblación y sociedad en la España cristiana medieval*. Madrid, 1979.

Munita Loínaz, José Antonio, ed. *Libro Becerro del monasterio de Sta. María de La Oliva (Navarra): Colección documental, 1132–1500*. San Sebastián, 1984.

Muñoz y Romero, Jesus. *Manual de paleografía diplomática española de los siglos XII al XVII*. 2nd ed. Madrid, 1917.

Muñoz y Romero, Tomas, ed. *Colección de fueros y cartas pueblas*. Madrid, 1847.

O'Callaghan, Joseph F. *The Cortes of Castile-León, 1188–1350*. Philadelphia, 1989.

Oceja Gonzalo, Isabel, ed. *Documentación del monasterio de San Salvador de Oña: 1032–1284*. Burgos, 1983.

Otto of Freising. *Gesta Frederici*. Ed. Franz-Josef Schmale. Berlin, 1965.

Pacaut, Marcel. *Louis VII et son royaume*. Paris, 1964.

Palacín Gálvez, María del Carmen, and Martínez García, Luis, eds. *Documentación del Hospital del Rey de Burgos, 1136–1277*. Burgos, 1990.

Pareja Serrada, Antonio, ed. *Diplomática Arriacense*. Guadalajara, 1921.

Parker, Geoffrey. *The Military Revolution*. Cambridge, 1988.

Paz y Melia, A., ed. *Series de los mas importantes documentos del archivo y biblioteca del Duque de Medinaceli*. Vol. 1. *Serie histórica, años 860–1814*. Madrid, 1951.

Peinado Santaella, Rafael Gerardo, and José Enrique López de Coca Castañer. *Historia de Granada*. Vol. 2. Granada, 1987.

Peña Pérez, F. Javier, ed. *Documentación del monasterio de San Juan de Burgos: 1091–1400*. Burgos, 1983.

Pérez Avellaneda, Marino. *Cerezo de Río Tirón*. Madrid, 1983.

Pérez Celada, Julio A., ed. *Documentación del monasterio de San Zoil de Carrión, 1047–1300*. Palencia, 1986.

Pérez de Urbel, Justo. *Sancho el Mayor de Navarra*. Madrid, 1950.

Pérez de Urbel, Justo, and Atilano González Ruiz-Zorillo, eds. *Historia Silense*. Madrid, 1959.

Pérez Millán, Juan, ed. *Privilegios reales y viejos documentos de Santiago de Compostela*. Madrid, 1965.

Pflugk-Harttung, J. V., ed. *Acta Pontificum Romanorum Inedita*. 3 vols. Graz, 1958.

Pino Rebolledo, Fernando, ed. *Catálogo de los pergaminos de la Edad Media, 1191–1393. Transcripción y notas críticas*. Valladolid, 1988.

Portela Silva, Ermelindo. *La colonización cisterciense en Galicia, 1142–1260*. Santiago de Compostela, 1981.

Powell, James M., ed. *Muslims under Latin Rule, 1100–1300*. Princeton, 1990.

Powers, James F. *A Society Organized for War*. Berkeley, Calif., 1988.

Procter, Evelyn S. *Curia and Cortes in León and Castile, 1072–1295*. Cambridge, 1980.

Pulgar, Pedro Fernando del. *Historia secular y eclesiástica de la ciudad de Palencia*. Vol. 1. Madrid, 1680.

Quintana Prieto, Augusto. *Monografía histórica del Bierzo*. Madrid, 1956.

———. *El obispado de Astorga en el siglo XII*. Astorga, 1985.

Quintana Prieto, Augusto, ed. *Tumbo viejo de San Pedro de Montes*. León, 1971.

Recuero Astray, Manuel. *Alfonso VII, Emperador*. León, 1979.

———. "El Reino de León durante la primera mitad del siglo XII." In *El Reino de León en la Alta Edad Media*, Vol. 4, *La Monarquía, 1109–1230*, pp. 9–75. León, 1993.

Reilly, Bernard F. *The Contest of Christian and Muslim Spain, 1031–1157*. Cambridge, Mass., 1992.

———. *The Kingdom of León-Castilla under King Alfonso VI, 1065–1109*. Princeton, 1988.

———. *The Kingdom of León-Castilla under Queen Urraca, 1109–1126*. Princeton, 1982.

———. "The Chancery of Alfonso VI of León-Castile, (1065–1109)." In *Santiago, Saint-Denis, and Saint Peter. The Reception of the Roman Liturgy in León-Castile in 1080*, 1–40. New York, 1985.

———. "Rodrigo Giménez de Rada's Portrait of Alfonso VI of León-Castile in the 'De Rebus Hispaniae': Historical Methodology in the Thirteenth Century." In *Estudios en Homenaje a Don Claudio Sánchez Albornoz en sus 90 años*, 87–97. Vol. 3. Buenos Aires, 1985.

Ribeiro, Joao Pedro. *Dissertaçoes chronologicas e criticas sobre a História e jurisprudencia ecclesiastica e civil de Portugal*. 5 vols. Lisbon, 1856–1896.

Richard, Jean, ed. *Le cartulaire de Marcigny sur Loire, 1048–1144*. Dijon, 1957.

Risco, Manuel. *Historia de Alfonso VII el Emperador*. Madrid, 1792.

Risco, Manuel, ed. *España Sagrada* Vols. 28–42. Madrid, 1774–1801.

Rivera Recio, Juan Francisco. *Los arzobispos de Toledo en la baja Edad Media*. Toledo, 1969.

———. *La iglesia de Toledo en el siglo XII*. Vol. 1. Rome, 1966.

Rivera Recio, Juan Francisco, ed. *Privilegios reales y viejos documentos, I, Toledo*. Madrid, 1963.

Robert, Ulysse, ed. *Bullaire du Pape Calixti II*. 2 vols. Paris, 1891.

Robinson, I. S. *The Papacy, 1073–1198: Continuity and Innovation*. Cambridge, 1990.

Rodrígues Gil, Magdalena. "Notas para una teoría general de la vertebración jurídica de los concejos en la Alta Edad Media." In *Concejos y ciudades en la Edad Media hispánica*, 321–45. León, 1990.

Rodríguez, Raimondo, ed. *Catálogo de documentos del monasterio de Santa María de Otero de las Dueñas.* León, 1948.

Rodríguez de Diego, José Luis. *El tumbo del monasterio cisterciense de La Espina.* Valladolid, 1982.

Rodríguez de Lama, Ildefonso, ed. *Colección diplomática medieval de La Rioja: Documentos, 923-1168.* Vol. 2. Logroño, 1976.

Rodríguez Fernández, Justiniano. *Las juderías de la provincia de León.* León, 1976.

———. *Palencia: Panorámica foral de la provincia.* Palencia, 1981.

Rodríguez González, Angel, ed. *El tumbo del monasterio de San Martín de Castañeda.* León, 1973.

Rodríguez López, Pedro. *Episcopologio asturicense.* 2 vols. Astorga, 1907.

Rogers, Randall. *Latin Siege Warfare in the Twelfth Century.* Oxford, 1992.

Rosell, Francisco M., ed. *Liber Feudorum Maior.* Barcelona, 1945.

Rubio, Luis, ed. *Documentos del Pilar.* Zaragoza, 1971.

Ruiz de Loizaga, Saturnino, ed. *Los Cartularios Gótico y Galicano de Santa María de Valpuesta, 1090-1140.* Alava, 1995.

Russell, Josiah Cox. *Medieval Regions and Their Cities.* Bloomington, 1972.

———. *Twelfth Century Studies.* New York, 1978.

Säbekow, Gerhard. *Die päpstliche Legationen nach Spanien und Portugal bis zum Ausgang des XII Jahrhunderts.* Berlin, 1931.

Sáenz de Aguirre, Joseph. *Collectio Maxima Conciliorum Hispaniae.* Vol. 5. Rome, 1755.

Sáez, Emilio, and Sáez, Carlos, eds. *El fondo español del Archivo de la Academia de las Ciencias de San Petersburgo.* Alcalá de Henares, 1993.

Sagredo Fernández, Felix. *Briviesca antigua y medieval.* 2nd ed. Madrid, 1979.

Saínz Ripa, Eliseo. *Colección diplomática de las colegiatas de Albelda y Logroño; Tomo 1: 924-1399.* Logroño, 1981.

Sánchez-Albornoz, Claudio. *Despoblación y repoblación del valle del Duero.* Buenos Aires, 1966.

———. "El fuero de León." In *León y su historia,* 11–60. Vol. 5. León, 1972.

———. "Notas para el estudio del 'petitum.'" In *Homenaje a Don Ramón Carande,* Vol. 2. 383–418. Madrid, 1963. Reprinted in *Viejos y nuevos estudios sobre las instituciones medievales españolas,* Vol. 2. 929–67. Madrid, 1976.

Sánchez Alonso, Benito, ed. *Crónica del Obispo Don Pelayo.* Madrid, 1924.

Sánchez Belda, Luis. "La cancillería real castellana durante el reinado de doña Urraca. In *EDMP,* 587–99. Vol. 4. Madrid, 1953.

Sánchez Belda, Luis, ed. *Cartulario de Santo Toribio de Liébana.* Madrid, 1948.

———. *Chronica Adefonsi Imperatoris.* Madrid, 1950.

Sánchez Maya, Antonio, and Juan Gil, eds. "Chronica Adefonsi Imperatoris." In *Chronica Hispana: Saeculi XII,* 109–296. Turnholt, 1990.

Sandoval, Prudencio de. *Antiguedad de la ciudad y iglesia catedral de Túy.* 1610. Reprint; Barcelona, 1964.

———. *Chronica del inclito y bienaventurado famoso emperador de España, Don Alfonso VII deste nombre, rey de Castilla y León, hijo de Don Ramón de Borgoña y de Dona Urraca, reyna propretaria de Castilla.* Madrid, 1600.

———. *Historia de los reyes de Castilla y de León.* 2 vols. Pamplona, 1634.

Santacana Tort, Jaime. *El monasterio de Poblet, 1151-1181.* Barcelona, 1974.

Sanz y Sanz, Hilario, ed. *Privilegios reales y viejos documentos de Segovia*. Madrid, 1977.

Segl, Peter. *Königtum und Klosterreform in Spanien*. Kallmünz, 1974.

Serrano, Luciano. *El obispado de Burgos y Castilla primitiva desde el siglo V al XIII*. 3 vols. Madrid, 1935.

Serrano, Luciano, ed. *Cartulario de San Millán de La Cogolla*. Madrid, 1930.

———. *Cartulario de San Pedro de Arlanza*. Madrid, 1925.

———. *Cartulario de San Vicente de Oviedo, 781–1200*. Madrid, 1929.

———. *Cartulario del monasterio de Vega con documentos de San Pelayo y Vega de Oviedo*. Madrid, 1927.

———. *Colección diplomática de San Salvador de El Moral*. Madrid, 1906.

Serrao, Joaquim Veríssimo. *História de Portugal*. Vol. 1. Lisbon, 1976.

Soldevila, Ferran, ed. *Historia dels Catalans*. 2nd ed. 3 vols. Barcelona, 1962–1964.

Sousa Soares, Torquato de. "O governo de Portugal pela Infante Rainha d. Teresa." In *Colectanea de Estudios im honra do Prof-Doutor Damiao Peres*, 99–119. Lisbon, 1974.

Spufford, Peter. *Money and Its Use in Medieval Europe*. Cambridge, 1988.

Stalls, Clay. *Possessing the Land: Aragón's Expansion into Islam's Ebro Frontier under Alfonso the Battler, 1104–1134*. New York, 1995.

Suárez de Alarcón, Antonio. *Relaciones genealógicas de la casa de los Marqueses de Trocifal*. Madrid, 1656.

Tapía Garrido, José Angel. *Historia general de Almería y su provincia*. 3 vols. Almeria, 1976–78.

Ubieto Arteta, Antonio. *Historia de Aragón: Creación y desarrollo de la Corona de Aragón*. Zaragoza, 1987.

———. *Historia de Aragón. La formación territorial*. Zaragoza, 1981.

———. "Los primeros anos de la diócesis de Siguenza." In *Homenaje a Johannes Vincke*, 135–48. Vol. 1. 2 vols. Madrid, 1962–63.

Ubieto Arteta, Antonio, ed. *Cartulario de Santa Cruz de la Serós*. Valencia, 1966.

———. *Colección diplomática de Cuéllar*. Segovia, 1961.

———. *Crónica Nájerense*, 2nd ed. Zaragoza, 1985.

———. *Documentos de Ramiro II de Aragón*. Zaragoza, 1988.

———. *Listas epicopales medievales*. 2 vols. Zaragoza, 1989.

Ubieto Arteta, Augustín, ed. *Cartularios (I, II, y III) de Santo Domingo de la Calzada*. Zaragoza, 1978.

Vaamonde Lores, César, ed. *Colección de documentos históricos*. Vol. 1. La Coruña, 1915.

Vajay, Szabolcs de. "Ramire le moine et Agnès de Poitou." In *Mélanges offerts à René Crozet*, 727–50. Vol. 2. 2 vols. Poitiers, 1966.

Valdeavellano, Luis G. de. *Historia de la instituciones españolas*. Madrid, 1968.

———. *El mercado en León y Castilla durante la Edad Media*. 2nd ed. Seville, 1974.

Vázquez de Parga, Luis, José María Lacarra, and Juan Uría Ríu. *Las peregrinaciones a Santiago de Compostela*. 3 vols. Madrid, 1948–49.

Vigil, Ciriaco Miguel. *Asturias monumental, epigráfica, y diplomática*. 2 vols. Oviedo, 1887.

Vignau, Vicente, ed. *Cartulario del monasterio de Eslonza*. Madrid, 1885.

———. *Indice de los documentos de la monasterio de Sahagún*. Madrid, 1874.

Viguera, María J. *Aragón musulmán*. Zaragoza, 1988.

Villar García, Luis-Miguel. *La Extramadura castellano-leonesa: Guerreros, clérigos y campesinos, 711–1252*. Valladolid, 1986.

Villar García, Luis Miguel, ed. *Documentación medieval de la catedral de Segovia, 1115–1300*. Salamanca, 1990.

Vivancos Gómez, Miguel C. *Documentación del monasterio de Santo Domingo de Silos; 954–1254*. Burgos, 1988.

Vones, Ludwig. *Die "Historia Compostellana" und die Kirchenpolitik des Nordwestspanischen Raumes, 1070–1130*. Cologne, 1980.

Wasserstein, David. *The Rise and Fall of the Party-Kings: Politics and Society in Islamic Spain, 1002–1086*. Princeton, 1985.

William, Archbishop of Tyre. *A History of Deeds Done beyond the Sea*. Vol. 1. Trans. Emily Atwater Babcock and A. C. Krey. New York, 1943.

Yepes, Antonio de. *Corónica general de la Orden de San Benito*. 7 vols. Irache and Valladolid, 1609–21.

Periodical Literature

Alamo, M. "Diocèse de Calahorra et la Calzada." *DHGE* 11 (1949): 275–95.

Alonso, Benito F. "Monasterio de Santa Maria de Osera. Privilegio de fundación." *BCM Orense* 1 (1900): 281–93.

Alonso Alonso, Manuel. "Notas sobre los traductores toledanos Domingo Gundisalvo y Juan Hispano." *Al-Andalus* 8 (1943): 155–88.

Andrés, Alfonso. "Documentos inéditos de Alfonso VII y Alfonso IX de León." *HS* 11 (1958): 401–9.

Bachrach, Bernard. "The Angevin Strategy of Castle Building in the Reign of Fulk Nerra, 987–1040." *AHR* 88 (1983): 533–60.

Barrero García, Ana María. "Los fueros de Sahagún." *AHDE* 42 (1972): 385–597.

Barton, Simon. "Sobre el conde Rodrigo Pérez 'el Velloso.'" *Estudios Mindonienses* 5 (1989): 653–61.

———. "Two Catalan Magnates in the Courts of the Kings of León-Castile: The Careers of Ponce de Cabrera and Ponce de Minerva Re-examined." *JMH* 18 (1992): 233–66.

Bishko, Charles Julian. "Peter the Venerable's Journey to Spain." In *Petrus Venerabilis (1156–1956): Studies and Texts Commemorating the Eighth Century of His Death*, 163–75. Rome, 1956. The latter is volume 40 of the *Studia Anselmiana*.

Bouchard, Constance B. "The Geographical, Social and Ecclesiastical Origins of the Bishops of Auxerre and Sens in the Central Middle Ages." *Church History* 46 (1977): 277–95.

Bravo, Miguel. "Monasterio de Eslonza; adiciones al cartulario de Eslonza de V. Vignau." *AL* 2 (1948): 89–111.

Bujanda, Fernando, ed. "Archivo catedral de Calahorra." *Berceo* 27 (1965): 417–78.

Camara Pina, Luiz María da. "A batalha de S. Mamede (24-VI-1128): Subsidios para su história militar." *RPH* 17 (1977): 199–229.

Canal Sánchez-Pagín, José María. "Casamientos de los condes de Urgel en Castilla." *AEM* 19 (1989): 119–35.

———. "La Infanta Doña Elvira, hija de Alfonso VI y de Gimena Muñoz a la luz de los diplomas." *AL* 33 (1979): 271–87.

———. "Jimena Muñoz, amiga de Alfonso VI." *AEM* 21 (1991): 11–40.

Canal Sánchez Pagín, José María, ed. "Documentos del monasterio de Carrizo de la Ribera (León) en la Colección Salazar de la Real Academia de la Historia." *AL* 32 (1978): 381–403.

Castro y Sueiro, Manuel, ed. "Documentos del archivo catedral de Orense." *BCM Orense.* 2 vols. Orense, 1922–23.

Cocheril, Maur. "L'implantation des abbayes cisterciennes dans la péninsule ibérique." *AEM* 1 (1964): 217–87.

Collins, Roger. "Sicut Lex Gothorum continet." *EHR* 100 (1985): 489–512.

Constable, Giles. "A Note on the Route of the Anglo-Flemish Crusaders of 1147." *Speculum* 28 (1953): 525–26.

Crosby, Everett U. "The Organization of the English Episcopate under Henry I." *Studies in Medieval and Renaissance History* 4 (1967): 3–88.

Defourneaux, Marcelin. "Louis VII et les souverains espagnols: L'énigme du pséudo-Alphonse." *EDMP* 6 (1956): 647–61.

"Documentos para la historia de derecho español." *AHDE* 2 (1925): 462–526.

Durán Gudiol, Antonio. "La Santa Sede y los obispados de Huesca y Roda en la primera mitad del siglo XII." *AA* 13 (1965): 35–134.

Duro Peña, Emilio. "El monasterio de San Pedro de Ramiranes." *AL* 25 (1971): 9–74.

Erdmann, Carl, ed. "Papsturkunden in Portugal." *AGWG* 20 (1927): 198–203.

Fernández Catón, José María. "Documentos leoneses en escritura visigótica." *AL* 27 (1973): 224–26.

———. "El llamado Tumbo Colorado y otros códices de la iglesia compostelana: Ensayo de reconstrucción." *AL* 44 (1990): 9–291.

Fernández Conde, F. Javier. "La Reina Urraca 'La Asturiana.'" *AM* 2 (1975): 65–94.

Fernández Martín, Luis, ed. "Colección diplomática del monasterio de San Pelayo de Cerrato." *HS* 26 (1973): 281–324.

———. "Colección diplomática del monasterio de Santervás de Campos." *AL* 32 (1978): 183–214.

———. "Registro de escrituras del monasterio de San Salvador de Celorio, 1070–1570." *BIEA* 78 (1973): 33–139.

———. "Villafrades de Campos: Señorío del abad de Sahagún." *AL* 27 (1973): 227–77.

Fita, Fidel. "Concilio nacional de Burgos (18 de Febrero de 1127)." *BRAH* 48 (1906): 387–407.

———. "Concilios nacionales de Salamanca en 1154 y de Valladolid en 1155." *BRAH* 24 (1894): 449–75.

———. "Dos bulas inéditas de Honorio II." *BRAH* 7 (1885): 414–23.

———. "Primera legación del Cardenal Jacinto en España. Bulas inéditas de Anastasio IV. Nuevas luces sobre el concilio nacional de Valladolid (1155) y otros datos inéditos." *BRAH* 14 (1889): 530–55.

———. "San Miguel de Escalada. Antiguos fueros y nuevas ilustraciones." *BRAH* 32 (1898): 367–427.

———. "San Miguel de Escalada: Documento apócrifo del siglo XII, auténticos del XIII." *BRAH* 32 (1898): 25–64.

———. "Variedades: Bernardo de Perigord, arcediano de Toledo y obispo de Zamora." *BRAH* 14 (1889): 456–66.

Fletcher, Richard A. "The Archbishops of Santiago de Compostela between 1140 and 1173: A New Chronology." *Compostellanum* 17 (1972): 45–61.

———. "Diplomatic and the Cid Revisited: The Seals and Mandates of Alfonso VII." *JMH* 2 (1976): 305–38.

Floriano Llorente, Pedro, ed. "Colección diplomática del monasterio de Villanueva de Oscos. Primera serie; años 1136–1200." *BIEA* 102 (1981): 127–90.

———. "El fondo antiguo de pergaminos del Instituto Valencia de Don Juan: Documentos reales, primera serie, 875–1224." *BRAH* 168 (1971): 441–513.

García Gallo, Alfonso. "El fuero de León." *AHDE* 39 (1969): 5–171.

———. "Los fueros de Toledo." *AHDE* 45 (1975): 341–488.

García García, Elida. "El conde asturiano Gonzalo Peláez." *AM* 2 (1975): 39–64

García Sáinz de Baranda, Julián. "El monasterio de monjes bernardos de Santa María de Rioseco." *BIFG* 156 (1961): 633–42.

Gautier-Dalché, Jean. "L'histoire monétaire de l'Espagne septentrionale et centrale du XI au XII siècle." *AEM* 6 (1969): 43–95.

González, Julio. "Repoblación de las tierras de Cuenca." *AEM* 12 (1982): 183–204.

Grassotti, Hilda. "Una 'convenientia' prestimonial entre un arzobispo y el emperador." *CHE* 51–52 (1970): 5–23.

———. "Dos problemas de historia castellano-leonesa, siglo XII." *CHE* 49–50 (1969): 135–97.

———. "Homenaje de García Ramírez a Alfonso VII." *CHE* 37–38 (1963): 318–29.

———. "Sobre una concesión de Alfonso VII a la iglesia salmantina." *CHE* 49–50 (1969): 323–48.

Guallart, Julieta, and Laguzzi, María del Pilar R. "Algunos documentos reales leoneses." *CHE* 2 (1944): 363–81.

Hiestand, Rudolf. "Reconquista, Kreuzzug und heiliges Grab." *GAKS* 31 (1984): 136–57.

Huici Miranda, Ambrosio. "Un nuevo manuscrito de al-Bayan al-Mugrib: Datos inéditos y aclaraciones sobre los ultimos años del reinado de Alfonso VII, el Emperador." *Al-Andalus* 24 (1959): 63–84.

Kehr, Paul, ed. "Papsturkunden in Spanien, I: Katalonien." *AGWG* 18 (1926).

———. "Papsturkunden in Spanien, II: Navarra und Aragon." *AGWG* 22 (1928).

Lacarra, José María. "Alfonso el Batallador y las paces de Támara." *EEMCA* 3 (1947–48): 461–73.

Lacarra, José María, ed. "Documentos para el estudio de la reconquista y repoblación del valle del Ebro." *EEMCA* 2 (1946): 467–574; 3 (1947–48): 499–727; and 5 (1952): 511–668.

———. "La iglesia de Tudela ante Tarazona y Pamplona." *EEMCA* 5 (1952): 417–26.

———. "La restauración ecclesiástica en las tierras conquistadas por el Batallador, 1118–1134." *RPH* 4 (1947): 263–86.

Ledesma Rubio, María Luisa, ed. "Colección diplomática de Grisén, siglos XII y XIII." *EEMCA* 10 (1975): 691–820.

Lomax, Derek. "Catalanes en el imperio leonés." *Toletum* 17 (1983–1984): 201–16.

Lourie, Elena. "The Will of Alfonso I, *el Batallador*, King of Aragon and Navarre: A Reassessment." *Speculum* 50 (1975): 635–51.

Lucas Alvarez, Manuel, ed. "La colección diplomática del monasterio de San Lorenzo de Carboerio." *Compostellanum* 3 (1958): 221–308.

McCrank, Lawrence J. "Norman Crusaders in the Catalan Reconquest: Robert Burdet and the Principality of Tarragona, 1129–1155." *JMH* 7 (1981): 67–82.

Mañaricua, Andrés E. "Provisión de obispados en la Alta Edad Media española." *Estudios de Deusto* 14 (1966): 61–92.

Martín, José Luis. "La orden militar de San Marcos de León." *León y su historia* 4 (1977): 19–100.

Martín Postigo, Maria de la Soterrana. "Alfonso I el Batallador y Segovia." *Estudios Segovianos* 19 (1967): 5–79.

Martínez, Gonzalo. "Diplomatario de San Cristobal de Ibeas." *BIFG* 55 (1975): 690–720.

Martínez, Marcos G. "El convento benedictino de Villanueva de Oscos." *BIEA* 8 (1954): 279–93.

———. "Regesta de Don Pelayo, obispo de Oviedo." *BIEA* 18 (1964): 211–48.

Martínez Díez, Gonzalo. "Fueros de La Rioja." *AHDE* 49 (1979): 327–454.

———. "Fueros locales en el territorio de la provincia de Santander." *AHDE* 46 (1976): 527–608.

Menéndez Pidal, Ramón. "Sobre un Tratado de paz entre Alfonso el Batallador y Alfonso VII." *BRAH* (1943): 115–31.

Millares Carlo, Agustín. "La cancillería real en León y Castilla hasta finales del reinado de Fernando III." *AHDE* 3 (1926): 227–306.

Miret y Sans, Joachim. "Le roi Louis VII et le Comte de Barcelone." *Moyen Age* 25 (1912): 289–300.

Montero Díaz, Santiago, ed. "La colección diplomática de San Martín de Jubia." *Boletín de la Universidad de Santiago de Compostela* 7 (1935): 1–159.

Nesbitt, John W. "The Rate of March of Crusading Armies in Europe." *Traditio* 19 (1963): 167–81.

Pascua Echegaray, Esther. "Hacia la formación política de la monarquía medieval. Las relaciones entre la monarquía y la iglesia castellano-leonesa en el reinado de Alfonso VII." *Hispania* 172 (1989): 397–441.

Pastor de Togneri, Reyna. "La sal en Castilla y León." *CHE* 37–38 (1963): 42–87.

Portela Silva, Ermelindo. "La región del obispado de Túy en los siglos XII a XV." *Compostellanum* 20 (1975): 1–325.

Powers, James. F. "The Creative Interaction between Portuguese and Leonese Municipal Military Law, 1055 to 1279." *Speculum* 62 (1987): 53–80.

Prestwich, J. O. "The Military Households of the Norman Kings." *EHR* 96 (1981): 1–35.

Quintana Prieto, Augusto. "Los monasterios de Poibueno y San Martín de Montes." *AL* 22 (1968): 63–131.

Rassow, Peter. "La Cofradía de Belchite." *AHDE* 3 (1926): 200–226.

———. "Die Urkunden Kaiser Alfonso VII von Spanien." *AU* 10 (1928): 327–468, and 11 (1930): 66–137.

Reilly, Bernard F. "The Chancery of Alfonso VII of León-Castilla: The Period 1116–1135 Reconsidered." *Speculum* 51 (1971): 243–61.

———. "The Court Bishops of Alfonso VII of León-Castilla, 1147–1157." *Medieval Studies* 36 (1974): 67–78.

———. "On Getting to Be a Bishop in León-Castilla: The 'Emperor' Alfonso VII and the Post-Gregorian Church." *Studies in Medieval and Renaissance History* n.s. 1 (1978): 37–68.

Represa Rodríguez, Amando. "Genesis y evolución urbana de la Zamora medieval." *Hispania* 32 (1972): 525–45.

———. "Palencia: breve análisis de su formación urbana durante los siglos XI–XIII." *En la España Medieval* 1 (1980): 385–97.

———. "La 'tierra' medieval de Segovia." *Estudios Segovianos* 21 (1969): 227–44.

Rivera Recio, Juan Francisco. "El 'Liber Privilegiorum' de la catedral de Toledo y los documentos reales en el contenidos." *HS* 1 (1948): 163–81.

Rodríguez López, Amancio. "Los fueros de Villadiegos inéditos." *BRAH* 61 (1912): 431–37.

Ruiz de la Pena, Juan Ignacio. "El coto de Leitariegos." *AM* 3 (1979): 173–215.

Sánchez Belda, Luis. "Notas de diplomática. En torno de tres diplomas de Alfonso VII." *Hispania* 11 (1951): 47–61.

———. "Notas de diplomática: La confirmación de documentos por los reyes del Occidente español." *RABM* 19 (1953): 85–116.

Sánchez Doncel, Gregorio. "Historia de Vertavillo." *Publicaciones del Instituto Tello Téllez de Meneses* 4 (1950): 63–132.

Serrano, Luciano. "Los Armíldez de Toledo y el monasterio de Tórtoles." *BRAH* 103 (1933): 69–141.

———. "Bérengère." *DHGE* 8 (1935): cols. 411–413.

———. "Fueros y privilegios del concejo de Pancorbo (Burgos)." *AHDE* 10 (1933): 325–32.

Serrano y Sanz, Miguel, ed. "Documentos del monasterio de Celanova, 975–1164." *Revista de ciencias jurídicas y sociales* 12 (1929): 5–47, 515–24.

Simon y Nieto, Francisco. "Nuevos datos históricos acerca del sepulchro de la reina Doña Urraca en la catedral de Palencia." *BRAH* 30 (1897): 379–99.

Todesca, James J. "The Monetary History of Castile-Leon (ca. 1100–1300) in Light of the Bourgey Hoard." *American Nuismatic Society Museum Notes* 33 (1988): 129–203.

Torres Balbás, Leopoldo. "Almería islámica." *Al-Andalus* 22 (1957): 411–53.

Ubieto Arteta, Antonio. "De nuevo sobre el nacimiento de Alfonso II de Aragón." *EEMCA* 6 (1956): 203–9.

———. "Homenaje de Aragón a Castilla por el condado de 'Navarra.'" *EEMCA* 3 (1947–48): 1–22.

———. "Navarra-Aragón y la idea imperial de Alfonso VII de Castilla." *EEMCA* 6 (1956): 41–82.

Ubieto Arteta, Augustín, ed. "Documentos reales del archivo catedralicio de Calahorra." *Berceo* 83 (1972): 195–262.

Vaamonde Lores, César. "Santa Marina de Gomáriz." *BCM Orense* 4 (1910): 8–15, 34–42.

Vázquez Núñez, Arturo. "Documentos históricos." *BCM Orense* 1 (1901): 393–96; 2 (1903): 169–71; 3 (1905): 343.

Vázquez Saco, Francisco, "Un diploma de Alfonso VII." *BCM, Lugo* 2 (1947): 285–98.

Vones, Ludwig. "Die Diplome der Könige Alfons VII von Kastilien-León und Ferdinands II von León für das Kloster San Pedro de Rocas (Prov. Orense)." *GAKS* 31 (1984): 158–80.

Yáñez Neira, Damián. "Aproximación al abadologia de Santa María de Meira." *Compostellanum* 33 (1988): 531–610.

Index

Pedro, bishop of León, 249, 251
Pedro, bishop of Lugo, 248, 264
Pedro, bishop of Mondoñedo, 116n, 258
Pedro, bishop of Oporto, 251
Pedro, bishop of Orense, 259
Pedro, bishop of Oviedo, 130, 259
Pedro I, bishop of Palencia, 18, 31, 235
Pedro II, bishop of Palencia, 251, 255
Pedro, bishop of Pamplona, 26n
Pedro, bishop of Roda, 43
Pedro, bishop of Segovia, 102, 247, 248, 251, 255–56
Pedro, bishop of Sigüenza, 196, 257, 258
Pedro, bishop of Zaragoza, 120, 127, 129, 260, 304
Pedro, candidate for bishop of Salamanca, 247
Pedro, nephew of a canon of Toledo, 372
Pedro de Barcelona, prior of the Holy Sepulchre, 68n
Pedro de Fania, 328
Pedro de San Pablo, 388
Pedro de Tolosa, 117, 380
Pedro de Torroja. See Pedro, bishop of Zaragoza
Pedro Alfónsez, 15, 20, 31, 33, 34, 42, 46, 127, 163, 167, 168, 177, 346
Pedro Alva de San Justo, 373
Pedro Annáiz. See Pedro, bishop of León
Pedro Ansúrez, 47, 121, 165, 288
Pedro Apulichen, 383
Pedro Balzán, 198–99, 204
Pedro Braólez, 16, 142, 328
Pedro Brimón, 353, 388
Pedro Bruno, 380
Pedro Burrín, 377
Pedro Cídez, 207n
Pedro Cristiano. See Pedro, bishop of Astorga
Pedro Cruciato, 386
Pedro Díaz, 39–40, 367, 376
Pedro Díaz de Marros, 372
Pedro Díaz de Valle, 32, 40, 193, 237
Pedro Domínguez, 328, 336, 360, 361, 370
Pedro Domínguez. See Pedro, bishop of Burgos
Pedro Domínguez de Nava, 381
Pedro Elias. See Pedro, archbishop of Santiago de Compostela
Pedro Fernández, 337
Pedro Froílaz, 8, 11, 17, 18, 166
Pedro García, 164, 324, 333

Pedro García, alcalde de Baeza, 393
Pedro Girberti, 362
Pedro González, 16, 192–93, 333, 344
Pedro González, chancellor, 148
Pedro González de Lara, 13, 18, 20, 22, 25, 27, 31–32, 136, 166, 172, 186, 237, 307, 316
Pedro Gordón, 361
Pedro Gudestéiz. See Pedro, bishop of Mondoñedo
Pedro Gutiérrez, 208
Pedro Gutiérrez, canon of Burgos, 378
Pedro Ibañez, 363
Pedro Isidoro, 397
Pedro Jiménez, 195, 301, 391
Pedro Leonis, 360
Pedro López, 17, 47, 172, 248n
Pedro Manga, 202–3, 367
Pedro Martínez, 323, 379, 382
Pedro Micháelez, 205, 386
Pedro Muñoz, 211, 326, 334, 345
Pedro Ovéquez, 327
Pedro Peláez, 201, 208
Pedro Peregrino, 327
Pedro Pérez, 69n
Pedro Pérez. See Pedro, bishop of Burgos
Pedro Rodríguez, 355, 360
Pedro Sánchez, 95n
Pedro Sanz, 391
Pedro Seguini. See Pedro, bishop of Orense
Pedro Taresa, 48, 64, 69n, 235
Pedro Vélaz, 325
Pedroche, 127, 131, 314
Pedroso, 329
Pelayo, abbot of Celanova, 36
Pelayo, archbishop of Compostela, 122–23, 126, 178n, 256
Pelayo, bishop of León, 195n, 237
Pelayo, bishop of Mondoñedo, 250, 257–58
Pelayo, bishop of Oviedo, 23n, 30–31, 33, 41–42, 245, 253, 294–95
Pelayo, bishop of Túy, 178n, 246–47
Pelayo Alfónsez, 396
Pelayo Arias, 148
Pelayo Caamundo. See Pelayo, archbishop of Compostela
Pelayo Cabecha, 394
Pelayo Calvo, 235, 366, 372
Pelayo Captivo, 81n, 192, 372
Pelayo Curvo, 161n, 189, 354
Pelayo Domínguez, 349